PRAISE FOR THE FIRST EDITION

'This book is a magnificent achievement. Ex[pertly] written and scrupulously scholarly, it is a fitt[ing tribute to one of the finest] historical action films ever produced. ... It i[s superbly] crafted, beautifully produced and h[ighly recommended.]'
Jeffrey Richards, Professor of Cultural History, Lancaster University

'...the #1 film book of the year. No reader of *Cinema Retro* will want to be without this volume on their bookshelf.'
Lee Pfeiffer, Cinema Retro

'A class act from first page to last... the author truly does the movie proud in his fastidious coverage, which is exhaustive throughout. A joy to read; movie books really don't come much better than this!'
Howard Maxford, Film Review

'A delight of a book: rich, exhaustive and entertaining...will delight fans, cineastes and history buffs alike.'
Ian Knight, author of Rorke's Drift: The True Story

'*Zulu* has been the door through which many entered the Anglo-Zulu War... Sheldon has opened another door into the film-maker's world...for which the film's devotees should be equally grateful.'
Peter Weedon, rorkesdriftvc.com

'It is possible to dip into any page and find yourself totally engrossed in what you find... You'll be delighted, amazed, intrigued but never ever bored!'
Roger Morgan, The Assegai

"The epic book about the epic movie' roars the blurb – but for once the hype matches the material... Quite literally everything you ever wanted to know about the 1964 classic.'
Quentin Falk, Academy Magazine

'...arguably the best book ever written on the making of a feature film.'
Tony Earnshaw, tonyearnshaw.com

WITH SOME GUTS BEHIND IT

THE MAKING OF THE EPIC MOVIE

EXPANDED AND REVISED 50TH ANNIVERSARY EDITION

Sheldon Hall

Second Edition published in 2014
First published in 2005
Tomahawk Press
PO Box 1236
Sheffield S11 7XU
England

www.tomahawkpress.com

© Sheldon Hall 2014/2005

The right of Sheldon Hall to be identified as the author of this work is hereby asserted in accordance with the Copyright, Designs and Patents Act 1988.

All rights reserved. No part of this publication may be reproduced or transmitted in an form or by any means, electronic or mechanical, including photocopy, recording, or other information retrieval system, without permission in writing from the publisher.

ISBN 13: 978-0-9566834-6-5

Edited by Bruce Sachs. Copy edited by Sheldon Hall
Designed by Tree Frog Communication 01245 445377
Printed by Gutenberg Press, Malta

Picture Credits
Tomahawk Press and Sheldon Hall would like to thank the following for supplying and giving permission to reproduce images: *bfi* Stills, Posters and Designs, British Board of Film Classification, Curtis Brown Ltd., Cineteca di Bologna, Michael Coate, Henry Coleman, Tony Earnshaw, Emap Metro Ltd, Maureen Endfield, Bill Fine, Bruce Forsyth OBE, Andrew Gryspeerdt, Hammersmith Actors and Writers Group, Thomas Hauerslev, Doreen Hawkins, Ian Knight, Brad and Eden Lochore, Colin Mathieson, Mike Siegel Archive, Steve Moore, Jay Pinto, Jan Prebble, Robert Porter, Royal Regiment of Wales Museum, Jürgen Schadeberg, George Smith, Leigh Tarrant, Larry Taylor, Jennifer Thompson, Glenn Wade, Dave Worrall.

Copyright Notices
Extracts from the papers of Cy Endfield are copyright © Estate of Cy Endfield. Used with permission. Extracts from the papers of John Prebble are copyright © Estate of John Prebble. Reproduced by permission of Curtis Brown Ltd, London, on behalf of the copyright owner. Extracts from *Anything for a Quiet Life* are copyright © Estate of Jack Hawkins. Used with permission. Extracts from *In Darkest Hollywood* are copyright © Peter Davis and Villon Films Ltd. Used with permission. The script of *Beyond Our Ken* is copyright © Estate of Eric Merriman. Used with permission. Interviews for the BECTU Oral History Project are copyright © BECTU. Used with permission. All quotations from published material are copyright © their owners. All rights reserved.

The author and publisher have made every attempt to trace and acknowledge the copyright holders of the images reproduced in this book. If any have been unwittingly omitted, they are invited to contact the publisher and the necessary rectification will be made in subsequent printings.

ZULU courtesy of Paramount Pictures. Used with permission.
© Paramount Pictures. All Rights Reserved

A catalogue record for this book is available from the British Library.

CONTENTS

Introduction to Second Edition IX
Foreword by John Barry, O.B.E. 1
Statement by His Excellency Prince Mangosuthu Buthelezi, M.P. 2
Message from Stanley Baker 4
"So what am I doing here?" – Introduction 6
Rorke's Drift, by John Prebble 12

PART I: PREPARING FOR BATTLE

1. "All's up with us!" – Researching the story 26
2. "You're a soldier now!" – John Prebble 42
3. "We can co-operate, as they say" – Developing the screenplay 50
4. "I suppose you have seniority?" – Cy Endfield 76
5. "Because we're here, lad" – Creating the characters 90
6. "Welshmen will not yield" – Stanley Baker 114
7. "I came up here to build a bridge" – Making the deal 126

PART II: DISPATCHES FROM THE FRONT

8. "Fall them in, call the roll" – Casting the actors 136
9. "Do carry on with your mud pies" – Locations, props and costumes ... 160
10. "Thousands of 'em" – Working with Zulus 180
11. "It's your country, isn't it?" – Filming under Apartheid 198
12. "Damned hot work" – Lights, camera, action 214

13. "Like a train in the distance" – Editing and sound 238
14. "Sing!" – Music and narration 252

PART III: VICTORY AND AFTERMATH

15. "Stuff me with green apples!" – Censorship 266
16. "Dwarfing the mightiest!" – Publicity, promotion and premieres 282
17. "Well, we haven't done *too* badly" – Release and box-office 300
18. "Volley fire present!" – Reviews and criticism 318
19. "No comedians, please" – Myths, gaffes and spoofs 344
20. "They're saluting you!" – The legacy of *Zulu* 360
"A final redoubt" – Afterword 376
The First Time 380

PART IV: MORE GUTS

The Film Finances Files 386
An Assistant's Saga, by Ian Fawne-Meade 402
Defending *Zulu* 426
Buthelezi Honours *Zulu* 445

APPENDICES:

Costing Documents 448
The Production Schedule 456
Location Call Sheets 463
Cast and Crew 467
Bibliography 472
Acknowledgements 477
About the Author 480
Index 481

Bourne
Sentries report that the Zulus have gone – all of 'em. It's a miracle.

Chard
If it's a miracle, Colour Sergeant, it's a Boxer-Henry .45 calibre miracle.

Bourne
And a bayonet, sir. With some guts behind it.

DEDICATION

With love and gratitude, to my parents, Maureen and Tom, who first took me to see *Zulu*. They didn't know what they'd started...

...and with thanks and respect, to three gentlemen without whom there would have been no *Zulu* to see:

STANLEY BAKER (1928-1976)

CY ENDFIELD (1914-1995)

JOHN PREBBLE (1915-2001)

INTRODUCTION

TO SECOND EDITION

'*Zulu* tributes – thousands of 'em!' So ran the speech-bubble for a still from the film in the satirical magazine *Private Eye*, published in the summer of 2014. There has indeed been many a celebratory encomium for *Zulu* appearing in the British media in this, its fiftieth-anniversary year. There will doubtless be more before the twelve months are out. Indeed, this book is another of them.

The film's world premiere took place on 22 January 1964, itself the 85th anniversary of the Battle of Rorke's Drift. A flurry of commemorative publications and broadcasts appeared around that date in 2014, including one written by the present author for a Sunday newspaper. Over in America, where the film has a somewhat lower profile but is hardly unknown, a new limited-edition Blu-ray was released on the anniversary date itself by the boutique label Twilight Time. But perhaps the most important and spectacular event of the half-centenary was a charity 're-premiere' of the film on 10 June at the Odeon, Leicester Square, in the West End of London before a packed audience including celebrities and royalty. There cannot be many fifty-year-old films to have achieved this level of public salutation.

Is it merited? Well, of course I think so. I would not have spent more than three years working on this book if I didn't consider the subject worth the effort. There are few if any other movies for which I would want to undertake a similar task – and in response to all those readers who have enquired, no, I will not be doing a follow-up on *Zulu Dawn*! So this Second Edition will have to suffice as a sequel.

Come to think of it, we are now approaching the tenth anniversary of the book itself. I began my research in 2001 and finally saw *With Some Guts Behind It* published in September 2005. I'm unabashedly proud of what I achieved with it. Responses from both reviewers and readers have been overwhelmingly, almost embarrassingly, positive – even those which expressed reservations did so while acknowledging the work that had been put into it. If my postbag is anything to go by, the book has been read by many people who would not normally pick up a hefty tome by a Film Studies academic. It succeeded in everything I wanted it to do. So why revisit it?

A word which cropped up in many of the book's reviews is 'definitive' – a gratifying thought, to be sure, but really there can be no such thing. No matter how exhaustive one tries to be, any research project reflects the sources and resources that are available at a given time. As I point out in one of the original chapters, history as a scholarly field, including film history, is constantly changing and developing, so no knowledge achieved can ever be final, no understanding complete. This much became apparent in the course of writing, when at various points new information came to light that I had not known about before. A crucial discovery, though it came at a very late stage just prior to publication, was the existence of a substantial cache of *Zulu* production documents held in the Paramount Pictures Collection at the Margaret Herrick Library in

X INTRODUCTION to Second Edition

Left: The author interviews special guests at the launch of the *Zulu* exhibition at the London Film Museum, County Hall, in July 2010. Front row, left to right: Dickie Owen, Rusty Coppleman, Denys Graham, Jennifer Bates and Maureen Endfield, with members of the Endfield family.

Los Angeles – a place of pilgrimage for all dedicated film researchers. I made what use of it I could in the brief time that I had available, and the insights thus gleaned formed a valuable corrective and addition to the mostly oral accounts I had previously assembled.

However, this material was itself limited in nature and scope. In the years since, other scholarly work has been published on *Zulu* and other primary source material has become accessible for the first time. The most important of this newly discovered material lay in the archives of Film Finances Ltd., a British-based company that provides completion guarantees for film productions throughout the world. I was fortunate enough to be one of a small number of historians invited to explore a selection of files pertaining to more than 600 films for which Film Finances had made guarantees between 1950 and 1979. Naturally, *Zulu* was one of the films whose files I chose to examine. They enabled numerous fresh insights which I have tried to convey in one of the additional chapters for this Second Edition.

In addition to scouring the libraries and archives for written documentation, I had also endeavoured when researching the book to contact every surviving member of the film's cast and crew that I could locate. Most of them came through with interviews, but there were inevitably some who proved elusive. One of them was Ian Fawne-Meade, assistant to the film's producers, who had decamped to America some years before. Ian got in touch after reading the finished book and has now contributed a major first-hand account of his own. (He was also responsible for the book's only negative review on Amazon, but his one-star rating was for the retailer's non-delivery of the goods, not the text!) Also missing in action first time around was actor Dickie Owen (Schiess in the film), who I'm delighted to say has since turned up alive and well. Dickie has attended a number of recent *Zulu*-related events, including the re-premiere, and has also been interviewed for the book.

The one figure who remains conspicuous by his non-contribution to these pages is Sir Michael Caine. I have made several attempts over the years to request his participation either as an interviewee or the author of a preface, but the only responses I have received were from secretaries who said that his work schedule was too crowded to accommodate me. This may well be the case, of course, as he is famously busy even in his eighties. But a number of people have told me that Caine would not want to be involved in any project concerned with *Zulu*. Although he agreed to record an introduction to the re-premiere screening, I have been given to understand that a certain amount of persuasion was required to get him to accede. Is there a reason for this reluctance beyond busyness? Perhaps the answer to this mystery will be uncovered in time for the Third Edition, if there is one.

The saddest news I have to report is the loss of so many people who *were* interviewed for the book the first time around. It is a heartbreaking task to record the passing of Bert Batt, Ivor Emmanuel, Mike Ewin, Geoff Freeman, Peter Hammond, Doreen Hawkins, David Jones, Basil Keys, Alan Strachan and Sergio Strizzi, all of whom gave generously of their time and whose contributions to my research were invaluable.

The final major addition to the book is a reflective account of the film itself, drawing

INTRODUCTION to Second Edition XI

on work previously published elsewhere but adding some new afterthoughts. I have often been asked why I didn't include a critical review or analysis of *Zulu* in the First Edition, and while my reaction to this has usually been 'Have a care! What more do you want?' I can see that the question is not unreasonable. So my 'defence' of the film is a concession to these queries and to offer, for whatever it is worth, a somewhat different approach to the subject than is contained in the rest of these pages.

One rather arcane avenue of enquiry that I have not been able to pursue might be of interest to other prospective researchers. As the film's dialogue tells us, Lieutenant Gonville Bromhead, the real-life character played by Caine, came from a long line of distinguished military officers. But the name of Bromhead also belonged to several figures who were pioneers of the film industry. Lieutenant-Colonel A.C. (Alfred Claude) Bromhead was a founder and chairman of the London branch of the Gaumont Company, originally a French firm, which went on to become one of the largest studio corporations in the early British cinema. The Bromheads – Alfred, his brothers Reginald and Herbert, and later their nephew Ralph – were major executives in the British film industry, and Alfred's own military career was reflected in his advisory role with the Films Division of the Ministry of Information during World War Two. Coincidence, or a shared family tree? A biography awaits!

I hope readers enjoy the new material, and also the many extra images – including a new colour section – that accompany it. I look forward to hearing your thoughts and thank everyone who has contacted me already either to offer their compliments on the First Edition or to press me for a publication date of the Second. To all of you, I say: 'Bayete!'

Sheldon Hall
October 2014

FOREWORD
by John Barry, O.B.E.

Reading Sheldon Hall's wonderful book has brought back so many happy memories of *Zulu*. There are certain things about the production that I will always remember.

The movie was Stanley Baker's 'baby'. It was Stanley who first asked me to work on the film and everything came together in an extraordinary way under his devoted guidance. We stayed friends and I later bought an apartment on the floor beneath his offices in a tower block called Alembic House overlooking the Thames.

At that time, I didn't know that Michael Caine didn't speak like his character Bromhead until I met him on the set of *The Ipcress File* and heard his authentic cockney accent. I was happy to witness the beginning of Mike's gifted career. *Zulu* was the first of five movies that we worked on together.

Cy Endfield was an unusual director in that he had a charming and curious habit of mumbling to himself and at the same time making sure that we would always understand what he was saying. Cy was involved in every aspect of the production from beginning to end. He and Stanley had recorded some of the Zulu tribal songs that I thought were very effective. I took some of these themes and adapted them into the score. The end result was that it all worked in the most dramatic and meaningful way.

The score for *Zulu* has always been popular at concerts and when I give interviews people always remember it. The soundtrack is a favourite of mine. I only have the fondest recollections of my time spent on the film, and of the great cast and crew that I had the good fortune to be a part of.

Sheldon Hall has written an incredibly thorough book which goes into every aspect of the production in fascinating detail. It provides a splendid read and many of the marvellous illustrations that I had never seen before will delight readers as much as they delighted me. I think that *Zulu: With Some Guts Behind It - The Making of the Epic Movie* is a worthy tribute to a film that continues to enthral audiences over forty years after it was made and to the efforts of all of us who worked on it.

Oyster Bay, New York
June 2005

Unable to visit South Africa personally during the course of research, I wrote to His Excellency Prince Mangosuthu Buthelezi to request that he make a statement concerning his involvement in *Zulu* for inclusion in this book. Although heavily involved in the national elections and suffering a recent personal bereavement, His Excellency was kind enough to respond. Opposite is the complete statement, as received by the author.

PROVINCE OF KWAZULU-NATAL ISIFUNDAZWE SAKWAZULU-NATALI PROVINSIE VAN KWAZULU-NATAL

INDLU YABAHOLI BOMDABU
THE HOUSE OF TRADITIONAL LEADERS
DIE HUIS VAN TRADISIONELE LEIERS

STATEMENT BY HIS EXCELLENCY PRINCE BUTHELEZI, MP

In 1963, the King of the Zulu Nation, King Cyprian Bhekuzulu Nyangayezizwe ka Solomon, and I as well as other traditional leaders (AMAKHOSI) in the districts of Nongoma and Mahlabathini were informed that a film company intended making a film on the battle of Rorke's Drift, which took place during the Anglo-Zulu War of 1879.

The main reason for informing us was because the film needed our people to act as 'extras' in the film when battle scenes were filmed. We undertook to cooperate with the film company. Both the King and I were great grandsons of King Cetshwayo, whose subjects fought that war against British invasion.

It came as a surprise to me when I was approached by Mr Cy Endfield, the director of the film, and the then Mr Stanley Baker (later Sir Stanley Baker) who asked me to participate in a short scene in the film and act the part of King Cetshwayo, my maternal great grandfather. They stated to me that they had already found a radio announcer in Durban by the name of Hubert Sishi who was going to play the part of the King but that when they saw me they were so struck by the family resemblance that they decided to request me to play the part of my great grandfather. I agreed to play the part.

I had to go to the Drakensberg, where the filming took place, for a few weeks. It was quite an interesting episode in my life to be on set. Sometimes it was a bit boring when one had to do a part over and over again until the director shouted: 'Cut'. But it was a fascinating experience to play in that scene with film heavyweights such as Jack Hawkins. It was also an experience I will always cherish to participate in the film in which Sir Stanley Baker participated and in which Michael Caine participated. This was his debut.

My late mother was also on the set to give advice on some of the indigenous music that was to be used in the film. My mother, Princess Constance Magogo ka Dinuzulu, was the granddaughter of King Cetshwayo. At times we were not very happy when some quite racy modern music was preferred by the director, who said that he was catering for western audiences. It was not the kind of indigenous songs that could have been sung during the time of the Anglo-Zulu war in 1879. At one time I had to write a statement for the record distancing myself from such choice of music in the film.

The film was supposed to pay tribute to brave people on both sides of the conflict, the Zulu regiments and the British soldiers. It will be remembered that eleven British soldiers were awarded the Victoria Cross in that battle, an all time record.

As Zulu people we wished that the battle of Isandlwana was portrayed, not just its end as was the case in the film. There were some things where they took licence as happens in most films portraying historical events.

Prince Mangosuthu G. Buthelezi, MP
The House of Traditional Leaders – Province of kwaZulu-Natal
July 2004

The message opposite was printed in the World Premiere programme brochure.

MESSAGE
from Stanley Baker

I give you ZULU, my first motion picture – a simple statement, but how much it means to me and what a complexity of intent and effort lies behind it.

The intent began three years ago when Cy Endfield and I decided that ZULU would make a great, exciting motion picture.

ZULU was conceived – and hopefully executed – as a unique epic. Unique because its spectacular qualities stem from the truth of its story, from its inherent attribute of human courage, from the grand sweep of its exciting adventure.

Truth is stranger than fiction, and the violent battle of Rorke's Drift fired imagination the world over. For us British the battle is as important a chapter in history as the Battle of the Alamo is to Americans. Thus, we were charged with making ZULU authentic, a true recreation of colourful history. In itself, the story supplied the adventure, the excitement, the drama, the scope that makes entertainment demanded by motion picture audiences.

And now the job is completed. How we acquitted ourselves, of course, will be judged by what we have accomplished on the screen.

And you will be the judges.

"SO WHAT AM I DOING HERE?"

INTRODUCTION
TO FIRST EDITION

'Be careful what you say about it,' Larry Taylor told me on the phone from Johannesburg. '*Zulu* is one of the greatest films ever made!' Sadly, Larry – like so many others in this story – is no longer with us; but I hope he would have agreed that he had nothing to worry about. This book is written by a lifelong fan of *Zulu* in the hope that it will reach like-minded people, and perhaps help to persuade a few others to look again at the film or even see it for the first time. My aim throughout has been both to celebrate *Zulu* and to document it as thoroughly (not to mention exhaustively) as I am capable of doing. It has not always been easy, but the journey thus far has been a most enjoyable and rewarding one. Just being able to talk to people like Larry – he played Hughes, the hospital patient with the neckbrace, if you've forgotten – has been reward enough.

Like many of its devotees, I first saw *Zulu* at an impressionable age. To the best of my recall, I was seven or eight years old when I was taken with a group of friends to see the film at the Carlton in Front Street, Tynemouth – long since gone, of course, and replaced by an estate agent's offices. I certainly remember gazing with eager anticipation at the colour lobby cards in the display case outside the cinema, and afterwards waiting – appropriately enough – by the nearby statue of Queen Victoria for the bus home, in a state of considerable excitement after the awesome spectacle I'd just seen. This was during *Zulu*'s 1972 reissue, not its original release (I was actually born in that year, 1964), and in the next few months I dragged my parents back twice more to see the film again on the big screen. At school, I wrote an essay about it ('My Favourite Film'), probably the first time in my life I ever sat down to write about a movie – a sign of things to come. What impressed me even then was not just the impossibly heroic real-life saga at its core – though that in itself was surely enough to stir the schoolboy imagination – but the air of gravitas the film achieved, and its palpable respect for the 'enemy,' which placed it above so many of the comic-strip adventure movies I'd already seen. I sensed myself in the presence of a 'grown-up' movie, and felt that in responding to it I had begun to grow up too.

At that time it had not yet been shown on television, and I had to wait four more years before *Zulu* made its British network debut, which I watched with my Grandma on New Year's Eve 1976 while Mam and Dad were out partying. (Grandma, let it be noted, found the action too bloodthirsty and occupied herself with her knitting.) There were no video recorders then which would have allowed me to keep a permanent copy of the film, so for years afterward I had to remain patient until it came round on television again – and again, and again. Once, I had the bright notion of creating the next best thing to a video and placed my audio cassette recorder under the television set to tape the soundtrack; I even had the nerve to shush my Grandad when he talked too loudly during the broadcast (he thought the battle scenes lack sufficient 'venom').

By special order from my local record shop, I purchased the Ember LP album of John

Barry's magnificent score, thus beginning a collection of movie-related music to which has since been added several CD reissues and re-recordings of *Zulu*. I also followed up my interest by reading about the history and culture of the Zulu Nation and subscribing to a part-work magazine about the British Empire, in the process discovering that the real Battle of Rorke's Drift was not exactly like the film's depiction of it. Not that this bothered me much, and the reader had better be forewarned that when, in the text, I refer to the disparities between film and history, no automatic criticism is implied. *Zulu* is a drama, not a documentary, and deserves fair consideration in its own terms.

When VHS finally arrived in my household, *Zulu* was of course one of the first films I decided to record and preserve, though I had to pause the tape during the adverts and the panning-and-scanning destroyed the film's glorious Technirama compositions. In later years, when I came to teach Film Studies professionally, I often used it to demonstrate the artistic havoc which can be caused by arbitrarily reframing and cropping the sides of a widescreen image. When W.H. Smith exclusively stocked a 'letterboxed' pre-recorded videotape of *Zulu* I was in seventh heaven. That has since been joined on my shelves by a laserdisc (remember them?) and two different DVD editions, on one of which my own voice can be heard in an audio commentary with the film's second unit director, Bob Porter.

At the beginning of that commentary I introduce myself as the author of this book – though at the time of recording I had not yet begun writing it and my background research was still in its infancy. 'Why a book about *Zulu*?' people have often asked me since. For the very simple reason that there isn't one, and there ought to be. Indeed there ought to be several, and I hope and expect that the present volume will be followed by others examining the film from different angles and perspectives (some of them may even be written by me). I first had the idea for it in early 2001 when preparing an article, 'Monkey Feathers: Defending *Zulu*,' for an academic tome entitled *British Historical Cinema*. I discovered that there had been scandalously little of any substance written about a movie which certainly deserves to be scrutinised in depth and breadth. Talking to Bruce Sachs of Tomahawk Press at an event publicising one of their books, I mentioned my interest in the film. He and his business partner Russell Wall were also enthusiasts and I was virtually commissioned on the spot.

My first real interview, in July 2001, was with Ellen, Lady Baker, widow of Sir Stanley. Arriving at her charming suburban home (surprisingly devoid of showbiz memorabilia) around lunchtime, I expected to be there only an hour or two. Nine hours later, having sunk a bottle of chilled white wine and exhausted my stock of audio cassettes, I made my way back to the train station in the gathering darkness, my head full of the marvellous stories I'd heard, not just about *Zulu* but about Ellen's life with Stanley and his whole career. That memorable day was but a foretaste of the immense courtesy, hospitality and generosity, in both time and the sharing of memories, which I was to experience with all my subsequent interviewees, more than two dozen of them, many of whom seemed – I trust my perceptions are correct – not only willing but glad and grateful to be asked to talk about their own work on the film or that of their departed loved ones.

Of the cast and crew members who agreed to be interviewed by me, I am particularly indebted to Bob Porter, with whom I have spoken on numerous occasions over the last few years, often in international telephone calls lasting an hour or more. But I cannot fully express my gratitude to everyone who has helped with or contributed to this book, as it could not have been written without them. Indeed, in a very real sense it has been co-written by them, as wherever possible I have used their own words in telling the story behind *Zulu*. All quotations not attributed to a specific published source derive from personal interviews conducted by me between July 2001 and August 2004. It should be emphasised that all the opinions quoted or cited herein are those of the individuals responsible, and are not necessarily shared or endorsed by the author or publisher

Of course, time plays tricks and recall can be blurred, partial or inaccurate, especially when the events concerned took place four decades ago. Some of my interviewees unwittingly contradicted one another and sometimes even themselves, disputed the testimony of others, or could not provide full answers to all my nit-picking questions. To supplement these oral histories, therefore, I tracked down as many contemporary print sources as I could locate, travelling not only to London from my base in Sheffield, three hours away from the British Film Institute's offices, but also to libraries and archives in California, Wisconsin, Oslo and Bologna (though not, alas, to South Africa). I am thankful to the many individuals working in these and other institutions who helped me trace contemporary writings about *Zulu*, in trade papers, critical journals, newspaper cuttings files and in the censorship records of the British Board of Film Classification and the Production Code Administration.

Primary research on *Zulu* was made especially difficult by the paucity of substantial archival records of either the production or those principally involved in it. There are no collections of corporate files for Stanley Baker and Cy Endfield's small, short-lived independent company, Diamond Films; nor did Baker, Endfield or their families donate their personal or business papers to a library for scholarly research. Only towards the end of writing and editing did I come across a collection of production documents held by the Academy of Motion Picture Arts and Sciences in Los Angeles (see the Appendices). There were, also, two rich sources of material which came to my rescue.

Jan Prebble, widow of screenwriter John Prebble, opened up John's files to me and allowed me access to several drafts of the script, sheaves of detailed research notes and personal correspondence, all of which proved invaluable. Unfortunately, *Zulu*'s co-writer and director Cy Endfield did not keep many

mementoes of his film career, most of it having gone the way of the skip or the shredder over successive changes of location. But his widow Maureen ('Mo') showed me what she had left, among which were several unique documents which filled in some important gaps in the record, while Cy's daughter and son-in-law, Eden and Brad Lochore, unlocked a trunk in their cellar which yielded some unexpected treasures. (My sincere apologies, though, for spilling black coffee on their white rug.) Both Jan and Mo were also, along with Doreen Hawkins, forthcoming in their recollections of their late husbands, and I cannot thank them – along with all my many interviewees – sufficiently for their many hours of delightful reminiscence.

Many friends and colleagues have also performed valuable services in carrying out research on my behalf or passing on to me leads and titbits which they thought might be of interest (they all were). Their names can be found listed in the Acknowledgements section, but I would like to single out here a few individuals who shared with me their own writing and research materials in a particularly selfless manner: stand up and take a bow, Diana Blackwell, James Chapman, Stephen Coan, Michael Coate, George Flaxman, William Hall, Ian Knight, Peter Krämer, Lawrence Napper, Brian Neve, John Oliver, Robert Shail and George Smith. I hope you realise how much your efforts are appreciated.

How to use this book

To assuage any possible confusion at the outset, this is *not* a book specifically about the Battle of Rorke's Drift or the Anglo-Zulu War of 1879: there are many such books available already, written by people far better qualified in those subjects than me.[1] It is, rather, about the film *Zulu*, those who made it and how they set about doing so.

The book is divided into three parts. Part I, 'Preparing for Battle,' examines the researching and writing of the magazine story on which the film was based, and the writing and rewriting of the screenplay in its various successive drafts, as well as the circumstances through which the production of the film was set up. Here you will also find biographical accounts of John Prebble, Cy Endfield and Stanley Baker, the prime movers behind the project. Part II, 'Dispatches from the Front,' details the making of the film itself in all its many aspects, from casting and location-finding to staging, shooting, sound-recording and editing. Part III, 'Victory and Aftermath,' deals with its passage through the censorship system and subsequent promotion, distribution, exhibition and reception by the public and by critics. The final chapters assess the legacy the film has left us and its influence on viewers and other filmmakers. Inset boxes throughout offer biographical information on the supporting actors, while the major players have a chapter to themselves.

Notes at the end of each chapter indicate my sources of information and also provide some interesting sidelights which, for one reason or another, I was not able to incorporate into the main text. Included as Appendices are selections from materials located in the Paramount Production Records Collection in Los Angeles, as mentioned above. This is followed by a cast and crew list (as complete as I have been able to make it, and far more comprehensive than any yet published for the film) and an extensive Bibliography listing all the relevant published works I consulted in my research, along with suggestions for further reading. The Bibliography also contains notes on John Prebble's own research materials used in writing his article about Rorke's Drift (and by extension the *Zulu* screenplay), the un-edited text of which is included here by way of a prologue – to my knowledge, the first time it has ever been published in full.

The chapters, though they seem to me arranged in a logical order, are to an extent self-contained, so that readers more interested in some topics than others can jump straight to where their enthusiasm takes them. I have assumed that anyone reading the book will already have seen the film, but for certain chapters it may useful to have access to a copy on DVD or video for purposes of reference and clarification. The illustrations may help to jog the memory: I have tried to select the rarest and most unusual pictures available, rather than those images most often reproduced in books and magazines mentioning *Zulu*. Some of these images are rare archival artefacts, and should be regarded as such. The less than perfect quality of some of them is more than compensated for by their historical value

A note on spellings and vocabulary

Throughout this book I have chosen, for the sake of clarity and consistency, to retain the spellings of Zulu words as used at the time the film was made rather than to substitute the more up-to-date, currently approved forms. Isandhlwana, for instance, is now usually spelled Isandlwana. The same principle goes for vocabulary: many of the words used belong to the Apartheid period and may offend modern readers. 'Kraal,' for example, often used to refer to the Royal homestead of King Cetewayo (itself now usually spelled Cetshwayo), derives from the Afrikaaner word for a cattle enclosure and would now be regarded as insensitive to use in respect of a human residence. However, rather than censor language in the interests of political correctness I have left words to stand as used by their original speakers and writers, without further comment or apology.

Notes

[1] The most recent, just published when this book was about to go to press, is Saul David's 'revisionist' account, *Zulu: The Heroism and Tragedy of the Zulu War of 1879* (London: Viking, 2004). David makes much of the 'whitewashing' of Rorke's Drift by both the British government of the day and by *Zulu*. His claims are not discussed in the present volume, but they have already been challenged by other historians as, among other things, one-sided, partial and inaccurate. David's arguments also formed the basis of the BBC's *Timewatch* programme *Zulu: The True Story* (2003), and are summarised in his article of the same title in *BBC History Magazine*, vol. 4, no. 11, November 2003.

This illustration appeared in *Lilliput* **alongside** *Slaughter in the Sun*.

"BAYETE!"

RORKE'S DRIFT
by John Prebble

> The original article on which the screenplay of *Zulu* was based has never, to my knowledge, been published in full. As will be explained in the following chapters, a shortened version appeared in the April 1958 issue of *Lilliput* magazine under the title *Slaughter in the Sun* and the pen-name John Curtis. This is the unexpurgated text, taken from a carbon copy of the typewritten manuscript in John Prebble's files. The passages in *italics* were deleted from the published version and appear here in print for the first time.

There was much killing that day. On the plain between the hills eastward from the Buffalo, in the shadow of the mountain called Isandhlwana, there was much killing.

The battle was forced upon the army of King Cetewayo. For two nights the moon had been full of bad omens, but when the British challenge came the Zulus did not avoid it. Their general, Tshingwayo, sent one impi to lure away the main body of the red soldiers and, when this was done, ten thousand warriors fell upon the remainder and destroyed them. The red soldiers died well. 'Ha, they die well!' cried an induna of the Royal Corps, 'They fell like stones where they fight!'

The soldiers stood in squares, and while they had ammunition for their Martini-Henry rifles the Zulus could not close with them, but when the cartridges were exhausted victory was quickly decided by the assegai. Eight hundred British soldiers and four hundred of their native levies were killed, and if people in England were to call this a massacre they were not to know, or were perhaps to forget, that three thousand Zulus were also killed, by the volley-firing of the scarlet squares.

The right and centre only of the Zulu Army were engaged that noon, the Umcityu, Nodwengu and Nokenke Regiments, the Mbonambi and the Nkobamakosi. These were all young and unwed warriors, and they fought for many reasons – to keep the white men from the Blood River Territory, to win the right to marry, to obey King Cetewayo who could do what he wished with their lives.

The left wing, men of the Royal Regiment of Tulwana under Cetewayo's ugly and fiercely ambitious brother Dabulamanzi, formed the reserve at Isandhlwana. The King had once served in their ranks and so they were now part of his Royal Undi Corps. They were veterans, scarred and skilful. Their average age was 45, but this did not mean that were past their strength, for Cetewayo had other valiant regiments with an average age of 55 or 60. The Tulwanas' brave record had won them the right ti marry, and the whole regiment had been wed in one afternoon, to maidens chosen for them by the King. Each soldier wore a leather head-ring to show that he was no longer a callow bachelor.

This day at Isandhlwana the Tulwana sat in a circle on a hill, crouched behind their white shields, and enviously they watched the fighting of their comrades in the regiments called **The Sharp-pointed Ones, The Dividers, The**

Leopard's Den, and *The Evil-seers*. They grumbled that the best of the day was going not to them the Tulwanas, but to the other regiment of the Royal Corps, to the arrogant young men of the Nkobamakosi who called themselves **Benders of Head-Rings** in high contempt for married men.[1]

But when the last British square had been destroyed, and the Nokenke were pursuing fugitives into the hills, Tshingwayo called to the Tulwana, and they stood up and quivered their stabbing spears in response. He told them to go now to Tshiwane, to the ford over the Buffalo at Rorke's Drift, and to destroy the garrison of red soldiers they would find there. He ordered the young Qikazi Regiment to accompany the Tulwana and to learn from the courage of the older men.

The two regiments stamped their right feet once in thunderous salute, and they raised their shields to Tshingwayo and cried '**Bayete!** *Thy Will be done!*'

In column of regiments they turned to the west, two thousand four hundred and fifty of the Tulwanas, and one thousand two hundred and twenty of the Qikazi. They marched at the double which was the Zulu way, and the ten miles they had to run to Rorke's Drift was nothing, for a Zulu **impi** could march fifty miles a day and fight at the end of them.

They ran company by company, and the dust rose up about the nodding ostrich plumes, the swinging kilts of civet and green monkey-skins. The sun shone on the shaven heads of the married veterans and on the uncut hair of the Qikazi. They reached the Buffalo some miles to the south of the British garrison. Here the water was deep and in near-flood, but the Zulus did not pause. They locked their shields together, the black shields of the Qikazi cadets and the white shields of the veterans, and they plunged in, each rank forcing on that before it, and thus carrying themselves across by their own impetus.

The day was bright with sun and warm. It was nearly high summer. It was Wednesday, January 22, 1879.

At three-fifteen in the afternoon Lieutenant John Chard, Royal Engineers, was standing on the sandy bank of the Buffalo,

above the ford and a mile to the north of the stores and depot at Rorke's Drift. Out on the river Sergeant Milne of the 3rd Buffs, a civilian ferryman called Daniells, and half a dozen swearing privates of the 24th were making a bridge from large ponts. Both banks of the river were deeply scarred with ruts, cut by the wagons of Lord Chelmsford's Third Column which had gone over into the Blood River country some days before and pitched camp at Isandhlwana.

Chard had, himself, come down from Isandhlwana early that morning and was now, by chance, commander at Rorke's Drift. At two o'clock Major Spalding, the DAQMG in charge of lines of communication in this area, had ridden off to Helpmakaar. It had been in Spalding's mind that B Company, 2nd Battalion, 24th Regiment[*] was scarcely strong enough to hold the depot should an **impi** filter past Chelmsford. He told Chard that he would return from Helpmakaar the next day with a reinforcing company of the 1/24th.

Chard had been a lieutenant for a long time and command was not unwelcome. He was a quiet, reserved man in his early thirties. The great, hooked nose that fell over his walrus moustache gave him an expression of resigned melancholy. He was a good engineer officer and took pains with the making of the bridge. So concerned was he with the work that he did not see the approaching riders until they were almost upon him. They came from the east, from the Zulu side of the river, forcing their tired horses into the water and beating its surface into yellow foam. One rider was a Carabineer, the other Chard recognised as Adendorff, a lieutenant of the Natal Native Contingent.

The Carabineer's face was white, and his eyes had the expression of a man who had seen too much and was afraid that he might

[*] The South Wales Borderers. [Prebble's footnote]

never forget what he had seen. Adendorff's pistol was swinging from his neck by its lanyard, and his mouth was open, yelling long before the words could have been understood by Chard. When he dismounted on the Natal side of the river he said that there had been a great fight at Isandhlwana, the First Battalion of the 24th had been over-run, and the whole of Cetewayo's Army must now be marching on the Buffalo.

Even as Chard was sending the Carabineer on to Helpmakaar, and was trying to dredge details from Adendorff's near-hysterical story, a B Company corporal came doubling down from the post, rifle at the trail, red tunic open at the throat, pith helmet thrust back from his forehead.

Lieutenant Bromhead's compliments, Sir! A Basuto had arrived at the camp with news from Isandhlwana.

Sergeant Milne waded inshore with the bridge party. If Mr. Chard thought well of the idea he would be glad to moor all the ponts midstream and hold them against the Zulus. Chard shook his head. He thought it unlikely that the Zulus would cross the river here. They would, he said, ford it further down and attack the camp from the granite hills to the south. He told Milne to anchor the ponts, inspan the wagons and bring them in as quickly as possible. Then, with Adendorff, he galloped up to B Company's lines at the mission station.

The white bell-tents that had been erected outside Mr. Otto Witt's little mission were already falling, and the men of the 24th were leaving them where they lay. Chard saw other parties erecting a parapet of mealie bags about and between the two stone buildings, and he was striding over to this when Gonville Bromhead called to him.

Bromhead was 33, and he too had been a lieutenant for a long time. He looked surprisingly young despite the enormous sideburns that curtained his vaguely effeminate chin. He was neat and smart, and his red tunic, green cuffs and collar, looked as if they had been freshly brushed. He was excited, but it was the excitement of anticipation, and perhaps beneath it was the realisation that being left behind the Column in charge of a depot company was not to prove dull after all. He told Chard that his orders from Isandhlwana had been to hold the post, and perhaps Chard would care to inspect its defences…?

Chard nodded and now things began to happen quickly. Mr. Witt, a short, spare Swedish missionary with a fair beard and moustache, came hurrying down from the shoulder of Tyana Hill to the south. Behind the concern on his face was his affectionate attachment to the Zulu people and his deep disapproval of this war. He tugged at Chard's sleeve. He said that from the hill he had seen the black, bobbing wave of the Zulu advance. No, he could not say how many, he was not skilled at such judgments. *He began to saddle his horse.*

But the Reverend George Smith, of the Army Chaplain Department, coming from the hill too with his spyglass, had such a skill. There were, he said soberly, *perhaps* four thousand Zulu warriors coming.

From the south came a short rattle of musketry.

The reason for this was plain in a minute. A hundred troopers of Durnford's Horse rode up to the mission. Some were wounded, some had lost arms and equipment. Panic was rippling among them, and many of them, ignoring the mealie-bag parapet and the hard-eyed infantrymen behind it, began to heel their horses down the Helpmakaar road. The troopers' captain was a man called Stephenson and he returned Chard's salute wearily. *He tried to explain what had happened at Isandhlwana, but let the sentence hang unended.*

Would he, asked Chard, throw out his troopers in a screen across the dongas to the south, the Zulus feeling as they did about cavalry? Stephenson looked at his men and then back to Chard. He could not, he said. His troop had been in the saddle since dawn. It was

exhausted and it was dispirited by the death of Durnford, and, in any case, it would no longer obey him. He turned his own horse and followed his men to Helpmakaar.

When the men of a detachment of the Natal Native Contingent saw the troopers retiring they climbed over the parapet and ran too, leaving Adendorff swearing in grief and anger.

It was now 4.20 p.m. Mr. Witt said goodbye sadly, and the clip of his horse died away to the south-west. In the sudden silence it may have occurred to Chard and to Bromhead, to the able-bodied men at the barricades and to the sick in the hospital, that they were terribly alone and could not have long to live.

Chard walked quickly about his post. Mr. Witt's mission consisted of two stone and thatched buildings standing on high ground, with a rock terrace to the north and a sloping bank to the south. Beyond this rock terrace, which was less than the height of a man, was a scrub of bush and rock, an orchard, a ditch, and a sunken road that led to the Buffalo. *All this made Chard uneasy, and he wished that there had been time to level the bush and the trees.*

The bank to the south was two feet high, and beyond this was a ditch and a scrabble of lean-to huts which B Company had been using as a cookhouse. These too, Chard knew, should have been levelled, had there been time.

Nor had there been time to get the wounded away, and now the wagons, in which he had thought this might have been done, were brought up, overturned and incorporated in the eastern rampart. He told Sergeant Milne to bring the water-cart into the perimeter, and he walked again about the defences with Bromhead, making alterations, making improvements.

The two buildings were awkwardly sited. The western building, sixty feet by eighteen, had been Mr. Witt's house, but with the arrival of the soldiers had been converted into a hospital. The eastern building, eighty feet by twenty had been his church and was now a stores. Outside it was a stone cattle kraal.

This second building, the onetime church, lay a little to the south of the first so that its north-western corner was opposite the south-eastern corner of the hospital. Between these corners had been built a wall of mealie-bags and the wagons, four feet high. The wall was 39 yards long, and this, Chard knew, must take the first assault of the Zulus.

The northern wall was the longer but, because it lined the lip of the rock terrace, might have been considered the stronger. The parapet here was also made of mealie-bags, and was also four feet high. It curved out in a salient from the north-western corner of the hospital and then ran eastward along the terrace to the cattle kraal. Chard walked along it two or three times and then asked Commissary Dunne to get a section of men and build an inner retrenchment of wooden biscuit boxes, from the north wall southwards to the north-western corner of the storehouse.

If any of the 24th wondered at this, and correctly gauged its inference, there was little time left to be worried by it.

Hastily, Chard heard Bromhead's report on the garrison's strength, and what that officer told him can have given him little comfort.

To defend these six hundred square yards against four thousand Zulus he had eight officers and 97 other ranks. To add to the problems this imposed he had the further concern of 36 sick and wounded men in the hospital.

The bulk of his fighting strength rested in Lieutenant Bromhead, Colour-Sergeant Bourne, four sergeants, one lance-sergeant, four corporals, four lance-corporals and 69 privates of B Company, 2nd Battalion of the 24th Regiment. They were well-trained, red-coated men. On their green collars and on the star-plates of their khaki helmets they carried a golden sphinx and the title EGYPT. They wore blue trousers with red piping on the seams, heavy ammunition boots and gaiters of leather. *They wore pipe-clayed belts with a cartridge-pouch on the right side, water-bottle on the right hip, haversack and bayonet on the left. The grey blanket which they usually carried in a roll on their shoulders had been discarded this day, and they were glad of it, for they knew that a man was* going to need his muscles free for this fighting. They were mostly short, stocky men from the Welsh borders, anonymously hidden under names like Jones and Williams and Roberts. Their drill, discipline and words of command had scarcely changed since the Peninsular War, nor, for that matter, had their courage.

They were armed with the Martini-Henry rifle, recently issued to the British Army and now getting its first test in this way. It had a hinged falling-block breech, operated by a lever beneath the butt. It fired short-chamber Boxer-Henry ammunition, .450 calibre, and it was sighted to 1,450 yards. It was a light and short weapon, but when fitted with two feet of narrow needle-bayonet it had a reach of some six feet, longer than a Zulu assegai.

Bromhead had posted his company in strength along the two walls of mealie-bags, and there the men stood now at the High Guard... left foot forward, right foot back, right-hand grasping the small of the butt and lowered to the right hip, left hand holding the stock below the upper sling-swivel and level with the chest. Cartridge pouches were open, ammunition boxes broached behind them.

Colour-sergeant Bourne, Sergeants Windridge, Gallagher, Smith and Saxty, Lance-sergeant Williams all walked steadily behind the parapets, repeating and repeating calmly 'Look to your front... Mark the orders... Mark your target when it comes... Look to your front...'

Bromhead had also posted sharp-shooters at the windows and hastily-cut loopholes of the storehouse and hospital. Chard could find no complaint with these arrangements. They were, in any case, more Bromhead's responsibility than his. The infantry officer was experienced, and at the back of his experience lay the moral influence of a long family history in the Army. He had three brothers serving. His father had fought at Waterloo. His great-grandfather, one hundred and twenty years before, had been the ensign who knelt beside the dying Wolfe on the Plains of Abraham and brought the news that the French had broken.

But beyond the men of the 24th Chard had few others fit for fighting. There were six casuals from the First Battalion. There was a bombardier of the Royal Artillery. There was a sergeant from Chelmsford's staff. There was Sergeant Milne of the Buffs, and a corporal of the Commissariat Corps. There was his own sergeant of the Engineers and the ferryman Daniells. He could not count the four men of the Army Medical Department.

His officers, apart from Bromhead, consisted of Adendorff, and Commissaries Dunne, Dalton and Byrne. Surgeon Reynolds and Chaplain Smith were his other non-combatants besides the four men of the A.M.D.

In the hospital at the west of the perimeter were 36 sick or wounded men; most of them belonging to the First or Second Battalions of the 24th, but some of the Royal Artillery, the 90th Light Infantry, the Natal Mounted Police and the Natal Native Contingent. It was a small garrison at Rorke's Drift, yet ten units were to share the honour that was to come from defending it.

It must have been at 4.28 p.m., with the inner retrenchments no more than two boxes high (despite Commissary Dunne's sweating efforts), that the men of Rorke's Drift heard a peculiar sound, coming from the saddle of the two hills to the south, a rhythmic thunder, a hissing call. The Tulwana veterans and the Qikazi cadets had risen from **ukumbi**, the ritual circle in which they received their orders for battle, and now they were flooding to the attack.

They came forward as yet unseen by the garrison, but they came in order of companies, each with its captain and three lieutenants. They came at the run, in step, with kilts swinging, plumes nodding, shields going up and down, and the sun running along the blades of their quivering assegais. About the necks of many of the Tulwana hung necklaces of sinew, threaded with pieces of willow-wood, one for each killing in battle. In the hearts of the Qikazi was a burning desire to wash their spears in blood, to win such necklaces, to change their shields from black to white.

It was a wall of shields that the 24th saw first, coming up and over the yellow stones and yellow grass of the saddle below Tyana Hill.[2] Fifty white shields of the first wave. Shields five feet high and three feet wide, made of tough bull-hide, tufted with wild-cats' skins and bullocks'-tails. Behind each shield was a hand's-grip of assegais and knobkerries. Behind that grip was a tall warrior with furred ear-flaps, white cow's-tails swinging across his breast, and his throat throbbing with a war-cry **'Usuto! U-su-to!'**

They were led by an **induna** astride a grey mare, a rifle in his hand, a band of leopard-pelt about his brows, two plumes of Kaffir finch above his head-ring. Then came the rest of Dabulamanzi's regiments, over the rise and down in a dark cataract. The soldiers behind the mealie-bags watched it flood toward them, washing into and out of the shallow dongas.

On a hill-top to the southwest Mr. Witt had paused and looked back. He saw the Zulu charge and waited until it had almost reached the parapet. Then he turned and urged his horse at the gallop for Helpmakaar. It would seem that he scarcely stayed there, for in less than two months he was in England, lecturing on the defence of Rorke's Drift.

Gonville Bromhead gave his first order when the Zulus were first sighted. **Fix Bayonets!** The response was instinctive, a drill-book response. *Place the socket of the bayonet on the muzzle, flat part of the blade to the front. When it falls on the foresight turn it with the thumb from left to right and press it home. Turn the locking-ring in the same direction.*

As the attack came on Bromhead have his second order: 'Load!'

Thumb inside the lever, open breech by strong downward pressure. Put cartridge into breech. Press home with the thumb. Close breech by placing fingers under lever. Press home.

'At five hundred yards!'

Adjust backsight by moving bar with forefinger and thumb.

'Volley firing. Present!'

Rifle to the hollow of right shoulder, check along the butt.

Bourne and his sergeants walked behind the ranks intoning steadily 'Take your mark... Take your sight an inch below your mark...'

'Fire!'

The volley tore away the front rank of the first wave, but it did not halt the rest. They came on at the run, spears quivering and shields bobbing. A second volley at shortened range cut down still more, but still the Zulus came on, narrowing the distance between them and the mealie-bags. Private James Dunbar leaped on the parapet after the volleys. He shot the **induna** from the grey mare and, loading and firing calmly, he shot down eight other Zulus with eight consecutive shots.

'Independent... Fire at will!'

And now the platoon sergeants began again. 'Fix your mark... Take your time... Squeeze slowly!'

The centre of the Zulu attack rushed to within fifty yards of the parapet before it was halted, caught in cross-fire from the windows of the storehouse, and the warriors took cover below the bank and behind the cookhouse. But the left and right wings did not halt. They swept behind the flanks and fell upon the north wall until the sustained fire of the Martini-Henry drove them back into the cover of the orchard trees, the bush and the stones.

It was 4.40 p.m. and there was a second's lull. Word went round the parapet from man to man 'Old King Cole's dead!' Tom Cole of B Company, first casualty, shot through the head as he rested his rifle on a mealie-bag for better aim.

For the Tulwana were not just spearmen. Cetewayo had equipped many of them with fire-arms, old flintlocks, Snider percussion-caps that his agents had bought from the Portuguese at Delagoa Bay. When Dabulamanzi saw that his frontal assault had failed to over-run the garrison he put his musket-men in the caves and on the ledges of Tyana Hill, and they kept up a steady, if inaccurate, fire on the perimeter. *The white smoke of the muskets and the blue smoke of the Martini-Henries drifted together in the windless air.*

Company after company of the Tulwana assembled in the cover of the orchard and then began assault after assault on the rock terrace and the north wall. They sang as they pranced, high-stepping, from cover, hidden behind their shields, their short-hafted assegais jerking. They threw few spears, for they were Zulus nor bushmen, and they struggled to get close to stab. They ran forward and they trod their dead into the earth. They filled the orchard and the sunken road with bobbing shields and fluttering plumes. They beat furiously against the north-western salient where, six times, Bromhead sallied out and drove them back. And then it was impossible to drive them back. They held one side of the north wall and the 24th held the other. Zulus and white men stabbed and lunged across it, spear against bayonet.

When the Zulus leaped upon the mealie-bags the 24th instinctively met the assault as the drill-book laid down for repelling mounted swordsmen. Point lifted... Butt lowered. Engage... Disengage... Throw the bayonet at the mark, holding the rifle with the right hand at the small of the butt...

It was growing dark, yet it was too early for sunset. But the roof of the hospital was afire and laying a ceiling of smoke across the perimeter.

Corporal Schiess, a Swiss by birth and a member of the Natal Police, went a little mad. He had an injured ankle and before the attack he had been lying on his bed with the rest of the sick. Now he was there on the south wall, with rifle and bayonet, his hat blown off by a Zulu musket ball. He jumped on the mealie-bags, bayoneted one warrior, jumped down and shot a second, leaped up again and bayoneted a third.

Calm as usual, Colour-sergeant Bourne paraded the north wall. 'Keep the point high… Deliver the point…' Inside the perimeter the blue-coated officers of the Commissariat Department, big, well-covered men in round caps and flowing beards, did what they could. Commissary Dalton was very excited. His pockets were full of cartridges and he walked along the infantrymen, filling their pouches. If a Zulu leaped on to the wall he shouted 'Pot that man, someone!' and he was calling this when a musket-ball from the caves struck him in the shoulder. He handed his rifle to Storekeeper Byrne and, disregarding his own wound, caught hold of Corporal Scammel of the Natal Native Contingent who was staggering back, hit in shoulder and thigh.

Scammel pushed Dalton aside and crawled to where Chard was calmly standing. He handed up his cartridges and asked for water. Storekeeper Byrne brought it, and this was the last action in Mr. Byrne's life, for he had no sooner put the bottle to the corporal's lips when another wave of the Tulwana struck both north and south walls and Byrne was shot in the head.

'Eyes off the point!' shouted Colour-sergeant Bourne, but less calmly now.

From an eminence Dabulamanzi saw the terrible waste of his warriors in these frontal assaults, destroyed by volley-firing and bitter bayonet work. He saw that if the hospital were taken the Tulwana would be able to flood across the perimeter. Coincidentally he sent an assault against the hospital and against the north-western salient. At the latter point Bromhead held the attack, and Corporal William Allen and Private Fred Hitch, although badly wounded, crawled on their hands and feet about the stamping legs of their comrades, dragging ammunition boxes and handing up cartridges.

For half an hour the Zulus tried to force an entry into the burning hospital, through the western and southern doors or windows.

A handful of privates held the buildings stationed in the rooms along both walls, firing steadily from the narrow windows as each wave of Zulus came prancing and singing out of the smoke. At such close range the .450 bullets easily penetrated the tough bull-hide of the shields, but this did not halt the incredible and demoniacal courage of the Zulus. *They beat at the walls with their knobkerries and spear hafts until they were shot down.*

Behind the far window of the hospital, on the western wall, was stationed a young soldier with less than two years' service – 1398 Joseph Williams from the border. There were two sick men in the ward he was defending, and as he fought he shouted for someone to take them to safety. So well did her fight that in the morning fourteen dead Zulus were found below the window, and many more further out within his line of fire.

He fought until his cartridge pouch was empty, and over his head he heard the crackle and the hiss of burning thatch, and his eyes were full of tears from the smoke. He kept his window with the bayonet until the Zulus broke down the door. He called to the sick men to take an axe and hack their way through the wall to the next room, and while they were doing this he faced the Zulus, left foot forward, right foot back, point twelve inches from the ground. The Tulwana pushed into the tiny room, their shields clattering together, the broad blades of their assegais stabbing. 1398 Williams fought them as he had been trained not long before. **Point... Engage... Disengage...** He fought until there was no strength left on his arms and the Zulus twisted the bayonet from his rifle and threw it behind them.

They caught him by the hands and dragged him into the darkening evening outside, and there they plunged their assegais into him. But this, they always claimed, they did with honour *and respect* for his courage.

Meanwhile, the two sick men had crawled through their well-hole into the next room. There, with rifle and bayonet, stood Henry Hook and 1395 John Williams, and these two kept back the Zulus with lunge, point and throw until the patients hacked and tore another hole in the next wall. The room was full of smoke, noisy with grunting and swearing, the stamping and thudding of feet.

Hole by hole, room by room, 1395 Williams and Henry Hook retreated, bayonet against bullhide shield and stabbing spear. The tall warriors of the Tulwana called out their admiration for the red soldiers. Hook and 1395 Williams did not understand the praise, but lunged and parried and swore in English and lilting Welsh. Although they fought well, they could not prevent the Zulus from dragging Private Jenkins from his sick-bed, thrusting him through the hole like a bale of straw, and spearing him outside.

Each tiny room of the hospital had its private of the 24th holding back the Zulus until the sick and wounded (or some of them at least) could crawl through to the east wall and escape. In one room were seven men. One of these was Gunner Howarth of the Royal Artillery. He took the rifle of Sergeant Maxfield who lay beside him and he stood up, none too steadily. He joined 593 William Jones and 716 Robert Jones, and he fought with them. *Through his mind (as he later remembered it) kept running the words* **All's up with us!**

While he and 716 Jones held the hole in the wall, one on each side, delivering the point each time a Zulu tried to burst through, 593 Jones quickly dressed the sick men and forced or pushed them through the next hole to safety. This went on until there were none left in the room to save but Sergeant Maxfield.

The sergeant was ill with fever, delirious, screaming, laughing and talking by turns while the naked feet of the Zulus and the ammunition boots of the infantrymen stumbled over his blankets and the narrow space of the room was cut and crossed by the swing of bayonet and stab of spear.

Howarth, 593 Jones and 716 Jones were forced into the next room where 716 Jones shouted angrily that the sergeant had been left behind. He dropped his bayonet to the charge and went back through the hole. But the room was now full of warriors and each was burying his assegai ritually in the body of Sergeant Maxfield of the Second Battalion, 24th*.*

It all happened very quickly and the wounded and the unwounded were never very clear about what happened, how they got out of the east wall into the barricaded perimeter. Each man had to fall down from a high window, and then run, crawl or stumble to the inner retrenchment. Some of them climbed out of the wrong window and found themselves outside the perimeter altogether, in a nightmare atmosphere of smoke, flames, and leaping Zulus. They ran round the south and west walls of the hospital and tried to climb over the mealie-bag salient at the north-west. Three of them were speared, and a fourth, a gunner of the Royal Artillery, ran straight through an advancing line of Zulus until he found himself stumbling in the bush and stones below the orchard.

There he lay all night, fearful of discovery,

afraid that the red piping on his overalls would betray. More afraid, still, when a wounded pig from Mr. Witt's sty, dropped squealing beside him.

But out of the far window to safety was got most of the wounded. The two Joneses stood one on either side the window helping the sick men through and down. Old Soldier Hook stood at the hole in the wall swinging his bayonet, and shouting aloud with each lunge and parry. Thus escaped Corporal Mayer of the Natal Native Contingent, crawling on one undamaged knee. Thus escaped Bombardier Lewis, pulling himself on his belly because both legs had previously been crushed in a wagon accident. Thus escaped Corporal Graham of the 90th, four corporals of the Natal Native Contingent, and the sick and wounded of the First and Second Battalions of the 24th.

Trooper Hunter, a tall, young member of the Natal Mounted Police, got out of the window too, and ill though he was he refused to crawl across the enclosure. He stood up and ran, and he was shot before he reached the entrenchment.

Henry Hook was perhaps the last man to leave the burning hospital, standing at the hole with arms tired and bayonet bent, until he was alone in the last room, with 716 Jones and 593 Jones calling to him desperately from the other side of the window. Hook listened to the Zulus in the other room. There they had found a wounded native levy, a man whose name has been lost, who appears on Chard's nominal roll merely as 'a member of Umkungu's tribe'. Hook had been unable to get this man through the hole, and he felt badly about it.

He heard the Zulus talking to this member of Umkungu's tribe, mocking him before they speared him. Then Henry Hook climbed through the window and ran, bent double, to the inner retrenchment.

Now Chard's wisdom in preparing this secondary line of defence was proved. While the hospital was being evacuated, while Bromhead, with sideburns singed and helmet lost, was holding the north-western salient, Chard had further strengthened the biscuit-box line. Within it he ordered Commissary Dunne and four slightly wounded privates to erect two redoubts of mealie bags, five feet high and large enough to hold the wounded and a section of sharp-shooters. From this redoubt the riflemen had an elevated line of fire controlling the whole perimeter.

At last the outer compound was abandoned. Black smoke from the hospital rolled and bounded across it, and the sky above was dark too with night. For two more hours the hospital continued to burn and in the red light of it the battle became easily confused. Sudden and desperate assaults were made across the perimeter by the Zulus. They came screaming '*U-su-to!*' but most of them were cut down by the fire from the redcoats before they could reach the biscuit boxes. Those who did reach the line, and leaped upon it, were bayoneted.

On the eastern end of the perimeter sections of the 24th held the cattle kraal, firing from behind the stones, but slowly they were beaten back from its outer wall to its inner wall, and them to the biscuit box entrenchment, until all that the garrison held was little more than one hundred square yards.

Chard had no worry about ammunition. There was enough and more of this, but he knew that there was a limit to the courage and strength of even the greatest of men.

The vigour of the Zulu attacks was maintained until well after dark, and then the intervals between them became longer and longer. That the 24th was able to hold and beat back the attacks was due much to the fact that the head-rings of the Tulwana and the cadets of the Qikazi scorned to creep up stealthily to the barricade, but came as they believed warriors should, with a war-cry, *with a rattle of spear on shield, in a phalanx*, shoulder to shoulder.

As each of these charges flowed over the far mealie-bags and came at the run for the biscuit-boxes, Bromhead gave his volley-orders calmly, and then, soon after midnight by Chard's watch, the heart went out of the Zulus. Firing still came from the musket men in the caves and along the ledges, and now and then a section of warriors would make an insane assault across the compound, but the real battle was over. The mission was still surrounded, the singing and the shouting and the stamp of feet in the darkness beyond continued for three hours.

Dawn came at 4 a.m. and silence with it.

One by one the men of the 24th stood up behind the biscuit boxes. They wiped their eyes and stared northward to the bush and the orchard, southward to the saddle below Tyana. They could not see a living Zulu. They climbed over the boxes with rifles at the trail, walked to the broken ramparts of mealie-bags and they wondered to find themselves still alive.

Surgeon Reynolds wiped bloody hands on his apron, and Chaplain Smith prayed.

The sun came up strongly over Tyana. The bush came alive with the sound of birds and a wind began to move across the yellow grass. Chard, his eyes even more melancholy behind that hooked nose, sent a patrol to scout the dongas and the streams to the south, The men left in the garrison watched the line of red tunics in open order going up and down across the broken land, and then saw them returning, with rifles lifted and waving in delight.

Another patrol was sent out and returned at 6.30 a.m. to say that it had counted over 350 dead Zulus about the post. Another patrol found a hundred more further out, and fifty blood-stained shields on which the Zulus had carried their wounded. One hundred rifles and muskets, and four hundred assegais were piled inside the compound, and the men of the 24th looked at them and realised that a miracle had been performed. They swore and they laughed, they punched each other. Some wept without knowing why, and others put cold clay pipes between their teeth.

Chard and Bromhead called Colour-sergeant Bourne to them, and the three men checked the nominal roll. Fifteen of the tiny garrison had died in the attack, most of them sick in the hospital. Twelve more had been wounded and Surgeon Reynolds was doing what he could for them, although it was his opinion (to be proved correct) that Sergeant Williams of the Second Battalion and Private Beckett of the First could not survive another twelve hours.

Among so small a company these losses were sad, yet a great and terrible thing had happened. A garrison of 97 fit men and 36 wounded had, for twelve hours, repelled the attack of three thousand and more of Africa's greatest fighters. It was to be many weeks before England was to hear of this, and hearing was to take away some of the sting and bitterness of the massacre at Isandhlwana. Ten V.C.s were to be awarded to the defenders of Rorke's Drift, and all ten believed they held the medal on behalf of the rest.[3]

Yet even at seven o'clock on the morning of Thursday the men at the Drift did not believe they were really to survive, for as Chard's watch marked that hour a wave of Zulus appeared again above the saddle below Tyana, rattling their shields, calling their war-cry, and preparing once more to attack. Chard called his men back inside the biscuit-boxes and waited.

The attack did not come. The Zulus remained against the sky-line, the sun behind them and shining on plumes, shields and spears. At eight o'clock they went and the garrison soon understood why. Galloping hard down the road from the river came a relief force under Lt.-Col. Russell of Lord Chelmsford's Third Column.

Two days later the Tulwana returned to the military kraal at Nodwengu where sat King Cetewayo, fat and splendid on his Royal Stool. He called for the regiments that had scattered the red soldiers at Isandhlwana. They came before him, **The Sharp-pointed Ones, The Evil-seers, The Benders of Head-Rings.** *They stamped the right foot and called* **'Ba-ye-te!'**

He asked for the Tulwana. At first the regiment would not come before him, refusing sullenly. When what was left of it stood before him he looked at it and cried bitterly 'But where are the others? Where are the rest?'

Then the Tulwana stamped and answered **'Ba-ye-te'** *Thy Will be done!*

Copyright © Estate of John Prebble. Reproduced by permission of Curtis Brown Ltd, London, on behalf of the copyright owner.

2nd Battalion "24th Regiment."

ROLL OF "B" COMPANY who defended "RORKE'S DRIFT" against the Zulu attack on the night of the 22nd-23rd January, 1879.

Regtl. No.	Rank	Name	Remarks	Regtl. No.	Rank	Name	Remarks
	Lieutenant	BROMHEAD, GONVILLE (V.C.)	Mentioned in Dispatches. Awarded the Victoria Cross.	2429	Private	GEE, E.	
2459	Color-Sergt.	BOURNE, F.	Mentioned in Dispatches. Awarded the Distinguished Conduct Medal.	1362	Private	HITCH, F. (V.C.)	Wounded Severely. Awarded the Victoria Cross.
735	Sergeant	WINDRIDGE, J. L.	Mentioned in Dispatches.	1373	Private	HOOK, H. (V.C.)	Mentioned in Dispatches. Awarded the Victoria Cross.
81	Sergeant	GALLAGHER, H. L.		1061	Private	JOBBINS, J.	
1387	Sergeant	SMITH, G.		1428	Private	JONES, E.	
849	Sergeant	SAXTY, A.		970	Private	JONES, J.	
1328	Lce. Sergt.	WILLIAMS, T.	Mentioned in Dispatches. Died of Wounds 23rd Jan., 1879.	1179	Private	JONES, J.	
				716	Private	JONES, R. (V.C.)	Mentioned in Dispatches. Awarded the Victoria Cross.
82	Corporal	TAYLOR, J.		593	Private	JONES, W. (V.C.)	Mentioned in Dispatches. Awarded the Victoria Cross.
1240	Corporal	ALLAN, W. W. (V.C.)	Wounded Severely. Awarded the Victoria Cross.	2437	Private	JUDGE, P.	
582	Corporal	FRENCH, J.		972	Private	KEARS, P.	
2350	Corporal	BUSH, J.		1386	Private	KILEY, M.	
1283	Lce.Corpl.	HALLEY, J.		963	Private	LEWIS, D.	
1287	Lce.Corpl.	BISSELL, W.		1409	Private	LLOYD, D.	
2389	Lce.Corpl.	KEY, J.		1304	Private	LODGE, J.	
1618	Lce.Corpl.	SHERMAN, G.		942	Private	LYNCH, T.	
2067	Drummer	HAYES, P.		756	Private	MARTIN, H.	
2381	Drummer	KEEFE, J.		1284	Private	MASON, C.	
912	Private	ASHTON, J.		1527	Private	MINEHAN, M.	
1381	Private	BARRY, T.		968	Private	MOFFATT, T.	
918	Private	BENNETT, W.		525	Private	MORRIS, F.	
2427	Private	BLY, J.		1342	Private	MORRIS, A.	
1402	Private	BUCK, W.		1371	Private	MORRISON, T.	
1184	Private	BUCKLEY, T.		1257	Private	NORRIS, R.	
1220	Private	BURKE, T.		1480	Private	OSBORNE, W.	
2420	Private	CAINE, P.		1399	Private	PARRY, S.	
1181	Private	CAMP, W. H.		1286	Private	ROBINSON, T.	
1241	Private	CHESTER, T.		1065	Private	RUCK, J.	
755	Private	CLAYTON, F.		914	Private	SHERGOLD, J.	
801	Private	COLE, T.	Killed 22nd January, 1879.	1005	Private	SMITH, J.	
1396	Private	COLLINS, T.		1812	Private	TASKER, W.	
1323	Private	CONNORS, T.		973	Private	TAYLOR, F.	
2310	Private	CONNORS, H.		889	Private	TAYLOR, T.	
470	Private	DAVIES, G.		879	Private	TOBIN, M.	
1363	Private	DAVIES, W. H.		1281	Private	TODD, W. G.	
1178	Private	DAW, T.		1315	Private	TONGUE, R.	
1467	Private	DEACON, G.		1497	Private	WALL, J.	
1357	Private	DEANE, W.		977	Private	WHITTON, A.	
1697	Private	DICKS, W.		1187	Private	WILCOX, W.	
971	Private	DRISCOLL, T.		1395	Private	WILLIAMS, J. (V.C.)	Mentioned in Dispatches. Awarded the Victoria Cross.
1421	Private	DUNBAR, J.		1374	Private	WILLIAMS, J.	
922	Private	EDWARDS, G.		1398	Private	WILLIAMS, J.	Killed 22nd January, 1879.
969	Private	FAGAN, J.	Killed 22nd January, 1879.	1060	Private	WILLIAMS, T.	

The following Officers and N. C. Officers were attached to above Company.

1st Battalion, 24th Regiment.
Private W. BECKETT .. .. Killed—H.
Private W. HARRIGAN .. .. Killed—H.
Private M. JENKINS .. .. Killed—H.
Private W. NICHOLAS .. .. Killed—H.
Private J. WILLIAMS .. .. Killed—H.
Private ROY .. Mentioned in Dispatches.

2nd Battalion, 24th Regiment.
Sergeant R. MAXFIELD .. .. Killed—H.
Private R. ADAMS .. .. Killed—H.
Private J. CHICK .. .. Killed—H.
Private G. HAYDEN .. .. Killed—H.
Private J. SCANLON .. .. Killed—H.

Royal Artillery.
Bombardier LEWIS .. .. H.

Royal Engineers.
Lieutenant JOHN R. M. CHARD (V.C.)
Mentioned in Dispatches.
Awarded the Victoria Cross.

The Buffs.
Sergeant MILNE.

Commissariat Department.
Asst. Commissary DUNNE, Mentioned in Dispatches.
Acting Commst. Officer DALTON, Severely Wounded. Mentioned in Dispatches.
Acting Store-keeper BYRNE .. .. Killed. Mentioned in Despatches.
Corporal ATTWOOD. Awarded the Distinguished Conduct Medal.

Army Hospital Corps.
Surgeon REYNOLDS (V.C.), Mentioned in Dispatches. Awarded the Victoria Cross.
Private McMAHON, Mentioned in Dispatches.

Natal Mounted Police.
Trooper HUNTER .. .. .. Killed—H.
Trooper GREEN .. .. .. Killed—H.

Natal Native Contingent.
Corporal SCHIESS (V.C.) .. Severely Wounded. Mentioned in Dispatches. Awarded the Victoria Cross.
Corporal MAYER .. .. H.
Corporal SCAMMELL.

Chaplain's Department.
Revd. C. SMITH .. .. Acting Chaplain.

Civilian .. Mr. DANIELS.

Note.—Those N. C. Officers and Men marked with an "H" indicate they were patients in Hospital.

By Special Request, and in order to preserve a record of those who took part in the Defence, this Roll was prepared by Major F. Bourne (late Color-Sergeant "B" Company) from the Regimental Pay List for January, 1879, kindly placed at his disposal by the Public Record Office, Chancery Lane, London.

BECKENHAM, KENT,
4th July, 1910.

The official regimental roll of defenders present at the Battle of Rorke's Drift. Note that Acting Commissariat Officer Dalton (bottom centre) is not identified as a recipient of the Victoria Cross, an omission which led to confusion in Prebble's research.

Notes

[1] Note the modern spellings of Tshingwayo as nTshingwayo and Tulwana as uThulwana. Prebble took the name Qikazi from the *Narrative of Field Operations connected with the Zulu War, 1879* (HMSO, 1907), but observed in his notes on another source, the *Précis of Information concerning the Zulu country, etc.* (HMSO, 1879): 'There is no record in the précis or elsewhere that I can find of this regiment. It may not have been the name of a regiment. Some accounts say that the Tulwana made the attack on Rorke's Drift with a mixed group from other regiments.' More recent sources indicate that the other regiments present at Rorke's Drift were the uDloko, iNdlondlo and iNdluyengwe: see, for example, Ian Knight and Ian Castle, *The Zulu War – Then and Now* (London: Plaistow, 1993), p. 47.

[2] Shiyane Hill, known to the garrison as Oskarsberg Hill.

[3] Eleven Victoria Crosses were actually awarded to the defenders of Rorke's Drift. For an explanation of this discrepancy, see Chapter 1.

PART I: PREPARING FOR BATTLE

John Prebble kept a framed reproduction of Alphonse de Neuville's famous painting of the Battle of Rorke's Drift on the wall of his home. Lieutenant Chard (without helmet) is at the far right and Lieutenant Bromhead stands in the centre, with arm outstretched. Just below him, Surgeon Reynolds tends to Commissary Dalton, while the evacuation of the burning hospital goes on in the background.

An alternative contemporary representation of the battle: 'The Defence of Rorke's Drift' (1879) by W.H. Dugan.

"ALL'S UP WITH US"

RESEARCHING THE STORY

> The Victoria Cross was created in 1856. In a century of wars since, only one thousand three hundred and forty four have been awarded for valour and extreme courage.
> Eleven of them were won in a single day in January of 1879.
> This is the story of that day.
> (Epigraph on title page of *Zulu (The Battle of Rorke's Drift)*, Final Shooting Script, 25 February 1963)

It is often assumed that history is somehow always there, just waiting for anyone who wants to take a book off the library shelf. The facts are available for the finding, their meaning self-evident. Everything is known or knowable, and only the lazy ignore the obvious truths. It's not really like that, of course. History is not just a body of facts but a process – both one of discovery and of interpretation – and it is constantly ongoing. Even the bare facts themselves don't just leap out at the casual inquirer: they may have to be dug up from slow and painstaking research, by scouring obscure primary sources and sifting through disordered masses of data. Interpretation involves weighing arguments, assessing testimony and, where the evidence is contradictory, trying to decide which version is the most reliable.

The above is a fair description of the author's work while compiling the present volume; but it also describes that of John Prebble in preparing his own books and articles. Even though Prebble preferred to be called a writer and story-teller rather than a historian, his literary reconstructions of past events were always rigorously researched. Among the principal sources listed in his masterwork *Culloden* (1961), for example, are many eighteenth- and nineteenth-century manuscripts, magazines and books, unpublished letters and papers, and regimental manuals, as well as a few more recent histories. In addition, a thirty-four-page index provides the reader with detailed factual and biographical information on many of the names and places which appear in his account of the eponymous battle.[1]

The origins of *Zulu* lay in a series of magazine articles Prebble was commissioned to write in the mid-50s called 'Stories of Endurance.' When he was trying to find suitable subjects, Jan Reid (then a friend and fellow journalist, who later became his second wife) suggested looking up books about recipients of the Victoria Cross: the highest British military decoration, awarded for extreme gallantry above and beyond that normally expected of the British soldier. Prebble read about the Battle of Rorke's Drift at the British Library and it became the basis for a short story, published in the April 1958 issue of a general-readership magazine called *Lilliput*. 'The other articles were insignificant,'

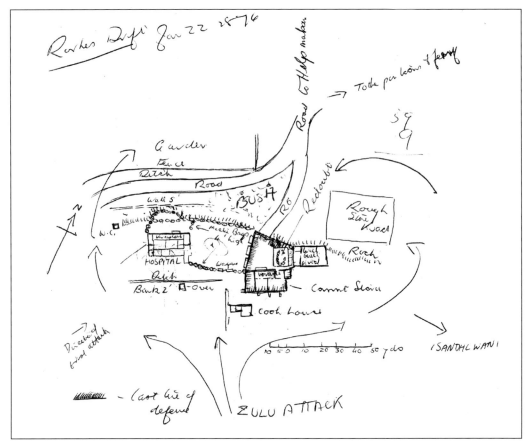

John Prebble's sketch of the layout of Rorke's Drift (based on Chard's own drawing), indicating the direction of the Zulu assaults during the battle. In the film, the ground plan is reversed, with the hospital at right and the church/store-house at left.

says Jan. 'He got more money for that than the rest of the series.'²

Because it was intended for a short article rather than a full-scale volume – or, indeed, a screenplay – Prebble's research on the Battle of Rorke's Drift was nowhere near as extensive as that which he would later do on Culloden. It was not feasible in the time and with the space available to him to explore the life and character of each of the mission station's defenders, or even of just those eleven who received the VC for their part in the action, as many have done since. Nor was there a readily available stack of modern secondary sources recounting the events and analysing the context of the battle as there are today. In fact, much of the research that has since been conducted into the chronology and the causes of the Anglo-Zulu War of 1879 has been undertaken in large part *because* of *Zulu*: the film has effectively helped to create several new generations of scholars, both amateur and professional, many of whom saw it as children and wanted to know more. The pity is that many of these experts now find it hard to forgive or understand the film's historical 'errors,' even though they owe their own discipline and much of the knowledge it has produced to its influence.

However, small-scale though his initial assignment may have been, Prebble was determined to research it as properly as he could. He spent five days at the British Library in December of 1957 and January of the following year, making detailed notes on the events of the battle, the composition of the

British garrison and Zulu regiments, their fighting tactics and equipment, the layout of Rorke's Drift and the surrounding terrain and so on (see the Bibliography for a detailed breakdown of Prebble's sources and the structure of his notes). On the basis of this material, Prebble wrote an initial draft of approximately 7,000 words, entitled simply *Rorke's Drift*. This was apparently never published in full; John kept no print copy of any publication under that title, only a carbon of the original typewritten manuscript. For its appearance in *Lilliput* the story was cut by a little more than a third and re-titled *Slaughter in the Sun* (a handwritten note on the pages Prebble tore from the magazine reads, 'See folder "Stories of Endurance" for full account'). Nor is it clear if the shortening and re-naming were the author's responsibility or the work of the magazine's sub-editors; however, I am inclined to think the latter because of the nature of the material excised.

The full draft begins with a prologue briefly describing the Battle of Isandhlwana and the composition of the Zulu forces, and giving an indication of Cetewayo's motives and methods in ordering his troops to attack the British column. It is also asserted here that the regiments attacking Rorke's Drift, as the

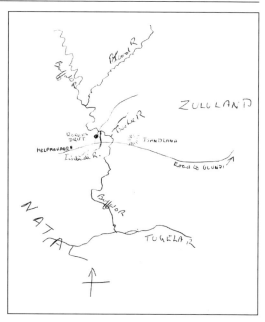

Prebble's roughly drawn map shows the location of Rorke's Drift on the Buffalo River, which marked the borderline between Zululand

Zulus' reserves, had not fought at Isandhlwana, and that they were subsequently ordered by the general Tshingwayo, not the King, to wipe out the garrison. All this was deleted from the published version, along with the short epilogue in which the Zulu survivors

Prebble made these sketches of British Army bayonet drill while conducting research in the British Museum Library.

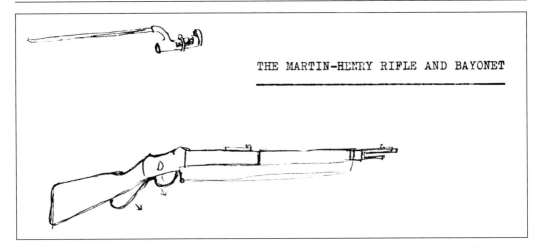

Prebble's drawing shows the bayonet fitting and lever action of the single-shot Martini-Henry rifle used by the defenders of Rorke's Drift.

return after the siege to the military kraal. Thus, the cuts made to Prebble's original draft effectively removed the Zulu viewpoint from his narrative, just as it is absent from *Zulu*.

Other material missing from *Slaughter in the Sun* includes bits and pieces of factual information culled directly from Prebble's research notes, such as the names of the different regimental units (other than the 24th) represented at Rorke's Drift; detailed descriptions of the British soldiers' field uniforms, weaponry and drill (all presumably deemed too 'technical' for the general reader); and Bromhead's family background (the references to his ancestors being at Waterloo and Quebec) which were later to find their way into the *Zulu* screenplay. By far the most surprising and substantial deletions, however – those which particularly lead me to believe that the cuts were the sub-editors' work and not Prebble's – are the lengthy passages recounting the events inside the besieged hospital involving Privates Henry Hook and 612 John Williams, neither of whom receives even a passing mention in the published version, though they figure prominently in the film.[3] One of the defenders of the hospital omitted entirely from *Zulu* (though he appears in drafts of the screenplay) does feature strongly in both *Rorke's Drift* and *Slaughter in the Sun*: Private 1398 Joseph Williams, who after putting up a valiant struggle met his death when he was dragged out of the burning building and assegaied.

It should be said that both versions of the story, despite occasional inventions such as Prebble's speculations on the thoughts and feelings of the participants and the Zulus' shouts of admiration for the defenders of the hospital, stick rigorously to the known facts of the battle as gleaned from the author's research. The chronology of events, statistics of the garrison and its casualties, descriptions of the appearance of characters and landscape, weapons and fighting tactics, were all taken directly from the sources he consulted. Scenes and incidents are described in such a way that the reader is invited to participate imaginatively in the action, but always the events themselves derive faithfully from the historical record. The film frequently departs from it and invents many details and characterisations (liberties for which it has not always been forgiven), but retains the story's essential structure and sequence of events.

While much of what Prebble discovered during his research has now become common knowledge for those with an interest in Rorke's Drift and the Anglo-Zulu War, there inevitably remained gaps in the record that he was not able to fill in the time and with the resources available to him. I have already mentioned the paucity of information on individual soldiers, beyond their role in the fighting, but there was even a lack of such a basic item of data as a full list of all the recipients of honours. Prebble's initial sources suggested that only *ten* men were awarded the Victoria Cross, not eleven as was actually the case. This was an omission not rectified until long after the publication of *Slaughter in the Sun* and the completion of the early drafts of the *Zulu* screenplay: the epigraph to the shooting script quoted at the head of this chapter originally referred to ten awards rather than eleven, an error which remained in every screenplay draft until the final one. On 1 June 1962, Prebble wrote to Cy Endfield: 'In one part of my research notes I have Colour-Sergeant Bourne as a V.C. winner and not the D.C.M., but I think this is wrong.' Six months later, with less than three months to go before the start of filming, Prebble wrote again to the director, having finally solved the mystery of the missing VC:

> I have also been able to determine at last the identity of our eleventh V.C. I thought for a long while he might have been Colour Sergeant Bourne, but he won the D.C.M. The eleventh man was in fact Commissary Dalton, who was killed or appears to be killed in the script as it stands. Since he survived the action I have made it plain in the roll of honour at the end that he lived. Fortunately we have scenes showing every one of our eleven V.C.s in action.[4]

It will be seen from his Bibliography that almost all the sources Prebble used in his research were primary documents roughly contemporary with the Anglo-Zulu War itself or secondary histories published shortly afterwards. Only C.T. Atkinson's *The South Wales Borderers* (1937) and E.A. Ritter's *Shaka Zulu* (1955) – the latter of which is in any case concerned with the history of the Zulu Nation *before* the war of 1879 – were remotely 'modern' scholarly texts. The best-known popular account of the war and of Zulu history, Donald R. Morris's *The Washing of the Spears* – whose narrative method is very similar to Prebble's in his books, and for which Morris has also been criticised, for much the same reasons as Prebble – was not published until 1965, the year after *Zulu*'s release (it was read avidly by Cy Endfield, who drew on it extensively in his own script for the 1979 'prequel,' *Zulu Dawn*). Three other relevant secondary texts appeared in 1963, while the film was in production.[5]

When commenting on *Zulu*'s historical errors, distortions and omissions, few modern observers have taken such matters into account. Indeed, much of the criticism directed at the film has been decidedly *ahistorical*, in the sense that *Zulu* has not always been placed in the context of its own historical moment of production, either in relation to the then-current state of knowledge about Rorke's Drift (both in academic circles and amongst the general public) or to the commercial/industrial circumstances within which the film was produced. A full and detailed account of these matters is beyond the scope of even the present book, but in the following pages I hope to indicate at least some of the important factors bearing on a fair assessment of the film and its achievements.

An instance of the kind of approach I will *not* be taking is provided by a recent article in a specialist journal, which offers a demonstration of some of the dangers which lie in wait for a too-literal attitude towards history on film. In this book I have elected not to provide a minutely detailed accounting of each and every disparity between the real Battle of Rorke's Drift and *Zulu*'s cinematic reconstruction, partly because this has already been attempted and accomplished far more thoroughly than I could hope to achieve. John McAdam's 'Observations on the film *Zulu*'[6] was clearly as much a labour of love for its author as my own work; but despite the copious military scholarship on display, it seems to me that it does little or nothing to address the central issues concerning historical adaptation and dramatisation. A major limitation of the article is that McAdam offers no theoretical framework to explain the many discrepancies between film and history, beyond the vague notion that Hollywood will do anything to appease the American audience in its search for a quick buck. Always the *American* audience, mind you: we Brits apparently have much higher standards.

Among the numerous egregious errors McAdam identifies in *Zulu* are the following: the opening caption giving the date of receipt of Lord Chelmsford's telegram is wrong (it should have read 11 February 1879, not 23 January), as is the wording of the dispatch itself; the topography of the film's Isandhlwana and Rorke's Drift is wrong; the bore of the cannons on the Isandhlwana battlefield is wrong; the Reverend Witt would not have been allowed to attend the Zulus' wedding ceremony and the (Christian) wedding song heard there is wrong; the term by which the Zulus are heard to describe Rorke's Drift – Shiyane, referring to the Oskarsberg Hill – is wrong (it should have been kwaJimu – Jim's Place); the river ponts are too small and the river both too narrow and too close to the mission station; the design and layout of the mission buildings are wrong, as is the height of the hospital beds therein; the details of the soldiers' uniform pouches, belts, collar and helmet badges, pistols, rifles, bayonets, tunics, insignia and markings are often wrong; the number of wagons and their placement in the perimeter are wrong; the direction of the first Zulu attack is wrong; the design of the ammunition boxes is wrong, and so is the packaging of the bullets; and so on and so forth.

By now the reader will have got the general idea – that *Zulu* gets a lot of things wrong and that Mr McAdam has been exceptionally meticulous in his cataloguing of them. Just how meticulous is suggested by the following characteristic observation:

> We then see a "Low-angle-Big Close Up" of Bromhead in the person of (Sir) Michael Caine ordering his troops to "*FIRE*" and in so doing exposing his amalgam filled upper right side teeth. I have checked with the British Dental Association and they have confirmed that in 1879, dental amalgam, which is a mixture of mercury, silver, tin & copper, was in its infancy and that a Lincolnshire gentleman of Bromhead's social standing would have had gold fillings in his teeth.[7]

This is madness. I mean no disrespect to Mr McAdam, who in his own way shows a commendable enthusiasm for his subject and a thorough command of his field of expertise, but none of the 'faults' of the kind mentioned above, no matter how galling they may be for military buffs, is of the slightest consequence to serious criticism of *Zulu* either as a work of art (or entertainment), or as a representation of history. The article represents an extreme case of what the historian Robert A. Rosenstone has called the '*Dragnet* approach' to history ('Just the facts, ma'am'). With this approach, factual minutiae take on an importance out of all proportion to their place in the bigger picture. Any number of ill-chosen costumes, weapons, collar badges or, indeed, tooth fillings would not alone be sufficient for the film to constitute a major misreading of the events of Rorke's Drift or their wider significance (within certain limits, of course: if Bromhead had carried a *Star Wars* light sabre instead of a nineteenth-century sword even I would have raised an eyebrow).

A related problem is McAdam's apparent inability to recognise the very practical – and literal – nature of film as an artistic medium (though he claims to be a filmmaker himself). Even with an unlimited budget, which the makers of *Zulu* did not have, compiling an entirely accurate set of props and uniforms would have been a near-impossible task. Those used have a *generic* appropriateness, sufficient to satisfy the expectations of a general audience if not the eye of a trained specialist. Just as impossible would be the complete transformation of an existing landscape to match another setting; given that it was not possible to shoot at the real Rorke's Drift, one could hardly expect its topography to be exactly reproduced elsewhere. The appearance of the mission

"Hold them! *Hold* them!" Michael Caine as Bromhead.

Commissary Dalton (Dennis Folbigge, left) and Byrne, the company cook (Kerry Jordan).

station is briefly described in all the various script drafts:

> the two buildings that make up the mission station ... are rectangular stone and mud and wood erections with thatched roofs, single-storeyed. Beside one of them is a stunted tree with branches spreading over the roof. The buildings stand about 30-40 yards apart and on a slight promontory. On one side, toward the river is a small orchard. On the other side, where the ground falls away more gently, are the fallen bell tents of B Company, 2nd Battalion, 24th Regiment.[8]

When it came to shooting on actual locations, rather than in landscapes imagined by the writers, it was not possible for the production team to create the 'slight promontory' (a shelf of rock with a steep incline separating it from the approaching plain) or the orchard, so these historically authentic details are missing from the film.

Filmmakers do have to make pragmatic decisions about such matters, but absolute historical fidelity is not necessarily their first priority. Consider this discussion by McAdam of details of the real Chard's uniform and its appearance in the film: 'As Chard was working in and around the Buffalo river building a pontoon, he may well have been wearing an undress frock or even a blue patrol jacket ... However, there is no evidence to confirm just which dress Chard was wearing at the time and any conclusions would be pure conjecture.'[9] Perhaps so, and historians working in a print medium have the choice of making such a conjecture or remaining silent. Filmmakers, however, have no such luxury: if a character is to be shown at all, he *must* be shown wearing *something* (if he were not, everyone's eyebrows would be raised). To be fair, McAdam does acknowledge that 'a red coat is much more attractive and dashing than a blue patrol jacket,' and as it happens the film's costume suppliers concurred:

> Bermans and Nathan had carried out their usual meticulous research and discovered that, in fact, as an engineer officer Stanley Baker would have worn a *blue* uniform. But in order to get the dramatic effect for the film Monty Berman and Stanley Baker decided to have *all* the major characters (including Baker) in the red uniforms that made the picture so memorable.[10]

So in this instance the filmmakers were aware of their 'error' yet made a deliberate decision – for *aesthetic* reasons – to depart from the historical record. This case is repeated in numerous instances throughout the scripting and realisation of *Zulu*.

For the record, the historian Ian Knight disputes McAdam's claim that the details of the officers' uniforms at Rorke's Drift cannot be verified: 'I have looked at this in great detail, and there is considerable circumstantial evidence to suggest both men [Chard and Bromhead] were in red on the day. Both de Neuville and Lady Butler had access to veterans of the battle when producing their paintings (including Chard himself) and showed them dressed the same (in red). Of course they could have made the same artistic choice as the movie! But the only photos of either men actually taken in the field shown them in red undress frocks, which suggests to me that is what they preferred to wear on the

Dafydd Havard (Gunner Howarth)
One of my regular visits to a popular internet website uncovered the following intriguing nugget: 'While in the "Llew Aur Tafarn" [Golden Lion] a few years back I made friends with an older wee fellow hustling the saesneg kids at bumper pool. When in the course of conversation he hit me up for a pint as royalties for a movie! Dafydd Havard himself!' ('Lanky Yankee,' http://www.rorkesdriftvc.com/discussion/, posted 6 January 2002). Digging further, I was put in touch by the pub landlady with Mr Havard's cousin John Havard, who vouchsafed further information about his late relative.

Regarded by Richard Burton (with whom he appeared in the 1971 film version of Dylan Thomas' *Under Milk Wood*) as the finest radio actor in Wales, Dafydd (Dai) Havard may be the only *Zulu* cast member with a direct connection to the regiment which fought at Rorke's Drift: one of his ancestors had been chaplain to the South Wales Borderers (though not at the time of the Anglo-Zulu War). On the wall at the right of the altar in Brecon Cathedral, where the 24th Regiment has its chapel, is the Havard family emblem, a bull's head with three stars, and its motto, 'Hope in God.' Dai's other films include *The Cruel Sea* (1953) with Jack Hawkins and *Where's Jack?* (1969) with Stanley Baker.

Dafydd Havard (left) as Gunner Howarth, with Richard Davies as 593 Jones.

campaign. So – one up to the film!' (email to the author, 27 April 2005).

One brief example may demonstrate something of the creative processes of condensation, dramatisation and interpretation involved in adapting the raw material of history into a film. Prebble read in another of his sources, Sir Henry Hallam Parr's *Kafir and Zulu Wars*, about an unnamed Royal Artilleryman who escaped from the hospital only to find himself trapped, unnoticed, among the Zulus in the orchard outside the barricades. This became a brief episode in Prebble's original manuscript: 'There he lay all night, fearful of discovery, afraid that the red piping on his overalls would betray. More afraid, still, when a wounded pig from Mr. Witt's sty, dropped squealing beside him.' The writer also came across a letter in the *Daily Telegraph* of 25 March 1879 from another of the surviving hospital patients, Gunner Arthur Howard, recalling how he borrowed the delirious Sergeant Maxfield's rifle and, when he saw the Zulus approaching, said to himself, 'All up now!'[11] The incident is again related in Prebble's original draft: 'He took the rifle of Sergeant Maxfield who lay beside him and he stood up, none too steadily. He joined 593 William Jones and 716 Robert Jones, and he fought with them. Through his mind (as he later remembered it) kept running the words *All's up with us!*' Both these anecdotes were cut from *Slaughter in the Sun*, but in Prebble and Endfield's screenplays the two incidents are combined: the unnamed Artilleryman became Gunner Howarth (played in the film by Dafydd Havard) and the scene of his concealment in a ditch outside the camp perimeter was written into the action. It remained there as late as the final shooting script, but like many another incidental scene it does not appear in the completed film. In a curious quirk of fate, it was later confirmed that the historical Gunner Howard and the anonymous Artilleryman were in fact one and the same – though Howard had chosen not to mention it in his letter to the *Telegraph*, he had lost his way in the confusion of fire and smoke and found himself outside the lines, hiding until it was safe to emerge – so in this instance the screenwriters' dramatic construction happened to square with history after all.

Wales Prevails

In amongst the nit-picking, McAdam does make a few salient points which have also concerned more substantive critiques of the film. These include, notably, the treatment of the personalities and actions of individual defenders, and certain other aspects of the film's representation of events which have a material bearing on our understanding of the battle (such as the order to attack Rorke's Drift being implicitly attributed to Cetewayo rather than his brother Dabulamanzi). One issue which receives surprisingly little coverage in McAdam's article, though it is mentioned in passing, is the film's misleading presentation of the 24th Regiment of Foot as a Welsh regiment, rather than – as it was at the time of the battle – an English one with a recruiting depot based in the Welsh border town of Brecon since 1873. In 1879 the 24th Foot's county name was the 2nd Warwickshire Regiment; only in 1881 was it designated the South Wales Borderers. According to Adrian Greaves, only five soldiers of B Company at Rorke's Drift were of Welsh origin, while five others hailed from the English border county of Monmouthshire.[12] Because it has concerned a number of commentators – especially those who have a personal and/or political stake in identifying the regiment as predominantly Welsh or English – it is worth exploring this matter a little further.[13]

The change in regimental name was certainly known to John Prebble: in a letter to Cy Endfield written while conducting further research for the screenplay in 1962, he says that the 24th was *'later known* as the South Wales Borderers' (my emphasis).[14] The Warwickshires are not mentioned as such in story, scripts or film, and partly because of this, historical purists have taken *Zulu* to task for its mystification of the issue and its perpetuation (or creation?) of the myth of the soldiers' Welshness. Prebble's original article makes very little play with either the name – the regiment is identified as the Borderers only in a single footnote, and is otherwise referred to throughout simply as the 24th – or its supposed Welsh connections, aside from a couple of passing references.

Undoubtedly Prebble's footnote drew Stanley Baker's eye and fed his imagination when he was conceiving his epic. In a television interview conducted during pre-production on the film in 1963, Baker explained that it was about 'an action that the South Wales Borderers fought in 1879 at the beginning of the Zulu War, in which they won, fantastically, eleven VCs.'[15] (Confirming the vague public awareness of this issue, the interviewer suggests that some people say seven or thirteen VCs; Baker, of course, had only recently had the true figure confirmed.) Prebble, interviewed in 1996 for a documentary about Baker, acknowledged the importance of the Welsh theme for the actor-producer and admitted the historically dubious grounds for it: 'Of course, what had caught him, I think, is the fact that the regiment involved, the 24th, was generally regarded as being a Welsh regiment. Certainly the South Wales Borderers eventually came from it, but in the company that was at Rorke's Drift about half of them, I think, were English. But Wales prevailed everywhere when Stanley was working.'[16]

Even so, despite Baker's nationalistic passion, the film is careful to remain relatively discreet. Of the principal characters, only five soldiers (Owen, Thomas, 612 Williams and the Joneses) are actually portrayed as Welsh – by a curious coincidence, the same number that Greaves was able to identify among the real B Company, though the film does of course imply that there were more. Though both Privates Owen and 593 Jones describe the 24th as a 'Welsh regiment,' none of the characters mentions its county name. Only Richard Burton's closing voice-over refers to the South Wales Borderers. This is consistent with the two volumes of regimental history Prebble consulted in his research – both entitled *The South Wales Borderers* and published in 1892 and 1937, respectively – whose titles identified the regiment by its *present* designation.

Few of those who have objected to the film's nationalistic distortions have acknowledged their thematic significance: the officers and NCOs are all English, whereas all the Welshmen are lower-ranks. Glynn Edwards, who played Corporal

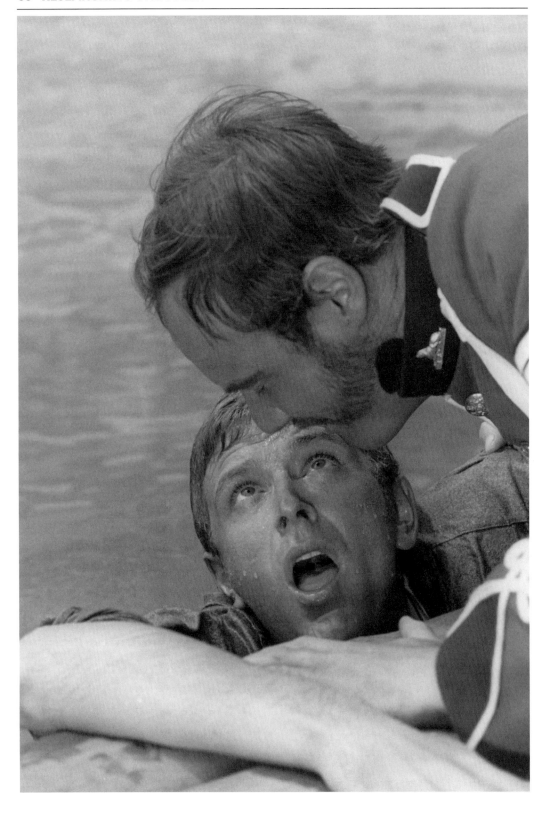

Allen, confirms that this was a conscious choice in Endfield and Baker's approach to the casting, and indeed dialogue to this effect was included in early drafts of the screenplay:[17]

612 WILLIAMS
I tell you, boyo. You notice all the N.C.O.s in this *Welsh* regiment are English? There's a carry-on.

HITCH
What's the matter with you, Dai? I'm English.

612 WILLIAMS
Aye, but you're not a Corporal now, are you, Fred boy?

A distinct ethnic/class hierarchy can thus be inferred, which finds an ironic echo in the martial affinities the soldiers share with the Zulus in the climactic 'battle of song.' Prebble later described the origins of this sequence, perhaps the most memorable and affecting in the film: 'I'd written a piece about the soldiers singing. This came out of a report from someone who was there, who said a lad sang a bit – he doesn't dwell on it or develop it or [say] what they sang. So I got them singing "Men of Harlech" in the script. I also said they make a bad attempt at it: they've been fighting all day long, their mouths are dry, they've scarcely got wind in their lungs. I think on the screen they start like this, but Stanley didn't want to use the actors singing, which I thought would have made a dramatic moment. He made it a great poem to Wales. He got a good choir from South Wales and dubbed it on the top, so that these lifeless figures who've been half dead suddenly spring into life with great tenors and great bass baritones. But that was how he saw it. To him the film was a tribute to Wales.'

In fact, the song title was not specified in any of the script drafts, which indicate only that Private Owen 'sings an old Welsh march.' The plausibility of the singing has often been disputed by sceptics, but Jeffrey Richards has persuasively invoked an authentic historical precedent for the film's dramatic licence: 'contemporary Matabele accounts of the massacre of Major Allan Wilson's patrol in Rhodesia in 1893 record that the survivors shook hands and sang "God Save the Queen" before being slaughtered to the last man. The scene entered popular folklore and many Victorian melodramas featured a scene in which singing British tommies fought off chanting natives – for example Walter Howard's *Midst Shot and Shell* (1899) in which the song was "Soldiers of the Queen" '.[18] The *Zulu* sequence is also strikingly anticipated in Hugo Fregonese's fine low-budget Western *Apache Drums* (1951), in which a community of Welsh settlers, trapped in a church besieged by Apaches, ward off their fears and reply to the sound of the eponymous war drums by singing 'Men of Harlech' – in Welsh![19]

Notes

[1] John Prebble, *Culloden* (Harmondsworth: Penguin, 1967), pp. 320-60.

[2] Contrary to popular belief, Rorke's Drift does not hold the record for the largest number of Victoria Crosses awarded for a single action; for its part in the battle, the 24th Regiment did, however, earn the largest number of VCs awarded for one action to a single regiment.

[3] One minor matter of historical dispute was later addressed when Prebble wrote to Cy Endfield to say that Private John Williams (also known as John Fielding), whose serial number is given in the draft article as 1395 and was variously identified in successive script drafts as either 612 or 395, should correctly be referred to throughout as 395 – though it was later changed again to 612 for the final draft and the film itself.

[4] Letter, John Prebble to Cy Endfield, 7 January 1963. Prebble's research notes indicate that he eventually identified Dalton as the eleventh VC from an issue of the *London Gazette*. Dalton's VC had been awarded much later than those of the other recipients, in January 1880, hence the ease with which he was overlooked. Prebble's own letter (the same one cited above) is dated 7 January 1962, though other remarks contained in it suggest the date is a typo and that it was actually written in 1963. It is a common error for correspondents to write the date of the year just ended at the start of a new one, but mistakes such as this are among the traps lying in wait for the unwary researcher!

[5] Donald R. Morris, *The Washing of the Spears: A History of the Rise of the Zulu Nation under Shaka and its Fall in the Zulu War of 1879* (first published by Jonathan Cape, 1965; revised edition, London: Random House/Pimlico, 1989). The other books were: C.T. Binns, *The Last Zulu King: The Life and Death of Cetewayo* (London: Longmans, 1963); R. Furneaux, *The Zulu War: Isandhlwana and Rorke's Drift* (London: Weidenfeld and Nicholson, 1963); and Sir John Smyth, *The Story of the Victoria Cross* (London: Muller, 1963). All three were included in an extensive Bibliography in the Production Information Dossier on *Zulu* issued to journalists. Prebble recommended the Furneaux text in a letter to one correspondent asking for further information on the War.

[6] John McAdam, 'Observations on the film *Zulu*,' *The Journal of the Anglo Zulu War Historical Society*, no. 9, June 2001. After this chapter was written, when the book was in the final stages of editing, Mr McAdam contacted me with an offer of help in further research. His unsolicited gesture was much appreciated, but in fairness to both him and myself it should be said that the passages concerning his article have not been altered in consequence.

[7] Ibid., pp. 52-3. One error that McAdam curiously does not mention is that the command 'Fire' was not incorporated into Army Orders until July 1879. Until then, British soldiers fired by rote three beats after the command 'Present' (David Rattray and Adrian Greaves, *David Rattray's Guidebook to the Anglo-Zulu War Battlefields*, Barnsley: Leo Cooper, 2002, p. 205).

[8] Note that the script does not identify the regiment as the South Wales Borderers, but simply as the 24th. The 'stunted tree' described here was designed to be used as a prop for the (wholly invented) sequence in which the soldiers engage in close combat with Zulus on the roof of the hospital. Sergeant Windridge, played by stunt specialist Joe Powell, was given an elaborately athletic piece of business in which he was to climb onto the roof from a tree branch, and thence to help others up after him. In the completed film, Windridge can be seen rounding the building to stand beside the tree and look up at the roof, but the climb itself, though most likely filmed, was eliminated, doubtless to save time and speed up the action.

[9] McAdam, p. 49.

[10] Elaine Gallagher, *Candidly Caine* (London: Robson Books/London Weekend Television, 1991), p. 73. Gallagher also recorded: 'In Monty Berman's office there hangs a colour picture of the *Zulu* cast in all their finery, inscribed: "Dear Monty, thanks to you *Zulu* looks magnificent. Yours, Stanley [Baker]."'

[11] Prebble apparently mis-transcribed the spelling of Howarth from the published letter; in the rolls and in modern histories of Rorke's Drift he is listed as Howard. His letter is reprinted in Alan Baynham Jones and Lee Stevenson, *Rorke's Drift: By Those Who Were There* (Brighton: Lee Stevenson Publishing, 2003), pp. 159-60, and Ian Knight and Ian Castle, *The Zulu War – Then and Now* (London: Plaistow, 1993), p. 57

[12] Adrian Greaves, *Rorke's Drift* (London: Cassell, 2002), pp. 328-9. See Chapter 13 of Greaves' book for biographical details of many of the defenders, and Chapter 16 for a brief history of the 24th Regiment and its Welsh connections. The actual number of Welshmen at Rorke's Drift has been the subject of much speculation. Alan Critchley has claimed that there were 32 Welshmen present (http://rorkesdriftvc.com/zulu.html), while Saul David puts the figure at 27 (*Zulu: The Heroism and Tragedy of the Zulu War of 1879*, London: Viking, 2004).

[13] For discussion of this issue, see the responses to the posting by Mark Hepworth ('Historical accuracy and the Media,' 4 February 2004) in the Discussion Forum at http://rorkesdriftvc.com/discussion.

[14] Letter, John Prebble to Cy Endfield, 1 June 1962. Changes in regimental names over time was a matter to which Prebble gave detailed consideration in *Culloden*: see the Appendix on pp. 317-8 of the Penguin edition.

[15] Interview for Television Wales and West, 1962. I am

grateful to BBC Wales producer Steve Freer for access to this and other television interviews quoted throughout this book. In a further television interview after completion of the film, Baker joked that it was about 'a famous battle fought by famous Welshmen, and I play the only Englishman in the script!' The importance of this aspect of the story for Baker is explored by Robert Shail in 'Stanley Baker's "Welsh Western": Masculinity and Cultural Identity in *Zulu*,' *Cyfrwng/Media Wales Journal*, vol. 1, 2004. I am grateful to Dr Shail for allowing me to read a pre-publication draft of his article.

[16] This interview was conducted for *Stanley Baker: A Life in Film* (1996) but not included in the finished programme. Subsequent quotations from John Prebble also derive from this source unless otherwise noted.

[17] The notion of an ethnic/class hierarchy is raised in the website Discussion Forum postings previously cited. Mark Hepworth considers this one manifestation of what he sees as the film's 'Anglophobia,' by which the English are seen as responsible for the oppression of Welshmen and Zulus alike.

[18] Jeffrey Richards, *Visions of Yesterday* (London: Routledge and Kegan Paul, 1973), p. 210.

[19] John Young has also suggested to me that *Apache Drums* has certain thematic parallels with *Zulu*. Possibly by coincidence, a review of this film (the last to be produced by horror maestro Val Lewton) is included in a clipping from *Variety* pasted in one of Cy Endfield's scrapbooks.

John Prebble, clutching a copy of the paperback edition of his best-known book.

"YOU'RE A SOLDIER NOW!"

JOHN PREBBLE
SCREENWRITER/ORIGINAL AUTHOR

> My sympathetic interest is always with the losers.
> A lost race – such as the Gaelic – dies with its virtues and its innocence intact. The winners become arrogant, overbearing, and aggressive.
> (John Prebble, quoted in Sally Brompton, 'The man who writes words fit for a Queen,' *Sunday Express*, 21 February 1971)

Some understanding of John Prebble's methods and the principles behind his approach to historical writing can be gleaned from comments he wrote in a letter to Cy Endfield some time after their collaboration on *Zulu*. They concerned the director's reworking of a draft screenplay inspired by Prebble's book *Glencoe*, which the writer felt had violated the spirit of the original:

> I know my character of Glenlyon was not historically true, but he was historically right, the quisling rejected by both sides and the embodiment of much of the tragedy of Highland history. Equally, I believe, the atmosphere of my version was historically right ... whereas I believe history must sometimes be bent for dramatic effect it must always have historical relevance. I suppose the best illustration of this is the quite fictitious meeting of Gordon and the Mahdi in *Khartoum* [the 1966 film]. What your treatment does is to create a string of non-factual events and people which, although entertaining, do not satisfy me that they improve on actuality. I know, as I said earlier, those events did occur at this time or that, and to this man or that, and I suppose that what is non-factual about them is the mortar that holds them together. Not only did they not happen, they could not have happened, and what did happen, to my mind, is much more dramatic and moving.[1]

Thus, while Prebble acknowledges that different ground rules apply in scholarly history as distinct from drama, he still insists that the latter does *have* rules and asks that they be respected. In making these stipulations to Endfield, Prebble was in essence employing the same distinction which the American historian Robert A. Rosenstone makes between 'false invention' and 'true invention' in dramatic representations of history.[2] It could fairly be said of *Zulu* that while much of it is not literally *true* in the strictest sense or in many of its details, for the most part it is imaginatively *right* in its dramatisation of the past.

John Edward Curtis Prebble was born on 23 June 1915 in Edmonton, Middlesex, and grew up in Sutherland, Saskatchewan. His family had emigrated to Canada following the First World War when his father, after being discharged from the Navy, could find no work except as a Smithfield porter. They returned to Britain when John was twelve and he completed his education with a scholarship at Latymer's School, London.[3] He got his first job, following eighteen months' unemployment, collecting rent from slum properties. The poverty he encountered persuaded him to join the Communist Party, but his offer to fight in the Spanish Civil War was rebuffed when he was told that the cause needed no more 'middle-class martyrs' – though his mother was a maid and his father an unskilled labourer. He was a journalist from 1934 until being called up at the outbreak of World War Two.[4]

Prebble spent six years in the services and for most of the war served in the Royal Artillery and as a radar operator in the Anti-Aircraft Command, based mainly in Rhyl, North Wales.[5] He was selected for officer training but dropped out; his political activism, which included raising petitions, organising debates and selling copies of the *Daily Worker*, cannot have endeared him to the top brass. In 1944, not long after D-Day, he unofficially boarded a troop ship taking soldiers who had been wounded back to France to rejoin their regiments. As his widow, Jan, recalls: 'When the holding camp officials called out "Normandy wounded" he joined them. He then fought in some fairly bloody battles through France and Holland into Germany.' John had married his first wife, Betty Goldby, by whom he had two sons and a daughter, in 1936, but he knew Jan Reid from 1952, when they met as journalists on the *Sunday Dispatch*. They eventually married in 1994 following Betty's death a year previously. John later took Jan to Calais to show her the site of a battle in which he had been involved in September 1944, 'providing artificial moonlight for the troops and fighting off Germans at the same time.'[6]

After the war's end Prebble spent nearly a year in Germany with the army of Occupation, writing for army newspapers. He then returned to Fleet Street as a reporter, feature writer and columnist for the *Sunday Express* and, briefly, the *Dispatch* before going freelance in 1953. His first published novel, *Where the Sea Breaks*

Sergeant Prebble (in spectacles) relaxes off-duty with his fellow servicemen while stationed in Germany. The writer's caption on the back of this photograph reads: 'A simulated exposure of drunken liberators/occupiers/barbarians (according to the German staff of *Soldier* magazine).'

John Prebble in 1948.

(1944), was set in Scotland, the history of which became his abiding passion. It had been formed by the influence of a Scottish schoolteacher in Canada, though he did not actually visit Scotland until he was 21. After several other volumes, including an account of the Tay Bridge disaster, *The High Girders* (1956), and an award-winning Western novel, *The Buffalo Soldiers* (1959), he published the book which made his reputation. *Culloden* (1961) was not 'another history of the Forty-Five,' he wrote, but 'an attempt to tell the story of the many ordinary men and women who were involved in the last Jacobite Rising, often against their will.'[7] It was followed by a series of companion books, including *The Highland Clearances* (1963), *Glencoe* (1966), *The Lion of the North* (1971) and *Mutiny* (1975), which collectively rediscovered a forgotten history of oppression and near-genocide in Scotland, and which sold in millions. 'Above all, John Prebble has interested more people than anyone this century in Scottish history,' remarked Professor Edward Cowan when proposing him for an honorary degree of Doctor of Letters at Glasgow University in 1997. 'His contribution has been as immense as his achievement.'[8]

Prebble attempted to recreate the past with a combination of meticulous factual detail and evocative, novelistic description – though it was the latter which vitiated his work for many more orthodox scholars. He tried to see an event through the eyes of its participants, or imagine himself in the position of a first-hand observer, in order to bring history vividly to life for his readers. As one of his obituaries put it, his aim was 'to personalise and dramatise the past.'[9] Some of his critics made political as well as methodological objections to his work, though his primary sources were impeccably researched. 'He didn't see himself as a historian but as a writer with an interest in history,' says Jan Prebble. 'In Scotland the academics didn't care for his method of writing: they thought he thought he made it all up. He did an immense amount of research, but there were no footnotes. He wanted to tell a rattling good story rather than have a lot of ifs and buts with notes at the bottom of the page. He was still pretty particular about the facts and figures but he wanted to paint a picture in words. *Zulu* is a very good example of what he was trying to do, and though he might not like me saying it, he possibly succeeded better there than in some of the books – in getting across the feeling of the event.'

Prebble's article on Rorke's Drift, *Slaughter in the Sun*, was published in *Lilliput* in April 1958. It was printed under the pseudonym John Curtis – Curtis being one of Prebble's middle names – because he had another article under his own name in the same issue. Some time later, this led to a problem over proof of his authorship when the contract for writing the screenplay was being drawn up. He eventually had to declare under oath at London's American Embassy that he and John Curtis were one and the same. Another version of the article was later printed to coincide with the US release of *Zulu*. This was rewritten by other hands and published in the American magazine *Argosy* under another name and title, for which Prebble was paid a licensing fee of $150.[10]

In a 1996 interview, he described the sequence of events which ultimately led to the production of *Zulu*: 'There was an article I wrote in the late 50s, published in *Lilliput* magazine. During the year that followed, a television producer, Douglas Rankin, approached me and asked me if I'd write a screenplay from it. I said I'd never written one before but I was willing to try. I didn't hear from him for about six months and then he came up with Cy Endfield, who of course was the eventual director, and he was very enthusiastic about it. I wrote, I think, about two or three drafts, which he would cut or advise me on, but there was no indication anywhere that anyone was going to make this film. He had no money, and I think I was paid two hundred quid in the hope of making more should it ever get on the screen. And about a year after that Stanley came into it.'[11]

The script, provisionally entitled *The Battle of Rorke's Drift*, was his first full-length screenplay, but Prebble was not entirely a novice dramatist, having already written scripts for radio and five drama-documentaries for television. The long delay in bringing *Zulu* to the screen meant that his interim work with two other scenarists on Endfield's fantasy adventure *Mysterious Island* (1961) marked his first screenwriting credit, though his story *My Great-Aunt Appearing Day* had previously been adapted by Delmer Daves as the Hollywood Western *White Feather* (1955, directed by Robert D. Webb).[12] *Culloden* was also adapted as a BBC television film, directed by Peter Watkins – who is perhaps best known for the controversial *The War Game* (1965) – and first broadcast in December 1964, after *Zulu* had completed its initial theatrical release. Though its 'docudrama' form is quite different from the approach taken by Prebble and Endfield in their screenplay, *Culloden* is nonetheless consistent with the model of 'faction' pioneered in Prebble's books.[13]

Prebble was never able to visit the set of *Zulu* during its location filming in South Africa. 'I was promised I would go on the first Press plane,' he said, 'but either there wasn't a Press plane or they forgot all about me, so the film was made without me there.'[14] His first sight of *Zulu* was therefore in a rough assembly shown to him by Cy at Twickenham Studios after the unit had returned to London. The director repeatedly stopped the screening as he patiently explained the reasons for the many changes, major and minor, which had been made to the script during filming. A writer is usually the first to object when his

Title page of the magazine article on which *Zulu* was based. This copy was kept by John Prebble in his personal files. Note the author's signature beneath the by-line.

work has been altered for the screen, but Prebble was more than satisfied with the job Endfield and his crew had done. 'He went to see it expecting to come back in pieces, and was there for hours,' says Jan, 'but he came back quite cheerful.'

Years later he described his first reaction to the picture: 'I was greatly impressed by it. I would have liked the uniforms to be a little dirtier: I spent a year in the army myself, and I know that when you're in the forward area you don't actually look smart and pukka, and the photographs of the period show much rougher-looking soldiers. But that's a detail.' After the premiere, which he attended with his wife and family, Prebble took Jan and a party of other journalist friends to a public matinee performance during its West End run at the Plaza cinema. As the film unspooled he repeatedly made comments about what he saw as the shortcomings of his own work, pointing out where the writing could have been better. Eventually, recalls Jan, an irritated punter from the row behind tapped him on the shoulder to complain: 'If you think *you* can write a script like that, laddie, you ought to try!'

In the wake of the film's success, and largely thanks to Stanley Baker's influence, Prebble was awarded a contract by executive producer Joseph E. Levine for four more screenplays. Yet though he wrote many scripts for Levine's company Embassy in the next few years, none was ever produced. These unrealised projects included, according to Prebble's surviving files: *When the Lion Feeds*, from Wilbur Smith's novel set in South Africa, intended for Baker and Endfield; *Glencoe*, inspired by his own book, also in collaboration with Endfield; *Death Watch*, alternatively titled *Blind Rage*, based on a story by Hitchcock's regular collaborator John Michael Hayes; a historical drama set in India, *Mutiny for a Cause*; John Masters' *To the Coral Strand*; and two Westerns, *Rebel Troop* and *The War Horses*, the latter adapted from a story by John Weston about 'how the Western cowboys helped Britain against the Boers.'[15] Another epic historical subject written by Prebble, *Isabella and Ferdinand*, was due to be made in 1971 by

Prebble (left) and Michael Caine chat to a journalist at the London press launch of *Zulu*.

Samuel Bronston – Spanish-based producer of *El Cid* (1961), *55 Days at Peking* (1963) and *The Fall of the Roman Empire* (1964) – whose ongoing financial troubles led the project to collapse only days away from filming.

Amid these disappointments, John wrote a number of well regarded pieces for BBC television, including episodes of the celebrated historical drama series *The Six Wives of Henry VIII* (1970) and *Elizabeth R* (1971); a feature-length John Buchan thriller, *The Three Hostages* (1977); and the rather less well received serial *The Borgias* (1981). Prebble was not primarily a screenwriter, though even unproduced screenplays earned him a healthy living to sustain him when writing his books – somewhere between £25,000 and £50,000 in the case of the Bronston fiasco. 'Films buy me time to do the things I want to do,' he said in 1971. 'I live on films. Over the years I must have bought a complete Polaris submarine for the tax people.'[16] For his work on *Zulu*, he was paid a fee of £2,000, including £200 for the rights to the original story, and two per cent of the profits, royalties from which are still being received by his estate. In his later years Prebble suffered from cancer, and he died in a London hospice on 30 January 2001, shortly before I began researching this book.

One of the most striking features of the creative partnership at the core of *Zulu* is that Baker, Endfield and Prebble should all have held such strong left-wing allegiances, motivated in part by the experience of their parents' poverty and their witnessing the deprivations of others. These politics are only dimly reflected in the film itself, primarily in the characterisation of the private soldiers and in Chard and Bromhead's class antagonism. Though Endfield and Prebble moved away from their hard-line Communist sympathies later in life, they shared with Baker a common hostility to the established social order and the oppressive British class system, and a sympathetic understanding of the life of the ordinary working man. Yet none of them seems to have been drawn to the subject of Rorke's Drift for the wider ideological issues of imperialism and racial disharmony. In contrast to his concern with the political and economic struggles of Scottish history, 'John never talked about a political interest in the Zulu War,' says Jan. He was preoccupied instead with 'the portrayal of the ordinary soldier,' something she considers the film's chief strength, and which may partly account for its popular appeal. 'One of the things John liked about *Zulu* was that ordinary people talked to him about it. He always said he'd bored more people at Christmas than anyone else alive!'

Perhaps surprisingly, John did not think of the film as one of his major works and would gently chide Jan whenever she brought it up in conversation with friends and acquaintances:

'Why do you go on about *Zulu*?' He did, however, discover how much the Zulus thought of it when he and Jan were guests at a performance by an African dance troupe at the Edinburgh Festival. Going backstage afterwards, John introduced himself to the lead dancer, who was carrying a long spear; in a gesture of respect, he laid it at Prebble's feet and embraced him. He then explained to the other performers who John was, and they gathered round to shake his hand. 'There was a great deal of excited talk,' says Jan. When the festival organisers tried to lead John away, the dancers would not let him go; they wanted to talk about film-making and the writer's knowledge of their history. 'They didn't understand how he knew so much. He didn't look very old, so they wanted to know who had told him. They didn't believe he had got it all from written records and couldn't quite grasp the concept of research.'

Prebble's memoir *Landscapes & Memories* covers mainly the earlier parts of his life and entirely omits mention of *Zulu*. However, readers might wish to ponder the relevance to the film of the following passage, in which he discusses the historical matter on which his Western novel *The Buffalo Soldiers* was based. Is there a clue here to the attitudes and values underlying his portrayal of both the Welsh and the Zulus?

> The writing of this book, more gratifying than others, was inspired by a terrible irony. Much of the 'pacification' of the Plains Indians was carried out by two regiments of United States Cavalry, the 9th and 10th. They were black, freed slaves enlisted at the close of the Civil War. Since most American officers were unwilling to serve in such units, some commissions were given to sergeants from the white regiments, and many of these were Irish. Thus men who were once slaves, commanded by junior officers who were the sons of evicted immigrants or had themselves been dispossessed, were now used to subdue, remove or confine a free people.[17]

Notes

1 Letter, John Prebble to Cy Endfield, 27 October 1967.

2 See Robert A. Rosenstone, *Visions of the Past: The Challenge of Film to Our Idea of History* (Cambridge, Mass., and London: Harvard University Press, 1995).

3 Following his return to Britain while still at school and his subsequent membership of the Communist Party, Prebble was never to revisit the United States as an adult. Though he ceased to be a Communist sympathiser during the Second World War he never formally resigned from the Party. This meant that he was unlikely to be granted an entry visa to the US, so he did not bother to apply for one.

4 These details of Prebble's early life have been compiled from his *Landscapes & Memories: An intermittent autobiography* (London: HarperCollins, 1993), and the following obituaries and appreciations: Dennis Barker, *The Guardian*, 31 January 2001; Angus Calder, *The Independent*, 3 February 2001; Brian Wilson and David Craig, *The Guardian*, 9 February 2001.

5 This may partly account for John's interest in the Welsh, as displayed in *Zulu*. He apparently developed a slight Welsh accent when he returned to Rhyl to write *Landscapes & Memories*.

6 Letter to the author, 26 October 2003. All other quotations from Jan Prebble derive from personal interviews with the author.

7 John Prebble, *Culloden* (Harmondsworth: Penguin, 1967), p. 10.

8 Prebble had this encomium inscribed on a coffee mug in his home.

9 Dennis Barker, 'John Prebble: Historian and writer who dramatised Scotland's struggles,' *The Guardian*, 31 January 2001.

10 Letter, Kenneth N. Hargreaves (Director, Anglo Embassy Productions) to John Prebble, 23 April 1964.

11 Though it is unlikely that anyone involved in *Zulu* was aware of it, the Battle of Rorke's Drift had in fact been represented at least once before on screen. The South African-made silent film *Symbol of Sacrifice* (1918) interweaves a melodramatic fictional narrative with the events of the Anglo-Zulu War, including the siege of the mission station. Only a fragment of the film now survives, in poor condition; I am grateful to Ian Knight for the loan of a videotape copy. See Peter Davis, *In Darkest Hollywood: Exploring the jungles of cinema's South Africa* (Athens: Ohio University Press, 1996), pp. 135-141, for further discussion, and the rest of this chapter – entitled 'Zuluology' – for details of other relevant films, including *Zulu* and *Zulu Dawn* (1979).

12 *My Great-Aunt Appearing Day* is collected in Prebble's anthology *Spanish Stirrup and Other Stories* (Harmondsworth: Penguin, 1975); *White Feather* is discussed by Michael Walker in 'The Westerns of Delmer Daves,' in Ian Cameron and Douglas Pye (eds.), *The Movie Book of the Western* (Studio Vista, 1996). There is a striking sequence in *White Feather* in which a large party of Indians appears from an empty landscape to fill the hero's, and the camera's, field of vision. The coincidence with *Zulu* is all the more remarkable in that the Zulus' first appearance on the ridge overlooking Rorke's Drift was conceived quite differently in all the versions of Prebble and Endfield's script, the final version having been improvised during filming. Sequences of this sort are a generic staple in the Western. In George Sherman's *Comanche* (1956) there is a similar face-off between a line of cavalry in the foreground and a line of renegade Indians in the middle ground. The surrounding hilltop is then filled by a row of peace-seeking Comanches, preceded by the sound of ululating voices, seemingly from out of nowhere

13 For a comparative discussion of the TV film of *Culloden* in relation to *Zulu* and the later 'New History film,' see James Chapman, *Past and Present: National Identity and the British Historical Film* (London: I.B. Tauris, 2005). For further background information, see Nicholas J. Cull, 'Peter Watkins' *Culloden* and the alternative form in historical filmmaking,' *Film International*, vol. 1, no. 1 (2003).

14 Prebble later spent several weeks on location in Namibia during the shooting of Endfield and Baker's next picture, *Sands of the Kalahari* (1965), by way of compensation for not having visited the *Zulu* set. 'I think Stanley thought I'd been hard done by,' he said.

15 'Joe Levine's plans for 1964,' *Films and Filming*, July 1964, p. 30.

16 Sally Brompton, 'The man who writes words fit for a Queen,' *Sunday Express*, 21 February 1971.

17 Prebble, *Landscapes & Memories*, p. 140.

52 Continued   23

                    CHARD
                 (gently)
            Your runner bring orders, Brommy?

                    BROMHEAD (nods)
            Something from Durnford, he said. To
            hold this station. Will they attack it?

                    CHARD
            Wouldn't you?

53 DISTANCE SHOT – BUGGY

    being driven at speed toward the station, WITT lashing at the
    horse. CAMERA HOLDS it until it swings up to the hospital
    and halts. WITT gets down and offers his hand to MARGARETA.

54 TWO SHOT   BROMHEAD AND CHARD

    Looking toward approaching buggy

                    CHARD
                 (looking toward buggy o.s)
            Who the devil's that, Brommy?

                    BROMHEAD
            Witt and his daughter. The missionaries
            here. Not English. Swiss, or German
            or something.

                    CHARD
            Get them out of here!

                    BROMHEAD
            You'll take command, won't you, John?
            You're senior to me.

                    CHARD
                 (pointing o.s)
            What's that sergeant's name?

                    BROMHEAD
                 (looking)
            Windridge

                    CHARD
                 (shouting)
            Sergeant Windridge.

                    SERGEANT WINDRIDGE
                 (o.s.)
            Sir.

                    CHARD
            Put two men on the hill up there. And tell
            them to keep their eyes peeled. Face them north
            and south.

This page from the first draft of the script carries extensive revisions and annotations in John Prebble's handwriting.

"WE CAN CO-OPERATE, AS THEY SAY"

DEVELOPING THE SCREENPLAY

> I'm a writer, and a writer who owes more than he can adequately express to Cy Endfield. I was not a writer in the late 50s, early 60s that was much interested in films, but I had written a short account of the defence of Rorke's Drift for a magazine called *Lilliput* which came to Cy's notice, and Cy had the great idea of turning that into a film. For about six months when we worked together I was sceptical about this – I didn't think it was possible to reproduce visually all the pictures I had in my mind about Rorke's Drift, but he did. I think our relationship was very intense at that time – frequent meetings, frequent rewrites, a great deal of despair, and then the sudden realisation that it was going to be made. I count that experience, and I count *Zulu*, as one of the little mountains in what are the arid plains of the average writer's life.
> (John Prebble, address given at Cy Endfield's memorial tribute, National Film Theatre, London, 15 June 1995)

It has been difficult ascertaining what particular contributions Prebble and Endfield each made to the writing and rewriting of the screenplay, a process which began in 1959 and continued until the film was in production in 1963. Jan Prebble recalls it as largely a solo exercise: 'It wasn't a collaboration. Cy wanted to reinstate himself after the McCarthy period and so John agreed to a co-screenwriter credit. The only things Cy did were changes made during shooting when John wasn't there.' However, Endfield's widow Maureen remembers the writing as a joint effort: 'There were lots and lots of meetings with John Prebble,' says Maureen. 'I think there was the usual friction with writers – one coming from a filmic point of view and the other from a historical point of view. A great deal of the *Zulu* screenplay was Cy's. Cy wrote on all his scripts; it was a necessity. He was really a director, but he had to write.' In their contract of 10 November 1962, assigning to Endfield all film, television and ancillary rights in the property, Prebble is described as sole owner of the screenplay, suggesting that he should indeed be regarded as substantially its author – though undoubtedly the numerous rewrites reflect Endfield's considerable input. The last-minute changes made during shooting were certainly the director's responsibility, as Prebble was not on hand in South Africa to make them himself. In a letter to Endfield, Prebble agreed that the script credit should be: 'Screenplay by John Prebble and Cy Endfield, from an original story by John Prebble.'[1] The final on-screen title in fact reads: 'Original screenplay by John Prebble and Cy Endfield. Suggested by an article written by John Prebble.'

From its earliest incarnation as Prebble's article, the *structure* of *Zulu*'s narrative – its overall shape and scene-by-scene progression – remained relatively constant. What changed most through the rewriting were the details:

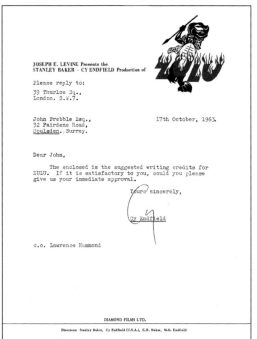

the characterisations, phrasing of dialogue and the inflection of particular scenes. Throughout all of this, the basic construction provided by Prebble's story, and indeed by the battle itself, remained a solid framework permitting ever greater refinement and reinforcement. However, with each successive draft the script moved gradually further away from the historical record and towards fictionalisation. While purists and pedants may protest, such a process is inevitable in filmmaking, for reasons which may be variously commercial, logistical, economic, artistic or all four in combination. This chapter considers the development of the narrative and of selected sequences through each script draft, paying particular attention to material which was substantially revised or ultimately deleted; a later chapter will deal with the development of the major characters.[2]

The first stage of the adaptation was a forty-page 'treatment' (scene breakdown and description) written by Prebble, also entitled simply *Rorke's Drift*, which divided the narrative into forty scenes, preceded by a brief prologue suggesting the aftermath of Isandhlwana as a background to the main titles. Though a very rough sketch for what was ultimately to become *Zulu*, the Treatment nonetheless contains indications of dialogue which survives largely unchanged in the finished film. They include, for example, the description of the Reverend Witt's diplomatic response to Cetewayo's query about his enjoyment of the Zulus' wedding ceremony: 'Witt answers gently that he is sad to see so many wives who may soon become widows.' Other lines retained with only minor variations include Chard's sarcastic query, 'Are you sure you're on the right side of the river, Mr. Witt?'; the exchanges between Schiess and the Joneses ('What do you know about Zulus?'); Bromhead's revelation of his family's military heritage (about which more will be said later); Bourne's instruction to Hitch to do up his tunic buttons, Allen's admonition when he drops his bayonet ('You slovenly soldier'), and Hitch's plaintive request to undo his buttons again when hit by Zulu musket-fire. Also included was seemingly the only line to be taken verbatim from the historical record: Dalton's 'Pot that man, somebody!'

The Treatment was followed by at least five full screenplay drafts. Prebble's files contain complete copies of three of these – the first, last and middle versions – together with two sheafs of pages detailing changes to be made to selected scenes (the scripts are also covered with handwritten annotations which indicate sundry other emendations and

DEVELOPING THE SCREENPLAY

corrections). I shall refer for the sake of brevity to the available scripts as the Original, Revised and Final versions and to the notes as the first and second revisions. The Original draft is entitled *The Battle of Rorke's Drift*, while the Revised and Final versions both carry the new title *Zulu*, with the original title after it in brackets. There is considerable variation between them in length as well as content: the Original script runs 121 pages, the Revised version 168 pages and the Final draft 123 pages. The usual rough rule of thumb is that one page of script equals a minute in screen time, so the Revised draft was somewhat overlong for a two-hour movie. The Final version is the shooting script, but even this is not quite as definitive as it sounds. (It is the only draft to carry a date: 25 February 1963, a month before filming began.)

As with any film, a great many changes, major and minor, were made during shooting. A further set of script revisions was typed up on location, and separate pages covering the changes made to the final sequence can be found enclosed with the two copies of the Final script deposited in the British Film Institute Library by associate producer Basil Keys.[3] The exact phrasing of dialogue, bits of business, details of action and the layout of shots were all subject to the interpretation of actors, director and crew, and in many cases the content, tone and emphasis of key sequences changed significantly in the filming. Some scenes were even wholly improvised or substantially rewritten shortly before the cameras rolled. Yet more changes were made during editing, as scenes or parts of scenes were eliminated and others rearranged. In

Jack Hawkins and Ulla Jacobsson as the Reverend and Margareta Witt, with Chief Buthelezi as King Cetewayo and Daniel Tshabalala as Jacob.

concentrating on such changes I do not, of course, mean to imply either that the original script material was deficient, or that its progressive alteration was a simple matter of compromise. I wish merely to demonstrate that the making of a film is a gradual process of evolution through collaboration – of imaginative conception subtly modified by practical as well as aesthetic considerations, before reaching concrete realisation.

Zulu Marriage Ceremony

The first full scene following the opening titles is set during a mass wedding in King Cetewayo's Royal homestead or 'kraal.' Here we are introduced not only to the Zulu chief and the warriors who will attack Rorke's Drift, but also to the Reverend Otto Witt and his daughter.[4] Margareta Witt was one of the few wholly invented characters that Prebble allowed himself: the historical Witt had a wife and three daughters, but they were all of school age and had already departed the mission before the battle commenced. Second unit director Bob Porter claims that Prebble 'insisted on putting female interest in the film as it would otherwise be all war.' Nonetheless, he confirms that Joseph E. Levine's company Embassy also 'wanted a woman in the picture.' Jan Prebble believes that the writer 'wouldn't have made changes to the historical record for commercial reasons,' and that the insertion of a female lead had not been at the insistence of the money people: 'It was his idea to use Margareta. He wasn't keen on having things put upon him.'

Another significant, if minor, figure in all the screenplay drafts is a young Zulu interpreter who mediates between Witt and Cetewayo. This is Jacob, whom Witt has taught English, dressed in European clothing and apparently converted to Christianity. The scripts give him several lines of English-language dialogue which, had they been retained, would have been the only intelligible (to a non-African audience) dialogue spoken by a Zulu character in the entire film. The scene includes the following exchange from the Final draft:

JACOB
The great Nkosi Cetewayo is angry. He says the red-coated soldiers are already upon his land and wish to take all the hills between the Blood River and the Buffalo ... The great Nkosi Cetewayo says that white-skinned farmers have made a ring about his land like jackals, waiting for the red soldiers to do their killing among the Zulus...

WITT
It does not please God, I know it does not.

JACOB
Then the great Nkosi Cetewayo asks why your God has not destroyed the red soldiers.

WITT
Tell him it is not for us to question the will of God. Only He knows what He will decide.

JACOB
The great Nkosi says that in that case he will help the white God to make up his mind.

During shooting, it was found that the process of translating dialogue back and forth from Zulu to English wasted screen time and delayed the progression of the scene. Assistant editor Jennifer Thompson recalls: 'They had a lot of bother with the king speaking Zulu, then a translation, then Jack [Hawkins] speaking and then a translation, and so on. It was an absolute nightmare.' The solution was to have the Zulu-language dialogue exchanged between Witt and Cetewayo inaudible to the audience, with Witt then explaining to his daughter what has been said. Jacob (played by Daniel Tshabalala) is still present and visible in the scene, wearing a broad-brimmed hat and white shirt and standing between the king and the Witts, but he no longer has a role in the drama. When Red Garters arrives with news of the massacre at Isandhlwana, Jacob was to translate this too: 'They fell like stones when their bullets were gone. Ten tens of them died ten times!' He then casts off his given name and reclaims his Zulu identity: 'And my name is no longer Jacob! It is again Sabeka, which means Making-Men-Afraid!'

While these deletions resulted in greater dramatic economy, moving the story along more swiftly in its opening stages, it is a pity that the stabs of irony, and the brief indications of legitimate political motivation for the Zulus, had to go. The whole sequence is in fact historically misleading on several counts: it presents the King's homestead as being closer to Rorke's Drift than was in fact the case (Ulundi, the seat of the Royal household, was several days' march away); and it implies not

Art director Ernest Archer's pre-production sketch offers an early vision of the wedding scene.

only Cetewayo's knowledge but also his approval of the attack on the British garrison (he had in fact forbidden his warriors to cross the Buffalo River – the boundary line between Zululand and Natal – or to attack entrenched positions). These matters will perhaps concern historians more than general viewers, but they are worthy of mention as the most serious and consequential of the film's alterations of history for purposes of narrative expediency. Elsewhere in the scripts there are vague references to the reason for the British soldiers' presence in Natal: in the Original draft Chard tells Margareta that 'Zulus have been killing White settlers' while in another version he comments bitterly that the battle has 'made South Africa a safe place for white men to fight among themselves.' These seem rather perfunctory attempts to provide some token generic motivation in the absence of any consideration of the genuine root causes of the Anglo-Zulu War. The excision of all such material from the film, though it leaves the battle without any informing context, cannot but be seen as a wise move. At least, if the film misinforms its audience about the history of colonialism in South Africa, with the exception of the wedding scene it does so largely by omission rather than by outright distortion and without imposing an explicit message on the material.

River and Ponts

The Original script version of this lengthy scene, which introduces Lieutenant Chard and his assignment to build a bridge across the Buffalo River, included a character deleted from later versions of the script and from the finished film. This was Sergeant Milne of the Buffs, described as an old soldier smoking a clay pipe, 'with the easy confidence of a long-service N.C.O.'[5] Chard asks him his opinion of the war, and Milne corrects him: it should properly be called a *campaign*. Their discussion continues as they haul on a rope, tethering the loose ponts to a post. It draws out Chard's ambivalent feelings towards military authority, a recurrent theme throughout all the script drafts:

Corporal Allen (Glynn Edwards) offers to hold the ponts.

MILNE
(sharing an old army joke with the lieutenant)
Am I supposed to think, sir?

CHARD
(standing up)
That ought to stop someone else going for an unexpected swim.
(returning to question)
There's nothing in Queen's Regulations that says you haven't the right to think.

MILNE
I know a soldier's rights, sir. Twenty-four inches in the ranks and the right to breathe, that's all.

CHARD
(smiling)
Allright. But what about this campaign?

MILNE
Bunch of savages murdering white people. So they call for the foot-soldier to stop them. That's it, isn't it?

DEVELOPING THE SCREENPLAY 57

Later in this scene, Prebble used an exchange of dialogue inspired by the historical Milne's main claim to fame, when he offered to defend the ponts from the approaching Zulus with the aid of a small party of riflemen. In later drafts this line was passed on to Corporal Allen (though it is quickly broken off by Chard's 'This a situation you think an *Engineer* officer can't handle, Corporal?'). Similarly, it was Milne who was initially given the remark, eventually spoken by Colour-Sergeant Bourne, that the successful defence is 'a miracle.' Prebble's characterisation of Milne bears a strong resemblance to Bourne and clearly *two* veteran NCOs would have been one too many for dramatic purposes. Milne was therefore

Peter Gill (left) as 612 Williams and David Kernan as Hitch in a deleted scene.

> CHARD
> (testing post with his foot)
> All the wood in this country's eaten by ants.
> Better replace it soon, sergeant.
>
> MILNE
> Yes, sir.
>
> CHARD
> That all a campaign is to you, sergeant? March to your front and soldier on?
>
> MILNE
> Better sore feet than a sore head. That's all a squadee knows, sir.
>
> CHARD
> That's all a lot of generals know, too, sergeant.
>
> MILNE
> (slightly shocked by the heresy)
> Yes, sir.

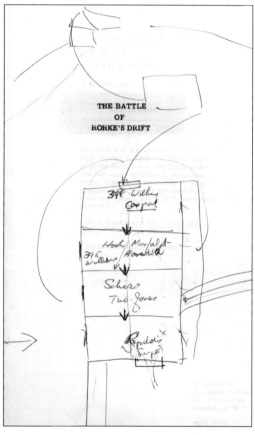

On the front page of the first version of the *Zulu* script (still bearing the project's original title) John Prebble sketched the layout of the hospital building, showing the direction of the Zulu attacks and the occupants of each room (altered in subsequent drafts).

eliminated from later drafts of the screenplay and his dialogue dispersed between Bourne, Allen and Private Owen.

Other passages of dialogue in the Final version of the river scene were shot but cut from the film. They included several exchanges between Privates Hitch and 612 Williams when they are plunged into the water to haul the ponts. This scene was filmed on the first day's location shooting but, according to actor Peter Gill, deleted because Endfield had 'crossed the line' (confused screen directions by putting his camera in positions which did not allow the shots to cut together smoothly). David Kernan, however, thinks the material was simply irrelevant, a thought which occurred to him even while shooting it: 'I don't know what we were chatting about, but it didn't seem to have anything to do with Rorke's Drift or Her Majesty's Army. I just remember thinking, this is totally extraneous, this stuff. It was just establishing the two of us as slightly foolish – one Welshman, one Cockney.' In fact, their conversation served to continue the anti-military theme suggested by Chard's dialogue with Milne. At one point Williams says to Hitch: 'Ah, my Mam said I'd be sorry for taking the shilling. And she was right, you know.'

Hospital Rooms

All the scenes set in the hospital underwent considerable change from the short story and Treatment through the successive drafts of the screenplay. In all the scripts, the patients are described as lying on blankets on the floor, not in bunk beds – in the actual Rorke's Drift infirmary, patients lay on beds only a few inches high. In the film, only two hospital rooms are presented in any detail. Room One houses Privates Hook and Hughes, Gunner Howarth and Sergeant Maxfield, among others. The Original script has Howarth and two other soldiers, Jenkins and Nicholls (both deleted from later drafts), sharing this room with the delirious Maxfield. It is Howarth as much as Hook who is given to expressions of irritation with Maxfield. A far more fleshed-out character in all the script drafts than the

Hook (James Booth), Hughes (Larry Taylor) and Howarth (Dafydd Havard) .

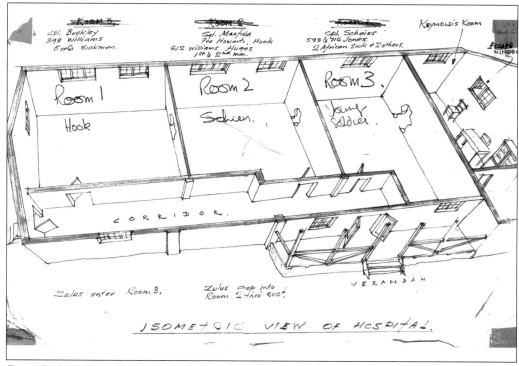

Ernest Archer's design for the hospital set also indicates the location of the patients and gives an indication of the action to be staged.

comic stooge we see in the film, he also plays a more active role in the fighting later. Hook himself is fit for duty in this first version, and more jovial in personality than in the film.

Room Two in the film is occupied by Corporal Schiess and sundry patients, among whom one is identified in the scripts and the film credits only as 'Sick Man' (played by Harvey Hall). They are later joined by Privates 593 Jones and 716 Jones. All the script drafts also introduce Surgeon Reynolds with the first scene in this room, which includes a short dialogue in which Reynolds tells Schiess to stay off his feet if he doesn't want to lose his injured leg: 'I'm a glad man with a knife, Corporal Schiess. I do more execution with it than any of your Zulus.' The film instead introduces Reynolds with the later scene in which he lances Hook's boil. (In the Revised script, which for the first time finds Hook as a patient in the hospital, Hook runs out of the room before the Surgeon can go to work.)

Other hospital rooms were also depicted in earlier script versions. In the Original draft, Margareta Witt is described tending patients in as many as five different rooms; Hughes occupies a separate room with a fever case, and four unnamed patients (one of whom speaks only in Welsh) are in a further room. But the most significant additional hospital scenes involved yet another room, housing an injured Corporal named Buckley and defended by a young, nervous Welsh soldier with a recurrent nosebleed, Private 398 Joseph Williams. The first major scene involving them (again in the Original script) contained a tender exchange between Buckley and Margareta:

CORPORAL
Why'd you come here, Miss?

MARGARETA
To help you.

CORPORAL
No, to Africa.

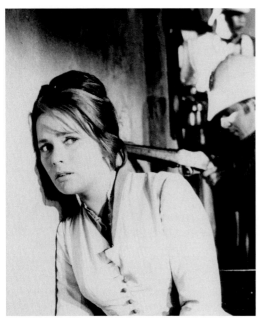

MARGARETA
To help my father. He was alone. I was alone. We were needed here. Among the Zulus.

CORPORAL
Not much appreciation they're showing.

MARGARETA
It will take time.

CORPORAL
(sceptically)
Yes.
(he studies her; then)
You walking out?

MARGARETA
(puzzled)
I'm sorry?

CORPORAL
(trying to explain)
You got a… well, you got a man? I mean…

MARGARETA
(smiling)
Oh, I see… I'm afraid the answer's no.

CORPORAL
Should have. You're a good-looker.

MARGARETA is embarrassed, and she turns her attention to the sick man. Then she looks back.

MARGARETA
Why did you ask that? About a… about a man, I mean?

CORPORAL
(finding it hard to explain)
Well… A moment like this, a man feels alone see. Feels half of himself missing. You know?

MARGARETA
I… well, yes, I think I understand.

CORPORAL
No offence took?

MARGARETA
Of course not.

CORPORAL
(looking at her hard)
Would you… You know, just for the nominal roll, think of walking out with me? I won't hold you to it later.

MARGARETA
You'd like to *think* of it. Is that what you mean?

CORPORAL
Yes, that's it.

MARGARETA
(moved)
I consider it an honour.

CORPORAL
No real honour. You know how the regulations go?
(quotes)
'Officers' – ladies. 'Sergeants' – wives. 'Other ranks' – women.

> MARGARETA
> It's an honour, Corporal.

This conversation may have seemed to the writers a little too sentimental, and in the Revised version Buckley's intentions are made more cynical and calculating:

> THE CORPORAL nods slowly. He is thinking of something. Then he grimaces points to his side.
>
> CORPORAL BUCKLEY
> Can you loosen that? Down my side. The bandage.
>
> Cautiously, as BUCKLEY leans over to expose his naked chest beneath the tunic that is draped over his shoulders, MARGARETA loosens the bandage. BUCKLEY looks full at her and grins, enjoying her touch and discomfort. She sees the grin and sits back quickly.
>
> CORPORAL BUCKLEY
> Thanks… Proper treat!

Though Buckley himself ultimately disappeared, a remnant of this business survives in the film with the Sick Man's half-conscious attempt to molest Margareta.

Subsequent dialogue between Buckley and 398 Williams – who occupy more space in the Treatment than Hook and Maxfield – mainly involves the teenage soldier's memories of his girl in Brecon and his fear that he will not be up to fulfilling his duty in the battle. When the Zulu attack comes, Williams watches the wood of the door splintering under the assault of assegais (much as Hook does in the film when he goes into the corridor during the battle); after killing a number of Zulus while Buckley helps other patients escape through a hole in the wall, Williams is eventually dragged out of the doorway and assegaied. These scenes had been present in Prebble's short story and Treatment and had survived through the Original and Revised scripts but were eliminated from the Final draft, with the exception of a couple of brief references to a 'Young Soldier' who sights the column of Stephenson's horsemen from his window. In the film, this latter bit of business is given instead to 593 Jones, who spots their arrival from the hospital verandah. The change was decided on during shooting at Twickenham Studios, when Stanley Baker nominated Richard Davies to deliver an extra few lines to save the company the cost of hiring another actor. Room Three now exists in the film only as the space through which Hook makes his escape in the fire sequences.

The reduction in the number of hospital rooms in the Final draft obviously avoided repetition and reduced the risk of the audience becoming confused about which room was which. It also made for budget economies, as the film's art department only had to build three interconnecting rooms and an adjoining corridor rather than five. The reasons for the elimination of 398 Williams and Corporal Buckley surely also lie in the necessity to avoid dramatic repetition. The relationship between the two men has close parallels with the father-son bonds which develop between Maxfield and Hook, Allen and Hitch, and even between Bourne and Private Cole. Two of these relationships were therefore dropped or diminished and the Hook/Maxfield and Allen/Hitch pairings correspondingly enlarged and strengthened.

Defence Plan

As other writers have noted, Adendorff's role in *Zulu* echoes that of the 'frontier scout' in

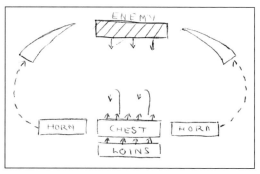

John Prebble's sketch of the Zulus' traditional 'fighting bull buffalo' attack formation.

traditional American Westerns: the White man who has lived with and understands the Indians and who therefore appreciates better than most their special qualities.[6] The sequence in which he explains the Zulus' characteristic attack formation in the shape of a 'fighting bull buffalo' helps establish them as a formidable military force, educating the audience in its strategies as much as the British officers. Though no Zulu figures are singled out as individuated characters, the army is characterised in the film by its strategic intelligence, fighting skill and bravery in battle. Adendorff's explanation also serves the necessary purpose of demonstrating what is about to ensue – and what the defence must avoid – in order to instil in the audience a sense of anticipation. This is followed by Chard's working out of his plans for the defence, ordering the construction of outer and inner ramparts and the final redoubt as well as explaining his defensive tactics.

The scene posed a number of problems for the filmmakers. It was rewritten in every successive script draft, none of them conforming exactly to the one which appears in the film. All the script versions called for Chard's plan of the defences, in which he orders

Filming the 'fighting bull buffalo': Bob Porter (in dark shirt at left) directs the second unit for this deleted scene.

the construction of outer and inner ramparts and the final redoubt as well as explaining his defensive tactics, to be shown first, followed by Adendorff drawing his diagram of the Zulus' attack formation and the officers' argument about the most effective defence strategy, in which Bromhead favours aggressive guerrilla tactics. However it was written, the scene involved lengthy verbal explanations among three people crouched in a group on the ground, with the only visual interest provided by the rough diagrams drawn in the dust. Endfield and his crew resolved this on set by having Chard draw his defence plan as a *response* to Adendorff's explanation of the Zulus' attack formation, and by having him get up and walk around the camp to demonstrate the location and purpose of the redoubt – thus he *shows* us his ideas rather than simply describing them. Bromhead's sense of exclusion and his opposition to Chard's plan are conveyed by having him standing above and to one side on the hospital verandah, then running ineffectually after Chard as the engineer paces out the ramparts.

There was an additional danger of *over-explicitness* in the scripted discussions about what would happen in the event of the Zulus coming over the barricades. The dialogue in the Revised draft reads as follows:

CHARD
(drawing quickly with bayonet)
Get a party to build an inner redoubt. Here at the corner. Six feet high, with a fire-step inside.

BROMHEAD
I don't see...

CHARD
When they come we'll have them trapped *inside* the perimeter, won't we?

ADENDORFF
(sarcastically)
Of course. Stupid of me. I thought they would have *us* trapped.

CHARD
A surprise party, hidden *in* the redoubt see? Twenty men will be enough.
(with brisk enthusiasm)
Men who can fire well, and quickly...
(sketches with bayonet)
Zulus come over. Perimeter defence hold as long as possible, then retire on the double at signal, leaving the Zulus concentrated *inside* the perimeter, to face the point blank fire of the surprise party. That'll hold them till our own men reach the redoubt, reload and add their own fire.

BROMHEAD
It's a gamble taking almost a quarter of our fire power off the perimeter...

ADENDORFF
(more thoughtfully)
It's still a way to handle them when they do come over.

CHARD
That's right.

ADENDORFF
How do we put the plan in action?

CHARD
On bugle-call. When I see we can't hold them any longer, I'll give the word. Or one of you if I'm dead. Or Colour-Sergeant Bourne if none of us is around.

ADENDORFF
(wryly)
You're certain that covers the possibilities?

CHARD
Let's assume so, shall we?
(stands up)

ADENDORFF
(drily)
Do the British always fight on assumptions?

CHARD
(a bleak smile)
One, anyway. They always assume they're going to win. It's a national conceit. Ask Bromhead.

Of course this dialogue describes with admirable clarity what eventually happens – but that is its weakness. It gives away too much, too early. Left in this form, the scene would have reduced the suspense and surprise experienced by the audience in the climactic assault. As the film now has it, Chard's plan is revealed to us, vividly and excitingly, *in action* rather than talk.

Adendorff's presence as the 'token' Afrikaaner in the camp is also used in this scene to invoke the future conflict between the British and the Boers over control of South Africa – the only reference scripts or film make to issues outside the specific events of Rorke's Drift. The Revised script includes an extra few remarks on this subject:

ADENDORFF
We haven't a chance, you know. It doesn't matter to me. I'm a Boer and I'll stay because this is my country and the Zulus are enemies of my bones. But why should *you* be here?

CHARD
Because there aren't enough of you.
(smiles a little)
And weren't the Zulus here before your people?

Now ADENDORFF is angered.

DEVELOPING THE SCREENPLAY 65

More deleted action.

> ADENDORFF
> If that's your point of view, what *are* you doing here?
>
> CHARD
> Do you object to the help?
>
> ADENDORFF
> (wryly)
> It depends on what you British expect to take for it afterwards.

Battle Scenes

Scenes of physical action must be amongst the most difficult to script in advance of production. Only when the director has the opportunity to stage them in front of the cameras can he know whether or not the envisaged business will 'play.' Even then, the finished shots may not cut together, or the sequence may take up too much time in relation to the whole and may have to be reworked or jettisoned entirely, as second unit director Bob Porter explains: 'On every film, there's material which finishes on the cutting room floor. There was some that I'd shot with the second unit of the approach of the "bull's horns" and the advance of the Zulu regiment. But they take an awful long time actually to take place physically on the ground and by the time you've got the whole scene on film you're talking about five or six minutes, so they were the first to go.'

Descriptions of scenes involving the Zulus' approach, showing them travelling across country on their way to Rorke's Drift, were included in both the Revised and Final scripts:

> FULL VISTA SHOT – VALLEY
> High in the hills above the mission station. First nothing but the wind moving across the grass in waves. Then over the ridge comes a line of ZULU warriors, sixteen abreast, and behind that another, in unending sequence. Each warrior with a black shield, behind each shield a hand's-grasp of assegais.
>
> ANOTHER ANGLE – HIGH SHOT
> As another column of ZULUS comes over the ridge, about fifty yards to the right of the first. These are younger men with longer hair, their shields are white.
>
> MED. SHOT – ZULUS
> From the hill itself, as the columns swing by. Now can be heard the drum-thud of pounding feet, the rhythmic hiss as the prancing legs come down. CAMERA PANS to follow the mighty columns down the hill. As they reach the shallow saucer of the valley each begins to turn on itself to form a circle.
>
> CLOSE SHOT – ZULU GENERAL DABULAMANZI
> A magnificent figure, in profile, watching the milling circle beyond him. The pounding feet, swinging kilts, nodding feathers and rising dust. Rhythmical hiss of voices. Abruptly, as DABULAMANZI raises an assegai, stabbing the air and yelling.

Some of this material was also filmed by Porter and his second unit crew, but it too ended up on the cutting room floor. Later in the scripts, after Bourne brings the sentries' report of 'Zulus to the south-west,' they are described awaiting the attack in a valley near the soldiers' camp, sitting in circles and chanting, before rising to move on, 'not as a disorderly mob, but with tight, practised

Bob Porter (at left) directs the second unit, utilising the VistaVision camera.

discipline, company by company, eight abreast, turning out of the sacred circles until they look like a great snake unwinding.'

All this was to be shown prior to the defenders' own first sight of the approaching Zulus, which was described in the various scripts quite differently from that scene's eventual realisation in the film. The Zulus' now-famous first appearance, lining the hillside overlooking Rorke's Drift, was actually an improvisation added during shooting (to be described in a later chapter). The scene of their arrival at the camp as originally intended is described in the Final draft script:

P.O.V. SHOT – THE PLAIN
seen beyond the shoulders of the men at the ramparts, their bayonets held forward like a glistening thorn bush. At first there is nothing on the yellow grass, then the hillside seems to break open and empty a black cataract. It is a wall of shields that the men of the 24th see first, coming up and over the yellow stones and the yellow grass. Fifty white shields on the first wave and behind them each company of the impis coming in perfect order. The mass is thickest at the centre, but on the flanks curve the two horns. They are still far off, but coming quickly, the sun running along the blades of their assegais, kilts swinging, feathers dancing, voices hissing and breaking.

ZULUS
U-su-to…! U-SU-TO…!

CLOSE SHOT – COLE
at the ramparts. He is staring, terrified, at the advancing ZULUS. The noise of their coming is thunderous.

GROUP SHOT – THE ZULUS
They are much closer now, coming shoulder to shoulder in superb order, knees going up and down regularly. At their head is an *induna*, a regimental commander on a grey horse. A monumental feathered figure waving a musket above his head. Dust is swirling; the ZULUS seem inexorable, invincible; triumphant as they begin to sweep up the long, gentle slope toward the southern rampart of the perimeter.

This description is in fact closer to the historical actuality of Rorke's Drift (compare the relevant passage in Prebble's article), in which the Zulus first appeared to the defenders approaching at a run from around the Oskarsberg (Shiyane) Hill. But the film's version is an inspired invention, albeit one dictated partly by necessity. The script's descriptions of Zulus deploying across the landscape in large numbers could not have been filmed exactly as specified because the production team simply did not have as many Zulu extras available as Prebble and Endfield had originally envisaged. Similar logistical considerations also ruled out certain other details described in the screenplays. The Original script refers to 200 horsemen arriving at the camp under Stephenson's command; the Revised and Final scripts, however, scale this down to fifty horsemen, and in the film itself there are only thirty seven – all that the budget would allow.

One scripted piece of business directly inspired by historical accounts of the battle (notably Chard's own) was Corporal Schiess's display of skill with the bayonet.[7] After hobbling out of the hospital, adjusting his foot-bandage and tackling one Zulu with a haymaker's throw (much as in the film), Schiess was to climb onto the barricades:

> There, with a wild yell, he leaps on to the bags, fires his rifle into the chest of a ZULU below him. He leaps down to the far side of the bags, swinging his bayonet and killing a second warrior. He jumps back on to the rampart, looks down, and comes down from behind on to the back of a ZULU who has got over the wall. Both men go down, but SCHIESS rises first, hammering down the butt of his rifle on the prostrate Zulu. SCHIESS straightens his body and breathes in deeply and desperately. He stares into the face of CHARD who is beside him. CHARD nods with the faintest of smiles.
>
> CHARD
> Reporting for duty, Corporal?

Dickie Owen in action as Corporal Schiess.

> For a reply SCHIESS yells incoherently and lunges past CHARD at another Zulu who, having broken over the wall, has a spear raised at CHARD's back.

The Revised and Final scripts simplify this action somewhat, removing the business on the ramparts but adding a line of rhetorical dialogue after Schiess has tackled three Zulus following his rescue of Chard: 'Come on, you bloody red-necks! Let's see some of you do that!' The scripts describe him as 'grinning down like a madman, his face full of bloodlust,' and though the line was cut in the editing, the beginning of this shot can still be seen in the finished film, as Schiess appears to stagger back from the body of the Zulu lying against the mealie bags.[8]

Other figures from the historical record were also given specific roles in the film's battle, but were deleted or reworked for later drafts. The deaths of Corporal Scammell of the Natal Native Contingent and Assistant Storekeeper Louis Byrne, for example, formed the basis for the scene in which Commissary Dalton and the company cook are respectively wounded and killed.[9] Other bits and pieces subsequently eliminated from the Original script include Surgeon Reynolds throwing himself protectively over the wounded Cole when a Zulu is pushed against his operating table (set outside the surgery rather than indoors), and a brief vignette during the evacuation of the burning hospital in which a trooper of the Natal Mounted Police dies in Chard's arms after bayoneting a Zulu. The scene of volley-firing as the Zulus come over the south rampart ('Form two lines – on the double!') was included only in the Final script, as was Bromhead's involvement in the combat on the hospital roof. The Revised and Final scripts give more business to Privates Thomas and Owen during the stampede of cattle, though it may have proved a little too outlandish for use in the film. Owen gives 'a mad, hysterical laugh' as Thomas is described 'with arms outstretched, dancing insanely about on the fringes of the cattle, cooing and crying to them,' before leading the beasts back into their kraal. However, the major change to the battle scenes from the Original draft involved the complete restructuring of their later stages to create a more satisfying climax.

In the first script, the Zulus' last full charge and the defenders' retreat to the inner redoubt take place at dusk. The final volley-firing is followed by the collapse of the burning hospital, whose flames illuminate the piles of Zulu corpses. But the Zulu attacks still continue, in more desultory fashion. As dawn breaks, Chard sends out a patrol led by Sergeant Gallacher (another character present in all the script drafts but eliminated from the film). The patrol comes back to report that it has found nothing but 400 Zulu corpses; 'They've gone. Divil a one left!' says the Irish Gallacher. There follows a description of the surviving defenders emerging, grimy, dazed and disbelieving, from the redoubt. Prebble appended a note to explain the intended tone of this sequence: 'The important climate of feeling in all these shots must not be one of triumph but of tremendous anti-climax.'

If the battle had ended this way in the finished film, audiences too might have felt a sense of anti-climax. The Revised and Final scripts postponed the final assault till daylight, added the 'duel of song' and reduced the number of night-time scenes. Though most of the historical battle had been fought during the hours of darkness, it was clearly felt that this would be visually unappealing as well as arduous to shoot: the preliminary production schedule allowed only a single night for filming the exterior night scenes, including the collapse of the burnt-out hospital. The Final script also permitted Private Owen a last bit of comic relief during the roll call, in which we learn the fate of Private Davies ('a fine bass baritone' who has been wounded in the throat):

> BOURNE
> Davies, four seven oh.
>
> A voice croaks unintelligibly. BOURNE looks up.

BOURNE
Speak up!

TWO SHOT – OWEN AND DAVIES
Standing in ranks. DAVIES's throat is bandaged.

OWEN
He's here! Wounded in the throat!
(to DAVIES, reassuringly)
You'll sing again, boyo…

Alternative Endings

All the script drafts contain versions of the aftermath of the battle, including the reflective dialogue between Chard and Bromhead, the sudden reappearance of the Zulus on the hillside, and the arrival of the relief column, as well as a further tying-up of loose ends, eventually deleted from the film during final editing, which will be described later. There are, however, considerable variations in the way the various scripts dramatise these scenes.

For Bob Porter, the passage in which Chard and Bromhead take stock and Chard reveals his own inexperience in combat provides the core of the film's meaning: 'The scene with Michael and Stanley portrayed to us what the film was all about: that war is an obscenity, a waste of time, a waste of life. That scene brought out everything that we tried to do throughout *Zulu*.' The precise tone of this scene changed somewhat in successive drafts before reaching its present one of grave irony. The Original version reads as follows:

CHARD
(with a look at the other man)
Well, you've fought your first action, Brommy.

BROMHEAD
Yes. I wonder if all men feel like this after it.

CHARD
How do you feel?

BROMHEAD
(quietly)
Sick. Disgusted. Damn silly, isn't it? Was that how it was with you, John? The first time?

CHARD
(almost angrily)
The first time? What the hell's the matter with you Brommy? Did you think I'd been in action before this?

BROMHEAD
(catching fire too)
Well of all the confounded cheek! You strutting about, putting on side!

CHARD
(taking a step toward him)
You infernal pipsqueak! Who the hell do you think you're talking to?

He stops and the two men stare at each other, each suddenly conscious of what they are doing and ashamed. There is strain and weariness in each face. After a pause –

CHARD
(pushing a fist against BROMHEAD's shoulder)
Allright, Brommy.

The Revised script removes the air of embarrassed humour maintained here to make the tone of the discussion more

mordant and to give Bromhead a new-found maturity. This version gives Chard a tougher retort to his innocent query: 'The first time? You damned fool. Do you think I've been in action before? Do you think I could stand this knacker's yard more than once?' (This was wisely altered to 'butcher's yard' in the Final draft.) Here Bromhead's reaction is one of shocked disbelief rather than comic outrage, in keeping with the shift of tone. The Final script adds a further gloss on this dialogue, echoing the anti-military theme associated with Chard, who responds to Bromhead's remark that they haven't done too badly: 'Not too much blood on our commissions, you mean? Do you think they'll make *you* a colonel now?'

When the Zulus make their final appearance, all the script drafts describe the despairing reaction of the now demoralised and dispirited soldiers:

> They are frozen in exhaustion. They can't move. They have done all and more than could have been expected of them. They stare up to the hills. ONE SOLDIER breaks down, his head in his hands. They are finished.
> BOURNE and the SERGEANTS move among them, shaking them, coaxing them, threatening them. It is no good ... CHARD swings round. He is no longer a human being, but an iron automaton red-eyed, fierce. He alone is the only man in the defence able to stand on his feet with the will left to fight.

Prebble took his inspiration for this scene from the aftermath of the actual battle, when on the morning of 23 January a large force of Zulus was spotted by the defenders on a hill some distance from the camp; they were, apparently, observing the distant approach of the relief column from a position of safety. The decision to turn this into a deliberate 'salute' to the surviving defenders was a brilliant conceit. The soldiers' realisation that the Zulus are not about to attack again is, however, given a different cast in the film by comparison with the scripts. All three drafts segue directly to the arrival of the relief force (in the manner of the last-minute cavalry rescue of the traditional Western), suggesting that this is the reason for the Zulus' retreat rather than a dignified voluntary withdrawal.

The arrival of the relief column was followed by the return to the camp of Otto and Margareta Witt – leading to perhaps the most significant and substantial of all the scenes cut from the completed film. It reunites Chard and Margareta and suggests a grudging rapprochement between them, perhaps even the beginnings of a tentative romance. It is present, with certain variations, in all the versions of the screenplay and was actually shot, though of all the crew members I have interviewed for this book, only actor Richard Davies (who was not on location but who saw the rushes back in London) and sound technician David Jones remember it. The decision to remove what is virtually a dramatic postscript was evidently made at a very late stage of post-production. It was included in the printed synopsis sent to the American Production Code Administration to assist the film's passage through the US censorship system: 'a stirring of dust appears on the horizon, followed by a charging column of British cavalry and missionary Witt and his daughter, who have returned, chastened, to do what they can.' Stills of the scene were even made available to exhibitors for publicity purposes, albeit supplied with a caption which fails to describe accurately what the picture shows (see illustration on page 72).

What follows is the unexpurgated version of this deleted scene from the on-location revisions to the shooting script:

> CHARD AND BROMHEAD
> They are standing, feet astride, hands behind their backs, watching a GRAVE-DIGGING PARTY, at work beyond the broken perimeter. They look up to the hillside.
>
> WIDE SHOT – SOUTH VIEW
> THE CAVALRY coming on screen from the left at the gallop breaking from column into skirmishing line, and at last halting in a screen beyond the station and the hill where the ZULUS were last seen.

BROMHEAD
Well, well, your cavalry has arrived.

CHARD looks at the watch in his hand and sniffs wryly.

BROMHEAD
A relief column with nothing to relieve. How disappointing for them. Perhaps they'll take on a bit of Guard duty while we get forty winks.

Meanwhile CHARD has turned around, in back-ground we see the Buggy arriving from the South. It halts. WITT and MARGARETA alight.

CHARD
I don't think our time is our own, yet.

BROMHEAD
(moving off)
Oh…. Yes, I've suddenly thought of something urgent that needs attention.[10]

BUGGY in distance. MARGARETA walking towards CHARD. He turns his head, sees her. Slowly, wearily he leaves the DIGGING PARTY and walks towards her.

TWO SHOT – CHARD AND MARGARETA
as they meet. WITT APPROACHING in background.

CHARD
(not understanding)
Why… what do you want?

MARGARETA
This is my home!

WITT arrives, his face haggard. He looks about him, and then:

WITT
You're alive…

CHARD
You were a bad prophet, Mr Witt.

WITT
(exultant)
I thank God with you all!

CHARD is about to answer this, then he looks at the distant hills. There is a wondering admiration in his tone.

CHARD
Your Zulu parishioners did well.

He turns back to WITT, his tone hardening.

The arrival of the relief column was filmed but deleted in the editing.

CHARD
They've seen the Bible in your hands and the Martini-Henry rifle in ours. What are they supposed to make of that choice?[11]

WITT
(hurt and confused)
Mr Chard, it is written that we must all walk in newness of life…

CHARD cannot argue. He nods wearily, walks off.

WITT
Mr Chard…!
(moves forward)

MARGARETA
(stopping him)
Father… *No!*
(and then, as if giving an order to a child)
Go to the wounded!

WITT looks at her, not understanding the change in her. He takes a step backward, turns and walks toward the church. She watches him.

TWO SHOT
Chard has reached the mealie-bag ramparts, facing CAMERA. In B.G. [background] WITT is walking toward the church. MARGARETA is coming toward CHARD. CHARD takes off his helmet and wipes his

This publicity still issued to journalists was captioned as follows: 'As the Battle of Rorke's Drift begins, Margareta Witt (Ulla Jacobsson) makes one last effort to persuade Lieutenant Chard (Stanley Baker) to allow her father to evacuate the mission hospital.' The fact that the relief column is visible in the background, and that Chard's uniform bears the blood-stain from the wound he received *after* the Witts' departure from the camp, should have alerted careful observers to the deception being attempted here: it actually shows the deleted scene of Margareta's return and reunion with Chard.

forehead with the back of his hand. He turns to MARGARETA as she reaches him. He glances toward WITT in distance (c.s.) [close shot] and looks back at her. She answers the unspoken question.

MARGARETA
He's gone to help your wounded. Will they understand?

CHARD
He'll be surprised. The men will like him now they know he has a weakness… That's the way it is…

MARGARETA
It might be better if they admired him for his strength.

CHARD
It might be better, but it wouldn't be natural.

He looks down, MARGARETA shakes her head upset.

MARGARETA
You can't talk of weakness as if it's a virtue… It's not! Either a man is good or….

He stops. He is too tired to talk to her. He squints up to the sky, then down again.

CHARD
It's going to be hot again today. There are almost four hundred dead Zulus out there, Miss Witt. By noon you should be able to smell them.

MARGARETA
Why are you trying to shock me?

CHARD
Am I?
(looks at her and smiles quickly)
If you want to understand men, Miss Witt, you must first accept the feelings you arouse in them….
(He has said too much)
Excuse me. I must see to my command……

FULL SHOT – PERIMETER
Now the men of the 24th break into delirious joy, yelling, throwing up helmets, flood out to greet the CAVALRY.

TWO SHOT
MARGARETA
No! Wait…
(then uncertainly)
What was it…? I mean…

CHARD
What was it like? I suppose we behaved as you said we would. Like animals, wasn't it.

MARGARETA
And you'll think all this has been glorious?

CHARD
(with disgust)
Glory's a cheap thank-you from those who profit by a soldier's death!

MARGARETA
Then the soldier's a fool!

CHARD
(gently)
Yes, he's a fool or he wouldn't have enlisted.
(harshly)
I'll tell you something…
(then softening)

Perhaps Man is an animal, Miss Witt. But black or white what distinguished him from the rest of the jungle here today was his courage, his willingness to give his life. Can you understand that? That he was sacrificing something he cherished?

MARGARETA
For what?

CHARD
(a short, bitter laugh)
For what?
(and then only half-cynically)
Rorke's Drift will probably become a page in the regimental history, Miss Witt. Something to stiffen a recruit's courage in the next war to which some damn fool commits us.

MARGARETA
(almost crying in bewilderment)
Is that all there is to it?

CHARD
(breaking momentarily)
Good God, isn't it enough?
(then gentler, wanting to understand it himself)
Now and then all men wonder how much courage they have. And now and then a soldier shows them. Perhaps that's his only purpose.

MARGARETA
(protesting)
No! A man's life should be worth more than that!

CHARD
(shaking his head)
Not a soldier's life. His country told him the value of that when he enlisted. It's a shilling. *One shilling a day.*

He slowly raises his hand to the peak of his helmet, turns away from her and begins to walk down the hill toward the SOLDIERS.

Another moment from the deleted final scene. The shooting script describes Chard's demeanour as he sits exhausted after the battle: 'His face has undergone a remarkable change. As if the muscles and bones that had held together his customary expression of defensive reserve [have] now dissolved. His face shows a sickening exhaustion and disgust, a great sense of isolation and loneliness.'

MARGARETA stands quite still watching him. Then, on impulse, she follows. Over the scene we hear the beginning of the NARRATOR'S VOICE. As the CAMERA MOVES BACK to show the battle-torn setting of Rorke's Drift.

The length of time it will have taken to read this scene should indicate clearly enough why it was necessary ultimately to remove it. Left intact, it would have added perhaps five minutes or more to the film's running time. The weakness of the material lies not just in over-length but also in the fact that it is too 'on the nose,' spelling out a moral paradox or humanist message which is already implicit in the preceding drama. To have a lengthy dialogue at this point, after the unexpected tension of the Zulus' sudden reappearance and their neck-prickling salute, and at a moment when many in the audience would already be reaching for their coats, would surely have invited disaster. Whoever made the decision to axe this scene – Endfield, Baker, editor John Jympson or Prebble himself – may well have saved the entire picture.

Notes

[1] Letter, John Prebble to Cy Endfield, 7 January 1963. Note again the apparent typo mentioned previously: the date on the letter is actually 1962.

[2] First assistant director Bert Batt recalls seeing an early version of the script (circa 1959) which was virtually all battle, with no sympathetic figures to root for, and suggested to Endfield that the characters needed to be more developed if the film was to have audience appeal.

[3] These copies of the shooting script are available for consultation in the British Film Institute Library's Special Collections.

[4] In the Treatment, Margareta is absent from the wedding dance, making her first appearance later at the mission, but she is by the Reverend's side in all the script versions of this scene.

[5] The correct spelling of the historical figure's name was Millne. Prebble received a friendly letter (dated 19 February 1964) from his daughter-in-law, Henrietta Millne, after she had read about him in an exchange of correspondence about the film in the *Daily Telegraph*. In his reply, Prebble apologised for the misspelling in his letter to the *Telegraph* – though, as he pointed out, the spelling 'was that used by Lieutenant Chard in his dispatch and nominal roll.' Referring to Mrs Millne's anticipation at being invited to attend the first-night screening in Manchester, Prebble added: 'I hope, when you see the film, that it does him and his comrades proper credit' (26 February 1964). Millne's own account of his experiences at Rorke's Drift is reproduced in Alan Baynham Jones and Lee Stevenson, *Rorke's Drift: By Those Who Were There* (Brighton: Lee Stevenson Publishing, 2003), pp. 183-5.

[6] See Christopher Sharrett, '*Zulu* or the limits of liberalism,' *Cineaste*, vol. XXV, no. 4 (2000), p. 30.

[7] The longer of Chard's two accounts of the battle, prepared at the personal request of Queen Victoria, includes the description of Schiess's actions; it can be found in Baynham Jones and Stevenson, p. 29.

[8] Bruce Dettman wrote to inform me that he recalls seeing a slightly extended version of this scene on the film's original US theatrical release, in which Schiess 'turns all the way and faces the camera with a maniacal grin on his face' (email to the author, 19 May 2004).

[9] See for example the Reverend George Smith's eyewitness account in Baynham Jones and Lee Stevenson, pp. 185-92. For the reasoning behind Prebble's decision not to include Smith among the defenders to be dramatised, see the chapter 'Creating the Characters.'

[10] A handwritten annotation at this point on one of the copies of the script held by the *bfi* reads: 'Presumably he wants to pee!' As the scripts were donated by associate producer Basil Keys, I suspect this is a sample of Basil's acerbic sense of humour.

[11] The first set of revision notes substitutes the following lines at this point: 'They've seen the Bible in your hands and the Martini-Henry rifle in ours. Between us I think we've made this country safe for white men, don't you think?'

"I SUPPOSE YOU HAVE SENIORITY?"

CY ENDFIELD
DIRECTOR/CO-WRITER/CO-PRODUCER

> I have always been in showbusiness in one form or another ... as a conjuror, or directing stage plays and musicals ... but to me film directing is the most fascinating business of them all. One must use every sense and every talent as a director – composition, motion, mathematics – in the working out of movement not only of the actors but of the machinery and equipment used.
> (Cy Endfield, *Zulu* Production Information Dossier, p. 21)

First assistant director Bert Batt remembers visiting Cy Endfield at home to talk about the film before going on location and found the director teaching himself to play the flute. 'He'd got the stand, and he had one of these classical records in which the flute part was missing. He had the music for the flute and was playing it.' An authentic polymath and Renaissance man, in addition to his film career Endfield enjoyed myriad interests in science and literature, chess and sports, sculpture and painting, wood-carving and silver-smithing, and especially conjuring and card tricks. Publicity for *Zulu* called him 'an expert sculptor, painter, flautist, squash player, caber-tosser, hammer-thrower, to mention but a few of his accomplishments.' During his lifetime, Endfield was regarded as one of the world's leading magicians and card tricksters. On the plane to South Africa, Bert recalls, his 'eyes were almost out on stalks' at Cy's skill with cards: 'It was sheer magic. Before continuing on to Durban we overnighted in Johannesburg and waiting at the airport to meet him were members of the South African Magic Circle.'

Cyril Raker Endfield was born in Scranton, a mining town in Pennsylvania, on 10 November 1914. He passed the entrance exam for Yale University in 1932 but his entry was delayed by a year when his father's business, selling fur coats, went bankrupt. Years later, Cy identified this, along with the Depression, as the initial cause of his sense of grievance against society: 'I was looking around for something to be wrong with it,' he told Brian Neve.[1] In his first year at Yale, Cy joined a small progressive theatre company in New Haven, Connecticut. He became briefly involved with the Young Communist League, though he never formally joined the Party: 'I just didn't have the personal discipline, nor, most important, the desire to part with dues.' His student political activity was limited to supporting unions in local industrial disputes, picketing in demonstrations and occasionally organising militant action on behalf of the poorly paid and under-privileged; he described himself as an 'incorrigible experimenter' rather than a revolutionary. According to his widow, Maureen, 'At Yale he would think the women workers weren't paid enough and he'd go into the street on strike for them. He just had a sense of justice.'

Having switched from science to philosophy and then to an arts course – the arts faculty was nearer home – Endfield left

Yale before graduating. 'He was too impatient,' explains Maureen. He moved to New York, where he would live on friends' couches and hound agents to get him onto the 'Borscht belt' circuit of Jewish cabaret clubs in the Catskills Mountains. He eventually succeeded when he answered the phone in his agent's office while the agent was out. The client was looking for a director-choreographer and Endfield successfully recommended himself for the job: 'We have this great young man called Cy Endfield....' Cy later worked for left-wing organisations like the New Theater League, where he associated with the future film director Joseph Losey and such performers as Shelley Winters (a close friend) and Martin Balsam, played night-clubs, weddings and bar mitzvahs with his own satirical revue troupe, performed a magic act and ran an amateur theatre company in Montreal.

Endfield moved to Los Angeles in September 1940 and struggled to get into the film industry. He worked in the Hollywood Magic Store on Hollywood Boulevard, whose frequent customer Orson Welles was so impressed by his card skills that Cy was able to wangle a job as an assistant in Welles' production company, Mercury, which was then making *The Magnificent Ambersons* (1942) at RKO Radio studios. At the rival MGM, studio executive Dore Schary was instrumental in enabling Endfield to direct his first film, a twenty-minute short called *Inflation* (1942), starring Edward Arnold and the future star of aquatic musicals, Esther Williams ('I directed Esther Williams before she swam,' Cy later recalled). A witty propaganda exercise, commissioned by the Office of War Information to warn the wartime public against the dangers of excessive materialism, it was nonetheless condemned as subversive by the US Chamber of Commerce and the Treasury and all prints were withdrawn before release.

Endfield's career suffered a further setback when, after only eight months in the film industry, he was called up for service in the Army Signal Corps in Missouri. 'He was overweight and the army sergeants loved having a rookie film director on their patch,' says Maureen. 'They made his life hell. He finally got an honourable discharge because of a spastic colon.' When he returned to Hollywood Cy made eight other short subjects for MGM before leaving the studio to make his debut feature, *Gentleman Joe Palooka* (1946). This, like most of his subsequent American films, was destined for the lower half of a cinema double bill: a low-budget affair made in a few days for Monogram, one of the many small 'Poverty Row' studios which lived in the shadow of the majors. Its successors, the comedies *Stork Bites Man* (1947) and *Joe Palooka in the Big City* (1949), were regarded as negligible even by Cy himself, though he thought more highly of *The Argyle Secrets* (1948), a mystery based on his own script for the radio series *Suspense*. He tried and failed to secure a starring vehicle for a young actress whose talent he believed in and who was briefly his assistant in his stage magic act. According to Maureen, 'Marilyn Monroe was a very close friend of Cy's. He desperately

Cy Endfield in 1939, when he was living in Montreal.

wanted to use her in something, but he was never able to pull it off. Somehow the people he took her to just couldn't see it.'

Cy did achieve a measure of success with two powerful independent productions of 1950. *The Underworld Story* is an extraordinary film noir thriller with Dan Duryea as one of the least sympathetic protagonists in Hollywood history. *The Sound of Fury* (also released in America as *Try and Get Me!*) is perhaps Endfield's most celebrated work besides *Zulu*. The story of an ordinary man (Frank Lovejoy), drawn into crime to help his family, who ultimately becomes the victim of a lynch mob, it offers little in the way of easy comfort, despite a preachy message tacked on by the producer over Cy's objections. Though neither of these films was a commercial hit, they did get Cy noticed and he was hired by producer Sol Lesser to direct the latest in his long-running Tarzan series for RKO, *Tarzan's Savage Fury* (1952), starring Lex Barker.

While it was being filmed, on 19 September 1951 Endfield was identified before the House Un-American Activities Committee as a Communist by screenwriter Martin Berkeley. Cy was in good company: among the 161 other people named as Communists by Berkeley, who has been described as HUAC's number one 'friendly witness,' were writers Carl Foreman, Dashiell Hammett, Lillian Hellman, Dorothy Parker, Budd Schulberg and Dalton Trumbo, and directors Herbert J. Biberman, Robert Rossen and Bernard Vorhaus.[2] Cy had been expecting and dreading such an exposure for some time, but the charge that he was the treasurer of the

Endfield (in spectacles) clowns around with actors Charles Korvin, Patric Knowles and Lex Barker on the RKO studio jungle set of *Tarzan's Savage Fury* **in 1951, the director's last film in Hollywood before his exile to England.**

Party's Hollywood branch was trumped up and the extent of his involvement in politics grossly exaggerated. His Communist associations were by now ten years old and he had already begun to have his doubts about Communism after the Hitler-Stalin pact, though he still considered himself a progressive. 'The reason he became involved with the Communist set in Los Angeles,' comments Maureen, 'was because they had something known as the "Red table" in the MGM studio commissary, where all the bright minds would sit, and he wanted to be among them. But he was never really a political animal. It was a mistake.'[3]

Cy had determined that he would not sacrifice his career on a point of principle. His agent asked if he would become a friendly witness before HUAC to identify other present or former Communists, and he considered naming only those who had already been named; but conscience got the better of him and Endfield found that he couldn't do it. In 1989 he told the BBC: 'In addition to the political question of whether you had the right to have your ideas, you had the moral question: do you snitch, do you become an informer – a dreaded, hated word, especially in the film business, because they made a picture called *The Informer*. I think there's a tradition that you don't rat on a fellow human being [with] whom you've had a common purpose at one time, no matter what the pressure.'[4] His directing contract having been bought out, Cy decided instead to leave the country (he had successfully applied for a passport several months before being named). 'He always said, you never know what you're going to do until the moment hits you,' says Maureen. 'His only options were to go to Mexico or France or come here. He didn't speak French, so he went from Los Angeles to New York and then to London.' In later years, when the political temperature had cooled sufficiently, Cy was able to revisit America without fear of persecution, though contrary to reports in some sources, Maureen insists that he never resorted to identifying other former Communists to restore his professional

The recently married Maureen and Cy Endfield.

standing, and despite continuing to reside in Britain he always retained his American citizenship. 'On a professional level I feel very bitter because I feel I was cheated by hostile forces,' he said, looking back on this period in 1989. He also resented the fact that many people whom he had helped get a start in the industry no longer wanted to be associated with him after he was named.

Endfield embarked for England on the *Queen Mary* in December 1951, arriving in Southampton on New Year's Eve after a particularly rough sea crossing. He met Maureen Forshaw, his second wife, six weeks later, though they didn't become romantically involved for another couple of years. They were always bumping into one another in the company of mutual friends – 'I think we started going out together because we had nothing else to do!' she jokes – and married in 1956, subsequently giving birth to two daughters (he already had one daughter from an earlier marriage). Cy's working life in London was not at all easy at first, as he was constantly threatened with deportation. 'Policemen would actually come to the door saying he had to leave the country by the end of the week, and he'd rush around to some producer who was going to make a film and would write letters saying he was going to give work to seventy people, and somehow he would manage to stay.'

Like Joseph Losey and many other victims of the Communist blacklist resident in Britain, Cy found work in television. In 1952 he helped producer Hannah Weinstein find financial

Cy directs *Hell Drivers* in VistaVision.

backing for three pilot episodes of a television mystery series, *Colonel March of Scotland Yard*, starring Boris Karloff as an inspector in the 'Department of Queer Complaints.'[5] Cy directed these himself and they were joined together to form his first British feature, *Colonel March Investigates* (1953). Four other B-movie thrillers followed, all starring second-rank American leads: *The Limping Man* (1953), *The Master Plan* (1954), *Impulse* (1955) and *The Secret* (1955). In order to avoid distribution problems in the US, where cinema projectionists in the right-wing technical union IATSE would refuse to run films bearing the names of blacklisted writers and directors, Endfield was forced to hide his identity behind professional pseudonyms. For *The Master Plan* he became Hugh Raker (Raker being his mother's maiden name), while on *The Limping Man*, *Impulse* and *Child in the House* (1956) he used a friend, Charles de Lautour, as a standby or 'front,' whom Cy paid the union minimum of £35 per week from his own salary for the use of his name on the credits. 'Charles de Lautour was a dear, sweet man with no ambitions,' recalls Maureen. 'He'd sit on the set not doing a thing.' Endfield also took on other work without credit, including rewriting the screenplay of the occult classic *Night of the Demon* (1957, known in America as *Curse of the Demon*) for its American producer Hal E. Chester, a former Poverty Row associate.

Child in the House, a sentimental drama featuring child star Mandy Miller, was also notable as the film which introduced Cy to Stanley Baker. The actor starred in Endfield's next three films, made for Cy's own

Baker and Endfield in conference on *Zulu*.

production companies, Aqua and Pendennis.[6] *Hell Drivers* (1957) is a vigorous action melodrama about fiercely competitive road haulage workers, with a remarkable cast of up-and-coming actors including Patrick McGoohan and Sean Connery. *Sea Fury* (1958) stars Baker, Victor McLaglen (his last film role) and the young Robert Shaw as tugboat seamen in action off the Spanish coast. *Jet Storm* (1959) is an all-star 'group jeopardy'

Cy on the set of *Zulu*.
(Jürgen Schadeberg)

suspense thriller, in which mad bomber Richard Attenborough threatens to blow up pilot Baker's airliner.[7] Endfield tested IATSE's reaction by using C. Raker Endfield as his directorial credit on all these films, and as the composer of the title song for *Jet Storm* (performed by Marty Wilde) he allowed himself to be billed as Cy Endfield for the first time, having used Cyril while directing in Hollywood. He then accepted an offer from producer Charles Schneer to direct *Mysterious Island* (1961) – a Jules Verne fantasy set during the American Civil War, starring Herbert Lom as Captain Nemo and featuring stop-motion monsters created by Ray Harryhausen – solely because it presented the first opportunity to use his own name on an American-produced film. Cy followed it with *Hide and Seek* (1962), a Cold War comedy-drama starring Curt Jurgens and Ian Carmichael, which sat on the shelf for nearly two years before being released in 1964.

While directing for the cinema, Endfield also kept busy with other activities. In 1955 a three-volume collection of his card tricks, *Cy Endfield's Entertaining Card Magic*, was published and he was also involved in theatre, television and advertising.[8] Some of his TV commercials, such as the 'People Love Player's' cigarette campaign, won awards, and Endfield later 'discovered' the 1960s' leading fashion model, Jean Shrimpton. Among the West End stage productions he directed were a one-woman show featuring Cornelia Otis Skinner at the St. Martin's Theatre, the plays *The Teddy Bear*, *Paris '90*, *Midnight Hour* and an adaptation of his own screenplay for *The Secret*. He enjoyed a major hit with Neil Simon's first stage comedy *Come Blow Your Horn*, starring Bob Monkhouse and Michael Crawford, which from 1962 ran for two years at the Prince of Wales Theatre (during which time the cast auditions for *Zulu* were held in the theatre's bar).

In 1959 Endfield began his association with John Prebble on the project which, after five years of arduous work, would become *Zulu*. It was a rare project for Endfield in that, in tandem with his star and co-producer Stanley Baker, he enjoyed full creative control. 'Cy always said that *Zulu* was the only film where he'd been left to get on and do what he wanted,' says Maureen. 'Joe Levine was a very good producer in that respect. You must remember that Cy's background was one of bitter disappointment. Throughout his career he was always worried about the next job because no-one ever brought projects to him. So he had a discipline of getting on with the job.' Cy worked punishingly long hours on location: 'He'd be up at the crack of dawn. Cy always insisted on having breakfast with the children before he went off to the set. At the end of the day he'd have to see rushes or there'd be one of the interminable union meetings or things to discuss about the next day's shooting. Then we'd have dinner and slink off to bed. Cy at that time also developed a very bad back for several weeks. I cried because he'd be in such agony that he had to be carried to the set on a stretcher.'

Bert Batt has his own memories of one of Cy's afflictions: 'Cy came out one morning and he obviously hadn't done his homework. He didn't know what he was going to do with the sequence, but the crafty bugger came with a stick – he pretended he'd hurt his back. I knew it was absolute codswallop, but it was thinking time! We eventually got a couple of set-ups done, and we were getting another one ready and I couldn't find Cy. The hospital building was made of tubular steel inside with planks around the side and straw on top – there was no interior as such. I happened to

Cy plays checkers with African crew members.

Cy addresses the audience of a retrospective season of his and Stanley Baker's films at the Cinémathèque Française in October 1964. The cinema's curator, Henri Langlois, stands at right.

walk round the back of the church and saw Cy inside – the walking stick's on the floor and he was doing pull-ups on a tubular bar. I said "Cy!" and he turned round so fast he hit his head on another bar and knocked himself out!' Although she laughs at the thought, Maureen insists that Cy would never have faked a bad back just to make time for himself. 'He was not a good invalid. He really did have serious back problems. He had a tubular frame at home on which he always exercised. I nearly broke *my* back on it once!' Sound technician David Jones (who remembers him as 'a bit of a strange beast – a rather eccentric director') also says that Cy injured his back for quite a long period and had an upright board made to lean against while on set.

Despite the rigours of filming, Endfield still managed to keep up his other interests during the shoot and amazed the crew with his varied abilities, as James Booth recalls: 'Cy was always inventing conjuring tricks. Most of the time he didn't seem to be directing a movie at all. He was a very quiet, introspective kind of genius. He had the mind of a conjuror and his direction was like conjuring. He used to create things out of nothing.' Ellen Baker remembers that 'Cy used to do a coin-rolling trick with his fingers – all day long on the set of *Zulu*. He was an astonishing man. He was incredibly talented.' The Bakers' eldest son, Martin, who, aged ten, stayed on location with his two younger siblings and Cy's own two daughters, Susannah and Eden, recalls the director as a yo-yo and ping-pong champion who would always make time during breaks in shooting to entertain the children with magic or a yo-yo trick.[9]

Batt found Cy 'fine to work with – a very easy-going guy, very gentle and clever,' while

Glynn Edwards also remembers him fondly: 'He was very sensitive to artists – a good guy. He was what I thought an American director would be like. He came on set with a baseball cap, tee-shirt and sneakers. "Go out there and do it!" – that was Cy. He was good to relax with at the hotel afterwards. But don't play a game of cards with him! He could make cards get up and walk if he wanted to.' Sound editor Rusty Coppleman, who worked with the director during post-production in England, was struck by Endfield's air of diffidence: 'Cy was a strange man really. He never seemed obstinate about getting his own way; he would always listen, but he was very persuasive.'

Yet despite his geniality with some of the company, to others Cy could be (in Edwards' words) 'a bit of a bully.' Bob Porter's wife at the time, Nan, describes Cy as 'a very complex man,' intense and fiercely competitive, who 'sank into the ground' if he lost a game of chess. Assistant editor Jennifer Thompson says that 'Cy was difficult – he was not the easiest of men. I remember the day we went to Technicolor to do the titles, he lost his cool.' Maureen Endfield suggests that the abrasive relationships with Cy suffered by some of the actors and technicians may have resulted from his frustration at being unable to explain his ideas precisely. 'He lived in his head. Cy always had a picture in his own mind of his concept, but maybe he was not always so good at communicating to other people what he had in mind. This was what particularly amazed the crew about *Zulu* when they first saw it, because to them it was disjointed and not cohesive and suddenly this amazing film came out of it all. They said to him, we'd have behaved a bit better if we knew what you were at! Even Joe Levine, when they ran the first screening at Paramount, said, "Gee kid, I didn't know you were going to make a *good* film out of it!" He thought he was just *selling* a film.'

Zulu was Cy's greatest popular success, and it also won him critical attention of a kind he rarely enjoyed during his lifetime. In October 1964, to coincide with the film's opening in Paris, the Cinémathèque Française hosted a season of films by Endfield and Baker, including all the films they had made together and several they had made separately. Cy pronounced himself delighted and flattered by the honour because 'while the Cinémathèque has previously honoured individual artists in this way, this is the first time a director-actor team has been recognised.'[10] However, the team's next film together, their sixth, was also to be their last. *Sands of the Kalahari* (1965) suffered numerous production difficulties from the outset, including the withdrawal of its original casting choices. 'It was originally meant to be with Richard Burton and Elizabeth Taylor,' recalls Maureen, 'and though Cy never liked the book that it was based on, it was quite a good career move to work with them. When they left Cy felt he should have too, but he had a commitment to fulfil.'

Despite its many problems, the film is an impressively stark adventure about the struggle for survival and supremacy between

Cy in later life, pictured with his most successful invention, the Microwriter.

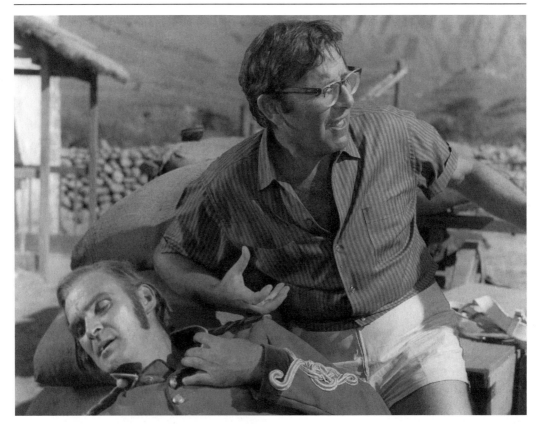

plane crash victims in the African desert. Nonetheless, it flopped critically and at the box-office, scuppering Endfield's chances of realising a number of other projects. 'The film didn't do well and it was a disaster because Cy had various projects that he wanted Paramount to do, and Joe Levine was very anxious to work with him again, but he had a lot of people who turned down whatever Cy wanted to make. It was a very difficult time for him. Cy was going to do three films in one year and was wondering how he would fit them all in, but none of them happened. He was going to do a film with Richard Harris, who went off to do *Caprice* with Doris Day, and he was going to do *The Seagull* with Rudolf Nureyev, who then got the chance to direct his first ballet abroad, so these things would disintegrate. Terence Stamp desperately wanted to make *Precious Bane* with Cy and Julie Christie. He was so excited about it he knocked on the door at 5.00am after he'd read the script.' But then he and Cy fell out over an abortive business deal of Stamp's and this film too was abandoned; the two friends never spoke again. 'This is probably why Cy developed a nervous disposition, because so much effort and creativity goes into making a film and you're at the mercy of so many elements.'[11]

Cy considered moving back to the US, though Maureen says she 'dampened that idea – from what I'd seen of Hollywood I didn't think it was a good place to bring up two children. But as a career move it would probably have been very good.' Cy was eventually able to direct again when he replaced the scheduled director, Michael Reeves, on *De Sade* (1969), a biography of the notorious Marquis starring Keir Dullea. But this too was a troubled production. It was an attempt by American International Pictures, a company better known for horror and exploitation movies, to make a 'prestige' picture, but screenwriter Richard Matheson disliked Cy's restructuring of his screenplay. The director fell seriously ill while on location in Europe, and the film was completed, without credit, by Roger Corman. The rushes of this material – mainly orgy scenes, according to some observers – were viewed by Endfield from his hospital bed.[12] 'He should never have made *De Sade*,' believes Maureen. 'We were in Germany for three months and Cy couldn't be moved. He'd taken the project just to make a film – he liked the idea of working with [co-stars] John Huston and Lilli Palmer. We never really discovered the nature of the illness. It was possibly some kind of hepatitis.'

Endfield's final film as director, *Universal Soldier* (1971), starred one-time James Bond George Lazenby as a mercenary seduced by the peace movement. It was barely released, though the director himself appeared in a small role with some tellingly autobiographical dialogue about political exile. After its failure, Cy turned his attention to other projects. He designed a commemorative portable chess set in gold and silver for the 1972 World Tournament. 'That was such a roaring success that he started to invent other things,' says Maureen. 'If he'd done it earlier he wouldn't have bothered about films. He probably should have been a scientist. Film was his main occupation, but he kept up to date with developments in science. He had a fantastic brain. He taught himself to play musical instruments, loved sport and had many diverse interests. He had a brain that was literally bursting with ideas.' Cy's most famous inventions were the Microwriter, a five-key pocket typewriter, and the Agenda, a computerised personal organiser.[13]

Cy returned to film-making for one last venture when he co-wrote (with Anthony Storey) the screenplay of *Zulu Dawn* (1979). This was initially meant as a reunion project with Stanley Baker, but advance preparations in 1975 coincided with the first signs of what was to be the actor's terminal illness. Endfield withdrew and the film was eventually directed by Douglas Hickox. Disappointed with the finished picture, another box-office failure, Cy turned his screenplay into a novel. He took out an apartment in Monte Carlo and wrote the entire manuscript on his own invention, the Microwriter. Published the same year the film

Affectionate testimony to Cy Endfield's penchant for shooting multiple takes is provided by the following ditty, circulated amongst the crew during the shooting of *Zulu*. It should be sung to the tune of 'As Time Goes By.'

THE TWIST

You must remember this
The twist is just the twist
And Cy is just a Cy,
There are many versions of the twist
But there's only one Cy.

The Unit groans in pain
When he says we'll go again,
For on that you can rely
He's never got a shot in one,
Because he's Cy.

We wake up bright and early,
To get a shot at dawn
By the time he's made his mind up
The dawn has been and gone.

But Bert and Stanley Baker
Are pushing things along
And no one can deny.

And now that *Zulu*'s over,
And we are on our way,
And we have time to think
He's never bought the boys a drink,
Still then – he's only Cy.

Anonymous
(Courtesy of Jennifer Thompson)

was released, the book sold 250,000 copies in Britain alone.

In his remaining years, with his eyesight failing, Endfield largely retired from showbusiness, apart from unsuccessfully attempting to set up a television series, *Superbrain*, with the magician Chan Canasta. 'Cy was not a self-promoter at all,' says Maureen. 'If he'd only had a bit of Michael Winner's chutzpah he could have been well-known. He didn't like to revisit his old films – he was always much more interested in moving forward. He was born too early – he should have been part of this generation.' Belated recognition was awarded him at the 1992 Telluride Film Festival in Colorado, including the first public screening after half a century on the shelf of Endfield's debut film *Inflation*. A programme note for the retrospective was provided by Jonathan Rosenbaum, film reviewer of *The Chicago Reader* and perhaps the only major critic to have celebrated Endfield as a serious filmmaker, albeit one whose socially critical work is not always easy to take:

> [T]hough Endfield's films are usually entertaining, viewers who expect to find the security blankets of charismatic heroes and neat psychological explanations are likely to be perturbed – at times even scared and shaken – by their relative absence in his work. With rare exceptions, these are upsetting movies with values that are often difficult to separate from Endfield's negativity and his capacity to depress us. People who go to movies in order to flee distress – and who no doubt expect their evening news to be cheerful and easily digestible as well – are advised to stay miles away from Endfield's corrosive work.[14]

Cy Endfield died of cerebral vascular disease in Shipston-on-Stour, Warwickshire, on 16 April 1995. A memorial celebration was held two months later at London's National Film Theatre, where *Inflation* was shown along with clips from *The Sound of Fury*, *Hell Drivers* and *Zulu*, and tributes were paid by Hal Chester, Martin Baker and John Prebble (both Baker and Prebble read extracts from Michael Caine's autobiography in the actor's enforced absence). Cy's own assessment of himself and his greatest success was related to interviewer Brian Neve in 1989:

> I think my talent for making pictures was best expressed in two pictures, *The Sound of Fury* and *Zulu*, because I think the one big talent I have is to make big pictures. There is a sense of structure about something of dimension that I have found lacking even in pictures that were supposed to be big ... *Zulu* is a two hour twenty minute picture, of which an hour and twenty was battle. The battle only consisted of two things – the Zulus coming up and being shot down. Two movements, and they had to be made into a symphony, and linked with a small theme. This had to be made into a unit. I know that it succeeded. I was really amazed that it did what I meant it to do.

Notes

1 Interview with Brian Neve, 19 December 1989. Unless otherwise noted, subsequent comments by Endfield derive from this source (unpublished at time of writing), courtesy of Professor Neve.

2 For a nearly complete list of the showbusiness personnel Berkeley identified as Communists see Robert Vaughn, *Only Victims: A Study of Show Business Blacklisting* (New York: G.P. Putnam's Sons, 1972), pp. 275-7. Endfield was also named by two other witnesses: Pauline Swanson Townsend on 12 March 1953 and David Andrew Lang on 24 March, by which time Cy had been in exile for more than a year (pp. 285, 290). However, in an interview for a 1989 BBC documentary, *The Fellow Travellers*, he mentions only Lang as the person who had identified him.

3 On this period of Endfield's life, see Brian Neve, *Film and Politics in America: A Social Tradition* (London and New York: Routledge, 1992); Jonathan Rosenbaum, 'Guilty by Omission,' *Film Comment*, September-October 1991, revised and reprinted as 'Pages from the Endfield File' in Rosenbaum, *Movies as Politics* (Berkeley, Los Angeles and London: University of California Press, 1997). Cy's own response to Rosenbaum's original article was printed in *Film Comment*, March-April 1992, p. 79.

4 Interview recorded for *The Fellow Travellers* (broadcast 14 December 1989). Only a brief snippet was included in the programme; videotapes of the full interview can be consulted by arrangement with the British Film Institute National Film and Television Archive. Endfield's next comment also derives from this source. *The Informer* (1935) was directed by John Ford.

5 For further information on Weinstein and her subsequent productions, often using blacklisted writers and directors working pseudonymously, see Steve Neale, 'Pseudonyms, Sapphire and Salt: "un-American" contributions to television costume adventure series in the 1950s,' *Historical Journal of Film, Radio and Television*, vol. 23, no. 1, 2003. Explaining his non-involvement in Weinstein's later series, which included *The Adventures of Robin Hood* (1955-9), *The Adventures of Sir Lancelot* (1956-7), *The Buccaneers* (1956-7), *Sword of Freedom* (1957-8) and *Ivanhoe* (1958-9), Endfield told the BBC in 1989 that there were 'one or two rough spots in our personal relationship. It wasn't a love match, that's for sure – on a personal basis.'

6 Production designer Ken Adam wrote about working with the director on *Child in the House* in 'Designing sets for action,' *Films and Filming*, August 1956. Endfield discussed his work on *Hell Drivers* and *Sea Fury* in Andrew Peters, 'Natural drama is just waiting to be found,' *Films and Filming*, May 1958.

7 In *Jet Storm*, Baker's airline pilot recalls his only previous rough flight, when two Zulu chiefs came on board complete with spears and lion-manes 'and a lot of trouble.' 'Ever since,' he tells the stewardess, 'everyone knows that one Zulu chief equals one bad motor.' Coincidence or in-joke? The film's release coincided with the writing of the first drafts of *Zulu*'s screenplay, prior to Baker's involvement.

8 On Endfield's work directing commercials, see Brian O'Brien, 'Private Lives', *Films and Filming*, April 1964.

9 Tribute to Cy Endfield at the National Film Theatre, London, 15 June 1995; tape recording courtesy of Maureen Endfield.

10 Press release, 'Unusual honour for Stanley Baker and Cy Endfield,' 23 September 1964.

11 On yet another unrealised project, a science-fiction thriller called *Only Tomorrow*, see Brian Aldiss, 'Cy's matters,' *The Guardian*, 25 June 1999. Aldiss also describes the 'dismayed' reaction to the first insider preview of *Sands of the Kalahari*: 'By the end of the movie, Levine's golden carpet was slithering away from under our feet with a tinkle of ice cubes.'

12 For further comment on the production of *De Sade*, see the interviews with director Gordon Hessler, producer Louis M. Heyward and screenwriter Richard Matheson in Tom Weaver (ed.), *Science Fiction Stars and Horror Heroes: Interviews with Actors, Directors, Producers and Writers of the 1940s through 1960s* (Jefferson and London: McFarland, 1991). Though they were unhappy with Endfield's work on *De Sade*, Heyward thought *Zulu* 'a brilliant piece of picturemaking' (p. 170) and Matheson considered it 'the best action movie ever made' (p. 313).

13 See Adrian Berry, 'Film director invents pocket typewriter,' *Daily Telegraph*, 23 May 1978; Roger Green, 'Big business for computer in the pocket,' *The Times*, 14 September 1982; Victor Keegan, 'Enter the keyboard virtuoso,' *The Guardian*, 27 October 1983.

14 Rosenbaum, 'Pages from the Endfield File', *Movies as Politics*, p. 332. This article remains the best single source for anyone interested in the director's work. Its author told me in conversation (Bologna, July 2004) that Endfield considered that Rosenbaum over-rated him!

Lieut. John Chard VC

Lieut. Gonville Bromhead VC

Col-Sgt. Frank Bourne DMC

Pte. Alfred Henry Hook VC

"BECAUSE WE'RE HERE, LAD"

CREATING THE CHARACTERS

> Though never a foot-soldier himself, [John Prebble] remembers what he saw of World War II infantrymen in N.W. Europe, British, American or German. [He] believes that such men are in a sense eternal, that the men he saw in slit trenches along the Maas in the winter of 1944-45, or rode with across the Rhine in the Spring of 1945, were the same men who marched in Roman Legions, who [were] sent up Cemetery Ridge with Pickett at Gettysburg, or stood behind the mealie-bags at Rorke's Drift. Perhaps the world will never need them again, and so it is to be hoped, but they should not be forgotten. At the end of *Zulu*, the commander, Lieutenant Chard, says: 'Men sometimes wonder now and then how much courage they have. And now and then a soldier shows them. Perhaps that's his only purpose.'
> (*Zulu* Production Notes)

'Creating' may seem rather an odd term to use in relation to names and figures most of whom actually existed and who are part of the historical record of Rorke's Drift. But in constructing *Zulu* as a dramatic entertainment, so many liberties were taken by the writers with the defenders' personalities that it would be fair to say that the film characters are to all intents and purposes original creations. This has, understandably, been a point of contention for many historians and, most especially, for the relatives and descendants of some actual participants in the battle. Nonetheless, I believe it is not only defensible but *necessary* to reinvent real-life figures for their new role in a drama. If this is accepted – and I realise it will *not* be accepted by many purists – then the critical questions then become what purposes the characters are designed to serve and how well they fulfil these functions. It is not my purpose here to compare John Prebble's creations with the reality, but rather to examine the construction of character within the film itself and in the various script drafts preceding it.[1]

Enthusiasts of military history who are familiar with the historical Battle of Rorke's Drift have often expressed disappointment not only at the distortion of those figures who are dramatised, but also at the omission of others they consider equally, or more, important (though there is no reason to believe that, had they been included, other figures would have been any less fictionalised than those who are). In the months following the release of the film, Prebble received letters from relatives of several of the Rorke's Drift defenders, including the descendants of Lieutenant Bromhead, Sergeant Frederick Millne of the Buffs, Corporal Francis Attwood of the Army Service Corps (one of several recipients of the Distinguished Conduct Medal) and two civilian ferrymen, George Brown Kennedy and Charles Kennedy, who claimed to have been at

Rorke's Drift, though they do not appear in any of the official rolls and were probably not present at the battle itself.[2] Prebble wrote detailed replies to each of these correspondents, but usually included a standard explanation in which he regretted 'the impossibility of naming or presenting on film all those who were there that day,' and added: 'I hope that when you see the film you will feel that it does [your ancestor] and his comrades proper credit.'

While working on the screenplay, Prebble wrote brief character sketches for nine of the main figures to provide thumbnail biographies or 'back-stories,' presumably for reference for himself and his collaborator Cy Endfield, and/or for the convenience of anyone reading the script. (These notes are undated, so it is difficult to be certain exactly when they were written, but comparison with the various script drafts and revised pages leads me to believe that they were prepared between the second and third Revised versions of the screenplay.) In the following pages I have reproduced (unedited aside from the correction of a few typos and the tidying up of punctuation) Prebble's original character descriptions for four of these: Chard, Bromhead, Bourne and Hook (Adendorff, Allen, Hitch, Owen and Thomas were the others). I then go on to compare each of them with the characters' development in successive drafts of the screenplay and the film.

Among the principal characters about whom Prebble did *not* write character sketches are the Witts. The Reverend Otto Witt had been present at Rorke's Drift until just before the commencement of the Zulus' assault, whereupon he had left to join his family in Helpmekaar, the nearest township to Rorke's Drift. There was, however, another parson present throughout the battle: the garrison's chaplain, the Reverend George Smith, who played a very active role in supporting the defence. When the film was released, his omission from the film was the subject of letters to the *Daily Telegraph*, to which Prebble responded with an explanation which can stand as an answer to most such objections:

As the author of the story on which the film *Zulu* was based, and as the co-author of the screenplay, may I reassure some of your correspondents?

Chaplain Smith, of whose existence we were well aware, was not replaced in our story by the "fictional" character of Witt. Rorke's Drift was the Rev. Otto Witt's mission. He was a friend of the Zulus, and violently opposed to the war. He left the Drift before the attack really got under way, and in the shortest possible time arrived in England where he lectured on the defence of the station and against the war. His was possibly the first full account of the action (if somewhat second-hand) to reach Britain.

Any attempt to concern ourselves with *two* ministers would have been dramatically unsuccessful. Witt, by his disapproval of the action and the campaign in general, was the more effective character. There were more than 140 men behind the ramparts, and to name or represent them all in two and a quarter hours is obviously impossible. Our story and our cameras were concerned particularly with the winners of the V.C., not because we believed those men exceptional that day, but because we know that their courage was representative of all, white and Zulu.

In that sense we do not consider that we ignored Chaplain Smith any more than, by the omission of their names, we were forgetful of the valour shown by, say, Sergeant Milne of the Buffs, Private McMahon of the Hospital Corps, or Corporal Attwood of the Commissariat Department.[3]

John Chard
Lieutenant, Royal Engineers

A square-set man in his mid-thirties, hair greying above a positive, determined, and rough-hewn face. His manner and aloofness are a defensive wall protecting a sensitivity of which he is somewhat ashamed and which he endeavours to subdue by a bluntness of speech and attitude. He is thus a solitary man, outwardly self-reliant and self-composed. But there are inner tensions, of which the only physical manifestation is his habit of winding and rewinding his watch when under stress. Although a professional soldier he is primarily an engineer, and it is the physical and mental engineering problems of his profession that really interest him, not the purely military side of it. Not being a regimental officer he is able to view the rest of the Army with a critical detachment, and he prefers it that way. So he is reluctant to accept responsibility for duties outside what he considers to be his particular concern. Thus, although seniority of rank makes him automatically the commander of the garrison at Rorke's Drift, at the beginning he thinks it more logical that this duty should be taken by the infantry officer Bromhead. He is impatient with Bromhead's insistence that he [Chard] take command, particularly since he knows that the infantry officer would give his eye-teeth for the chance of command. But Bromhead is a man who lives by the book, with a great deal of courage if no imagination.

Chard[4] has no roots in the officer-class of his age, is both envious and critical of it. He has no relations close enough to him in England to make that country mean 'home' to him. He feels, if anything, closer to the BOR [British other ranks] than his fellow officers, but with both of them he is short, incommunicative, even faintly aggressive.

Lieutenant Chard was from the beginning constructed by Prebble as the lead protagonist. He was equally clearly modelled on the archetypal he-man hero of the traditional war movie, and as such provided an obvious starring role for Stanley Baker: it is not difficult to picture Baker from the details of the pen portrait quoted above, even if one did not have his portrayal in the film already in mind. The scripted Chard shares a number of traits with the heroic Hollywood tough-guy: in all the various drafts he is constantly described as having a dead or unlit cigar clamped in his mouth (for purposes of comparison, see Robert Mitchum's cigar-chewing Brigadier General Norman Cota in the 1962 D-Day reconstruction *The Longest Day*). A second behavioural quirk invented by Prebble is the one described here: his obsessive winding of a pocket watch, another detail largely eliminated during filming.

Instead of these rather self-conscious devices the filmmakers found other ways to convey Chard's inner life. The screenplay included a moment of insight in which his hand shakes as he tries to light one of his ever-present cigars. In the film this was altered to the officer's attempt to load his pistol, his hand unsteady as he tries to insert a bullet. Prebble noted later that Baker 'hadn't been sure about his part until [that] particular moment, which interested me. He said, that was the moment when I understood that I had to be afraid, and show it.' The writer himself confessed that he had not expected the scene to be used at all.

Despite his suitability as an audience identification figure, Chard is by no means a wholly likeable character and could even be described as something of a martinet. Certainly Baker's hard-bitten performance refuses to soften or sentimentalise him, and it is only towards the end of the film, in his response to Bourne's 'with some guts behind it,' that Chard relaxes sufficiently to allow himself a wry smile. Indeed, so unyielding is Baker's portrayal that some commentators have been led to see Chard as virtually a fanatic, a quality suggested by a brief description in the Final shooting script as he contemplates the defences: 'His face has a wild, fixed, dedicated passion.'5 The same passage includes the observation, after Chard has given Bourne the order to continue building the inner redoubt no matter how tired the men might be, that the soldiers 'look almost venomously' at him.

A further aspect which made the part ideal for Baker is the implication of a working or lower-middle class background, and the consequent sense that Chard has a chip on his shoulder at the domination of the military establishment by members of the aristocracy and the landed gentry who have passively followed family tradition or paid their way into the service. This is brought out, for example, in his cutting remark to Bromhead that the officer at Isandhlwana who issued the orders to hold Rorke's Drift was probably 'somebody's son and heir, given a commission

before he has learned to shave.' The various drafts of the script elaborated upon this notion by stressing Chard's credentials as a man who has earned his position, rather than a scion of privilege. In the Revised script, for example, Private Owen tells Chard in the early scene at the river that 'there's something to be said for an officer who gets his hands dirty like a private soldier.' In a rare moment of openness, the officer responds that he has worked with his hands all his life (the film, of course, *shows* him working with his hands at the ponts). Chard's down-to-earth quality even earns him the respect of Hook, who says in the first set of revision notes: 'Least he takes his coat off and does a turn, which is more than our flaming Mr Bromhead would think of … He takes the flaming army seriously, that's how he's allright.'

However, there is also the suggestion in this script that Hook regards Chard as being as much of a careerist as Bromhead, and therefore ultimately just as deserving of his contempt. Passages of dialogue originally written for Hook and Williams were later abbreviated and transferred to the two Joneses in the Final script (though they too were ultimately deleted from the film). 593 tells 716: 'That Mr Chard, he's got a headache with all this, hasn't he? And only a lieutenant still. He's a long way to go to be a general now … So you and me have got to be very brave today. With Mr Chard's career to think of.' Both the Original and Revised scripts contain a brief scene in the surgery during the battle in which Chard tries talking to the wounded men, including Hitch, but can make no contact with them. A trace of this can still be discerned in the film when Chard pauses at the surgery door and glances uncomprehendingly at the injured Allen and Hitch after his own wound has been treated. In the Revised draft this scene also becomes the occasion for the demonstration of a streak of cruelty in Chard, as he takes out on Bromhead his own frustration at the evident limits to his affinities with the ordinary soldiers. Chard ('with deep, controlled anger and bitterness' according to the script instructions) at one point tells his junior: 'They're your men, aren't they? Find something to say to them! Something one of your high and mighty ancestors would have said.' In the film, Chard's testy, brittle manner with Colour-Sergeant Bourne carries some of the same charge, when he loses his patience at the NCO's failure to carry out orders instantly and in his brutal retort when told how tired the men are ('I don't give a damn').

Prebble's descriptive sketch of Chard stresses his *reluctance* to take command of the post, and suggests that he does so only because of Bromhead's by-the-book insistence – quite the contrary of the impression given by the film, in which Chard forcibly asserts himself. This was a matter over which the screenwriters clearly had differing ideas, as successive drafts and notes offer both variations in the discussion which takes place between the two officers about who has the right to command. The following version appears in the first set of revision notes:

> BROMHEAD
> Just a minute. I said there's something we have to settle, Chard.
>
> CHARD
> (still walking)
> Well?
>
> BROMHEAD
> Who's to command here?
>
> CHARD halts, turns to face BROMHEAD squarely.
>
> CHARD
> I am.
>
> BROMHEAD
> We're both lieutenants.
>
> CHARD
> (making the point bluntly)
> And I'm senior to you.
>
> BROMHEAD
> (dawning understanding)
> You found that out? Before you came down here?
> (a short laugh)
> You're a damned ambitious fellow!
>
> CHARD
> The Army's my job.
>
> BROMHEAD
> Do you think it isn't mine? My family were serving officers when yours....
> (He stops, ashamed)
>
> CHARD
> (coldly)
> You aren't the first *gentleman*...
> (a slight pause)
> ...to point that out to me.

Bromhead's social gaffe here in referring to his superior breeding, and Chard's hurt response, clearly point up the class hostilities in the officers' relationship and are amplified elsewhere.

In the second set of revision notes, the officers' respective positions have changed considerably; Bromhead makes a greater effort to be supportive and solicitous, while Chard is self-effacing. This is the discussion which ensues when Bromhead asks whether Chard's recommendation to evacuate the Witts is a direct order:

CHARD
An order? You command this post, not me.

BROMHEAD
Well that's just the point, isn't it? You see, you are senior to me, old fellow.

CHARD
You found that out? The hell with seniority. You're the line officer, not me. I build bridges.

BROMHEAD
And jolly good ones too.

CHARD throws him a glance of contempt, then looks up to hill.

The Final script changes this around yet again, and for the first time includes dialogue revealing the respective dates of the officers' commissions: May 1872 for Bromhead, February 1872 for Chard.[6] The Final script also adds Chard's despairing exhortation to Bromhead when he is wounded, echoing their earlier conflict of opinion: 'You're the professional! Take command!'

All the scripts imply that there is a certain meeting of minds between Chard and Surgeon Reynolds, another 'working officer' with a similarly jaded view of the army. This is rather suppressed in the film, and indeed Reynolds' exclamation to Chard at the height of the battle ('Damn all you butchers!') suggests that the Surgeon simply regards him as just another member of the war-mongering military establishment. The first revision notes introduced the following conversation, some of which was retained as far as the Final shooting script, but which did not make the final cut of the film:

REYNOLDS
Why didn't you let Bromhead take command? Nobody would have blamed you.

CHARD
(lifting scalpel again)
I have the seniority. A man climbs in this Army by taking opportunities like that.

REYNOLDS
(he is genuinely surprised)
Is that all it means to you?

CHARD
It's enough, isn't it? I've no blood lines, no family acres, no influential friends.

REYNOLDS
(nodding to door)
And those shilling-a-day devils out there?

CHARD
What about them?

REYNOLDS
I'll have some of them on this table soon. Maybe you, too. Or Bromhead. Now tell me, how am I going to know the difference?

CHARD
(shortly)
The difference is, I command.
(turns away, then back)
Do your best for them.

REYNOLDS
(smiling)
Careful! Your humanity's showing.

CHARD
I said do your best for them.

REYNOLDS
Trouble is, if my best were good enough I wouldn't be in the Army at all.
(a tired smile)
But keep the numbers down if you can, there's a good chap.[7]

This conversation takes place in the presence of Margareta Witt, who quizzes Reynolds about Chard's character after his departure from the surgery before the dialogue turns to her own motivation. Reynolds answers: 'An ordinary man. Ambitious. Afraid of feeling. Afraid of losing. Afraid of himself probably. Just an ordinary man.'

Patrick Magee
(Surgeon James Henry Reynolds)

'Patrick Magee was a lunatic, insane, but a fantastic actor,' says James Booth. 'I loved old Pat, he was full of great Irish anecdotes. He had a brother who'd had infantile paralysis or polio when he was young, and lived up in the attic and was never seen. But he had a walking stick and now and again you could hear tap – tap – tap, and Pat would say, "He's up again! He's waaalkin'…!"'

The unmistakable, inimitably sepulchral face and voice of Patrick Magee enlivened – if that is the word for an actor whose most natural home seemed the mausoleum or morgue – more than fifty films in a little over twenty years. Their titles make for a startling set of contrasts: on the one hand respectable adaptations of stage classics like *The Marat/Sade* (1966), *The Birthday Party* (1968), *King Lear*, *The Trojan Women* (both 1971), *Luther* (1973) and *Galileo* (1975); on the other, the hand-me-down Gothic horrors of *Die, Monster, Die!*, *The Skull* (both 1965), *The Fiend* (1971), *Demons of the Mind*, *Tales from the Crypt* and *Asylum* (all 1972).

He was born Patrick Joseph Gerard McGee in Armagh, Northern Ireland, on 31 March 1922, and after gaining theatre experience he travelled to Britain in the early 50s when offered the chance to perform on radio. It was through this medium that he first encountered the work of the playwright with whom he would be most closely associated: his fellow countryman, Samuel Beckett. In 1958 Magee made his West End stage debut in *Winter Garden* and the same year appeared in a play especially written for him by Beckett, *Krapp's Last Tape*, which he would later reprise for television in 1972. His many other Beckett performances included the radio plays *Embers* (1959, also written expressly for him), *Cascando* (1964) and *Rough for Radio* (1976), and on stage *Endgame* (1964) and *That Time* (1976). In 1964 he joined the Royal Shakespeare Company; also among Magee's theatre work were Peter Weiss's *The Marat/Sade* (which marked the actor's Broadway debut) and Harold Pinter's *The Birthday Party*, both of which he later recreated on film.

Magee made his movie debut in 1960, when he was cast by Joseph Losey as the prison warder Barrows in *The Criminal*, a character described by one critic as 'a remarkably vivid snapshot of authority turned discreetly but utterly monstrous' (Bob Baker, 'Patrick Magee,' *Film Dope*, no. 38, December 1987, p. 11). His first appearance as Surgeon Reynolds in *Zulu*, when he lances Hook's boil, evokes the sadistic relish of the authoritarian Barrows but Reynolds is later called upon to express – somewhat anachronistically, but powerfully – the humanist's distaste for slaughter, as he shouts 'Damn all you butchers!' at Chard while bloodily operating on the wounded Cole. According to Lee Stevenson, the Surgeon's descendants were deeply upset by Magee's portrayal. Reynolds' eldest grand-daughter, now aged 92, attended the premiere in London and told Stevenson 'that she was so unhappy with what they'd done to "Grandfather" that she went and spoke to Cy Endfield about it at the after film party' (email to the author, 25 February 2004).

Magee worked again for Losey on *The Servant* (1963) and *Galileo*, and again with Stanley Baker in *A Prize of Arms* (1962). Stanley Kubrick gave him perhaps his best-known big-screen roles, as the writer in *A Clockwork Orange* (1971) and the Chevalier in *Barry Lyndon* (1975), but he became regularly associated with horror films after appearing for fledgling director Francis Ford Coppola and producer Roger Corman in *Dementia 13* (1963), a low-budget thriller made in Ireland. Thereafter he made another dozen shockers, including his last theatrically released film, Walerian Borowczyk's *The Blood of Dr. Jekyll* (1981). Magee died of a heart attack on 14 August 1982.

It has already been mentioned that every version of the script includes the stirrings of a romance between Chard and Margareta. All trace of this was ultimately deleted from the film. In the Original script, Chard and Margareta already know one another at the outset, but the Revised version alters this by having them meet for the first time: Chard is described 'looking curiously' at Margareta and mistakenly addresses her as Mrs Witt. (A note in the screenplay says that she is 'disturbed by the stare' and that Chard's faux pas 'strangely angers' her.) Margareta's own reason for being in Africa, it is suggested, is flight from an unfulfilled relationship in Europe, perhaps prompted by her disturbed feelings towards men generally.8 Aside from introducing a romantic subplot, Margareta's function in his scenes with her is seemingly to bring out Chard's latent humanity and to prick the officer's conscience over his initial cynical disregard of the Zulus as 'animals' (as he describes them to Witt in one draft). Conversely, Margareta's tendency to regard *all* men as animals is gradually modified by her philosophical conversation with Chard on her later return to the camp, as discussed earlier. These themes are at their most explicit in a long scene (six pages) in the Original draft between Chard and Margareta just prior to her departure. Later versions shorten it considerably, and by the Final draft the almost tender exchanges of affection and understanding between the two have become near-total hostility. The first version contains dialogue in which Chard lets down his guard and at last admits something of himself and his background:9

MARGARETA
I'd like to know this. Is being a soldier so important?

CHARD
To me, yes.

MARGARETA
And to your men?

CHARD
They're not my men, they're Bromhead's. An Engineer officer like myself stands isolated. He...
(recovers himself)
England, below my class, Miss Witt, is no paradise for them. In civilian life these men might live and die desperate and alone. In the Army they get self-respect... they get comradeship and they get a shilling a day. They consider it a good bargain. They are good men.

MARGARETA
Aren't the Zulus good men too?

CHARD
Probably. Good soldiers of a kind, anyway. I heard Cetewayo once ordered a whole regiment to march off a cliff. They did it, too. Without a murmur.

MARGARETA
And you despise them for that...

CHARD
(stopping)
No. I think it is a superb example of military discipline. And equally a demonstration of its stupidity.

Gonville Bromhead
Lieutenant, 24th Regiment

A boyish, naïve, brightly enthusiastic man in his early thirties. A professional soldier without reservations. His family has served the Army for two centuries and Bromhead is aware that back in England are scores of relatives who will not only expect him to conform to the code this day at Rorke's Drift but add further standards for future generations of Bromheads to live by. He is ambitious and acutely aware of the fact that he is still a lieutenant (at an age when his grandfather, who fought at Waterloo, was commanding a regiment). His desire would be to have overall command of the garrison, [but] his almost religious respect

for the book insists that Chard, senior officer, takes command.

Bromhead has a girl in England, whose picture he carries. Her father is a general, and Bromhead is aware that his conduct this day will be carefully noted by the general. He admires his men but does not understand them. In their turn they are indifferent to him once they sense the authority of Chard.

Bromhead believes that Chard has seen action before, and this too is one of the reasons why he insists that Chard takes command. It is not until later, after the action, that Bromhead discovers that this had been Chard's first action, too. This results in an outburst of boyish indignation from Bromhead.

Perhaps no character changed as much from conception to final realisation as Lieutenant Bromhead. Prebble's decision to present him as something of a fop may have derived not only from the writer's discovery of Bromhead's family lineage but also from a picture he found in *The Illustrated London News* which, according to Prebble, showed Gonville had a 'weak chin' (he also noted that a photograph of Chard in the same magazine showed 'a man with a resolute expression [and a] large hooked nose dominating his face,' which doubtless also influenced Prebble's characterisation of that officer).

Michael Caine recounted to his biographer William Hall how he approached Baker on the plane to South Africa with his ideas for playing Bromhead: 'Listen, Stan, your character has to overpower him in the end, because that's the story. Wouldn't it be better to overpower a man who is strong and who believes in himself, rather than a fellow who comes on like Jeremy Lloyd and says "Hello, chaps" and all that – the kind of fellow everyone knows immediately that Stanley Baker could wipe the floor with? There's no clash of personality.'[10] Caine was given permission to go ahead with his more assertive interpretation, but in fact this strengthening had already been anticipated by the gradual evolution of the character throughout the successive script drafts.

In the film, Bromhead's first appearance is at the river where he introduces himself to Chard. But in the Treatment and Original script, as in Prebble's story and according to the historical record, Chard and Bromhead already know each other at the outset. They are on familiar, if testy, terms and Bromhead addresses Chard by his first name throughout; Chard in his turn calls him 'Brommy' or 'Gonny' (the loss of this detail in later drafts was a fortunate development) and appears to regard him with the irritability one might reserve for an excitable puppy. Bromhead is first encountered in the Original draft when Chard has returned from the river to the camp and received news of the massacre from Adendorff. In the Revised script, Bromhead is instead introduced out hunting with his native bearers, and encounters Chard when he crosses the river, where he is described 'sauntering with the casual self-satisfaction of an English gentleman returning from a good day's sport.'

In this draft the officers are still already acquaintances, though their relationship is now a more spiky one, characterised by overt mutual dislike. Bromhead is described as having a look of 'amused contempt at the sight of a brother officer working like a private with

Adendorff (Gert van den Bergh) disapproves of Bromhead's attitudes towards the native levies.

his coat off.' Their dialogue at the river largely follows that in the finished film, but includes a blunter exchange of insults than the film allows: Chard tells Bromhead that he is an 'ass' who has 'never done a day's work in [his] life.' Bromhead also remarks that Chard has got 'pretty filthy' (the engineer replies that it 'goes with the job') and the first revision notes give him an extra few needling lines as he gestures disdainfully towards the ponts: 'You don't really soldier, do you? I mean, this sort of thing....' The gist of this material, which draws out the incipient class resentments between the officers, was retained in the film, where the decision to have Bromhead on horseback further accentuates his air of smug superiority.[11]

Great emphasis was placed in early drafts on Bromhead's boyish enthusiasm. He is described in the Original script as seeming 'more excited than alarmed' by the news from Isandhlwana and in the Revised script as 'excited' by Bourne's report of Zulus to the south-west. At one point in the Original, Chard is forced to tell him: 'It's not a game of cricket.' Later in this draft, Bromhead remarks to Adendorff after the repulse of the Zulus' assault on the north rampart: 'Three times they came over. Did you see anything like it? Adendorff, did you see it… By God, our chaps are wonderful! … Damn it all, Adendorff, there's never been anything like it. It was glorious!' Prebble's thumbnail description of Bromhead gives him a girlfriend back in England, but no mention of this can be found in any of the script drafts. Indeed, the screenplays tend to throw the very nature of Bromhead's sexuality into question.[12] The

Final script includes an exchange after one of Chard's rows with Margareta, when the engineer remarks to Bromhead: 'What the hell's the matter with her. You'd think a man had never touched her before. Or would you know?' He gets the cryptic reply: 'Couldn't say, old chap. You may be the better man… *there*.' However, despite these suggestions of immaturity and 'inferior' masculinity, even the early drafts grant Bromhead a measure of military know-how appropriate to his rank. In the Original and Revised scripts, the flying platoon designed to plug gaps in the defences is his idea, not Chard's.

From the Treatment onwards, Prebble had tried to incorporate into the dialogue the information he had discovered about the military background of Bromhead's family. The Original script includes the first full version of dialogue which would be much reworked in subsequent drafts, but the core of which remains in the finished film:

CHARD
(as he and BROMHEAD walk on)
Yours is an Army family?

BROMHEAD
In the blood, you know? Box of lead-soldiers at Christmas before I was out of the cradle.
(he pauses, speaks to a SOLDIER)
Get your pouch round to your front, 294 Thomas. Where your right hand can reach it.

294 THOMAS
(obeying)
Sir!

BROMHEAD
(as they walk on)
I've three brothers serving. How about you, John?

CHARD
I'm just an Engineer. The red coat came with the work.

BROMHEAD
You know, my father was at Waterloo? He died long ago. He was an old man when I was a boy. I scarcely knew him, but he was at Waterloo. Damned funny. And my great-grandfather was the Johnny who knelt beside Wolfe at Quebec. You know, the chap who said 'They run, sir!' or something like that.

CHARD
(drily)
Quite a tradition, Brommy.

BROMHEAD
(earnestly)
Bit of a responsibility to live up to, though. A chap doesn't seem his own master. I mean, my father had his own regiment at the time he was my age. I'm glad that… you…
(he halts and stares at the hills. CLOSE ON his face. Beneath the jolly-ass front the tension breaks through)
Where are they, John? Why don't they show themselves?

The first set of revision notes moves this discussion forward to the moments of tension immediately preceding the Zulus' first appearance above the camp. Placed here rather than earlier, the conversation brings out Bromhead's anxiety about his ability to live up to the family tradition.

The veracity of the information about Bromhead's family background was doubted even by members of the family itself. On New Year's Eve 1964, Prebble received a letter from a Mrs K. Preston (née Bromhead) in Llandudno Junction, North Wales: 'My husband assures me that the remark of my Gt Uncle Lieut. Bromhead to Chard was a piece of nonsense – I would like to prove him wrong.' In his reply of 21 January 1965, Prebble could not disguise his pride in the rigour of his research:

I am afraid I am going to disappoint your husband. Indeed, the actual facts quoted in the authority we used are even more remarkable. We did our best in *Zulu* to keep as close as we could, within the limits of drama and film-making, to the truth of

shown in the film' (Caine was 30 at the time of shooting) and added cuttingly that the real Chard was also 'well versed in the proper etiquette of command.'

Bourne
Colour-Sergeant, B Coy [Company], 2/24th Regiment

A man in his fifties. Professional soldier since his youth. Married to the Army, honouring the union with a selfless fidelity. Son of a lay-preacher, he mixes profanity, discipline and the Psalms with, to him at any rate, logical homogeneity. He is not uncommon in the British Army of his day, where the long-service NCO was often inclined to live happily by the Bible and Queen's Regulations.

If he has a philosophy it is 'my officer right or wrong.' His type no longer exists. It got itself killed with a blind obedience at places like Balaclava. Towards the ranks he acts paternally and harshly in turn. It is doubtful whether he ever considered the rights or wrongs of the war he now finds himself engaged in; the colour of the enemy's skin is immaterial to him. Company Orders brought him to Rorke's Drift, and Company Orders will be obeyed by him.

the affair. I don't think I would have invented Bromhead's remark about Waterloo and Wolfe, it would have seemed to me (as it obviously did to your husband) as being a little far-fetched.

However, in the issue of the *Daily Telegraph* for March 7, 1879, there was published a letter from the Rector of Bassingham. This was about the time when full news of the defence of Rorke's Drift, a couple of months earlier, was reaching England. The Rector said in his letter that Bromhead came from Thurlby Hall in Lincolnshire, and that he was one of four soldier *sons* of a Waterloo veteran, and that his *great-grandfather* was the ensign who told the dying Wolfe at Quebec that 'They run, sir!'.

The tone of Bromhead's great-niece's letter was friendly, but the *Daily Telegraph* of 28 February 1964 had printed a much more hostile response to the film from the officer's great-nephew, a serving officer who had been an invited guest at its World Premiere a month earlier. Lieutenant-Colonel Sir Benjamin Bromhead was contributing to the correspondence about the portrayal of the Reverend Witt cited earlier (he sympathised with the complainants), but he was clearly more aggravated by the characterisation of his own ancestor. He pointed out that at the time of the battle Bromhead was aged 35, 'a mature man, unlike in character to the foppish youth

Though no film characterisation can truly be said to be complete until the part is cast and realised on screen, there are few better examples in cinema history of just how much an actor can bring to a role than Nigel Green as Colour-Sergeant Bourne. On the page, Bourne is little more than an archetype, one of several sergeants in the scripts along with Windridge, Milne and Gallacher. Only when Green was cast did the part properly spring to life. Given comparatively little to work with, it is he who was largely responsible for creating Bourne. Indeed, so definitively does Green seem to embody the popular conception of the stern but benignly paternal NCO that it comes as something of a shock – and an acute disappointment – to be told that, at 24, the real Frank Bourne was fifteen years younger than Green and about a foot shorter.

Nigel Green as the archetypal Colour-Sergeant Bourne. Note the fly on his otherwise immaculate tunic.

Bourne's first appearance in the film, patrolling the camp grounds and having a brief exchange of dialogue with Hughes at the hospital window, was not included in any of the screenplay drafts and appears to have been entirely improvised on set – doubtless to give Green more to do. In the Revised and Final drafts Bourne is first shown directing the work of building the ramparts, but in the Original draft, his introduction is postponed until even later, to the store room scene with Witt. Green also benefited from the temporary indisposition during shooting of Joe Powell. Powell, playing Sergeant Windridge, was obliged to spend ten days in hospital after suffering an insect bite and contracting an infection. Bourne therefore inherited several lines of dialogue and bits of business intended for Windridge, such as leading the tired men into the inner redoubt, and his apology to Chard for having fallen asleep on duty.

One of Bourne's own major scenes was apparently filmed intact (first assistant director Bert Batt remembers it being shot), but was later abbreviated in the editing. The following is the full version, from the Final draft, of the scene in which Witt speaks to the frightened Private Cole from his makeshift prison inside the store room. Its intended function was apparently mainly to inform the audience about the soldiers' firepower and weaponry, and though it provided Green with an additional set-piece it was probably judged excessive to requirements:

WITT
Will you be like Cain and kill your brother? Don't you understand what they are asking you to do?

COLE
(desperately)
Sir, I understand. Only you don't see…

WITT
(his voice rising)
Throw down your weapon and go. The Lord shall be with you. Thou shalt not kill, saith the Lord. Sorrow and sighing shall flee away, saith the prophet Isaiah!

COLE
(almost hysterically)
It's wrong what we're doing, isn't it?… Somebody ought to do something…

WITT
(realises he's making headway)
The Book says, put up thy sword into its sheath…. Obey the Word, boy… Obey the Lord! Go to the others. Go.

COLE takes a step in one direction, halts, looks desperately about him. Turns to door, bending down, almost whispering to it.

COLE
Mr Witt, you got to help. Tell me what I should do. Not just say things out of the Bible, Mr Witt…

Two pairs of legs, in blue trousers, black gaiters, come on screen beside him. He stops, looks at them, and then up. He gets to his feet, CAMERA RISING with him. There are COLOUR-SERGEANT BOURNE and CORPORAL ALLEN.

BOURNE
(firmly but softly)
Put your helmet on, lad. And pick up your rifle.

COLE
(looking from BOURNE to ALLEN)
He says… Mr Witt says…

BOURNE
(to COLE)
Never mind him, boy. What's your name?

COLE
(surprised)
You know, Colour Sergeant.

ALLEN
Answer the question, soldier.

COLE
One-three-two-one Cole, Colour Sergeant.

BOURNE
(nodding)
What's your rifle sighted to, Cole?

COLE
One thousand, four hundred and fifty yards.

BOURNE
Right. And what's its muzzle-velocity, boy?

COLE
One thousand, three hundred feet per second.

ALLEN
(in disgust)
One thousand three hundred <u>and</u> fifty.

COLE
Yes, Corporal.

BOURNE
What's your ammunition, boy?

COLE
Short-chamber Boxer-Henry, point four-five calibre.

BOURNE
And what are the Zulus armed with?

COLE
(puzzled)
Spears, Colour Sergeant?

BOURNE
(nodding)
Good boy. Now you cut along to the ramparts with your mates.
(to ALLEN)
See him along, Corporal.

BOURNE watches ALLEN and COLE leave, then he bends down to grating.

BOURNE
(earnestly)
Mr Witt, sir. Be quiet now, will you, there's a good gentleman? You'll upset the lads.

WITT
(through door)
Is that Colour-Sergeant Bourne?

BOURNE
It's me.

WITT
You said you prayed. Are you praying?

BOURNE
(standing up and speaking as if to a child)
That's all right sir. I'll attend to that.

The paternal relationship between Bourne and Cole suggested here was more developed in earlier versions of the script than in the film

itself. In the Original draft, Bourne's lines to Cole about the capabilities of the Martini-Henry come after Witt's departure, as Bourne patrols the perimeter. He then adjusts Cole's chin strap before moving on. After the Witts leave the camp Cole asks of Bourne: 'What're we doing here? ... I never seen a Zulu in the Brixton Road, have I? So what we got to fight them for?' A variation of these lines subsequently found its way into Hook's mouth, while the essence of Bourne's reply – 'Because we're here, lad ...and nobody else is now...' – was retained in the film. Later in the Original script, when Cole is hit by a bullet from a Zulu sniper, Bourne catches him and calls for an orderly. At the end of the battle, Bourne is described tending Cole as he dies:

[CHARD] looks down. BROMHEAD's head is already on his knees. CAMERA PANS from him to BOURNE who is kneeling by the side of the boy COLE who is dying. COLE is staring upward.

BOURNE
You want anything, lad?
(no reply)
I say you want anything, lad? Anything I can do?
(no reply)
Can you hear me?

COLE turns his head slowly to stare at the

Colour Sergeant. He does not speak but his face is full of fear.

BOURNE
You want to say something, boy?

COLE still does not answer. The fear in his face is now terror.

BOURNE
Nothing I can do for you, boy?

Still staring in desperate terror, COLE dies.

BOURNE (looking up)
Sir?

SURGEON REYNOLDS crouches beside the dead soldier, takes his pulse, puts a hand inside his shirt. Then he closes COLE's eyes with his thumb. He looks at BOURNE.

BOURNE
(calmly, without emotion)
His name was Cole.

HOLD ON BOURNE's plain, sad face.

In later script drafts and in the film, Cole dies much earlier, on Reynolds' operating table without the Colour-Sergeant being present, but Bourne's affection for him is still registered in his grave expression and the grim finality of his voice when speaking the boy's name at the roll-call and crossing out his name in the register.

The night-time scene quoted above is immediately followed (again in the Original script) by a dissolve to the silent camp at dawn. Chard and Sergeant Milne 'stand in the central ground, covered with shields and spears,' and exchange the following dialogue which will surely strike a chord with frequent viewers of the film:

CHARD
They've taken away their dead.

MILNE
Yes, sir.

CHARD
(straightening shoulders)
You think they've gone?

MILNE
Looks like it, sir. It'd be a miracle.

CHARD
(in bitter weariness)
A miracle, sergeant. A short chamber Boxer-Henry point four five calibre miracle.

MILNE
Yes, sir. And, sir…

CHARD
What?

MILNE
Perhaps some guts behind the bayonet points, sir?

With the elimination of Milne from the later scripts, it is Windridge who is given a version of this dialogue in the Revised draft: 'And some muscle behind the bayonets too, sir?' Not until the Final draft was Bourne eventually assigned the lines for which he is perhaps best remembered, although in the film they are very slightly altered and given a more assertive reading than the quizzical one suggested in the script: 'And some guts behind the bayonet, sir?'

Gary Bond (Private Cole)

The actor playing the nervous paperhanger who asks 'Why us?' and is shot by a Zulu sniper early in the battle actually came from a staunch military family. Gary Bond's father and his mother's brothers were all soldiers, and he too was expected to join the army. But after his father's death when Gary was 16 he trained to be an actor at the Central School of Speech and Drama, making his first stage appearance in the same year he filmed *Zulu*.

Gary James Bond – the name suited his dashingly handsome appearance – was born on 7 February 1940 in Liss, Hampshire. He was primarily a theatre actor, and apparently had only two other feature film roles besides *Zulu*: as Smeaton, the courtier tortured into a false confession of adultery with Anne Boleyn in *Anne of the Thousand Days* (1969); and the jaded hero of the Australian drama *Wake in Fright* (released in Britain as *Outback*, 1971). He also made a number of appearances on radio and television, including a leading role as an army officer in *Frontier* (1968), a short-lived ITV adventure series set in India but filmed in Wales, and guest spots in episodes of *Hammer House of Horror* and *Roald Dahl's Tales of the Unexpected*.

However, it was in the theatre that Bond made his reputation and spent most of his career, acting in the works of Shakespeare, Shaw, Ibsen, O'Neill, Wesker, Coward, Wilde and Anouilh, and winning his greatest fame in the musicals of Andrew Lloyd Webber. Gary played Joseph in the original stage production of *Joseph and His Amazing Technicolor Dreamcoat*, which debuted at the Edinburgh Festival in 1972, going on to great West End success, and in 1978 he took over as Che Guevara from David Essex in *Evita*. He also toured with concerts of Lloyd Webber songs, and created the lead role of *Aspects of Love* on a demonstration album in 1988 before appearing in the stage production the year before his tragically early death.

Following a long illness, Bond died on 12 October 1995, aged only 55. The official cause of death was cancer, though according to David Kernan it was actually AIDS. 'He was a charming, charming man, and a very talented actor,' says Kernan, who got to know him well after they worked on *Zulu*. Gary's obituaries (*Daily Telegraph*, 16 October 1995; *The Independent*, 17 October 1995; *The Times*, 14 October 1995) described him as 'a gentle man of great integrity,' with 'a twinkling sense of humour and a sometimes wicked sense of fun.' He was 'the complete company man, bounding across the stage at every performance with the vigour of one half his age, and diffusing any tension backstage with paternalistic advice and an endless store of jokes.' How very different from the image of him created by Private Cole.

Henry Hook
Private, B Coy, 2/24th Regiment

London guttersnipe. Took the shilling to get one step ahead of the peelers. Never could remember his parents. Began life more or less as a 'sweeping boy,' living on the edge of the Thames and going aboard ships in the pool on the pretext of sweeping them for a penny or two, but in fact using the opportunity to steal anything he could lay his hands on. Although he looks thin and wizened, survival of this early life made him tough as a whip. He graduated from this to stealing from shop-doors and windows, and served his first prison sentence for this.

He regards the Army as a form of

imprisonment, only just that much better than a real gaol. He is an amiable fellow, but not above twisting any duck he thinks worth the try. Before he joined the Army he was a 'magsman,' a professional cheat working the three-card trick, the thimble-and-pea trick, and the lock trick. For the first two of these he needed a confederate, and had one in a woman he claims was his wife. His colleagues in B Coy know every trick he can pull, but among the men of other companies in the hospital he finds his dupe, and is busy relieving the fellow of money up until the moment of the attack.

His courage, and he has an immense amount of it, springs from his refusal to believe that there is anyone who can get the better of Henry Hook.

The most controversial of all Prebble's fictionalised characters is Private Hook – in reality a model soldier, teetotaller and the company cook, who did indeed defend the hospital but was not a patient in it, much less a malingerer. For some viewers, Hook's characterisation in the film goes beyond creative licence or permissible liberties to become a libel on the man often seen as the true hero of the battle. Several of Hook's relatives – including his daughter – invited to early screenings of the film were reportedly appalled. After its release, Prebble received a query from one George Robinson, who asked if the real Hook was indeed a 'bad soldier' as the film made him out to be. Prebble replied:

Very little is unfortunately known about the personalities and background of the people who took part in the defence of Rorke's Drift, and in writing a script one has to use intelligent deduction or imagination. Hook is perhaps a case in point. In those days the Army contained many men who had to choose between prison or enlistment, and it seemed dramatically effective to make Hook one such. I don't think he was in fact a 'bad soldier' as you put it, and I hope the film did not make him seem one, only a real man.[13]

Contributors to the internet website http://rorkesdriftvc.com/ have shared some anecdotes and comments of their own on this matter (it is a popular topic on the site's Discussion Forum). 'Dave' reports that the local city guide book for Monmouth, Hook's birthplace, declares that his descendants 'refused to view the local screening of the film because of the way his character was portrayed.' On the other hand, webmaster Alan Critchley claims to 'have had correspondence from one of Hook's descendants who was quite happy with the rogue image as portrayed in *Zulu* even though it's not accurate.' Disinterested viewers have usually concurred with this latter view, as Vaughan Birbeck testified: 'I once attended a screening of *Zulu* where the audience broke into a spontaneous cheer when it was announced that "Hooky" won the VC. Obviously a successful cinematic character however unhistoric!'

Eddie Saunders makes a more pragmatic point: 'I wouldn't have even known of Hook or Bromhead or what "Rorke's Drift" was if it hadn't been for watching the film *Zulu*. If by means of its "poetic licence" it is keeping the names of these men alive in our memories then it's not all bad is it?' This is a viewpoint shared both by myself and Diana Blackwell, one of the film's most articulate apologists: 'Despite its historical basis, *Zulu* is a work of art, not a documentary. It takes quite a few liberties with the facts, but always in the interest of strengthening the story. Those who object might take comfort in the ironic fact that the film's dramatic power (arising partly from inaccuracy) has probably drawn more attention to the historical battle than all other sources combined.' Diana was so impressed by the film, and especially by Hook and his portrayal by James Booth, that she was moved to construct her own tribute website, http://www.jamesbooth.org/.

Booth himself naturally has his own views on the appeal of the character: 'He was a villain, a rebel – a guy who stuck his fingers up at the world, and didn't like discipline, which most people don't like, and liked to drink. He saw the ludicrous side, but when it came down to it he fought the good fight and helped save the day. It may be something to do with the British character. When you've lived abroad for twenty-five years as I have and come back, you see what a strange lot the Brits are – they really are odd. I think that's why they liked Hook, he was such a cheeky bastard, but when it came to it he fought and saved his mates. The British cinema-going public recognised a bit of themselves in that character. There is quite a lot of the layabout in the old British character.'

As mentioned previously the Original script does not show Hook as a hospital patient or present him in quite such colourful terms as later drafts. In this version he first appears in the hospital with 395 Williams (later corrected to 612) when they come to issue rifles to the patients and knock loopholes in the outer walls. It seems likely that Prebble was encouraged to play up the roguish elements in Hook's character – the name itself suggests such traits, no matter how inaccurately in the case of the real Hook – and to amplify the love/hate relationship with Sergeant Maxfield, who has sent money to Hook's wife while he was on field punishment for stealing brandy from the Surgeon's medicine cabinet (details added in the Revised version of the script). In the Revised and Final drafts Hook is introduced complaining about the noise from his senior officer's blood sports and trying the cup-and-bullet trick on Gunner Howarth.[14] Dialogue in these scripts indicates that Hook was meant to be working at the river when he reported sick; that he is malingering to avoid the guardroom; and that he has previously been imprisoned in Marshalsea and Southwark. He exclaims at one point: 'Gawd! What a place for a gentleman magsman,' and shares with Howarth his philosophy of life: 'Always cheat. Never leave nothing to chance, Gunner. That's a mug's way.'

When Hook later proves his mettle in combat, it is not from any sense of duty or patriotism, or even self-preservation, that he fights so furiously, but by way of fulfilling a personal indebtedness to Maxfield. All the script drafts emphasise Hook's grief at the Sergeant's death in the burning hospital. The Original draft is, as usual, closest to the historical record:

HOOK
Maxfield. We've left the sergeant in there.

INTERIOR SHOT – OTHER ROOM
HOOK coming through into the smoke and the room crowded with triumphant warriors. He heads for three who are plunging their spears into MAXFIELD's writhing body.
HOOK kills one with a terrific lunge, wrenches the weapon free and knocks another man down with a brutal butt stroke. The third is about to stab him when he falls from a shot fired by 395 WILLIAMS who has also come through the hole. Smoke has now almost darkened the room. 395 WILLIAMS grabs HOOK's arm and pulls him to the hole. As they force their way through HOOK is yelling.

HOOK
They killed my sergeant. They killed my bloody sergeant!

The Final script replaced the last line with the less hysterical 'Where's that bloody sergeant?' as Maxfield yells out for help; Hook can be seen shouting it in the film, from behind a wall of flames as the roof collapses,

"Brandy's for heroes, Mr Hook."

though the words are barely discernible. Other subsequent revisions have Maxfield still alive when Hook goes back to rescue him, exhorting Hook to greater effort in the struggle, before he dies – as in the film – under falling timbers from the burning roof. The Revised and Final drafts also introduce Hook's typically nose-thumbing gesture of stealing brandy while attempting to escape the flames and his drinking an ambivalent toast to the Sergeant. The scripts describe his close-up: 'The brandy is wet about his mouth. But his cheeks are wet too, as he turns to face CAMERA. He is crying.' In the Revised script Hook escapes the hospital by falling backwards through the upstairs window into the arms of the waiting Sergeant Windridge, who takes the brandy bottle and throws it away (in the film Hook's exit from the hospital is not shown).

For budgetary purposes, all Hook's scenes (and those of several other characters, including Reynolds) were designed to be shot in the studio rather than on location. Hence, Hook is largely conspicuous by his absence from most of the later scenes, though during the brief night assaults he is seen talking to Williams behind a wall of mealie bags and asking if Maxfield 'wanted it that way.' This scene remained fairly constant throughout all the major script drafts, though it was progressively shortened; it includes Hook's tender expressions of regret over the Sergeant's death: 'He was a right mucker that one. All brass and the drill book. But it was no way to die.' In the film Hook makes a very brief appearance during the roll call and all the scripts describe him reacting to the sudden return of the Zulus, with a cry of 'It's not fair. It's not bloody fair!' The Revised script adds a brief comment on his dejected appearance: 'The picture of a soldier with duty done and no relish for any more. He is staring up at the hills and his face, losing the cocky arrogance, indicates that he has taken his limit, albeit well. Now he almost cracks.'

Diana Blackwell has detected a homoerotic subtext in the film's relationship between Hook and Maxfield, which has some justification in the text but which has predictably not gone down too well with some of the film's more conservative adherents. I would like to end this chapter by quoting at length Diana's account of the fire sequence in her own website discussion of the film, in a passage which can hardly be bettered for its eloquence and passion:

> Hooky's spectacular display of heroism, when it finally arrives, feels believable and right precisely because it *doesn't* come out of the blue, but rather is the fulfillment of our half-conscious expectations …
>
> More Zulus pour in and beset him, but Hooky is an aggressive fighter, always on the offensive. Throughout the defense of the hospital, and especially as he fights his way to Maxfield's side, he seems to have the lethal power of several men. In this *Zulu* does no more than justice to the historical Hook, who is widely considered the überhero of Rorke's Drift, conspicuously brave even by the high standards of that battle. To underscore his special status, *Zulu* makes Hooky's combat moves the most picturesque and ferociously driven in the film. His explosive energy, hitherto only hinted at, here achieves frenzied, dionysian release. Booth gives the scene everything he's got and makes Hooky an exhilarating vision of in-the-Zone empowerment and near-invincibility …
>
> The climax of the Hooky subplot occurs during the celebrated brandy-drinking scene. Though Hooky is amusingly funky earlier (boil, latrine, sock), here he is freighted with extravagant spiritual meaning and glorified almost to apotheosis. Like some pissed-off phoenix reborn from the flames, he's running for his life through the burning hospital when he passes the cabinet containing the medicinal brandy he wanted earlier – the brandy the surgeon said was 'for heroes.' He smashes the glass door and takes the bottle. Williams returns and warns him, 'That's a flogging offense! Get out for God's sake, man!' Suddenly Hooky turns all sublime and Promethean. Surrounded by leaping flames, his grime-streaked face blazing with power and defiance, his torn red tunic glowing in the firelight, he smashes the bottle open with one blow and very deliberately raises the jagged opening to his lips for a deep, ecstatic draught that leaves him shuddering.
>
> Wow! That scene is so fantastically beautiful it gives me chills to this day. It reminds me of Gericault or Beethoven, with overtones of Nietzsche, Blake, and 19th Century romanticism generally. It suggests that Hooky recognizes the supreme event in his predominantly loser's life, and it also somehow makes him seem magnificently free on the inside, noble and exemplary.

Paul Daneman (Sergeant Robert Maxfield)

'When I was at RADA,' says James Booth,'I used to go to the Old Vic where Paul was one of the leading actors and I saw him play all the great roles. I became a great admirer of his. He was an immensely likeable man. I knew people who used to go to him for acting lessons and they couldn't have found anyone better. He knew the business inside and out. He never applied himself to making movies

Paul Daneman (centre) as the fever-stricken Sergeant Maxfield.

and I don't think he had the personality – he thought it was all rather silly, he was a bit of an intellectual. In my view, he was badly under-used [by the film industry].'

Another of the *Zulu* actors to shoot his scenes exclusively at Twickenham Studios, Paul Daneman was better known as a stage and television actor than for his occasional film work. Born in Islington on 26 (some sources say 29) October 1925, he began acting while studying fine art at Reading University and gained further experience in troop shows during and immediately after the Second World War. Following demob he won a scholarship to RADA, acting professionally from 1947 (his first role was as the front legs of a pantomime horse in a production of *Alice in Wonderland*) and making his West End debut in 1949. Daneman quickly established himself as an extremely versatile actor with the Bristol Old Vic and the Birmingham Repertory Company. As well as appearing in stage musicals, thrillers and farces, he performed numerous Shakespearean and other classical roles, and played Vladimir in the first English-language production of Samuel Beckett's *Waiting for Godot* (1955), at London's Arts Theatre under the direction of Peter Hall. The following year he made his first film, Joseph Losey's *Time Without Pity*, and from 1959 he often appeared on television, including regular roles in the drama series *An Age of Kings* (1960) and *Spy Trap* (1972-5), and the situation comedies *Corrigan Blake* (1963), *Not in Front of the Children* (1967) and *Never a Cross Word* (1968-9). Among his few other films following *Zulu* were *How I Won the War* (1967) and *Oh! What a Lovely War* (1969), in which he played Czar Nicholas II.

When Daneman suffered a heart attack at the age of 53, he wrote a TV sitcom based on the experience, *Affairs of the Heart* (1983), and a novel, *If Only I Had Wings* (1995). His later television roles included *Thatcher: The Final Days* (in which he played Douglas Hurd) and Alan Bleasdale's *G.B.H.* (both 1991), and he appeared as Bilbo Baggins in a BBC radio adaptation of J.R.R. Tolkien's *The Hobbit*. He died of heart disease on 28 April 2001.'We all know that's it not only acting ability that takes you to the top,' reflects James Booth.'There are many actors around who are supposed to be stars but who aren't really very good actors at all. But, in my lifetime anyway, Paul Daneman was one of the good actors – kind, unassuming and a *good* actor.'

Notes

1. For more detailed biographical information on the personalities of the historical participants, see: Adrian Greaves, *Rorke's Drift* (London: Cassell, 2002); Alan Baynham Jones and Lee Stevenson (eds.), *Rorke's Drift: By Those Who Were There* (Brighton: Lee Stevenson Publishing, 2003); Ian Knight and Ian Castle, *The Zulu War – Then and Now* (London: Plaistow, 1993).

2. I am, as always, indebted to contributors to the Discussion Forum at http://rorkesdriftvc.com/, especially Peter Ewart, who answered my queries about the Kennedys.

3. Letter, *Daily Telegraph*, 17 February 1964.

4. Prebble's manuscript here says 'Bromhead,' but this is clearly a typo.

5. See Geoffrey Macnab, 'Valley boys,' *Sight and Sound*, March 1994, and the correspondence which followed in the issues for May and June over Macnab's account of Baker's characterisation of Chard.

6. In fact, the historical figures had been in the army a little longer: Bromhead had purchased an Ensign's commission in April 1867 but was not given a full officer's commission until October 1871; Chard had entered the service as a full Lieutenant in April 1868, hence his superiority and right to command as determined by Major Spalding, the senior officer at Rorke's Drift prior to his departure for Helpmekaar before the start of the battle. I am indebted to John McAdam, 'Observations on the film *Zulu*,' *The Journal of the Anglo Zulu War Historical Society*, no. 9, June 2001, p. 50, for this information and for comments on the social standing of engineer officers in the Victorian era.

7. The Final draft gives Reynolds an additional line which echoes the conversation between the Joneses quoted earlier: 'And how much of their blood has to go on your commission, or Bromhead's, before they make you a captain?'

8. In the scene just cited Reynolds tells Margareta: 'Don't be afraid of men, my dear. Or what they want. We owe our lives to that. You should have married him.'

9. In this scene Chard also refers to his boyhood in Sussex, though the real Chard was brought up in Plymouth.

10. William Hall, *Raising Caine: The Authorized Biography* (London: Arrow Books, 1982, p. 105.

11. In *Past and Present: National Identity and the British Historical Film* (London: I.B. Tauris, 2005), James Chapman offers the intriguing interpretation that the opposition between Chard and Bromhead mirrors that between the opposing party leaders in the 1964 British general election. He suggests that Bromhead is the equivalent of the Tory aristocrat Sir Alec Douglas-Home and Chard that of Labour's Harold Wilson, the provincial grammar-school boy and ultimate election victor. Chapman might have added that Stanley Baker actively supported Wilson's 1970 election campaign and was later knighted in the outgoing Prime Minister's Honours List. I am grateful to Dr Chapman for allowing me access to a pre-publication typescript of his chapter on *Zulu*.

12. Christopher Sharrett argues that there is still sufficient substance to the 'contrasting masculine styles' represented by Chard and Bromhead for the film to be guilty of homophobia. See '*Zulu* or the limits of liberalism,' *Cineaste*, vol. XXV, no. 4 (2000), pp. 32-3.

13. Letter, 6 June 1964.

14. This game, with thimbles and a dried pea replacing cups and bullet, is also practiced by a character in an episode of the Walt Disney television show *Davy Crockett, King of the Wild Frontier* (broadcast in 1954-5 and released as a theatrical feature film in 1955). This is Thimblerig, played by Hans Conried, a genial con-man and card-sharp who ends up sacrificing his life with the other defenders of the Alamo, somewhat against his better instincts. The character is played by Denver Pyle in John Wayne's *The Alamo* (1960), albeit without these same traits.

"WELSHMEN WILL NOT YIELD"

STANLEY BAKER
LIEUTENANT JOHN CHARD/CO-PRODUCER

> I'm the son of a Welsh coal miner. From the age of 13 I have been an actor. I've been married for 14 years to a wife I love. I'm the father of four children. That's who I am.
>
> A working-class background can give you security. You remember what life was like. You *appreciate* that your life is better now – and it's *you* who've made it so. That gives you confidence – and a sense of values.
>
> (Stanley Baker, interviewed in Susan Barnes, 'How I hate flattery grumbles Mr. Baker,' *Sunday Express*, 2 February 1964)

Stanley Baker always looked a decade older than his real age, in life as much as on screen. His wife Ellen had assumed he was in his thirties when she met and began courting him; only when she heard the banns read in church following their engagement did she discover that he was a mere 22. Baker's typecasting as a heavy in most of his early movies was dictated by his brusque, surly manner, deep-set brown eyes, bony brow and strong jaw. 'I have the looks that bring out the worst in people in pubs,' he said.[1]

Baker was born on 28 February 1928 in Ferndale, in Wales' Rhondda Valley. His father had been a miner, like almost all working men in his home town, until losing a leg in a pit accident. With few other jobs around, the Baker family struggled to put food on the table. Stanley recalled with bitterness having to borrow £5 to pay for his father's funeral, and throughout his life he stayed loyal to his Welsh roots, his working class upbringing and his socialist beliefs.

As a boy, Baker was, as he later put it, 'a wild kid,' unpromising as a scholar and interested only in sport – football, boxing, swimming and athletics – until he was taken up by an inspiring teacher, Glyn Morse: 'He took immense pains with me. He taught me elocution, gave me books to read and generally encouraged me to make acting my career ... Make no mistake, I was very lucky to get the right start.'[2] Morse encouraged Baker to act in school plays, and one such show was attended by the producer-director of an Ealing war picture set in Yugoslavia but to be filmed partly in Wales. 'I was thirteen at the time,' Stanley recalled, 'and really believed it to be my last acting fling before going down the mines. In the audience was film producer Sergei Nolbandov. He must have liked my performance for he offered me a screen test at Ealing for the film *Undercover* ... I got the part – despite the fact that I competed against a juvenile actor named Richard Attenborough.' Already Baker's performance in *Undercover* (1943) suggested the intensity he would bring to his most characteristic later work. Film-making was, said Baker, 'another world altogether – a world I hardly dreamed existed.'

He left school at fourteen and found a job as an electrician, but Morse persuaded him to

audition for Emlyn Williams' play *The Druid's Rest*. He didn't get the part, but instead became the understudy for another teenage Valleys boy who did: Richard Burton. This sealed Baker's professional future and also created a lifelong friendship between the two lads. Burton said later that, when the play opened in Liverpool, Stanley introduced him to sex.[3] Stanley then gained two years' experience in the Birmingham Repertory Company before spending the next two years doing his National Service in the Royal Army Service Corps, achieving the rank of sergeant. After demob he went back to London, living at the YMCA and working as a waiter while looking for acting work. His big theatre break came with a role in Christopher Fry's *A Sleep of Prisoners*, which he played in both London and New York. In 1950, within six weeks of their first meeting at the Apollo Theatre, he married actress Ellen Martin. 'I would be nothing without her,' he later said. 'She's given me the security of a home, and without that you can't take chances. It's the base you can go back to after the battles.'[4] They had four children and remained together until his death.

After small parts in various movies, including the Bosun in *Captain Horatio Hornblower R.N.* (1951), Baker won a plum supporting role as the boorish First Officer Bennett in another Ealing war picture, *The Cruel Sea* (1953). Acting as 'stooge' in a screen test for co-star Donald Sinden, Baker persuaded director Charles Frend to test him too and, he later said, knew instantly that he would get the role. This character set the tone of Baker's future screen persona, not just in the vigour and flamboyance of his performance but also in the way class background is used as motivation: Bennett is a former used car salesman who resents his fellow junior officers and whose vulgarity reveals his lack of breeding. Between-class characters became Baker's forte, as borne out in *Zulu* by the rivalry between the engineer Chard and the blue-blooded Bromhead. (One might say that, in *Zulu*, the likes of Bennett get to win out over the hereditary officer class.) Baker did not fit the middle-class, Home Counties, pipe-and-tweed mould of male British stardom in the mid-50s – in *The Red Beret* (1953) his voice was dubbed over with a more English-sounding accent – so in most of his early pictures he appeared as a glowering heavy.

Baker won a contract with the producer Alexander Korda, for whom he played Henry Percy in Laurence Olivier's film of *Richard III* (1955), but after Korda's death in 1956 he was 'sold' to the Rank Organisation. This was perhaps the worst fate which could befall a promising young actor at the time, leading to such pallid vehicles as *Checkpoint* (1956), *Campbell's Kingdom* (1957) and *Violent Playground* (1958). Despairing at the short-sightedness of the studio's management, which after two years could find little to interest him, Baker bought his way out of the contract. 'They have no plans as an organisation,' he explained. 'They change attitudes week by week, almost day by day.'[5]

However, he fared better at the hands of American directors, who seemed to appreciate and exploit his rugged Celtic masculinity more successfully than domestic filmmakers. 'Americans saw Stanley as more American than British,' believes Ellen Baker. 'They all said, "We can work with you." Maybe it was the Welsh thing.' Baker won a number of key character parts in Hollywood-financed epics

Baker and Patrick Magee in Joseph Losey's *The Criminal*.

and action films made in Britain and Continental Europe: he replaced George Sanders as the evil Modred in *Knights of the Round Table* (1953), was Achilles in *Helen of Troy* (1955), supported Richard Burton in *Alexander the Great* (1956) – their only on-screen appearance together – and played an oddly sympathetic Nazi in *The Angry Hills* (1959). Most significant, however, were the long-term associations he formed with two left-wing American émigrés, both refugees from the Communist blacklist.

The first of Baker's six films with Cy Endfield was *Child in the House* (1956), and in close succession there followed *Hell Drivers* (1957), *Sea Fury* (1958) and *Jet Storm* (1959). These films presented the actor more sympathetically than in any of his previous work to date, giving him his start as a leading man. He gradually earned a loyal following, even becoming seen as a sex symbol. *Hell Drivers*, reported *Films and Filming*, 'showed an enormous increase in his fan mail from girls between the ages of 17 and 20.' The magazine considered that he represented 'the new breed of British actor: the realist,' and offered this assessment of his evolving image as he moved away from purely villainous roles:

> Baker in recent years has been conscientious in his choice of parts. He has played a waiting game for scripts which give him a chance of showing that ordinary men, doing everyday jobs, can be exciting and often are ... This full-blooded and two dimensional approach to the part that he is playing, has kept Baker's audiences from wholeheartedly accepting him. They can't love him. They can't hate him. He defies being pigeon-holed.
>
> It is in this refusal to be categorised that the secret of Baker's success and slow development as a box-office name lies.[6]

This may also help to account for his lack of full critical recognition during his lifetime.

Though a product of the 50s, Baker, with his barely disguised working class origins, stood out from his contemporaries as a harbinger of the 60s and such socially mobile stars as Albert Finney, Peter O'Toole, Sean Connery and Richard Harris (according to Ellen, he was the initial casting choice for the 1963 film of *This Sporting Life* as well as an early contender for James Bond).[7]

Despite his long association with Endfield, it was Joseph Losey whom Baker most credited with teaching him to take the cinema, and screen acting, seriously. He was impressed by Losey's 'total involvement in film making ... for the first time in my life I really became properly aware of an actor's total responsibility when acting on a film. It was still as enjoyable as it was before but it was something else, it was something better.'[8] The four films they made together – *Blind Date* (1959), *The Criminal* (1960), *Eva* (1962) and *Accident* (1967) – arguably contain Baker's finest performances, in which he was able to explore his characters' psychological makeup with greater depth and complexity than in anything else he attempted.[9] The experience of working with Losey also provided the initial impetus for Baker to turn producer: 'I thought there's a better and a bigger thing to do than just acting in a film and that is to make a film,' he told Clive James in 1972. Ironically, Losey himself – a prickly personality – disapproved of *Zulu*; he once told Ellen: 'I thought that film was disgraceful. I thought I'd taught Stanley better than that. I'm bitterly disappointed in him.' When Stanley was dying from cancer, she recalls, 'Joe wrote him a letter telling him off: "How dare you get ill?" But Joe taught Stanley everything he knew about filmmaking.'

In 1959 Baker told *Films and Filming* that, 'British producers are becoming more enlightened by the hour,' and indeed the calibre of his films showed considerable improvement with *Yesterday's Enemy* (1959), *Hell is a City* (1960) and *A Prize of Arms* (1962). *Yesterday's Enemy*, a war picture set in the Burmese jungle but made by Hammer Films entirely on interior studio sets, is particularly remarkable for Baker's role as a ruthless officer who executes civilians in order to extract a confession from an informant. A few lines of dialogue indicate the character's attitudes: 'Never mind the padre. I don't want any nonsense about a service. My concern is with the living, not the dead.' 'There's only one way to fight a war, and that's with the gloves off.' Baker's Chard is clearly cut from the same cloth; one feels he too would not stop far short of summary execution if the situation called for it.

A supporting role in the huge international hit *The Guns of Navarone* (1961) gave Baker valuable exposure and he was offered a long-term contract by Columbia but declined to move base to Hollywood – an environment which, according to Ellen, he detested. He never made a film in America. Stanley sought instead to extend his career in his native industry by moving into production. He later told *Photoplay* magazine: 'I became a producer because whenever I read stories or scripts that seemed worthwhile material for films, I used to pass them on to other people. It was the other people who made them into films. I began to wonder: why not me? Why shouldn't I make these films myself?'[10] In 1960 he set up Stanley Baker Arts to develop his own projects, and later formed a film production company, Oakhurst. Though many Hollywood stars had been setting up their own companies for both tax and creative purposes since the mid-40s, actor-producers were still relatively uncommon in the British film industry. Indeed, Baker's co-star in both *Zulu* and *The Cruel Sea*, Jack Hawkins, had been one of the first to move in this direction when, with fellow actors Richard Attenborough and Bryan Forbes, he set up Allied Film Makers in 1959, the first project of which was *The League of Gentlemen* (1960).

Baker wanted his own inaugural producing venture to have some personal significance, and when Cy Endfield and Douglas Rankin showed him John Prebble's screenplay adaptation of his magazine article about Rorke's Drift, it clearly fit the bill. 'I liked him immediately,' said Prebble about his first meeting with the actor. 'He was a very kind and courteous man, but a bit cold. I was never sure whether he liked the script at that time, or liked the idea.'[11] Prior to shooting, Baker told a television interviewer: 'The first thing that attracted me to the subject was that it was about the South Wales Borderers.'[12] But his imagination was also fired by the Zulus themselves. 'Suddenly I became interested not only in the film, but in the people we were making it about,' he said later. 'I financed two years of research and preparation out of my own pocket.'[13]

In early 1962 he successfully pitched *Zulu* to yet another American, the impresario Joseph E. Levine, while in Rome shooting *Sodom and Gomorrah* (1962), and with Cy Endfield he formed a new company, Diamond, to get the film made. 'He had gone to Rank for finance,' says Bob Porter, Baker's close friend and colleague, 'but they and most people in England didn't reckon him as a star. If he'd been in America he'd have been another Humphrey Bogart. In England he was seen as a "second" man.' As a first-time producer, Porter remembers, Stanley was 'green as a duck – he was an *actor*.' Stanley himself told the London *Evening Standard* that potential backers may have been put off by this: 'They may very well have thought, he's had no experience of producing and he'll probably just live it up.'[14] But unlike some stars who take producer status to enhance their prestige and profit without assuming the day-to-day responsibilities of the job, Baker was determined to have a hands-on role in making the picture.

'Stanley was 35 at the time,' recalls Ellen. 'That was very young for a producer on a big film.' The burden proved heavy for him at times. Ellen recalls that the strain showed in the early days of filming, 'but as the film went on he relaxed. He had always wanted to produce a picture. I was amazed at his talent for it, but I didn't like it. I'd married an actor, not a producer.' His wife was not the only person surprised by Baker's newly revealed abilities. 'There are those who looked upon Mr. Baker as an efficient actor but more at

home spending money around in a night club than working out budgets in an office,' said the *Evening Standard*. 'In fact he worked from 5.30 in the morning until bed time.'[15]

Stunt arranger and actor Joe Powell, who had worked with him on *Captain Horatio Hornblower R.N.*, says Baker clearly set his producer's stamp on *Zulu*: 'Stanley Baker was dead keen on getting the action absolutely right – he was very meticulous on the details. He had a tremendous interest in all aspects of the film all the way through.' Glynn Edwards recalls: 'Although he had the reputation of being a jack-the-lad, chatting and boozing, he was conscious that he had a tight ship to run. He mucked in but he was very aware he was the producer. He kept both flags flying very well. He'd come with us to drink in the bar, but when it went too far you knew – steady lads, he's the producer.' Sydney Chama, who as a boy visited the location to watch his uncle, Simon Sabela, act as a Zulu stuntman, remembered Stanley as 'Big Daddy – a very meticulous, hard-working person, a good sense of humour now and again, but you could feel that he had a very big burden on his shoulders. It was quite a challenge; he'd taken a giant step and he wanted to live up to it.'

Not all the *Zulu* crew have fond memories of Baker, however. According to camera technician Peter Hammond, he had a hot temper and his behaviour could be volatile and

unpredictable: 'We had a getting-to-know-you party at the beginning of the film, on our second night in Africa. I was sitting at a table with Brian Ellis, the clapper boy, and a few others, having a laugh. Someone told a joke and Brian just happened to look at Stanley Baker when he started to laugh. Stanley came over, pulled him up and was going to plant one on him.' Baker's favourite pastime in leisure hours was gambling; sound technician David Jones recalls the boom platform being used as a poker table: 'He was a great gambler. He played poker, but nobody ever wanted to play him because he would never give in.' John Prebble, who had been warned against playing cards with Baker, confirms that he was 'an inexorable poker player, with no mercy shown.' ('He didn't like losing!' adds Bob Porter.)

Baker himself looked back on the experience of producing with mixed feelings. In an article he wrote for the American trade journal *Motion Picture Herald* he commented: 'Surprisingly, I found no conflict between acting and producing. During the day, I acted; at night, I became a producer, attacking that job's problems. There were many.'[16] There were also many rewards, he told a British trade press reporter:

'It's the first film I've produced and it's not just a nominal title, either: I physically produced it and I found it stimulating.'

He became so closely identified with the physical production of the film that he was quite disturbed when it hit him one day that the sets were only temporary and would eventually have to come down.

'That was the only sad thing about it,' he said.[17]

Later, when the film had just gone into release, he told another journalist:

'I don't mind telling you I went through two of the worst months of my life.

'Suddenly someone had given me a million pounds to make a film with! All the fears and doubts and misgivings came

rushing in: was I capable of producing and acting? Could I do this, did I dare do that?

'Then one morning I woke up and thought: "What the hell! You're here to make a film so go right on and make it."'[18]

By the time of this interview *Zulu* was already 'a smash', and Stanley speculated that 'with any luck it'll be the biggest grosser of all time, bigger than James Bond, even.'

Zulu's success was rewarded by Joe Levine with a three-year, multiple-film contract for Baker as actor and producer.[19] Searching around for other projects to make in South Africa, Stanley followed *Zulu* with *Dingaka* and his final film with Cy Endfield, the ill-fated *Sands of the Kalahari* (both 1965). With the latter's box-office failure, other planned collaborations foundered, and Endfield and Baker went their separate ways. Oakhurst did eventually succeed in producing three more pictures. *Robbery* (1967), loosely based on the 1963 Great Train Robbery, was made for release through Embassy, while *The Italian Job* (1969), a more light-hearted caper starring Michael Caine, was released by Paramount (Baker appeared in the former but not the latter).[20] Both were highly successful in the UK, if not in the US, but *Where's Jack?* (1969) – a costume drama set in eighteenth-century London and filmed in Ireland, co-starring Baker with Tommy Steele – was an expensive flop. It was the last Oakhurst production, though Stanley continued to entertain the prospect of the company making up to three films a year.21 Producing, he said in 1970, had 'furthered my understanding and my need to understand film making and methods of film making and what I believe are the sort of films that should be made. It's got me more involved with acting because the more involved with a production you are, the better it is ... When I'm acting and producing, people ask if it's difficult to do the two things. My answer, if it's an honest answer, is no, it's a hell of a lot easier because you have to be on the set and you're totally involved in every aspect of the film all the time, and this helps you as an actor.'22

While Oakhurst was still a going concern, Baker became more ambitious and wide-ranging in his business ventures. He was a founder director and major shareholder of the Welsh commercial television station HTV (Harlech Television). In 1967 he bought Alembic House, a tower block on Albert Embankment, overlooking the Houses of Parliament. 'Buying it was part of Stanley's determination to ensure a future for the family,' says Ellen Baker. He installed various show-business friends in its luxury apartments: 'He wanted his chums around him. John Barry was living on the tenth floor with Jane Birkin. Stanley's offices were on the eleventh floor and his business manager John McMichael was on the twelfth. Richard Harris also lived on the twelfth floor.'

Stanley saw no contradiction between capitalist enterprise and his socialist principles. He became a prominent activist on behalf of the Labour Party, supplying production facilities for, as well as presenting, party political broadcasts in Harold Wilson's 1970 election campaign and frequently speaking at rallies and conferences. However, his financial resources were eventually over-extended when, along with Michael Deeley and Barry Spikings, his new partners in Oakhurst (Bob Porter having departed), he sold Alembic House in exchange for a controlling interest in the state-subsidised company British Lion, which owned Shepperton Studios. A stock market crash

resulted in heavy losses and he was forced to curtail his production activities.23 Baker's later British pictures, such as *The Last Grenade* (1969), *The Games*, *Perfect Friday* (both 1970) and *Innocent Bystanders* (1972), were relatively undistinguished. He subsequently acted mainly in European co-productions, such as *Popsy Pop* (1970), *Lizard in a Woman's Skin* (1971), *Zorro* (1974) and *Pepita Jiménez* (1975), though he remained resident in Britain. Indeed his most notable later work was done for British television, in single plays such as *The Changeling*, *Graceless Go I*, *Who Killed Lamb?* and *Robinson Crusoe* (all 1974), and in the BBC's serial adaptation of *How Green Was My Valley* (1975), which took him back to Wales for his last screen performance.

Zulu itself was financially a mixed blessing. In 1967 he had said ruefully: 'Every month I'm told: "You'll begin to see your profits soon." But nothing happens.' Another investment had an ironic conclusion after Stanley's death. At auction in 1972 he bought a box of medals belonging to the real Lieutenant John Chard for £2,700. They included what was thought to be a cast copy of his Victoria Cross, the original having been presumed lost. Ellen recalls: 'After he died we found the medals in a desk drawer and took them to Spink's, who gave me £5,000 for them on the spot.' Scientific tests later revealed that the VC was authentic. It was valued at £350,000 – the original budget estimate for *Zulu*.24 It since been sold several times at auction, fetching even higher prices; it may well be the single most sought-after Victoria Cross ever struck.

Stanley was re-united with Cy Endfield and Bob Porter when they tried to set up *Zulu*

Dawn in the mid-1970s, but before they could properly begin pre-production Stanley was diagnosed with lung cancer. 'Cy didn't want to do it without Stanley,' says Ellen Baker. 'Stanley got paid a little money and pulled out. Cy and I sold the rights to another company after his death.' In February 1976, Baker underwent an operation to remove the cancer and appeared to be recuperating well. He was given a fillip when, in May, he was awarded a knighthood in Harold Wilson's resignation honours.[25] But he did not live to have the honour conferred by the Queen. He contracted double pneumonia after swimming while on holiday at his Spanish villa, against doctors' advice. He was hospitalised in Malaga for three days and died on 28 June 1976, aged 48. Baker's body was cremated a week later, and his ashes scattered on a mountain top overlooking Ferndale. This occasion was recalled by his childhood friend Arthur Bowen:

Stanley shows off a few South African souvenirs before boarding the flight back to London.

> After the service finished I was walking back to my car and I met this coloured feller from Maerdy. I knew him well. I said to him, 'Well, what are you doing up here, then? What contact did you have with Stanley Baker, 'cause you are Maerdy man, and Stanley was a Ferndale boy like myself?' 'Well, it's like this,' he said, 'someone had to come up here to represent the Zulus at this funeral!'[26]

On 6 October a memorial service was held at St Martin's-in-the-Fields, attended by colleagues, family and friends including Endfield, Porter, Jack Hawkins' widow Doreen, Ivor Emmanuel and Harold Wilson. Harry Secombe led a chorus of miners in some Welsh songs, and tributes were made by Hammer's chairman Sir James Carreras and George Thomas MP, Speaker of the House of Commons.[27] Ellen, now Lady Baker, remembers that Prince Mangosuthu Buthelezi, with whom Baker had been friends since making *Zulu*, sent a wreath and a letter saying that Stanley was the finest white man he had ever met. Buthelezi himself offered these reflections for the BBC: 'He was a very humble person, and you really couldn't help just loving him. He was a very caring man, I'd say, because he was concerned about the happiness of all the extras and the people who were acting as stuntmen in the film. It was quite a wonderful thing to relate to him, and for him to relate to Black people at that time.'

Baker is remembered by those who knew him well as a mixture of toughness and sensitivity, earthiness and intelligence. 'He was a tough old sod,' says James Booth. 'But like a lot of seriously tough men, he had a soft centre. Like a lot of Welshmen he would burst into song and cry.' John Prebble spent several weeks with Baker on the set of *Sands of the Kalahari* and recalled his courtesy and concern for the writer's welfare: 'He was always deferential and polite; he always, if I was on the set, had me sit next to him when he was not acting, when he was resting. I was suffering from a peptic ulcer, which meant I didn't have anything on a six-week trip except bland fish and milk. Stanley instructed his wife and Cy's wife and Susannah York, who was playing the lead in it, to keep me from eating or drinking anything except milk and water; he would come round and check this. He talked quite a lot about his life and childhood in Wales. His house in Wimbledon was full of miners' lamps – mad about Wales.' Anthony Storey, co-writer of *Zulu Dawn* and author of what is still the only book yet published about the actor,[28] thought him 'a great man. He was a very *male* male – a clever man, but inarticulate. His sentences were usually only four or five words long, but straight to the point. Almost every acting professional I met said that Stanley was under-rated.'

Richard Burton paid his own, idiosyncratic tribute in a self-penned newspaper article he described as 'a murderous love letter;' Stanley's family were upset to find him characterised as 'a rough and terrifying old boot … with a face like a determined fist prepared to take the first blow but not the second.'[29] Ellen Baker prefers to remember the loving husband, father and family man, whose softer side the public rarely saw, as it did not make such good copy in the newspapers. The hard-man image was largely a myth, she says; though Stanley enjoyed his reputation, played up to it in interviews and was frequently challenged by drunks to prove that he was as tough as his screen persona, he always tried to dodge fisticuffs. Once, when a would-be assailant in a Soho dining establishment ended up charging through a plate glass window, Stanley picked him up and escorted him to Charing Cross Hospital. Following the sale of Alembic House, Ellen discovered that Stanley had secretly kept a cheque-book just to give money to out-of-work actors and broken-down boxers.

Bob Porter, who was with Stanley when he died, fondly recalls a man who was always true to his word: 'In all the years I was with Stanley we never had a contract between us – no piece of paper till the day I left the company, and he honoured every penny and shilling for everything we did, even after he died.' Baker took films seriously but suffered no pretensions. Bob remembers the advice Stanley gave co-star Susannah York when she wanted to know how to play a scene in *Sands of the Kalahari*: 'Stand in front of the camera and say the fucking words.' An editorial in the British trade journal *Screen International* remarked on his down-to-earth qualities: 'In The White Elephant or Les Ambassadeurs he would order a baked potato as his main course. As the waiter stood there slightly astonished, Stanley would add: *"And fill it with butter and a large portion of Beluga caviar!"* The baked potato reminded him of early life in Ferndale. The caviar was to celebrate his success.'[30]

Shortly before his death, while planning the shooting of *Zulu Dawn*, Baker himself had this to say about *Zulu* when interviewed by the BBC's Vincent Kane in 1975:

> I've made something like sixty-odd films since 1952 and none of them has affected me in the particular way this film has affected me. Not because of its critical and financial success, but because I was terribly involved *with* it – before I made it, during the time I made it, after it was shown, and I'm *still* involved with it.[31]

Notes

[1] Susan Barnes, 'How I hate flattery grumbles Mr. Baker,' *Sunday Express*, 2 February 1964, p. 3.

[2] This and the following quotations are taken from the *Zulu* Production Information Dossier, p. 12.

[3] Lester David and Jhan Robbins, *Richard & Elizabeth* (London: Arthur Barker, 1977), p. 34. Ellen Baker is sceptical of Burton's account of his sexual education and suggests that it was most probably the other way around, Stanley being fourteen years old at the time to Richard's sixteen.

[4] Robert Ottaway, 'How strange… that I may spend more in a minute than my father earned in a year,' *TV Times*, 14 March 1974, p. 4.

[5] 'Stanley Baker: Tough at the Top', *Films and Filming*, November 1959, p. 5.

[6] Ibid.

[7] For more recent appreciations of Baker's significance, see Andrew Spicer, 'The emergence of the British tough guy: Stanley Baker, masculinity and the British

crime thriller,' in Steve Chibnall and Robert Murphy (eds.), *British Crime Cinema* (London and New York: Routledge, 1999); and chapters in Geoffrey Macnab, *Searching for Stars: Stardom and Screen Acting in British Cinema* (London and New York: Cassell, 2000); Andrew Spicer, *Typical Men: The Representation of Masculinity in Popular British Cinema* (London and New York: I.B. Tauris, 2001); and Peter Stead, *Acting Wales: Stars of Stage and Screen* (Wales, 2002).

[8] Interview with Clive James for *Cinema* (Granada Television, broadcast 2 November 1972; transcript consulted in the British Film Institute Library Special Collections).

[9] Baker's films with Losey, along with *Zulu*, are discussed in David Berry, *Wales and Cinema: The First Hundred Years* (Cardiff: University of Wales Press, 1994), pp. 259-68.

[10] Des Hickey, 'Why I wanted to produce my own movies,' *Photoplay*, February 1969, p. 47.

[11] Unused interview recorded for *Stanley Baker: A Life in Film* (BBC Wales, 1996).

[12] Interview for Television Wales and West, 1962.

[13] Alan Road, 'Zulu bwana,' *The Observer Magazine*, 17 August 1975; Hickey, op. cit. 'News to me!' said Maureen Endfield when I showed her Baker's remark about his financing the research.

[14] 'Enter Mr. Baker, new role: tycoon,' *Evening Standard*, [?] September 1963.

[15] Ibid.

[16] Stanley Baker, 'Meeting the Challenge Of Producing an Epic As a First Picture,' *Motion Picture Herald*, 8 September 1963, p. 10.

[17] Derek Todd, '*Zulu* safari makes camp at Twickenham,' *Kine. Weekly*, 18 July 1963, p. 12.

[18] William Hall, 'The Lush Life – by Mr. Baker,' *Evening News*, 7 March 1964.

[19] 'Levine signs Baker to 3 year contract', *Daily Cinema*, 25 May 1964, p. 6; Robin Bean, 'Mud Victim', *Films and Filming*, July 1964, p. 50.

[20] In the background of a scene in *Robbery*, a policewoman puts in this call to a squad car: 'Calling Zulu Five, Zulu Five.'

[21] There is also *The Other People* (1968, also known as *I Love You, I Hate You* and *Sleep is Lovely*), co-produced by Oakhurst and Telstar for Paramount, which seems not to have received a theatrical release.

[22] Margaret Tarratt and Kevin Gough-Yates, 'Playing the game,' *Films and Filming*, August 1970, p. 33.

[23] For a concise discussion of this misadventure, see Alexander Walker, *National Heroes: British Cinema in the Seventies and Eighties* (London: Harrap, 1985), pp. 116-29.

[24] '"Lost" VC of Zulu battle is found,' *The Times*, 13 June 1996; Simon De Burton, 'Incredible journey of soldier's Zulu medals,' *Evening Standard*, 12 January 2001, p. 21. The medal has since been sold again, fetching twice this estimated value. For further discussion of this issue, see Oliver Bennett, 'How to make a heroic investment,' *The Independent*, 18 September 2004, pp. 8-9, which quotes medals collector Michael Hargreave Mawson as saying that Anglo-Zulu War medals 'are worth far more than other medals of the period, which is all the fault of Michael Caine in the film.'

[25] 'Sir Harold Productions is proud to present...', *Screen International*, 29 May 1976, p. 1.

[26] Interview recorded for *Stanley Baker: A Life in Film*. Prince Buthelezi's subsequent comments were also recorded for this programme.

[27] 'Memorial service for Sir Stanley', *Screen International*, 9 October 1976, p. 20.

[28] Anthony Storey, *Stanley Baker: Portrait of an Actor* (London: W.H. Allen, 1977).

[29] *The Observer*, 11 July 1976. For Ellen Baker's reaction to Burton's article, see Peter McKay, 'Town Talk,' *Sunday Express*, 18 July 1976.

[30] The Editor, 'A tribute to Sir Stanley Baker,' *Screen International*, [?] July 1976, p. 3.

[31] Interviewed in *Kane on Monday* (BBC Wales, first broadcast 1975 and repeated on 30 June 1976, two days after Baker's death).

Left to right: Ellen and Stanley Baker, executive producer Joseph E. Levine and second unit director Bob Porter.

"I CAME UP HERE TO BUILD A BRIDGE"

MAKING THE DEAL

7

> *The Battle of Rorke's Drift* was the less-than-catchy title of a filmscript which, by 1962, had been doing the rounds of the major film companies for a year or two. Co-written by director Cy Endfield and John Prebble (later historical adviser on the memorable BBC TV play *Culloden*), it had been through several 'almost' situations, but the film moguls were still wary. There were no big name stars involved; they argued; and they thought the budget was too large for a film that was unlikely to take off anywhere except Britain. Only one studio, Columbia, had shown any definite interest, but they said they would only make the picture if Endfield could get Burt Lancaster to do it!
>
> Most of these refusals seemed like stock answers to the experienced Endfield, who was convinced there was a much simpler solution to the problem of getting his script accepted. He'd suspected the cumbersome title might be putting people off, and he clearly remembers the day when, while crossing Grosvenor Square in London, the flash of inspiration came. He'd call it simply *Zulu*.
>
> (Elaine Gallagher, *Candidly Caine*, London: Robson Books/London Weekend Television, 1990, p. 69)

The deal to make *Zulu* was concluded, as it had begun, with a handshake. The terms were finalised in the gentlemen's rest room of London's Dorchester Hotel, with only one condition: 'First, wash your hands.' That, at any rate, is how Stanley Baker's friend and business associate Bob Porter remembers it. But it had taken three years to reach that final handshake and there would be another two years before the film itself would reach the public.

The actor had not in fact been brought onto the project until more than a year after Douglas Rankin, an advertising executive and a producer of television commercials, had commissioned John Prebble to write a screenplay after reading *Slaughter in the Sun* in *Lilliput*. Rankin took the draft script to Cy Endfield, who had directed TV advertisements for him, and Endfield in turn showed it to Baker. While working separately on other films over the next few years, they both tried to raise the necessary finance for the project. Rankin was subsequently rewarded with a screen credit as production consultant, though aside from attending some early pre-production meetings he seems to have done no more work on the picture.

The budget for the proposed epic was initially set at £350,000 (at that time the equivalent of around $1 million): modest by Hollywood standards but a hefty sum for Britain. To entice potential investors Endfield offered a choice of actors for the starring role: either Baker or Stanley's friend of many years and fellow Welshman, Richard Burton. In the manuscript of an unpublished article, the director recalled a meeting in 1960 with a recently formed producer-distributor, Britannia Films, which had backed his and Baker's previous film together, *Jet Storm* (1959), and whose board of directors was chaired by Sir Michael Balcon, until recently in charge of Ealing Studios. Endfield was handed a report on Britannia's judgement of *Zulu*'s commercial possibilities:

> In summary it was that they would take on the project if I could reduce my budget by one-third (knowing this to be impossible, I took it as a rejection). This made irrelevant their additional comment – they deemed the Richard Burton suggestion unacceptable, because, said they, they deemed that Burton was "finished" in films. Baker, though not really big-star casting had the virtue of being a "new face," with unknown potential, at least not – like Burton (in their opinion 1960) – a has-been.[1]

Burton had lately appeared in a string of box-office flops, including the screen adaptation of John Osborne's *Look Back in Anger* (1959). By the time *Zulu* was ready to shoot, he had become one of the most sought-after and highly paid actors in the world, in large part because of the scandal over his relationship with Elizabeth Taylor while they were making *Cleopatra* (1963), which was nearing completion as filming on *Zulu* commenced. Burton's career was then, as Endfield reflected, 'on such a level that his availability for casting in a modestly budgeted English film would quite simply be beyond the pale of possibility,' though he was later persuaded to supply the voice-over narration without taking a fee. Endfield does not say so, but the meeting with Britannia probably took place before Baker came on board. The company's preference for Baker over Burton no doubt influenced the director's decision to share the project with him, but had Britannia considered him viable it is quite likely that *Zulu* would have been Burton's vehicle instead of Baker's.

The project was first announced to the press, under its working title *The Battle of*

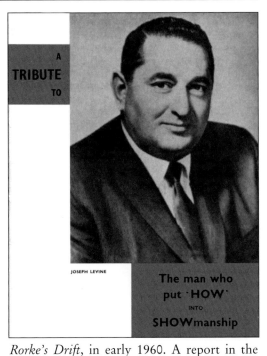

Rorke's Drift, in early 1960. A report in the popular British magazine *Films and Filming*, discussing Baker's producing ambitions, noted that he had 'plans for his company to make *The Battle of O'Rourke's Drift* [sic] with Donald Houston. This is the epic story of the Welsh Borderers.'[2] The vagueness of this comment suggests how little was generally known about the historical events before the film was released; Houston, for the record, was originally to play Colour-Sergeant Bourne. Baker and Endfield took every opportunity to pitch the story to potential backers, approaching as many as thirty production companies and distributors, but it aroused little interest – certainly not with an actor as its debutante producer. 'It took about two years of literally carrying that script under one's arm and being thrown out of every distribution office from here to California,' he later recalled in a television interview. 'Nobody wanted to know about that film – particularly companies in this country. They all said it was a non-commercial project – it was sort of dull and who wanted to know about the Zulu War in any case?'[3] The industry had been in recession since the late 40s and British film financiers were then, as ever, highly conservative and cautious about spending money on any picture without a guaranteed box-office return.

Several times the project came close to being made after it became known as *Zulu* from the screenplay's second draft onwards. One spurt of interest came from Warwick Productions, chaired by American expatriates Albert R. Broccoli and Irving Allen, with Columbia as its chief backer and distributor. Warwick specialised in formula action adventures with an international flavour; earlier in his career Stanley had acted in its first two productions, *The Red Beret* (1953) and *Hell Below Zero* (1954). Broccoli and Allen assigned the project to producer Harold Huth, who had recently made *The Hellions* (1961) for Warwick in South Africa, and agreed a budget of two million Rand. But *The Hellions* turned out to be the company's last film; indeed it did not go out under the Warwick banner, as even before its release the partners went their separate ways, Broccoli to form a new company, Eon, with Harry Saltzman to make *Dr. No* (1962), the first of the James Bond films.

Anglo Amalgamated, whose chief executives Nat Cohen and Stuart Levy had enjoyed success mainly with horror and exploitation pictures and the early *Carry On* films, then stepped in as a backer for *Zulu*. This company had recently closed down its domestic distribution arm in order to concentrate on production; it would subsequently release its product through Warner-Pathé, whose parent company Associated British Picture Corporation had a fifty per-cent stake in Anglo. But it too withdrew at the eleventh hour, after a production schedule had already been drawn up and a start date for location filming announced.[4] In the interim, however, Baker had found himself another sponsor.

Joseph E. Levine (1905-1987) was the Boston-born son of poor Russian-Jewish immigrants. After pursuing various business interests, including running a restaurant and a garment factory, Levine entered the film industry in 1938 when he bought a small 'art house' theatre in New Haven, Connecticut. He began by showing a mixture of old B-Westerns and European imports supplied by the small number of specialised distributors then in operation. In 1942 Joe formed his own company, Embassy, with his wife Rosalie as vice-president, to distribute pictures independently. His early successes included the Italian neo-realist classics *Rome – Open City* (1945), *Paisá* (1946), *Shoeshine* (1946) and *Bicycle Thieves* (1948), as well as more downmarket exploitation fare such as *How to Undress in Front of Your Husband*. He broke into the major league when he acquired the Japanese creature feature *Godzilla* (1954) and the low-budget Italian epics *Attila* (1954) and *Hercules* (1958), and using extravagant publicity methods turned these unpromising items into box-office giants. The rights to *Attila* cost Levine $80,000; he spent $590,000 promoting it and earned more than $2 million in US and Canadian rentals. *Hercules* was an even more spectacular hit: costing $125,000 to buy and $1,156,000 to promote, the film took $4.7 million in domestic rentals (though

---

We are very happy to announce our association with Stanley Baker and Cy Endfield to make

"ZULU"

the inspiring story of the heroic battle of Rorke's Drift to be produced in the Union of South Africa and in England early in 1963, in Technirama 70

Joseph E. Levine   *Nat Cohen Stuart Levy*
EMBASSY PICTURES CORPORATION   ANGLO AMALGAMATED

The collaboration of Embassy and Anglo Amalgamated as co-producers of *Zulu* was announced prematurely in this trade advertisement, which appeared in *The Daily Cinema* on 5 November 1962.

Levine often claimed that it had grossed more than $20 million). Its sequel, *Hercules Unchained* (1959), was named the number one general release in the UK for 1960 thanks to Joe's promotional tactics, and in spite of a total lack of critical acclaim.⁵ Levine's groundbreaking methods included the use of full-page newspaper advertising and television spots timed to coincide with the picture's opening. Perhaps most importantly, he pioneered the simultaneous saturation release of an unusually large – for the time – number of prints: some 600 in the US for *Hercules*, twice the usual inventory for a major feature.⁶

From 1960 Levine used his profits from distribution to invest in international production, especially in Italy, where he helped to finance such well-regarded pictures as the Oscar-winning *Two Women* (1960), *Divorce, Italian Style* (1961), *Boccaccio '70* (1962), *8½* (1963), *Yesterday, Today and Tomorrow* (1963) and *Le Mépris* (*Contempt*, 1963), in which the philistine film producer played by Jack Palance is supposedly based on Levine himself. He also began to get involved in upmarket domestic production with *Long Day's Journey Into Night* (1962) and in the same year he made the first of many deals for more mainstream commercial product with the major Hollywood studio Paramount. By this arrangement he agreed to supply the company with three pictures, all based on Harold Robbins properties – *The Carpetbaggers*, *Where Love Has Gone* (both released in 1964) and *Nevada Smith* (which was delayed until 1966) – which Paramount would finance and distribute worldwide.⁷

Paramount's executives soon came to regard Levine as an ally who might help to fill the gap left by the death in 1959 of its previous major supplier of large-scale spectacles, Cecil B. DeMille. Indeed in 1963 Levine received the DeMille Award as Showman of the Year from the Hollywood Foreign Press Association (the body which hands out the Golden Globes). By this time he had the most extensive production programme of any American-based independent: Embassy, which now had eleven branch offices in the US and four overseas, announced twenty-three new films for 1963-64, representing a combined production investment of $25 million and an advertising budget of $8 million. None other than President John F. Kennedy hailed Levine as 'the master showman of the world.' According to US trade paper *Variety*, Levine was 'perhaps responsible for the most excitement created by an individual on the business end of the film business in some number of years. His bids for overseas productions have made him a household world [sic] in foreign production circles and he has become significantly known in the U.S. for his merchandising methods along with the product he has to offer.'⁸ Levine in his turn saw the association with Paramount as a way of easing Embassy's distribution load as well as a source of finance for its more ambitious ventures. Their partnership was, however, non-exclusive: despite persistent rumours that Embassy and Paramount would merge, Levine retained his numerous links to other producers and distributors as well as full autonomy over his own company's in-house production and distribution activities.⁹

A co-production between Embassy, Twentieth Century-Fox, Britain's Rank Organisation and the Italian company Titanus, *Sodom and Gomorrah* (1962) was an expensive Biblical epic with locations in Morocco and interiors shot in studios in Rome. Levine

> 21, Oct. 1964
>
> Welcome, dear Joe, and the very best wishes to THE CARPETBAGGERS
>
> from the ZULUs
>
> Stanley and Cy

The producers of *Zulu* paid for this advertisement in *The Daily Cinema*'s special supplement on the occasion of the UK release of Joe Levine's production of *The Carpetbaggers*.

visited the studio in early 1962 to see how the picture was getting along, and after watching some of the filming he attended a screening of the rushes, where he met one of its stars, Stanley Baker. Stanley often liked to tell the story by which he got a verbal agreement from Levine to back *Zulu* and it appeared with numerous variations over the years. Here are three such versions:

> When we got out of the theatre he [Levine] put his arm around my shoulders and said, 'If you ever want to make anything talk to me.' It was a heaven-sent opportunity for an actor who was sitting on a great story budgeted down to the last penny and ready to go.
>
> I sent him the script. He read it that night, called next morning to ask what it would cost. When I told him he said, 'We have a deal.' He was willing to take the risk although we were going 8,000 miles away, taking 11 actors and a crew of 70 from England.

> We were together, quite accidentally, in a lavatory in Rome and Levine turned to me and said: 'Baker, how's about that script you've been talking about? We'll do it.' He hadn't read it, he didn't know the cost, but he seemed to have confidence in me. But if I had shown doubts about myself, he wouldn't have been convinced. Belief in yourself is the essential quality.

> At the end of a week's rushes he came to me, flamboyantly, magnanimously, and he said, 'If you ever want to do anything, you come to me.' And I said, 'Well, I've got this script in my pocket….' True! I went to the Excelsior Hotel the next day, on the Sunday morning at eight o'clock, with the script. He said, 'I don't want to look at the script, what's it called?' I said, '*Zulu*.' He said, 'Fine, you got a deal.' [10]

Whatever the particular circumstances were, several factors remain constant: Levine's willingness to take a gamble, his faith in Baker's determination, and the allure of the title, *Zulu*. As soon as he heard the word, Levine could envision it above a theatre marquee, spelt out in big letters alongside a giant poster of a belligerent African warrior. 'Joe Levine was a sort of fairground barker,' said John Prebble, 'and this was the sort of sign he could see – the word coming out in enlargement. I still don't think he ever read the script.' Levine had a record of buying potent titles around which he could construct an elaborate promotional campaign. The film itself mattered less in his eyes than its marketable image, as his success with *Godzilla*, *Attila* and *Hercules* – all one-word titles – had shown. Photographer Yousuf Karsh later recounted a further version of Baker's anecdote, as told to him by Michael Caine: 'Levine had received the script of *Zulu* from Stanley Baker on a Friday, and on Monday, called Baker to tell him he was buying *Zulu* and wanted to begin filming as soon as possible. "You liked the script that much," Baker asked incredulously. "I haven't had time to read it," Joe replied, "but I liked the title."'[11] In a seminar for the American Film Institute in 1979, Levine explained his habit of playing a hunch: 'If you stop to analyse a picture, with all these guys sitting around a board of directors' meeting and they don't want to make it because the wind is coming from the south-east – I mean, that's a lot of bunk. If you want to make it, *make* it.' Even he admitted, however, that there was only so much that advertising could do: 'After a while, they don't believe all the lies we tell them. You have to have a film to back it up.'[12]

Baker and Endfield had asked for a budget of $2.6 million, but Levine insisted on the picture coming in for under $2 million – though for publicity purposes it was inflated variously to $3 or $3.5 million.[13] The initial plan, settled in the last week of October 1962, was that *Zulu* would be a co-production between Embassy, Anglo Amalgamated, and Baker's company, Oakhurst Productions, with eleven weeks of location filming scheduled to begin in March 1963. British distribution would be handled by Anglo through Warner-

This trade advertisement appeared while *Zulu* was still in production. Note the misspelling of Cy Endfield's name and the erroneous description of the Rorke's Drift defenders as Lancers. (From a microfilm source.)

Pathé, and release in the rest of the world by Embassy. *Zulu* was envisaged as the first fruit of an extended relationship between Oakhurst and Embassy, but when Anglo pulled out early in 1963, with pre-production already underway in South Africa, a new partner had to be found as a matter of urgency.

The rescuer was Paramount. While other American studios had been investing heavily in the British film industry since the early 50s, Paramount had been only tentatively involved to that time.[14] *Zulu* would be its first British-based production in three years and the start of a more sustained programme of UK investment for the company. The film was added to the existing three-picture package with Levine; Paramount guaranteed one hundred per cent financing but shared fifty-fifty ownership with Embassy. According to John Prebble, Levine 'never put his own money up. Joe found money that someone else was able to put up. In this case it was Paramount.' His company was to handle distribution in the United States and Canada, with Paramount distributing in the rest of the world, though Levine retained full control of all advertising and merchandising, as was his custom, and was guaranteed a producer's fee of $250,000 for each of the four Embassy-Paramount pictures.[15] This was a somewhat different deal from those made for the three titles previously announced, which gave Paramount sole worldwide distribution, but *Zulu* – the first of the quartet to be produced and released – was decreed 'a natural extension of the previous associations … indicative of the flexibility of the relationship between the two motion picture companies.'[16] Baker and Endfield created a new joint company, Diamond Films, to co-produce the film.[17] These arrangements were concluded the very week that shooting commenced and were announced to the press when filming was already underway.

No doubt remembering his bitter experience with Anglo Amalgamated and his long months of shopping around domestic producer-distributors, Baker subsequently denounced British filmmaking attitudes as 'outmoded.' Visiting New York after the completion of shooting, he told the American trade press that British producers concentrated too much on small films and were too short-sighted to make the large-scale action pictures he felt the world market required. He described *Zulu* as the biggest British film made in the last ten years but claimed that 'you couldn't get the money for this kind of picture in England.' Baker was full of praise for Levine's hands-off approach during filming, as he later wrote: 'Through it all and perhaps this is what gave Cy and me our greatest peace of mind – we had several visits and many conferences with Joe Levine. But they were just that: visits and conferences. Constructive, helpful suggestions, yes but otherwise a free hand to produce our picture as we had

Left to right: Joseph E. Levine, Stanley Baker, Bob Porter, Cy Endfield, stunt director John Sullivan.

planned, without hindrance – that was what Joe provided us.'[18] He also promised to offer Embassy first look at all his future producing projects, as he felt a 'moral obligation' to Levine for having had faith in his first producing venture.[19]

Joe visited the South African location at Easter, in the third week of shooting, to check on the production's progress. After this, wrote Karsh, 'the effect of Levine's recent visit still lingered among the cast and crew. Although this was one of the smoothest-running productions I had ever seen, Levine's visit left a warm glow among the group virtually isolated at Mont Aux Sources in the Drakensberg Mountains, and seemed to provide the additional motivation for them to continue harmoniously.'[20] Yet according to camera operator Dudley Lovell, it wasn't until after Levine's visit, when he had seen the 'rushes' of what had been shot so far, that the unit knew the money was completely secure.[21] Nor was the shooting to be quite as harmonious as Karsh perceived it to be. The difficulties which then faced the production team were, however, practical and creative rather than financial ones. *Films and Filming* had already laid out the stakes: 'Baker's immediate production is to be *Zulu* for Joe Levine. This is the story of an historic incident when little more than a hundred men stood off the attack of a thousand natives [sic!]. A challenging subject, and Baker's problem will be to avoid the conventional extremes, either historical spectacle or a mere re-statement of the colour problem.'[22]

Notes

[1] Cy Endfield, 'The Coal Miner's Son,' unpublished manuscript, 1988.

[2] John Vincent, 'The "Scent" of Todd and "Lovers" of Wald,' *Films and Filming*, March 1960, p. 26.

[3] Interview with Clive James for *Cinema* (Granada Television, 1972).

[4] 'Anglo Amalgamated To Fold Pix Distribution In Britain, Keep Overseas,' *Variety*, 31 October 1962, pp. 23-4; trade announcement, *The Daily Cinema*, 5 November 1962, p. 9.

[5] 'The Year,' *Films and Filming*, January 1961, p. 29.

[6] On Levine's career and reputation, see *The Daily Cinema* Supplement, 'A Tribute to Joseph Levine: The Man Who Put "HOW" Into SHOWmanship,' October 1964, and various articles in *Variety*, 22 April 1964, pp. 14-5, 97, 99. On his publicity campaigns see, for example: 'Saturation release for *Hercules Unchained*,' *Kine. Weekly*, 5 May 1960; Robert Alden, 'Advertising Hard Sell for Motion Pictures,' *New York Times*, 29 May 1960; 'Mighty advertising campaign for *Hercules* gets underway,' *Kine. Weekly*, 4 August 1960; 'Long Shots,' *Kine. Weekly*, 25 August 1960.

[7] 'Levine's *Carpetbaggers* For Paramount Financing,' *Variety*, 26 September 1962, p. 5; 'Embassy Projects Figure Importantly In Perk-Up of Paramount Product,' *Variety*, 6 February 1963, pp. 3, 18; 'Levine's Latest on Hippodrome Track: Driving Home 36 Steeds In Tandem,' *Variety*, 15 February 1963, p. 5.

[8] 'Levine, Hub's Biggest Bean,' *Variety*, 30 October 1963, p. 7; 'Maybe: Par's 50% of Embassy,' *Variety*, 2 October 1963, p. 30.

[9] On Levine's relationship with Paramount, see Bernard F. Dick, *Engulfed: The Death of Paramount Pictures and the Birth of Corporate Hollywood* (Lexington: University Press of Kentucky, 2001), pp. 78-82.

[10] These accounts were taken from, respectively: Hedda Hopper, 'Stanley Baker gets $3 million for movie with a handshake,' *Los Angeles Times*, 27

October 1963; Robert Ottaway, 'How strange... that I may spend more in a minute than my father earned in a year,' *TV Times*, 14 March 1974, pp. 3-4; *Cinema* interview. Ellen Baker recalls that Joe and Rosalie had a love of old music hall songs and in social gatherings would sing them at any and every opportunity. One of them was an Edwardian song with the refrain, 'You can have Pearl, she's a darn nice girl, but I'll have Lulu!' One evening while out with the Bakers he burst into song with the replacement line 'I'll have *Zulu*!'

[11] Yousuf Karsh, 'Ottawa Photographer's Prose Impressions of Joseph E. Levine,' *Variety*, 22 April 1964, p. 97.

[12] Joseph McBride (ed.), *Filmmakers on Filmmaking: The American Film Institute Seminars on Motion Pictures and Television, Volume Two* (Los Angeles: J.P. Tarcher, 1983), pp. 31-3.

[13] *The Carpetbaggers* was originally announced as costing $5 million, though other sources suggest it actually cost $3.3 million.

[14] For further discussion of Hollywood involvement in British film production in this period, see Robert Murphy, *Sixties British Cinema* (London: British Film Institute, 1992), especially pp. 256-75; and Alexander Walker, *Hollywood, England: The British Film Industry in the Sixties* (London: Michael Joseph, 1974; reprinted London: Harrap, 1986).

[15] 'Paramount Set For 4th Feature From Joe Levine,' *Variety*, 3 April 1963, pp. 3, 18; 'Joe Levine a Man of Many Homes: Paramount Just One of His Ties; Numerous Production Projects,' *Variety*, 26 June 1963, pp. 3, 26.

[16] 'Paramount and Embassy Join Forces for *Zulu*', 4 April 1963 (in Margaret Herrick Library cuttings file on *Zulu*; publication title illegible).

[17] 'Lotsa Eggs But No Omelette?, *Variety*, 22 January 1964, p. 3; 'International Sound Track,' *Variety*, 6 March 1963, p. 22.

[18] Stanley Baker, 'A Handshake Deal That Paid Off,' *Variety*, 22 April 1964, p. 14.

[19] 'British Think "Too-Small" Pictures For World Playoff – Stanley Baker,' *Variety*, 7 August 1963, pp. 3, 28.

[20] Karsh, op. cit.

[21] Interview by John Taylor, 17 January 1990, for the BECTU Oral History Project; tapes available for consultation in the British Film Institute Library.

[22] Barrie Pattison, 'Cool man,' *Films and Filming*, October 1962, p. 59.

PART II:
DISPATCHES FROM THE FRONT

> ## "FALL THEM IN, CALL THE ROLL"

CASTING THE ACTORS

> Nine tough unshaven men all destined to win Victoria Crosses confronted Customs officials at Jan Smuts Airport today. They were some of the 50 actors and technicians who arrived in two charter flights in South Africa this morning to begin filming the R2,000,000 film *Zulu* in the Royal Natal National Park.
>   Led by the film's producer, Stanley Baker, the group left immediately for Natal. Baker will take the lead in the film. With him today was Michael Caine, the big blond 30-year-old West End actor who will take the part of Lt. Bromhead, V.C. Baker said of him today, 'Watch him, he is going to be a great star. I've taken him on for three years.'
> ('Tough, unshaven men arrive to film *Zulu*,' *The Natal Witness*, 27 March 1963)

One of the consequences of cutting back the budget of *Zulu* to under $2 million was that there was no money available to pay for the services of major international stars. The film would have to be cast largely with unknowns and newcomers if 'above the line' expenses were to be kept to a reasonable minimum. This pragmatic arrangement nonetheless fitted in with the way Baker and Endfield envisaged their streamlined epic. When the film was first announced for location filming in South Africa, speculation was rife that the likes of Jean Simmons, Deborah Kerr, Alec Guinness, Fredric March and Dirk Bogarde would soon be appearing in Natal, but Cy told a South African journalist while on location: 'The film is powerful enough in its subject matter. We are spending a lot of money to ensure dramatic action and authenticity in the huge cast. Rorke's Drift is not a big-star vehicle at all.'[1] Indeed, director Douglas Hickox's decision to fill the cast of *Zulu Dawn* (1979) with famous names and faces was one of the reasons for Endfield's dissatisfaction with that later film.

By contrast with other British war movies of the time, which tended to use the same old faces filling stock roles, the casting of *Zulu* has an invigorating freshness.

Stanley paid himself an acting fee of £30,000 (approximately $100,000) and gave the same to Jack Hawkins, the only other star name of comparable stature in the picture. Michael Caine, in his first leading role, was paid a mere £4,000, though after years of bit parts and frequent unemployment it must then have seemed a fortune. The remainder of the principal cast was made up of young theatre actors new to the screen, supported by a few established character players and veteran stuntmen. David Kernan says he was paid £750 for the whole job, while Ivor Emmanuel remembers getting £200 a week: 'It was not a lot of money for filming. In those days you'd do the part for nothing just to get it.' Before leaving for South Africa, Ivor met an old friend of Baker's, the Welsh actor Donald Houston, at a party. 'He was going to play the Colour Sergeant but he said he wouldn't do it because the money was terrible.'

According to the Production Information Dossier issued to journalists when the film was ready for release, the casting call for *Zulu* 'caught the imagination of nearly every actor in the British Isles, [and] Baker's office in London was inundated with enquiries.' It was one of the hallmarks of a Baker production that there was always work for his friends. 'I knew him from *Captain Horatio Hornblower*,' said Larry Taylor, 'and whenever he made a film he tried to push me into it.' James Booth claims that 'Stanley got all his mates in the cast – that's how it got made so cheap.' Careful viewing of other Baker films does indeed turn up many a familiar face. Joseph Losey's *The Criminal* (1960) probably holds the record for the number of actors shared with *Zulu*: in addition to Baker there can be spotted Nigel Green, Patrick Magee, Neil McCarthy, Dickie Owen and Larry Taylor. When it came to casting his own production, no doubt Stanley remembered them and saw that they each got a part. This jobs-for-the-boys approach was not mere favouritism, however, as Baker later explained: 'I choose people like Mike Caine and Jimmy Booth for my films because I know them and understand their potential. That's where the actor-producer has the edge on the layman. He understands just how much other actors can give.'²

Michael Caine
(Lieutenant Gonville Bromhead)

I was on holiday with my parents and Grandmother in the Drakensberg during the filming of *Zulu* – I was only about 8 years old. We were staying at the Cavern Holiday Resort which is situated about 10kms from Royal Natal National Park.

One day while we were visiting the film set, we happened to walk past a group of actors who were lying on the grass suntanning during one of their breaks, one of whom was Michael Caine. When he heard my Grandmother speaking he jumped up, came over, shook her hand and introduced himself (he had recognised her English accent – she was born in Gloucestershire). He took her arm and

helped her to our car and then asked if we would be so kind as to give him a lift back to the Hotel, which we did ... That incident has stuck in my mind, and as for my Grandmother (she was 79 years old at the time), she became an instant fan of Michael Caine and followed his career avidly after that.
(Wendy Hittler, email to the author, 18 September 2003)

Of all the personnel involved in *Zulu*, whether before or behind the camera, only Michael Caine needs no introduction for non-film buffs. Billed fifth in the opening credits ('And Introducing Michael Caine') he is now frequently promoted to first place in television listings magazines and on home video packaging, reflecting the global superstardom which he achieved shortly after the film was released and still enjoys today. 'How do you feel when someone comes bounding forward and says *Zulu* made Michael Caine?', Clive James asked Stanley Baker in a 1972 television interview. 'Well that's a lot of nonsense,' Baker replied, 'he made himself into a star through that film. The picture helped but no-one made him but him.'³

Caine's bright future was already evident to those who saw his performance as

Bromhead even before the film's release. Maureen Endfield often went with Cy to the cutting rooms to watch assemblies of footage: 'I remember my heart stopped the first time I saw Michael – the demeanour and his bearing and the way it was shot were incredible. It was obvious there was a star.' South African journalist Derrick Kain, who visited the set on several occasions during shooting, remarked at the time: 'A new film face is always a thrilling event, particularly to the teenage enthusiasts. In Michael Caine they will find someone to swoon over.'[4] British journalist and future Caine biographer William Hall also went on location to interview the established stars and instead found himself pointed in the direction of the newcomer:

'If I were you,' Jack Hawkins said quietly, 'I'd go over and talk to that young man.'
'Who is he?'
He told me.
'I never heard of him.'
'You will,' Jack Hawkins promised. 'You will. He's the best thing in this film. Just you wait and see.'[5]

Caine's own first sight of himself in the daily 'rushes' had a different effect than it did on Maureen Endfield: he promptly vomited over his military boots and vowed never again to watch dailies. Adding to his upset were the overhead comments of a technician who wanted to know why Caine often had his helmet pulled down low over his eyes, hiding them from the camera. The actor was rightly indignant:

I had decided to use this as part of my characterisation. I would say some of the lines with my eyes in the shade and when I wanted to make a strong point I would tip my head back slightly and catch the full glare of the sun in my eyes. This had been worked on with great skill, I thought, and here was someone misunderstanding and calling me a silly bastard into the bargain.[6]

Inspection of the film confirms Caine's skill, in this respect as in others. The shade of

his helmet gives Bromhead an air of confidence and when he shoots a direct glance at Chard his arrogance is clearly felt; only when the helmet is pushed back, away from his forehead, as it is when he first receives news of the massacre at Isandhlwana, does Bromhead appear rattled and insecure. This is the kind of 'invisible' technique that has sustained Caine throughout his career, yet which has often led to his being under-rated, especially in Britain, where subtlety is less often valued than stridency.

He was born Maurice Joseph Micklewhite in Rotherhithe, South East London, on 14 March 1933. The son of a Billingsgate fish porter and an office cleaner, he grew up in poverty in the working class Elephant and Castle district. He developed an ambition to be an actor – or rather a star – from his childhood enthusiasm for movies, and his first job on leaving school was as a clerk in the office of a small film production company. He also acted in an amateur theatre club before being called up for National Service at the age of seventeen. Maurice served in Korea in the Royal Fusiliers, where his commanding officer, Lieutenant Robert Mill, provided a model for his later characterisation of Bromhead.[7] After demob, he turned professional actor, initially taking Michael Scott as his stage name and working in repertory companies based in Horsham and Lowestoft before a second change of moniker was inspired by the marquee of a Leicester Square cinema advertising *The Caine Mutiny* (1954).

The offer of his first, small film role also led to his first meeting with Stanley Baker, on *A Hill in Korea* (1956). Set during the conflict in which Caine had recently served, it was filmed on location in Portugal; Caine thought Wales would have been a better match for Korea, but wisely kept his mouth shut. The film concerns a beleaguered army patrol surrounded by a much larger enemy force – another foreshadowing of *Zulu* – and its cast includes two other up-and-coming actors worthy of note: Robert Shaw and Stephen Boyd. Contrary to some reports, Caine did receive a screen credit (at the very bottom of the cast list) for playing Private Lockyer, though in many of his subsequent films he went unbilled. These other bit parts include fleeting appearances in war movies like *The Steel Bayonet* (1957), *The Two-Headed Spy* (1958), *Danger Within* (1959) and *Foxhole in Cairo* (1960); the comedies *The Bulldog Breed* (1960, in which he plays a sailor who rescues Norman Wisdom from hooligan Oliver Reed) and *The Wrong Arm of the Law* (1963); and as a police constable in the science fiction thriller *The Day the Earth Caught Fire* (1961).

The same year that he filmed *A Hill in Korea*, Caine also made his television debut. As Michael Scott he was 'Third Knight' in an episode of *The Adventures of Sir Lancelot* – Nigel Green also appeared, as 'Second Peasant' – and under his new name he was cast by Julian Amyes, who had directed him in *Korea*, in a BBC production of Jean Anouilh's play about Joan of Arc, *The Larks*. Over the next seven years Caine made, by his own count, over a hundred television appearances, many in unrecorded live broadcasts. They included episodes of series like *The Adventures of William Tell* (in which Nigel Green was a regular) and *Dixon of Dock Green*, and single plays such as Rod Serling's *Requiem for a Heavyweight* (1957, opposite Sean Connery in

his first leading role), Herman Wouk's *The Caine Mutiny Court Martial* (1958, adapted from the same novel which inspired the film from which he took his name), and Johnny Speight's *The Compartment* (1961). After completing *Zulu* he briefly returned to television, playing Horatio in *Hamlet at Elsinore* (1964) opposite Christopher Plummer and Robert Shaw, and the lead in a live science fiction drama entitled *The Other Man* (1964). Among the latter's distinguished supporting cast, portraying another Colour Sergeant, was the ubiquitous Nigel Green.

Though he remained set on a big-screen career, Caine also continued to act on stage, including an unhappy stint with Joan Littlewood's Theatre Workshop in *The Chimes* (1954); John McGrath's *Why the Chicken* (1961) in Golder's Green, with Terence Stamp and Peter Gill; and several months on tour understudying for Peter O'Toole in *The Long and the Short and the Tall* (1959). His first and only West End appearance came in James Saunders' highly acclaimed experimental piece *Next Time I'll Sing To You* at the New Arts Theatre, which opened on 23 January 1963. The play won him favourable personal notices and was seen, apparently at the recommendation of Michael's agent Dennis Selinger, by Stanley Baker and Cy Endfield. Caine was invited to read for the part of Private Hook at the auditions for *Zulu*, then being held in the bar of the Prince of Wales Theatre, where Endfield's production of Neil Simon's *Come Blow Your Horn* was enjoying a long run.

The story of how Caine came to play Bromhead has been told many times and with many variations, but it bears repeating.[8] Michael arrived at the audition to be told by Endfield that Hook had already been cast with James Booth. Caine turned to leave, but the bar was unusually long and before he had reached the end of it, Cy called him back. The director said that, to his untutored American eyes, Caine didn't look like a downtrodden Cockney but, with his tall build, long face and wavy blond hair, more like a blue-blooded officer; could he do an upper-class accent? Michael, ever the professional, replied in the affirmative and after discussing the matter with Baker, Endfield arranged a screen test at which he would read for Bromhead. (According to Booth, the role had previously been offered to Robert Stephens, who had turned it down.) Fellow actor Richard Davies claims that Baker couldn't at first see Caine in the part: 'Michael was in the West End in the Arts playing a Cockney lad like Alfie. Stanley saw him as that, but Cy saw him as a fey soldier. So it was Cy's idea to cast him – which I confirmed in the Salisbury pub, which all actors used to go to. Mike Caine was there after we'd shot the film – he gave me a little salute.'

Whatever Baker may initially have thought about the off-casting, he gave Caine the benefit of the doubt. The screen test was shot in a small studio in Fleet Street. For an hour, wearing his costume uniform for the film, Stanley fed Caine his side of the dialogue from behind the camera: a demonstration of professional respect which Michael appreciated and long remembered. 'There were only two screen tests for Bromhead,' says Ellen Baker. 'Terence Stamp was the other. Paramount wanted him but he was too well-known; Cy and Stanley wanted an unknown. Michael's test was no good but he was cast anyway.'9 Caine did not in fact learn that he had been chosen until he and Stamp – his flatmate and close friend of several years – both attended a party at which Endfield was also a guest. The director avoided Caine's gaze all night until Michael, his nerves sufficiently stiffened with drink, confronted him and demanded to know if he'd got the part. Cy confirmed that, despite the lousy test, indeed he had, whereupon Michael burst into tears; he had vowed to quit acting if he had not made a success of it before he was thirty, and the offer of *Zulu* came in February 1963, the month before his thirtieth birthday.10

Caine had already been able to perfect the upper-class accent needed for Bromhead through his experience in rep theatre, where 'you were always playing Lord Ponce or some bloody part like that.'11 The appropriate details of body language and military graces,

however, had to be gleaned from research. He took to observing the behaviour of real army officers, as he explained in a recent interview:

Because I'd been a soldier, I knew how officers behaved towards privates – I'd been on the receiving end of it all the time. And in a war situation you get to know the officers very well. But I didn't know how they were with each other, which I needed to because of my relationship [with Baker as Lt. Chard] in *Zulu*. So I used to have lunch at the guards officers' mess in the Mall by Buckingham Palace every few weeks just to watch how they behaved with each other.12

Caine has also described his reaction on learning that the film's financiers had failed to understand another of his deliberate gestures: Bromhead's habit of crossing his hands behind his back (a quirk borrowed from the Duke of Edinburgh), which signified an inbred sense of authority, even arrogance. 'They said, "Suggest you fire actor playing Bromhead – doesn't know what to do with hands." I thought, boy, I'm ahead here, I'm dealing with dummies here. This is the first positive thing; I thought, I can make a career in this because I'm actually smarter than the guys who are running this show – they don't know what I'm doing.'13 Later, when he was introduced to senior military guests of honour at social events, he always experienced a glow of triumph when, having assumed him to be one of their own, they were shocked to hear his natural South London vowels.14

For his first day's shooting in South Africa, Caine had to ride a Basuto pony as Bromhead returns from his animal hunt. Having had only three riding lessons, Michael was immediately thrown by his mount and had to be replaced for the long shot by a double, Jan Rossouw. After this and throwing up at the screening of rushes, he continued to doubt that he would keep the job and remained anxious about his future prospects. 'The officer was quite a character stretch for Michael,' says Glynn Edwards. 'He used to say, if it goes alright it'll be good for me, but he was never very sure he would be.' This is confirmed by Paul Blignaut, a young visitor to the film set with his sister, who had brought with her a pet Siamese cat. Journalist Stephen Coan picks up the story:

> They were walking along the path by the river to the set when they met Michael Caine coming towards them. He said 'Hang on, I want to take a picture of the girl with the cat.' He got a camera – he was a bit of an amateur photographer apparently – and took the picture. He then stayed and chatted for quarter of an hour, during which he said that the film was a big break for him but he was worried about how he was doing in it. Then Cy Endfield came along and called him back to work.[15]

'I was terrified,' Caine said later, 'because I'd always thought that I'd make it as a film actor, everybody does, thinks they can make it on screen, and here was the chance. And so now you're confronted with this chance and you've got to put up or shut up your big mouth about what you're going to do and what you could do if you had the chance – you've got the chance, and that's terrifying.'[16] Michael's insecurity came to a head when he happened to see a telegram sent by the film's distributors demanding that he be replaced. As he tells it, Michael then approached Stanley, demanding to know if he was going to be fired:

> 'Who is the producer of this movie?' he finally asked. 'You are, Stan.' 'Have I said that you are fired?' 'No,' I mumbled. 'Well, just get on with your job,' he said and walked away. Then he turned and said, 'And stop reading my fucking mail or you *will* get fired.' At last the weeks of agony and doubt were over; I knew that for better or worse, I had the part – and that was that.[17]

Joe Powell, who had worked with him in *The Steel Bayonet*, recalls that in the staging of the battle scenes, Michael was 'very keen.' Because he had served in the Fusiliers, unlike most of the cast he needed no instruction in how to use the bayonet, and entered vigorously into the action. This was not without risk, however; Marius Markgraaf, manager of the nearby Mont-Aux-Sources Hotel, claims that filming on the hospital roof set was interrupted when Caine's trousers caught fire from the burning thatch.

On the night of the World Premiere in London, Caine was accompanied by the future fashion designer Edina Ronay (though in his autobiography he claims not to remember his escort). He had invited his mother but she refused to go; on the way into the cinema, he spotted her in the crowd, standing amongst the other star-gazers to wish him luck.[19] Before leaving England to shoot the film, Caine had borrowed actress Liz Fraser's lucky

charm – a dead mouse – as a mascot, and kept it until the first night. Fraser sat next to him at the screening and later recalled: 'I asked him about my mouse but got no reply. At the end of the film there was a standing ovation, and only then did Mike turn round to me and say, "Here's your mouse back."'[20]

Caine was rewarded for his work in the film with two long-term contracts, from Twentieth Century-Fox and producer Harry Saltzman respectively, to add to the one he already had with Embassy and Diamond.[21] Elmo Williams, Fox's managing director of European production, said when announcing their three-year deal: 'We all think he is one of the greatest star bets for the future.'[22] Michael has since enjoyed telling how Joseph Levine, who had never been convinced of his rightness for Bromhead, soon cancelled his contract with Embassy because he thought Caine looked too gay to become a star. Ironically, stills photographer Yousuf Karsh, while paying his own tribute to Levine, wrote that Caine had 'spent one whole afternoon while we drove to Durban telling us about "Uncle Joe" and how encouraging he had been to this young actor just beginning his film career.'[23] The only other Levine-sponsored movies in which Michael appeared were his cameos in the all-star international comedy *Woman Times Seven* (1967) and the massive war epic *A Bridge Too Far* (1977). But Harry Saltzman saw what 'Uncle Joe' could not and cast him as the home-cooking, bespectacled spy in his adaptation of Len Deighton's novel *The Ipcress File* (1965). This at last gave Caine the launching pad for fully-fledged stardom, confirmed by his next film, *Alfie* (1966), which won him the first of several Oscar nominations as Best Actor.

The subsequent glittering career hardly requires detailed summary. Caine has on several other occasions played upper-class military officers, proving that his performance

Caine and Edina Ronay dance at the *Zulu* World Premiere party.

Michael's performance. David Kernan comments: 'I thought his work on the film was excellent. To become an aristocrat as he did was quite an achievement.' Unit publicist Geoff Freeman, who has worked on many of Caine's subsequent films, says that his favourite memory of *Zulu* was 'seeing this new guy – Michael – make a great success.' For Bert Batt, who worked as a first assistant director on several of Caine's movies at different stages of the actor's career (*The Bulldog Breed*, *Zulu*, *The Man Who Would Be King*), 'Michael Caine is what he has always been, a fine actor and a very nice man to know. The status changed but the man did not.' Stanley Baker, who might have been expected to share in the glory of his protégée's achievement, instead took a self-effacing view: 'I don't believe in people taking the credit for other people's success. If it hadn't happened in that film it would have happened in another. The time was right, and Mike was good.'[24]

Jack Hawkins (Reverend Otto Witt)

'I think it is charming that in England a man does not need to be either young or good-looking to be a star,' remarked Italian actress Gia Scala of Jack Hawkins, her co-star in *The Two-Headed Spy* (1958).[25] Perhaps she meant it as a compliment.

Born on 14 September 1910 in Wood Green, London, the son of a public works contractor, Hawkins made his acting debut aged only ten. He attended the Italia Conti Stage School, acted opposite Sybil Thorndike in George Bernard Shaw's *Saint Joan* as a thirteen-year-old student, and was appearing regularly on the West End stage in his late teens. He made his Broadway debut in R.C. Sherriff's *Journey's End* aged nineteen and his first film, *Birds of Prey* (1930), at twenty. Sixteen more movies – mostly 'major roles in minor films and minor roles in major films'[26] – and around fifty stage appearances in London and New York followed before Hawkins enlisted to serve his country in the war. The regiment he joined, the Royal Welch Fusiliers, was later represented at *Zulu*'s World Premiere. Unable to relinquish showbusiness

as Bromhead was no fluke: in *Play Dirty* (1969), yet again cast opposite Nigel Green), *Battle of Britain* (1969), *A Bridge Too Far* and, as a sympathetic German, *The Eagle Has Landed* (1976). He appeared again for Stanley Baker when the latter's company Oakhurst produced *The Italian Job* (1969), and was reunited with *Zulu*'s Bob Porter, Joe Powell, John Sullivan and Larry Taylor on the fine, unfairly neglected historical epic *The Last Valley* (1971). Caine donned the Victorian redcoat uniform once more to play opposite his own wife Shakira and Sean Connery in John Huston's *The Man Who Would Be King* (1975). Among his many honours are two American Academy Awards as Best Supporting Actor, for *Hannah and Her Sisters* (1986) and *The Cider House Rules* (1999), he was awarded a CBE in 1993, and a knighthood in 2000.

Other cast and crew members are generous and genuine in their compliments on even while in uniform, Jack found himself in command of the army entertainment service ENSA for India and South East Asia, leaving the military as a colonel. It was through ENSA that he also met his second wife, Doreen Lawrence (his first was the British actress Jessica Tandy, whom he had married in 1932 and divorced in 1940). Jack and Doreen ('Dee') met on New Year's Day 1944, married in 1947 and subsequently had three children.

Jack returned to the professional theatre after demobilisation, touring Europe in Shaw and Shakespeare and playing opposite Olivia de Havilland in *Romeo and Juliet* on Broadway. Up to this point, in common with most British stage actors, he had not taken the cinema very seriously: 'He didn't see films as a career,' says Doreen. 'He only did films to pay the tax on the money he'd made in plays.' This began to change when Jack was given a three-year contract with Alexander Korda's London Films, which gave him key supporting roles in such films as *Bonnie Prince Charlie*, *The Fallen Idol* (both 1948), *The Small Back Room* (1949) and *The Elusive Pimpernel* (1950). He made his last stage appearance in 1951 but it was not until the Royal Air Force drama *Angels One Five* (1952) that Hawkins established the solidly paternal officer persona which sustained him throughout a number of other war pictures, including the performance for which he is best remembered: as Captain

Ericsson in the Ealing production of Nicholas Monserrat's *The Cruel Sea* (1953). An earlier Ealing drama, *Mandy* (1952), gave Jack a personal triumph as the headmaster of a school for the deaf. '*Mandy* was the first film that brought Jack to the notice of both the public and the film business,' says Doreen. 'That's what got him *The Cruel Sea*. It changed our lives.' Ellen Baker recalls that the standing ovation at the *Mandy* premiere was the longest and loudest she has ever heard, even including the one for *Zulu*. As a result of these and other successes, Hawkins was voted the most popular star at the British box-office for 1954.[27]

In the later 50s Jack began acting on television and in big-budget international pictures for major directors, such as Howard Hawks' Egyptian epic *Land of the Pharaohs* (1955), David Lean's enormously successful *The Bridge on the River Kwai* (1957) and William Wyler's multi-Oscar-winning *Ben-Hur* (1959). Hawkins was awarded the CBE in 1958 and soon afterwards moved into production, setting up Allied Film Makers in partnership with fellow actors Richard Attenborough and Bryan Forbes, directors Guy Green and Basil Dearden, and producer

Makeup man Bob Lawrance adjusts Jack's hairpiece, watched by Tom Gerrard.

Michael Relph. AFM's first production was the popular bank robbery caper *The League of Gentlemen* (1960). This, however, was virtually Hawkins' last starring role; henceforward, he would concentrate on character parts, most notably in Lean's massive epic *Lawrence of Arabia* (1962). Hawkins shaved off his thick, wavy dark hair to play the balding Colonel Allenby and, though it had grown back by the time he made *Zulu* he found himself once again wearing an unbecoming hairpiece as the greying Swedish missionary Otto Witt. He had in fact visited the Drakensberg Mountains before, spending three months at the Royal Natal National Park Hotel while shooting his first top-billed role in *The Adventurers* (1951). Finding himself there again for *Zulu*, he told assistant editor Jennifer Thompson that she now had his old room.

Stanley Baker had made his first cinematic impression with the key supporting role of First Officer Bennett in *The Cruel Sea*, and it's possible that Baker saw *Zulu* as the opportunity to pay Jack back for helping him make a start in the industry. Undoubtedly the presence in the cast of such a distinguished veteran gave him reassurance. 'Actors like working with people they're comfortable with,' says Doreen. 'They nearly always try to work within the same group. And it *was* Stanley's first film as a producer.' However, the film was not a very happy experience for Jack. He was playing a clergyman for the first time and it seemed to many observers, possibly including himself, that the cloth was not cut out for him. 'It feels strange to be playing a man of God after causing death and havoc in all my previous films,' he was quoted as saying at the time, and he later claimed that the part appealed to him 'because it was so unlike all the parts I was known for.'[28] In one respect at least he entered into the spirit of his role as the bibulous Bible-thumper. 'Jack was dead right for what he played,' said Larry Taylor. 'He was pissed all the time in the film. We couldn't get him up in the morning. But he was liked by everyone.' Jennifer Thompson, who got to know Jack well during the shoot, recalls: 'He was about the same age as my father at the time. He was very like my father – it was uncanny to me. I loved the film, but that drunken part upset me – I never liked it. That I'm sure is what he must have felt.'

Other members of the cast and crew also remember Hawkins chain-smoking while standing off camera or relaxing at the on-site social club. Jennifer recalls: 'He smoked so much – I'd see him in the canteen in the evening and he'd always be smoking.' This was tempting fate: Hawkins had already had cobalt treatment for cancer of the throat three years earlier, and when the condition returned in 1966 he was forced to undergo an operation to remove his larynx. Doreen had been unable to join Jack in South Africa (she was busy doing up a villa they had just bought in the South of France) and was anxious about his going on location for *Zulu* without her: 'He was already having voice problems and I was worried about Jack for various reasons. When they got together he and Stanley would always smoke too much and drink too much. Jack loved South Africa and so did I, but that particular location I don't think he enjoyed. I'm not sure anyone did. It was very hard work. He said the dust was terrible, and when I met him at Nice my fears were confirmed – he was very husky. He'd also been shouting a lot.' (As Private Owen remarks to Chard in the film: 'The heat and the dust, sir – very nasty on the larynx.')

Maureen Endfield remembers that the director had his misgivings about Hawkins' performance: 'Some people think that it was rather hysterical and that if it had been toned down a bit it would have been an even better film. I know Cy thought that. But sometimes if you're on a schedule you don't realise until it's too late.' Jack described his own disappointment with the film in his autobiography, in which he claimed that Endfield had in effect 'cheated [him] out of a good performance':

What I did not know then was that Cy was a great prestidigitator, a man who, in the kindest interpretation of the word, is a skilled conjurer. Had I realised this I might have been rather more careful but, as it was, I believed that my interpretation of the role was being taken seriously, and so I played it with this conviction.

During my scenes, Cy had arranged a number of covering shots which, for example, showed various other characters laughing at me; in other words, sending me up as a misguided buffoon. The performance that appeared on the screen bore no relationship whatever to the

performance I gave in front of the cameras. When I saw it on the first night, I was so annoyed that I got out of my seat and walked out of the cinema – the only time I have ever walked out on any première.

However, thinking of my friends, Stanley Baker and Michael Caine – and of my astonished wife, left alone in the front row of the circle – I recovered my good humour sufficiently to collect her and take her to the traditional first-night party. All my protests achieved was that Dee thought I must have suddenly been taken ill, and everyone else – if they thought anything at all – believed I'd simply gone to the loo![29]

The strange thing about this account is that the cutaways Hawkins describes are nowhere evident in the film. There are reaction shots, certainly, but no-one is shown laughing at him. If anything, Witt's words strike home as intended, especially on the unfortunate Private Cole. I suspect that what Hawkins really objected to in the finished film was the shortening of his part in the editing, and especially the deletion of his last scene, when a chastened Witt returns with his daughter to the camp after the battle. In the film as it stands, the Reverend disappears halfway through the running time, and this cannot have been welcome for an actor billed second down the cast list. Doreen Hawkins offers her own explanation of Jack's reaction to the film: 'When he got the role he thought he could do something good with it. I seem to remember him saying, "I really think I can make something of this role." But he expected it to be taken more sincerely than it was. I think he was a bit fed up that he ended up as the sort of comedian of the whole thing. They needed a laugh, obviously, in such a film, and I think that there was a bit of light relief when he was bundled off in the wagon. I thought he was being sensitive. Actors grumble away – they're terribly sensitive about everything they do. Their best work is always the stuff that ends up on the cutting room floor. David Lean almost came to grief over something that was cut in *Lawrence*. All directors will tell you that when a film is too long, something has to go. Jack felt it was unfinished: he was disappearing on the wrong note.'

Aside from Doreen, none of those who attended the premiere were aware of Jack's being upset on the night. To Ellen Baker, who danced with him afterwards, he seemed to be in a perfectly cheerful, upbeat mood. James Booth, who had not been on location and did not share any scenes with Hawkins in the film, also recalls chatting with him at the party: 'Jack Hawkins was a great drinker and full of stories. I met him for about an hour at the premiere and got pissed with him. He said he'd been a colonel in the army and thought it was a bit of a comedown to be an actor. I said, think of the money; he said, "That's what I keep telling myself."' Jack's hurt was evidently short-lived and not taken personally. 'Don't ever think that he held anything against Stanley,' says Doreen. 'He was delighted for him that it was a success, very happy. He wasn't *that* upset, you know. We all sat having supper afterwards. I still think it was a wonderful film. I don't think Jack's role mattered a whit, but it mattered to *him*.'

After *Zulu* Hawkins made six more films before his career-threatening laryngectomy, including *Guns at Batasi* (1964) and *Lord Jim* (1965), in both of which his voice sounds very

(1970) and *Nicholas and Alexandra* (1971), though in Richard Attenborough's *Young Winston* (1972) his role as a public school headmaster was entirely wordless.

Desperately seeking a way to restore his natural voice – one of the most distinctive in British cinema, after all – Jack underwent an operation in New York to install an artificial voice-box which would allow him to speak normally. However, the incision in his throat developed an infection and refused to heal. With the wound repeatedly haemorrhaging, Hawkins died in a London hospital on 18 July 1973, aged 62. Jack's final screen role was in the American TV mini-series *QBVII* (1974), but among his last public appearances was the February 1972 press launch for the reissue of *Zulu* where, apparently in good humour, he was pictured toasting a dummy dressed in the uniform of the South Wales Borderers with a glass of brandy.

Private Cole (Gary Bond) and the Reverend Witt in a deleted shot.

hoarse. 'Jack had a marvellous sense of humour and a great wit,' says Doreen. 'Losing his voice was a great tragedy.' Jack's humour was evident in his choice of title for his (posthumously published) autobiography: *Anything for a Quiet Life*. Following the operation Jack was employed by American director Henry Hathaway as production liaison on the Africa-set adventure *The Last Safari* (1967). He was eventually able to resume acting, but only his first post-op film, *Great Catherine* (1968), used his new voice, produced in the oesophagus by belching wind from the stomach. Usually thereafter he was dubbed by either Charles Gray or Robert Rietty. He made fifteen films in this fashion, including *Oh! What a Lovely War* (1969), *Waterloo*

Ulla Jacobsson (Margareta Witt)

'In keeping with the noted histrionic tradition established by her countrywomen, Ulla regards herself as a serious actress (which she is), and declines firmly but politely when asked to wear bikinis in pictures. "I am a dramatic actress," she declared. "I don't want the audience to think of me in any other way."' So said a press release for *Zulu*, a film in which bikinis were hardly required, though Jacobsson did at least agree to pose for photographs with Stanley Baker and a tame cheetah.

Ulla Jacobsson was born on 23 May 1929 in Gothenburg, Sweden. After leaving school she became a secretary but successfully auditioned for a part with the Royal Swedish Theatre, beating over fifty other applicants. Within two months of joining the company she was playing leading roles in productions such as *Gigi*, *A Midsummer Night's Dream*, *The Glass Menagerie* and *The Rose Tattoo*. Spotted on stage by film director Arne Mattson and cast as the female lead in his *One Summer of Happiness* (1951), Jacobsson scandalised the film world by appearing nude in an open-air sex scene. 'That scene caused a furore and

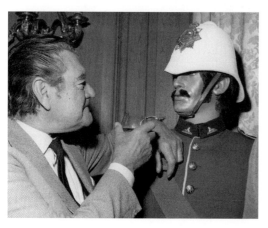

everyone was talking about me,' she said later. 'I suppose that was fame – but I didn't enjoy it. The thing pursued me for years and now I want to forget about it. I'd never strip again.'[30] The most celebrated of Ulla's subsequent Swedish films are Gustav Molander's *Sir Arne's Treasure* (1954) and Ingmar Bergman's wry, bitter-sweet comedy *Smiles of a Summer Night* (1955). She married an Austrian entomologist, Dr Winfried Rohsmann, and the couple lived with their two children in a converted 600-year-old monastery in Vienna.

Ulla was fluent in English, German, French and Italian, and appeared in films in France and Germany as well as Scandinavia. In the early 60s she guest-starred in episodes of American television series such as *The Virginian* and *Ben Casey* before winning a small role in her first Hollywood feature film, the sex comedy *Love is a Ball* (1963) – on the posters for which she was pictured wearing a bikini. But it was after seeing her in 'A Wednesday Night Story,' a 1961 episode of the

Ulla Jacobsson is fitted for her costume by the *Zulu* wardrobe staff.

crime series *The Naked City*, that Baker and Cy Endfield cast her as the prim, puritanical, possibly neurotic Margareta Witt in *Zulu*, after both Jean Simmons and Deborah Kerr had turned the role down.³¹

'I love the outdoors,' she was quoted as saying on location for the film, where she was accompanied by Winfried. 'Whenever I get a chance, my husband and I like very much to climb mountains, swim and enjoy nature. I can't stand being cooped up.' The anonymous, but evidently male, copy-writer commented: 'The mind's eye would rather imagine the delicate Swedish beauty seated on a rug, in front of a cozy fire, seductively munching chocolates.'³² Yet Ulla is remembered by several members of the production team as being a rather chilly and remote personality. Richard Davies says that, 'Ulla was very aware that she was in something that was going to be popular. She was very serious, in herself. She didn't go and chat with all the boys.' Denys Graham feels that 'she was a bit "the star",' while sound technician David Jones recalls that she 'didn't have much to do with anyone.' Bob Porter believes that her role as the uptight Margareta may have been too close to home: 'I don't think she liked the way Cy got her to react to the Zulu wedding dance. She was a bit of a holy roller – a very intense, religious person.'

James Booth received an even less favourable impression of his co-star: 'She was the queen egomaniac and she tried to get me off the picture. I had a scene with her and the first time I appeared she said, "Who's that man, who's that man? He can't play the role!" Cy took me aside and said, she's very insecure and anybody who seems a threat to her of any sort, she's frightened of. I had no idea I was a threat to her, I hadn't been a threat to anybody up to that time and haven't been since. But with that particular lady, I seemed to be a threat.' He may not have been the only one. Interviewed after four months of shooting in Norway on her next film, the war adventure *The Heroes of Telemark* (1965), Ulla said that she needed 'a long rest cure' after suffering the clash of personalities between male leads Kirk Douglas and Richard Harris:

> They are so extrovert in personality that it was a battle from beginning to end.

Jacobsson poses for an uncharacteristic glamour shot back in England.

They were both fighting for position – camera position – and neither was prepared to give way to the other.

I have never known anything quite like it before. Even when this battle for supremacy did not result in an explosion the tension remained.

I had a taste of this kind of temperament when I was filming with Stanley Baker on *Zulu* – but then he was also the producer and he had it all his own way.[33]

The same voluminous collection of press and publicity material which contains these reminiscences also helpfully informs us that Jacobsson stood a mere five feet tall (when standing next to Michael Caine in *Zulu* she is visibly at least a foot shorter), with honey-blonde hair, blue eyes and vital statistics of 34-23-35. Also included are her recipes for Swedish meat balls, reindeer heart and glogg (mulled wine with brandy, whiskey and sherry), along with various articles – presumably intended for placement in women's magazines – in which Ulla is interviewed on such subjects as 'Brush Up On Your Hair Beauty,' 'Women Don't Want Sex Equality,' 'Here is How They Celebrate Christmas in Sweden,' and 'Ulla Jacobsson Keeps in Great Shape.'

'If I do become an international star, it will not be because I have gone out for it,' she said at the time. 'It will happen naturally. I couldn't bear to go out for publicity, or take anything that was offered, in the hope that sooner or later I would catch on. To begin with, I'm too shy to push myself. I just can't do it.'[34] In fact, *The Heroes of Telemark* proved to be the last of Jacobsson's three English-language films and marked the end of her half-hearted bid for the big time. She subsequently appeared in only six more European-made films, including three more directed by Arne Mattson and Rainer Werner Fassbinder's *Fox and His Friends* (1975), before her premature death from bone cancer on 20 August 1982, at the age of 53.

James Booth (Private Henry Hook)

'I didn't do any research on the real Hook,' James Booth admits. 'I just played him the way it was written. Cy wanted a sort of ne'er-do-well, which suited me – it was the sort of character I played. When the picture came out most people liked that character, except the Hook family – they hated it. The company got a letter from the family complaining about the way that I'd played him. They actually sent me a photograph of him – even now it's up in my hallway. He looked like a typical working class Victorian gentleman, a big fat guy with a big bushy moustache, and not the layabout that I played.' In most of his films, *Zulu* included, Booth has not looked or behaved like a gentleman, Victorian or otherwise. That is part of his appeal, though it has not often been fully exploited by filmmakers.

He was born David Geeves-Booth in Croydon on 19 December 1927. The family spent some time in the East End of London and then moved to Southend after the death of his father, a probation officer. At seventeen Booth entered the army for his National Service and stayed on, receiving officer's training at Sandhurst and rising to the rank of captain before leaving the service at 24. Taking an office job in London, he also enjoyed amateur acting and later won a scholarship to

study at the Royal Academy of Dramatic Arts. James graduated in 1956, in the same class which produced Alan Bates, Albert Finney, Richard Harris and Peter O'Toole. He did a season as a spear carrier at the Old Vic and was then taken up by Joan Littlewood's London Theatre Workshop at Stratford East. His first major success came in 1959, as the Cockney spiv Tosher in Frank Norman and Lionel Bart's musical *Fings Ain't Wot They Used T' Be*, which later enjoyed a two-year West End run at the Garrick Theatre.

In 1958 Booth began appearing on television in series such as *The Adventures of William Tell* and made his film debut in *Jazz Boat* (1959). He had a striking small role as the weaselly blackmailer, Alfred Wood, opposite Peter Finch in *The Trials of Oscar Wilde* (1960), and for *The Hellions* (1961) he travelled to South Africa. Before appearing in *Zulu*, James had the lead roles in Joan Littlewood's only film as director, *Sparrows Can't Sing* (1963) – based on her stage production of Stephen Lewis' *Sparrers Can't Sing* – and in Ken Russell's first theatrical feature, the frenetic comedy *French Dressing* (1964). Booth also acted at the Royal Court, the Oxford Playhouse and the New Arts Theatre; when he was approached to play Hook he was appearing as Edmund in *King Lear* for the Royal Shakespeare Company in Stratford-on-Avon. 'I'd been introduced to Stanley Baker by a guy called John McMichael, who was his agent and also my agent. We'd become quite good friends. Stanley called me up and said, did I want to play Hook in *Zulu*? He said, come down and meet the director – an American called Cy Endfield. So I went and met him, and that's how I got the part. I was only on the picture for about a week or ten days.' All his scenes were shot at Twickenham Studios, and after filming was over he said that Hook had been 'an actor's dream ... and I only hope that I did full justice to it. I'd hate to let Stanley down.'[35]

James was accompanied to the World Premiere by his wife Paula, whom he had met and married in 1960 when she was a stage manager. 'I liked the premiere because everyone said, "Oh Jimmy, you were *wonderful*!" When the film came out and was a huge success it was such a surprise.' On the strength of his performance major stardom was predicted for Booth, but bad choices marred his career. In 1965 he worked again for Joan Littlewood, playing opposite his *Sparrows* co-star, Barbara Windsor, as Robin Hood in Lionel Bart's disastrous stage musical *Twang!!*, which closed after only a ten-week West End run. James had turned down two film offers in order to get it: the title role in *Alfie* and Willie Garvin in Joseph Losey's spy spoof *Modesty Blaise* (1966), a part eventually taken by Terence Stamp. As he later ruefully acknowledged, *Alfie* could have been his big break instead of Michael Caine's, but at the time he described the role as 'a spiv all over again,' and dismissed the film before its release as '*Sparrows Can't Sing* in colour.'[36]

On the recommendation of novelist Harold Robbins, who had been impressed by Booth's work in *Zulu*, he was given a three-year contract by Joseph E. Levine. 'Now there was a character and three-quarters,' says James of Levine. 'Very uncouth, very coarse man, but very smart, street-smart – that's why he got on so well with Stanley. He was a man with an incredible personality – incredible drive, and an incredible vocabulary of swear words: he was the greatest swearer I ever came across. Joe Levine was a one-off.' The contract, however, didn't work out: 'It was the worst thing I ever did. I got screwed over – they wouldn't let me appear in any parts.' James was at one time lined up to star in an adaptation of Robbins' novel *Stiletto* (1969), but it never happened. The only film he completed under the Levine contract was *Robbery* (1967), in which he and Glynn

Privates 612 Williams (Peter Gill) and Hook defend the hospital.

Edwards played police officers doggedly on the trail of Stanley Baker's criminal mastermind.

For other producers James made *Ninety Degrees in the Shade* (1965) in Czechoslovakia and the heavy-handed British comedies *The Secret of My Success* (1965) and *The Bliss of Mrs Blossom* (1968). In the latter, set in Swinging London, he appears in one scene wearing the redcoat tunic of a Victorian soldier – an in-joke for *Zulu* fans, perhaps? He also went to Yugoslavia and Hungary to star in *Fräulein Doktor* (1968) opposite Nigel Green, who had not shared any scenes with Booth in *Zulu* (happily, neither actor played the fräulein, a Mata Hari-esque spy incarnated by Suzy Kendall). All of these were leading roles, but thereafter James mainly played supporting parts in a series of increasingly undistinguished films, such as *The Man Who Had Power Over Women* (1970), *Rentadick* (1972), *Percy's Progress* (1974), *Brannigan* (1975) and *I'm Not Feeling Myself Tonight* (1976).

There were a few superior assignments, such as David Essex's estranged father in *That'll Be the Day* (1973), *Gentlemen Prefer Anything* (1974) at Stratford East, and other stage roles as Archie Rice in John Osborne's *The Entertainer* (1973), James Joyce in Tom Stoppard's *Travesties* (1975) and Pompey in *Measure for Measure* for the RSC. James also appeared on British television in Johnny Speight's short-lived series *Them* (1972) and in John Vanbrugh's Restoration romp *The Confederacy of Wives* (1975). But after his property business went bust in 1974, leaving him with massive debts, and acting offers in the UK had all but dried up, he went to live and work in America. There he reflected on his fortunes in an interview for the British magazine *TV Times*:

'I started off in this business with a bang,' he says, toying with a half-pint of beer, his end-of-the-day treat. 'I started off with a great God-given gift but I abused it. I didn't work hard for the first 15 years of my acting life and now I'm going to try and make up for it for the next 15.

'God, I regret those wasted years. I would turn up not knowing my lines; turn up drunk. I used about 10 per cent of the talent I had. It was all too easy. I made a lot of money and had a ball. Then one day it suddenly wasn't so easy. I got a reputation as a drunk, a hell-raiser ...

'I woke up one day flat broke, with a wife, four kids, a big house in the country and little men in bowler hats knocking on the door. I worked for the Royal Shakespeare Company, where I'd spent some of the happiest days of my life, but there was no way I could earn enough money to pay off my debts.'[37]

In Los Angeles, James turned successfully to screenwriting with *Sunburn* (1979), his first of several scripts, as well as acting in films such as *Airport '77* (1977), *The Jazz Singer* (1980) and *Zorro, the Gay Blade* (1981), and on television, including the mini-series *Wheels* and *Evening in Byzantium* (both 1978) and a recurring role in *Twin Peaks* (1990-91). He revisited Britain intermittently for appearances in long-running TV series such as *Bergerac*, *Lovejoy*, *The Bill*, *Minder* and *Auf Wiedersehen, Pet*. My own first meeting with James was in fact on one of these visits, circa 1987, when he starred in a Christmas production of *Peter Pan* at Newcastle upon Tyne's Tyne Theatre and Opera House, playing – of all characters – *Captain* Hook. He eventually made a permanent return and now lives with Paula in Benfleet, Essex.

One of our interviews took place in a famous London actors' bar, Gerry's of Dean Street, where James refused the offer of a cognac ('Brandy's for heroes, Mr Hook!') in favour of a lime cordial. Of *Zulu* he says: 'I'm amazed that people still remember me for it. Walking down the street in New York and other places in the world, they still recognise me, even though I've got white hair now. I haven't seen it in years – after you've seen it twenty-eight times you get bored. If it's on TV I prefer to turn it off. But it's a great adventure story, very well done. When the Brits see it they feel good about themselves.'

Nigel Green
(Colour-Sergeant Frank Bourne)

Perhaps no actor in *Zulu* is so closely identified with his screen character as Nigel Green is with Colour-Sergeant Bourne. 'He brought such a presence to what could have been a nothing role,' remarks John Barry. Green had previously appeared alongside Stanley Baker in Joseph Losey's *The Criminal* (1960) – he is one of the goons employed to beat up the hero in the closing scenes – and in *The Man Who Finally Died* (1962), and he had worked for Cy Endfield on the Jules Verne fantasy *Mysterious Island* (1961). All his acting scenes in the latter – in which he played a sailor called Tom, killed off before reaching the eponymous island – were cut from the finished movie, though he can still be seen floating face downward in the surf in the background of one sequence. No doubt both Baker and Endfield remembered him and gave Green the role of his career when they cast him as Bourne.

He was in fact born in South Africa – in Onderstepoort, near Pretoria, on 15 October 1924. His father, Dr H.H. Green, was, according to the *Zulu* Production Information Dossier, 'Deputy Director of the Animal Research Station and the first man in the world, by fourteen years, to apply biochemistry to animal health.' The family emigrated to Britain when Nigel was five, settling in Weybridge, Surrey, where Dr Green had accepted a position in the Ministry of Agriculture. Nigel was educated at King's College School, Wimbledon, and studied chemical engineering at London University. Aged eighteen, he enlisted in the Fleet Air Arm, becoming a Sub-Lieutenant Observer for torpedo bombers. After the war he studied at RADA on a scholarship, and subsequently acted opposite Edith Evans in *The Way of the World* at the Old Vic and John Gielgud in *King Lear* in Stratford-on-Avon.

Green began acting for the cinema and television in 1952, accumulating bit parts in such films as *The Sea Shall Not Have Them* (1954, as a Met Officer delivering such deathless lines as 'It'll be pretty grim'), *Reach for the Sky* (1956), *The Gypsy and the Gentleman* (1958) and *Beat Girl* (1960). He had a recurring role as 'The Bear' in the television series *The Adventures of William Tell* (1958), played Little John opposite Richard Greene's Robin Hood in Hammer's TV spin-off *Sword of Sherwood Forest* (1960), and was Hercules in *Jason and the Argonauts* (1963). But the most remarkable of Green's early film roles is in Nicholas Ray's World War Two drama *Bitter Victory* (1957). His Private Wilkins is a perversely Puckish, jester-like figure, forever mocking the antagonistic officers (Richard Burton and Curt Jurgens) leading a mission in the North African desert by seemingly peering into their souls and seeing the baseness at the heart of all would-be heroes. It's an extraordinary performance, which makes one wonder why major roles did not come Green's way earlier; perhaps he just seemed too dangerously strange. Peter Gill comments that 'there were rumours that he had offended Binkie Beaumont,' the influential theatre impresario, which may possibly explain what Gill calls Green's 'chequered career.'

Certainly he seems not to have been the easiest of people to get along with in the *Zulu* company. Assistant editor Jennifer Thompson – who drove out into the South African countryside with him one night to shoot rabbits by the glare of car headlights ('It was something to do!') – says that, 'Nigel Green was a nightmare after a few drinks. He lost his temper and went a bit barmy. But he was a very nice man and had a wonderful presence on screen.' David Kernan concurs: 'There were two Nigel Greens, no doubt about that. He was gentle, charming most of the day, but got a little argumentative after a few drinks.' Bob Porter recalls one fierce argument that broke out in the location bar between Green and stunt arranger John Sullivan. Coming to Sullivan's defence, Porter raised a fist to lash out at the actor, but Stanley Baker yelled from across the room: 'Don't! You'll kill him!' In 1956 Green had suffered a serious skull fracture after slipping on ice, subsequently spending many weeks paralysed in hospital and suffering from amnesia. He recovered but had had a metal plate fitted in his head, and a heavy blow would have been lethal.

Green could be volatile on set, too. 'A madman' is how sound technician David Jones recalls him. 'He got carried away in the fight sequences. They had to tell him, look, it's only a film. He'd have killed someone.' Joe Powell remembers Green having 'a tremendous row' with Cy Endfield over the interpretation of Bourne. 'That evening Nigel was sitting on his own eating and Cy approached him to pacify the situation and calm him down. Nigel put his knife and fork down with a tremendous clatter and said, "Cy, you're an intellectual cripple!"' Green's sharp tongue almost led to his being replaced, as Ivor Emmanuel recalls. 'He was nearly out of the film. One night he crawled back from a party, covered in mud. He was incapable – I had to wash him down. He'd been complaining about Stanley. He had been an alcoholic but had pulled himself out of it. But he was a charming guy and a bloody good actor.' Ellen Baker recalls that one post-prandial 'walkabout' lasted three days, and that on his return Stanley sat Green down for a serious talk about his attitude problems.

All was forgiven when the film came out. Nigel earned more favourable mentions in reviews of *Zulu* than anyone else in the cast,

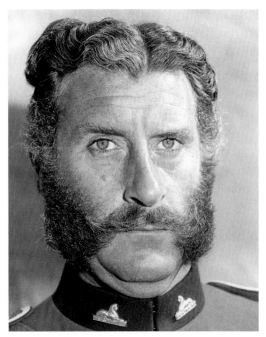

A rare publicity portrait of Green as Bourne without his helmet: the Colour-Sergeant is never shown bare-headed in the film.

and his performance seems to have gained him belated recognition from his industry peers. He subsequently won a number of major supporting roles, including the arrogant, antagonistic intelligence officer opposite Michael Caine in *The Ipcress File* (1965); detective Nayland Smith in *The Face of Fu Manchu* (1965); General Sir Garnet Wolseley in *Khartoum* (1966); unsympathetic army officers in two more desert warfare movies,

Tobruk (1967) and *Play Dirty* (1969), the latter also co-starring Caine; and a striking cameo appearance in John Huston's Cold War thriller *The Kremlin Letter* (1970).

There were also lesser parts in weaker movies, such as the villains in the spy spoofs *Deadlier Than the Male* (1967) and *The Wrecking Crew* (1968). But Green's career was cut tragically short at the age of 47 when he died from an accidental overdose of sleeping pills. He was discovered dead at his Brighton home – which he had named Bourne House in honour of *Zulu* – on 15 May 1972. He had separated from his wife, Patricia Marmont, his skull injury caused him continual pain, and he suffered from depression and insomnia. Because of these circumstances there are some who believe Green committed suicide, but the coroner recorded a verdict of death by misadventure.[38] His last film, the low-budget Arthurian fantasy *Gawain and the Green Knight* (1973), in which he appropriately played the Green Knight, was released posthumously.

Notes

[1] D.N.E. Kain, '*Zulu*: A Film Completed,' *Personality*, 3 October 1963, p. 57. Kain commented of the rumours: 'South Africans seem to be a trifle old-fashioned in their concept of film-making. The trend today is away from the star system.'

[2] Des Hickey, 'Why I wanted to produce my own movies,' *Photoplay*, February 1969, p. 47.

[3] Interview for *Cinema* (Granada Television, broadcast 2 November 1972).

[4] Kain, p. 62.

[5] William Hall, *Raising Caine: The Authorized Biography* (London: Arrow, 1982), p. 3. For more material on the making of *Zulu*, see pp. 100-11.

[6] Michael Caine, *What's It All About?* (London: Random House/Arrow, 1993), p. 177. Allowing for some raconteur's embellishments, Caine's account of the filming of *Zulu* provides many valuable insights and amusing anecdotes. On acting technique, see also his excellent BBC television masterclass, *Acting in Films* (1987), and the spin-off book of the same name.

[7] Elaine Gallagher, *Candidly Caine* (London: Robson Books/London Weekend Television, 1990), p. 13. For this account of Caine's professional career Gallagher makes use of wide-ranging interview material originally compiled for a TV special, *The Trouble With Michael Caine* (1987). There is also an excellent reference section giving details of Caine's television, stage and film work, including his early, unbilled appearances, many of which she has actually bothered to view. On *Zulu*, see pp. 69-78.

[8] For slightly different versions of this story and its aftermath, see Caine, pp. 162-5; Gallagher, pp. 70-2; Hall, pp. 101-3.

[9] Though Bob Porter confirms that Stamp had been considered for Bromhead, Maureen Endfield does not recall his actually being approached: 'I don't think Cy had met Terence then. I think we only met him through Michael, because they lived together.' Stamp has not commented publicly on the matter and I have not been able to quiz him about it.

[10] In his own memoirs, Terence Stamp claims that the party was on 13 March, the very eve of Caine's birthday, but by then Endfield had already left London for the South African location. See *Double Feature* (London: Bloomsbury, 1989), pp. 85-7

[11] Richard Porton, 'The Character Actor as Movie Star: An Interview with Michael Caine,' *Cineaste*, vol. XXIX, no. 2 (Spring 2004), p. 4. In an earlier interview, Caine had commented: 'Afterwards some people said they thought I'd overdone the accent, slurring the vowels and that … But they do, those people. That's how they talk' (Anne Billson, *My Name is Michael Caine*, London: Muller, 1991, p. 27).

[12] Graham Fuller, 'Ordinary Bloke,' *Film Comment*, March-April 2004, p. 30.

[13] Interview for *The Man Who Would Be Caine* (BBC, 1998).

[14] Caine, pp. 177-8; Gallagher, pp 74-5, 78.

[15] Stephen Coan, email to the author, 19 January 2004. As Coan says, the anecdote 'gives a poignant picture of a lonely Brit far from home.'

[16] *The Man Who Would Be Caine*.

[17] Caine, p. 179.

[18] For a fan's appreciation of Caine's performance, see Pete Clark, 'My local hero,' *Evening Standard*, 4 March 1998, p. 29: 'He is the sort of man who makes young boys want to grow up to be film stars.'.

[19] Caine, p. 194.

[20] Gallagher, p. 77.

21 'Michael Caine signed by Fox;' 'International Sound Track,' *Variety*, 19 February 1964; 'Caine signed by Columbia,' *The Daily Cinema*, 10 June 1964, p. 7; 'New York Sound Track,' *Variety*, 17 June 1964.

22 'Michael Caine signed by Fox,' *The Daily Cinema*, 12 February 1964, p. 7.

23 Yousuf Karsh, 'Ottawa Photographer's Prose Impressions of Joseph E. Levine,' *Variety*, 22 April 1964, p. 97.

24 Untitled newspaper interview, c. 1966-67; in British Film Institute Library microfiche on Baker.

25 'Cuttings,' *Films and Filming*, August 1958, p. 17.

26 Dennis John Hall, 'Gentleman Jack,' *Films and Filming*, September 1970, p. 75. Biographical information on Hawkins derives from this article, the actor's own memoirs *Anything for a Quiet Life* (London: Elm Tree, 1973), and Alvin H. Marill, 'Jack Hawkins 1910-1973,' *Films in Review*, January 1976, which contains a detailed Filmography.

27 See 'Jack Hawkins: Mr. Box-Office, 1954,' *Films and Filming*, March 1955, p. 3.

28 *Zulu* South African programme brochure; Hawkins, p. 131.

29 Hawkins, pp. 131-2.

30 John Webster, 'Ulla Jacobsson,' *The Heroes of Telemark* programme brochure (London: Sackville Publishing, 1965). Biographical information on Jacobsson derives from publicity material produced for *Telemark* and *Zulu*.

31 'Jean Simmons not for Rorke's Drift film,' *The Natal Mercury*, 26 February 1963, p. 3.

32 *Zulu* Pressbook.

33 'Tension? It was like sitting on a volcano,' in John Willis, Saul Cooper and Laurie Bailey, *All About The Heroes of Telemark*, Rank Organisation, 2 September 1965, pp. 114-5.

34 Webster, op. cit.

35 South African programme brochure.

36 Gerard Garrett, 'There's something odd about Robin Hood,' *Evening Standard*, 24 September 1965.

37 Lesley Salisbury, 'James Booth's new beginning – when he put down a pint and picked up a pen,' *TV Times*, 2 November 1978, p. 11. Other biographical material on Booth derives from: Lesley Salisbury, 'Why haven't I been on the box for three years? No one asked me,' *TV Times*, 8 March 1975; Bill Hagerty, 'The crooked finger of fame beckons,' *Daily Mirror*, 25 October 1976; Maureen Paton, 'Fings look up for the crafty Cockney,' *Daily Express*, 15 March 1986.

38 David McGillivray, 'Now You Know,' *Films and Filming*, April 1988, p. 47.

"DO CARRY ON WITH YOUR MUD PIES"

LOCATIONS, PROPS AND COSTUMES

> That director Cy Endfield, my co-producer, and I were able to bring in *Zulu* under budget and under the shooting schedule was entirely due, I hasten to state, to thorough pre-planning.
>
> Faced with the great trust of spending an enormous amount of other people's money, and getting its value all on the screen, Cy and I, with our staff, tried to anticipate every possible contingency in filming *Zulu* 6,000 miles away from London on location in Africa. Not a camera rolled until everything was ready; until every problem was solved, from building virtually complete studio facilities in Natal, to supplying the best possible working conditions and leisure-time comforts for our cast and 63-man crew.
>
> (Stanley Baker, 'Meeting the Challenge Of Producing an Epic As a First Picture,' *Motion Picture Herald*, 18 September 1963, p. 9)

Though it now seems the obvious course of action, it was by no means a foregone conclusion that *Zulu* would be shot almost entirely on location in South Africa. In the 1950s it was still common practice for companies producing movies with exotic settings to send a second unit on location to shoot extensive background footage, with doubles standing in for the principal actors. The bulk of the film would then be shot on studio sets in Britain (or America, as the case might be), with the location footage used for long shots or as 'plates' for use with back projection or blue-screen special effects techniques. These methods were used, for example, for the British production *Simba* (1955) and the American *Untamed* (1955), on both of which the stars, in all probability, never set foot in Africa (though for its large-scale action scenes *Untamed* used many more Zulu extras than were subsequently available for *Zulu*).[1]

When Cy Endfield and Stanley Baker began to prepare *Zulu*, however, they were determined from the outset that it should substantially be filmed overseas. 'Adhering to historical fact,' wrote Baker later, 'made it mandatory to film *Zulu* where it happened, in Africa, and to use real Zulus to portray their warrior ancestors.'[2] First assistant director Bert Batt recalls receiving a phone call from Endfield as early as 1959, shortly after returning to London from filming Ken Annakin's *Nor the Moon by Night* (1958) in Natal, just a stone's throw away from what would later be the location for *Zulu*.[3] 'Cy wanted to know what it was like making movies in South Africa. I told him that if he and his crew could keep their eyes closed and their mouths shut there would not be any problems.'

On 24 August 1962, unit manager and second unit director Bob Porter set out to scout the southern part of the continent to find an appropriate location where the filming could take place. The actual site of the battle was considered, but swiftly rejected. The

Unit manager and second unit director Bob Porter

landscape there around the Shiyane (Oskarsberg) Hill was mostly flat and, from a cinematic viewpoint, uninteresting. There were additional problems which prevented its use, as George Smith explained in his retrospective article on the making of the film: 'None of the original buildings had survived – a modern school and monuments to the battle had been erected over the mission and battlefield. But the greatest obstacle to filming there was that the missionary society who had bought the land from Jim Rorke's widow still owned it. They would in no way allow a film to be made on their property that, in their eyes, glorified war.'[4]

With the real Rorke's Drift ruled out, Porter's recce involved three separate trips and several thousand miles of travelling, taking in Namibia and the Transvaal before he came across the Drakensberg mountain range in the Royal Natal National Park (a distance of about 160 kilometres as the crow flies from the real Rorke's Drift). He saw the dramatic rock-wall Amphitheatre for the first time from the front seat of a jeep – 'It was like an opera stage' – at which point he knew immediately that he had found the right site for the picture. Soon after, as the press office's Production Information Dossier put it, 'Western man and his modern machine invaded Royal Natal National Park, a vast picturesque nature reserve, established by the South African government on a plateau 6,000 feet below the Drakensberg Mountains, and the animals, birds and snakes indigenous to the area fled before them.' As far as the crew was concerned, it was a pretty remote location, as unit publicist Geoff Freeman recalls: 'We were very isolated in the Drakensberg National Park. People passed through it, they didn't *go* there. You had to drive up to Johannesburg the night before, stay over in a hotel, and drive up to the location the following day. [Journalist] Bill Hall went there. His first words to Stanley Baker after a long trek to the mountain were, "Ah, Stanley I presume!"'

While Endfield worked on the script with John Prebble in London and Baker continued acting in other films, Porter set up the production with the aid of local contacts. Josh du Toit was the location manager, who scouted locations with Bob and collaborated on all the preparatory work needed to put the film together. Andre Pieterse's company S.A. Films (Pty), and its South African Film Studios at Lone Hill on the outskirts of Johannesburg, supplied production facilities, including personnel and equipment.[5] While visiting Zululand to arrange for tribesmen to be used as extras, Porter stayed and became friendly with Chief Mangosuthu G. Buthelezi, who became a key figure behind the scenes as well as in front of the camera. Other key members of the unit included associate producer Basil Keys, production manager John D. Merriman and Colin Lesslie, brought in by the completion guarantors to see that the film was made on budget and on schedule.

Basil Keys (born on 16 July 1919) came from a notable film-making family: his brothers were Anthony Nelson Keys, an executive producer at Hammer Studios, and John Paddy Carstairs, director of many popular comedies, including Norman Wisdom's early vehicles. Basil entered the industry as an assistant director in 1936, became a producer with Hammer and Walt Disney in the 50s, and subsequently racked up a formidable list of credits as a freelance production manager and supervisor, including *The Naked Prey* (1965), *Monte Carlo or Bust!* (1969), *O Lucky Man!* (1973), *Aces High* (1976) and several of the *Carry On* films. He hired Bob Porter to direct behind-the-scenes documentary footage for Disney's television show on Ken Annakin's large-scale live-action pictures *Third Man on the Mountain* (1959) and *Swiss Family Robinson* (1960). Porter returned the compliment by inviting Keys to oversee preparations in the Natal National Park while he was in Zululand.

After army service during the war, Bob Porter (born on 8 August 1924) had started in the film industry as assistant casting director at Shepperton Studios and as a stunt performer in such large-scale pictures as *Bonnie Prince Charlie* (1948), *The Black Rose* (1950), *Knights of the Round Table* (1953), *The Dark Avenger* (1955) and *Moby Dick* (1956). After doubling for stars like David Niven and Tyrone Power, Porter embarked on a seven-year contract with Stewart Granger, serving as his stunt double and stand-in on such films as *Beau Brummell* (1954) and *Bhowani Junction* (1956). With *Carve Her Name With Pride* (1958) Bob became an assistant director, and after working as location manager on *HMS Defiant* and *The Man Who Finally Died* (both 1962) he was invited by Stanley Baker to join Diamond Films in setting up *Zulu*. 'Bob was such a good control on the film,' says sound technician David Jones, 'such a good support for Stanley.' Porter describes his own role as being 'like the wristwatch on Cy's arm.'

Bob's main initial task was to get the film's budget down to under $2 million, as Joe Levine had stipulated. This was done partly by

Bob Porter relaxes between takes.

using mostly unknown actors in the cast, as discussed in the last chapter, and partly by cutting back on the cost of sets, props and costumes. While Baker and Endfield supervised the casting, Bob did the costing. By way of example, he says that the leading British theatrical and film costume house Bermans, run by the late Monty M. Berman, wanted around $150,000 to supply the British and Zulu costumes. Rather than accept this, Porter negotiated more advantageous terms with his South African contacts: 'I did a deal with Gatsha Buthelezi to have the Zulu costumes and props made locally. We made them for around $15,000 using the Zulus, and they were pre-sold for $20,000 to S.A. Films after I showed them the quote from Bermans.' Bob also visited an abattoir to pick out cows due to be slaughtered and bought their hides for the Zulu shields and costumes, while a hundred cattle for use as livestock were hired from local people near the location site.

Though the Drakensberg location was ideal pictorially, it was not quite ready for filming. The script called for the opening scenes to be set in and around the fast-flowing Buffalo (Mzinyathi) River, and while the Natal National Park's Tugela (Thukela) River could in theory serve as a substitute, in mid-winter it was actually no more than a small stream at the spot where the production unit was based. In order to create the semblance of a river in need of bridging, Porter had to use bulldozers and a force of several hundred local labourers to move 400 tons of earth to alter the stream's course and dam it to hold 5,000 square yards of water.[6]

164 LOCATIONS, PROPS AND COSTUMES

The Tugela River before and after damming.

Accommodation also had to be found for the cast and crew for the duration of the fourteen-week shoot. There were two large tourist hotels within easy reach of the location site: the Royal Natal National Park Hotel, which was only a short walk from the set, and the Mont-Aux-Sources Hotel, a few miles away uphill. 'They booked the whole hotel,' comments Marius Markgraaf, still the owner-manager of the Mont-Aux-Sources some forty years later. 'As usual [with filmmakers] they wanted everything for nothing.'[7] Even though the lodgings were designed for overnight stays rather than for long vacations, rooms were booked in both hotels for over one hundred personnel for three months of shooting; motor transport was provided to and from the set each day in the form of 'combis' (people-carriers). To accommodate the Zulus – whom South Africa's racial laws prevented staying in the hotels – a pre-fabricated village compound, comprising dormitories, kitchens and dining rooms, toilets and showers, wardrobe, laundry, and so forth, was built over the hill from the set, to and from which the Zulus marched each day. Accommodated in their own military encampment nearby was a company of white South Africans receiving their Active Citizen Force training – the equivalent of the British National Service – made available as extras by

LOCATIONS, PROPS AND COSTUMES 165

The Mont-Aux-Sources was the more distant of the two hotels used by the *Zulu* cast and crew.

the Department of Defence.

Other facilities also had to be provided in the absence of a permanent studio: offices for the production staff and their secretaries, carpentry workshops for the building of sets and manufacture of props, stores for the props, costumes and other equipment, secure armouries to hold the many weapons, wardrobe and hair-dressing departments, an editing room, and so on. With the assistance of a Durban-based timber company and three hundred labourers, a complex of some thirty small buildings was therefore constructed between the set and the hotels, and camouflaged so that it would not be caught accidentally on camera. This was described in the Information Dossier as an 'administrative village' and was known to the crew as 'the Colony' (apparently named after a hotel night club in Johannesburg). The offices were air-conditioned and fitted with electricity and running water, and had to be inspected and approved by Natal's Chief Medical Officer before use. 'I paid $120,000 to build the facilities,' says Bob Porter, 'and sold the whole lot at cost before they were built to a road-building company.' By selling off props and materials to local businesses and independent film producers, Diamond was reportedly able to recover as much as 15% of *Zulu*'s production cost.[8]

In total, some one thousand people were employed at the location before and during the shoot. Catering for their everyday dietary needs was a massive (and expensive) task in its own right. A staff of thirty-five Asian and African cooks and waiters regularly served hot coffee and other refreshments on set. Endless crates of Coca-Cola and other soft drinks were also on hand, left immersed in the shallows of the Tugela to keep them cool. South African journalist Derrick Kain offered his own first-hand report on the catering:

A Pretoria man, Mr. Tony Allchurch accepted the challenge to cater for the film 'army'. His restaurant in the film village was open until late at night. He was proud of the fact that fresh South African fruit, most of it sent up from the Cape, appeared on the menu. The cost of a typical day's food orders was between R500 and R800.

And a typical day's food order would be 1,500 cups of tea, 1,100 cooked meals, 220lb. of meat, 20 dozen eggs, 15 dozen loaves of bread and 60 dozen cups of lime juice.[9]

Part of the purpose-built production village.

Supplying the set with these and other materials was a small armada of vehicles, including pantechnicons, three-ton trucks, station wagons, jeeps and helicopters. Each day the exposed film was carried by former racing drivers in a pair of 'souped-up' Volkswagens, travelling the 250-mile journey to Johannesburg at high speed so that the rushes could be shipped out to the laboratories in London, then making the return journey with cans of developed footage for the editors to view on location. According to the Information Dossier, the cars 'travelled an estimated 40,000 miles before the film was completed.'

The largest of the pre-fab buildings – and possibly the most important from the crew's point of view! – was a bar/canteen designed as a recreation facility for use in the evenings and during breaks in filming. Bob Porter hung a tongue-in-cheek sign outside the canteen designating it 'The Talk of the Town' after the currently fashionable London restaurant and stipulating that ties should be worn (they weren't). Maureen Endfield says that, 'You could get a large brandy there for about fourpence, and nights were so cold everyone was knocking them back.' Geoff Freeman recalls spending 'wonderful evenings playing pool and darts in the recreation room. We worked hard by day and it was nice to relax in the evening. Being our own place we could go in in our jeans and so on, we didn't have to dress up. It all worked like a dream, even though it was in the middle of nowhere. It wasn't primitive at all.' David Jones also enjoyed the experience: 'It was a very pleasant location, a South African holiday resort. You were mixing with tourists on holiday. We used to spend our time playing table tennis. Michael Caine was a very good player.' The nearest large towns, such as Durban and Ladysmith, were many miles away, but at least some members of the unit

'The Talk of the Town.'

Art director Ernest Archer

tried to keep in touch with the outside world. Maureen says that 'Michael would go off at every opportunity to Durban – he used to bring back loads of records from DJs there.' On one occasion, noted the Information Dossier, 'Twenty-five members of cast and crew, led by Stanley Baker, made a 500-mile round trip to support the Tottenham Hotspurs football team playing the National League Eleven in Durban. Spurs won 5 to 2.'

In addition to the production and administration facilities, the film's sets also had to be built from scratch. These were designed by art director Ernest Archer (1910-90), a veteran of Gaumont-British and Gainsborough Studios, who had worked with Cy Endfield on *Hell Drivers* (1957) and *Mysterious Island* (1961). Archer's work on *Zulu* earned for him the only nomination the film received for an industry award: the British

168 LOCATIONS, PROPS AND COSTUMES

Ernest Archer at work in his location office, joined by Bob Porter. The drawings on the wall are production designs, not story-boards: no story-boards were used on *Zulu*.

Local inhabitants, dressed in tribal costume for a pre-production publicity shoot, observe the construction of the buildings for the Rorke's Drift set.

Film Academy's Best Colour Art Direction (won that year by *Becket*). A team of builders and carpenters, led by construction manager Dick Frift and head 'chippie' John Paterson, arrived on site early in 1963, well before the arrival of the rest of the crew in March, to begin building the replica of the Rorke's Drift mission station. The small interior set representing the chapel storehouse was also built close to the production offices. Cetewayo's Royal 'kraal' or homestead, comprising a village of small thatched huts made of plaster, wood and straw over a steel frame, was built on the other side of the Tugela, where the aftermath of the battle at Isandhlwana was also shot. The throne used to seat Chief Buthelezi (playing the Zulu king) was reportedly the one actually used by the real Cetewayo, which had been 'located at a mission near Eshowe in Zululand and permission was obtained for its temporary removal to the film set. It was insured for R10,000.'[10] A week after shooting in the village set had been completed, it was occupied by a colony of baboons driven down from the mountains by heavy snow.

Arthur Newman was overall wardrobe supervisor for the film, but while the British soldiers' uniforms were supplied by Bermans of London, responsibility for the Zulus' costuming was largely in the experienced hands of the Pretoria-based Hilda Geerdts. *Zulu* was her sixteenth film in southern Africa; according to the Exhibitors' Campaign Book (or Pressbook), she was 'one of the world's outstanding authorities on African tribal life [and] had to draw heavily upon her knowledge of Old Africa to design authentic costumes.' According to Derrick Kain, Geerdts found that she had to educate the Zulus in how their

The church and store-room sets designed by Ernest Archer.

Bob Porter directs a group of local servants, gardeners and labourers – most wearing traditional costume for the first time – in this pre-production publicity shot. *The Natal Mercury* reported that Porter 'was bowled over twice yesterday morning by over-exuberant "warriors" who could not halt their combined charge in time' ('Zulus Charge Again,' 26 February 1963, p. 3).

Hilda Geerdts and Bob Porter dress Vimba Mkize with a costume of leopard skin and plastic animal teeth. The caption to this picture, which appeared on the front page of *The Natal Mercury* on 26 February 1963, read: 'Perhaps yesterday, as he posed for the cameras, Vimba recalled stories of the days when to be a Zulu was to be invincible. But the dreams soon faded... less than an hour later he was back at his job as a pantry-boy in the Royal Natal National Park Hotel.'

ancestors dressed, using her own sketches to demonstrate.[11] Interviewed about the particular demands of the production, she said:

> Fashions may not always be functional here [in Britain], but in Natal everything a Zulu wears has a meaning and a purpose.
>
> The Zulus had the right idea about clothes. For instance, the Indunas – tribal chiefs of high birth – wore plumed headdresses of red, white and black ostrich feathers – the red feather representing their battle honours.
>
> In addition to the feathers, they also wore a full leopard skin draped around their bodies and a leopard tail 'mutsha' – a type of loincloth worn in front – which is exclusive to the Zulu Royal family during the 19th century.
>
> For the Zulus clothes were more than fashion. Each piece had a meaning and a protection, both spiritual and physical. It might not be such a bad plan to subscribe to in these days of fashion fad and fancy.[12]

In manufacturing the costumes Hilda preferred traditional materials to synthetic modern substitutes, so all the Zulu regalia and adornments worn in the film were made by hand by some twenty local men and women. Among the accessories were 'necklaces of baboon teeth (plastic), belts of woven grass, decorations from seeds, horns of dried roots, long strings of animal hair, ankle rings of porcupine quills, skirts of animal skin,' head rings and loincloths made from the skins of leopard, springbok, impala and wild cat.[13] For the wedding dance sequence, according to the Pressbook,

> Specially chosen virgin girls wear thousands of hand-made beads and a headdress of leopard skin and vari-coloured ostrich feathers with white pompom-like balls of feathers attached. They also have copper bracelets and ankle rattlers – called 'umface'.
>
> The small coloured beads – more than 100 pounds of them – were made by a contingent of local Zulu craftswomen working together for many weeks.
>
> A further 100lbs of wild syringa beads were dyed in many colours and strung together into necklaces by use of sinews taken from animal skin and rolled together by hand – into a material stronger than the toughest fishing twine. This primitive

Vimba Mkize, here dressed 'in his everyday servant's uniform,' told *The Natal Mercury*'s reporter 'that he had never worn the traditional Zulu uniform until yesterday. "It makes me feel like a man," he said' (26 February 1963, p. 3).

Ngofiza Majola makes 'riempies' from strips of animal hide.

method dates back into antiquity but is still used today in Zululand.

A complete single costume could cost up to R100. The Zulus themselves, however, were not always familiar with the old customs and costumes, needing Geerdts' help to put them on the right way. A local newspaper wryly observed that 'few Englishmen sitting safely at their firesides will realise that the "bloodthirsty warriors" were as unfamiliar in tribal dress as they would be themselves.'[14] One of the craftsmen, Ngofiza Majola, was described as shaking his head 'in sorrow for the "good old days"' when he saw young extras 'wearing their head-dresses back-to-front or with shorts peeping from below the animal-tail skirts.'[15]

Assegais and shields were also made locally. The assegais had rubber tips and, recalls camera technician Peter Hammond, 'when we used them on the first day they wobbled. The [Zulu] chief called Cy and said, we've been using spears for thousands of years – the only people we hurt are the ones we want to hurt!'

Derrick Kain reported on the manufacture of the warriors' shields:

> The back garden of a Pietermaritzburg home resembled the headquarters of an impi. Lying in heaps and propped up against a fence were 350 authentic oxhide shields. A Pietermaritzburg firm under the management of Mr. A.J. Harborth undertook the job, and the Harborth family and neighbours were roped in to add the finishing touches to the fighting equipment. Fourteen-year-old Glyn Harborth and his friends made the sticks for the shields, and Mrs. Harborth canvassed old fur coats from her friends. The coats were cut into strips and wound round the tops of the shield sticks.[16]

Once they had been issued with their costumes and decorations, the Zulus kept them for the duration of the shooting, taking them back to their accommodation at night to save time the following morning. When not wearing their costumes on set, they were provided with white boiler-suits which, along with their bedding, they took back with them to their homes in Zululand at the end of shooting. As the Pressbook described it, getting them properly set up for filming was still a lengthy procedure: 'Long after the professional cast was ready for the cameras ... the Zulu actors were still being made-up. Cow tails, worn back-combed and fluffed out around their legs had to be affixed by the experts ... Particular attention was given to the hair-styling of the Zulu soldiers, for in actual combat this was as distinguishing as a British soldier's uniform marks.' The White soldiers were also marched back to their camp wearing their uniforms and came to the set each morning already dressed; only their makeup and false whiskers had to be applied once there.

The company's main properties supplier was Dawie van Heerden (born 1928), who had begun his career in the South African film industry as a child actor in the British production of *King Solomon's Mines* (1937) and had also worked in various capacities on such other location-shot films as *The African Queen* (1951), *Mogambo* (1953), *Duel in the Jungle* (1954) and *The Hellions* (1961). Van Heerden brought many of the props from his own vast collection of artefacts, including '100 spears, dozens of rifles, swords, revolvers, cavalry equipment for 50 horses, two Cape carts, a wagon, soup tureens, and horses which he has trained to fall and plunge,'[17] and even a lizard for the script's opening shot (never actually filmed).

Bob Porter fondly recalls van Heerden's propensity for accidents, such as shooting himself in the foot while trying to impress Stanley Baker with a fast draw. Bob remembers that he insisted on testing one of Dawie's rifles

172 LOCATIONS, PROPS AND COSTUMES

– which were supposed to be loaded with harmless blanks – by firing at an empty cardboard cereal box placed halfway up a tree. 'After one shot the box disintegrated. We kept trying to get the powder charge down, and it took three hours to get it down to just a puff a smoke.' Dawie also hired around eighty rifles from the London-based armourer Bapty. Not all the firarms used were the authentic breech-loading Martini-Henry, however. A number of those visible in the film are instead bolt-action Long Lee-Enfield or Lee-Metford rifles, which the company attempted to disguise by removing the magazines, though they are still recognisable to eagle-eyed military buffs.[18]

One contributor to the Discussion Forum at http://rorkesdriftvc.com/ has questioned the authenticity of another of the props: the bags of mealie meal used to form the perimeter of the defences. Sergeant Windridge is at one point shown carrying one on each shoulder, and according to 'Miguel' the 'actual mealie bags were said to be "very heavy affairs" weighing 200 pounds (100 kgs.) each. No way in hell could a sergeant have carried TWO of them on his shoulders…' (posted 22 April 2003). For the record, the film's mealie bags were filled with wood shavings.

Among the more bizarre props required – though in the end they did not actually appear on screen – were papier maché dummies of a number of dead animals, including horses and oxen, intended to be seen scattered around the devastated Isandhlwana battlefield. Production assistant Ernest Bisogno arranged for these to be made by a local couple, Ken and Pam Coughtrie. Pam picks up the story: 'The unit had tried injecting live animals with darts but they kept getting up and walking around. [Production manager] John Merriman just wanted to use old sacks but Ernie Bisogno contacted me to make some mock-ups. I had made one cow and took the udders off and put some horns on it to make a bull. They liked it and gave me the go-ahead to make the other eighteen or whatever it was. My husband Ken and I made them at home using wire mesh and plaster. The back yard looked like an abattoir. A big white pantechnicon with "SA Films" painted on the side arrived to pick them up and they were strapped down. But when they arrived they had all been flattened, so my husband and I went down to the location for a weekend or so to repair them.' No dummies were used for the dead bodies of the soldiers and warriors, because, says Pam, 'there were many willing extras for both roles. I certainly did not have to manufacture them personally!'

Among the live animals used in the film was the cheetah Bromhead is shown hunting in the opening scenes. This was a one-year-old called Chita, which had been obtained on loan from the South African Air Force. He was squadron mascot to Number Two Squadron, the Cheetah Squadron of the Korean War, and was often pictured posing with the film's stars for publicity photographs.[19] It was returned safely to the squadron at the end of the shoot: the trophy carried by Bromhead's bearers was a pair of stuffed leopard skins sewn together, courtesy of prop master John Poyner.[20]

A Cruel Country

Setting up the location site and the production unit was largely accomplished by Bob Porter, Basil Keys and their team in the months before shooting commenced. Cy Endfield had visited South Africa for a week in September 1962, prior to the drawing up of the shooting schedule, and went again in February 1963 to check on progress ('I remember Cy was scared stiff because he hated flying,' says Maureen).

On 7 March he arrived for final pre-production preparations and remained for the duration of filming (until 28 June). With him were first assistant director Bert Batt and director of photography Stephen Dade, and together they spent the next three weeks laying out the shots and planning the action scenes.

On Tuesday, 26 March, some fifty actors and technicians arrived at Johannesburg's Jan Smuts Airport on two Lufthansa charter flights, after a twenty-hour journey from London. Among them were Stanley Baker and Michael Caine, as well as Nigel Green, Glynn Edwards, Ivor Emmanuel, Neil McCarthy, David Kernan, Peter Gill and Larry Taylor.[21] Some had not shaved for weeks, as it had originally been planned to have most of the officers and NCOs – including Chard and Bourne – wearing full beards. They were quickly clean-shaven, though Green was allowed to keep a handsome set of mutton-chop whiskers and Baker sported long sideboards.

There followed another long journey in a coach from the airport to the location hotels. 'It seemed endless,' recalls David Kernan. 'We were in the air for twenty-four hours, and then it seemed we were in the bus for twenty-four hours.' Nor did he find the accommodation luxurious: 'The Mont-Aux-Sources Hotel was a bit rough, I thought. Maybe the crew stayed at the better-class hotel – isn't that always the way? I remember the very gloomy dining room; the food was atrocious, but the white wine was good.' As shooting progressed, there was, as usual with filming, much waiting around between shots. During one break in shooting Bert Batt told David and some other actors to relax by going to the bowling green of the Royal Natal National Park Hotel and

An unused long shot of the devastated Isandhlwana battlefield. Note the bodies of the livestock, built in papier maché.

South African Actors

Gert van den Bergh (Lieutenant Josef Adendorff) was the real star of *Zulu* for many locals. 'South African people visiting the set would always rush over to get Gert van den Bergh's autograph,' recalls Glynn Edwards. 'He used to act in Afrikaans and do stand-up comedy. He was always being dragged up on stage to do it.' A prolific actor in his home country, Gert's other films before his death in 1968 included *The Hellions* (1961), *The Diamond Walkers* (1965), *The Naked Prey* (1965) and *Seven Against the Sun* (1966), on all of which he worked with other *Zulu* personnel.

According to journalist Derrick Kain, Dennis Folbigge (Acting Assistant Commissary James Langley Dalton) was at the time 'well known on South African radio and has also taken leading roles in stage productions. He has written several plays; in fact, acting and writing are his spare-time activities. He is employed by a Durban advertising agency as a radio account executive' ('*Zulu*: A Film Completed'). Folbigge's other films include *American Ninja 2: The Confrontation* (1987), written by *Zulu*'s James Booth. David Kernan stayed often with Dennis at his home in Pietermaritzburg, on weekends off during the *Zulu* shoot and in later years: 'I remember him being a very gentle actor, immensely hospitable, and I saw him many times when I went back to South Africa.'

Kernan also visited Kerry Jordan (Byrne, Company Cook) at his home in Johannesburg and remembers that 'he had 22 dogs running all over the place.' Originally from New Zealand, Kerry also appeared in the American TV mini-series *Shaka Zulu* (1986). Both Folbigge and Jordan are now deceased.

"Who do you think is coming to wipe out your little command – the Grenadier Guards?": Gert van den Bergh

"About the soup, sir...": Kerry Jordan.

"Pot that man, somebody!": Dennis Folbigge.

sitting in the shade of its thatched roof. 'There were about six of us and we ordered some tea. The waiter arrived with the tea tray and he looked above our heads, dropped the tea tray, screamed and ran. About ten minutes later one of the stunt guys arrived with a double-barrelled shotgun. He said, "Now boys, just carry on quietly – don't look up, don't cause any stir." He raised this gun just above our heads, fired and two green mambas fell out of the thatch – two of the most lethal snakes known to man.'

There were other less-than-welcome encounters with the local wildlife. On one of Joe Levine's visits, Bob Porter drove him and Stanley to the location from Johannesburg. 'We went through a swollen river and the car sank in too deep. As the water came over the wheel arches, I said, "Don't worry, the crocodiles can't get in with the window up!" Of course, there were no crocs in the river.' Maureen Endfield remembers that she was nearly killed when she was out horse-riding with Stanley's ten-year-old son Martin and saw a wild pig: 'Martin shouted out and it ran between the horse's legs, throwing me off and landing me face first in the gravel. I was given a facepack by some local women and stayed in bed for three days. Cy gave me no sympathy: "It serves you right!"'

Ellen Baker had her own brush with death, albeit with a bizarre twist: 'I had a wonderful hairpiece from Vidal Sassoon. Joe Levine came for Easter and the party was on the Saturday. So we go down in a car, rather late, with Nigel Green, me and Ivor Emmanuel in the back, Stanley's driving, with Caroline Murray, his secretary, in front with Stanley. We're going along the escarpment when Stanley suddenly says, "My God, the brakes have gone!" This was two o'clock on Easter Sunday morning. He pulls the car over into the ditch and the car rolls over. I'm wedged between Nigel and Ivor so nothing happens to me at all, except I lose my hairpiece. We were totally shocked at what could have happened if we had gone over into the escarpment. I didn't realise

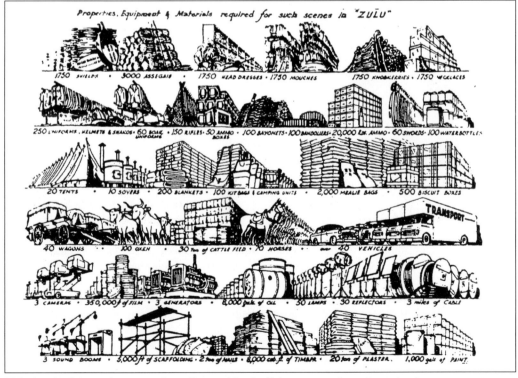

This sketch of the equipment and supplies used by the *Zulu* company throughout the shoot represents typical publicity hyperbole and should be taken with a large pinch of salt.

Ivor Emmanuel walks back to his hotel after a hard day's work.

Gert van den Bergh.

for days that my hairpiece was missing. It was found in a field – the local people thought someone had been scalped.'

Another incident had a more tragic outcome, as David Kernan again recalls: 'I remember a pit where you could go and view poisonous snakes and learn to distinguish between poisonous and non-poisonous snakes, and that you mustn't kill non-poisonous snakes, or indeed the poisonous snakes unless they're rather unhappy with you. There was a very sad experience. There was a little kid who was sort of a groupie; he was always hanging around, and we got rather chummy with this kid. One day he was missing and apparently he was bitten by a snake. He was found dead in the bushes a week later. It's traditional in Africa that you just walk away and die because there's no cure. It's an extraordinary country, a cruel country. It was beautiful and I've been back many times to work. I love it, but there is a sort of cruelty there.'

Despite his close involvement in helping to set up virtually every shot taken by the main unit, first assistant director Bert Batt claims his chief memory of *Zulu* has 'nothing to do with the shooting. There came a day when Cy was in agony with a raging toothache and the production office had a car ready to take him to a dentist in Middleberg, the nearest small township, at the end of the day's work. He attended, for a few minutes, a meeting in the production office and then got in the car with a Black driver. Night was about to fall. The meeting proved to be a long one and about two hours later the door crashed open and Cy was standing in the doorway ready to commit murder. The office had hired the car but had forgotten to tell the driver where to go. Things being in South Africa as they were at that time the Black servant took off, waiting for the White master to tell him where he wanted to go. Cy found himself on a night tour of the S.A. countryside (the only thing to be seen was what was in the headlamps), with a driver whose English was non-existent. All Cy had been told was "Cy, there's a car to get you to the dentist." He didn't know that he should have been going to Middleberg. Had he known, that single word might have got him there and an inquiry would have, in that very small township, led him to the dentist. His problem then was to get the driver to take him back to where they had started from. I have often pictured in my mind what went on in that car and I can still see Cy standing in that doorway. There was a lot of bad language.'

When the unit was almost ready to pack up and go home, one G. Vernon Essery of the Natal Provincial Council publicly criticised the Natal Parks Board for allowing the company to use the National Park as a location for a 'ridiculous' charge of only R1,500: 'What are they paying for – nuisance value?' he asked rhetorically. He thought that it would cost more than that to clean up the site after the unit had left, and demanded that in future commercial enterprises wishing to use the park should be charged a larger deposit, 'to cover all damage to the property – say a sum of R4,000 – which could be held by the Board until they have left and the place has been restored.' Essery also questioned whether the publicity value brought to the Park by the film was worth the upset caused to holiday-makers: 'He said he had received complaints about the many cars, the sightseers and other developments caused by "the whole circus of people" who had gone there.'[22] A few weeks later, at the very end of shooting, publicist Geoff Freeman responded by saying that the film had 'drawn thousands of visitors to the reserve in what is normally recognised as a slack season,' and that the unit would clean up the site at its own expense: 'We undertook to leave the film location exactly as we found it, and we will.'[23]

Accordingly, when the rest of the company had set off on the long return flight to London, Bob Porter remained behind with

178 LOCATIONS, PROPS AND COSTUMES

Dennis Folbigge, Stanley Baker and Kerry Jordan on set. Note the microphone boom, small lights and reflector in the background.
(Jürgen Schadeberg)

bulldozers and a demolition crew to dismantle the sets and office buildings, and to return the site, including the man-made river, to its former state. He eventually returned home on 16 August 1963, almost a full year after his arrival in South Africa.

Notes

[1] Richard Dyer discusses *Simba* in 'White,' *Screen*, vol. 29, no. 4, Autumn 1988, pp. 49-54. On *Untamed*, see Peter Davis, *In Darkest Hollywood: Exploring the jungles of cinema's South Africa* (Athens: Ohio University Press, 1996), pp. 149-52; for background material on its production, see Stephen Coan, 'When Hollywood Came to Cato Ridge,' *The Witness*, 10 May 2004, p. 10.

[2] Stanley Baker, 'Meeting the Challenge Of Producing an Epic As a First Picture,' *Motion Picture Herald*, 18 September 1963, p. 10.

[3] According to Dudley Lovell, camera operator on both films, *Nor the Moon by Night* was filmed twenty miles from Pietermaritzburg, in the Valley of a Thousand Hills in what is now KwaZulu-Natal, from October 1957 to March 1958.

[4] George Smith, '*Zulu* – Behind the Scenes,' *Movie Collector*, vol. 1, no. 4, 1994, p. 11.

[5] 'Films Made in South Africa,' *Variety*, 29 April 1964, p. 136.

[6] *Zulu* Production Information Dossier; D.N.E. Kain, '*Zulu*: A Film Completed,' *Personality*, 3 October 1963, p. 50.

[7] Interview with Stephen Coan, 27 June 2003; I am grateful to Stephen for sharing his notes with me. The Royal Natal National Park Hotel, so named because it had played host to the British Royal Family on their visit to the Park in 1947, closed in 2000.

[8] 'British Think "Too-Small" Pictures For World Playoff – Stanley Baker,' *Variety*, 7 August 1963, pp. 3, 22.

[9] Kain, '*Zulu*: A Film Completed,' p. 103.

[10] Information Dossier.

[11] Kain, '*Zulu*: A Film Completed,' p. 63. According to another report, the chair, 'carved from a solid tree trunk,' was ensconced in the Natal Museum ('Eleven VCs in Technicolor,' *Soldier*, February 1964). The Information Dossier also claimed that the 'officer's sword and scabbard used in the film' (presumably the

one carried by Bromhead) was 'taken from the body of a dead British officer killed at Isandhlwana.'

[12] Kain, 'Zulu: A Film Completed,' p. 62.

[13] *Zulu* Exhibitors' Campaign Book, p. 11.

[14] D.N.E. Kain, 'Zulu,' *South African Panorama*, September 1963, p. 27.

[15] 'War Regalia Puzzled The Zulus,' *The Natal Mercury*, 26 February 1963, p. 3.

[16] 'Warrior Of A Day,' *The Natal Mercury*, 26 February 1963, p. 1.

[17] Kain, 'Zulu: A Film Completed,' p. 62.

[18] I am grateful to Tony Watts of Bapty Limited for information on the armaments supplied for *Zulu*. After pointing out that many of both the British guns and the Zulu shields were not properly in keeping with the period, Mr Watts admitted to me that it is still his favourite film; he is particularly impressed by the retractable assegai blades employed in some of the gorier killings. Around fifty of the weapons used in the film are still kept in stock by Bapty, along with the fibre-glass elephant tusks (purchased from Diamond Films) which appear behind Cetewayo's throne in the wedding dance sequence.

[19] Information Dossier. Michael Caine gives an amusing account of his hair-raising encounters with Chita, and with the local baboons, in *What's It All About?* (London: Random House/Arrow, 1992), pp. 171-2, 179-80.

[20] John McAdam, 'Observations on the film *Zulu*,' *The Journal of the Anglo Zulu War Historical Society*, no. 9, June 2001, p. 49.

[21] D.N.E. Kain, 'Tough, unshaven men arrive to film *Zulu*,' *The Natal Witness*, 27 March 1963. See also Caine, pp. 169-71, for the actor's account of the long journey and his unpleasant experiences on arrival in Africa.

[22] 'Natal Parks Board condemned for *Zulu*,' *The Natal Witness*, 6 June 1963.

[23] 'Film man contests allegation,' *The Natal Witness*, 27 June 1963.

Simon Sabela and Cy Endfield supervise the wedding dance.

" THOUSANDS OF 'EM "

WORKING WITH ZULUS
10

> 'I can remember when the extras arrived by bus for the first day of shooting [says Stanley Baker]. They queued up in their shirts and jeans to go into the wardrobe department and emerged in their tribal costumes and carrying assegais.' They were truly Zulu warriors.
>
> It was not necessary to explain to them the background to the filming. The Zulus know their own history. A proud people, says Baker, they are not the sort to work in the mines of South Africa. The four million Zulus live on reservations and tend their cattle and corn. 'It seemed to me as an outsider that they cared more about their culture than their corn,' says Baker.
>
> Despite their aversion to mining, they reminded him of his Welsh compatriots. On his first visit, he recalls, it was like going home to Ferndale, in the Rhondda Valley, where he was born 46 years ago.
>
> (Alan Road, 'Zulu bwana,' *The Observer Magazine*, 17 August 1975)

Contemporary newspaper reports and publicity bulletins frequently inflated *Zulu*'s production statistics wildly. Consider, for example, an outlandish claim printed in the American trade press: '*Zulu*'s location sheets … show things like 200 soldiers, 100 Levies, 2,500 Zulus, 550 horses, 200 head of cattle, 200 men for local labor, 12 soldiers for radio communication, aircraft, six cheetas [sic], four leopards, two lions, six elephants, 40 giraffes [and] six zebras.'[1] One wonders where they all went. (There were actually only forty horses, a hundred cattle and one cheetah.) Those involved in making the film willingly went along with this benign deception to help sustain the illusion of vast numbers of natives, on which the credibility of the battle scenes depended. Stanley Baker, for example, wrote that the crew worked with 'an elite corps of 750 Zulus, at times we used as many as 4,000;' while Cy Endfield quipped to reporters, with tongue evidently in cheek: 'There isn't a shot with less than 300 people in it!'[2]

In fact, there were rarely this many Zulus involved at any one time in the movie. For most of the shoot there were only 240, with an additional 280 extras and 100 dancing girls for the mass wedding scene.[3] The reasons for this small number are open to speculation. Bob Porter, Basil Keys, Geoff Freeman and Maureen Endfield all maintain that the accommodation built in the Zulus' compound could hold no more than they had, and that it was full throughout the filming. This may indeed have been the case, and as each Zulu extra had to be paid individually, small as their wages were, so was the film's budget. Yet first assistant director Bert Batt offers an intriguing alternative explanation: 'The gathering of the Zulu warriors was attended to by the South African authorities. We had nothing to do with it and accepted what we were given. We had weapons and shields for something like 750 and we got 250. That could only have been a

political decision and from the moment that the warriors arrived we had, until the end, plain clothes police supervision.' The government did not want any more Zulus than this gathered together, he believes, because, 'they just didn't want a rampaging mob.' No doubt the Sharpeville massacre of 1960, in which sixty-seven civilian demonstrators were shot and killed by the military, was also at the back of officials' minds.

Most viewers in my experience don't notice the deception, and are more than ready to accept that there really were vast numbers of Zulus appearing in front of the cameras; Cy Endfield's reputation as a conjuror was well deserved. But in Batt's opinion the meagre Zulu forces are a major weakness of the movie. The extras they had, he says, were 'nowhere near enough. You miss a great deal in the film because of that – you can see always see off the edges and back and beyond. There's no way 250 can look like 4,000, so it was a great, great shame. With 750 we'd have really made it look something, so for me it's a continual failure through the picture. And we didn't have any dummies. With 250 you couldn't leave the dead lying on the battlefield. That place would have been heaped with bodies. You never saw anyone going out to pick them up – and in any case they wouldn't have done that, because they would have been an obstruction to the others coming forward. So the bodies would have piled up and piled up. They were killing and killing and killing but there was never a body on the ground, never any dead. Someone should have thought of this, but it was too late to do anything about it and you would have needed a great amount of them.'

In order to recruit genuine Zulus to work on the picture, the company had to secure the permission and co-operation of a number of people in high places. They had, first of all, to get the approval of the national government. However, because the administration was keen to attract overseas filmmakers to a country which, due to its policy of racial apartheid, was becoming increasingly politically isolated, it was positively eager to help. The Zulus themselves also had to give their consent, and therefore a meeting was arranged between Baker, associate producer Basil Keys, the Head of Bantu Administration and Mangosuthu G. Buthelezi, hereditary chief of the 12,000-strong Buthelezi tribe of Mahlabathini. Despite Chief Buthelezi's prominence among his own people, which led to his being treated with greater deference than was granted to most Blacks in South Africa, the unavoidable fact of his race led to an awkward problem. The meeting was to take place in Nongoma in Zululand, but where could Whites and Blacks sit together socially? As Basil Keys recalls, only one place was available for a formal meeting: the county court-house. Approval was finally given on all sides for a party of Zulus to leave their tribal home and travel to the Natal National Park to appear in the film as their warrior ancestors. South African journalist Derrick Kain reported: 'The Paramount Chief of the Zulus, Cyprian Bhekuzulu, pledged complete co-operation in the production of the film ... Africans clamoured to take part in the film, as the thrill of wearing the insignia of an induna of the Royal Kraal, or becoming a warrior under the great strategist, Dabulamanzi, fired their imagination.'4

The Ministry of Bantu Affairs and the Departments of Information and Defence lent keen assistance to the production but also kept a close and watchful eye on the unit from the outset. They wanted to know in advance every aspect of how the Zulus would be treated: where they would sleep, what games they would play, what food they'd eat, how they'd be looked after, and so forth (the company had to make them their usual tipple of mealie beer at weekends). Particular concern was expressed about the prop weapons that would be used in the film: not just the rubber-tipped assegais, but also the very real vintage rifles. The Zulus were forbidden by law from carrying firearms, so to prevent any weapons getting permanently into their hands, said Baker in an American magazine interview, the unit 'had to build an armory of concrete and

steel, and every man was checked in the morning and at night. We wouldn't want a repeat of 1879.'[5]

This same interview – conducted by the noted columnist Sheilah Graham, whose articles were widely syndicated (the interview appeared, for example, in both the *Los Angeles Citizen News* and the *New York Mirror*) – was greeted with scorn by some South African commentators, who considered that it displayed the typical outsider's ignorance of the Zulus and their traditions.[6] As an outsider myself, I am in no position to judge, but readers can make up their own minds with the following extracts from Graham's article:

> Nothing has changed in the Zulu's customs since 1879 [said Baker]. 'They still live in straw huts. The men wear brief skin loin cloths; the women are naked except for a beaded G string. And virginity is prized, because an untouched maiden will bring her father a larger number of cattle from the man who wants to marry her. They have as many wives as they can afford in cattle. The women do all the work, tilling and sowing, while the men do absolutely nothing except singing and dancing.' …
>
> 'The native,' continued our man Stanley, 'in his own surroundings, is a wonderfully happy man. They are mostly vegetarians. When we roasted a couple of oxen for a special treat, they went crazy with joy. Meat is only eaten at a feast, and they sing and dance around the meat before eating it.
>
> 'The girls in our picture were aged from 12 to 16. They had beautiful figures. But because they start bearing children at 13, the figure doesn't stay too good too long. When I asked one man who had eight wives, "When is a woman too old for you?" he replied, "At 22 a girl is finished." It's funny that the women are working so hard for the men so that they can buy cattle to get another wife who will replace them.
>
> 'But don't get the Zulus wrong. They are a very moral race. And very proud. They will not accept gifts without giving something in return. They carved beautiful meat platters for us. They were in seventh heaven because we allowed them to wear the "mouchis," the fancy G-strings the women wore in our film. The men wore necklaces of claws from wild animals. …
>
> 'They don't use money as such. They wouldn't know what to do with it. For working in the film we paid them $40 a month each, but they wanted us to pay them in cattle. A cow costs $30 and we would have had to go into the cattle business, so we paid them and let them make their own arrangements about cattle. They want cattle for breeding so that they

can buy more wives. They only kill the cattle after ten years. They use the ox for tilling the land, the cows for milk. And they trap wild game.'[7]

Contrary to popular belief, the Zulus were *not* paid for their services with wristwatches. The monthly wage of $40 paid to each of them was also subject to official approval.[8] Unit publicist Geoff Freeman comments: 'We might have been paying them a bit less than what they would have earned in this country [Britain], but they were still paid five or six times what they were used to. The fact that we had Chief Buthelezi on our side was a tremendous help. He wasn't there to exploit his fellow Zulus, he was there to ensure things went smoothly.'[9] Buthelezi was himself given a small acting role, though this was not pre-arranged when the film went into production. Indeed, the film had already begun shooting when Bob Porter was interviewing prospective actors to play both Cetewayo and the Zulu general commanding the forces at Rorke's Drift, Dabulamanzi (who was identified by name in the screenplay but not in the film).[10]

Perhaps the surprise casting choice of Buthelezi as Cetewayo was intended as compensation for a gaffe the filmmakers made early in the shooting schedule when the Chief was invited one evening to view the first rushes of the battle scenes. The crew used the dining room of the Royal Natal National Park Hotel as a makeshift viewing theatre, but the laws of apartheid prevented even Buthelezi from entering the hotel. Assistant editor Jennifer Thompson recalls that, 'We had to smuggle him and his entourage in through the french windows. No-one at the hotel knew he'd been in.' The occasion was described by Michael Caine's biographer, journalist William Hall:

> By some oversight, or maybe simply someone's very thick skin, the footage that unrolled was the scene of the first mock Zulu charge, when the front-line warriors flung themselves at the British guns to draw their fire and judge the strength of the resistance in the mission.

Accordingly, with whoops from the redcoat camp of 'Here they come! Mow 'em down!' and the like, scores of Zulus were seen biting the South African dust before the rest fled in apparent terror under a hail of bullets from the cheering soldiers.

The smile of the Zulu chief faded like the sky darkening outside the windows. The women who had been chattering so animatedly fell silent at the base imagery of their forebears in full flight. The screening ended in a stony silence.

'Well, Chief,' said Stanley Baker as the lights went up. 'What did you think of that?'

'Interesting,' said the chief impassively.

And left.[11]

Training the Warriors

As a boy, the late Sydney Chama took every opportunity he could to watch the staging of the battle scenes at the film location, 200 miles away from where he went to school in Durban. Chama was the nephew of Simon Sabela, one of the professional Black actors working on *Zulu* as a stuntman, who also led the wedding dance in the opening sequence. 'I was one of those little kids who are very star-struck, wanted to be in the movies,' Sydney told BBC producer Steve Freer in 1996 in an interview

Chief Buthelezi (King Cetewayo)

Chief (now Prince) Mangosuthu Gatsha Buthelezi was born on 27 August 1928 in Mahlabathini, KwaZulu-Natal, to a house of Royal blood. His mother, Princess Constance Magogo ka Dinuzulu, was the daughter of King Dinuzulu and the granddaughter of Cetewayo. His father was Chief Mathole, the grandson of Chief Mnyamana Buthelezi, Cetewayo's prime minister. Cyprian, the Paramount Chief (or King) at the time *Zulu* was made and father of the present King, Goodwill Zwelithini, was Mangosuthu's cousin. Prince Buthelezi studied at Fort Hare University – he was the first tribal chief to attend university – and briefly became a lawyer until ascending to the acting chieftainship of the Buthelezi tribe in 1953, becoming fully recognised as hereditary chief in 1957.

The real King Cetewayo.

He has held numerous political offices, including Chief Executive Officer of the Zulu Territorial Authority and Chief Executive Councillor of the KwaZulu Legislative Assembly, and he is hereditary Chief Minister of KwaZulu-Natal. As founder of the mass Inkatha movement and leader of the Inkatha Freedom Party, Buthelezi frequently opposed the African National Congress and has often been the subject of political controversy. From 1994 to 2004 he was Minister of Home Affairs in the South African Government and a member of the National Assembly, and was several times appointed Acting President of the Republic by Nelson Mandela, formerly his political rival. He has also published widely and received many honours, including Knight Commander of the Star of Africa (1975), humanitarian and outstanding leadership awards, and honorary doctorates from five universities.

According to his biographer, Ben Temkin, 'For Buthelezi not to have accepted the invitation to play the part of King Cetshwayo in *Zulu* would have been unthinkable. Not only was Cetshwayo his great-grandfather (there is a strong facial resemblance and they have similar tapering, sensitive fingers), but the chief was in one of his "plump" phases, which meant he was in the right shape for the part as well' (*Buthelezi: A Biography*, London and Portland: Frank Cass, 2003, p. 84). Temkin says that, in talking about the filming, Buthelezi used such phrases as: 'It is amazing; it is remarkable; it is unbelievable.' Interviewed by the BBC in 1996 for the television tribute *Stanley Baker: A Life in Film*, Buthelezi himself recalled: 'It was the first experience [of filmmaking] for all of us, including myself ... They [the Zulus] acted within their culture, so it became a lot of fun from that point of view. Although I don't think that they cherished the idea of, for example, getting up at the crack of dawn to do some of the scenes, very early, before daybreak.' Of his own acting, Buthelezi said: 'It was funny, in the sense that it was something out of my normal routine. But you know, directors are very fussy people. Sometimes you'd do the scene, and they'd say "cut" and you'd do the same scene all over again, to get exactly what they want.'

John Prebble was under the impression that Buthelezi 'took a very amused view of it all. Stanley was perhaps a bit awed by him at the beginning, and pointed out that there was no cause

Chief Buthelezi as Cetewayo.

for worry because the rifles used by the actors playing British soldiers would not be loaded with real bullets. Buthelezi said, well that's quite alright, we're not allowed real spears!' Buthelezi remained on good terms with both Endfield and Baker long after the end of filming. Interviewed for BBC Wales by Vincent Kane shortly before his death, Baker described Buthelezi as 'a close personal friend of mine, a man I have a high regard for because of what he's doing, and the way he's doing it, and the kind of person he is ... He's the kind of man that knows exactly what he wants, not for himself, but for his nation, and you can be sure he's going to get it ... I promise you he's the kind of man who, if I'd ill-treated his people, his nation, in any way whatsoever, we'd be enemies rather than friends.'

Zulu is not Buthelezi's only film appearance: he also acted in the local production *Tokoloshe* (1965, but given a limited release overseas in 1971) opposite the South African-born actor and comedian Sid James. He was later instrumental in helping to set up and provide Zulu extras for *Zulu Dawn* (1979). Buthelezi was asked to reprise the role of Cetewayo, but according to co-producer Nate Kohn he was obliged to decline. 'He said he'd like to, but his position was different now and politically he couldn't. He had a lot of responsibilities. It was shortly after the Soweto riots and it wouldn't have looked good for him to go off to appear in a film. But he was very happy with Simon Sabela in the role.'

Buthelezi's opinion of *Zulu* itself seems to have changed somewhat over the years. In the 1996 interview quoted earlier he said: 'At the time, racism in South Africa was at its height, so the human approach that he [Baker] had was something that is not common. The approach both of Sir Stanley Baker and of Cy Endfield was really of respect – they approached the subject with great respect. I think the aim was to portray the bravery of both sides.' Seeing the film again, he said, was 'very touching – quite nostalgic and very moving when you think of all those people who are no more.' But in recent years his views seem more tinged with regret for what might have been. In 2003, interviewed for the BBC's revisionist documentary on the Anglo-Zulu War, *Zulu: The True Story*, he said of the film's representation of Rorke's Drift: 'It is very, very painful, especially as my great-grandfather was not spoiling for any war; in fact he was totally against the war himself, he did not want any war, he wanted negotiations ... We as Zulus felt it distracted from the importance of Isandhlwana, which was a Zulu victory, because Isandhlwana was more important for the Zulu people, as much as it still is even for generations of Zulus like us who are living in this time.'

conducted at the *Zulu* location site. He recalled the intense excitement among the local population at the prospect of watching the filming: 'Everybody came from everywhere. That's the funny thing about movies – you can go anywhere and always find a crowd. The scenery was so breathtaking that you just couldn't resist it. Everybody just wanted to come out here.'[12]

The Zulu extras' first arrival at the Drakensberg, two weeks before the scheduled start of shooting, is remembered vividly by several members of the film company. They were brought in on coaches and were wearing ordinary everyday clothing rather than traditional tribal costume (one report in the trade press claims that many of them were 'domestic servants and laborers from nearby farms').[13] George Smith quotes Baker's disappointed reaction to his first sight of them: 'They looked absolutely nothing. Even those who normally wore blankets in their kraals had bought or borrowed trousers because, I learned later, they didn't want us to think them primitive ... But when we gave them leopard skins and assegais, they were suddenly transformed. They began leaping about and dancing like Dervishes. Most of them had never held a real spear before and they were ecstatic.'[14] Ivor Emmanuel also recalls his first encounter with the Zulus: 'They were all coming over a hill and chanting. When they came into view they all looked like a bunch of tramps. One had on a string vest and a bowler hat, and another one was wearing a mac. Then they were given their costumes and spears and

they started with the war chants and you got a bit scared.'

Bert Batt gives his own recollection of the occasion: 'The company had built accommodation for them, and outside it we dumped the two hundred and fifty foreground cowhide shields, assegais and clothing. They almost fought each other to take what they thought were the most attractive shields and with weapons and clothing they entered the accommodation and togged up. When they came out they formed three lines and, stamping their feet and banging on the shields, they launched into all the old battle songs. It went on for about forty-five minutes and the Afrikaaners [in the unit] were not at all amused.' Stanley and Cy had their wives and families with him throughout the shoot, and Ellen Baker remembers: 'The first time we saw the Zulus they did the charge at us and stopped a few feet away from me and my children – they were terrified.'

The Zulus were, by all accounts, pretty scared themselves at first and had to be shown that they had nothing to fear from the staged battles and the guns firing blanks. Bob Porter tried to demonstrate the artifice of movie violence when he and Baker visited the tribes in Zululand: 'I used to give Stanley the blank rifle, and I would come rushing at him with the spear. He'd fire the blank and I'd go up in the air in a very dramatic death scene. Then of course I'd stand up, and they'd all burst out laughing.' James Booth tells an amusing story, possibly apocryphal (he was not on location in South Africa), that is nonetheless worth repeating: 'Stanley explained to the old Zulu chief that they should use rubber-tipped spears as the Whites would be using blank ammunition. The chief said they could use live ammo as it would take a silver bullet to kill a Zulu and he knew the budget wouldn't stretch to that!'

The crew still faced real difficulties in gaining the Zulus' trust and co-operation in the early days of staging the battle, as camera operator Dudley Lovell recalled in 1990: 'They were very tentative about making the attack on Rorke's Drift and they used to get within

Chief Buthelezi (wearing his own tribal regalia rather than the movie costume) inspects still photographer Yousuf Karsh's camera.

about a hundred yards and stop; they wouldn't come any further. We used to say, come on, you can charge us, and they'd say, no, we've heard that what's going to happen is, as soon as we charge the lines you'll be firing at us and then you'll go and send for some more natives, and because we've been shot somebody else will come along. It took a couple of days before they were really happy to come and

attack us, or pretend to attack, with their make-believe shields and spears.'¹⁵ Nor did many of the Zulus find it easy to grasp the mechanics of filmmaking. Geoff Freeman remembers that a group of Zulus 'passed the editor's room one day and heard voices on the moviola – they tried to see where they were coming from.' One of Geoff's press releases stated that editor John Jympson had the 'difficult task of convincing terrified Zulu that his editing machine did not contain 500 [sic] mangled Zulu warriors. Only their voices were in the "Magic Box".'

Sydney Chama also recalled the filmmakers' frustrations in explaining to the Zulus the nature of dramatic reconstruction: 'A lot of people had to be trained and they had to use some urbanised people because there were certain problems. Some people were not quite used to the camera, they kept on looking at the camera, and there had to be people to coach the warriors because some of them were kind of bloodthirsty, they just got sort of wild and got carried away. They actually believed they were fighting a real war. And when they were given rubber spears they threw them away and they wanted the real thing. But they had to be convinced, look, this is make-believe, it's not the real thing.'

Doubtless some readers will regard these anecdotes as instances of patronising stereotypes being perpetuated at the Zulus' expense. That is filmmaker and historian Peter Davis's view of another oft-repeated story, though everyone involved that I have spoken to agrees that it happened.¹⁶ At some point it was realised that, coming from the rural tribal areas, most of the Zulus had never been to a cinema or seen a motion picture, and therefore they did not fully understand what they were doing or what the cameras did. Glynn Edwards pithily sums up the problem and the solution: 'The Zulus didn't know initially what they were there for. We ran them an old Western and they got the message – they were going to be the Indians.' A 16mm film was hired in – most seem to agree that it was a Gene Autry 'singing cowboy' musical Western – and a projector, screen and sound speakers were set up in the open air one night in the Zulu compound. Baker told Sheilah Graham: 'We showed it to the men first, and they couldn't stop laughing. Their eyes were popping. I have never heard such unrestrained laughter.' Geoff Freeman recalls that 'they kept running around the back of the screen to see where the gunfire was coming from.' Sydney Chama says that 'there was quite an improvement after that,' and henceforward there were regular screenings in the Zulu compound. The Production Information Dossier states that the Zulus always 'watched with noisy appreciation and animated enthusiasm. Their favourite films were "Cowboys and Indians".' Ellen Baker remembers that they also enjoyed silent comedies, particularly the films of Charlie Chaplin, Buster Keaton and Harold Lloyd. Cy Endfield chose a photograph of the Zulu men watching their first movie as the cover image of his Christmas card for 1963 (see illustration).

The Zulus were, in David Kernan's view, 'terribly superior in comparison to the rest of the Black races in South Africa. They were all very eloquent.' Joe Powell comments about working with them: 'I had a great respect for the close association of the Zulus. I remember setting up a screen to show them the action they'd shot so far. They were like children, laughing and pointing each other out. They had no animosity about how we showed them. I asked them how they felt [about the real battle] and they shrugged their shoulders and said, "We lost some, you lost some." And that was it. Cy was keen to portray the Zulus in a good light – not like the Indians in American Westerns. He didn't want to show how *we* smashed the Zulus but how *they* put up a tremendous fight.'

There was one thing about which the film company could teach the Zulus very little: the traditional tribal dances and wedding rituals seen at the beginning of the picture. Although John Prebble had researched the movements for the dance in an old book he had located, he was not on hand to supervise the choreography. Chief Buthelezi's mother, Princess Constance Magogo ka Dinuzulu, a tribal historian with a detailed knowledge of Zulu music, was therefore brought to the location to coach the dancers.[17] In casting the female dancers for this sequence, Stanley Baker had the pleasure of auditioning off-duty office workers and night-club dancers from Durban or Johannesburg, who were to join those bussed in from Zululand. Mixing women from different backgrounds caused a few problems: those from the city were lighter-

Cy Endfield used this photograph of the Zulu menfolk enjoying their first experience of movies as the cover of his personalised Christmas cards for 1963. The greeting inside read: 'Zulus, during the location of *Zulu*, watch their first motion picture ever.' Note the 16mm projector in the centre of the image.

Simon Sabela (Dance Leader/ Stuntman)

It has been predictably difficult locating much information of any kind on the indigenous African actors appearing in *Zulu*, Chief Buthelezi always excepted. But one of the Zulu stuntmen went on to become the most famous Black performer in the South African film industry and the country's first Black film director.

Simon Mabunu Sabela was born in Durban on 19 March 1931, the youngest of five sons of a minister and a schoolteacher living in Eshowe in Zululand. Despite growing up in rural surroundings, he was playing jazz trombone by the age of seventeen and later sang and performed in a variety group called the Durban Jazz Sledge. When he saw an all-Black stage play called *King Kong* (apparently unrelated to the well-known story and film of the same name), he determined that he could do better and subsequently directed, produced, choreographed and starred in his own play, *Chief Mamba and the Slave*. After a year's rehearsal, it ran at Durban City Hall for a week, where it was seen by Bob Porter while he was scouting local talent for *Zulu*. Interviewed by Chris van der Merwe in 1977, Simon recalled: 'I was invited to play in this international film. I started as a link between the director and the Zulu extras. Then I became assistant director – then stuntman.' ('My movies click,' *South African Panorama*, September 1977, p. 25).

'Simon Sabela was a lovely, charming man,' recalled Larry Taylor. 'They liked him – he was used a hell of a lot. He did four close-up shots of stabbing and so on. It was his big break.' Whereas most of the indigenous actors were unbilled, Sabela earned a credit as the Zulu Dance Leader for his starring role in the wedding dance sequence, where his bearded figure can be seen at the forefront of the lines of male dancers. A South African trade paper profiling Sabela's career subsequently commented: 'Simon has not forgotten the excitement he experienced when working opposite Jack Hawkins, Michael Caine and Stanley Baker, who offered him a scholarship in London. Cy Enfield [sic], who directed *Zulu* advised Simon not to take the scholarship since he felt that Simon was a "natural" and could become stereotyped if he took lessons' ('Portrait of a Filmmaker,' *South African Film & Entertainment Industry*, August 1982, p. 4).

Ten years later, Simon had still not ventured outside South Africa, but he had appeared in many films made there, including *Diamonds are Dangerous* (1961), *Death Drums Along the River* (1963), *The Diamond Walkers*, *Tokoloshe* (both 1965), *Seven Against the Sun*, *Africa Shakes* (both 1966), *King of Africa* (1967), *Strangers at Sunrise* (1968), *Katrina* (1969) and *Satan's Harvest* (1970). It was while publicising *Gold* (1974) that Sabela revealed his great ambition: 'to become South Africa's first Black movie director' ('Actor in the Black,' *Sunday Times*, 17 February 1974). That same year he made a documentary on family planning for the National Film Board, and was then offered the chance by a local company, Heyns Film, to direct low-budget pictures aimed at Black audiences. He was placed in charge of an all-White crew, the necessary technical skills to be learned on the job. Simon's directorial debut, *u-Diliwe* (1975), based on a popular radio drama serial, was seen by an estimated two million people, several times the usual audience for Black films. In the next five years, he directed

Director of photography Stephen Dade, Simon Sabela (in tee-shirt) and Stanley Baker discuss the wedding dance.

thirteen more features, including *Inkedama* (*The Orphan*, 1975), *I-Kati Elimnayana* (*The Black Cat*, 1975), *The Boxer* (1976), *Ngwanaka* (*My Child*, 1976), *Ngaka* (*The Doctor*, 1976) and *Setipana* (*The Blanket Story*, 1979).

With the development of South African TV in the early 80s, Simon was appointed associate producer of Heyns' television productions, which included a spin-off series of *u-Diliwe*. However, the company's reputation was tarnished when it was revealed in 1979 that its films were being part-funded by the Department of Information with the aim of indoctrinating Black audiences in the desirability of separate development. The scripts for Sabela's films, usually written and/or selected by Whites, had also been subject to the approval of a pro-apartheid ethnologist, married to the company director (see Keyan Tomaselli, *The Cinema of Apartheid: Race and Class in South African Films*, London and New York: Routledge, 1989, pp. 65-8).

Simon continued to act, and among his later films are *é Lollipop*, *Tigers Don't Cry*, *Shout at the Devil* (all 1976), *Game for Vultures* (1979), *Skeleton Coast* (1987), *Scavengers* (1988), *The Gods Must Be Crazy II* (1989) and *The Rutanga Tapes* (1990). He also played Nelson Mandela in *Der Rivonia-Prozeß* (1966) and portrayed three Zulu chiefs: Dingaan in *Die Voortrekkers* (1973), Cetshwayo in *Zulu Dawn* (1979) and Dingiswayo in *Shaka Zulu* (1986). He died in 1994.

skinned than the tribal dancers, having had less exposure to the sun, and had to be darkened with body makeup. As Michael Caine recalls in his autobiography, contrasting standards of decorum in dress also caused confusion: the tribal women were used to wearing little clothing, while the urban women preferred to cover up. A delicate balance had to be struck to reconcile the demands of modesty and authenticity, wrote Caine:

> There was an almighty row between the two sets of girls, with Cy in the middle trying to get the pants on one side and the brassières off the other lot. Peace was finally restored and we shot the sequence once, but had to shoot it again because as the camera tracked along the line of dancing girls, the camera operator suddenly shouted, 'Cut!' He pointed at one of the girls and said, 'That one's got no drawers on,' and indeed she hadn't. Her reply was translated back to Cy: 'I am sorry,' she had said. 'I'm not used to them and just forgot.'[18]

A whole week in May was spent rehearsing and shooting the dance to get it exactly right and to provide enough 'coverage' for the editor. The wedding scene was the high point of the shoot for many. Marius Markgraaf, manager of the Mont-Aux-Sources Hotel, claims that Baker was so moved by the experience that he was 'almost in tears' afterwards: 'He said it was the most beautiful thing he had ever done in his life.'[19] Although Maureen Endfield did not often visit the set during filming ('I've never felt comfortable being on a film set – it's very boring and repetitive'), she was persuaded to go with her two young daughters to watch the great spectacle: 'Cy insisted I take the children to see the dancing sequence – he thought this was quite miraculous.' Other set visitors came from further afield: famed still photographer Yousuf Karsh arrived hotfoot from Moscow, and Joe

Levine flew in from New York. Maureen recalls Joe's nervous reaction to the tremendous energy of the dancing: 'He clutched my children, he was so frightened for them.' She and Cy were keen dancers and made an attempt to join in: 'They said we danced like Zulus. They were such joyous people.'

Other members of the company also attempted a bit of tentative cultural exchange, teaching the Zulus how to dance to 'Knees up Mother Brown,' the Hoki-Koki and the Conga. 'But when their turn came,' noted the Information Dossier, the Cockney crew 'didn't find it so easy to follow the Zulu dances.' Ellen Baker remembers that the Zulu compound and the main set 'were at opposite ends of a field, separated by a kind of stream. It was the time of the Twist, and we would set up a tannoy and show them how to do it! We played Tom Jones's "It's Not Unusual" and had the Zulus doing the Twist by the time we left.' Stanley wanted the Zulus to share the music of his own people, as Ivor Emmanuel recalls: 'One day when it was raining and we couldn't shoot, Stanley said, come with me down to the Zulus' camp and sing for them. I tried to sing something that was in keeping with their culture.'

The wedding dance was not the only sequence in which the necessity of repeating action until it was just right caused frustration amongst the Zulu performers. Cy Endfield was a meticulous director who asked for multiple takes of each shot. Sydney Chama recalled watching the filming of the closing sequence in which the Zulus reappear on the top of the ridge overlooking Rorke's Drift:

'They had to do it a couple of times. They had to climb over the mountainside and get there, do it once, go back – that was for a rehearsal. But when they did it again for another rehearsal, and then a third time, and they're told, this is now the actual shot, there would be trouble. They'd say, listen, are you guys playing games here, what's going on? But eventually Big Daddy himself [Buthelezi] would talk to them and convince them.'

Endfield's usual method of directing the Zulus en masse, according to John Prebble, was to blow a whistle as the signal to charge: 'If Cy didn't like the shot, he blew the whistle and they stopped, sat down and started playing games among themselves. Blow a whistle and they'd leap up and charge forward yelling. That sympathy and obedience they got from people who really couldn't be asked to do something like this [recreating the battle], which is a slaughter of them, was due to the influence that both Cy and Stanley – principally Stanley – had over them.'

The biggest problem Bert Batt found in working with the Zulus was that they didn't care much for the sun. 'We were scorching and they were hiding in every nook and cranny they could find. We had to dig 'em out to get them back on set.' Bert also gives generous credit for ensuring a harmonious relationship with the Zulus to the film's third assistant director, who also functioned as translator: 'I was lucky in having at my side a White South African by the name of Howard Rennie who spoke word-perfect Zulu. He also had great affection for them as a race, or tribe, and they returned it. He was about twenty years old and there's a case to be made that he was the most important person on the unit and he had never worked on a movie before.' Because he was not an Afrikaaner like many of the other White South Africans employed on the picture, Rennie was 'a godsend. He had an incredible rapport with the Zulus. He absolutely loved them; they respected him too, so we got an awful lot of work with him.'

The Zulus gave honorary names in their own language to several members of the company. Endfield was called Manxugela – 'Big Thinker,' and Stanley Baker was Imehle Kwa

Chief Buthelezi, dressed in formal business attire, visits Cy Endfield on set.

Mamba – 'The One with the Eyes of the Mamba.' Michael Caine was disgruntled to learn that he had been dubbed Indoda Enezinwele Ezinde Nyengomnbazi – 'The One with the Hair of a Woman.'[20] Continuity girl Muirne Mathieson became known as Sapata Ndaba wa Zonke – 'The One who Carries the Troubles of All,' while cinematographer Stephen Dade was Mpunsi – 'The Little Buck.'[21] The Zulus also presented Endfield with a gift of a lion's tail; intended 'to give its owner strength and courage.' Baker in turn gave the director a 'lucky' Zulu bracelet made from the hairs of an elephant's tail. Both of these charms Cy carried with him throughout the shooting.[22] Stanley remarked on the Zulus' habit of using just about anything as personal adornments, for which there is ample photographic evidence in production stills: 'They have big holes in their ears and they wear as earrings anything that takes their fancy. We found some men wearing spare film spools in their ears. And one had a cigarette lighter from one of our crew members. And some had pipes in their ears. We had to check them carefully before each scene for incongruous elements.'

Looking back on the experience of working with the Zulus, Cy reflected: 'We were plunged into a completely different world … The Zulu culture has a thousand interesting facets. They are completely governed by ritual. They have ritualistic modes – chants and dances – for everything, one for approaching a place, one for leaving, one for going into battle. Then I realised that the soldiers had their rituals, too, drill and so on. And I was able to contrast the two.'[23] Baker felt that the 'neophyte' actors 'put more heart and guts into their work than do many professionals,' and looked forward to showing them the completed film: 'I believe they will like it. Even though their ancestors lost the Battle of Rorke's Drift, the encounter, to them, was an honourable one, lost, when they voluntarily retreated for the first time in their history, to a brave group of British soldiers.'[24] As for the reaction to the film of the Zulu participants themselves, Sydney Chama said: 'It was so genuine, everybody was very, very pleased with it. Now and then people would say, when is he [Baker] going to make another one?'

Notes

[1] 'South African Government a Lulu For Cooperation on Levine's *Zulu*,' *Variety*, 1 May 1963, p. 3.

[2] Stanley Baker, 'Meeting the Challenge Of Producing an Epic As a First Picture,' *Motion Picture Herald*, 8 September 1963, pp. 9-10; Derek Todd, '*Zulu* safari makes camp at Twickenham,' *Kine. Weekly*, 18 July 1963, p. 12. Michael Caine also did his bit to perpetuate – and further exaggerate – the myth when, years later, he wrote in his memoirs: 'The script called for six thousand [sic] Zulus to line the top of the hills surrounding the British. I wondered how we were going to accomplish this with only two thousand warriors [sic!]' (*What's It All About?*, London: Random House/Arrow, 1992, p. 183).

[3] The same extras playing the attacking Zulus doubled up as the British Army levies who flee the camp

following the Reverend Witt's exhortation (stunt performers Simon Sabela and John Marcus are easily recognisable in their khaki uniforms, the former wearing a black and white headband).

[4] D.N.E. Kain, '*Zulu*: A Film Completed,' *Personality*, 3 October 1963, pp. 62-3.

[5] Sheilah Graham, 'African Zulus Moral and Proud,' *Citizen News*, 19 August 1963.

[6] See Peter Davis, *In Darkest Hollywood: Exploring the jungles of cinema's South Africa* (Athens: Ohio University Press, 1996), pp. 156-7.

[7] Graham, op. cit. After reading Baker's interview, Bob Porter wrote to me: 'Most Zulu men would work for De Beers in Jo'burg on a six month contract and then return home. Of course they knew about money.' His notes in the margins of the copy of the Graham interview I sent him for perusal include such comments as 'rubbish,' 'not true' and 'bollocks.'

[8] According to a contemporary British magazine, the 'Zulu extras were hired at £12 a month,' which seems to equate roughly to US$40 under the exchange rate of the time ('Eleven VCs in Technicolor,' *Soldier*, February 1964).

[9] Freeman, who was unit publicist on both *Zulu* and *Zulu Dawn*, says: 'We were told by Chief Buthelezi on *Zulu Dawn* to pay [the Zulus] no more than this and no less than this. He didn't want them leaving the land. We were accused of under-paying them but we could only do what he allowed us.' This is confirmed by producer Nate Kohn, who stated in his article 'Glancing Off a Postmodern Wall: A Visit to the Making of *Zulu Dawn*' that the *Zulu Dawn* extras each earned $7 per day (Davis, p. 65). For comparison, director Zoltan Korda claimed that the thousand African extras appearing in his *Sanders of the River* (1935) were each paid the equivalent of sixpence per day for ten days ('Filming in Africa,' *Film Weekly*, no. 338, 1935; quoted in *Film Dope*, no. 31, January 1985, p. 30).

[10] It was reported in the South African press on 29 March, the day after the start of shooting, that Porter had 'already interviewed two Zulus in Durban for the part of the great Zulu strategist, Dabulamanzi, and two additional Zulus, one in Durban and the second in Johannesburg, for the plum part of Cetewayo. No decision on these roles has as yet been made, however' ('S.A., London, New York premieres for *Zulu*?,' *The Natal Witness*, 29 March 1963).

[11] William Hall, *Raising Caine: The Authorized Biography* (London: Arrow Books, 1982), p. 110.

[12] Interview for *Stanley Baker: A Life in Film* (BBC Wales, 1996). Interviews recorded for this programme are also the source of the comments from John Prebble and Chief Buthelezi quoted in this chapter.

[13] 'Embassy's Joe Levine Fixes World Distrib For *Zulu*, Africa Pic,' *Variety*, 22 May 1963, p. 13.

[14] George Smith, '*Zulu* – Behind the Scenes,' *Movie Collector*, vol. 1, no. 4, 1994, p. 14.

[15] Interview by John Taylor for the BECTU Oral History Project, 17 January 1990.

[16] See Davis, pp. 157-8, who quotes a press release for a local production, *Jim Comes to Jo'burg* (1949), describing the reaction of a party of Zulus to seeing a film for the first time.

[17] D.N.E. Kain, '*Zulu*,' *South African Panorama*, September 1963, p. 27.

[18] Caine, p. 181.

[19] Interview with Stephen Coan, 27 June 2003.

[20] See Caine, p. 181.

[21] Kain, '*Zulu*: A Film Completed'; Production Information Dossier.

[22] Ibid.

[23] Todd, op. cit.

[24] Baker, op. cit.

" IT'S YOUR COUNTRY, ISN'T IT? "

FILMING UNDER APARTHEID

> This was my first visit to South Africa and I had no preconceived notions about their politics or racial policy – nobody had. However as I worked and watched what was going on around me I was uncomfortable, then concerned and finally downright angry. Most of the workers on the set were Black, but they were not tribal – simply ordinary carpenters and electricians from the city, just like anybody else. But all the foremen were White Afrikaans and they treated the Black workers with an incredible rudeness the like of which I had never seen before. They literally talked to them as though they were dogs.
>
> One day I saw a Black worker make a mistake and I stopped to watch him getting a real telling off, just as an English worker would in the same situation. To my astonishment, the foreman didn't reprimand him; he smashed a fist into his face instead. I was so shocked at this I couldn't move, and then suddenly I started to run towards the man, screaming at him, but Stanley got there first. I had never seen him so angry. He fired the man on the spot and then gathered all the White gang bosses together and laid down the law on how everyone was going to be treated on this film set from then on. He was in an absolute fury and so were the rest of the British contingent. It brought home for the first time what this word 'apartheid' really meant. (Michael Caine, *What's It All About?*, London: Random House/Arrow, 1992, pp. 181-2)

The signs of South Africa's segregationist political regime were, quite literally, visible from the moment the cast and crew arrived at Johannesburg's Jan Smuts Airport. Waiting for the unit when they stepped off the aircraft, as Michael Caine described in his memoirs, were the Chief of Police and his assistant. They were carrying a bundle of forms detailing the country's race laws and warning of the dire repercussions which would follow if anyone were found guilty of contravening them. The punishments for miscegenation ranged from imprisonment to flogging. The police officials were not amused when Stanley Baker quipped: 'If I get caught, can I have the twelve lashes while I'm still doing it?'[1]

Baker nonetheless took the law very seriously. At the government's insistence, the members of the company were contractually bound to obey the country's race laws, as the consequences of any White person being caught fraternising with a Black woman – or man – could have been disastrous for more than just the individuals concerned: the entire production might have had to be shut down and the unit forced to return home. Glynn Edwards remembers some of the local temptations which had to be resisted: 'It was virtually an all-male film. Then one day they brought in seventy or eighty girls, boobs glistening in the sunlight, and Stanley would say, "Remember the contract lads!"' In fact, one crewman did fall foul of the law and had to be hustled out of the country with great speed

Baker and director of photography Stephen Dade greet state officials on an inspection of the location site.

and secrecy. 'One day he was there, the next day he was gone,' says unit publicist Geoff Freeman. 'And no-one said why. They just told us to keep out of politics.' Depending on whose account you believe, he had either been caught selling the property department's spare weapons to the Zulus, who were forbidden to carry arms of any kind; or he had 'gone native' and taken a Black mistress (if not several).

Long before the location had even been decided on, first assistant director Bert Batt had advised Cy Endfield to keep a tight lip if he wanted to film in South Africa. But they and other members of the company found it impossible not to notice what was going on around them. Batt, who made four movies in the country, told me: 'You feel ashamed of yourself for what you had to shut your eyes and ears to.' Everyone from the crew I have interviewed has at least one chilling – or sometimes darkly amusing – memory of the everyday realities of apartheid. On his very first day in the Royal Natal National Park, David Kernan was standing at the reception desk of the Mont-Aux-Sources Hotel, 'when an Afrikaaner who'd had two glasses of brandy too many came bursting through and pushed us all aside and said to the receptionist, "Will you get that kaffir out of my room? I want to sleep!" So the receptionist, in all her haughtiness, said [here Kernan adopted a thick Afrikaans accent]: "Mr xxx, in front of our guests you speak like that! You make me so ashamed I want to put my head under a boulder!"' When David travelled outside the Park he 'couldn't actually believe [his] eyes' at the sight of cordoned-off beaches and separate park benches for White and Black people.

It was not just sexual contact which was forbidden: even ordinary social interaction was banned beyond certain prescribed limits. Only children were allowed to fraternise with the Zulus, according to Ellen Baker. 'Our three children wanted to dress up as Zulus, which they did all the time. My son Glyn was allowed to have his sixth birthday party with them.' The White adults on the unit, however, could not even socialise on equal terms with non-Whites. 'We could only work with the Zulus,' says Bert Batt, 'we could not in any way befriend them. We couldn't offer them cigarettes, put an arm around a shoulder, sit and chat with them through an interpreter.' Assistant editor Jennifer Thompson remembers talking to John Marcus, one of the professional Black stuntmen, while walking through the production village one evening at the end of a day's shooting. 'I asked him to come and have a drink and of course he said he couldn't. And this was in our own canteen.' Ivor Emmanuel recalls: 'There were a lot of Asians who used to work at the hotel and I got friendly with them. I was invited by one to come back home for a curry and Neil McCarthy was the only one [from the film unit] who would come with me. We took some wine and he made us a lovely curry. He asked me to sing, and as soon as I started the door burst open and there was Stanley Baker. He said, "You stupid bastard, you could get put into prison for this!"'

Some cast and crew members did manage to bend the rules, however. Stunt arrangers John Sullivan and Joe Powell played rugby with the Zulus between bouts of battle drill, while Glynn Edwards recalls that he and a few others 'misbehaved ourselves and had a glass of beer with them, which we weren't supposed to do.' David Kernan adds: 'While we were filming, the Zulus were kept very much to themselves and we kept to ourselves, but we were very naughty and crept down to the Zulu compound to drink the Zulu beer and smoke a little "dagga" [marijuana]. No-one actually told us that we shouldn't but it was not welcomed that we fraternised with them. But we just took it upon ourselves because we wanted to.' Bob Porter says that even Baker dropped his guard to discuss politics with the Black actors: 'I know for a certainty that there were members of the ANC who were actually in the cast and talked to Stanley about their struggle, and he was very sympathetic to it. It used to worry me. But if the authorities knew it, I think that because of the impact of us being there, making a film in an apartheid country, they allowed him to skate near the edge.'

Unit members agree that there was a constant presence of plain-clothes policemen at the location, and Michael Caine claims that spies had even infiltrated the labour gangs to observe activities on set and report anything untoward to the authorities. There were also more formal inspections, as when helicopters brought a visit one day from General Hiemstra, second-in-command of all Army forces, and Colonel Frazier, Chief of Natal Command.[2] They were greeted by Baker and Endfield before being shown around the set and allowed to observe some of the filming. The tone of the meeting was amicable enough, despite its formality, and may have helped smooth out subsequent relations between the film company and officialdom.

On 12 June, towards the end of filming, a particularly unpleasant incident occurred when Chief Buthelezi, who was soon due to make his first trip out of the country to attend an Anglican Church conference in Canada, was arrested by police on suspicion of trying to rob a petrol station. Bob Porter called General Hiemstra to ask him to intercede; he in turn called the arresting officer to authorise

Ellen Baker, daughter Sally and son Glyn mingle with the Zulus.

Buthelezi's release. When the case, apparently a put-up job, was heard in the local magistrate's court, the Chief was acquitted of all charges. The Afrikaaner petrol attendant who made the accusation – that 'he had an altercation with Buthelezi over change and the chief had snatched money from him and driven off' – turned out to have a police record, and a member of the Security Police called to the scene had told Buthelezi, 'that he would not be flying to Canada but would be flying to jail.' His biographer, Ben Temkin, notes: 'The implication of the police in this case was not clear, although it appeared there was some doubt – at least in Buthelezi's mind – about their motives in allowing the case to be brought to court.'[3]

Many members of the unit found the experience of witnessing legalised oppression deeply upsetting. Maureen Endfield recalls: 'I came down with our two children, aged six and three at the time, and we stayed for the duration. It was incredibly depressing. I didn't want to have a nanny for the children but they said, if you don't you'll be depriving someone of a job. The conditions that they were kept under were just terrible – just like hutches. We all hated the way they were treated.' Ellen Baker says that the Afrikaaners in turn disliked the 'visitors from England' with their attitude that the Blacks should be on a par with the Whites. Bob Porter comments: 'I don't think the English crew were worried about mixing with the Black extras but some of the South Africans were, because it was totally alien to everything that they'd done for a hundred years.'

Camera technician Peter Hammond still remembers his experiences on location with great bitterness and anger. 'South Africa was a lovely place but the people there were horrible. [Camera operator] Dudley Lovell and I were

Stanley Baker explains a point to General Hiemstra and Colonel Frazier.

invited to somebody's house one weekend – a lovely house with a pool and servants. We were sitting at the pool and a servant brought a tray of drinks. We said thank-you and the woman of the house said not to say thank-you, as they'd lose all respect for you.' Some of the White South Africans working on the production were no better, he says. 'An Afrikaaner asked if we'd like some Zulus employed on the camera crew. We asked for two, but he said that we ought to have four because a Zulu is only worth half a one. So we had four, and they arrived with tags around their necks – white discs with a number on. He said, just call their number and they'll come running. We soon stopped doing that. They spoke English, Afrikaans, Zulu and a couple of other native languages – and he said they were thick! The Zulus were amazed at seeing White guys actually working – normally they sat around doing nothing. Instead of *telling* them to do things, we'd *ask* them to do things.'

Some of those who worked on *Zulu* but did not accompany the unit on location nonetheless had other opportunities to visit South Africa and see for themselves the sort of conditions that prevailed. Sound editor Rusty Coppleman went with Stanley Baker to work on *Dingaka* (1965) for local director Jamie Uys shortly after they had completed *Zulu*: 'I was doing some revoicing using a man from Bantu radio. It came to lunch-time and we went into a canteen. I was offered my lunch on a china plate and he was offered his on a tin plate; I could have my lunch inside and he had to go outside. I was horrified, but I didn't do the right thing – I should have gone outside with him. I did question him about it afterwards and I apologised; he said, don't worry about it, but it still haunts me. All the other people I was working with were sitting at the table and it didn't occur to them there was anything unusual. But it occurred to me. If I had done the right thing they would have thrown me out [of the country]. I've lived to regret not following my original instinct. I've been offered a few opportunities to stay in South Africa and my attitude was, I couldn't live under that regime at the time.'

Despite their draconian regulations, the government authorities were nonetheless eager to help the *Zulu* unit and to attract other overseas filmmakers to the country. On returning to America following one of his set visits, Joseph Levine praised the efforts on behalf of the production of both official state departments and the local commercial company S.A. Films. He had been impressed by the eager assistance afforded by the government in making available the White soldiers, Zulus, labourers and equipment, looked forward to working again with the fledgling industry entrepreneurs and noted that there was 'a strong interest on the part of Johannesburg financiers' in setting up international co-productions to be made in South Africa.[4] Levine subsequently sponsored *Dingaka*, while other pictures made in South Africa by members of the *Zulu* company include *The Diamond Walkers*, *Tokoloshe* and *The Naked Prey* (all 1965).

Readers today might be surprised that apparently liberal White filmmakers should have chosen to go back to work in a country they knew to be oppressive. Yet at a time of deep recession in the international film

industry – which only worsened in the 1970s, especially for the British industry – the economic and practical advantages of filming in South Africa were not to be ignored. Nor was there as yet any official opposition to working there from trade organisations such as the craft and technical unions. David Kernan reflects of his participation in *Zulu*: 'It was interesting that there was no caution from [actors' union] Equity about it, which I thought rather odd at the time. I remember that when I went on my second trip in 1973, certainly Equity made it very clear that you go out under your own banner, with no support from us.'

In 1970, the film technicians' union ACTT (later incorporated into the present-day union BECTU) introduced a ban on working in South Africa, but this was lifted in 1977 in the face of the increasing unemployment of many of its members.[5] Even so, other British-backed films made there during the period of the ban included *Gold* (1974), *Shout at the Devil* (1976) and *Golden Rendezvous* (1977), while Baker and Endfield began pre-production on *Zulu Dawn* in South Africa in 1974. Michael Caine, however, vowed not to return while apartheid was still in force and kept to his word. He made *The Wilby Conspiracy* (1975), an anti-apartheid political thriller set in South Africa, on location in Kenya, and after the fall of the White minority regime he shaved his head to play President F.W. de Klerk, who helped pave the way for the end of apartheid, in the American TV movie *Mandela and de Klerk* (1997).[6]

Yet even as early as 1963, controversy was fomenting in America about the South African racial policy, and some of this was inevitably directed towards *Zulu*. Levine's company Embassy was forced to issue a formal denial that it had received complaints from the South African government itself in response to reports that the company had allegedly tried to hush up the fact that the film was made with official co-operation. It had been pointed out

Peter Gill (Private 612 John Williams)

When Peter Gill discovered that *Zulu* was to be made in South Africa, he did not want to go, 'because of the apartheid thing. But I'm glad I did go. Seeing it all was much more shocking. I remember being very angry that the White "liberals" that we met, who'd been there for a very long time, while despising the Afrikaaners, were seen to go "boy" [he clicks his fingers] at the Blacks. I wasn't there long but it was real enough just coming out of the aeroplane and seeing the notices.'

Gill says he has 'no idea' why he was cast. 'I can remember going for an interview in filmland, somewhere off Old Compton Street or maybe Wardour Street, and getting the part. My Welshness must have had something to do with it. But I'm not a real Valleys boy – I'm not the real McCoy.' He was born in Cardiff on 7 September 1939. *Zulu* was only his second feature film, and his last; indeed, it was the last time he ever acted. Previously he had played a tiny supporting role as a Napoleonic naval officer in *HMS Defiant* (1962). After completing *Zulu* Gill decided against following an acting career and turned instead to writing and directing plays: 'I didn't have the temperament to be an actor. It was impossible to do everything I wanted to do and remain an actor.'

In 1964 he became an assistant director at the Royal Court Theatre, where the first of more than twenty plays he has authored, *The Sleeper's Den*, was staged in 1965. His other performed works include *Small Change* (1976), *Kick for Touch* (1983), *Cardiff East* (1997), *Friendly Fire* (1999), *The York Realist* (2001) and *Original Sin* (2002). Gill has also directed over eighty productions in Britain and America, received acclaim as one of our finest living playwrights, and been recognised with an OBE for his services to theatre. He was a founder director of both London's Riverside Studios and the Royal National Theatre Studio, and has been an associate director of both the Royal Court and the National Theatre. Our interview took place in the bar of Sheffield's Crucible Theatre in the summer of 2002, during a retrospective season of his early plays – in itself a rare accolade.

Peter was on location for *Zulu* for only one week, and completed his part in the studio at Twickenham. 'I wasn't involved in the battle scenes. I was shot very quickly and sent home. They used a double for me when they come out of the hospital window – it's not me. The African making a hole in the roof is not the African who jumps in and I shoot – we did that in the studio. I wasn't in the square or all that kind of thing; all I got was pushed in the water at the beginning.' He recalls being impressed by the scale of the film. 'It seemed like a big production to me, because I was only a boy; I was 24. I went onto a daily rate because we overshot, and I don't think they do that anymore. Film pay and the way you were treated began to change after that year. I remember being astounded at having a daily rate.' Though they shared no scenes in the film, Peter already knew Michael Caine from the theatre: they had both been understudies in *The Long and the Short and the Tall* (1959) and had appeared together, with Terence Stamp, in John McGrath's play *Why the Chicken* (1961). Cy Endfield was, he says, 'very nice – to me!' but he found Stanley Baker 'rather dour and off-putting.'

Peter didn't go to the premiere and first saw the completed film during its regular cinema run with a friend, the stage director William Gaskill. 'He loved it because it was pure narrative. I think that's why it's so popular. It's a strong story about blokes. It doesn't involve you in any romantic interest. The only detour is the conscience of the vicar. Otherwise it simply follows the two protagonists and then there's a lot of good characters. They're British and they're in peril, and there's this noble element – the worthy enemy. I do think the redoubt is a brilliant scene.' He received letters from viewers who knew the history of the battle, saying that 'the character of John Williams wasn't who we said he was. I didn't do any research at all – I was too young to know anything. I never quite understood why I won the VC to be honest with you.' The film,

Above: Peter Gill (right) as 612 Williams, with James Booth as Hook.

Right: Press kit for the Crucible Theatre's tribute season of Gill's work as a playwright.

Peter says, has 'a huge effect on people. It's only now that very young people don't see it. Until recently it was a film that *all* young boys had seen.'

When I raised the issue of the political criticism the film has sometimes received, Peter seemed taken aback that anyone could attack *Zulu* in such terms. 'Ipso facto a commercial film will have a political theme,' he conceded. 'But I don't you think you could say it's overtly racist or imperialist. Considering how long ago it was made it's rather not: it's about the noble savage and the noble working Welsh boy. You can smell that 60s liberal flavour.' Gill became more animated as he pondered the matter further. 'Look, I don't give a fuck about this film, but I'm getting my gander up! Your only argument could be that there was no portrayal in depth of the other soldiers. I think it would be hard to dredge up anything other than that it's bound to be jingoistic in some way. But you couldn't accuse *Zulu* of what you could accuse all those terrible American Vietnam films of. There's not one that isn't about America. If Americans had made it [*Zulu*] you'd be drowning in your own nausea, wouldn't you?'

by critics (in South Africa and elsewhere) that in Sheilah Graham's newspaper interview with Stanley Baker, the film location had been wrongly identified as *East* Africa and no mention was made of either apartheid or government help. In fairness to the actor, it was Graham herself who named the location site as being in East Africa, and Baker referred more than once to its having been in Natal, as Embassy's executives pointed out. The company also denied that the government had invested financially in the film and even suggested that it might receive its world premiere in Johannesburg; it was not in fact shown there until December 1964, much later than most countries had received the film.[7]

Race, Politics and History

'Our picture shows the horror, filth and dirt of warfare itself – face to face, with direct, thrusting steel. It's war between two nations – British invaders and the proud nation of great Zulu warriors fighting for their land. Not between two races.'
(Stanley Baker, quoted in Howard Thompson, 'Stanley Baker: Peripatetic Actor-Producer', *New York Times*, 1 September 1963.)

With the benefit of hindsight, a number of recent critics have accused the filmmakers and even the film itself of complicity with apartheid.[8] Christopher Sharrett, for example, in discussing the supposed '"burden of guilt" *Zulu* might share for actual existing policies on race in the South Africa of the 1960s,' has claimed that it would be 'not unreasonable for a film pretending to acknowledge the dignity of a colonized people at least to allude to these realities' – though he does not say how this could have been achieved in dramatic terms by a film set more than half a century before the policy of apartheid was instituted.[9] Peter Davis suggests that such an allusion to the contemporary political situation is in fact present in the film at some level, albeit veiled and probably unintentional. He sees in the mass slaughter of Blacks an echo of news images of the Sharpville massacre: 'These were again the result of a Black and White clash, where the Whites were outnumbered, and undoubtedly felt themselves threatened by the hordes surrounding them, and tried to defend themselves – only the hordes were unarmed, and they were not marauding, they were demonstrating.'[10]

Davis also argues that Chief Buthelezi's real-life political image was effectively both echoed and enhanced by his participation in the film:

His presence in the frame signifies his approval of the project ... Depending on where you stand, this can be seen as seizing an opportunity to bring cash and jobs to the homeland, on whatever ephemeral basis location filming brings; or it can be seen as a cynical selling-out of Zulu heritage and history.

For Buthelezi, there was a bonus both from the filming and from his role-playing in some of those films in that through his on-screen persona, the historical figures he portrayed fused with his image as a legitimate modern leader, in much the same way as the panoply and ritual of royalty give a mystical legitimacy to the individual holding the office.[11]

When *Zulu* was screened on South African television in November 1993, in the week of the signing of the new constitution which introduced non-racial democratic elections, one journalist drew an analogy between the film's portrayal of Cetewayo as a leader whose forces are about to be defeated and Chief Buthelezi's own real-life political position as one of several factions which opposed the constitution.[12]

It is the position of Davis's book, *In Darkest Hollywood*, and his 1993 television documentary of the same name, that any filmmakers who did not actively oppose the apartheid regime were effectively complicit with it and implicitly endorsed its legitimacy. This is a perfectly tenable argument, though not one shared by the present book, which takes a more pragmatic and non-judgmental view: without the co-operation of the South

African government of the day, there would not now be a *Zulu* to write about. In that respect, I believe the filmmakers' ends justified their means. They also, of course, brought work and additional income to members of the local population, many of whom would have lived in poverty. Nonetheless, it is worth quoting Davis's querulous comments on the Zulus' participation in the film – and that of other indigenous peoples in other Western films – and its implications for their grasp of their own heritage and history:

> The educational system of [apartheid] South Africa had been deliberately structured to deprive Africans of a sense of continuity, of a past in which they could take pride, and a movie offered, in a graphic way, some access to their own history, however inaccurately presented. Never mind that the film glorified White heroism and conquest: there were images of African warriors on the screen. As contemporary cinema in America has revealed, Black people would rather have images of Black villains than no images of themselves at all …

Why has it always been so easy to find masses of extras willing to re-enact the defeats of the Zulu nation, preserving past humiliations and thereby contributing to the continuance of White hegemony? Not least must be counted the attraction of play-acting itself, of appearing before the camera in a role that offers escape from the humdrum. It is not hard to imagine the glee of mineworkers offered the recreation of play, even at the sacrifice of a day off, to be part of the glamour of cinema. To this must be added the strong sense among Zulus of belonging to a warrior nation, and the pride and social bonding this entails; the traditional dances are still alive, and were often incorporated into the films. It

was only a short step from there to fall into the part of the charging warrior, thus reliving the glories of the past – ignoring that on the screen these became the humbling of the Zulu *impis*.[13]

In a recent article entitled 'We, "The Children of Isandlwana": Isandlwana and Rorke's Drift Revisited', published on the internet website http://rorkesdriftvc.com/ under the rubric 'A Zulu Perspective,' Black African scholar Themba Mthethwa compares *Zulu* to the later wave of American films about the conflict in Vietnam, and argues that it 'failed dismally to capture moments of glory of the People's Army.' Seeking further elucidation on this issue, I spoke to two Zulus who, escaping apartheid in the 1970s, now live and work in Britain, both of whom separately agreed to watch and discuss *Zulu* at my invitation. Not surprisingly, they each have a very different take on the film from my own, but they do not themselves agree in every particular.

Paul Matewele is the great-grandson of Tshingwayo, the Zulu commander at the Battle of Isandhlwana. He has lived in the UK for 28 years and now lectures in micro-biology at London Metropolitan University. He first saw *Zulu* in the 1970s, and does not believe that the film is straightforwardly racist. 'They [the filmmakers] were clearly more interested in portraying one side than the other. But I wouldn't say the film was racist per se – it just didn't emphasise the Zulu side. They did try to portray the bravery of the Zulus, and some of the Zulu battle strategies were authentic, but some of the fighting strategies that one would have expected to see were not shown. Some of the young men could crawl for five miles on their shields to surprise the enemy – literally "marching on their stomachs."'

Paul also points out that some of the specific incidents shown in the film are unlikely; by way of example, he cites the misrepresentation of Zulu customs in the wedding dance scene. 'The translator [Jacob] would have stood in front of the King and bowed; he wouldn't be wearing a hat in the King's presence. The messenger would have been an older person. Blood was not allowed to be shed in the Royal homestead; the offending warrior [who accosts Margareta] would have been taken outside the walls to be disciplined. It's unlikely that he would have been killed, though this could be argued either way – it's not clear if he had disobeyed the King's order.' Also unclear, even to a Zulu viewer, are the meaning of many of the Zulu chants and songs performed in the film. 'If only we could hear the words we could put into perspective how authentic they are. All they wanted was people to say Zulu things without our hearing the actual words. They are noises rather than words.'

Elliot Ngubane was born in 1947 into the Amabovu clan of KwaZulu-Natal; Emsinga-Top, his mountain-top village, was within walking distance of Isandhlwana. His grandfather had fought there, while his great grandfather had been defeated in battle and was subsequently blinded by King Shaka. Elliot was leader of the traditional dance and music for the acclaimed musical production *Iphi Ntombi*, which played at Her Majesty's Theatre and then at the Cambridge Theatre, London, from 1975 to 1982. He has also worked on several films in South Africa, including *Zulu Dawn*, for which he composed all the Zulu songs and chants, performed in a London recording studio by members of the *Iphi Ntombi* cast. On the walls of his home in North London (where he keeps his traditional shields, weapons and regalia in the garden shed), Elliot has pictures of the Battle of Ulundi and of Zulus mustering for attack. There is also a photograph of him meeting Queen Elizabeth II at the Commonwealth Institute two years ago; inserted in its frame is a small portrait of King Cetewayo, whom he played in the dramatised documentary *Rorke's Drift 1879: Against All Odds* (Cromwell Films, 1994).

Under apartheid, he says, 'Blacks weren't allowed to have pictures of the historical battles against the British or the Boers. Our children were not allowed to learn the history – people today don't know it. Most of the writers of history were Whites. Our people got their information from here [Britain].' The Zulu culture instead favoured oral story-telling: 'My people were "Amasomi" – a group of the last people who could tell the story, who were there. They told us how they fought the war. The history of the war is very powerful. When the war dance is done today, these people are still thinking about the wars – it's no joke. My grandfather told me, don't ever work for White people: they killed us. He talked every day about Isandhlwana. He talked about the strategies and technology of the war: we only had spears, they had guns. Christianity tore our people down: it brain-washed everybody, affecting every Black man on Earth.'

The *Iphi Ntombi* cast saw *Zulu* together, in a hotel room, on its UK television premiere on New Year's Eve 1976. 'It was around the time of the Soweto riot.[14] It gave a terrible feeling to Black people. A lot of us felt it was a lie – not a true story. They said, can this really have happened?' The film, Elliot believes, was made 'to show how the British Empire was powerful; English people wanted to be seen as supreme. I think that's a little bit sad. The film was made to be suitable for them, not us – it was not meant for showing in South Africa.' The main problem, he argues, is a lack of detail and authenticity in the film's portrayal of Zulu culture. 'We see the drama on the English side, but not on the Zulu side. The drama is hidden. It doesn't matter if the Whites won the war – but show it properly, show *how* they won. The Zulus were as well organised as any army in the world. We need to see their training, strategy, culture – to see them as a people. The general's orders aren't explained. We don't see them planning or preparing the attacks. There's no sense of pride, and not enough beauty in the costumes. We don't know what the shields and costumes mean. It could be in English, it doesn't have to be in Zulu; we just need to see them as themselves.

'There are also a lot of mistakes. Buthelezi couldn't have been involved – he obviously had no say in the making of the film. "Bayete!" is a greeting to the Zulu King – like "My Lord" – not a war cry. Meat is not roasted on a spit like in the film: it should be on sticks. And how can the King sit with his enemy [the Reverend Witt]?' Elliot doubts that all of the Black extras employed on the film were tribal. 'You can see from the Zulus running on the stones in the river that they don't belong there. They don't run with confidence; real Zulus wouldn't run like that. They were probably taken off the streets of the townships, or from Durban or Johannesburg.'

Elliot is equally unhappy with *Zulu Dawn*, despite working on it himself. 'I was very disappointed. They didn't show the Blacks stabbing the Whites – just the Whites killing the Blacks. After that I stopped being interested [in making films].' By contrast, Elliot believes the TV mini-series *Shaka Zulu* (1985) 'was very good at showing the Black people's side. Shaka gave Zulus pride, but the leadership after him was weak; Cetewayo failed as a King.' He concedes that *Zulu* has its redeeming features: 'The film is promoting the Zulu name, which is good. If it could be done again with the true story, that would be very good. *Zulu* should be remade, now that Black people have won their freedom. Things are very different now. In those days there were no Black filmmakers – none whatsoever. For a remake you would need Black crews, Black producers, to remind Black people of their history – so they can worship their history. It would be good to have a working committee to approach our government to renew it as part of the heritage industry, to encourage Black people to be proud of their culture. Oral history is not a good way of telling history, and Black people have a distrust of books written by the White man. We need films.'

Zulu Songs and Chants

I have often been asked during the preparation of this book if I would be providing translations of the tribal music and martial chants performed by the film's Zulu cast. I had always thought it unlikely, until in the final stages of writing I was put in touch by John Young with two expatriate Zulus who were able to help. Neither Elliot Ngubane nor Paul Matewele could provide full translations of all such material, the inadequacies of either the original recording or the sound playback on home video preventing many of the lyrics from being clearly audible. But Elliot gave me detailed interpretations of many of the songs and chants, while Paul explained the origins and significance of the Zulus' oft-heard war cry 'Usuthu!' I am most grateful to both these gentlemen, who were extremely generous with their time and knowledge, for providing what I believe to be a unique insight into these aspects of Zulu history and culture.

Wedding songs

In the first song heard during the wedding dance at the Royal homestead, a harmonist leads a chant in which each girl chooses the partner she wants:

Hamba naye, hamba naye (Harmonist: Go with her, she is yours)
Soka lakhe
Intombe ikhetha emthandayo (Answer: Of course, she is yours)

The second song is relatively modern, performed in the Umbolohlodlo (a capella) style of music, which would not have been heard during Cetewayo's reign. According to Elliot Ngubane, 'Weddings changed after the Christian influence, when they got married in a Christian way. Traditional Zulu women don't sing like that.' The chant relies, like most of these songs, on simple repetition:

Gwaza ngomkhonto ka Shaka ma (Step with Shaka's spear)
Gwaza ngomkhonto ka Shaka ma

The third wedding song, performed by the men, is a war chant intended to scare the enemy:

Jojum-thakathi, Jojum-thakathi (Stick it up his arse, witch doctor!)

The levies' work chant

The chant shouted by the native levies working at the ponts on the river was actually performed impromptu by the Zulu extras and incorporated in the film by Cy Endfield on the spur of the moment. Actor Glynn Edwards recalls: 'The Zulus' singing at the river wasn't in the script but when Cy heard them singing on set he shoved it in. Cy was like that.' The chant gives an insight into the regular work done by many of the Zulus, as according to Elliot it is a work chant usually sung by miners:

Khuluma nobani (Who do you speak to?)
Kuuluma lepoyisa (I'm talking to the police.)
Elesaba insimpi (Who's afraid of picking up the metal?)
Move suka nsimbi (Move, stand up, metal.)

War songs

'You can't tell what they're singing,' comments Elliot of the song (at first mournful, then aggressive) performed at daybreak by the Zulus at Rorke's Drift. 'The sound is terrible, you can't hear the lyrics. But it's a war song: it comes from the area of the Kumalos. Buthelezi sings a similar song on Shaka's Day every September. This is a festival event – all the chiefs of the Zulus are there.' In the film, it is accompanied by the sound of assegais hammered rhythmically against shields, and is of course answered by the defenders' rallying chorus of 'Men of Harlech' ('The Welsh song makes me laugh,' says Elliot).

When the Zulus perform their gesture of respect on the hillside after the battle, the following chant is heard:

Hebe wusuthu

This incorporates *usuthu*, the war cry with which the Zulus are commonly associated. I had always assumed this to be the rough equivalent of the Japanese 'Banzai!' – childhood reading of war comics stays long in the memory – but Paul Matewele recounts the little-known historical and mythic background to this symbolic cry: 'Its literal meaning derives from King Mpande's reign. There were some Zulu troops on a raid in what is now Lesotho, who came back with some cattle. When they got to the Nondweni River and the cattle drank from it, the river stopped flowing. It was said that if the contingent which came back with the cattle could stop the enemy as the cattle had stopped the flowing of the river ("Liyowaminya amanzi") then nothing could stop them. The cattle came from the Usuthu people – hence the word is used like a slogan to remind warriors of this story.'

Notes

1 Michael Caine, *What's It All About?* (London: Random House/Arrow, 1992), p. 171.

2 See Caine's remarks on both the surveillance and the official visit on pp. 182-3.

3 Ben Temkin, *Buthelezi: A Biography* (London and Portland: Frank Cass, 2003), p. 85.

4 'South African Government a Lulu For Cooperation on Levine's *Zulu*,' *Variety*, 1 May 1963, p. 3. See also Eddie Kalish, 'South African Film Production On Increase; Gold Mining Firm "Diversifies" Into S.A. Studios,' *Variety*, 31 July 1963, pp. 7, 22.

5 'British union ban on South Africa lifted', *Screen International*, 9 April 1977, p. 1.

6 See Caine, pp. 183, 373-80. Caine's autobiography was published shortly before the end of the apartheid system.

7 '*Zulu* Gets Full Levine Promo Tactics; Deny Any South African Complaints,' *Variety*, 18 December 1963, p. 11.

8 In his influential book *A Mirror for England: British Movies From Austerity to Affluence* (London: Faber and Faber, 1970), Raymond Durgnat comments of the film's ending, in which the Zulus and British go their separate ways: 'Real understanding is attained through – apartheid, might one say?' (p. 82).

9 Reply to letters, *Cineaste*, vol. XXVI, no. 2, 2001, p. 60. The liner notes for The Voyager Company's US laserdisc edition of *Zulu*, released in 1990, include a disclaimer which seems to imply that the film itself expresses pro-apartheid attitudes: 'The Criterion Collection seeks to publish important cinematic works of which *Zulu* is one. The philosophies expressed in the film are in no way representative of the beliefs of our company. We firmly believe the policy of apartheid should be stopped.'

10 Peter Davis, *In Darkest Hollywood: Exploring the jungles of cinema's South Africa* (Athens: Ohio University Press, 1996), p. 155. The Sharpeville massacre took place on 21 March 1960, resulting in the deaths of 67 protestors and the wounding of 200 more.

11 Ibid., p. 161.

12 Buthelezi eventually agreed to participate in the elections less than a fortnight before they were held, and drew 51% of the vote in KwaZulu-Natal (Anthony Sampson, *Mandela: The Authorised Biography*, London: HarperCollins, 1999, pp. 484-6, 491).

13 Davis, pp. 159-60.

14 The violent suppression by armed police of a student demonstration in Soweto took place on 16 June 1976; the subsequent riots continued for several months, ultimately leading to some 1,000 fatalities (Temkin, pp. 186-7).

"DAMNED HOT WORK"

LIGHTS, CAMERA, ACTION

> Shooting for the film began yesterday at the dammed up Tugela River under overcast skies. In the middle of it all, perhaps the calmest person was Mr Cy Endfield, the Director, who was dressed in a natty pair of swimming trunks, gum boots and a red sweater.
>
> Smart, red-coated 'British' soldiers with White pith helmets (the dress of 1879) marched along a Drakensberg rough road nearby, carrying their Martini-Enfield [sic] rifles. Their rehearsal ground was high up on a hill overlooking the river…
>
> Several scenes in *Zulu* were shot at the Royal Natal National Park yesterday, but the one that took the longest went like this:-
>
> 'Corporal!'
>
> 'Sah!'
>
> 'Get some men into the river.'
>
> 'Sah!'
>
> ('S.A., London, New York premieres for *Zulu?*,' *The Natal Witness*, 29 March 1963)

The storm clouds which cast their shadow over the location on Day One might have been taken as an omen by the superstitious. The more literal-minded simply saw bad weather coming. David Kernan was involved in the first day's shooting – as Hitch, he was one of the men plunged into the river – and he was less than delighted by the inclement conditions. 'I looked around and I said, we could be in Scotland, couldn't we? It was freezing cold and covered in snow. They were deeply worried – it was just sort of a freak weather. There was a lot of sitting around the first week because of snow. It was Africa, but we had blankets around us, waiting for our cues.'

The *Zulu* unit was on location for fourteen weeks from 28 March. This was the South African winter, when the grasslands are dry and the weather often cold. Ironically, in view of Private Thomas's morose observation that the landscape surrounding the film's Rorke's Drift is 'not really green, like – no moisture in it,' if the company had been shooting a few months earlier the Drakensberg grass would have been as verdant as that in Wales.[1] The crew usually worked six days a week, sometimes seven. A typical working day for the actors began with a call for 6.00am and into makeup by 6.30, but the technicians had to be up by 5.30 so that the company could make the best use of the available light. The days were short and night fell very quickly: it was usually dark by 6.00pm.

The production schedule was continually threatened by the weather, especially heavy rains in April; Cy Endfield was told by the Black African labourers that it was King Cetewayo weeping.[2] Stanley Baker later remarked: 'We studied weather reports for the past 13 years before we went out there to pick

Cy Endfield directs the first day's filming.

the best period for shooting. Then we had rain! It meant that we lost 20 days but we were able to catch up and finally finished only a week behind schedule.'3 The company made the best of the bad weather by using the spare time to make additional props and to rehearse the complex battle scenes. As the shoot progressed, the weather improved and, said Baker, 'temperatures reached 110 deg. [Fahrenheit] in the daytime, but at night we slept under blankets with temperatures falling to 34 and even 22 at times.'4

Zulu was filmed in a wide-screen process called Technirama, introduced by the Technicolor Corporation in 1957. Technirama was a development of VistaVision, which employed 35mm film stock running horizontally through the camera (rather than vertically as with normal cameras). The negative film exposed a frame twice as large as that of standard 35mm film, the extra surface area giving sharper resolution and a brighter, clearer image. With the addition of an anamorphic lens, which slightly 'squeezed' the visual information recorded on the film, Technirama gave an aspect ratio (relative width to height) of 2.35: 1, the same proportions as CinemaScope. The opening titles for *Zulu* actually have a credit for Super Technirama 70, which meant only that the film was designed to be blown up to 70mm for exhibition purposes to give a vastly superior picture quality.

However, the company had brought no high-powered lighting equipment on location with them. Cinematographer Stephen Dade was therefore required to light the entire film using small lamps, reflectors and battery-powered 'sun-guns' which depended on a steady supply of strong sunlight. (Light bouncing from the reflectors can clearly be seen in the first shot of the cheetah being hunted by Bromhead.) 'There were no big Brutes or 10-Ks,' says Bob Porter, 'just mirrors and dinkies and in-fills. The unit was powered by an ex-army generator dug into the ground three or four hundred yards from the set. One night there was a fire – the generator had been set on a coal seam which had caught light. It took two days to put out.'

Stephen Dade (1909-1975) entered the film industry as a camera assistant in 1927 and became a director of photography in 1940. He began by shooting low-budget comedies and worked his way up to bigger things like *Knights of the Round Table* (1953), *The Angry Hills* (1959) and *The Man Who Finally Died* (1962), on all of which he worked with Stanley Baker. Despite the limited lighting equipment at his disposal on *Zulu*, Dade performed wonders in giving the film's images a remarkable, almost three-dimensional depth of field. His eldest son Richard recalls that when his father was away on location he would send the family audio tapes of recorded messages.

The Technicolor camera in operation.

LIGHTS, CAMERA, ACTION 217

Dudley Lovell lines up a shot with the Technicolor Technirama camera. Note the modest lighting rig and the large reflectors. Cinematographer Stephen Dade stands at left with hands on hips.

Two cameras are used to capture this action scene.
(Jürgen Schadeberg)

218 LIGHTS, CAMERA, ACTION

For the tracking shots during the Zulu assaults, a trench was dug and a platform laid to carry the camera dolly.

Stephen found Cy Endfield a hard taskmaster and framing the shots was difficult, but according to Richard he thought that the sun-guns were 'marvellous as a way of getting contrast in the bright African sun.' Some shots were achieved the hard way, simply by waiting for the right light: perhaps the most remarkable is the first shot of dawn breaking, with Chard entering the frame from off-screen right as the light gradually comes up from the distant horizon. This beautiful image was done for real, says Richard, without using filters or optical effects to create an artificial sunrise.

Three cameras were used on the film: an adapted VistaVision camera, a converted Technicolor three-strip camera (the three-strip colour format having been obsolete since the mid-1950s), and another used for action shots which camera technician Peter Hammond calls 'a lightweight.' Hammond (born 1928) worked for the Technicolor Corporation, and his special duties on *Zulu* involved running the Technicolor camera, focussing it and carrying out maintenance. He remembers Stephen Dade as 'a very quiet man. He spent all Saturday evening in his hotel room trying to phone his wife. It took three hours to get through to her for a ten-minute conversation.'

Camera operator Dudley Lovell (1915-1998) was also an industry veteran, having started out at Gaumont British studios in 1931. He became an operator in 1945 after leaving the Army and from 1948 went freelance, later working on such films as *The Cockleshell Heroes* (1955), *Battle of the Bulge*, *Those Magnificent Men in Their Flying Machines* (both 1965) and *The Wild Geese* (1978). Lovell described his work as varying 'from being constructive, helpful, artistic, to a pure camera pointer. The American style was a camera pointer. They didn't really want you to provide anything, they would definitely tell you exactly what they wanted … I preferred the other way.'5 Though Dudley counted *Zulu* among his personal favourites, he too found the experience of making the film rather trying at times, especially in his prickly relationship with the director, as he recalled in a 1990 interview:

Cy Endfield, script in hand, and camera operator Dudley Lovell set up a shot.

> I had problems with Cy Endfield, but Cy did a good job of directing. We had this crane, and we hadn't got any generators so it had to be moved by hand, and it was very hot in the midday sun. I'm up this crane with a viewfinder and Endfield's down below. And he said, give me a long shot with the mountains. So I said, I've got a long shot with the mountains. He said, what have you got? I said, I can see the mountains and it's a long shot. So he said, well, move two or three feet back. What have you got now? I said, well, you can't see it but I must have a little bit more mountain. So he said, well move in a bit then, move in. So the boys are all pushing this crane, sweating like anything. After about a quarter of an hour I said, look, wouldn't it be a good idea if I came down, put the crane at the back of the tracks, we'll get a pair of stepladders and you come up with the viewfinder and decide what you want visually through the viewfinder? He said, what did you say? I said, I thought it would be a good idea if the crane came down and we got a pair of steps. He said, that's what I thought you said. So we got the steps and we did the shot with the crane.

Later that day Stephen Dade, the lighting cameraman, said, Cy Endfield wants to see you in his office. Well, the office was a shed. So I go along and he's in one of those lean-back, whirl-around chairs behind a desk. He said, you know I would like to have a cooperative, friendly spirit on this picture. I said, great, that's what you need in pictures, that's important. He said, but I can't if you're rude to me, can I? I said, rude to you? When have I been rude to you? I've never said a rude word to you. He said, today, up the crane there, you were most sarcastic and rude! I said, I wasn't being rude, I was being helpful. If I sounded rude I'm sure it was in your mind, I wasn't being rude. I was only trying to save you time, to stop pushing backwards and forwards with the crane. He said, yes, I've heard about you operators in England, you've got an over-estimated sense of your own importance, and I like to work in the Hollywood style. I said, fine, I've worked with a lot of American directors and cameramen, I'll work in the Hollywood style. You tell me what to do, where to put the camera and where to point it. I'll keep my mouth shut. He said, well I didn't really mean that…! And this was the problem I had … it's so difficult, isn't it?

While the producers gave Dade and Lovell a hard time, the unit electricians made sure that they did the same to Baker and Endfield. Maureen Endfield says: 'Because they were away from their families for so long it was difficult for them, so there was quite a lot of grumbling and complaining, especially as Cy and Stanley had their families with them. There were lots and lots of union meetings, with everybody calling each other "brother." I think it must have been over hours and not wanting to do overtime. If there'd be a shot at the end of the day that was perfect and the crew packed up and said that was it, it was something you'd never get again. In those days unions were so powerful. After that the film industry hit a low, and I thought, well, it just serves them right, they behaved so badly.'

Even now the electricians' attitudes and activities provoke strong reactions from members of the *Zulu* production team. Bob Porter comments: 'The sparks were a disgrace. They had lived for years with the union being the Big Brother and the power was beginning to wane.' Some other crew members, such as sound technician David Jones, could at least see the electricians' point of view and shared their grievances at the situation: 'We all got a bad deal on it. It was an all-in deal, with no overtime. The producer could work you as much as he liked.' Dudley Lovell was also sympathetic:

> We were up in the highlands in Natal in the 'Berg and we were in a hotel for fourteen weeks, with no transport out. It was like being in an open prison, really. I was lucky because I'd been there before on *Nor the Moon By Night* and I had friends in Natal who would come up occasionally ... but the other boys, and especially the electricians, weren't getting any overtime because the whole thing was shot by Stephen Dade with sun-guns, in the African sun. It was ridiculous – if they'd had some real lamps they'd have had some work to do. So what happened was that when the sun went down about half past five or six – it was the winter – that was the finish ... you went to the hotel and you didn't come out again till seven o'clock [next morning]. You were getting seven guineas a week, in those days, allowance, and you can't live in a hotel and find your amusement for seven guineas a week. It was impossible, so there was a lot of bolshy feeling among the electricians.
>
> They were [electrical company] Mole Richardson's and ... when they came back ... Stanley Baker really tore them apart because of the behaviour of the crew. I will say that people don't go away for fourteen weeks to live on a mountain for basic wages, live an anti-social life and leave your family for fourteen weeks and not expect some good money or some overtime. And it would have been possible to give them some basic overtime of some kind which would have obviated the situation, I think. It was really a most unhappy picture, most unhappy.

On occasions, however, the electricians' behaviour simply appeared bloody-minded, as Peter Hammond recalls: 'One of them decided he wanted to get his hair cut. He came to breakfast and stood in front of the production manager's office and said he was going to sit there until he got his hair cut. They had to get a car to take him to the nearest town for a haircut.'

South African Chris Dresser had been interviewed by Bob Porter for the job of third assistant director, though it eventually went instead to Howard Rennie. Dresser nonetheless visited the location during shooting with a friend, stills photographer Dennis Bughwan, and provides an intriguing sidelight on attitudes among the British crew: 'In South Africa, for all our faults during those years, most people in the film industry had a working knowledge of nearly all the jobs in a film crew. We had no trade unions in those days and so became all-rounders. At one stage Dennis went over to one of the British lighting hands and asked him some fairly technical question about the lighting set up. He was shocked when the man replied "Dunno mate, I just put 'em up where the gaffer tells me to." Dennis could not believe that someone could

Joe Powell (Sergeant Joseph Windridge)
John Sullivan (Captain Stephenson)

'Normally I tried to avoid dialogue,' says ace stunt performer and action arranger Joe Powell. He was persuaded by Stanley Baker and associate producer Basil Keys to take on a rare acting role as 'the sergeant with the muscles,' but it was the local wildlife, not a stunt, which put him temporarily out of commission during the location shoot. 'Halfway through my part I got bitten by something, my leg got poisoned and I was put in the hospital for a week. I recovered and went back to the film, but I didn't get to do a lot of my lines.' Some of his missed dialogue was given instead to other characters, including Nigel Green's Colour-Sergeant Bourne.

Zulu's stunt director, the late John Sullivan (1924-1996), also had a small acting role, as the commander of the troop of horsemen who stop briefly at Rorke's Drift. Powell and Sullivan had worked together before on such large-scale pictures as *The Crimson Pirate* (1952), *Helen of Troy* (1955), *Moby Dick* (1956), *Exodus* (1960) and *The Longest Day* (1962). They were later reunited on *The Heroes of Telemark* (1965), *The Last Valley* (1971), *Golden Rendezvous* (1977), *Caravans* (1978), *The Passage* (1979) and *Flash Gordon* (1980).

"The sergeant with the muscles": Joe Powell.

After serving in Italy during the war, Sullivan made his reputation as a stuntman on *Ivanhoe* (1952), impressing American stunt director Yakima Canutt with his readiness to fall off a horse, in full armour, onto hard ground. On *Moby Dick* he made a 110-foot dive from the mast of the Pequod into the sea. 'He was as thick in the legs as he was in the shoulders,' comments Bob Porter, who, then a stuntman himself, had refused to perform this same action. 'John Sullivan was very erudite. He could do the *Times* crossword in ten minutes, the *Telegraph* in five. He was the best stuntman leader in England at the time: a very decent, talented, intelligent feller.' John doubled for Kirk Douglas in *The Vikings* (1958), for Peter O'Toole in *Lawrence of Arabia* (1962) and *Lord Jim* (1965), and for Richard Burton in *Alexander the Great* (1956) and *Cleopatra* (1963). He had the looks, says Porter, to be a star in his own right and his many other films as stunt co-ordinator, assistant director or occasional bit-part player include *John Paul Jones* (1959), *Tarzan the Magnificent* (1960), *Those Magnificent Men in Their Flying Machines* (1965), *The Tamarind Seed* (1974), *Barry Lyndon* (1975) and *The Pink Panther Strikes Again* (1976). He also wrote two unproduced scripts, including *Osmosis*, an interracial love story set in Africa, intended to star Burton and Elizabeth Taylor.

Joe Powell was born on 21 March 1922 and joined the army at seventeen. He became a sergeant in No. 4 Commando and saw action in Normandy on D-Day. London's Imperial War Museum has film footage of him carrying a wounded comrade to safety, and Joe later helped recreate his unit's part in the battle in *The Longest Day*. After the war, he and Captain Jock Easton, formerly of the Special Air Services, formed the first professional stunt team in Britain, employing several other ex-servicemen including Joe's brother Eddie Powell. Joe's first film stunt, for *The Small Voice* (1948), involved riding a motorcycle into a tree at forty miles per hour – twice! – for a fee of £25. Captain Easton told journalist Andrew Peters that 'the best [stuntmen] are ex-regular servicemen. He explains that it is not enough for a stuntman to be tough and courageous. He has to be well-trained and disciplined, too, so that he can respond readily to the precise requirements of the director and cameraman' ('Playing Safe – With Danger,' *Films and Filming*, June 1956, p. 6).

Easton and Joe Powell effectively created the stunt profession in the British film industry, though not without a struggle. According to Joe, they 'fought the British Film Producers Association, which suddenly realised that Jock and I had found a niche in the industry they had overlooked. They had started their own crowd casting agency, known as the Film Casting Association. They attempted to push us out of business by starting their own stunt register. They couldn't however match the quality of the work or the artists we provided.' The opposition eventually gave up when Easton and Powell succeeded in persuading Actors' Equity to admit stuntmen into its membership and to recognise stunt work as a legitimate branch of the profession.

John Sullivan leads the Boer horsemen as Captain Stephenson.

Joe's first big film assignment was *Captain Horatio Hornblower, R.N.* (1951), in which Stanley Baker also had a small role. The following year he was responsible for organising 'the first group of stuntmen ever to be taken abroad to work on a film,' for *The Crimson Pirate*. 'As a direct result of the work we did, further locations followed. Having established ourselves in the industry, on future films abroad stuntmen were taken on locations

Joe Powell in action as Sergeant Windridge.

with the main units.' In addition to its film work, the Easton/Powell agency also provided acts for fêtes, carnivals and open-air shows, such as trick riders, sway pole artists, car stunt and motorcycle teams, dental acts from tethered balloons, bucking bronco acts and a stage act called Stuntmen of the Films. Joe also cast the Chinese extras for the crowd scenes in *The Inn of the Sixth Happiness* (1958), *The World of Suzie Wong* (1960), *55 Days at Peking* (1963) and *Genghis Khan* (1965).

Among the countless other films on which Joe has worked, performing and arranging stunts around the world, are *The Guns of Navarone* (1961), *633 Squadron* (1964), *Khartoum* (1966), *Where Eagles Dare* (1968), *Murphy's War* (1971), *Young Winston* (1972), *The Man Who Would Be King* (1975, in which he doubled Sean Connery's fatal fall from a rope bridge strung across a crevasse), *Top Secret!* (1984), many Hammer productions and several of the James Bond films. At time of writing he still goes to the gym, keeps fit and has just completed writing his memoirs. My interview with him took place on 21 March 2002 – Joe's eightieth birthday, although, with characteristic modesty, he did not reveal this fact until the interview was over.

First assistant director Bert Batt (left) with Stanley Baker.

work with lights and have no idea how they were set up.'6

Staging the Battle

Much of the work of staging the action scenes fell to first assistant director Bert Batt. 'The bits that took a lot of working out,' he says, 'were the really close bits. The most difficult thing was setting up foreground action where guys were fighting.' Assistant editor Jennifer Thompson recalls that Batt 'had the loudest voice as an A.D. People shook when he shouted "Be quiet!"'

Bert has worked as an assistant director on more than fifty major films over a span of nearly half a century, including *Victim* (1961), *The Dirty Dozen* (1967), *The Return of the Pink Panther* (1975), *Cross of Iron* (1977), *A Bridge Too Far* (1977), *The Sea Wolves* (1980), *Enemy Mine* (1985), *Robin Hood* (1991) and *Les Misérables* (1998), as well as many Hammer horror movies; he also wrote the screenplay for one of the best of these, *Frankenstein Must Be Destroyed* (1969). He has made several other films in Africa besides *Zulu*: *Nor the Moon by Night* (1958), *The Diamond Walkers* (1965), *The Naked Prey* (1965) and *The Man Who Would Be King* (1975), the last filmed in Morocco by the distinguished American director John Huston. Huston's description in his autobiography, *An Open Book*, of the role of the first assistant director in the production process, and his centrality to the success and efficiency of a film shoot, cannot be bettered:

> I've had two great assistant directors in my life: Tommy Shaw is one, and the other is Bert Batt. The rest range from good to fair to very bad indeed. Whatever is good about *The Man Who Would Be King*, Bert Batt had something to do with it. Bert's ideas were always well thought out, and usually they were good ideas. If you didn't go for what he proposed, he didn't turn petulant, but addressed himself to the next problem. He would sometimes be up two days and three nights running, arranging something complicated like a whole troop movement; not only was he a powerhouse of energy, but he was resourceful to an amazing degree ...
>
> The great first assistants are all well known. They are like great top sergeants, often valued more highly than the director. When I find such an assistant, I put all my trust in him. First assistants are basically 'company men,' and one of their primary responsibilities is to protect the interests of the studio. Some of them carry this to extremes, basing every decision on immediate monetary savings, regardless of quality. Then there are those, like Tommy Shaw and Bert Batt, who understand that cutting corners doesn't necessarily save money. They have the ability to perceive what a director is after, and the judgment

to decide whether it's good enough to warrant added expense. If it is, they are the director's champions.

A first assistant worth his salt takes over the details, leaving the director free to make creative decisions. The first assistant decides when the company moves; whether or not there should be a second unit working on the preparation of the so-called action shots; whether the action scenes should be shot together or broken up. He is a specialist in such back-up people as stunt men; he knows them by name, and knows who is best for what falls, horses, rope-climbing, driving, piloting or motorcycling. When it comes to explosives, he picks the powder man. A good first assistant is a first-rate diplomat as well as a disciplinarian. He has the ability to command without offending people. Along with his authority he has a sense of fitness and good taste. He is able to go to the stars' dressing rooms and persuade them to his course of action without toadying to them or seeming too authoritarian. There aren't many like this.[7]

Though he is characteristically modest about claiming credit for it, Bert was largely responsible for devising one of the most important, powerful and memorable shots in

John Sullivan dispenses advice on weapons to the boiler-suited Zulus.

John Sullivan rehearses combat moves with a warrior.

LIGHTS, CAMERA, ACTION 225

Simon Sabela performs a spectacular hundred-foot fall.

the film, the one which more than any other creates the illusion of great numbers: the first appearance of the massed Zulu ranks atop the hillside overlooking Rorke's Drift. This was not in fact written into the screenplay, but was improvised on the spur of the moment as a way, Bert says, of making use of the many spare shields and props the company had left over. He describes how it came about:

I saw all these shields lying on the floor and said, what are we going to do with them all? I had the idea to put them on batons. I got them all rigged up on a Saturday afternoon, after we'd finished shooting, with my two assistants. What we did was put the shields on the baton, all at different angles and heights. Then we banged a knobkerry to the back to break up the outline. We got it all up there and saw how it worked. I got Cy and Stanley to come down on Sunday and have a look at it. Cy said, 'Jesus Christ, that's terrific! How many more shields have we got left?' We had about 120, so he told me to put them on posts and hammer them into the ground, so you've got a battery of shields. They were so far away and so small you couldn't tell there weren't men standing behind them. [Cy said] 'When we get to the end of the panning shot, we'll come off your lot and go down to my lot and we'll have the 250 Zulus tucked round the corner. As we come onto the static shields, run the 250 in.' Cy's was a great idea – when you've done that and set that up before you've seen them arriving to fight, then you've got 250 to do it with.

When the operator panning the horizon for this shot could not hold focus and turn the camera on its axis at the same time, Bob Porter held onto a broom handle inserted in the lens mount to give the movement leverage and keep the camera steady. On the hillside, the pop-up 'Zulus' were operated by two men per baton of shields, and so effective is the result that very few viewers realise the deception. After this shot, the audience simply accepts without question the size of the Zulu force and requires no further demonstration of their numbers.

Although stunt arrangers John Sullivan and Joe Powell also took acting roles in *Zulu*, their main tasks involved rehearsing the scenes of close combat and training the cast to perform the action convincingly. 'It was continuous action rather than stunts,' says Powell. 'I'd been in the Guards so the fighting

Unit nurse Anne Nickson examines an injury sustained in 'battle.'

with bayonets was what I dealt with. The military experience was very useful to me. We had to set up scenes showing continuous fire but all the rifles were single shot, so we set up a rolling fire with volleys.' Joe recalls that he and Sullivan were assigned to take the Zulu extras away from the main unit to rehearse up in the hills surrounding the location site. 'The Zulus were initially suspicious of us in case we were taking the mickey. After a couple of days they realised we weren't and got into it. After that you couldn't hold them back.' Joe describes his and Sullivan's methods of preparing the Zulus for their part in the action: 'We'd each take a different group to rehearse. We helped the Zulus practising their fighting ability. They were very pleased with that and that gained their confidence. We had the Zulus sitting in a big circle and we'd pull them out one at a time. When they got used to us they would shove their shields in the ground and stamp their feet, challenging us. At the end of the day John and I were knocked out!'

Key to the operation were seven professional Black stuntmen from Johannesburg, all 'boxers, wrestlers and body-building experts,' who were needed for foreground and close-up work while the mass

of Zulu extras were featured in the backgrounds or long shots. Derrick Kain reported on their part in the production:

Able to speak English fluently and with fine physique they were soon on first-name speaking terms with the film crew. In fact, Solomon, Morgan, John and Osborn were found to be born actors.

Osborn Mbili, to single out one of them, is a judo and physical training instructor in one of the municipal African clubs in Johannesburg. He is a First Dan in Judo.[8]

These men were taught the more dangerous work of high falls, necessary for the action which took place on the roof of the hospital. In order to train them for this, a high platform was built on metal scaffolding, with a pile of mattresses placed below it for a soft landing. 'They were afraid at first,' said Stanley Baker, 'and then they thought it was great fun and they were running up to the top of the high rostrum and falling down with great glee.'[9] Ivor Emmanuel recalls: 'they were having great fun until one of them fell off the blanket and ran away screaming.' By the time it came to filming, Joe Powell feels, 'They tumbled off our Rorke's Drift hospital roof quite happily.'[10] Simon Sabela, cast as the Dance Leader in the wedding scene, also did his share of stunts, including a hundred-foot fall from the hillside in which he narrowly avoided hitting a ledge on the way down. 'Nobody would fall down this 30-metre cliff,'

he said in 1977. 'But I felt responsible. If you aimed right you would be all right. So I did it.'[11]

There was some anxiety amongst senior members of the crew about what consequences might ensue if any of the Zulus suffered serious injury during the shooting of the action scenes. Bob Porter recalls: 'I know that Basil Keys, the associate producer, was very worried that if there was any kind of accident where a bayonet from one of the soldiers would go into one of the Zulus, we'd have trouble. But I think because of Johnny Sullivan and Joe Powell playing rugby with them, rehearsing with them – there'd already been one or two minor accidents in training – they were all actors; they were all Stanley Bakers!' Despite the inherent risks, no serious injuries were inflicted on anyone during the filming (most of the bayonets were, like the assegai tips, made of flexible rubber). Bert Batt believes that, 'The warriors enjoyed the shoot except on occasions, rare, when one or two of them got too close to an exploding rifle and had their chests peppered with hot powder.' According to the Information Dossier, one Zulu warrior 'had his leopard skin "loin cloth" pulled from [his] waist during [an] energetic battle scene. "But how can you tell if a Zulu blushes?" asked Stanley Baker afterwards.'[12]

Few of the British actors had any experience with a rifle and bayonet, and all were required to practice their combat skills with Zulu partners. David Kernan had escaped National Service (which had ended in Britain in 1959) by six months, and was also left-handed, making it even more difficult for him to handle a rifle. 'I said, I don't want to do this because I'm left-handed. They said, oh I'm sure we can find a left-handed Black warrior. And indeed they did. He was enormous, must have been six foot six tall. I said hello, and he said [adopting a camp, effeminate voice], "You won't hurt me, will you? I'm very frightened…." He was as gay as they come! It caused quite a lot of mirth. I was absolutely shaking in my boots.' Once trained, the actors and extras entered vigorously into the spirit of the battle.

Derrick Kain was also able to observe at close quarters the work of the expert make-up team headed by veteran Charles E. Parker (1910-1977):

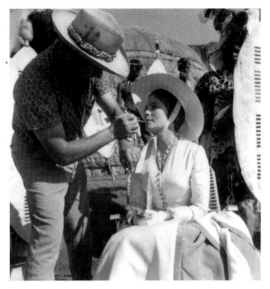

> It was all very realistic, so much so that the unit doctor and nurse went into action after each 'battle' asking if there were any casualties. 'Business is bad,' the doctor remarked jokingly as the 'dead' Zulus cheerfully got to their feet and walked away to prepare themselves for the next call.
>
> Ace make-up artist, Charlie Parker, who worked on *Ben-Hur*, fooled even the doctor with his realistic bullet wound on one of the Zulu's [sic] bodies. The doctor took one look at the warrior and said 'Get him to surgery!'
>
> When he made a close inspection, however, he found no bullet entry or exit holes, only some expert work with – well, with whatever expert things Charlie uses.[13]

Parker seemed to specialise in epics and period subjects: his many other pictures include such blockbusters as *Quo Vadis* (1951), *Ivanhoe* (1952), *Knights of the Round Table* (1953), *Moby Dick* (1956), *Ben-Hur* (1959), *King of Kings* (1961), *Lawrence of Arabia* (1962), *Becket* (1964), *Lord Jim* (1965), *2001: A Space Odyssey* (1968), *Ryan's Daughter* (1970), *Murder on the Orient Express* (1974) and *Star Wars* (1977). However, he was unable to remain on location for the whole of the shoot and after his departure to work on another movie, Richard Mills took over, along with Michael Morris, Bob Lawrance and South African Judy Cadman.

Aside from applying fake blood, one of Parker's main tasks had been to improve the way Michael Caine appeared on camera. Ellen Baker explains: 'He was very blond, almost albino, and photographed badly. Stanley asked Charles Parker, a wonderful makeup artist from MGM, to design Michael's makeup. Charles had done Stanley's makeup on *Knights of the Round Table*. It had got him the part – he walked straight onto the set in it. So Charlie Parker flew out especially to do that makeup for Michael. He looks very pretty in it!' Morris recalls that 'Michael Caine was so fair I had to put fake eyelashes on him and darken them.' These false eyelashes also had to be imported from England.

The battle was shot largely in story order to help maintain continuity. Other scenes were filmed out of chronology, depending on the availability of the cast. Ulla Jacobsson did not arrive until 20 May, shortly after Jack Hawkins, and their scenes, were shot over the next three or four weeks.[14] This interruption in script chronology threatened to create a logistical problem: the burning down of the hospital was due to be shot before their arrival, but as the Witts needed to be seen in and around their hospital mission it was planned to rebuild the set after the conflagration.[15] However, when Derrick Kain visited the location a month into shooting, one-third of the way through the schedule, only one-fifth of the film was in the can. Filming on the battle continued after Hawkins' and Jacobsson's departure and the hospital was destroyed only

A Soldier's Story

Standing in as the soldiers of B Company, 2nd Battalion, 24th Foot were the men of A Company, 5th South African Infantry Battalion. Most were undergoing their National Service for the South African Defence Force. Journalist Derrick Kain claimed that some 135 were used for ten weeks in the film, though eighty soldiers would be a more accurate figure. Kain talked to some of the troops while visiting the location, including Allan Perel and Gordon Atkins, in civilian life both professional actors from Durban, who found the atmosphere of the film set 'just fine, thank you!' ('Zulu: A Film Completed,' *Personality*, 3 October 1963). Among the other conscripts was Don McArthur, who wrote to me from South Africa to describe the experience of filmmaking from the perspective of a 'grunt.'

Stunt director John Sullivan instructs the new recruits.

I was a member of A Company, SAI Ladysmith, seconded to the film as extras while undergoing nine-month citizen force training. We were encamped in a field below the hotel next to a dam and about one kilometer from the film set. This was not particularly comfortable as we were in two armies at the same time and had to perform normal SA Army duties in the evenings after coming off the set. These were company parades, guard parades plus standing guard, and a number of night exercises. Two sets of uniforms had to be kept spotless plus beds made up and the tent kept immaculately clean, not to mention the rifles. Showers and loos were in uncovered hessian enclosures and the former only had cold water for the first three weeks. The kitchen and mess were in a wood and iron prefab. When we arrived many of us contracted a form of dysentery known as 'Berg guts, which was pretty persistent and caused belching H2S.

We rose very early, made our own breakfast and marched up to the set before dawn (daylight hours were very precious) to the make-up prefab where sideburns were stuck on for the day. Thereafter we were under instructions from Stanley Baker and Cy Endfield. We were not required for about 50% of the time (or so it seemed) and we used to laze about in the sun and drink Coke, which was in unlimited supply. When required, however, the activities were pretty intense and we were expected to act like stars. Many scenes were repeated until perfection was achieved and a record number of 23 'takes' of one particular scene sticks in my mind. Most of us were involved in all the action from the defence of the maize bags and biscuit box walls to the final 'firing' squad which did the 'front rank fire, rear rank load' and so on bit. This after singing 'Men of Harlech' (rousing stuff).

The stunts crew were very impressive and 'fell' off the cliff-top on to boxes and mattresses on a scaffold half-way down. Also interesting was the way the cameras ran along a wooden platform next to the running Zulus and in the same direction but not as fast in order to create the illusion of great numbers (I think). When the Zulus attacked the fortresses they were inclined to become over-zealous and run on over us and the barricades, which was a bit nerve wracking at times. They also threatened to strike because the blanks fired at them were wads of paper which stung and in some cases caused minor injury.

Filming the scenes of the Isandlwana aftermath, when we were required to play dead, draped over the sides of wagons, rocks and maize bags, was cause for some amusement. At one point someone swatted a worrisome fly at a critical moment. A friend, Ralf Zunckel, and I were the two riders who came down the distant hill on horseback at the beginning of the film. We had to gallop down the slope bashing bags of fuller's earth to create dust plumes. Ralf was a better rider and went ahead with my mount objecting to the dust in his face, throwing his head and playing up. How I didn't come off I don't know.

Bad weather held up the filming on a number of occasions when cold fronts came through and it snowed on the mountains at least once. As a result of the delays we were told to work over week-ends and on public holidays for very little extra. One of our members, called Rusty, exhorted us to go on strike and ended up negotiating a much better deal. When we were not filming we used to sit around in groups and chat. I hung out with the farmers and learned a lot about practical aspects of agriculture, having graduated in pasture science before undergoing army training. We spent hours scoring the oxen on the set for conformation and condition and every tuft of grass was identified and discussed. We also became experts at spotting dassies (rock rabbits or hyrax) on the cliff face behind the hospital. One of the more pleasant duties was to go up to the hotel and play table tennis with the dignitaries at night and have the odd beer. I seem to remember Cy Endfield, Michael Caine and Tom Gerrard as being very good players.

We only saw the 'rushes' once towards the end when I think they wanted to boost morale because time was dragging. We were very impressed. It was some years before I actually saw the film but my sister was in London when it was released and shouted out when she recognised me, causing some consternation.

once, towards the end of shooting. This is confirmed by David Jones: 'It was what we call a one-timer. When the hospital was set alight, we had to do a scene with Michael Caine and Stanley Baker in the foreground and the hospital burning in the background. When it burnt down it got so hot that we had to move away from it – it was singeing the back of our necks.'

There were other difficulties with shooting the burning of the hospital set, as Dudley Lovell recalled. The VistaVision camera was difficult to operate because the viewfinder was on top of the camera, not at the side, and there was no parallax correction: in other words, the image which appeared in the camera viewfinder was not exactly the one which would be recorded on film, so the camera operator 'had to guess at the correct framing.' He oversaw all three cameras, which were set to run automatically while the burning was in progress, though he constantly had to adjust their position and framing, as he explained:

So before it got dark we lined up our shots on the hospital which was going to be burned down. The main three-strip camera we used around the corner on the main shot, and there was another camera somewhere which we had to run to, so once we started shooting we were running from one camera to another as the fire progressed in the hospital. Well I ran from the main camera … to the VistaVision camera with the viewfinder on top and turned over some film there. We ran back again to the other camera, and in the meantime … somebody had messed about with the other camera. I ran back again, and when I looked at it I thought, my God, somebody's changed the set-up … It was dark by now, it was night, you see. And so I readjusted the frame to where it should be. Then I ran back again to the main camera and we did some more shooting as the fire went on in the hospital and the fire started to burn down. Then we rushed back again and when I rushed back again to the second camera it was panning down on the floor. And I thought, how on earth did that happen? I've done the whole sequence looking down at the ground.

I said nothing about it because there was no time to say anything about it. I panned up again to the right frame and we shot, everything went on shooting and the place burnt down. Now, rushes took about a week to come back … and I thought, now, my God, we're going to find this shot is no good, and suddenly on comes the shot where the camera's now pointing down. There'd been water from hoses and we had a huge puddle and shooting down into the thing was the whole hospital, on fire, beautifully framed in the pond! And they all said to me, oh … you didn't tell us, what a fantastic shot, a beautiful shot, thank you very much indeed! … I nearly had my mouth open to say, I'm sorry about this next shot, and it turned out to be the best shot they had – absolutely fantastic! I never said a word about it. It shows you – it's better to be lucky than clever!

Don't bother looking for this shot in the completed film: it was deleted from the final cut, presumably because the pool of water was not supposed to be there (though it can be seen in the backgrounds of some shots during the night sequence).

At the end of the location shoot, Michael Caine and other members of the unit spent the last night in a club in Johannesburg before

Ulla Jacobsson and Cy Endfield on the studio set at Twickenham.

flying back home to England. The Lufthansa charter flight carrying the cast and crew – along with their souvenirs, including many a Zulu shield – took off on 28 June, exactly three months after the start of filming. The plane did not land at Heathrow until the following day, which happened to be the birthday of Stanley Baker's secretary, Caroline Murray; on arrival at the airport she was presented with a cake in the shape of a Zulu drum. Two days later, the *Zulu* crew was at work again in Twickenham Studios, south of London, for four more weeks of shooting on interior sets.

Studio Shoot

Though he has made a number of other films in South Africa, James Booth was not among the cast members who went on location for *Zulu*. All his scenes were filmed at Twickenham, as were those of Paul Daneman, Patrick Magee, Richard Davies, Denys Graham and Dafydd Havard. 'If they'd taken me and Paul, Pat and all the others, they'd have had to pay our fare to South Africa, paid us a per diem and so on,' Booth says by way of explanation.

Compared to the other major UK studio facilities like Pinewood and Shepperton, Twickenham was rather a modest space. It was once described as being 'like a red barn,' with offices 'which look for all the world like converted bedrooms.'[16] It had only three stages, all quite limited in size: number 1 stage measured 116 feet by 62 feet; number 2 measured only 50 by 40 feet; while number 3 was 95 by 60 feet. (For purposes of comparison, Pinewood's largest stage at that time measured 165 by 110 feet; while Shepperton's largest, then the biggest stage in Europe, was a massive 250 by 119 feet.)[17]

'Twickenham is quite a small studio, but the real hospital was also fairly small,' says Booth. 'It was quite cramped. But it was the most relaxed movie I ever worked on. The actors were terrific, we got on great as a team. For any film you need that kind of camaraderie. We did so much in such a short time that we didn't have time to think about it. It was fun playing soldiers – having a laugh with the Cockney Zulus.' The 'Zulus' James fought in his scenes of claustrophobic hand-to-hand combat were not, of course, the genuine article. 'All the Zulus came from Brixton and Notting Hill Gate. We used to go over to the pub at lunchtime. We had about twenty or thirty – they turned up looking like anybody else. Some they had to "black up" – urbanised Black people are not as dark as those who live in kraals. They were guys off the streets – I think we got them from the Labour Exchange. They all had a West Indian patois and drank Guinness, as I remember. They were all cricket fans – supporters of the West Indian cricket team.'

For the action scenes, James drew on his own military experience. 'I'd been a small arms instructor in the army and the actual combat – coming through the windows and my bayonet fights, all that stuff – I mainly did myself, showed them how to do it, how to use a rifle and bayonet. It's just playing Cowboys and Indians, playing soldiers, and trying to make it look real. You just do what you did when you were twelve, except you've got real fire and real guns and bayonets and Zulus. It was great fun. The problem was, after we'd all been up the pub, the Zulus had had about six pints and it all became a bit real!'

The hospital scenes also involved the extensive use of fire and smoke effects. James explains the tricks of the trade: 'They put a gel, like a napalm jelly, on the wood, and have firemen standing around with fire extinguishers, and they set fire to it, add a lot of smoke and you just run through it. It might look dangerous but there's no danger whatsoever. Maybe a bit dodgy for the Zulus – with all those feathers, they might get seriously singed up the rear end.' Though James denies that it happened, others recall that the fire briefly got out of hand when the studio's roof insulation caught light. Sound editor Rusty Coppleman says: 'They set fire to the straw roof, which was an interior set, which created a fire hazard and set alarms ringing, to the point where the local fire brigade was called out. I don't think they had any input in putting it out – it was put well under control by the security people, but there were lot of

Larry Taylor (Private Hughes)
'The battle scenes in *Zulu* were so good,' said actor and sometime stuntman Larry (Laurence) Taylor of his favourite among the 96 films he claimed to have appeared in. 'It had a good beginning, a bloody good middle and a fucking good end. A lot of films die in the middle.'

Born on 13 July 1918 in Peterborough, Taylor spent twelve years in the army, serving in India and Palestine before the Second World War. After demob he got a job in the film industry, 'teaching people how to be soldiers,' and made his screen debut as a sergeant in *The Captive Heart* (1946). He toured in variety in 1947-48, and appeared in legitimate theatre from the early 50s. Stand-out films in his seven-page CV include – deep breath – *The Glass Mountain* (1949), *Helen of Troy* (1955), *Alexander the Great* (1956), *The Gypsy and the Gentleman, Carve Her Name With Pride, A Night to Remember* (all 1958), *Swiss Family Robinson, Exodus* (both 1960), *Lawrence of Arabia* (1962), *Cleopatra* (1963), *King and Country* (1964), *Khartoum* (1966), *Chitty Chitty Bang Bang, Carry On... Up the Khyber* (both 1968), *Cromwell* (1970), *The Last Valley* (1971), *Brannigan* (1975), *Golden Rendezvous* (1977) and *Zulu Dawn* (1979).

Though many of these performances were bit parts and walk-ons, Larry is always instantly identifiable by his swarthy complexion, sprouting eyebrows and the wide gap between his front teeth. With his army background, he tended to specialise in military roles – never higher in rank than NCO – and when he wasn't acting he found plenty of work as a stuntman with Joe Powell's agency: 'I was a boxer and a karate and judo man. I was a good horseman but I only stuck it a couple of years. I made a name for myself and started playing villains.' Sound technician David Jones recalls that on *Zulu* Taylor was 'the laugh of the unit. He kept our morale up – a good joker.' Bob Porter knew him for many years, and says that despite his proficiency with stunts Larry was not at ease with dialogue; cast for once in a leading role, as Mexican revolutionary Pancho Villa, he had to be replaced when he fumbled his lines.

As Hughes, a patient in the hospital, Larry has probably the longest speaking part of his career. He wears a heavy neck brace throughout: 'The neckpiece made it look good,' he told me. 'I spent ten weeks on location, and another two weeks in Britain to finish off.' He had fond memories of everyone involved in the film, with the exception of Cy Endfield: 'I didn't get on with him. We started out alright but he took a dislike to me. Cy was a good director, but very aggressive.' Larry had close friends in Stanley Baker and Richard Burton – 'whenever they made a film they tried to push me into it' – and benefited from Baker's generosity while on location in South Africa. 'The accommodation was fabulous. I had a room on my own – everyone else was sharing, but Stanley worked a little one for me.' Indeed, Taylor should not have been on location at all: his scenes were originally scheduled to be shot at Twickenham.

Larry kept a memento of the film when he married a receptionist from one of the location hotels who had found additional work as Bob Porter's children's nanny. Larry and Ann returned to South Africa in November 1974 on a late honeymoon and stayed to live (though they were to divorce in 1980). Ann became a leading film makeup artist and their son Rocky a movie stuntman: he was Stanley Baker's stand-in on the BBC TV movie *Robinson Crusoe* (1974) and doubled for Glynn Edwards in an episode of the television series *The Paper Lads*.

Though he continued to appear in local television commercials until well into his eighties, Larry made his last film in 1992 and died, aged 85, of a heart attack on 6 August 2003, a year after I interviewed him for this book. The most notable of his later films is the 1979 prequel to *Zulu*. 'Every actor in South Africa was in *Zulu Dawn*. I was there for ten weeks and only worked eight days. For my money it didn't work – the direction was up to shit and people didn't seem to bother with it much.'

When Rocky Taylor bought an English pub called The Slug on the River, he decorated it with stills from *Zulu*. The shrine quickly developed a loyal following which turned out in force whenever Larry came to visit. 'There was a regular crowd of fourteen people who were *Zulu*-mad and so pleased when I went there,' he said. 'Every time I walked in they'd salute me.'

James Booth and a 'Cockney Zulu' go hand-to-hand.

charred sound-proofing panels on the ceiling of the studio.'

Peter Gill remembers shooting the final scene which plays during Richard Burton's VC roll-call voice-over, as the surviving soldiers are shown walking, standing or lounging around what remains of the mission. Each actor was asked to improvise an appropriate bit of business as the camera panned onto him. 'I'd seen James Booth work at Stratford East,' says Gill. 'I remember thinking that he had a lot of brass neck when Cy took these close-ups of us when we come back at the end. We all had to choose something to do, and I couldn't think of anything so I picked up a Bible. When the camera came to him, he was carving the name of his character in the post!'

All shooting on *Zulu* was completed by the last week of July, under budget and only a week behind schedule despite the weather delays on location. A first rough cut of the assembled footage was screened in London for Joe Levine and Paramount vice-president George Weltner on 23 July. The following day, Levine wrote Endfield and Baker a letter on headed note-paper from his suite at Claridge's Hotel. He could scarcely contain his delighted reaction: 'to say that I am thrilled beyond words, would be putting it mildly ... *Zulu* is my kind of picture. It is big, it has guts and it has all kinds of exploitation values that we can really sink our teeth into.'[18] Work on the picture was far from finished, however: ahead lay another six months of post-production and pre-release preparations.

CLARIDGE'S LONDON

TELEPHONE, MAYFAIR 8860   TELEGRAMS, CLARIDGES LONDON

Messrs. Stanley Baker & Cy Endfield, 24th
Diamond Films Limited, July,
London.

Dear Stanley & Cy:

The shooting is over — the shouting begins! And there is so much to shout about, thanks to you.

Last night, in the company of George Weltner, Executive Vice President of Paramount Pictures Corporation, and Charles Boasberg, President of Paramount Film Distributing Corporation, I saw a rough cut of ZULU and, to say that I am thrilled beyond words, would be putting it mildly. As a business man, I was delighted that you were able to overcome such tremendous obstacles to bring ZULU in ahead of schedule and under budget. As a Showman, I am thrilled beyond words to have a picture that tells a powerful story of a band of gallant British soldiers who, in one memorable day, won 11 Victoria Crosses at the Battle of Rorke's Drift; told against the most breathtakingly exciting background a film ever had, magnificently captured by Stephen Dade's colour cameras.

As an epic, ZULU ranks with BEAU GESTE and FOUR FEATHERS — the acting, of you Stanley, Jack Hawkins, Ulla Jacobsson, James Booth, Michael Caine and everyone else in the cast, is superb.

ZULU is our kind of picture. It is big, it has guts and it has all kinds of exploitation values that we can really sink our teeth into.

On behalf of George Weltner and myself, sincere thanks and congratulations to you, your entire crew, and all who have contributed to what will surely be the big picture of 1964.

Sincerely,

JOSEPH E. LEVINE

P.S. I have just read this letter to George who is as excited about ZULU as I am.

Cy Endfield kept this congratulatory letter from Joe Levine framed behind glass.

Notes

[1] I am grateful to Stephen Coan for information about South African winter weather conditions. 'Bala, and the lake there,' as described by Private Thomas, can be seen in a brief location sequence in Michael Powell and Emeric Pressburger's *The Small Back Room* (1949).

[2] D.N.E. Kain, '*Zulu*: A Film Completed,' *Personality*, 3 October 1963.

[3] Derek Todd, '*Zulu* safari makes camp at Twickenham,' *Kine. Weekly*, 18 July 1963, p. 12.

[4] Hedda Hopper, 'Stanley Baker gets $3 million for movie with a handshake,' *Los Angeles Times*, 27 October 1963.

[5] Interview by John Taylor, 17 January 1990, for the BECTU Oral History Project; audio tape consulted at the British Film Institute Library, London. Subsequent comments by Lovell also derive from this source.

[6] Email to the author, 16 September 2003.

[7] John Huston, *An Open Book* (London: Macmillan, 1980), pp. 357-8.

[8] Kain, p. 103.

[9] Sheilah Graham, 'African Zulus Moral and Proud,' *Citizen News*, 19 August 1963.

[10] Kain, op. cit.

[11] Chris van der Merwe, 'My movies click,' *South African Panorama*, September 1977, p. 25.

[12] Another information pack, produced for American journalists, claimed with distinctly dubious authority: 'Although the film version of the battle was being fought with "harmless" weapons, the Zulus suffered 47 broken-bone casualties and 69 cases of muscle-strain and ligament tears against no casualties for Baker's British forces' (Production Information Guide, pp. 9-10). As a further instance of its hyperbole, the corps of 250 fighting Zulus mentioned in the UK Information Dossier was expanded to 550 for American consumption.

[13] 'Battle scenes from *Zulu*,' *The Natal Witness*, 27 April 1963.

[14] 'Three Now Shoot, Six Prime to Go For Embassy Slate,' *Variety*, 3 April 1963, p. 14; 'Film star arrives,' *The Natal Witness*, 21 May 1963; 'Great film potential in S.A.: Jack Hawkins,' *The Natal Witness*, 4 June 1963.

[15] Picture caption, *The Natal Witness*, 5 April 1963.

[16] A.L. Graham, *World Film Encyclopaedia* (1933); quoted in Geoff Brown with Tony Aldgate, *The Common Touch: The Films of John Baxter* (London: National Film Theatre, n.d.), p. 37.

[17] 'British & Irish Studios,' *Variety*, 29 April 1964, p. 35.

[18] Levine's letter was published in its entirety in the UK trade journal *Kine. Weekly*, 1 August 1963, p. 2.

"LIKE A TRAIN IN THE DISTANCE"

EDITING AND SOUND

> One scene was rehearsed and rehearsed and finally everyone was ready. Dudley Lovell was peering through the viewer of his mammoth camera ready to press the button when suddenly assistant director Bert Batt shouted 'Hold it, I hear bells.'
>
> 'The silence was profound and then everyone heard it. 'Yeah,' said Cy Endfield. 'I can hear it too. Has someone got a transistor radio on?'
>
> Through the loud hailer, Bert roared: 'If anyone has a radio on please turn it off.' Everyone listened. Still the bells.
>
> A lone cow came ambling along the road from the mountains, a bell tied underneath its neck, swinging from side to side as it walked. The culprit was found... so was a Zulu herdboy to shoo the offending animal away from the set.
>
> On another occasion a woman on a horse thoughtfully parked herself on the road right in view of the camera. She would have made a most incongruous background to the 1879 scene. She, too, was asked to 'move on.'
>
> (D.N.E. Kain, 'Zulu: A Film Completed,' *Personality*, 3 October 1963, p. 63, p. 103)

Approximately five thousand feet of Technirama film stock passed through the *Zulu* cameras each day of shooting. A total of 350,000 feet and 560 'slates' had been exposed by the end of the location shoot, for a film which in its final form ran 12,150 feet (a screen running time of 138 minutes). In order to begin cutting and assembling the mass of footage, a month into shooting film editor John Jympson and his assistant Jennifer Thompson flew to South Africa to join the crew.

An editing room had been constructed on site in the Drakensberg production village, equipped with a moviola and cutting bench, while the dining room of the Royal Natal National Park Hotel was converted into a makeshift screening room so that Cy Endfield, Stanley Baker and key members of the unit could watch the daily 'rushes.' The processed footage, however, took a week to return after being despatched to the Technicolor laboratories in London. The delay meant that problems with shots already taken could not be identified and rectified immediately, and retakes had to be arranged whenever the shooting schedule permitted. Endfield recalled that Baker and Michael Caine's first scene together by the river, filmed early in the schedule, had to be reshot:

> Both Mike and Stanley looked awful. There was an exchange of close shots; and I kept running them and running them, and then it dawned on me. Mike's face had been lit from one side to give it shape, as otherwise it tended to get washed out; and Stanley's craggy features had been lit more square on, to flatten them out a

little. So, of course the shots didn't match.

We were behind schedule, but I asked for all these close-ups to be re-shot. Of course there had also been a lot of first-day tension, so this was a most beneficial thing from Mike's point of view, because by now he was much more into the picture.[1]

John Jympson (1930-2003) was sought out by Baker to work on the film after he had edited two of the actor's previous pictures, *A Prize of Arms* and *The Man Who Finally Died* (both 1962); they subsequently worked together again on *Dingaka* and *Sands of the Kalahari* (both 1965). Jympson had entered the industry at the age of 17 and learned his trade in the cutting rooms at Ealing Studios, where he worked as an assistant on such classics as *Scott of the Antarctic* (1948), *Kind Hearts and Coronets* (1949) and *The Lavender Hill Mob* (1951). While doing his National Service in the Royal Air Force he was put in charge of making training films. Returning to the industry, his first assignment as full editor was *Suddenly, Last Summer* (1959) and John's many other pictures include *A Hard Day's Night* (1964), *Where Eagles Dare* (1968), *Kelly's Heroes* (1970), Hitchcock's *Frenzy* (1972), *Little Shop of Horrors* (1986), *A Fish Called Wanda* (1988) and *Mad Cows* (1999).

Bob Porter describes Jympson as 'a fantastic aid to the film – one of the best cutters in the business. I was in contact with him every day. I had this second unit crew, and Johnny and I worked closely in the cutting rooms. Anything that was hiccupping in the cutting rooms, he would call me in, put me on the seat and show me the shot that was needed to go into whatever cut he had. Myself and the crew would go out and organise it and we'd bring back whatever he wanted in that second cut.' John's editing of the movie was, he says, 'a masterful job, a wonderful job, considering the complexity of the battle scenes.'

Assistant editor Jennifer Thompson had also worked with John on *A Prize of Arms*, as well as on *The Treasure of Monte Cristo* (1961), *Stork Talk* (1962) and *It's All Happening*

Mr and Mrs John Jympson.

(1963). Among Jennifer's other films before her early retirement from the industry in 1965, when she married the distinguished sound editor Jonathan Bates, were *Whistle Down the Wind* (1961) and *The Loved One* (1965). 'It's very different now, but in those days you marked up the script for the editor, looked after the trims and generally looked after the editor,' she says of the assistant's duties. 'You had to know exactly where the trims are so they could be found instantly if the editor needed something back. On location the editors worked seven days a week. I remember there were masses of shots of charging cattle for Johnny to play with.'

Sound editor Rusty Coppleman describes the collaborative nature of the cutting process. He believes that, as a producer, 'Stanley was on a learning curve, so he was particularly prepared to listen to John Jympson. John had a very good brain, a good feeling for the film and for films generally. I think Stanley would use John as a sounding board. From time to time we would have screenings of cut material, and both Stanley and Cy would be involved in those screenings with John and Jennifer, who was usually taking notes. So whatever discussion they had about possible changes or altering the balance of a sequence in terms of using a close shot or a long shot or whatever, that would almost be done under John's guidance but with some input, certainly from Cy if not Stanley. But Stanley wasn't the sort of man to insist on his close shots being used, or "Stay on me, stay where the money is!" – I don't think he had that sort of paranoia about his career.'

When John left *Zulu* towards the end of post-production to move on to another film, Jennifer was left with Endfield to supervise the making of the opening and closing titles. The main title sequence had proved a major headache for the production team. Several different possibilities were mooted before the final version, in which all the credits appear simply as yellow letters against a black background, followed by the dispatch from Lord Chelmsford which dissolves to the scene of the battlefield at Isandhlwana. The title itself is displayed in blazing letters, zooming towards the camera over a shot of the Zulus on a hill overlooking the battlefield.

Throughout all the various script versions the aftermath of the battle had been conceived as a pre-credits sequence; in John Prebble's first Treatment it had even been envisioned as a background to the titles. The battle itself was never intended to be shown, though the Treatment suggested that the sounds of the battle be heard over shots of circling vultures. In all the screenplays, the first image the audience is meant to see is a close-up of a lizard on a rock, followed by a panning shot across the hand and face of a dead British soldier. The legs of a Zulu then come into shot as the warrior reaches down to pick up the man's Martini-Henry rifle. The camera pulls back to show more bodies of the slaughtered troops and the Zulus arrayed on top of the hill. (In the Original draft, one redcoat remains alive and runs in terror from four pursuing Zulus only to be brought down by an assegai in the back; this did not survive the various script revisions.) A commander then sends a messenger, Red Garters, to report the victory to the king. The main titles were intended to appear over images of Red Garters as he runs across country to deliver the news. In the film as it stands, only the final shots of the messenger (played by Ephraim Mbhele) arriving at the royal homestead are retained.

During the editing, a further variation on the idea of a pre-credits sequence was tried by splitting the scene of the wedding dance into two parts, with the titles sandwiched in between. But this was soon discarded, as

Stanley Baker explained to a BBC radio interviewer after the film had already proved itself at the box-office:[2]

Q: How did it work?
A: It didn't! That's why we scrapped it and decided to begin right at the beginning with the title and credits. You remember we opened the film with a tribal dance – quite a long sequence, about four and a half minutes of it. Our first idea was to split it up, so we showed the first three minutes before the title and credits and the rest after we'd told the audience what they were seeing. But then we ran it through and it seemed not only pointless but confusing.
Q: You found it more effective to show the dancing all in one piece, after the credits had gone up?
A: Much more.
Q: Well it obviously did the film no harm, because I believe it turned out to be one of the big box-office blockbusters of all time.
A: Yes, it's been quite extraordinary, not only in Britain but all over the world. We're still getting the receipts in from most parts of the world and they're quite fantastic.
Q: Why did you try this pre-credit idea in the first place?

A: Well, I'd seen it used in one or two other films and it seemed to give them a sort of sharp kick-off.
Q: *Ah, yes, and like so many good cinema tricks it's now been worked to excess.*
A: Yes, just an over-worked gimmick, and in most cases I find it's just a gimmick for gimmickry's sake. As a novelty it was fine at first but now it's become routine, well it's just a bore.

Yet another alternative credits sequence had been scripted by Prebble and submitted to Endfield in early September, when post-production was in its final stages. This shows Prebble's experience as a radio dramatist: it called for several off-screen vignettes establishing the reaction in Britain to news of the massacre at Isandhlwana, while the credits would appear against period prints setting the scene of Victorian London. The following is the complete script of this unused (and in all probability unrecorded) sequence.[3]

1. BACKGROUND: CONTEMPORARY (1879) PRINT OF THE HOUSES OF PARLIAMENT

Effects: Murmur of voices, coughing, echo effect of the Commons chamber. Then a tense silence.

VOICE
Her Majesty's Secretary of State for War has received the following dispatch from Lord Chelmsford, Commander-in-Chief of her forces in Natal Colony, South Africa.
(pause)
I regret to report a very disastrous engagement which took place on the 22nd January between the Zulus and a portion of Number Three Column. The Zulus came down in overwhelming numbers, and in spite of gallant resistance made by five companies of the First Battalion, 24th Regiment, and one company of the Second Battalion, two guns, two rocket tubes, one hundred and four mounted men....

FADE VOICE to sound of MORSE KEY
and CUT TO

2. BACKGROUND: CONTEMPORARY
(1879) PRINT OF FLEET STREET

FADE MORSE KEY to

VOICE
Terrible Defeat of the British. Annihilation of the Column. The Colony in Danger. From your Special Correspondent:
(pause)
The disaster at Isandhlwana is without any parallel. I do not know about the survivors any more than has been publicly stated. I have been told by Mr Witt, the Lutheran missionary of Rorke's Drift that a thousand soldiers left their camp at Isandhlwana to attack more than ten times their number of Zulus, and after having shot away their ammunition fought for their lives with the bayonet…..

3. BACKGROUND: CONTEMPORARY
(1879) PRINT OF LONDON CLUBMEN READING

Effects: Angry rustle of newspapers

FIRST VOICE
Wiped out? British soldiers? Impossible!

SECOND VOICE
Fellow Witt says here the Zulus were fighting for liberty. What?

THIRD VOICE
Nonsense! Damned fuzzies!

FIRST VOICE
Where is the confounded place? Fawcett, pass the map, there's a good fellow.

4. BACKGROUND: CONTEMPORARY
(1879) MAP OF NATAL COLONY

FIRST VOICE
What was it? Eye-sand….

SECOND VOICE
…Wahnah, or something…

CAMERA closes on the spot marked Isandhlwana and Rorke's Drift

THIRD VOICE
I don't believe it, you know. There's some mistake….

FLAME spurts from the spot marked Isandhlwana and over the map into the title:
ZULU

Like the other pre-credits sequence described by Baker, the principal disadvantage of this material is its excessive length. A prologue of this kind would not only have delayed considerably the start of the main narrative, but would also have detracted from the sense of the isolation of the soldiers at Rorke's Drift. Confining all the action to the immediate environs of the mission station and the twelve or so hours of the battle, its build-up and aftermath, gives the film an Aristotelian unity and a dramatic concentration which would have been dissipated by the inclusion of scenes set on another continent and at a later time (the news of Isandhlwana did not reach England until nearly a month afterwards). The one element which was ultimately retained from this material was a device which does not appear in any of the screenplay drafts: the letter of dispatch from Lord Chelmsford.

Sound Recording and Mixing

'They were ideal conditions for recording sound,' says sound technician David Jones of filming in the Drakensberg Mountains. 'We had full control of the set. We didn't have any problems with background sound.' Jones was the boom operator in a four-man sound team led by recordist and mixer Claude Hitchcock. The 'sound camera' operator was Derrick Leather and the sound maintenance engineer Fred C. Hughesdon. All the 'live' sound from the main unit was recorded by this group; the second unit under Bob Porter shot without direct sound, its material either being additional coverage of first unit scenes or action and long shots for which sound effects would be added later. David particularly remembers the 'amazing' noise of the Zulus' rhythmic feet-stomping: 'It really got you in the ribs, that sound. A lot of dust was coming up.'

Claude Hitchcock had himself been a boom operator on one of Stanley Baker's early films, *Hell Below Zero* (1954), and subsequently worked extensively for Hammer Films as well as on such major international productions as *Born Free*, *The Blue Max* (both 1966) and *The Dirty Dozen* (1967). 'People like Claude Hitchcock would always come back with what they thought the sound editor would need for the final dubs,' comments Rusty Coppleman. 'Frequently they would go out on their own when no-one was working and record sound, atmospheres, set noises and so on.' As the sound editor on *Zulu*, Coppleman was based at Twickenham Studios while the unit was out in South Africa, servicing the unit by synchronising the rushes with the location sound and sending them back to be viewed by Endfield and his team. Once the company had returned to England, Coppleman and John Jympson worked in adjoining cutting rooms: 'I was in the studio and working alongside John, looking at whatever he was doing and working out what sounds I'd need, making sure I got them from the original sound recording or from sound libraries, or working out what I'd need to create. That's the way sound editors work normally – you were part of a team, with your individual responsibilities. John seldom ever interfered with the sound editing, though there were certain things he might request; he had a good sense of what was right and what was wrong and he trusted me. We did seven or eight films together.'

The sound editor's job, explains Rusty, 'involves replacing all sound that is unusable for final mixing as well as recording sounds that are deemed necessary. That encompasses things like atmospheres and removing any extraneous noises like modern traffic or aeroplane noises in a period film, or replacing dialogue that is obscured because of wind or any other noise. So what you have to do is start with a clean canvas. Certainly the most important thing is dialogue where it's necessary and any relevant movement like footsteps or the clatter of cutlery, the noise of eating or drinks being poured out, or general atmosphere like a clock ticking in the background. "Sound designer" is just another smart name for sound editor: I don't think they do anything today that a competent sound editor wouldn't do in my day.'

Starting out in the film industry by working in laboratories, Rusty became an assistant picture editor on *Alf's Baby* (1953), then worked for Ealing Studios before going freelance. The first film on which he became a sound editor – 'much against my better judgement' – was Joseph Losey's *Time Without*

Left to right: David Jones, John Sullivan, Cy Endfield, Bert Batt, Ulla Jacobsson.

Sound recordist Claude Hitchcock (left).

Neil McCarthy (Private Thomas)

'We had a piano in the canteen and everyone sang around it in the evening,' recalls Zulu's assistant editor Jennifer Thompson. 'Neil McCarthy had huge hands – outstandingly large fingers – and used to play the piano beautifully.' Instantly recognisable for what Ellen Baker fondly calls 'That Face' – long, horsey, with high cheekbones and a heavy jaw – McCarthy owed his unusual looks to acromegaly, a condition of the pituitary gland which causes excessive growth of the facial bones, hands and feet. 'I seem to have spent most of my life playing outcasts or sub-normals,' he told journalist Ivan Waterman. 'People say the most unpleasant things about the way I look anyway. Luckily I'm not a sensitive soul and it's better to be noticed than not at all' ('Monster of a role for Neil,' News of the World, 19 July 1981).

'What the 'ell do you think you're doing at a time like this?'

McCarthy was born in Sleaford, Lincolnshire, on 26 July 1933. The son of a dentist, he was educated in Dublin, developing a talent for languages (including Welsh) and gaining his first acting experience in the university dramatic society. He became a teacher of French and Latin in Nottingham but later took a professional interest in the theatre. He was assistant stage manager of the Oxford Playhouse, and when its production of Lysistrata moved to London he went with it and decided to become an actor. From the early 60s, Neil made many appearances in plays, films and television series, including small roles in The Criminal (1960) – as one of the two prisoners Stanley Baker beats up in his cell – and the B-movie Solo for Sparrow (1962), which also gave work to Michael Caine. Later

he was an early casualty among the commando team in Where Eagles Dare (1968) and, encased in heavy makeup, he played the monster Calibos in Clash of the Titans (1981).

'Sometimes I worry about growing old and having no one to love me but I've enjoyed my independence,' he told Waterman on the set of the latter. 'Something tells me I wouldn't make a good husband. But women don't exactly chase me in any case.' Neil was living in Greenwich at the time, with his cat and Alsatian dog. He never married and died, apparently of motor neurone disease, in Hampshire on 6 February 1995. Most of his later films, which included low-budget remakes of Agatha Christie's Ten Little Indians (1989) and Arthur Conan Doyle's The Lost World (1992), were made in South Africa.

Michael Caine prepares to deliver his lines off-camera for the benefit of Stanley Baker. Microphone boom operator David Jones stands at top left; continuity girl Muirne Mathieson sits with her copy of the script behind Cy Endfield, alongside John Sullivan.

Pity (1956), and among his fifty or so other films are *El Cid* (1961), *55 Days at Peking* (1963), *The Fall of the Roman Empire* (1964), *Frenzy* (1972), *Midnight Express* (1978), *Victor/Victoria* (1982) and *The Adventures of Baron Munchausen* (1988). Like Jympson he worked again with Stanley Baker on *Dingaka* and *Sands of the Kalahari*, and met and married his wife while on location in South Africa for *Tokoloshe* (1965). He retired after making *The Englishman Who Went Up a Hill and Came Down a Mountain* (1995).

'The one important thing with *Zulu*,' he says, 'is that because it was set in Africa, you couldn't just add English countryside birdsong or anything that wasn't indigenous to the area. Silence over there is really silent – there's a very occasional bird-tweet or insect noise, so those things were either recorded on location or obtained from sound libraries.' He lists some of the other sound effects that had to be created in post-production: 'When they turned the carts over to create the defensive wall, there was the original sound that needed additional weight. Also the sound of the fire in the hospital, straw crackling, body falls – when a stuntman takes a body fall he doesn't fall heavily, so we had to add all the body falls and make them sound authentic; spears going into

bodies, and in many instances replacing the gunshots of the Martini-Henrys. These things are rigged by armourers not to fire bullets so we had to create the sound of the guns being fired. Fortunately the libraries are well-equipped with a lot of sounds of old weapons, probably recorded over a number of years, and people like Bapty's the armourers have a selection of weapons that can be hired for both front of camera and behind the camera if you want to do some recordings.'

A great deal of post-synchronisation (also known as dubbing or 'looping') had to be done by the actors on their dialogue, along with the addition of a few other voices off-screen: 'I remember working with people like Glynn Edwards and Neil McCarthy – his very gentle voice when the calf is ill; certainly Stanley, Michael Caine and Patrick Magee. I hadn't heard of Michael then; he seemed alright, wasn't obnoxious or anything, turned up on time and did what he had to do. My own voice is in there somewhere, saying "Here they come again!" or something similar. It was pre-recorded in the theatre and then laid in at an appropriate place and mixed in with the rest of the dialogue tracks. Sometimes we had a problem where, with a change of angle, you get a big change in the level of background noises. With the river scene we had to create a cohesive single soundtrack for the water and replace the dialogue.'

The voices for the wounded and dying Zulus following the final assault were provided by Coppleman and his four assistants, one of whom almost passed out from hyperventilation because of breathing in and out heavily for the length of time needed to get the recording. Rusty and his team also had to enhance the Zulus' foot-stamping and shield-banging, for which they borrowed some shields and assegais which Baker had brought back and was keeping in his garage at home. The film is rich in incidental sound effects, such as the noise of wind and creaking wood in the tense interludes between Zulu attacks. Some sounds affect the viewer at a virtually sub-conscious level, such as the low, throbbing pulse underlying the wedding dance just prior to the arrival of the messenger bearing news of the massacre at Isandhlwana.

Perhaps the most memorable sound effect that Rusty created was the eerie noise of the approaching Zulus beating the hafts of their assegais against their shields, which Bromhead describes as being 'like a train in the distance.'[4] And that is exactly what it was, as Rusty explains: 'I got a soundtrack of a train going over rails and I used the mass beating of the shields and cut them into synch with the train's rhythm. I also used a deep thunder rumble under it to give it a deep bass; this was even more resonant than the train noise, which carried some high frequencies as well. It was coming in and out on the winds. So when Michael Caine hears it, we've only just heard it and then we hear it a little bit more later. So that was a combination of sounds that worked very successfully: the shields were on top of the sound, but the base sound was a train on rails. I remember another sound editor, Norman Wanstall, ringing me and saying, "Congratulations, I thought it was a great soundtrack, but the Zulus approaching was really imaginative." I thought it was lovely for another sound editor to be able to say that.' Bob Porter recalls how this scene was received by audiences: 'Stanley and I went to many, many premieres all over the world, and every time that train sound started, you could practically see the hairs go up on the back of the audience's necks – that really made them sit up and listen.'

For effects such as this, Rusty was given complete creative freedom by Endfield and Baker. 'The fact that they may not have liked everything I did would come out at different rough-dub screenings. They'd say, could you change that, or possibly enhance that? I don't think we had a difference of opinion or anything I had to change at the final dubbing. Also, I'd keep them informed during preparation about my intentions so I wouldn't hit them with any surprises. Sometimes I'd surprise myself because the results on screen would come across so well. I don't think I was ever disappointed with anything I added to the film. It was the effectiveness of the use of silence, particularly after the Boer farmers go off to defend their homes and Stanley is screaming after them, "Come back, we need you!" And then there's absolute silence for a moment until Sergeant Bourne says "Nobody told you to stop working!" It would have been so easy to spoil that moment by adding activity from the cattle in the background or even from a bird twittering; but it was just open air.'

In the final stages of dubbing, Rusty had to call in additional help from Len Walter and his assistant Alan Strachan to lay up and edit the dialogue tracks in order to meet his deadline. A temporary mono sound mix or 'rough dub' was created by Stephen Dalby at Twickenham Studios, and what was meant to be the final mix was made at MGM-British Studios in Borehamwood by J.B. Smith (whose affectionate nickname was 'Banana Fingers' because of his large hands) and his assistant Ray Palmer. But for the 70mm release prints they had in mind Endfield and Baker wanted a six-track stereo dub, comprising outer and inner left and right, centre and surround channels. According to Rusty, full stereo sound effects were not needed 'until the final chants; also the song "Men of Harlech" against the Zulu chanting. The most important scenes, where the use of stereo was paramount, were the approach to the final battle and the final battle itself.' In November, at Rusty's request, the producers therefore decided to re-record the last two reels in stereo. To do this they went to the man universally recognised as the British film industry's most skilful and experienced dubbing mixer, Gordon K. McCallum (1919-1989), based at Pinewood Studios.

McCallum was born in Chicago but had moved to the UK as a child. His first screen credit was on Michael Powell and Emeric Pressburger's *I Know Where I'm Going!* (1945), and for the next forty years he seemed to work on virtually every film that passed through Pinewood's sound department, his last being *Supergirl* (1984). The first stereo film he worked on was the epic *El Cid*: 'For me, the horizons opened up as we came to stereo – so much more opportunity,' he said in a 1988 interview.[5] Stephen R. Pickard, who worked at Pinewood from 1968 to 1974, had this to say about McCallum in a posting on the *Film Score Monthly* internet website: 'What an inspiration of a man Gordon K. McCallum was. I got to know him very well, and I am sure my prolonged passion for audio was because of him. At every opportunity I went into Theater #2 to watch him work. He was an extremely emotional man and would get very frustrated when the quality of the audio tracks did not meet his impeccable standards. He was very demanding on his co-workers ... He would often flare into a rage, disappear into the bathroom to cool off and then return to work as if nothing had happened. Everybody used to call him "Mac" and people held the very highest respect for him.'[6]

Though *Zulu* is not among the 320 titles listed in his filmography on the Internet Movie Database, McCallum was nonetheless crucial to its final sound mix. Rusty Coppleman recalls Mac's skill at mixing the tracks: 'We were handed mono tapes from the location, and when we came to making a stereo mix at Pinewood we had to fill the screen right across with the Zulus and their chants. McCallum was very, very adept at the controls on his desk. We laid up parallel tracks of the same thing, very slightly out of synch. The mono tracks we had and were using as our main dub were set centre screen. What McCallum was then doing was punching in and out of the induna doing his shout and the responses coming off the secondary tracks, which he then spread across the screen, left speakers and right speakers. During the

whole of that little sequence before the final charge of the Zulus he was punching in and punching out, and he timed it perfectly after a couple of rehearsals so that when we played it back there was just one induna doing the shouting – "Bayete!" – and then the responses came from 4,000 guys [sic] coming across the screen, and it was spine-tingling – really imaginative dubbing. Stanley was so pleased, he was delighted when he heard the stereo dub. He was totally knocked out by it; he said, "Fuck me, Rusty, that's what we should have had all along!" When J.B. heard McCallum's stereo mix even he admitted he couldn't have done it so well.'[7] Cy was equally impressed, and later tried to get part of the money paid to MGM for the first mix refunded for the budget.

Rusty is rightly proud of his own work on the film: 'When I see it on television I don't know what else I could have done for it. Maybe with modern digital equipment for bending sound I could have done something different with it, but bearing in mind that sound recording wasn't as sophisticated as it is now, I'm certainly not ashamed of it.' Sadly, the 35mm print used at *Zulu*'s world premiere was only monaural. A few four-track stereo 35mm prints were among those used for the British general release two months later, but the six-track 70mm prints were only used abroad until a UK reissue in 1972 was launched with a 70mm print at the London Casino Cinerama theatre. The few remaining mono 35mm prints still in circulation are not well served by modern multiplex sound equipment, which is generally ill-suited for anything but Dolby and its equivalents. Even more unfortunately, the film's original magnetic stereo masters now appear to be lost: the soundtrack on the Region 2 Paramount DVD release seemingly derives from a 35mm stereo print, but MGM's Region 1 DVD is in plain mono. Any reader who knows of an extant 70mm print is urged to contact the publishers of this book.

Notes

[1] Elaine Gallagher, *Candidly Caine* (London: Robson Books/London Weekend Television, 1990), p. 75.

[2] BBC radio interview, circa 1964 (programme title unknown); audio tape courtesy of Ian Knight.

[3] These script pages were enclosed with a letter from John Prebble to Cy Endfield, dated 5 September 1963, referring to discussions which had already taken place about this sequence and offering suggestions on where the prints to be used as backgrounds might be located.

[4] This line was added to the script in the first set of revision notes, as preserved in John Prebble's files. The sound is described as a 'distant, rhythmic, pumping.'

[5] Interview by Alan Lawson for the BECTU Oral History Project, 11 October 1988; transcript consulted at the British Film Institute Library.

[6] http://www.filmscoremonthly.com/ (posted 14 June 2003).

[7] In response to a question I posed on the Message Board at http://www.filmscoremonthly.com/ Stephen R. Pickard wrote: 'At the time Gordon McCallum mixed *Zulu*, Dubbing Room Theater #2 was only equipped to mix in 3/4-track stereo. The "spread" to 6-track was probably done at Technicolor who were equipped at that time with a simple formula that created "inside" left and right, derived from information in the other channels. This was done on all 70mm releases that did not have a "discrete" 6-track mix provided. Discrete 6-track dubbing could only be done in the US at the time' (posted 10 December 2003). Pickard believes that the final stereo mix was created *after* the British premiere run, but it was recorded over four weeks beginning 11 November 1963.

"SING!"

14
MUSIC AND NARRATION

MEN OF HARLECH

Men of Harlech stop your dreaming
Can't you see their spear points gleaming
See their warrior pennants streaming
To this battle field.

Men of Harlech stand ye steady
It cannot be ever said ye
For the battle were not ready
Welshmen never yield.

From the hills rebounding
Hear their cry resounding
Summon all at Cambria's call
The mighty foe surrounding.

Men of Harlech on to glory
This shall ever be your story
Keep these burning words before ye
Welshmen will not yield.

(Lyrics adapted for *Zulu* by Ivor Emmanuel and Cy Endfield)

Throughout the duration of filming, the Zulus' songs and chants were heard echoing around the Drakensberg location. 'Every morning the Zulus would come up from the camp in the valley where they stayed,' recalls Jennifer Thompson. 'They used to march the Zulus up the valley and they'd go past my room. Their singing was the most wonderful sound.' Joe Powell remembers that the Zulus 'used to run to the set, and chant all the way. After rehearsing all day or at the end of a day's shoot, they'd run *back* chanting.'

Visiting Zululand while setting up the film, Bob Porter was introduced to a great many traditional Zulu songs by Chief Buthelezi's mother, Princess Constance Magogo ka Dinuzulu, a tribal historian. Porter recorded performances of these for reference when it came to shooting those parts of the film which had been planned to include Zulu music – notably the wedding dance and the 'battle of song' (to use Rusty Coppleman's apt phrase) prior to the climactic assault. All the material of this nature heard in the film was recorded on location during shooting by Claude Hitchcock and his sound team, and mixed back in London by Rusty Coppleman and his collaborators.

The tapes of Zulu songs, which Bob brought back to England, also turned out to have another use. Cy Endfield gave the tapes to John Barry, who had been hired to compose the orchestral score for the film. 'One song was very repetitive,' says Barry. 'Doo-ap, doo-*ap*, doo-ap, doo-*ap*, and so forth. I liked that repetition.' The rhythm of this song – part of which can be heard in its original form in the wedding dance scene – gave Barry the inspiration for the principal leitmotif of his score, which he combined with a more traditional Western arrangement: 'The theme was a mixture of that and having spent three years in a military band – that martial sound.' In his sleeve notes to the soundtrack album, Endfield commented that Barry had 'used the themes of traditional Zulu music, [and] elevated them with his musical skill into thrilling and musical effects to support and give character to some of the mighty moments from the film's dramatic content.'[1]

Born on 3 November 1933 in York, England, Barry was the son of a Yorkshire entrepreneur, Jack Prendergast, who owned a chain of eight theatres in the region. The young John developed his fascination with movies by regularly visiting and working in his father's cinemas, combining this with a love of music to develop an early ambition to compose film scores. Three years of National Service in Egypt allowed him to hone his skills in a military band, and after leaving the service he found his way into the music industry.

Forming his own group, The John Barry Seven, John developed a distinctive sound which combined orchestral and jazz influences with a pop beat. He and the band enjoyed a number of hit records and regularly appeared on television pop shows such as *Drumbeat* and *Oh, Boy!* as well as in the 1958 feature film spin-off of another TV show, *6.5 Special*. He helped make a star of young singer Adam Faith when their song 'What Do You Want?' became the first of a series of top-ten hits for the pair. Faith repaid Barry by having him hired to compose and conduct the score of his low-budget film vehicle *Beat Girl* (1960). Its twanging guitar sound launched John's career as a movie composer, and after scoring several other minor British films he was asked to arrange the theme for a million-dollar action picture intended by its producers as the first of a series based on a popular character created by novelist Ian Fleming. The film was of course *Dr. No* (1962), and as well as being a box-office smash in its own right, with 'The James Bond Theme' it created a new trend in pop-influenced movie scoring.

Barry was assigned to compose the whole score for the second film in the Bond series, *From Russia With Love* (1963), which had a title song written by Lionel Bart, perhaps best-known as the composer/lyricist of the theatre and film musical *Oliver!*. Bart was also a friend of Stanley Baker's (Ellen Baker recalls that Stanley had been approached to play the role of Bill Sykes in *Oliver!*) and was asked by Baker to compose the score for *Zulu*. Sensing that he was not the right man for the job, Bart referred Stanley to Barry instead, having been impressed by his work on *From Russia With Love*.[2] 'It was the first big epic movie I'd done,' says John of *Zulu*. 'I'd never done anything in that vein before. I'm always interested when a subject comes up that I haven't done before. The others had been small, black-and-white movies. I read a screenplay and then met with them [Baker and Endfield] when they came back. I remember it as a very happy association.'

Once he had heard the tapes of Zulu songs, John set about orchestrating and Westernising the rhythms to suit a modern symphony orchestra. He told his biographer, Eddi Fiegel: 'I guess my role model for that was Prokofiev when he did [Sergei Eisenstein's 1938 film] *Alexander Nevsky*. He took very basic Russian folk tunes and set them in a large dramatic scale. There's a whole history of that with Stravinsky and Bartok and I was thinking along those lines.' Nonetheless, he credited the Zulu source material itself as his principal inspiration: 'those original themes were so good, so very basic, so wonderful and simple. Just two chord changes and yet so *good*.'[3]

No doubt partly because of *Zulu*, John was subsequently commissioned to write the music for a number of other films with African settings, including *Mister Moses* (1965), *Born Free* (1966) and *Out of Africa* (1985). His prolific career – he has composed over 120 scores – includes such varied material as *King Rat* (1965), *The Chase* (1966), *The Lion in Winter* (1968), *Midnight Cowboy* (1969), *Walkabout* (1971), *King Kong* (1976), *Robin and Marian* (1976), *The Black Hole* (1979), *Body Heat* (1981), *The Cotton Club* (1984), *Dances with Wolves* (1990), *Chaplin* (1992) and *Enigma* (2001), as well as a further ten Bond movies. For another film made and set in South Africa, the 1995 remake of Alan Paton's

Cry, the Beloved Country, John actually re-used the main theme of *Zulu*, albeit with a very different orchestral arrangement: suitably slow and melancholic rather than martial and epic. 'I don't remember using the theme again for *Cry, the Beloved Country*,' he told me on the phone from his home in Oyster Bay, New York. 'It's such a simple thing – just four notes. It's quite possible that I did it subconsciously.'

What is often overlooked is the brevity of Barry's score for *Zulu*: his music lasts for less than twenty of the film's 138 minutes. '*Zulu* was a short score, but it was enough,' he says. 'In no way did I skimp on it. I never got the feeling that it needed more. For an action movie it was a very wordy piece, with a lot of people spouting off. With the Bond movies I was always asked to score car chases. I said no, let's hold off rather than flogging a dead horse. I've always been a great believer that music should be doing a very specific thing. I hate the phrase "background music" – I believe in foreground music. With the Bond movies it really came out at you. Subtlety isn't an option: you hit the audience.' Indeed. Many of us vividly remember being hit by the *Zulu* soundtrack when we first heard it. The sweeping strings and pounding percussion over the opening titles immediately made one sit up and take notice, and *Zulu* remains among the most powerful of all epic scores.

To record it, John required the largest orchestra he had yet used: around seventy pieces. Uncertain about the pace of the recording schedule, he asked the advice of a veteran Hollywood composer. 'In England you had no rules about how much you should be recording in a session. I remember phoning up Henry Mancini. He told me to work at eight minutes of music a session. So we probably used only three sessions, at the CTS Studios in Bayswater, which are no longer there. It was an old church hall and had a natural sound to it – an echo in the sound of the room.' CTS Studios was the locale for many a film recording session; the recording engineer for *Zulu* was Eric Tomlinson and the orchestra was booked by Barry's regular 'fixer,' the late Sidney Margo. In an interview with Eddi Fiegel, Margo described the special equipment John needed:

> John used every conceivable type of percussion on that... He went down to a repository in Archer Street where they kept unusual musical instruments and said, 'I want African, African, African everything.' So in the end we had drums, bongos, bell belts and boobams. Boobams were like mini-tablas all laid out in a row, like a piano keyboard in half tones, but you played them with drumsticks. In the end, that studio was so packed with gear, there was hardly room for the orchestra with all that stuff in there. Also, normally you have three percussionists. On *Zulu*, John had six as well as a wacking great orchestra. But John always had large orchestras; he never stinted. He always said: 'Either you get the orchestra or I don't do it.' And it made sense, because if you start skimping on the orchestra, you can't get the colour you want.[4]

The rest of the orchestra for *Zulu* comprised four horns, three trumpets, four trombones, one tuba, and forty-eight strings. Several different versions of the soundtrack were issued, some in mono and others in stereo, but all based on the same recording sessions. Albums were released in the US by United Artists and in Britain by the

Now you too can do the Zulu Stamp! Choreographer Lionel Blair demonstrates the steps in the UK Pressbook.

independent label Ember, of which Barry himself had become creative director in 1963.[5] In whichever version it appeared, the soundtrack sold very well, says Barry. Enormously popular, the soundtrack has seemingly never been deleted, but, like the sound masters for the film itself, the original master tapes of the album recording sessions, as well as the arrangements for the score, have apparently been lost.[6]

As the score only took up one side of the album, the B side contained a further set of variations on the Zulu songs. A keen follower of pop music, Stanley Baker had proposed to Barry that he create modern instrumental versions of some of the tribal music. Barry therefore produced six additional tracks, which were recorded at Olympic Sound Studios by engineer Keith Grant.[7] They included 'Monkey Feathers,' adapted from the same wedding song which formed the basis of the orchestral score, and 'Zulu Stamp.' These two were recorded by The John Barry Seven and released as a single by Ember ('one of Britain's most "with it" recording companies,' according to the film's UK Pressbook). Baker also asked the popular dancer and choreographer Lionel Blair – whose first film appearance had been at the age of nineteen in Cy Endfield's *The Limping Man* (1953) – to devise the steps for a dance to go with 'Zulu Stamp.' The Stamp was promoted on television, in night clubs and even in schools, while a printed insert in the single's sleeve provided an instructional diagram so that listeners could learn the steps and join in at home (see illustration). At the supper party at London's Mayfair Hotel following the film's World Premiere, Baker and Blair showed other partygoers all the right moves. 'They had everyone up doing it,' remembers Maureen Endfield, while trade paper *Kine. Weekly* suggested that 'it was not difficult to imagine that it will oust the twist.'[8]

The other piece of music associated with *Zulu* which has captured audiences' imagination is the rendition by the British soldiers of the 'Men of Harlech', led by Ivor

Stanley Baker and Lionel Blair do the Zulu Stamp at the after-premiere party.

Lionel Blair leads Catherine Milinaire, Terence Stamp and Leticia Adam in the Zulu Stamp.

Emmanuel's Private Owen to rally the troops' morale in the face of the Zulus' own intimidating martial chants.[9] The performance of this 'ancient Welsh hymn' on location caused some consternation when, according to Joe Powell, it was realised that the company had not got copyright clearance on the lyrics. Emmanuel and Endfield therefore rewrote the song, 'to make it more relevant,' says Ivor. 'Years later Cy rang me up one day to ask me to confirm that he had written them. It was my song but I said okay, not realising that there might be a few bob in it.' (At this point in our telephone interview, Ivor began to recite and then sing his version of the lyrics!) Ivor also sang the song at the film's Welsh premiere: 'I went to quite a few premieres with Stanley – in Cardiff and in Ireland – and we got well-oiled every time.'

The recording of the song made on location was, however, unusable in the final sound mix. Among the cast only Ivor and David Kernan were trained singers and it had not been sung all the way through in any single take; so, like much of the dialogue, the song tracks had to be replaced by sound editor Rusty Coppleman. To re-record the song, Baker literally went back to his roots. He, Ivor, Rusty and publicist Geoff Freeman travelled one weekend to Stanley's home town of Ferndale in South Wales, where Ivor was to lead the local male voice choir, the Imperial Glee Singers, in an open-air performance in a valley near the village, watched by an audience of proud relatives, friends and neighbours. 'The choir drank about seventy-five crates of beer that day,' jokes the singer.

Rusty recalls the technical problems he faced on this occasion: 'When we went down, the sound department provided just one Nagra – a recording machine, but also a player, which has a synching device in-built which gives you the correct recording speed. Unfortunately we didn't have any other means of playing off the tracks: we had to play the original track so that the choir could hear something they could sing to. Stanley hunted around and through one of his contacts he found somebody who had a shop which sold tape recorders. He got them to open up and he rented a tape recorder that could run the quarter-inch tape that we had brought with us. That's the recorder we used to play off our original tracks. The conductor, myself and Ivor had headphones, and I would give a signal to the conductor to bring Ivor in at the relevant moments so he could sing in close-up while the choir was singing around him, and a point for cut-off where we'd just hear the choir with his voice within it. It was a lash-up job, but it's the one that's in the movie. Stanley was so pleased that we had a party in his working men's club that night – I got very drunk! Stanley put me up in his hotel suite because his family had insisted on him going home. I liked Stanley – he was one of those people who was very loyal to the people he thought he could trust.'

Recording the Narration

There remained one other crucial component of the *Zulu* soundtrack still to be recorded. Having rejected the notion of a sound-only sequence playing under the opening titles, Endfield and Baker needed an alternative way of setting the scene. John Prebble's device of

using a letter of dispatch from Lord Chelmsford to Queen Victoria, informing Her Majesty of the disaster at Isandhlwana, was retrieved from the rejected script pages. A closing narration, reciting the list of Victoria Cross recipients, had already been introduced into the final shooting script, incorporating the explanatory epigraph which appeared on the front page of every screenplay draft. Both this and the text of Chelmsford's letter, along with the closing VC roll, had to be read in a suitably authoritative voice-over – but whose?[10]

Rusty Coppleman recorded a temporary version for editing purposes, which remained in place for several weeks before the right person was found: Stanley's old friend Richard Burton (1925-1984). 'Not only did Richard readily agree to do the job,' recalled Endfield, he 'refused to take a fee for the work, which the picture couldn't have afforded in any event – testimony to the depth of friendship and loyalties between these two Welshmen of such excellent sentiment.'[12] Having met while appearing together in Emlyn Williams' play *The Druid's Rest* in 1943, when Burton was seventeen and Baker fourteen, the two remained close, lifelong friends, despite having their share of ups and downs. One of the downs was Richard's desertion of his first wife Sybil for Elizabeth Taylor, which had led to a temporary falling-out when the Bakers sided with Sybil and made clear their disapproval of the affair. Ellen Baker believes that Richard agreed to record the *Zulu* narration gratis out of a sense of guilt and to rebuild his relationship with Stanley. According to writer Anthony Storey, Baker had flown especially to New York to persuade him to do it. 'Burton kept Stanley waiting three days before meeting him,' says Storey. 'The shit.' Shortly before his own death, Stanley himself said affectionately: 'It's impossible to remain angry with Richard.'[11]

When the time came to make the recording, Burton was staying in Paris with Elizabeth Taylor, trying to avoid the massive media interest which had sprung up following their affair which began during filming of the just-released *Cleopatra* (1963). Endfield travelled to Paris with editor John Jympson (Cy's passport records that he passed through Orly Airport on 20 and 21 September 1963). Once this was done, the tapes would be brought back to London for Coppleman to lay into the soundtrack: 'My job as sound editor was to take

Ivor Emmanuel (Private Owen)

It is perhaps as much the presence of Ivor Emmanuel in the cast as the historical significance of Rorke's Drift for the South Wales Borderers which endears *Zulu* to Welsh audiences. 'I only did it originally to sing "Men of Harlech,"' he says. 'But Cy said, you can't just stand up and sing it out of the blue, it has to be established.' So the popular Welsh tenor was given a major supporting part as Private Owen.

Born on 7 November 1929 in Port Talbot, the son of a steelworker, Ivor grew up in Pontrhydyfen, Glamorgan, the same home town as Richard Burton and only ten miles away from Stanley Baker's home in Ferndale. Tragically, his entire family, apart from himself and his brother, were killed during a German bombing raid when Ivor was twelve. He became a coal miner at fourteen and two years later won a scholarship to study engineering at Neath Technical College, but he soon left to follow a long-held ambition to be a singer and actor. Emmanuel successfully auditioned for the London stage production of Rodgers and Hammerstein's *Oklahoma!* and later followed it with appearances in *South Pacific* and *The King and I*. He joined the D'Oyly Carte Opera Company in March 1950, remaining with the company for eighteen months, and after a six-year run in *Plain and Fancy* at Drury Lane he won a leading role in *Damn Yankees* at the Coliseum. Following a three-month theatre stint in Liverpool at Sam Wanamaker's New Shakespeare Theatre, Ivor was offered a job as resident singer on Granada Television's Welsh afternoon programme, and he was later given his own, enormously successful BBC TV series, *Land of Song*. His other stage appearances included the lead in a short-lived Broadway show, *A Time for Singing*; among the lucky few who saw it was Bruce Sachs, editor and publisher of this book.

Ivor's appearance in *Zulu* came about after a chance meeting with his old friend Stanley Baker. 'I got to know Stanley as early as 1949-50,' he says. 'In fact I danced with his wife. Stanley said, excuse me, this is an excuse-me dance, took her away and married her! I used to go to a

restaurant in London called the White Elephant. It was quite a privilege to get in, as all the big names used to go there, Sophia Loren and so on. And one night there were Stanley Baker and Cy Endfield. Stanley said, we've just been talking about you. I hadn't seen Stanley for some time and they invited me to a party and offered me the film.' *Zulu* is Ivor's only film appearance, but he might have had a longer big-screen career if he had followed Baker's advice. 'I sang on location when Joe Levine came there. He said to me, my God but you can sing. He didn't know I was mainly a singer. He said he wanted to use me in a musical, and Stanley said, you should keep in there, but of course I never did. I was basically a singer; I didn't have any ambitions to go into films. My roommate did: Michael Caine. He used to say, God, I want to be a film star – look at the money they get! At that time I didn't know him, but he knew me from television. He's a different kind of actor than Richard Burton or Stanley Baker: he's got this way about him.'

Ivor bought a holiday villa in Spain in 1972, moving there permanently when he retired ten years later. He says now that he doesn't miss being in showbusiness: 'I've fulfilled my dreams and more. I'd done everything and there was nowhere else to go, so I could leave it quite happily. I've been in six musicals in London, including a Command Performance, had my own television series for seven years and been on Broadway, but the one thing everyone says to me is, oh, *Zulu*'s on again! There are some who say it's the greatest film ever made, but I found it a bit slow – I don't know if it was because I wasn't in it enough.'

it and place it in the film, so that the key words hit certain shots,' he says. Rusty worked with John to match the narration to the images, 'by closing pauses or opening them up.'

In the manuscript for an unpublished article entitled 'The Coal Miner's Son' (a reference to Burton rather than Baker, though the description would have fitted Stanley too), Endfield described the intrigues by which he had first to avoid the pack of paparazzi lying in wait to observe the actor's every move – in the event Burton hid in plain sight by eating breakfast in the restaurant of the George V Hotel – and then to avoid getting drunk with Burton, whose early-morning meal of scrambled eggs was accompanied by three bottles of chilled white wine, each of a different vintage. Declining to join him and in an effort to save himself from indulgence, Cy instead showed Burton a 'wine divination' trick with three glasses.

From the George V, he, Burton, Jympson and Richard's agent Harvey Orkin made their way in the actor's chauffeur-driven car to 'a more remote location on the fringes of Paris where the sound-recording studio had been booked by *Zulu*'s editor for an 11.30am start.' Here, in Cy Endfield's own words, is the director's account of the rest of what turned out to be a memorable day:

On arrival, first stop was just inside the studio entrance, where, as in every Parisian film studio it seems, the bar-room can be found. He was greeted with enormous gusto and cries of love from the Patron and his wife, and at least three or more stiff brandies were quaffed by each of them before bonhomie and auld-langsyne were satisfied, and we moved out then up the staircase to the Sound Recording rooms.

Again, Richard was known to the staff and once this further set of effusions was completed and Richard met our film's editor John Jympson, work began.

It was only two pages of narration I'd extracted from the screen-script, which Richard glanced through, then tonelessly read out, in a manner that gave nothing away. Then he studied the text again, marking it out here and there.

Very politely he suggested a few deletions, mostly single word changes – each well chosen, none damaging the sense or dramatic intent, but invariably improving intonation.

I had in truth been moderately worried about the danger of pomposity, even pretentiousness, that this format of bracketing a visual work with explanatory narration might bring. Suffice to say, this concern fled the moment I heard Burton's treatment of the words.

In fact, I was thrilled and more than thrilled. Increasingly during recent weeks as *Zulu*'s editing had progressed, I'd begun to see the emergence of a major work, even that rarest event in one's directorial experiences, i.e., intention not only realised, but surpassed. And now this last touch, the Burton narration even on run-through exceeding all expectations and hopes. In Paris, what can one say but 'magnifique'.

More, it was a relief to find one was communicating with a man who had wholly objectified the task, did not personalise criticisms. His ear was impeccable in all instances. Occasionally I found the better word or phrase, just as often or more he did, as mutual vocabulary searching pyramided into the finding of the perfect word for each instance in the text. The same was true for his performance – suggestions for nuances of vocalisation, pauses here, an elision there, shadings of emphasis or de-emphasis, crescendo or decrescendo were accepted by him, ego-free about source.

Richard Burton in characteristic pose.
(Tony Earnshaw Collection)

And in an astonishingly few minutes a level of finesse was reached, agreed perfect, a judgement which has not changed for me throughout hundreds of occasions of listening to it over a more than 25-year period.

It was a wrap, time to leave – but [Richard] held back, asked tentatively, 'didn't you say we had this Studio until one o'clock?' (all had gone so smoothly it was only 12.30). He asked them if they were okay for tape. Of course they were. And what ensued for the next half-hour was remarkable.

Settling back into his seat at the microphone desk, he began reciting softly. Unsurprisingly with something from Dylan Thomas's *Under Milk Wood*, in fact conducting a duet conversation, then adding other roles, speaking all parts from memory, a virtuoso rendition. Breaking off, he asked for playback. Satisfied with what he heard, he launched into an ad lib medley: first, slabs of Shakespeare recited with an eloquence of meaning, and a resonance of sound and intonation familiar – but exquisite in its uniqueness, in this moment of spontaneous

```
THE SECRETARY OF STATE FOR WAR
                    February 11th 1879

I regret to report a very disastrous
engagement which took place on the
morning of the 22nd January, between the
Armies of the Zulu King Cetewayo and our
own Number 3 Column, consisting of
Five Companies of the 1st Battalion,
24th Regiment of Foot, and One Company of
the 2nd Battalion, a total of nearly
1,500 men, Officers and other Ranks.
The Zulus, in overwhelming numbers, launched
a highly disciplined attack on the slopes
of the mountain ISANDHLWANA, and in spite
of gallant resistance, the Column was
completely annihilated.
```

enjoyment. Then – ad lib – into other writings – the range of his memory seemed endless, from fragments only a sentence long, to lengthy epistles, items known and unknown to me, in each excerpt or piece the sensibilities and affects therein maximised by the man's most awesome, effortless yet forceful recitational Art. Indeed, if there is a separate art called 'Recitation' – and there must be, for this was it – here it was being rendered at some pinnacle of its capability to communicate, to stir, to reach mind and soul of listeners.

Some performing skills have been labelled minor by our culture – say juggling, ventriloquism, stilts-walking, shado(w)ography, and I imagine some would say 'recitation' and – woe – even conjuring. Yet selected practitioners of any of these minority Arts by reasons of some rarity of endowment, devotion, and extraordinary effort, transcend society's designation to stand equal with the more widely approved virtuosi artists who transport us using, e.g., violins, pianos, theatre and/or writing materials. Given the capriciousness and subjectivity of modern criticism, there will be disagreement as to rating of Richard Burton the Actor. But Burton the recitationist, on that day in that half hour, revealed to me that there stands a Himalayan range at its far horizon. …

All the tapes of that day of work were sent on to London, but when post-production was complete, the Burton recitation tapes were missing. Lost treasure.

The exit from the studio, via the bar-room again, brought a repeat of the love and libations exhibited upon Burton's arrival. The amount of morning alcohol was already impressive, but its only effect on his demeanour was an increase of mellowness and general loquacity.

We had about four more hours for our plane at Orly, but Richard insisted on being lunch host for myself and Jympson. He took us to a paradisially located restaurant, consisting of an automated roll-back canopy over an ascending set of exquisitely coloured floral terraces engraved in a hill along the roadside. Its ambience was unique, I'm certain the loveliest and most visually affable I'd ever visited. Richard of course was well-known here too, and the usual bevy of waiters and other attendants matched every whim and need with fulsome response. Richard whispered in the wine-waiter's ear (or vice versa, I can't quite recall) and three bottles of musky vintage 1943 claret, Mouton Rothschild I think I was told along with the tale that 1943, the year acknowledged as the greatest in French wine history, was also the year when the occupying Nazi army confiscated the entire crop and pressings, sent them all back to Germany. Except – well, naturally, a few hidden cases of the one being served us at that moment. Three bottles of the last dozen or so in all the known cellars of the world. And the greatest. And the costliest.

Whether it was the knowledge being imparted, or the actual uniqueness, my palate – a primitive detection instrument at any time – responded. I hadn't drunk the martinis that started the lunch nor the brandies still ahead but I drank my share of the '1943'.[12]

Notes

[1] Ember NR5012, March 1964.

[2] See Eddi Fiegel, *John Barry: A Sixties Theme: From James Bond to* Midnight Cowboy (London: Constable and Company), p. 117.

[3] Ibid., p. 118.

[4] Ibid., pp. 118-9.

[5] See the postings by Bob Bryden and 'woolston' on 7 and 10 June 2003 on the Message Board at http://www.filmscoremonthly.com/.

[6] John Clark, http://www.rorkesdriftvc.com/ Discussion Forum, posted 22 September 2002. According to Clark, 'In 1974, Barry left England to live and travel abroad. He couldn't take everything with him, so he left some antique furniture and the manuscripts for all his scores with his former business manager. When he returned in the 1980s, he discovered that the former business manager had died – no trace of his furniture or scores has ever been found.' Clark also comments on what he regards as the defects of both the original soundtrack album recording and its 1999 'reconstruction' by Nic Raine: 'the rerecording lacks all the drive and crashing power of the original – besides being plagued by orchestrations and tempos unfaithful to Barry's original.'

[7] 'Geoffers' http:// www.filmscoremonthly.com/ Message Board, posted 13 June 2003. See also Fiegel, p. 119. According to the liner notes to the 1988 Silva Screen reissue of the original recording (FILM CD 022), four of the six 'Zulu stamps' were original compositions by Barry and only two were based on 'authentic Zulu melodies.'

[8] 'Long Shots,' *Kine. Weekly*, 30 January 1964, p. 4. See also Observer, 'Commentary,' *The Daily Cinema*, 27 January 1964, p. 3.

[9] In his chapter on *Zulu* in *Past and Present: National Identity and the British Historical Film* (London: I.B. Tauris, 2005), James Chapman summarises the history of the song, which 'commemorates the defence of Harlech Castle (Gwynedd) in 1468 against the Earl of Pembroke. The music was first published in 1784; there are different versions of the lyrics, the most common English versions being by W.H. Baker (1860) and John Oxenford (1873), as well in Welsh by "Talhaiarn" and a German version by Heinrich Möller. The version sung in *Zulu* is peculiar to the film ... One of the delightful quirks of the scene is that all the men know these non-standard lyrics and join in.' (Chapter 9, footnote 44; as the book has not yet been published at time of writing, no page numbers are available for this reference.) I am informed by *Western Mail* film reviewer Gary Slaymaker that 'Men of Harlech' is the anthem of Cardiff City Football Club, and that the version sung at matches is the one written for *Zulu*.

[10] The device of ending the film with a recitation of battle honours in voice-over was introduced in the second set of revision notes, as included in John Prebble's script files; the narration was intended to begin over the shot of Margareta walking towards the soldiers in the ultimately deleted final scene (see Chapter 3). Bromhead was originally to be shown first, but the final order of the VC roll-call in the film is as follows: Schiess, Allen, Hitch, Dalton (added to the final draft screenplay after he was belatedly identified as the eleventh VC), 612 Williams, 716 Jones, 593 Jones, Hook, Reynolds, Bromhead and Chard. The last shot as described in the shooting script, not unlike that in the finished film, has Chard standing by the body of a Zulu, lighting a cigar and planting the Zulu's spear and shield 'upright into the earth' as a 'gesture of respect.'

[11] Lester David and Jhan Robbins, *Richard & Elizabeth* (London: Arthur Barker, 1977), p. 33.

[12] Cy Endfield, 'The Coal Miner's Son,' unpublished manuscript, 1988; reproduced courtesy of Maureen Endfield.

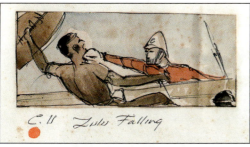

For many years I had assumed that no storyboards had been created for *Zulu*. But in 2009 I was contacted by Henry Coleman, who revealed that he was in possession of a set of original storyboards for one sequence, the Zulus' assault on the hospital, which had been discovered and acquired by his brother. This sequence involved elaborate stuntwork (some of it deleted in editing) on the hospital roof set, hence the need for shot-by-shot pre-planning. I am grateful to Henry for giving permission to reproduce the surviving storyboards here in their entirety.

330 A. C.U. Windridge & Bromhead.

330 B. Bromhead Fires at Zulus on End of Roof, Windridge Climbs onto High Roof.

330 C. C.U. Bromhead Firing

332 C.U. Bromhead as he pulls back Bayonet Zulu falls through Frame. Bromhead moves forward to Ridge of Roof.

331. Bromhead reloads as Zulu attacks down Roof. ONE SHOT Bromhead Lunges with Bayonet

333 Full Shot of Roof (Also 321) and intermittent Cuts.

334 Windridge Shouts to Bromhead "GET DOWN"

334 a Bromhead Fires at Zulus hacking hole thro' Roof. Bromhead now at Ridge of Roof.

334 B. Zulus Hacking Hole thro' Roof One falls Shot.

341. Thatch ignited STUDIO.

341 Zulus Stagger back from flames.

Windridge Butts 2nd Zulu with rifle

342 a Bromhead Fires at Zulus through Smoke.

342 B & 342 D. Bromhead fires again and proceeds down far side of Roof.

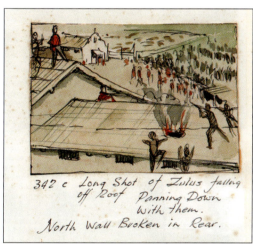
342 c Long Shot of Zulus falling off Roof Panning Down With them. North Wall Broken in Rear.

343 Windridge deals with Last Zulu.

343 A Windridge Runs along Roof

343 B. Windridge Slides Down Rope.

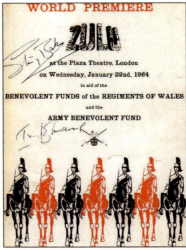

Top: Members of the crew pose following completion of the last set-up filmed on location. Wearing spectacles are Cy Endfield (foreground) and Stephen Dade. At right are Jennifer Thompson and Bob Porter. *(Courtesy of Jennifer Bates née Thompson)*
Left: Cover of the World Premiere souvenir programme, signed by Stanley Baker and Ivor Emmanuel. *(Courtesy of Bill Fine)*
Far Left: Costume design for the uniform of the 24th Foot. *(Courtesy of Maureen Endfield)*
Bottom: Reserved-seat ticket for the World Premiere. *(Courtesy of Royal Regiment of Wales Museum)*

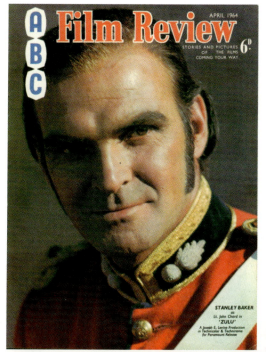

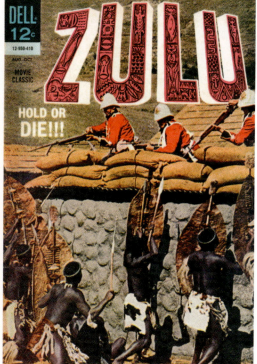

Above: Magazine and comic covers from the 1960s. The image of Gary Bond on the cover of Tyne Tees Television's listings magazine *The Viewer* is not in fact from *Zulu* but from the 1968 TV series *Frontier*. Overleaf (reading across the double page): actual frame blow-ups taken from a 70mm work print by assistant editor Jennifer Thompson. As these are 'trims' (frames cut from the beginning or end of shots) they do not correspond exactly to the shots used in the film. Shifts in colour between frames are caused by differential fading. Note the rubber bayonet bending on impact in Frame 14.

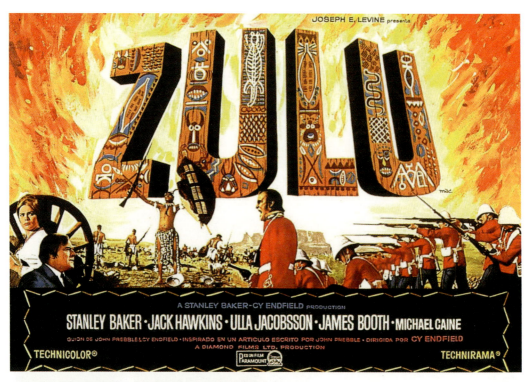

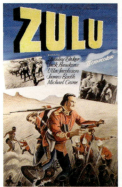
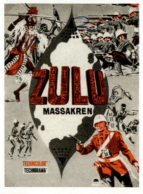

Advertising from around the world.

Above and below right: Spanish posters.
Far left: Hawaiian poster.
Left: Swedish flyer.
Below left: Australian poster.
Below middle: Australian poster.

Opposite top: original UK quad poster.
Opposite below: Japanese poster.

For other international ad materials, please visit www.zulufilmstore.com

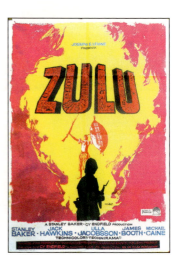

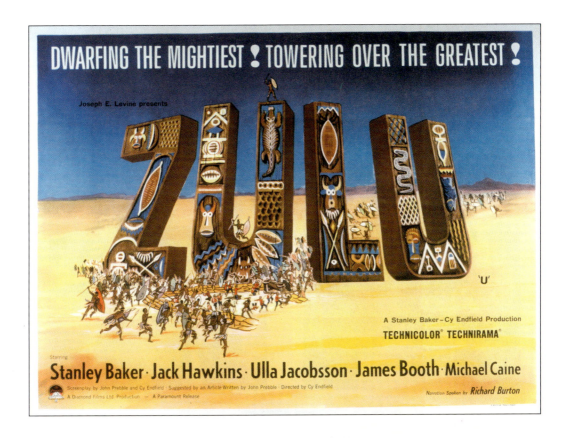

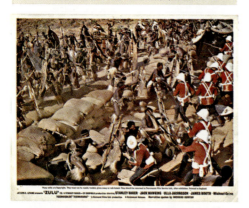

Original UK lobby card set from first release (1964).

Original UK lobby card set from re-release (1972).

Film buffs will be familiar with the stencil colouring used for old lobby cards. But the 'tinted' effect of these West German lobby cards is highly unusual and provides a striking contrast with the design of the UK lobby cards. *(Courtesy of the Mike Siegel Archive)*

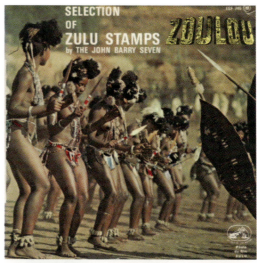
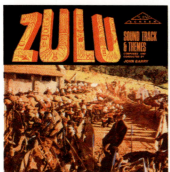
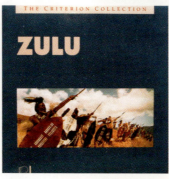

Top: spin-off records from Italy and France. Above left: CD edition of the soundtrack album. Above middle: US laserdisc. Above right: 78 r.p.m. single on John Barry's own record label. Below: US and UK DVD covers. Right: Music sheet for one of the six modern dance tunes composed by Barry for the B-side of the soundtrack album.

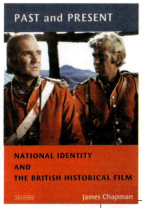

Above left: Magazine cover from 2013.
Top right: Books by British film historians.
Below: Posters for exhibitions of memorabilia organised by Henry Coleman.

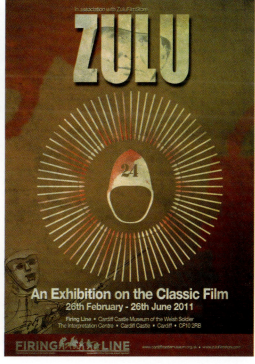

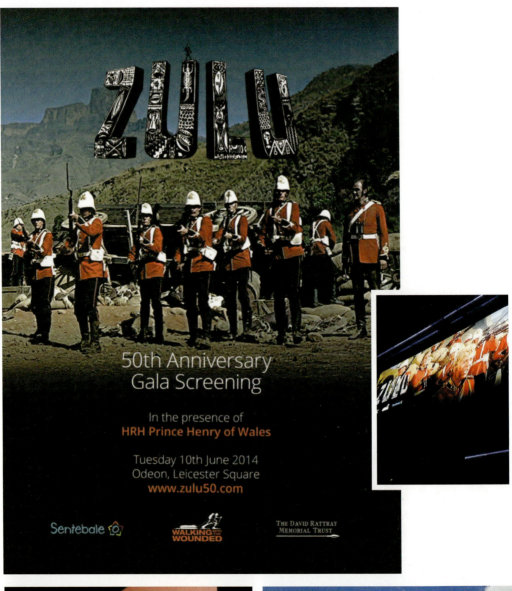

Images from the fiftieth anniversary charity gala at London's Odeon, Leicester Square.

PART III:
VICTORY AND AFTERMATH

The script directions for this deleted scene read: 'CORPORAL ALLEN breaks into a thick, retching cough. He spits. Before the spasm has passed a ZULU, who has been bayoneted at the bags above, falls across the CORPORAL – He yells in terror. HITCH leans forward and with great difficulty drags the dead warrior away. He then claws at the CORPORAL's head.' Hitch then echoes Allen's earlier comment on his inability to fix a bayonet properly: 'You slovenly Corporal you!'

CENSORSHIP

> [We] know what sort of film it would be to show to a race that has not yet reached the level of civilization that we have reached ... things which they cannot understand should not be shown to them ... there are some films which can be exhibited much more safely to a white child of fourteen years than to an adult Bantu.
> (South African Minister of the Interior, 1963; quoted in Keyan Tomaselli, *The Cinema of Apartheid: Race and Class in South African Film*, London and New York: Routledge, 1988, p. 22; ellipses in original.)

From 1951, when the X certificate (which originally allowed admission to over-sixteens only) was introduced, the British Board of Film Censors awarded three categories of certificate. The others were U, meaning that the film was passed for Universal exhibition (all ages were permitted entry); and A, meaning that the film was recommended for exhibition primarily to adults, and that minors under the age of sixteen had to be accompanied by a parent or guardian. Because the A and X implied the exclusion of part of the potential audience, it was desirable for most films to receive a U, which did not then have the stigma of suggesting a film meant largely for children, as it tends to have now. The subject matter of *Zulu*, however, presented several obstacles to its gaining a U.

Since the early years of sound it had been customary, though not compulsory, for British film companies to submit the screenplay of a proposed production to the Board for approval before shooting had commenced (and sometimes before the picture had even been 'green-lit'). In this way any potential censorship problems likely to be faced by the completed film could be addressed at the outset, and material unlikely to be passed could be altered or eliminated according to the script examiner's advice. This was a procedure encouraged by the Board's Secretary – the member responsible for the day-to-running of the Board, and its chief examiner – who in 1963 was John Trevelyan. Widely respected in the industry, Trevelyan had first joined the Board in 1951, been appointed to the senior position in 1958, and had established a reputation as someone inclined to deal leniently with what he perceived to be films of quality and filmmakers of integrity. Script examination effectively allowed censors to participate in the creative process when their suggestions for alterations were accepted, and some were also tempted to write as critics in their judgements on individual films.[1]

The final shooting script of *Zulu* was submitted to the BBFC in late February or early March 1963, and the Board's Reader's Report was delivered on 8 March. The authors of all such reports were identified in internal documents only by their initials, and even today researchers are requested not to disclose their identities. One of the Board's current examiners, Craig Lapper, explains the policy of the time: 'Because the five examiners then employed by the Board were advisory only – responsibility for classification decisions lay at a higher level – they were supposed to remain anonymous to outsiders. Accordingly, the Reader's Report was only seen internally by its other members.'[2]

The three-page report went into considerable detail on what the examiner felt to be the screenplay's 'danger' points for censorship purposes. Its principal concern was, predictably, the extensive use of bayonets in the battle scenes:

> The suicidal stand is the sort of thing we have often seen in films before, except that we do not usually have so much bayonet work in close shot, and that is going to be a problem here if they [the filmmakers] don't look out. It seems to me that there is bound to be too much of it for an "A" in the script as presented to us. Lunging the bayonet in, often from below with a cutting-up movement, wrenching it out again, bloodstained weapon in frame – the lot, over and over again, and often in c.s. [close shot], and usually accompanied by the inevitable screams. I append a list, to show that I am not exaggerating, but it is by no means complete, as I think a general direction to take care will have to suffice at this stage.

The examiner went on to note the particular instance of Schiess bayoneting a Zulu after his rescue of Chard:

> This kind of thing does not seem to be comparable to bow-and-arrow work in westerns: the film is meant to be a realistic presentation of the carnage of even old-fashioned warfare; moreover, this is what the audience are going to come to it for, not the preaching about 'God, isn't war brutal,' which (or something like it) the characters do say from time to time.

Other potential problems in the matter of violence included: the script's description of Zulu warriors advancing over the dead and dying bodies of their comrades ('We do not normally care for this sort of shot, especially if we can see details'); the Witts' carriage rolling over the fallen Zulu's body as it leaves the Royal homestead (again, 'We don't like this sort of shot'); Corporal Allen's retching cough from his chest wound ('Coughing blood, I wonder? If so, let them be careful'); the presence of corpses on the battlefields, both in the Rorke's Drift scenes and in the opening tableau showing the aftermath of Isandhlwana; the depiction of the makeshift operating theatre and details of Reynolds' surgery (including the lancing of Hook's boil); and the effects of the hospital fire. The examiner also considered that the climactic volley-firing at close quarters would give 'scope for a lot of non-"U" shots.' Her anxiety about what the camera would show also extended to the soundtrack: 'the company should be warned against too many blood-curdling screams of agony.'

Violence and bloody death were not the only cause for concern, however. The Report also remarked on the dance of the half-naked Zulu virgins in the wedding sequence ('We have seen this kind of thing often enough before, but when it comes into c.s. it is not unknown for us to cut it') and on the scene of Margareta's rough treatment by a soldier in the hospital ('care should be taken about what we see, no bare breasts'). The soldiers' coarse language was considered 'pretty mild on the whole for "A" … "Near the knuckle" lines are singularly few,' though objection was raised to Hook's use of 'Get knotted' ('If we can continue to resist this I shall be glad'), 'Mucking idiot' and another, more ambiguous exclamation ('I suppose "Stuff me with green apples" is a respectable sort of "stuff," like a roast?'). The more common swear-words were not deemed likely to present a serious problem unless the filmmakers were to ask for the lower certificate: 'If they should say they mean to aim at a "U", they should take out all the "bastards" and practically all the "bloodies" *now*. It is no good trying to have it both ways. Personally I don't see all this bayonet stuff in the "U" at all.'

The examiner also took the liberty of pronouncing critical judgement on what she saw as the script's artistic merits and demerits. Particular exception was taken to the Witts: 'I do not believe in these two, who are stock film characters: Otto preaches pacifism and gets drunk; his attractive daughter is afraid of men because of something unspecified which happened to her in England. However, we may be thankful for small mercies: no one has time to rape Margareta.' The Report also objected to the script's 'stereotyped characterisation' of Chard and Bromhead: 'We always have to have someone who is full of colour prejudice, and always jealousy about who is in command and why. In real life, there is a time and place for this, heaven knows, but about the one time and place there *isn't* is when there is imminent danger of death. However, this is not censorship, I just mention it with regret.'

On the whole, though, the examiner was upbeat in her assessment of the film's potential: 'I don't want to be unfair to this script, however, which should be a terrific spectacle if enough money is spent on it and enough care taken in marshalling the spectacular scenes of the Zulu phalanx advancing. For all I know, the fighting scenes, which occupy most of the script, are historically accurate; and there is effective use made of contrasts of battle sounds with birdsong and Welshmen singing.' A handwritten note added to the bottom of the typewritten report, dated 11 March, suggests that another examiner was moved to present

> NOTES ON SCRIPT OF "ZULU"
>
> In general the film should be suitable for the "A" category. Caution necessary about close shots of bayonetting, blood-curdling screams of agony and nasty shots of blood and wounds (particularly in the "operating theatre") and shots of corpses should not be nastily gruesome.
>
> Comments on points of detail:-
>
> Page 1 Scene 2 — The script direction refers to "still, twisted shapes of violent death". They should not look too nasty for children to see.
>
> Page 2 Scene 9 and 15-16 — Here we have the dance of the Zulu virgins, who are half-naked. If the conventional dance, it should be all right, but we have from time to time found it necessary to cut this kind of thing. There should be no unnecessary camera emphasis, especially in close shot on breasts and bottoms.
>
> Page 9 Scene 44 — We might have trouble with the shot of the buggy being pulled over the body of the fallen warrior. This might upset children.
>
> Page 11 Scene 47 — The phrase "wading in the river up to their asses" may be all right, but we might possibly ask for an alternation.
>
> Page 21 Scene 59 — We would not want to see any close or nasty shots of the lancing of the boil.
>
> Page 39-40 Scene 80 — The words "mucking" and "muck around" are used in this scene. The more dubious one is "you mucking idiot". We are always doubtful about the use of this word in this kind of way since it is so completely obvious that it is a substitute for "fucking". "Muck around" is used without this kind of interpretation.
>
> Page 42 Scene 80 — We think that Hook's line "Bet she's never had a man warm her up" may pass, but if it were possible to have some modification it might be helpful.
>
> Page 45 Scene 82 — Here the sick man grabs Margareta's dress "instinctively" and rips it down the front. What we see should not be censorable.
>
> Page 64 Scene 149 — The assault comes forward "trampling its dead into the earth". This suggests potentially nasty shots, and we would not want to see anything really nasty.
>
> Page 78 Scene 220-1 — The descriptive material in these two scenes suggests that they might give us trouble. Care should be taken not to have nasty screams, or too much blood, especially if the film is in colour. If Allen is to be seen coughing, we would prefer him not to cough blood, although it will probably be natural for him to do so.
>
> Page 80 Scene 235-7 — The script directions of this bayonet work suggest that it might be a bit too nasty.
>
> Page 81 Scene 238 — The same comment applies.
>
> Page 81 Scene 242 — The same comment applies.
>
> Page 81 Scene 244 — The same comment applies. Care should be taken with screams, grunts, etc. in the sound track.
>
> Page 82 Scene 249 — More bayonet trouble.

his own views on the subject. There are approving remarks on the script's general historical accuracy, though it is noted that 'Hook is considered the main hero in the books' and that 'Witt and his daughter may be real persons, however improbably they behave.' This second examiner expressed his agreement that the film was most likely to be in the A certificate category and added that 'as it will probably be in colour a warning is necessary about blood.'

A formal set of script notes was drawn up from these reports and handed personally to Stanley Baker on 13 March 1963 (see above). Two typewritten pages itemised points of detail and listed passages in the script which required careful attention. The censors expressed particular concern about the likelihood of younger viewers being admitted to the film, and 'nasty' is a term used repeatedly to stress what the filmmakers had to avoid. As in the Reader's Report, the bayonet work was the main subject of concern and the notes made direct recommendations on how to avoid problems with shots of graphic bloodshed. Specific comments were also made on the other potential areas of contention, such as the partial nudity of the women dancers and the opportunities for showing wounds and corpses in the hospital

```
                                    2.

    Page 82 Scene 254    The same again.  Here we get a bayonet straight in the
                         stomach which sounds even nastier than the others.
    Page 84 Scene 260    More bayonet work.  Provided this is the conventional kind
                         of fighting it would not be likely to run into trouble, but
                         the script suggests that the film is meant to be a realistic
                         representation of the carnage of this kind of old-fashioned
                         warfare.  I must make it clear that there are limits.
                         Perhaps some of the material could be done as intercuts which
                         are easily removable.
    Page 84 Scene 264-6  Care should be taken with the surgery sequences, and
                         especially with shots of blood and wounds.
    Page 84 Scene 266    The same comment applies to the shots of Cole's wound.
    Page 86 Scene 276    Here a Zulu plunges a spear into Byrne's back.  Care should
                         be taken.
    Page 87 Scene 280    More possibilities of trouble here.  Repeated bayonetting
                         of the same body may be unacceptable.  Here and elsewhere
                         sounds of screams, groans, grunts, etc. must be handled with
                         great care.  The sound track is important in this kind of
                         stuff.
    Page 88 Scene 283    Allen is doing his "retching cough" once again.  We would
                         prefer not to have blood coming out of his mouth as he does so.
    Page 94 Scene 322    Windridge using his bayonet.  Care as before.  What are we
                         to see when he pulls it free?  Not spurting blood I hope!
    Page 95 Scene 332    More bayonet work on the hospital roof.  We are to see the
                         thrust, and there is a wrench and a red weapon comes into
                         frame.  This sounds as though it might give trouble.
    Page 95 Scene 335    A Zulu stabs a screaming sick man.  This sounds particularly
                         nasty and should be shot as an intercut which can easily be
                         removed if necessary.
    Page 95 Scene 338    Howarth's bayonet is up to its hilt in a warrior's chest.
                         My previous cautions apply.
    Page 96 Scene 346    A Zulu body is pinned to the wall by bayonets.  We are not sure
                         about this one.  It might be nastier than we would like.
    Page 98 Scene 351    We try to keep the phrase "Get knotted" out of films -
                         certainly "A" films.
    Page 99 Scene 355    Care should be taken with this scene.  We would not want to
                         see shots of men on fire.
    Page 108 Scene 421   Care should be taken with the shots of dead people.  They can
                         look very macabre and gruesome.

    As will be seen, the main possibility of trouble lies in the bayonet work and its
    results.  Great care should therefore be taken in shooting these scenes, and you
    should provide either for the easy removal of any really nasty shots, and for
    alternative material to be available.
```

and battle scenes ('Care should be taken with the shots of dead people. They can look very macabre and gruesome.'). In the matter of coarse language, several uncouth lines or colloquial words and phrases were singled out as problematic; most of these were deleted from the film during shooting, and Hook's lascivious line about Margareta was changed to the equally suggestive 'Know what she needs.'

After shooting had been completed and the film was still in post-production, a print running 138 minutes 7 seconds (12,430 feet on fourteen short reels) was submitted for viewing by the Board on 18 September 1963.[3] It was common at the time for films to be seen by the censors while editing and sound dubbing were still in progress, so that potential problems could be addressed before the final edit and sound mix had been locked. In the event, the three examiners present – including the author of the original Reader's Report – were pleased with what they saw: the filmmakers had generally heeded the recommendations made in the script notes. A handwritten letter noted that only two small cuts were required, and that subject to approval of the still unfinished soundtrack the film would be acceptable for the U category. One of the three examiners had, however, 'expressed doubts about the sequences

```
BRITISH BOARD OF FILM CENSORS
            3, SOHO SQUARE, W.I

Telephone:          President: The Rt. Hon. LORD MORRISON OF LAMBETH, C.H.        Telegrams:
2677/8 GERRARD                                                                "CENSOFILM, PHONE,
                    Secretary: JOHN TREVELYAN, O.B.E.                              LONDON."

No.................Please Receive the following Films for Censorship   18th September 19 63.
```

No. For use by the Board only.	EXAMINER. For use by the Board only.	TITLE. To be filled in by the Publisher.	SCREEN TIME. To be filled in by the Publisher.	LENGTH: ft. To be filled in by the Publisher.	FEE. To be filled in by the Publisher. £ s. d.
33341	AOF. 13	ZULU Scope	12430	93	

FEATURE FILMS.—Not exceeding 3,000 feet, 75/- per 1,000 feet, 7/6 per 100 feet.
            Over 3,000 feet, 132/6 per 1,000 feet, 13/6 per 100 feet.
DOCUMENTARY FILMS AND CARTOONS.—20/- per 1,000 feet—minimum charge 40/-.
ADVERTISING FILMS.—40/- per 1,000 feet, 20/- per 500 feet.
TRAILERS.—4/- per 100 feet.
REISSUES.—40/- per 1000 feet, 4/- per 100 feet.
...bmit the above Film or Films under the terms and conditions of the Agreement already signed.
            Name of Publisher DIAMOND FILMS (Twickenham Studios).

---

showing Zulu "maidens" in deshabille.'

A formal letter was sent to *Zulu*'s production manager, John Merriman, at Twickenham Studios requesting that the two cuts be made, each of a single shot to be removed in its entirety: one in Reel 9, depicting 'an assegai thrust into the soldier with his mouth wide open,' and another 'almost identical' shot in Reel 10. In the matter of the soundtrack the following instructions were given, reiterating previous concerns the examiners had expressed: 'The sound track will be acceptable as far as gun fire and war cries are concerned, but it would be troublesome if it contained shrieks and groans of wounded men.

In the present track there is nothing we would worry about, but it might be wise for us to see later any parts of the film that might in this way produce problems for us.' When the final print was readied, the battle scenes were re-checked on 16 December. Another handwritten note, apparently initialled by Trevelyan, says that the sound was deemed 'perfectly acceptable – there are no shrieks or groans from wounded men – just a few mild gasps. The film is now cleared for the "U" category.' (Sound editor Rusty Coppleman confirms that there were no censorship problems with the soundtrack, adding: 'By and large my own sense of what was acceptable and

what wasn't would have taken over anyway.') Paramount was charged a fee of £93 for the examination process, at the Board's usual rate of 132 shillings and sixpence per thousand feet.

The oddity in the above account is that the first shot which the Board required to be cut, of the open-mouthed soldier being stabbed, remained in the film as released (it can be found at 86 minutes 40 seconds on MGM's Region 1 DVD, or at 83 minutes 11 seconds on Paramount's Region 2 edition),[4] though there is no other 'almost identical' shot, which presumably was indeed cut as requested. There is no correspondence in the Board's surviving files to confirm it, but it is probable that the producers were able to negotiate for the retention of one of the shots – the most graphic instance of bloodshed in the film – and still gain the desired U rating.

When *Zulu* was released in the UK on home video in 1989, in a widescreen 'letterboxed' edition in 1993, and on DVD in 2002, on each occasion it had to be resubmitted to the BBFC (an acronym which now stands for the British Board of Film *Classification* rather than Censors). In all of these versions the film received, not a U, but a PG certificate, standing for a recommendation of Parental Guidance – the rough equivalent of the A certificate after 1970, when it became a purely advisory rather than a restrictive category. The Board's more recent files are not open to public inspection, so one can only make an educated guess at the reason for the higher rating. Censors, who once regarded a reasonable amount of blood and gore, when suitably stylised, as fit for viewing even by very young children, are now more sensitive to concerns about the potential upset scenes of violence may cause, and even to their possible influence on more impressionable viewers.

United States

In the US, films also had to pass through a strict censorship procedure. The American film industry did not adopt a ratings system along the lines of the British one until 1968; before then, all films to be given public exhibition in mainstream cinemas (those whose owners were affiliated to the Motion Picture Association of America) were required to be given a Seal of Approval by the MPAA's Production Code Administration. The PCA, whose chief officer at the time was Geoffrey M. Shurlock, was charged with applying the principles of the Production Code: that set of strict censorship rules initially established in 1930, rigorously enforced from 1934 onwards and first revised in 1956. Each film was subjected to a systematic analysis of its content, in which significant story elements were categorised and evaluated for their potential offensiveness. Those which particularly concerned *Zulu* were its portrayal of professions (military, medical, the clergy and – in Schiess's case – the police), races and foreign nationals, along with 'miscellaneous sociological factors,' including the depiction of violence, drunkenness, and prayers or religious ceremonies.[5]

Characters identified as members of professions were checked against each of four categories. Examiners were required to note whether these characters were: (1) prominent, minor or incidental; (2) 'straight' or comedic; (3) sympathetic, unsympathetic, a mixture of the two, or 'indifferent'; (4) 'inefficient or dishonest in the performance of [their] duties.' (Examiners were also asked to record whether a character was '*both* of foreign birth and, in all probability, not a citizen of the United States' – which obviously applied in all cases for *Zulu*.) All the film's professional characters (which is to say, all the White male Europeans) were regarded as sympathetically portrayed, with the exceptions of Bromhead and Witt, who were judged to be both sympathetic and

Glynn Edwards (Corporal William Allen)

As one of the early casualties in the battle, Glynn Edwards found himself wearing blood-stained surgical dressings for most of the *Zulu* location shoot. He remembers having 'a lot of difficulty with the wounds. Once the makeup artists had put them on they had to stay on. They made it difficult to eat lunch.' The Zulus gave their own names to members of the British cast and crew, and Glynn became known as 'The Sorrowful One With The Bandages.'

Edwards' family origins lie in Cornwall but he was born, on 2 February 1931, in Penang, Malaya, where his father worked rubber plantations. His mother was an actress who died two days after Glynn was born. He was brought up back in England by his grandparents in Southsea, and in Portsmouth and Salisbury where his father became a publican. Glynn then relocated to the West Indies, getting a job in the sugar industry in Trinidad, where he also appeared in an amateur production of *The Chiltern Hundreds* which toured European oil bases and country clubs. Realising that his professional ambitions lay in the entertainment business, Glynn 'slid' (as he puts it) into London's Central School of Speech and Drama at the age of 21. He gained his most important theatrical experience at Joan Littlewood's London Theatre Workshop, where he appeared alongside James Booth in the Cockney musical *Fings Ain't Wot They Used T' Be* (1959).

'The first time I appeared in front of a camera,' Glynn says, 'was in the television series *Francis Drake*, starring Terence Morgan and Jean Kent, in the late 50s.' His earliest film part was a tiny role in *The Heart Within* (1957) as 'First Constable' – appropriately, as he went on to play at least a dozen more police officers in films and television. Glynn had briefly appeared with Stanley Baker in the army robbery thriller *A Prize of Arms* (1962), but it was Cy Endfield who cast

him in *Zulu* after seeing *Fings*. He read for several roles, including Colour-Sergeant Bourne, before being given Allen: 'They wanted Cockney NCOs and Welsh Privates,' he says. Glynn ultimately had to choose between doing the film and appearing in another Littlewood stage show, her celebrated production of *Oh! What a Lovely War*.

'Apart from doing my heroic bit carrying round the ammunition I didn't have to do any cut-and-thrust fighting,' he recalls. Despite enjoying a comparatively leisurely time in the battle scenes, Glynn nonetheless found the three months' shooting hard work. 'They had us on the bus at 7.00am to the location and by the time we got back in the evening there wasn't a lot of time left. When we weren't working we had a few drinks. There was quite a big chess school and Ivor Emmanuel would always start a sing-song in the bar.' It was not until the World Premiere – Glynn's first experience of one – that 'for the first time we could feel we had a hit on our hands. It was done in the big style.'

Edwards has worked prolifically in the years since *Zulu*, including film roles as a police station desk sergeant opposite Michael Caine in *The Ipcress File* (1965) and a senior detective (James Booth's superior officer) in *Robbery* (1967). He was also memorably knifed by Caine in a Newcastle back yard in *Get Carter* (1971) and later in the decade he returned to Tyneside to play a recurring character – a retired policeman – in the popular children's TV drama series *The Paper Lads*. In one 1978 episode involving a dangerous stunt, for which he was supposed to plunge over a cliff-top, Glynn was doubled by Larry Taylor's stuntman son Rocky. Among numerous other television appearances, however, he is perhaps best remembered as Dave the barman in the long-running (1979-1991) comedy-drama series *Minder*.

Zulu, he says, is 'one of those films that'll go on and on. People like it – it's a man thing, really, not a lady's. A lot of blokes just love to see it again and again and again. There are very few films I watch more than two or three times but when *Zulu*'s on….' He remembers going into a bar in Gibraltar and was surprised to be told by the barman: 'Do you know you're on the wall?' Expecting to see a still of himself from the film, he turned and instead found a photograph of 'a very hairy gentleman, with a VC round his neck. The barman said, that is my great-great-grandfather, who is in fact Corporal Allen! It was quite a buzz – he didn't look anything like me, but it's quite something to see a character you've played on film and know he actually exists.'

unsympathetic. None of the characters was seen to be depicted as professionally inefficient or dishonest. Similar categories were applied to the portrayal of races and nationals, and the Zulus were also seen as being portrayed both sympathetically and unsympathetically.

Although the examiners took note of the depiction of violence in the form of a 'native uprising,' the depiction of 'prayers and quoting scripture,' and the showing of drunkenness, none of these was signalled as a problem. The partial nudity of the female dancers was not even noted. The only other matter of concern to the PCA was the treatment of the animals used in the film. On 26 June 1963, Edward Schellhorn of the PCA forwarded to the American Humane Association (the US equivalent of the RSPCA, which monitors the use of animals in films) a covering letter from J. Stanton, Warden in Charge of the Royal Natal National Park, who made the following declaration:

I consider that in making the animal sequences of this film 'Paramount Pictures' acted in a humane and careful manner. They took all reasonable precautions to avoid cruelty or injury to the animals and ensured that at all times they had expert veterinary and technical advice available. They were also most meticulous in abiding by the game laws, and the directions and restrictions of the Game Division of the South African Government.

In addition such animals as were retained in captivity were well cared for,

fed and attended by expert staff, and regularly inspected by qualified Veterinary Surgeons.[6]

Thus satisfied, Shurlock and his three fellow examiners had no hesitation in granting *Zulu* a Seal of Approval on 3 January 1964; a certificate and a standard letter setting out its terms and conditions (including the stipulations that all copies of the film in circulation should conform exactly to the one examined and approved, and that all advertising and publicity materials should be submitted for approval to the MPAA's Advertising Advisory Council) were sent to Joseph E. Levine on the same day.

The PCA files on the film also contain documents recording the judgements of both the BBFC and several other American bodies which applied their own censorship standards: the two influential religious lobbying organisations, the Catholic Legion of Decency and the Protestant Motion Picture Council; and the Film Estimate Board of National Organizations, which represented a range of political interests. Unlike the PCA, all of these bodies issued ratings to the films they examined. The Legion of Decency, notorious for its conservative line on sexual issues in particular, gave each film a rating based on its acceptability on moral grounds: either AI, AII, AIII, AIV, B or C (the last indicating a Condemned rating). *Zulu* was awarded the AIII rating, meaning that it was considered 'morally acceptable for adults.' The Catholic examiners' principal concern was the 'irreverent portrayal of [a] minister of religion,' even though the minister concerned was of the Protestant faith. Curiously, the Protestant Motion Picture Council, which had its own classification system for the guidance of parents, did not appear to be bothered by this, classing *Zulu* as an unequivocal A, its highest rating.

South Africa

The only instance of significant censorship problems with *Zulu* I have discovered was in South Africa itself, where the film was not released until December 1964. Unlike Britain and America, film censorship in the Republic was controlled by law and administered by a government authority, the Publications Control Board.

Though legal censorship of films stretched back to 1916, the Board had been set up as recently as 1963 under provisions laid down in the Publications and Entertainments Act of that year. Its purpose was to rate films for their perceived suitability for local, specifically racial, audiences; it was concerned particularly to regulate the exhibition of films which might lead to civil disorder. Black South African émigré Lewis Nkosi, now a professor at the University of Wyoming, explained in a 1993 interview that under the apartheid system, 'for the Black African in South Africa it was not possible to simply go to any film that arrived in the country. The films were actually graded in accordance with a certain hierarchy. At the top you had the Whites and then in the middle you had the Coloureds and then at the bottom Blacks, and I remember that a White child was given the same grading, or permission to view, as a grown-up, adult Black African. This censorship was a source of bitter anger. For example, we were so mad about certain products from Hollywood being censored or unseeable by us because we were not "adult" enough as Blacks to see such products. I remember at times we petitioned the industry in Hollywood to intervene on our behalf against such censorship, and I don't remember them doing anything about it.'[7]

When it was submitted to the Publications Control Board, *Zulu* was declared 'unfit for black consumption' and awarded a D rating, which banned it for viewing by the country's indigenous population and by children under twelve.[8] It was far from alone in meriting this status: according to South African film historian Keyan Tomaselli, in the decade during which the Act was in force as many as one third of all films passed as suitable for White audiences were denied to Blacks.[9] The *Zulu* decision occasioned vigorous protests from liberal newspaper commentators. Dora Sowden's argument in the *Rand Daily Mail*, which opens by stating that 'politics and racialism are beginning to bedevil canned as well as live entertainment,' is worth quoting at length:

Whether ... the Rorke's Drift action was not a 'racial clash' or whether it was, it was history. Children who have to study history books also learn about Weenen and Blood River and Dingaan's Day, now 'Day of the Covenant'. Why should they not see British soldiers being brave against the Zulu enemy, and Zulus as great fighters?

It would surely do nothing to affect race relations adversely to let them see that Africans could salute an enemy as stout-hearted as themselves.

In the case of Africans, it would even be good racial policy to let them see that the White filmmakers are ready to do them justice as fearless warriors in their time – and to note the savagery of Cetewayo towards his own men as well as to the White enemy.

It would be good for them to see that credit is given to them for letting the missionary (unworthy and unaware as he was) and his daughter go in peace.

Americans do not mince matters about the clash between White men and Red Indians – as can be see in *Rio Conchos* and in *Apache Rifles*. Right and wrong are apportioned without fear or favour.

Covering up the facts of history only makes present truth ugly. South Africa is, alas, once again giving cause for the world to note that even its own story is meant

only for some of the people some of the time.¹⁰

Zulu's title itself, Sowden noted, belonged to the Africans, yet, 'concerned as they are in the episode by blood and history, they are denied the film.'

One of the saddest aspects of the ban, as Sowden pointed out, was that even the Zulu actors, stuntmen and extras who took part in the film were forbidden by law from seeing it. The injustice was registered strongly by Chief Buthelezi in a personal letter he wrote to Cy Endfield, in which he expressed his deep sorrow over the matter (see opposite), though Endfield and Baker were subsequently able to have a 16mm print of the film brought to Zululand to show the local actors the fruits of their work. The Zulu community's newspaper, *Umthunywa*, offered its own comments:

> There is widespread concern among the African cinema fans throughout the Republic of the decision taken by the Publications Board to ban Africans of all ages from seeing the much talked about film *Zulu*, the cast of which includes thousands [sic] of Africans ... The picture, we are told, depicts scenes of violence and bloodshed involving Whites and Africans. If the ban has been placed only because there is fear that such scenes might cause racial friction, these assumptions must be dismissed as nonsensical.
>
> Our African folk, we maintain, have as much decency as theatre-goers of other racial groups. With their many years as theatre patrons there is nothing to justify any assumption that they will suddenly turn savage and allow their feelings to run high at the sight of the war scenes to which one is much accustomed on the silver screen.
>
> If Africans in the rest of the Republic are prepared to tolerate this ban, those in the Transkei should not.
>
> At least the Republican Government has considered them mature enough to merit self-government. It is inconceivable that at that stage of their development they must not be allowed to see a film which adults of other racial groups are entitled to see, and thus be treated as non-African children under 18 years of age.¹¹

Newspaper advertisement for a Johannesburg cinema in 1969. Note the censor restrictions: 'No children 4-12 – No Africans.' (From a microfilm source.)

Three decades after its initial release, censorship of the film in South Africa still continued. A planned television screening by the state-run South African Broadcasting Corporation in 1993 was cancelled at the last minute because, argued critics, of 'the political ramifications of depicting black-on-white violence' at a time of real-life social and political unrest. The station offered the defence that it was simply responding to 'a perceived wave of viewer sentiment against TV violence,' and that it had received 'numerous calls from concerned viewers saying it would be insensitive to screen the movie with so much violence going on.'¹² Writer and film-maker Peter Davis – whose book and film about South African cinema, *In Darkest Hollywood*, are invaluable resources on this subject – supports the network's case. He

"UMTHIKASOMADAKA"

Phone Ngilazi 2

Chief/~~Mntwana~~
Mangosuthu Gatsha
Buthelezi

"KWAPHINDANGENE"
P.O. BOX 1
MAHLABATINI
ZULULAND

SOUTH AFRICA.
25th, January, 1965.

Dear Mr. Endfield,

    I hope Mrs Endfield the Kids and yourself are keeping well.
    We are keeping fine here except that we feel terribly upset about the news that we will not see the film 'ZULU'. I curse myself for having been such a fool as to miss the opportunity to see the film when you offered to run it for me when I was in London. We naturally feel very bitter about the whole thing and I spoke to the Commissioner-General on the 5th and was quite disappointed when he said to me in confidence:'There would be nothing wrong if a person like yourself sees the film, but I do think that it is bound to arouse feelings of excitement with the raw Africans'. I tried to point out that such feelings were not aroused on Location and that I could'nt see how they could be aroused by looking at the completed film on the screen. He changed the subject and from his attitude I concluded that the chances of us seeing the film were very slim. I just do not know how I am going to explain to my people that your promise to show them the film here will now not be fulfilled as a result of this ruling. We are very upset about it and that includes my cousin the Paramount-Chief.
    I wonder if you will ever come to South Africa in the near future it will be good to see you.
    Our regards to Mrs Endfield, the Kids and yourself.
        Yours sincerely,
        Mangosuthu G. Buthelezi.

suggests that 'the racial warfare portrayed in the film had to be viewed in the context of the massive letting of blood in contemporary South African society, and in that context, the decision to run the film in the first place seems criminally myopic.'[13] *Zulu* had already been shown on the network before, and was eventually shown again in November of that year – in the very week which saw the signing of a new constitution preparing the way for the democratic, all-races elections which would usher in Nelson Mandela as the Republic's next president. Even today, a decade and more after the death of apartheid, the country remains sensitive to the issues the film raises. Stephen Coan, a White journalist on KwaZulu-Natal newspaper *The Witness*, wrote to tell me: 'Though *Zulu* is one of my favourite films I would think long and hard before giving it a public showing here even now.'[14]

Interviewed by the BBC in 1996, when he was Minister of Home Affairs in the national government following the fall of apartheid, Prince Buthelezi remarked on the irony that he was now in charge of the ministry which had previously been responsible for censorship. He

280 CENSORSHIP

reflected: 'I'm not sure if this film touched a raw nerve in the sense that White and Black people were fighting in it, but for some reason it was banned before it was even shown. But because Sir Stanley Baker had promised that it would be shown to our people there was a special screening for those people who were actors in the film. That promise was kept.' Simon Sabela's nephew, the late Sydney Chama, recalled this same year that, under apartheid, the rule was 'if you're White, you're right, if you're Black, get back – that was it. Nobody could watch it. In fact a lot of people caught up with it later on in home movies. They were very lucky to get it. We found out there were some videos and everybody wanted to keep a copy. There are so many good memories with it, especially because, sad to say, everybody is now gone – everybody who was in that movie is just about gone. We are like the little lone survivors.'

Notes

[1] The BBFC files on *Zulu* were consulted in the Board's offices at 3 Soho Square, London, by courtesy of David Barrett and David Godfrey. Additional assistance and permission to reproduce extracts from the files were provided by Craig Lapper.

[2] Email to the author, 3 August 2004. For further insight into the Board's activities in the 1960s, see John Trevelyan, *What the Censor Saw* (London: Michael Joseph, 1973).

[3] Press and publicity materials issued at the time of the film's UK release gave an official running time of 135 minutes, which has led some commentators to assume that the British version was three minutes shorter than the version shown overseas (where press materials carried the correct running time of 138 minutes). This was not the case, however: my hunch is that the publicity information was prepared well in advance of the film's final cut and therefore carried only an approximate running time.

[4] The difference in running times is accounted for by the fact that the American NTSC video system replicates the running time of theatrical presentation, while the British PAL system, which runs at 25 frames per second, involves a slight speeding up; so that, for example, a 100-minute cinema film will run 96 minutes on video in PAL format. There are no significant material differences between the British and American home video versions (the opening Paramount logo is omitted from the American prints and replaced by a title card, in the same yellow-writing-on-black-background style as the other titles, identifying the film as an Embassy release).

[5] The PCA files on *Zulu*, held in the Margaret Herrick Library, Center for Motion Picture Study, Academy of Motion Picture Arts and Sciences, Los Angeles, were consulted courtesy of Janet Lorenz of the National Film Information Service. For further information on American censorship practices and the work of the Production Code Administration, see Murray Schumach, *The Face on the Cutting Room Floor: The Story of Movie and Television Censorship* (New York: William Morrow, 1964; reprinted by Da Capo, 1975), and Leonard J. Leff and Jerold L. Simmons, *The Dame in the Kimono: Hollywood, Censorship, and the Production Code from the 1920's to the 1960's* (London: Weidenfeld and Nicolson, 1990).

[6] The letter, a copy of which is included in the PCA files, is dated 17 June 1963 and printed on Diamond Films' official headed notepaper.

[7] Interview for *In Darkest Hollywood: Cinema and Apartheid* (directed by Daniel Riesenfeld and Peter Davis, Nightingale/Villon Films, 1993).

[8] Roderick Mann, 'Banned,' *Sunday Express*, 14 December 1964. Another journalist commented sarcastically that 'As the film shows 80 [sic] men of the South Wales Borderers repulsing 4,000 Zulus, it would be more logical for the apartheid government to make African attendance compulsory' ('More prejudice than pride,' *Sunday Telegraph*, 17 January 1965).

[9] For further details of censorship under the apartheid regime, see Keyan Tomaselli, *The Cinema of Apartheid: Race and Class in South African Film* (London and New York: Routledge, 1988), pp. 13-28.

[10] Dora Sowden, '*Zulu* ban is branded as political,' *Rand Daily Mail*, 11 January 1965.

[11] Quoted in *Johannesburg Star*, 21 January 1965, and reproduced in Peter Davis, *In Darkest Hollywood: Exploring the jungles of cinema's South Africa* (Athens: Ohio University Press, 1996), pp. 158-9.

[12] 'Violence Halts TV Screening,' *Los Angeles Times*, 3 June 1993; A.A. Gill, 'Is this the queue for *Zulu*?,' *Sunday Times*, 1 May 1994; Davis, pp. 159, 161.

[13] Davis, p. 159.

[14] Email to the author, 21 January 2004.

DWARFING THE MIGHTIEST! TOWERING OVER THE GREATEST!
The supreme spectacle that had to come thundering out of the most thrilling continent!

Joseph E. Levine presents

ZULU

A Stanley Baker - Cy Endfield Production

TECHNICOLOR® TECHNIRAMA®

The Massacre of Isandhlwana! The Mating Song of the Zulu Maidens! The Incredible Siege of Ishiwane! Night of the 40,000 Spears! Day That Saved A Continent! Mass Wedding of the 2,000 Warriors and 2,000 Virgins! Amid the Battle's Heat...the Flash of Passion!

Starring

Stanley Baker · Jack Hawkins · Ulla Jacobsson · James Booth · Michael Caine

Screenplay by John Prebble and Cy Endfield · Suggested by an Article Written by John Prebble · Directed by Cy Endfield · A Diamond Films Ltd. Production
A Paramount Pictures Release · Foreword Spoken by **Richard Burton**

"DWARFING THE MIGHTIEST!"

PUBLICITY, PROMOTION AND PREMIERES

> One November morning in 1963 four people sat in a chilly viewing theatre. Stanley Baker and Cy Endfield were the star/co-producer and producer/director respectively of a film they had just completed called *Zulu*. Esther Harris was the producer for National Screen Service, a company specialising in the making of cinema trailers and also stills, posters and all the other material essential for the promotion of feature films. Doug McCallum was the top editor for NSS, with a lifetime of experience in the film business.
>
> The lights dimmed and onto the screen was projected a scratched and patched black and white work print. Just discernible were shots of columns of Zulu warriors, advancing to the attack in the dawn's early night. Over the pounding of assegais on shields a voice was heard: '*Damn funny, like a train in the distance.*' Suddenly another voice boomed out '*Dwarfing the mightiest! Towering over the greatest!*'
>
> For the next three minutes images of charging Zulus, British Redcoats fighting hand-to-hand, a thundering cattle stampede and a spectacular wedding ceremony between 200 Zulu warriors and 200 Zulu maidens filled the screen. Stanley Baker jumped to his feet and shouted excitedly '*Is that our film, Cy?! Is that our film?*'
>
> (George Smith, 'Zulu – Behind the Scenes,' *Movie Collector*, vol. 1, no. 4, 1994, p. 11)

When released to cinemas, the *Zulu* trailer gave the general public its first glimpse of the now-completed film. Esther Harris had begun working at National Screen Service in 1926, aged sixteen, and was its senior scriptwriter and producer. In an interview recorded in 2000, Harris described her work and that of the company:

> National Screen used to see pictures before everyone else had a look at them. They were always in rough cut. Even when they went into colour I would see them in black-and-white. Because the trailer had to go to the cinema, particularly the West End before the premiere, you were selling the film before they had done any publicity. It was their main form of advertising in those days.
>
> We used certain voices which were not frightfully English and not frightfully American. You had to have a voice that was kind of common-denominator, you know, because if it was too American they wouldn't understand the damn thing – you had problems, you really did. And we had tremendous censorship problems – no matter what certificate the film was the trailer had to be 'U'.
>
> Frequently you'd have to follow the pattern of their publicity. I mean if they were going to stress the thing in a certain fashion they'd want you to do it in the trailer. But often they would pinch ideas I had already written in the trailer for their publicity, there's no doubt about that. They

```
                            353'       "ZULU"
                                   TRAILER CONTINUITY                    27.11.63
```

1. Open on L-S Zulus on hill at dawn. Zulu effects noise sounding like a train can be heard, and BROMHEAD says: (off)

    "Damn funny ...Like a .. Like a train in the distance."

    Cut to M-S Zulus moving through undergrowth. (Continue effects.)

   -

2. COMMENTARY: (Echo chamber)   TITLES   BACKGROUNDS

   DWARFING THE MIGHTIEST   (Zoom from behind hill to C-S)   Cut to further L-S Zulus on the hill as dawn breaks.

       DWARFING THE MIGHTIES!   (Continue effects.)

   TOWERING OVER THE GREATEST   (Zoom from behind hill to C-S)   - as above -

       TOWERING OVER THE GREATEST!

   -

3. TITLES   TRICKING

   JOSEPH E. LEVINE presents   Title rises from behind skyline and up to camera.   Continue effects, and dissolve through to L-S Zulus on hill at daybreak.

   -

4. "Z U L U"   Zoom up one letter at a time. As title is established, commentary says: -   Cut to L-S as Zulus commence attack, from left to right.

   -

5. COMMENTARY: (Echo chamber)

   ZULU   Cut to C-S panning along ranks of redcoats waiting. (Continue effects.)

   [struck through: Cut to L-S as the Zulus attack from left to right.]

   -

   [handwritten: SWAP 6 + 7]

6. Cut to C-S WITT shouting:

    "You're all going to die!...

   Cut to C-S Colour Sgt. and two redcoats.

    ... Don't you realise ...

   Cut to C-S CHARD.

    ... Can't you see ...

   CHARD slaps horse's rump and buggy moves off.

   Cut to M-S buggy moving away as WITT shouts: -

    ... Die!"

   Cut to M-S Colour Sgt. and two men.

   COLE: "Why is it us eh? Why us?"

   SGT. "Because we're here, lad, and nobody else."

   -

The first couple of pages of Esther Harris's continuity script for the *Zulu* trailer, prepared in November 1963.

- 2 -

7. **COMMENTARY:**

BACKGROUNDS

IN CLEAR: Cut to C-S CHARD as he turns to bugler and says: - "Now!"
Cut to M-S CHARD and bugler, who raises bugle to his lips.
Cut to C-S bugler sounding 'Retreat'.

THESE ARE THE DAYS AND NIGHTS OF
FURY AND HONOUR - OF COURAGE
AND COWARDICE THAT AN ENTIRE
CENTURY OF EMPIRE
MAKING AND FILM MAKING CAN
NEVER SURPASS.

Cut to M-S as redcoats retreat from front positions.
Cut to further angle of redcoats running to take up new positions.
Cut to C-S redcoats repulse Zulus at barricades.
Cut to M-S redcoats and Zulus fighting at barricades.
Cut to C-S CHARD as smoke wafts in front of him.
Cut to L-S of Zulu wedding dance.
Cut to C-S Zulu girls' legs as they dance.

THIS IS THE DAY
WHEN TWO HUNDRED ZULU VIRGINS
AND
TWO HUNDRED ZULU WARRIORS
PERFORM THEIR FANTASTIC
WEDDING DANCE.

Cut to C-S Zulu warriors as they move in towards girls.
Cut to C-S Zulu girls as they dance towards men
Cut to C-S Zulu warriors dancing.
Cut to C-S girls' legs as they dance.
Cut to C-S Zulu girl as she dances with warrior.
Continue above for short section.
L-S line of Zulu girls as they dance.

THIS IS THE DAY A WOMAN
FIGHTS FOR HER HONOUR ...
AMONG MEN
FIGHTING FOR THEIR LIVES.

Matte through centre screen to C-S MARGARETA's eyes.
Cut to M-S as MARGARETA struggles with man in hospital.
Cut to M-S two soldiers watching knowingly.
Cut to C-S as MARGARETA struggles with man and breaks free as her dress is torn.

----

8. **TITLES**
STARRING
STANLEY
BAKER

TRICKING
Wipe across on left.

Cut to three C-S's of CHARD, which are placed on right of screen. He shouts: "Fire!" three times.

----

9. MICHAEL
CAINE

Wipe across on right.

Cut to three C-S's of BROMHEAD which are placed on left of screen. He shouts: "Fire!" three times.

----

would incorporate that in their advertising jargon. That was fair enough.[1]

Harris's copy, used as narration for the trailer, did indeed appear on many of the film's advertising materials, in the US as well as in Britain. The UK trailer's voice-over was contributed by Robert Beatty, a well-known Canadian actor often used by National Screen for his mid-Atlantic accent, though he was replaced on the otherwise similar US trailer by a less ambiguous American narrator.[2]

The trailer was the centrepiece of an extensive publicity campaign which had begun with the first announcement of the production in the trade press in November 1962 and continued well after the film's eventual release in early 1964. Joseph E. Levine told his executives at Embassy shortly after shooting was completed: 'Every motion picture requires a tailor-made sales and merchandising technique. Everyone knows that but not everyone heeds that. You can't just distribute motion pictures any more. Distribution, as a term and a practice, is archaic and old-fashioned. This is a highly skilled and specialized field of bringing pictures to the public.'[3]

As was his wont, Levine personally orchestrated promotion for the film, visiting London in July and November 1963 for 'confabs' with Baker, Paramount world sales vice-president George Weltner, and the various sales managers and advertising directors whose combined job it was to coordinate world promotional activities. They included Paramount's Russell W. Hadley, Peter Reed, Günther Schack, Jack Upfold and Leslie Pound; Embassy's Kenneth N. Hargreaves and Bob Weston; and freelance publicist Theo Cowan.[4] Attending a pre-production press conference, one trade observer had fantasised that Levine was already hatching some typically outlandish, extravagant publicity stunts: 'As we left, Levine was beginning to visualize thousands of Zulus paddling their war canoes [sic] across the Atlantic to converge on US shores on opening day, egged on by drums pounded by Gene Krupa and other percussion greats, while overhead helicopters hovered and fireboats shot streams of water hundreds of feet into the air.'[5]

As unit publicist on location with the production crew, Geoff Freeman was in the front line, keeping up a steady supply of stories on all aspects of the picture which he filed with Theo Cowan's advertising agency in London's Half Moon Street, for distribution to the world's press. He explains: 'I filed stories about the Zulus, how they found them, the geographical location, Michael [Caine] as a new star, the supporting players – Nigel Green, Ivor Emmanuel – little snippets on them.' Freeman joined the location unit two weeks before shooting began, shortly after completing a lengthy stint in Rome on *Cleopatra* (1963). He chose the job from half a dozen international projects he was offered. Geoff's younger brother had been Cy Endfield's assistant on several films, but friendship with Cy was not the key factor in

The first logo design for *Zulu* was used as a letterhead on Diamond's office notepaper.

JOSEPH E. LEVINE Presents the
STANLEY BAKER · CY ENDFIELD Production of

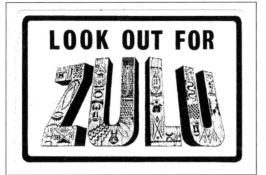

These sticky-backed labels, carrying the new title logo, were available as promotional items and were frequently attached by Paramount staff to envelopes carrying correspondence.

his decision. 'I liked the sound of the subject,' he says. 'Cy and John Prebble had done some marvellous research. They sent me that and that really swung it for me.'

Coincidentally, Geoff later served in the same capacity on *Zulu Dawn* (1979), though its producers were not aware that he had worked on *Zulu* when they offered him the post. He has been in film publicity since the age of sixteen, training at Associated British Picture Corporation and going freelance in 1958. Among his numerous other films are *Cromwell* (1970), *Shout at the Devil* (1976), *The Eagle Has Landed* (1977), *Victor/Victoria* (1982), *Aliens* (1986), *Shirley Valentine* (1989), *The Mummy* (1999) and many of the James Bond pictures, including all of Pierce Brosnan's. At time of writing Geoff is still very much active in the business: our interview took place at Pinewood Studios during the filming of *Die Another Day* (2002). Film publicity, he says, 'has completely changed now because of the internet. You don't have to release stories every week like we used to. On *Zulu* I was churning stuff out to send out to journalists. All of my stuff – copy, stills – went back to Theo; he placed them.' Geoff remained in South Africa until the end of location shooting, and continued to work on the picture for several weeks while filming was completed in London.

Geoff shared a room at the Royal Natal National Park Hotel with veteran stills photographer Norman Gryspeerdt (1911-1998). A former fashion photographer and subsequently a distinguished photographic artist, Fellow of the Royal Photographic Society and member of the London Salon of Photography, Gryspeerdt had learned his trade during naval service. After World War Two he entered the film industry, initially under contract to the Rank Organisation and later with Universal. As a freelance, he also worked on such films as *The Dirty Dozen* (1967) and *Scrooge* (1970).[6] For *Zulu*, Gryspeerdt took literally thousands of production and publicity shots, capturing both the action in each scene being filmed and the work of the crew behind the cameras (many of his pictures are used as illustrations in this book). Freeman had the stills printed by a South African laboratory before they were sent on to London and beyond.

Gryspeerdt's work was supplemented by two 'special' photographers who created portraits of the stars and other key advertising images. Sergio Strizzi started in the film industry in Italy in 1950, when he was twenty years old. He got to know Stanley Baker on Joseph Losey's *Eva* (1962): 'We were like

Unit stills photographer Norman Gryspeerdt poses with one of the Zulu stuntmen.

brothers,' he says, 'I loved him.' Strizzi later worked with Stanley on *Sands of the Kalahari* (1965), *Robbery* (1967), *Where's Jack?* (1969) and *Pepita Jimenez* (1975), among others. He has also shot stills for many films starring Michael Caine, including *Funeral in Berlin* (1966), *Billion Dollar Brain* (1967), *The Magus* (1968), *The Italian Job* (1969) and *The Last Valley* (1971). Sergio ('the best stills man *ever*,' in Bob Porter's opinion) is still active in his early seventies: when he spoke to me on the phone from Rome he had just completed work on *A Good Woman* and *Exorcist: The Beginning* (both 2004). *Zulu* is Sergio's favourite among his own films, along with *Zorba the Greek* (1964). He recalls that following the World Premiere of *Zulu* in London, fans smashed the glass in the cinema's front-of-house display cases to steal the lobby cards. Stanley, he says, was delighted.

Joining the location unit for a single week in May 1963 was Yousuf Karsh (1908-2002), an

Special photographer Karsh shoots a portrait of Hawkins and Baker.

Ottawa-based portrait artist regarded at the time as the 'world's most famous photographer.'[7] With his wife, Karsh flew to South Africa two weeks after photographing the Soviet Premier Nikita Khruschev in Moscow, arriving in time to capture shots of the Zulu wedding dance. He worked on *Zulu* at the express invitation of Joseph E. Levine, who paid him $50,000 for the privilege and told him: 'You can do anything you want … so long as it spells *Zulu*.'[8] Karsh's colour images were supposed to take priority when it came to placing photographic 'breaks' in the world's leading picture magazines, such as *Life*. His portraits were prized by their subjects: several of the cast and crew, including Cy Endfield and David Kernan, had them framed and hung on their own walls at home.

Like all film distributors, Paramount issued exhibitors with a press campaign book, produced by National Screen Service, for each of its releases. These pressbooks displayed the publicity material available for exhibitors' use, such as posters, stills, lobby cards, advertising blocks and behind-the-scenes stories (derived from Geoff Freeman's location reports) for placement in newspapers and magazines. They were also typically filled with ideas and recommendations for publicity stunts, promotional activities (such as tie-ins with local retailers and businesses) and 'exploitation' (the industry term for advertising of all kinds, though for most laymen the word tends to have unsavoury connotations). Not unnaturally, the pressbook for *Zulu* plays heavily on the film's military theme and recommends that cinema managers do likewise:

> War Heroes: The background of courage and valour that runs through the story of *Zulu* can be used as the theme of much of your campaign approach on the film. Tie-in with any local service organisations in your territory. Invite local youth movements such as the boy scouts, sea cadets, Boys' Brigade, etc., to co-operate with you on possible parades, foyer and stage presentations, etc. It might be possible to get the local press to run a series on heroes on heroes who live in your town. This could cover not only brave men in battle, but those who have won medals for other deeds of heroism.

Cover of the Exhibitors' Campaign Guide (Pressbook) for the 1972 UK reissue.

It might be possible to hold a special Hero Night at your theatre, with all its attendant publicity.

Army Co-operation: Any use you make of the war hero theme should be arranged, where possible, in conjunction with local army authorities. In addition, endeavour to tie up with recruiting drives, the Territorial Army, old soldier associations and similar bodies.

The recruitment campaign is known to have worked in at least one instance: the television chef Keith Floyd has admitted joining up the day after seeing *Zulu*.[9]

STANLEY BAKER PUZZLE BLOCK

The films of Stanley Baker form the basis of this puzzle block (Stereo No. 33). It is available from National Screen Service.

CLUES
1. S - - F - - y was a big hit for Baker.
2. Last word of a film which also co-starred Hardy Kruger.
3. Last word of an epic set in Greece.
4. The "Hills" were this. Two words.
5. One of Baker's greatest triumphs.
6. A war drama that made Baker a star.
7. This something was French. Last word of title.
8. A hat that was red.
9. "A Prize of A - - -"
10. Dirk Bogarde co-starred. Last word of title.
11. This has appeared in several Baker titles.
12. One of Baker's toughest films.

ANSWERS
1. SEA FURY; 2. Blind DATE; 3. Guns of NAVARONE; 4. ANGRY HILLS; 5. ZULU; 6. CRUEL SEA; 7. In the French STYLE; 8. The Red BERET; 9. A Prize of ARMS; 10. Campbell's KINGDOM; 11. HELL; 12 The CRIMINAL.

This crossword puzzle was one of a number of promotional items available for placement by exhibitors in local newspapers.

World Premiere

Pre-release publicity culminated in the night of the World Premiere, an event designed to garner the film valuable space in national and international newspapers and magazine columns.[10] The initial premiere date for *Zulu* had been announced by Joe Levine on one of his visits to South Africa, halfway through the production schedule. The film, he told a Johannesburg press conference on 14 May, would be premiered in New York and London at Christmas 1963 and released 'simultaneously in 12 other world capitals.'[11] A couple of months later, a week after shooting had finally wrapped, Levine and Stanley Baker gave a press luncheon in New York where a change of plan was announced: now the film would debut in London, with a Royal Command performance in February.[12] In the event, the final date chosen was 22 January 1964, the 85th anniversary of the Battle of Rorke's Drift. It was to be a charity benefit in aid, at Baker's suggestion, of the Army Benevolent Fund and the Benevolent Funds of the Royal Regiments of Wales: the Welsh Guards, the Royal Welch Fusiliers, the Welch Regiment and of course the South Wales Borderers.

A reception and luncheon were held the week before Christmas at the Council Chamber of the Royal Hospital, Chelsea, where plans for the premiere were discussed with members of the various organising committees.[13] Baker, Endfield, John Prebble, Michael Caine and James Booth were also present to mingle with journalists and other guests, including members of the various Welsh regiments, over a glass of champagne. Among the soldiers present was Ian Hywel-Jones, then a Captain with the South Wales Borderers, now a Lieutenant-Colonel (retired), holder of the MBE and Military Cross, and co-ordinator of the Victoria Cross and George Cross Research Project. Lt.-Col. Hywel-Jones recalls that at one point, 'Stanley Baker got up on a chair and said a few words of the sort you'd expect at one of those occasions. He said, "When you gentlemen of the regiment see it you'll notice we've included

Richard Davies (Private 593 William Jones)

Like Michael Caine, Richard Davies was initially sent by his agent to read for the role of Hook. He too was disappointed to be told by Cy Endfield that James Booth had the part, but on his way out of the Diamond Films offices he bumped into his old friend and fellow Welshman Stanley Baker. 'He said, Dickie, what are you doing here, boy? When I told him, he said, you can play one of the boys in the hospital.' And so he did. It's hard to imagine the short, balding Davies as the cynical, snarling Hook, but he was apparently a good likeness for 593 Jones: 'I got a letter from Jones' family saying they liked me playing the part,' he says.

Davies was born on 25 January 1926 in Dowlais, near Merthyr Tydfil, and started acting in the National Association of Boys' Clubs Theatre. He toured the country with a religious drama group before getting a job as assistant stage manager at Colwyn Bay Rep. During the war he joined the Military Police ('a peeler, 716') and the Army Topical Theatre, where he met and worked with actors such as Alan Badel, Clifford Evans, Bryan Forbes and Roger Moore. After demob he went onto the West End stage, joining the Old Vic in 1951. That same year he made his film debut with an uncredited bit part in the Ealing comedy *The Lavender Hill Mob*. Among his other films are *The Night My Number Came Up* (1955), *The Long Arm* (1956), *Twisted Nerve* (1968), *Oh! What a Lovely War* (1969) and *Under Milk Wood* (1971). But it was on television that Davies became a familiar face. In addition to many guest appearances, he had regular roles in the comedy series *Please Sir!* (beginning in 1968, and including the 1971 feature film spin-off), *Oh No, It's Selwyn Froggitt*, *Rule Britannia!*, *Whoops Apocalypse* and *Bottle Boys*, and played Idris Hopkins for two years (1974-75) in *Coronation Street*.

Prior to *Zulu*, Davies had worked on television with Stanley Baker and in the theatre with Nigel Green, when the latter was employed shifting scenery in a small venue on a corner of Leicester Square. Though he had previously toured southern Africa with the Old Vic, understudying Iago in *Othello* ('I was dying to do him as Welsh, but never got to play him'), Dickie shot all his scenes for *Zulu* in a couple of weeks at Twickenham Studios. Whenever it appears on television, he invariably gets shouts of 'Saw you in your film last night!' from his neighbours. Unlike some of his fellow cast members, the film's success did not take him by surprise. 'I thought at the time that this would do great at the box office. There's a lot of drama in the situation — guns and spears, and then when you get to the scene where they're firing like a machine gun — that's an eye-opener. It's a marvellous period for people scrapping with each other.'

292 PUBLICITY, PROMOTION AND PREMIERES

'ZULU' STARTS ITS ATTACK ON THE BOX-OFFICE

World premiere of the Joseph E. Levine presentation of "Zulu" at the Plaza Theatre, Piccadilly Circus, fired a new salvo in the big gun showmanship campaign for this Stanley Baker-Cy Endfield production. The premiere, which set a high standard for the coming year, was in aid of the Army Benevolent Fund and the Benevolent Funds of the Regiments of Wales.

A strong Army flavour was the keynote of the evening—the 85th anniversary of the day they won eleven Victoria Crosses were won at the Battle of Rorke's Drift, which is spectacularly re-created in the Paramount release. Men of the modern army wearing the uniforms of 1897 were on parade at strategic points throughout the theatre. The band of the Welsh Guards played prior to the performance, and there was a roaring reception for the choir of the 1st Battalion Welsh Guards.

In the foyer, leading trade personalities, headed by Joseph Levine, George Weltner, executive vice-president of Paramount Pictures Corporation, Russell W. Hadley, Jr., managing director of Paramount, and Kenneth Hargreaves, director of Anglo-Embassy Productions, greeted the many guests, who included three holders of the Victoria Cross.

The star contingent was headed by many of the cast of " Zulu "—Stanley Baker, Jack Hawkins, James Booth, Michael Caine, Nigel Green and Ivor Emmanuel. Director and co-producer, Cy Endfield, music composer John Barry, author John Prebble, and editor John Jympson were other personalities present.

Trade paper coverage of the World Premiere.

Local newspaper coverage of regional premieres. Note the unhappy expression of Henry Hook VC's daughter, Mrs J. Bunting.

some things you might not remember from the history; but what you must remember is that we've had to make some changes in order to recoup the investment from the world market." If one looks at the film now, at a distance, it does have clear characteristics of one of the Hollywood-style movies of that sort. But when the film was made, apart from holding Rorke's Drift Days, we in the regiment weren't the least bit knowledgeable about it. We just saw it as another film. As young officers we were busy doing other things. Those people who had a connection to those who were there [at the battle] would have taken a greater interest than we did. Older officers in the regiment would have been more aware than the young chaps who were learning to be officers.'

The premiere was held at Paramount's 1,889-seat London flagship, the Plaza, a short walk from Piccadilly Circus, from which the cinema's distinctive dome is still clearly visible despite its closure in 2002. (The site is now occupied by a Tesco supermarket with an adjacent multiplex cinema underground.) Rows of soldiers from the South Wales Borderers, all dressed in Victorian redcoat uniforms, stood guard in the theatre foyer and an additional escort was provided, as one trade paper put it, by 'Three "Zulu girls" [who] helped out with the atmosphere – Hazel Futsh, Mamsie Toboli, Patience Gwabi.'[14] No royalty appears to have been present, but among the patrons of the premiere were distinguished military personnel, including officers of the various regiments represented; members of the House of Lords and Commons, including the War Minister, James Ramsden; and noted Welsh celebrities, including opera singer Geraint Evans, actor Mervyn Johns, and singer and comedian Harry Secombe. One name that stands out from the list of military patrons is

Peeping over Michael Caine's left shoulder at the premiere party is his dynamic agent, Dennis Selinger. Cy Endfield can be seen between Michael and Edina Ronay; further to the right is Lionel Blair, dancing with Joe Levine's wife Rosalie. Dancing in the centre of the shot is Ian Fawne-Meade, assistant to the producers, and in glasses at the far right is publicist Theo Cowan.

that of Lieutenant-Colonel Sir Benjamin Bromhead, OBE, the descendant of Gonville Bromhead, whose unfavourable reaction to the film we have already encountered (see Chapter 5). Other invited guests included three holders of the Victoria Cross.

As well as Joe Levine and senior representatives of Paramount and Embassy, members of the film's cast and production team were present in force, along with their respective partners. 'There was a great feeling of excitement about it,' says Maureen Endfield. 'For the premiere I went to Yves St Laurent for the first and last time,' recalls Ellen Baker, 'and bought a very expensive black-and-white dress.' As well as the Bakers, the Endfields, and John and Betty Prebble, there were Mr and Mrs Jack Hawkins, James Booth and Nigel Green. Michael Caine was escorted by the future fashion designer Edina Ronay, and Ivor Emmanuel by his partner and later wife, Patricia Bredin. Also present were composer John Barry; actors Donald Sinden (with his wife and young son, the future actor Jeremy Sinden), Donald Houston, Ron Randell, Liz Fraser and Terence Stamp; showbiz personalities Lionel Blair, Alma Cogan, Barbara Kelly and Bernard Braden; and producers Albert R. 'Cubby' Broccoli and Nat Cohen, both of whom had turned down the opportunity to make the film for their own companies.

A musical concert was performed prior to the commencement of the film by the Band of the Welsh Guards and the Choir of the 1st Battalion Welsh Guards, whose repertoire inevitably included 'Men of Harlech.' Other pieces were chosen because of their popularity at the time of the Anglo-Zulu War, including a selection from Gilbert and Sullivan's *HMS Pinafore*, the waltz 'Tres Jolie,' the ballad 'In the Gloaming,' and what were described in the programme as a 'cavalcade' of martial songs and a 'pot-pourri' of regimental marches. The only concession to contemporary 1960s musical fashion was a medley from the current West End production of Richard Rodgers' show *The Boys from Syracuse*. The screening itself was accorded a rousing reception, being followed by a spontaneous, thunderous round of applause. George Weltner considered that 'he had never before heard such an enthusiastic reaction in his long experience of first nights.' It was 'like being at the opera,' said Levine; according to one trade paper, he was 'subdued in awe at the recollection.'[15] Following the screening, invited guests moved on to a party at the Mayfair Hotel where, at one o'clock in the morning, according to the *News of the World*, 'Baker and a couple of chums were roaring out Sospan Fach fit enough to bust.'[16]

Careful attention was also paid to giving the film a proper start in major regional centres. Press launches, attended by Baker, Endfield and others, were held in Glasgow, Manchester and Birmingham, and the national release at Easter was accompanied by an advertising campaign costing, said Weltner, up to £60,000. The first public screening outside the capital was a duplicate premiere on 23 March at the Olympia Theatre, Cardiff, also in aid of the Army Benevolent Fund and the Regiments of Wales, for which every seat was sold.[17] Baker was in America doing pre-release publicity but he flew back into Britain for one night only to be at the Welsh premiere. 'I've got to,' he told *Evening News* journalist William Hall. 'I wouldn't dare show my face again in Wales if I didn't.'[18] The programme included the Band of the Welch Regiment, performing martial and patriotic music including – of course – 'Men of Harlech,' plus 'The Leek,' 'Cambrian War Song,' 'Welsh Patrol' and 'Steps of Glory' (another 'march pot-pourri'). This was followed by the Ferndale Imperial Glee Singers, with Ivor Emmanuel singing 'Nidaros' and 'Sanctus.' The usherettes were dressed in traditional Welsh costume, while guests included members of Baker's own family (his mother, a brother, sister, uncle, aunt and assorted relatives and friends), four Welsh VC holders and Mrs L. Bunting, the daughter of Private Hook.[19]

Cinemas in other UK cities often arranged regional galas when their turn to show the film came around, inviting local military veterans as guests of honour, along with a star of the film if one was available and occasionally relatives of soldiers who had been present at Rorke's Drift. Mrs Bunting also attended the first screening at her local ABC cinema in Gloucester, where she was photographed looking somewhat less than elated at the occasion; presumably she had agreed to attend before witnessing her father's representation in the film, and was unable to cancel the engagement afterwards. Mrs Elizabeth Barlow, the daughter of another defender, Private William Jones (played in the film by Richard Davies), attended opening night performances in Manchester, Halifax and Huddersfield. She appeared much happier than Mrs Bunting: 'The film seemed very true to life from what I remember him telling me,' she told the local press.[20]

At the Scottish premiere at the ABC Regal in Glasgow, five Scottish VC-holders were accompanied by a guard of honour from HMS *Zulu*, a warship due to be commissioned on the River Clyde. At the ABC Sheffield, the opening performance in aid of *Sheffield Star and Telegraph*'s charity 'Old Folk's Fun' was attended by actor Patrick Magee, the Master Cutler, a 24-man guard of honour from the Hallamshire Regiment, and assorted veterans of the Boer War and the First World War. At the Westover Cinema, Bournemouth, the Victoria Cross Association arranged a special screening for representatives of African churches and missions, plus eighty African guests from universities, colleges and hospitals. At the ABC Southend, the manager arranged Army recruiting displays and a convoy of military vehicles carrying placards

Stanley Baker, Rosalie Levine, George Weltner and Cy Endfield attend the New York premiere.

advertising the film; on opening night the cinema was attended by veterans of African campaigns and its new Marine Club bar introduced a 'Zulu Cocktail.' The Regal, Chepstow, in the Monmouthshire borders region, stressed the local connection to the regiment depicted in the film and foyer displays were arranged with both the South Wales Borderers and the Royal Engineers; 'Men of Harlech' and 'Zulu Stamp' were played over loudspeakers in the auditorium for three weeks prior to the run, and each performance was preceded by Elgar's 'Pomp and Circumstance No. 4,' with 'Land of Hope and Glory' playing directly into the film's opening music.

Numerous cinemas arranged displays of military flags or African relics supplied by museums and collectors, attendance by local military bands, recruiting boards and veterans' associations, or tie-ups with South African wine merchants, airlines and travel agencies, gratefully supported by the South African Tourist Board. A *Zulu* showmanship contest between ABC managers was actively supported by Baker, Endfield and Levine. Some of the more outré publicity stunts tried by local managers to attract patrons are also worthy of note: a celebrity ventriloquist took a *Zulu* cake to a Blackpool hospital children's ward; seventy honeymoon couples were invited to see the Zulus' 'wedding with a difference;' Red Coats from a Butlin's holiday camp gave the film a uniformed escort; and a Zulu Stamp contest was arranged at a technical college's Rag Ball. These campaigns, bizarre as some of them may seem, apparently brought about an overall increase of 120.6% in average admissions to their respective cinemas, with some reporting that business for the film was triple the average take.[21]

New York Premiere

Having gone on national general release as an Easter attraction in Britain, *Zulu* was held back in the US until the summer 'to capitalize on the hefty seasonal biz potential for such a pic what with school out and other such factors.'[22] The extra time was used for careful planning. To coordinate activities among exhibitors in key cities, a 'showmanship caravan' toured the country between 16 December 1963 and 10 January 1964, beginning in New York and calling at Chicago, San Francisco, Los Angeles, Dallas, Atlanta and Kansas City. A convention of Embassy sales staff was held in New York over three days in May 1964 for planning of the company's advertising and publicity campaigns for its release schedule for the second half of the year, with a 'Showmanship Forum' putting special emphasis on the summer releases. Joe Levine was, as expected, fully prepared to put his own not inconsiderable weight behind promoting the picture on his home turf. Sometimes dubbed 'the Boston Barnum,' Levine had visited that city, his former stamping ground as an exhibitor, to announce

Denys Graham
(Private 716 Robert Jones)

'I was with Michael Caine in a stage play called *Next Time I'll Sing To You* by James Saunders,' remembers Denys Graham. 'We were at the Arts and [producer] Michael Codron was waiting to transfer it to the Criterion. Michael Caine and I both got called up for auditions for *Zulu* and he got offered this wonderful leading role. Michael Codron was thrilled for him but he said that if anyone else goes we'll not transfer it. I was originally offered a much bigger part in the film, but I'd never been that interested in films so I stayed in the play.' Caine joined the transfer to the Criterion before departing for South Africa, while Denys was given 716 Jones as a consolation part: 'I probably only worked on the film for a week – filming during the day and in the play at night.'

Denys Graham as he is today.

Graham was born on 29 June 1926 in Newport, Monmouthshire. After the war he took a postgraduate degree in chemistry and maths at Oxford and went to work in a factory at Hackney Wick, but he wanted to be in the theatre. He belonged to a number of acting groups and eventually won a scholarship to study at RADA. He started his professional career in the West End with the John Gielgud Company before going to Stratford-upon-Avon. Denys's big break came with the original stage production of Dylan Thomas's *Under Milk Wood* in 1954. Among his many other plays are Wyn Thomas's *The Keep*, William Trevor's *The Old Boys*, Sue Townsend's *Groping for Words*, and the musical *Grand Hotel*. His most recent professional stage appearance was in a revival of *Under Milk Wood* at the Royal National Theatre. Apart from *Zulu*, Denys has made only six other films: *Valley of Song* (1953), *The Dam Busters* (1955), *Fire Maidens from Outer Space* (1956), *Dunkirk* (1958), *Modesty Blaise* (1966) and as the Kaiser in the 1979 remake of *All Quiet on the Western Front*. He has also appeared often on television and had recurring roles in the drama series *On the Line*, *Rumpole of the Bailey* and *Lovejoy*.

'I was very surprised when it was so successful,' he says of *Zulu*. 'If you mention you were in it you immediately rocket up in people's estimation. It's a great film – I was amazed. It shows us in a good light – us and the Zulus. They're not put down or diminished. They're put on the same level and treated equally.'

that he would spend more money on advertising and promoting the film than had ever been spent there before.[23] He promised that a total of $1.5 million would be spent on national advertising for *Zulu* and the season's other big release, *The Carpetbaggers*. 60% of this would go on newspaper ads and 40% on TV spots. A brief promotional featurette, *Courageous Moments in History*, featuring 'six action stills from famous movie battle scenes,' had been shown on thirty-eight local television stations by late July 1964.[24]

The official US premiere took place on 7 July at the RKO Palace, a large (1,642 seats) Broadway first-run theatre. The event was fairly unusual for such an occasion in that attendance was not by invitation only. The general public was able to buy tickets to sit alongside invited guests, contrary to the usual practice for premieres. Present at the screening were Stanley Baker, for once unaccompanied by his family; Cy and Maureen Endfield, whose children were left in the care of a nanny at their Hampshire Hotel suite; Joe Levine and company executives including Paramount's George Weltner and Embassy's vice-president Leonard Lightstone. Outside the theatre, a Colour Guard from the British War Veterans of America and fourteen members of the Ulster Pipe Band – not exactly apposite, but perhaps the Welsh community was not strongly represented in the Big Apple – paraded down Broadway to the theatre past waiting crowds. Carroll Baker, star of *The Carpetbaggers*, was among the guest celebrities, along with Joey Heatherton from Levine's other current Harold Robbins property, *Where Love Has Gone*. Other invited guests included actors Anthony Perkins, Monique Van Vooren, Constance Bennett, Veronica Lake, Anita Louise, Red Buttons, Ann Sheridan, Bert Lahr and Darryl Hickman: not exactly an A-list line-up.[25]

One obstacle the film's Stateside publicists faced in trying to arrange merchandising tie-ins and other promotions with manufacturers and retailers was the unwillingness of some potential clients to be associated with a film known to have been filmed in, and with the co-operation of, a country operating a policy of apartheid. *Variety* reported: 'Reluctance seems to be coming from companies and individuals who are aware of the S. African racial policy. This is particularly true in attempted arrangements for national promo hookups. It is revealed that Embassy also had its troubles with some companies and individuals in the same field when trying to line up national promos for *The Sky Above, The Mud Below*, a documentary on New Guinea.'[26]

The politics of race was an especially potent topic in America at this time. Black militancy was on the increase, and in 1964 alone race riots occurred in New York, Chicago, Philadelphia, Rochester and Jersey City. The Civil Rights Act, introducing reforms in the areas of voting, education and the use of public facilities, was passed in July 1964, when *Zulu* was on release and race riots were breaking out in Harlem.[27] It is a matter for speculation whether such events, and the concurrent difficulties in securing publicity breaks for *Zulu*, contributed to its relatively disappointing box-office performance in the US. The film experienced no such problems in Britain however, where its release made box-office history.

Notes

[1] Interview by Denis Gifford, 18 January 2000, for the BECTU Oral History Project; audio tape consulted at the British Film Institute Library.

[2] The US and UK trailers can be viewed on the Region 1 and Region 2 DVDs released by MGM and Paramount, respectively. Doug McCallum, the trailer's editor, was the brother of Gordon K. McCallum, who, as previously discussed, created the final stereo mix of the *Zulu* soundtrack. George Smith, formerly of National Screen Service, currently works at the Imperial War Museum, London, and has supplied many of the illustrations for this book.

[3] 'Selling Haste Makes Waste,' *Variety*, 27 May 1964, pp. 7, 19.

4 'Levine to Europe – Again,' *Variety*, 24 July 1963, p. 3; 'Ballyhoolies a la Levine For British Campaign,' *Variety*, 27 November 1963, p. 10.

5 Mel Konecoff, 'The New York Scene,' *Motion Picture Exhibitor*, 10 April 1963.

6 For more information on Norman Gryspeerdt's life and work, see the website maintained by his family at http://www.gryspeerdt.co.uk/.

7 See, for example, D.N.E. Kain, 'I interview world's most famous photographer,' *The Natal Witness*, 30 May 1963. Kain elsewhere reported that Karsh was paid 'several thousand rand' for his photography on the film ('*Zulu*: A Film Completed,' *Personality*, 3 October 1963, p. 103).

8 Yousuf Karsh, 'Ottawa Photographer's Prose Impressions of Joseph E. Levine,' *Variety*, 22 April 1964, p. 97.

9 Elaine Gallagher, *Candidly Caine* (London: Robson Books/London Weekend Television, 1990), p. 78.

10 *Zulu* picture spreads appeared frequently in the British trade press; see, for example, *Kine. Weekly*, 26 December 1963, pp. 10-11 (press luncheon) and 30 January 1964, pp. 10-13 (World Premiere, regional press launch); and *The Daily Cinema*, 22-23 January 1964, p. 2 (press luncheon), 24-25 January, pp. 4-10 (showmanship luncheon, World Premiere), 29-30 January, pp. 4-5 (West End crowds), 5-6 February, pp. 8-9 (regional launches in Glasgow, Manchester and Birmingham) and 22 April, pp. 6-7 (letters from exhibitors).

11 'Embassy's Joe Levine Fixes World Distrib For *Zulu*, Africa Pic,' *Variety*, 22 May 1963, p. 13.

12 'Not Small-Minded; At *Zulu* Fertility Rites Levine Touts Bronston,' *Variety*, 7 August 1963, p. 4.

13 *The Daily Cinema*, 22-23 January 1964, p. 2. At a 'showmanship luncheon' for ABC cinema managers held at Quaglino's restaurant, also attended by Baker, Endfield and Joe Levine, the menus were printed on small cardboard Zulu shields held upright with a cocktail stick ('Launching *Zulu* with showmanship,' *Kine. Weekly*, 30 January 1964, pp. 12-13).

14 *The Daily Cinema*, 24-25 January 1964.

15 Observer, 'Commentary,' *The Daily Cinema*, 27 January 1964, p. 3.

16 Bryan Buckingham, '*Zulu* will pack 'em in,' *News of the World*, 26 January 1964.

17 According to *XXIV: The Journal of the South Wales Borderers and the Monmouthshire Regiment*, August 1964, p. 8, the Army Benevolent Fund 'decided to take 50 per cent of the takings from the London Premiere and to leave the whole proceeds from Cardiff to the four Welsh regiments.' The South Wales Borderers' Benevolent Fund alone received £500 from the two events. I am indebted to Martin Everett, curator of the Royal Regiment of Wales Museum in Brecon, for sending me copies of this editorial and other press clippings.

18 William Hall, 'The Lush Life – by Mr. Baker,' *Evening News*, 7 March 1964.

19 'Big night out for *Zulu* stars,' *Western Mail*, 24 March 1964.

20 'Film shows how her father won V.C.,' unidentified newspaper cutting (courtesy of Martin Everett).

21 Details of local premieres and publicity campaigns are derived from various issues of *The Daily Cinema* and *Kine. Weekly* for 1964. Additional information on the Sheffield event was provided by Clifford Shaw in a letter to the author, 16 July 2002. Joe Levine was canny enough to flatter his hosts during an interview with the UK trade press when he said that 'British theatre managers were far superior to those in America. With *Hercules Unchained* they had lorry loads of entries here but in the States a mere trickle and almost an indifferent response to showmanship ideas' (Observer, 'Commentary,' *The Daily Cinema*, 27 January 1964, p. 3).

22 'Foreign Production Still Significant On Embassy Slate For 1964,' *Variety*, 1 April 1964, p. 8.

23 'Just Tell Them – ,' *Variety*, 11 December 1963, p. 17.

24 'Embassy Keys To the Seller,' *Variety*, 20 May 1964, p. 7; Peter Bart, 'Advertising: An Uninhibited Film Producer', *New York Times*, 5 May 1964; 'The Love of Battles,' *Variety*, 20 May 1964, p. 17; '*Zulu* Featurette Shown On 38 Top TV Stations,' *The Hollywood Reporter*, 21 July 1964.

25 'Joseph E. Levine's *ZULU* in Gala N.Y. Premiere,' *The Hollywood Reporter*, 8 July 1964; 'Show People Are Due at N.Y. *Zulu* Bow,' *Film Daily*, 6 July 1964, p. 3.

26 '*Zulu* Gets Full Levine Promo Tactics; Deny Any South African Complaints,' *Variety*, 18 December 1963, p. 11.

27 Edward Mapp, *Blacks in American Films: Today and Yesterday* (Metuchen: Scarecrow Press, 1972), p. 83.

The Plaza cinema, Lower Regent Street, venue for the World Premiere engagement.

"WELL, WE HAVEN'T DONE TOO BADLY"

17 RELEASE AND BOX OFFICE

> Dear Exhibitors of the World,
> Zulu is the first film we have produced.
> We wanted to make a fine, uncompromising, honest film that would bring in a lot of fine, uncompromising, honest money. Joe Levine and Paramount backed us to reach this double goal. After the opening here in Great Britain, we know that we have done it.
> On the assumption that you would like to do the same, we would like you to exhibit Zulu wherever you are.
> Yours faithfully,
> Stanley Baker   Cy Endfield
> (Trade advertisement, Variety, 29 April 1964, p. 53)

'Remember it? I'll never forget it,' said Mike Ewin when I asked him about the British theatrical release of *Zulu*. Now the managing director of his own film distribution company, Winstone, in 1964 Ewin was UK circuit manager for Paramount Film Service, handling bookings with exhibitors around the country and keeping records of their box-office returns. He recalls being taken by the manager of the Granada cinema, Clapham Junction, into the auditorium to observe the audience at a screening of the film: 'There were about 2,500 seats in there and they were packed absolutely solid – there wasn't a murmur.'

In the 1960s, the British film exhibition scene was dominated by two extensive cinema circuits, Odeon and ABC, respectively owned by the Rank Organisation and the Associated British Picture Corporation. Films would typically play only one or other of these circuits, not both. In addition to being supplied by the production and distribution arms of their own parent companies, they each had long-standing exclusive ties with the other major distributors. Paramount, MGM and Warner-Pathé (a shareholder in ABPC) regularly released their films on the ABC circuit, while Columbia, Twentieth Century-Fox, United Artists and Universal (whose films were actually distributed by Rank) played theirs in Odeon houses. There was therefore never any question that *Zulu*, as a Paramount release, would play the ABC circuit, the weaker half of the duopoly in size and earning capacity.

National releases for both the two major circuits tended to follow a strictly defined pattern. Normally a film would open in London's West End for an exclusive run of four to eight weeks, or longer in the case of so-called 'roadshow' engagements.[1] The first stage of national release after the West End launch was a wave of openings in North London suburban cinemas coinciding with the start of regional first runs, usually in one flagship circuit cinema in each of the 'key cities,' or major population centres. These city-centre theatres typically played a film for one or more weeks, as long as its drawing power justified, but rarely for longer than a month, while the smaller local cinemas usually did not hold onto a film for more than a single week, in order to avoid a logjam of upcoming product. For the second week of release the film would move to the South London suburbs, followed in successive weeks by the rest of the country, also subdivided into regions. Simultaneous national releases such as those which are common today, with new films seemingly playing every cinema at once, were quite unknown at this time: the phased regional release made more efficient use of a comparatively small number of prints, though these would inevitably become increasingly battered as the release progressed and as the film eventually reached the more distant and less remunerative parts of the country.[2]

With the encouraging send-off of the World Premiere, *Zulu* was launched on the West End cinema-going public. They gave it an ecstatic welcome. The film grossed $4,172 in its first day at the Plaza, and the first week's box-office take was in the region of $26,000, the best of any film then in the West End.[3] The second week saw scarcely any falling off, with a gross of around $25,000 – still London's number one attraction when the main competition came from the newly opened *Dr. Strangelove Or: How I Learned To Stop Worrying And Love The Bomb* at the Columbia (later Curzon), Shaftesbury Avenue. The American trade paper *Variety*, which published these figures (hence their presentation here in US dollars rather than pounds sterling), called *Zulu* 'One of the hottest attractions at this theatre in years.'[4] Ellen Baker recalls that, despite the winter cold, she and Stanley stood across from the Plaza every night, watching the long queues snaking down Lower Regent Street.

The film ran for nine weeks before it had to vacate the Plaza to make way for another major Paramount picture, *Becket*, and by this time it had racked up a total gross of $155,000: an all-time record for the cinema, 50% higher than that achieved by any previous non-roadshow attraction.[5] Two days after the Plaza run finished on 24 March, *Zulu* moved over to the Ritz in Leicester Square, a small (only 430 seats) cinema immediately adjacent to the vast Empire and which now forms Empire 2. The film ran there from 26 March to 6 May: the first week gave the cinema its best overall take in two years and the run also registered an all-time four-week house record.[6]

Zulu began its national general release on the ABC circuit on 30 March (Easter weekend), with 29 engagements in North London and up to 75 prints in circulation nationwide. This was a large enough number for the time to be considered a 'saturation' release – a term now more usually applied to print runs of 400 or 500.[7] The holiday period was an ideal slot for the film, though it faced strong competition from the rival Rank Odeon circuit with the popular Cary Grant/Audrey Hepburn thriller *Charade*; the smaller independent chains led with a double-bill reissue of *From the Earth to the Moon* and *Enchanted Island* (both originally released in 1958). No-one need have worried, however: in its first week of London suburban release *Zulu* grossed $242,118. This was 25% above the North London earnings of the previous highest-grossing film shown on the circuit, the Cliff Richard musical *Summer Holiday* (1963), which in the same number of situations had grossed just under $200,000. 28 out of the first 29 *Zulu* engagements broke house records. The second week of London-area release, south of the city, brought the combined total to $428,400, breaking all ABC circuit records. 'In fact, it beat the previous best by no less than 12.1%,' wrote ABC's D.J. Goodlatte when informing Paramount of the good news. Combined with the nine-week Plaza run, the takings from the whole London area brought the film's total box-office take, after less than three months on release, to a huge $583,400. Already it was being claimed that *Zulu* was the biggest-grossing film Paramount had ever released in Britain, beating even its roadshow titan *The Ten Commandments* (1956). Joe Levine predicted that the film would earn back its entire production cost in domestic release alone (it did).⁸

More records were shattered in ABC cinemas in Birmingham, Liverpool, Manchester and Newcastle, among other cities. Cinemas in Welsh areas, in particular, reported unprecedented business. *Zulu* established the longest-ever runs for general releases in Cardiff and Newport, and in Swansea it took 'in excess of anything before' at the box-office.⁹ Letters and telegrams sent by cinema managers from across the country were reproduced in trade press advertisements testifying to the film's extraordinary pulling power: 'Twice the return expected!' 'Easily a record!' 'Broke standing record by 20%!' 'Absolute record!' 'Best-ever take!' *The Daily Cinema*, carrying a photo story of the crowds still flocking to see the film in the West End in its eleventh consecutive week, observed: 'Throughout the country it is the same heart-warming box-office story. Ask any exhibitor. Ask any member of the general public. Phenomenal? Fantastic? Such words are almost an understatement regarding the triumphant success of this truly remarkable British picture.' It was announced in a letter from Paramount, also published in the trade press, that as of 25 April 1964, '3,268,056 people in Great Britain had paid admission to

London West End cinema box-office grosses for week ending 4 February 1964:

Film	Cinema	Gross	Seats	Price Scale	Week
The Cardinal	Astoria	$7,800 ('steady')	1,474	$1.20-$1.75	6
Cleopatra	Dominion	$23,000 ('steady')	1,712	$1.45-$4.20	27
Dr. Strangelove	Columbia	$20,000 ('smash')	740	$1.05-$2.50	1
Fantasia (reissue)	Studio One	$5,300 ('brisk')	862	70c-$2.50	10
55 Days at Peking	Odeon, Haymarket	$5,000 ('steady')	690	$1.05-$2.80	28
How the West Was Won	Casino	$14,900 ('fancy')	1,155	$1.20-$2.15	66
It's a Mad, Mad, Mad, Mad World	Coliseum	$14,200 ('big')	1,795	$1.20-$2.40	9
Ladies Who Do	Odeon, Marble Arch	$4,300 ('fair')	2,200	70c-$1.75	3
Lawrence of Arabia	Metropole	$14,300 ('great')	1,391	70c-$1.75	51
The Leather Boys	Empire	$12,500 ('lively')	1,330	$1.70-$2.15	2
The Leopard	Rialto	$4,800 ('solid')	529	70c-$1.05	4
McLintock!	Leicester Square Theatre	$12,500 ('good')	1,375	$1.05-$2.80	2
Of Love and Desire	Carlton	$4,300 ('moderate')	1,128	70c-$1.75	2
The Pink Panther	Odeon, Leic'r Square	$20,000 ('big')	2,200	70c-$1.75	4
The Servant	Ritz	$5,500 ('sturdy')	430	70c-$1.05	4
This is My Street	Warner	$10,000 ('okay')	1,785	70c-$1.75	n.a.
Tom Jones	London Pavilion	$9,800 ('amazing')	1,217	70c-$1.75	31
The Wonderful World of the Brothers Grimm	Royalty	$8,500 ('okay')	862	70c-$2.50	9
Zulu	Plaza	$25,000 ('mighty')	1,889	$1.95-$2.20	2

Source: *Variety*, 12 February 1964, p. 35. The figures for box-office gross and seat price scales were converted by the journal to US dollars from pounds, shillings and pence. The exchange rate in 1964 was approximately $2.80 to the pound. The comments in brackets represent the reporter's own judgement on the performance of each film, relative to the potential gross of the theatre and the week of the film's run. Note that the apparent popularity of *Cleopatra* is exaggerated by the unusually high seat prices (the highest ever charged in the West End to that date).

304 RELEASE AND BOX OFFICE

LAUNCHING 'ZULU' WITH SHOWMANSHIP

Joseph E. Levine, president of Embassy Pictures, was the host at a combined ABC-Paramount showmanship luncheon in London to launch his presentation of the Stanley Baker-Cy Endfield production, "Zulu".

The luncheon, held at Quaglino's, St. James's, was attended by ABC managers from all parts of the Home Counties. The presentation of "Zulu" is to be backed by a big showmanship contest on the entire ABC circuit. Stanley Baker, star and co-producer of the film, Cy Endfield, director and co-producer, and Jack Hawkins, who also stars in "Zulu," were present at the luncheon and among the many top industry executives attending were George Weltner, executive vice-president of Paramount Pictures Corporation, Russell W. Hadley, Jr., managing director of Paramount in Great Britain, C. J. Latta, managing director of Associated British Picture Corporation, Kenneth Hargreaves, director of Anglo-Embassy Productions, D. J. Goodlatte, managing director of ABC, Howard Harrison, head of Paramount British Pictures, and W. Cartlidge, assistant managing director of ABC. Henri Michaud, Paramount's division manager for Europe, North Africa and the Middle East, was also at the luncheon.

Joseph Levine, D. J. Goodlatte, Kenneth Hargreaves, Stanley Baker, W. Cartlidge, Cy Endfield, and George Weltner; David Jones, Joseph Levine, Bill Cartlidge, George Weltner, and C. J. Latta

Jack Hawkins and Stanley Baker with theatre managers: J. Wright, A. Broadhurst, P. Jackson, A. Fowle, and J. Lewis; and also with S. H. Winterson, P. J. Murray, E. Cecil, S. Burgess, and E. V. Forgham

Joseph Levine speaking at the luncheon

D. J. Goodlatte, Kenneth Hargreaves, Stanley Baker, Peter Reed, general sales manager, Paramount, and Cy Endfield

Joseph Levine welcomes D. J. Goodlatte—in between is Russell Hadley, and on the right George Weltner; Bill Cartlidge speaking at the luncheon

Joseph Levine with D. J. Goodlatte and C. J. Latta; Joseph Levine speaking at the luncheon

Section of the top table at the luncheon; Peter Reed, Bill Cartlidge, Russell Hadley and Kenneth Hargreaves

Joseph Levine welcomes ABC managers R. H. Walker and B. W. E. Nethercote; Jack Hawkins, Stanley Baker and Cy Endfield with managers

The leading **British** trade paper reports on the *Zulu* exhibitors' launch.

RELEASE AND BOX OFFICE 305

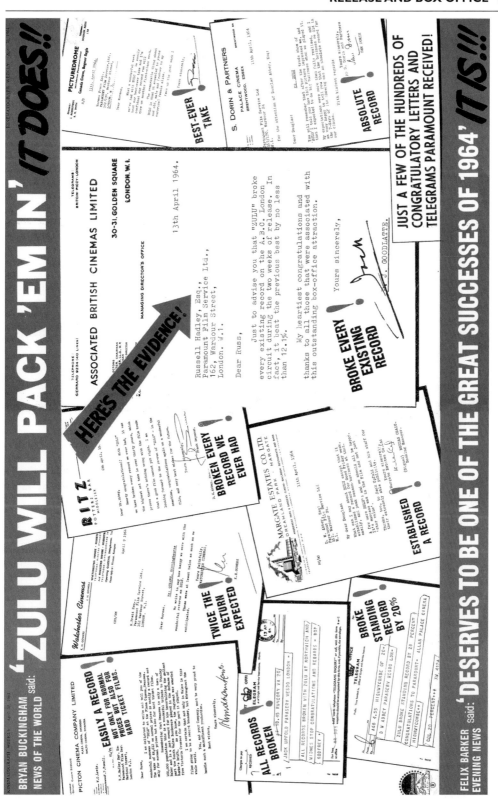

This trade advertisement appeared in *Kine. Weekly*, 30 April 1964.

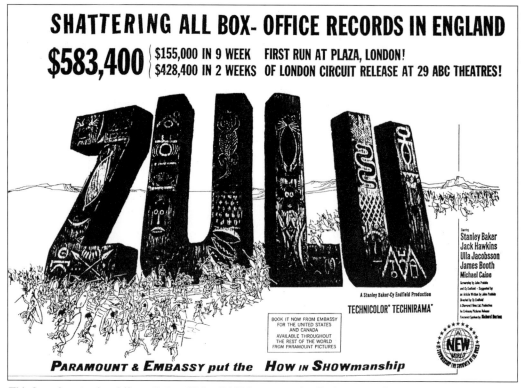

This American trade ad (from *Variety*, 22 April 1964) stresses the film's extraordinary commercial success in the UK. (From a microfilm source.)

see *Zulu* at a total of 224 theatres,' with 'at least 1,200 to 1,300 theatres to go.' It was thought likely that by the end of the year a new record would be established for the percentage of the population in Great Britain who would have seen the film.[10]

For a few months in 1964, as well as setting an all-time record for admissions on the ABC circuit, *Zulu* seems also to have become the highest grossing general release in British cinema history, surpassing the previous recent incumbent, the James Bond film *From Russia With Love* (1963).[11] However, this title was not held for long. In September, the next Bond film, *Goldfinger*, grossed $48,515 in its first week at the Odeon, Leicester Square, and went on to set a new gold standard with a UK gross of £1.25 million (approximately $3 million) before the year's end.[12] *Zulu* was ultimately placed 'a close third' in the ranks of general releases for 1964, after *Goldfinger* and The Beatles' vehicle *A Hard Day's Night*.[13] On the strength of this, the American trade paper *Motion Picture Herald* named Stanley Baker the third most popular star at the UK box-office for that year, behind Sean Connery and Cliff Richard but ahead of Elvis Presley, Peter Sellers, Norman Wisdom, Harry H. Corbett, The Beatles, Sophia Loren and Dirk Bogarde.[14]

Thanks to its historical setting, the popular appeal of *Zulu* did not date and the film was reissued several times over the next few years. A revival West End run at the Plaza from 25 May to 7 June 1967 preceded a full ABC circuit re-release from 30 July, followed by a smaller-scale reissue beginning on 22 March 1970.[15] The major revival, however, took place in early 1972 when, for the first time in Britain, a 70mm print of the film was exhibited at the Casino Cinerama (now the Prince Edward Theatre), Old Compton Street. Some members of the production team misremember the World Premiere screening as having been in 70mm. In fact 70mm projection equipment was not installed in the Plaza until after *Zulu* had finished its initial run, in preparation for the opening of *Becket*, which Paramount announced as its first 70mm release. The impetus for the upgrading of *Zulu* to 70mm was provided by the fact that, at a time of recession in the film industry, the Casino and other 70mm-equipped houses were starved of new product suitable for their vast screens and superior sound systems. *Zulu* was therefore one of a number of older films reissued in a 70mm version at this time. To mark the occasion, a press launch was organised, reuniting Baker, Michael Caine, Jack Hawkins, James Booth, Gary Bond, Peter Gill, Patrick Magee, Cy Endfield and John Prebble, all of whom posed for the cameras.[16] The film took a respectable £21,637 in its seven-week run at the 1,090-seat Casino between 3 February and 21 March 1972. There followed another ABC circuit release from 26 March, complete with a revised advertising campaign ('Now! It's Back!'), while at least two 70mm prints played special seasons over the next eighteen months in suitably equipped venues.[17]

A final ABC reissue came on 4 April 1976 ('It's Back – The Epic Adventure of All Time!'), preceded by a further two-week West End revival at the Ritz from 19 March. The box-office total for the Ritz run was a modest £5,545, but by then the film had already been sold to Britain's commercial television network, ITV. Though television screenings even of the biggest blockbusters are now inevitable, and usually follow within three years of theatrical release (much less in the case of cable and satellite channels), in the 70s the industry still liked to hold on as long as possible to its biggest earners in order to milk them for their last drops of box-office revenue.

Stanley Baker had wanted *Zulu* to be kept in permanent theatrical circulation, never to be diminished by a showing on the box. In fact, long before its eventual network debut, the film had already been telecast at least once, on 11 February 1968, on the capital's cable subscription channel, London Telemeter, though this would have played to a relatively small viewing audience. Perhaps deferring to Baker's wishes – but more likely waiting for an appropriate time-slot – ITV schedulers did not screen the film until following the actor's death. Six months after he passed on, *Zulu* received its national television premiere at 8.00pm on New Year's Eve 1976. ITV's programme planners had initially intended *Zulu* to form the centrepiece of their holiday schedule with a prime slot on Christmas night, but the network's watchdog body, the IBA, had interceded, claiming that this might upset diplomatic relations with South Africa! Another nineteenth-century battle epic, *Waterloo* (1970), was screened in that slot instead; presumably relations with France were considered of lesser political importance. *Zulu* was repeated nationally on Easter Monday 1978 before being syndicated to the various

Broadway's RKO Palace played host to the New York premiere. The event was accompanied by a parade led by a Color Guard from the British War Veterans of America and the fourteen-member Ulster Pipe Band. The entertainments offered on either side of the theatre seem rather less salubrious.

Advertisement from the *New York Times*, 5 July 1964, for the official US premiere and Gotham first runs. Note the supporting feature.
(From a microfilm source.)

regional ITV franchise-holders. It has cropped up at frequent intervals on British television ever since, usually in the key holiday periods and alternating between ITV, the BBC and the cable/satellite stations as the broadcast rights have changed hands. Many younger fans have, as a consequence, never had the opportunity to see it on the big cinema screen where it properly belongs.

United States

Stanley Baker was especially concerned about *Zulu*'s commercial prospects in the vital US market. The only British-made pictures which had broken through to major box-office success in the States had been financed and distributed by the Hollywood studios themselves, and therefore were claimed by them as their own: films such as Columbia's *The Bridge on the River Kwai* (1957), *The Guns of Navarone* (1961, in which Baker appeared) and *Lawrence of Arabia* (1962).

These pictures also had big American stars in front of the camera and big American producers – as well as big American money – behind them.

Aside from Cy Endfield, all the talent on *Zulu* was British, European or South African, and though Paramount was handling its release in the rest of the world, US distribution was in the hands of Embassy: an up-and-coming independent company but by no means yet a major. Baker was afraid that his film would simply not get the attention and the playing time that it deserved. This was an issue he was keen to discuss with the trade press while in New York on promotional duties. He told *Variety* that 'no British picture has been given a full job in the States' and added that with Levine in charge he felt confident that *Zulu* would prove an exception.[18]

In fact, once Paramount executives had seen some of the still unfinished film for themselves, they began to negotiate with Joe Levine to take over its US distribution to give them full world rights to the picture. Studio vice-president George Weltner told the press that the risk taken in financing a film shot on such a far-flung location had been justified ('all parties are highly satisfied with the result,' said *Variety*).[19] At a time when speculation was rife that Paramount and Embassy might permanently join forces, which would mean Levine in effect becoming an employee of the studio rather than an occasional partner and Paramount taking half-ownership of his company, the prospect of a renegotiated *Zulu* deal seemed to be a crucial indicator of the future path they would follow. The trade press speculated that if Embassy were to give up the film's US rights to Paramount, this would be an indicator that a permanent partnership or merger was in the offing.[20]

However, Levine resisted whatever blandishments Paramount threw his way and kept his independence – for a while. By 1966, his involvement with the studio was at an end, their only subsequent co-production being another Harold Robbins project, *The Adventurers* (1970), the result of an old arrangement. The late 60s saw a wave of

Advertisement from the *Los Angeles Times*, 13 July 1964, for the film's multiple LA first runs, often in lengthy double bills. (From a microfilm source.)

corporate takeovers of the Hollywood studios by international conglomerates with no particular interest in filmmaking beyond the bottom line. Paramount was bought up by Gulf + Western, an expanding corporation which had begun life as an auto parts company. That was in 1966; two years later Levine sold Embassy to the finance company Avco, remaining active in the newly named Avco Embassy until his departure in 1974.

Perhaps *Zulu* might have fared better in the US if Levine had accepted Paramount's offer. For though it started out promisingly, the film's Stateside release ultimately proved a relative disappointment. Following its gala Broadway premiere on 7 July, a regular public run commenced at the RKO Palace the following day, along with concurrent runs at around thirty other cinemas in the Century Theatres chain in the Greater New York area. This was the so-called 'Showcase' pattern, originally devised to give local exhibitors an early bite at the box-office cherry rather than their having to wait for the downtown picture palaces to get through with exhibiting a new picture on an exclusive basis.[21] However, *Zulu* had opened elsewhere in the US much earlier than its official start-date, playing in at least six other cities, beginning with Detroit on 17 June, before it reached New York. The Gotham premiere therefore became a regional event rather than a national one. It had also been announced that New York, Chicago and Los Angeles would have screenings in 70mm, though again it seems that America, like Britain, may actually have seen the film only in 35mm.[22]

Nonetheless, though it was only booked in for a two-week stay, *Zulu* prospered at the Palace, grossing an excellent $35,000 in its first week and a very respectable $25,500 in the second. *Variety* commented that it could have been held over for longer if the theatre had not already been booked for another attraction. Promising first-week grosses had also been registered by theatres in the other key cities in which *Zulu* had already opened: $20,000 in Detroit, $15,000 in Chicago, $14,000 in Boston – all at traditional 'hard-top' venues –

***Zulu* box-office gross for first eight weeks of release in selected US cities:**

Boston
July 1 $14,000 ('wow') at Pilgrim (1,909 seats) + 29 other sites
Buffalo
July 1 $6,800 ('good') with *The Hellfire Club* at Century (2,700 seats)
July 8 $5,500 ('modest') with *The Hellfire Club* at Century
Chicago
June 24 $15,000 ('wow') at Loop (606 seats)
July 1 $16,000 ('smash') at Loop
July 8 $7,500 ('good') at Loop
July 15 $6,200 ('bright') at Loop
Cincinnati
July 8 $12,000 ('swell') with *Bullet for a Badman* at Twin Drive-In (800 cars)
July 15 $5,500 ('hotsy') with *Bullet for a Badman* at Twin Drive-In
Cleveland
July 29 $8,000 ('fair') at Hippodrome (3,500 seats)
Aug 5 $5,000 ('thin') at Hippodrome - 5 days only
Denver
July 22 $2,000 at Towne (600 seats) + 8 other sites
Detroit
June 17 $20,000 ('boffo') at Palms (2,995 seats)
June 24 $18,000 ('lively') at Palms
July 1 $8,000 ('good') at Grand Circus (1,400 seats)
July 8 $5,000 ('okay') at Grand Circus
Kansas City
July 22 $60,000 ('big') from 13 sites
Los Angeles
July 15 $26,100 ('slick') at 4 sites with *55 Days at Peking* + $190,000 ('boff') at 30 other sites
July 22 $6,500 ('brisk') with *Ensign Pulver* at Hollywood (856 seats, second week)
July 29 $3,800 ('medium') with *The Long Ships* at Iris (825 seats)
Minneapolis
July 29 $6,000 ('sad') at Orpheum (2,800 seats)
New York
July 8 $35,000 ('smash') at Palace (1,642 seats) + 30 other sites
July 15 $25,500 ('socko') at Palace
Portland
June 24 $5,300 ('good') with *Shame of the Sabine Women* at Fox (1,600 seats)
Providence
July 1 $7,000 ('good') at Majestic (2,200 seats)
July 8 $5,000 ('nice') at Majestic
San Francisco
July 22 $21,000 ('fine') at 3 sites (1,829 seats/ 1,804 seats/ 925 cars)
Seattle
July 15 $6,000 ('dull') with *The Hellfire Club* at Paramount (3,000 seats)

Source: *Variety*, 24 June-19 August 1964.

and $12,000 from a Cincinnati drive-in. Buffalo, Portland, Providence and Seattle reported less favourable results, but the film did well when it opened in Los Angeles on 15 July in a saturation pattern, grossing $216,100 from a total of 34 theatres around the city.

Other multiple-run bookings also did fairly well, with $60,000 earned from thirteen sites in Kansas City and $21,000 from three in San Francisco. But later openings showed something of a falling off, with weak results reported from Cleveland and Minneapolis, and few of the individual runs lasted longer than a couple of weeks (the longest being four weeks at the 606-seat Loop in Chicago). After the eighth week of release *Zulu* simply stopped appearing in *Variety*'s box-office surveys of the key cities, suggesting either that the film lacked the 'legs' for sustained performance or that it simply wasn't getting the key playdates it needed to make a big enough impression on the market.

Interestingly, a number of *Zulu*'s American engagements were double bills, despite its already considerable length of 138 minutes. In its New York Showcase runs the film tended to play in tandem with either *Doctor in Love* (1960) or *Doctor in Distress* (1963). In both Buffalo and Seattle it was partnered with the period swashbuckler *The Hellfire Club* (1961). Cincinatti cinephiles could catch it with the Audie Murphy Western *Bullet for a Badman* while Portland patrons were treated to a pairing with Mexican epic *Shame of the Sabine Women* (1961). The most bizarre co-feature choices were in Los Angeles, where filmgoers had the option of seeing *Zulu* coupled with a variety of lengthy supports, including reissues of *Some Came Running* (1958) and *Rio Bravo* (1959), the Western *A Distant Trumpet*, naval comedy *Ensign Pulver*, Viking epic *The Long Ships* or, most often, second runs of *55 Days at Peking* (1963). This saga of the Chinese Boxer Rebellion, starring Charlton Heston and David Niven, stands worthy comparison with *Zulu*; at a combined running time of 300 minutes, the all-siege programme certainly offered value for money.[23]

The Motion Picture Herald regularly surveyed the experiences of exhibitors around the country to compile a chart of Film Buyers' Ratings as a guide for other cinema programmers. Film bookers were asked to 'rate current product on the basis of its performance in their theatres,' in the ranked categories Excellent, Above Average, Average, Below Average and Poor. *Zulu* received four Above Average ratings, two Average and one Below Average. It was not placed in *Variety*'s compilation of the nation's top twelve attractions for July, though the journal commented helpfully that it 'did some nice to big biz the last two weeks in July on a few playdates.'

Wherever *Zulu* opened, and whatever the local competition, one rival in particular always seemed to get the lion's share of the grosses (and perhaps publicity breaks): the other current Levine-Paramount collaboration, *The Carpetbaggers*. This lurid melodrama, adapted from Harold Robbins' best-selling novel, was Embassy's biggest money-maker and Paramount's biggest non-roadshow release to date, grossing $3,795,000 in only four weeks from 74 theatres in the New York area alone and racking up a number of other box-office

Guests including representatives of the South Wales Borderers attend the Hong Kong premiere on 31 July 1964 at the Princess Theatre, Kowloon. The great-grandsons of Privates Hook and Hitch were both soldiers in the Borderers, which was then stationed in Hong Kong. Corporal Hook was present at the premiere but Lieutenant (Quartermaster) Hitch was ill in hospital and unable to attend.

records.24 As a result, Embassy achieved its highest ever earnings in 1964, with revenues up 50% from the previous year.25 *Zulu* nonetheless made its own contribution to the companies' wellbeing, and certainly did not lose anyone money, as company executive Leonard Lightstone pointed out: 'It's not doing *Carpetbaggers* business, and I guess we've been spoiled. But it is doing very well.'26 *Zulu* was ultimately the second most profitable Embassy release of the year, after the Italian-made Sophia Loren sex comedy *Yesterday, Today and Tomorrow*.

Interestingly, analysis of *Zulu*'s balance sheet shows that, as of 1980, its combined US and Canadian earnings were almost exactly equal to those from Britain – though the North American revenue total includes an early 70s theatrical reissue and probably broadcast television and home video earnings, which may have contributed substantially. Certainly the film soon became a mainstay of US cable TV networks, where it gradually acquired a large, loyal and enthusiastic following far outstripping the public which attended its comparatively modest theatrical run.27

International Release

Throughout the second half of 1964, *Zulu* opened in most of the remaining major markets around the world, beginning with Japan in late June and Hong Kong and Sweden in July. Openings in Austria and West Germany followed in August, Finland and Australasia in September, France and Italy in October, Denmark in November, and South Africa in December. Further international distribution extended into 1965, mopping up all the various minor markets. Several countries, including Sweden, New Zealand and possibly France and South Africa, saw the film in 70mm on first release, unlike Britain (Australia had to wait until 1967 for a 70mm reissue).

A few figures are available for some of these foreign engagements. In Tokyo, *Zulu* earned a total 2,701,544 Yen on its opening day in four theatres. At the Palladium in

This advertisement from the *Cape Times*, 8 October 1968, for a revival screening in Capetown emphasises the presentation in 70mm and six-track stereo. (From a microfilm source.)

Cover of a German souvenir programme brochure.

Stockholm, it grossed the equivalent of $1,342 on opening day. The film was ranked sixth at the Italian box-office for October, the number one slot being held by *It's a Mad, Mad, Mad, Mad World*. Even so, Joe Levine was able to announce at a Paris trade conference that in its international release 'Zulu has been scoring tremendous business, and in some situations abroad has been running ahead of *The Ten Commandments*.'[28]

It may seem surprising that, of the key markets, South Africa should have been left till last. The South African premiere had originally been announced for 25 January 1964, a mere three days after the film's London debut, though this may have been a purely diplomatic move.[29] It had been decided as early as May 1963 that the South African release would be delegated to a local company, Ster Film-Import, controlled by Andre Pieterse, whose staff included several former members of Twentieth Century-Fox's local branch.[30] Pieterse was also, through his SA Film Studios, then lending practical help to the *Zulu* production unit during its location shooting, so it may have been decided that he had earned this participation in the film's fortunes. Of course, Paramount and Embassy may also have felt that his taking the distribution of the film in a politically controversial market off their hands was a welcome break. Ster later won the South African distribution rights of more of the two companies' product, including *The Carpetbaggers*, *A House is Not a Home* (1964), *Harlow*, *Sands of the Kalahari* and *The Naked Prey* (all 1965).[31]

Despite its geographical expanse, South Africa did not have a large film-going catchment. In 1964 there was a total national population of 16,236,000, of whom some 3,000,000 were White. The country had 368 cinemas, mostly in urban areas, with a total seating capacity of 210,000. The government imposed a 50% admissions tax on tickets, so revenues from the country were not likely to be large even if a film proved massively popular.[32] *Zulu* was nonetheless a box-office success: it opened at Johannesburg's Cinerama Theatre in the last week of December and was still running there six months later.[33] The cinema was the only one in southern Africa equipped to present the original three-strip Cinerama format projected on a vast, deeply curved screen, though by the time *Zulu* appeared the process had been replaced by a single-strip 70mm format. It seems likely that *Zulu* was shown there in 70mm (it certainly was when revived in 1968-9). Indeed, George Smith, formerly of National Screen Service, claims that the print screened at the London Casino Cinerama in 1972 was imported from South Africa, so it may very well have been the same one! Nonetheless, a misleading advertisement for '*Zulu* in Cinerama' led one disgruntled fan – identified only as 'Disgusted of Discovery' – to complain to the *Johannesburg Star* that *Zulu* 'was filmed in a process known as Panavision or Technirama, a process without even the added inducement of stereophonic sound,' and that the seat prices were 'much in excess of the prices expected to be paid for such a type of film.'[34]

Zulu world revenue and costs to 31 December 1980:

GROSS RENTALS	Avco Embassy	Paramount	Combined
United States and Canada	$1,867,289	$911,376	$2,778,665
Great Britain		$2,787,598	$2,787,598
Foreign		$2,570,343	$2,570,343
Outright Sales		$243,101	$243,101
Eady Money & Music Royalty		$890,022	$890,022
Totals	$1,867,289	$7,402,440	$9,269,729
DISTRIBUTION FEES			
US & Canada – 35%	$653,551	$318,982	$972,533
Great Britain – 35%		$975,659	$975,659
Foreign – 50%		$1,285,172	$1,285,172
Outright Sales – 10%		$24,310	$24,310
Totals	$653,551	$2,604,123	$3,257,674
NET AFTER DISTRIBUTION FEES			
	$1,213,738	$4,798,317	$6,012,055
DISTRIBUTION EXPENSES			
Preparation & Print Costs	$375,121		$375,121
Advertising & Publicity	$506,384		$506,384
Other Film Costs	$128,065		$128,065
Paramount Expenses		$1,390,648	$1,390,648
Totals	$1,009,570	$1,390,648	$2,400,218
NET AFTER DISTRIBUTION EXPENSES			
	$204,168	$3,407,669	$3,611,837
PRODUCTION COSTS			
Production Advances		$1,751,246	$1,751,246
Interest on Advances	$3,587	$165,888	$169,475
NET PROCEEDS AFTER DEDUCTION OF COSTS			
	$200,581	$1,490,535	$1,691,116

The balance sheet

In December 1964, Stanley Baker had predicted an ultimate world gross – meaning *distributor's* gross, or rentals, not *box-office* gross as mainly discussed thus far in this chapter – of $9 million for his movie.[35] After ten years in distribution *Zulu* had reached almost exactly that figure: $8,747,688 was the actual sum, roughly equally divided between income from Britain, America and the rest of the world. By 1980, with additional revenues from theatrical reissues and television sales, this had reached $9,269,729 and by the end of 1989, $10,186,216. The total profit at this stage – the latest date for which detailed figures are available – was $2,137,013. The rest of the grosses had been eaten up by distribution fees (which always take a hefty cut of the box-office) and the actual costs of distribution, the manufacture of prints, advertising and publicity, studio 'overheads,' and so forth. Nonetheless, it was a very healthy and gratifying return on a picture whose direct production cost had been a mere $1,751,246.

Notes

[1] A roadshow, in film industry parlance, is a film – usually a very expensive blockbuster or an exceptional prestige item – exhibited like a legitimate theatre presentation, with higher than usual ticket prices, reserved seats and a limited number of separate performances per day (in contrast to the continuous performances, without breaks between shows, which were then the norm). *Zulu* was presented on a roadshow basis in some overseas territories, but not on its first release in the UK.

[2] It may be necessary for the benefit of younger readers to point out that there were also no multiplexes in Britain at this time. Oxford Street's venerable 'art-house' venue, the Academy, became London's first two-screen cinema in 1965, while the Odeon, Nottingham, was subdivided into twin auditoria the same year.

[3] '*Zulu* London Lulu,' *Film Daily*, 27 January 1964, p. 2; London box-office report, *Variety*, 12 February 1964, p. 35.

[4] London box-office report, *Variety*. The release date of all films mentioned in this chapter is 1964 unless otherwise noted.

[5] London box-office report, *Variety*; trade advertisements, *Variety*, 22 April 1964, pp. 36-7, and 29 April 1964, pp. 38-9, 53. *Becket* subsequently matched *Zulu*'s grosses in its first two weeks, albeit playing at higher seat prices and in only two performances a day (*Variety*, 14 April 1964, pp. 23, 25). *Zulu* returned to the Plaza for a short pre-Christmas run from 17 to 30 December 1964, following the completion of its national general release.

[6] 'Commentary', *The Daily Cinema*, 8 April 1964, p. 2, and 20 April 1964, p. 3.

[7] In fact, it was Joe Levine's release of his two *Hercules* films in print runs of 60 or more which had initiated the saturation release pattern in Britain. For purposes of comparison, Levine and Paramount's release of *The Carpetbaggers* later in 1964 called for 110 prints while The Beatles' *A Hard Day's Night* was released the same year by United Artists on an extraordinary 180 prints (*The Daily Cinema*, 22-23 January 1964, p. 12).

[8] See 'Box-Office Business,' *Kinematograph Weekly*, 9 April 1964, p. 7, and 16 April 1964, p. 8; '*Zulu* New Record in 29 Brit. Spots,' *Variety*, 15 April 1964, p. 23; trade advertisement, *Variety*, 22 April 1964, pp. 36-7; D.J. Goodlatte, Associated British Cinemas Limited, letter to Russell Hadley, Paramount Film Service, 13 April 1964; 'All Ballyhoo Stops Out On *Carpetbaggers*,' *Variety*, 8 April 1964, p. 11; 'Joe Levine happy with Paramount', *The Daily Cinema*, 20 April 1964, p. 12.

[9] Trade advertisements, *Variety*, 29 April 1964, pp. 38-9, 53.

[10] Paramount International Films, letter to Joseph E. Levine, 25 May 1964, reproduced in a trade advertisement in *Motion Picture Herald*, 10 June 1964, pp. 15-6.

[11] *Motion Picture Herald*, 25 May 1964, pp. 15-16.

[12] Trade advertisement, *Variety*, 30 September 1964, pp. 10-11; William Pay, 'Great Britain's Top Pictures And Players for 1964,' *Motion Picture Herald*, 20 January 1965, p. 5.

[13] Bill Altria, 'British Films Romp Home – Fill First Five Places,' *Kinematograph Weekly*, 17 December 1964. See also 'Bond – Beatles – Zulus: what would you pick?,' *Films and Filming*, February 1965, p. 39, and Pay, op cit. All these lists excluded films playing only on a roadshow basis. Revenues for the most successful film roadshown in Britain to that date, the musical *South Pacific* (which began its roadshow runs in 1958, but was not generally released until 1963), far exceeded those for both *Zulu* and *Goldfinger*, though it too was soon to be surpassed, by *The Sound of Music* (1965).

[14] Pay, op cit.

[15] Mike Ewin, who arranged the 1967 reissue with ABC circuit booker Noel Ford, says that no additional advertising money was made available by Paramount for this re-release because, he was told, the film 'would take care of itself as it always has done.' Ewin claims that *Zulu* was never officially withdrawn from the release schedules, as normally occurred with most films, because it was constantly being booked by cinemas, especially in Wales and the West Country.

[16] See *The Daily Cinema*, 12 February 1972.

[17] George Flaxman reports 70mm engagements of *Zulu* taking place in Derby, Hanley, Leamington Spa, Bedford, Leeds, East Kilbride, Swansea, Perth, Coventry, Colwen Bay, Blackpool, Westcliffe, St. Ives and Newquay (http://www.instereo.com/). For the 1972 re-release an intermission was created (intermissions being a standard feature of 70mm roadshow presentations) by inserting an artificial break just after the series of four shots showing the Zulu snipers raising their rifles – thus creating a mood of

anticipation about how these will be used in the second half. Because it was not integral to the film the intermission is not included in DVD versions; it would have been placed at 75.23 on Paramount's Region 2 DVD or at 78.33 on the MGM Region 1 edition. The Paramount DVD also features the 1972 reissue trailer as an 'Easter egg.'

[18] 'British Think "Too-Small" Pictures For World Playoff – Stanley Baker,' *Variety*, 7 August 1963, p. 22.

[19] 'Not Small-Minded; At *Zulu* Fertility Rites Levine Touts Bronston,' *Variety*, 7 August 1963, p. 4.

[20] 'Maybe: Par's 50% of Embassy,' *Variety*, 2 October 1963, pp. 3, 30; see also '"I'm Too Busy To Run Theatres On The Side" – Levine,' *Variety*, 5 February 1964, p. 13.

[21] Eddie Kalish, 'Cry: "No Summer Widows, We",' *Variety*, 20 May 1964, pp. 7, 17.

[22] 'New African Pic By Baker-Endfield For Jos. E. Levine,' *Variety*, 27 November 1963, p. 3; '*Zulu* Into Palace, N.Y. In Public-Welcome Gala,' *Variety*, 17 June 1964, p. 18. 'I have time on my side and can wait and see whether I'll put it out in 70mm in the States,' Joe Levine had said after the UK premiere (Observer, 'Commentary,' *The Daily Cinema*, 27 January 1964, p. 3).

[23] Additional research on *Zulu*'s US exhibition was conducted on my behalf by Michael Coate.

[24] '*Carpetbaggers* Nears $4,000,000 in New York,' *Film Daily*, 5 August 1964, p. 2.

[25] 'Lovable Banks and Levine,' *Variety*, 14 October 1964, pp. 3, 28; 'Embassy Biz Up 50%; More to Come – Edele,' *Film Daily*, 28 December 1964, pp. 1, 6.

[26] 'Embassy Roadshow Policy Set But Release Plans Are Not,' *Film Daily*, 16 July 1964, pp. 1-2.

[27] The entry on the balance sheet (reproduced at the end of this chapter) indicating that a US-Canadian gross of $911,376 accrued to Paramount, despite the fact that Embassy was responsible for distribution in those territories, is an anomaly I have not been able to explain. Perhaps Paramount was entitled to a proportion of Embassy's income in return for having financed the picture.

[28] '*Zulu* a hit in Japan', *The Daily Cinema*, 1 July 1964, p. 9; '*Zulu* in Stockholm', *The Daily Cinema*, 29 July 1964, p. 5; '*World* Paces Italo Boxoffice, With *Rio*, *Marnie* in 2d and 4th places,' *Variety*, 21 October 1964, p. 31; 'Paramount soaring to new peaks Paris parley learns', *The Daily Cinema*, 3 October 1964, pp. 1, 4.

[29] 'New African Pic By Baker-Endfield For Jos. E. Levine,' *Variety*, 27 November 1963, p. 3.

[30] 'Embassy's Joe Levine Fixes World Distrib For *Zulu*, Africa Pic,' *Variety*, 22 May 1963, p. 13.

[31] 'S. Africa Outfit Lands Par Film,' *Variety*, 23 December 1964, pp. 17-18.

[32] Mike Mosettig, 'Average African Native Sees Only One Feature Film In Course of A Year,' *Variety*, 12 May 1965, p. 161.

[33] Evelyn Levison, 'South African Production Pace As Bigger Budgets Multiply; Government Posture Helpful,' *Variety*, 12 May 1965. p. 151; Evelyn Levison, 'Monthly, Not Weekly, Payrolls, Withholding Taxes Curb Films In Otherwise Booming South Africa,' *Variety*, 29 April 1964, p. 136. Remarkable as *Zulu*'s long run was, it was not a national record: that was held by the all-star Cinerama Western *How the West Was Won* (1962), which ran at the very same theatre for fifty weeks from April 1963

[34] '*Zulu* is not in Cinerama,' *Johannesburg Star*, 29 December 1964. Panavision and Technirama are *not* identical photographic processes, and if the print screened had indeed been 70mm it would have had six-track stereo sound.

[35] 'Baker-Endfield Back Filming In South Africa: It's for Par-Embassy,' *Variety*, 2 December 1964, p. 3.

"VOLLEY FIRE PRESENT!"

REVIEWS AND CRITICISM

> Why do I keep sounding off like a broken record about critical standards? Because I think that sound and effective criticism is absolutely essential in the contemporary world ...
> Roughly 90 per cent of what passes for film criticism in this country today is incompetent and without merit ... Until a substantial number of people, however, demand honest, competent criticism and learn to recognize it when they see it, the public, society at large, and to a certain extent the Church will continue to be manipulated to their detriment by the least scrupulous of commercial film operators.
> (Moira Walsh, 'Which *Zulu* Did You See?', *America*, 25 July 1964.)

In the week before Christmas 1963, *Zulu* was screened in London for the magazine and trade press in what was described by the latter as 'one of the most successful magazine screenings ever held by Paramount.'[1] A second press show, for the newspaper reviewers, was held the week before the World Premiere.[2] One scribe who had attended the earlier showing, Maryvonne Butcher of *The Tablet*, felt that this gave her an advantage over her peers: 'my part of the house happened to be packed with authentically Welsh Welsh Guardsmen. Since the film is about the battle of Rorke's Drift ... the comments of my neighbours (surprisingly complimentary) added greatly to my understanding and enjoyment of the picture.'[3]

The thirty-nine contemporary British reviews of *Zulu* I have sampled are about equally divided between those which are generally positive or sympathetic (nineteen) and those which are 'mixed' (eighteen); only two are wholly unfavourable. As Robert Shail has discussed in a recent article, British critical responses to the film were generally split between the popular press, which on the whole expressed uncomplicated enthusiasm for it, and the upmarket broadsheets, which were more ambivalent, perhaps confused and at times openly hostile.[4] (See the checklist at the end of this chapter for full details of all the reviews consulted.)

The trade press, whose main interest was in assessing the commercial viability of a new picture (though professional accomplishment was also a consideration), were united in pronouncing *Zulu* a solid hit. The anonymous reviewer for the Cinematograph Exhibitors Association's monthly newsletter *CEA Film Report* awarded a particularly high rating on its usual ten-point scale: '9 marks for general, more particularly masculine and better-class, audiences.' The trade reviewers also drew attention to qualities that were frequently to be praised in the mainstream press notices: the spectacle, excitement and 'realism' of the battle scenes; the tension and suspense of the preceding build-up; the film's air of period authenticity, enhanced by location shooting; and the high quality of the acting and

REVIEWS AND CRITICISM

British Press Reviews

POSITIVE	MIXED	NEGATIVE
CEA Film Report	Birmingham Post	Daily Worker
The Daily Cinema	Catholic Herald	Manchester Guardian
Daily Express	Daily Telegraph	
Daily Herald	Evening Standard	
Daily Mail	Liverpool Daily Post	
Daily Mirror	Monthly Film Bulletin	
Daily Sketch	New Statesman	
Evening News	The Observer	'Everybody liked it
Films and Filming	Punch	except the *Manchester*
Financial Times	The Spectator	*Guardian* ... and they
Housewife	Sunday Citizen	don't have much
Illustrated London News	Sunday Express	circulation.' (Joseph E.
Jewish Chronicle	Sunday Telegraph	Levine, quoted in
Kine. Weekly	Sunday Times	Katherine Hamill, 'The
News of the World	The Tablet	Supercolossal – Well,
The People	The Tatler	Pretty Good – World of
Sunday Mirror	Time and Tide	Joe Levine', *Fortune*,
Thames Valley Times	The Times	March 1964, p. 180)
What's On		

production values. Margaret Hinxman, writing in *The Daily Cinema*, commended Endfield and Baker for 'triumphantly juggling commercial and prestige values' to produce a film which was both 'an epic for the masses and a film for the connoisseurs.' She went on:

> The primitive splendour of the massed Zulus is stunningly contrasted with the puny contingent of British soldiers in their red, Victorian, pre-Boer War uniforms. And the tension within the camp leading to the explosively bloody battle action creates a throbbing suspense that never lags. Brilliantly sustained through well over half the film, the combat scenes achieve a relentless realism that few war films (ancient or modern) have managed to achieve.
>
> Yet the spectacle isn't allowed to obscure the integrity of purpose. With amazing restraint, the film despatches the heroine before she can so much as cast sheep's eyes at one of the besieged officers or cower shrieking before a marauding Zulu. Though the theme is one of death or glory, it doesn't prettify the bestial facts of even this comparatively gallant chapter in the annals of war.

A number of the mass-market and middlebrow critics saw the film primarily as a triumphant return to the tradition of the imperial adventure or war drama. Cecil Wilson of the *Daily Mail* described it as 'a classic piece of real-life Errol Flynnery ... [brought] nobly back to life.' John Sandilands in the *Daily Sketch* offered 'three cheers' for 'a picture that does the British Army proud ... as fine a memorial to the glorious battle of Rorke's Drift as any of the defenders ... could have wished,' while Felix Barker of the *Evening News* wanted 'to award this superb film a Victoria Cross of its own ... If ever the phrases "the Thin Red Line" or "last man, last round" had real significance, they get it in the film made by Stanley Baker and Cy Endfield.' The many similar comments included the following:

'This is every schoolboy's dream of magnificent defiance – and it makes a magnificent film. You'll know what I mean: you won't dodge out before the National Anthem is played.'
(*Daily Mirror*)

'Stanley Baker and Michael Caine give exactly the right touch of pride and glory to this old-fashioned but strongly exciting film.'
(*The People*)

'This picture will make a fortune ... And it's one of the most exciting adventure yarns I've ever seen.'
(*News of the World*)

'The battle scenes are truly magnificent. All in all, an epic of courage and fortitude that stirs the senses.'
(*Jewish Chronicle*)

'*Zulu* reflects an unusual amount of credit on everybody concerned. It thrilled and rejuvenated me.'
(*Illustrated London News*)

Several critics also linked the film to the currently fashionable genre of the large-scale period epic, but found that *Zulu* successfully avoided its worst tendencies. James Monahan in *Housewife* claimed that, despite the film's having a 'big out-of-doors' subject typical of widescreen spectacles, the result was far from 'a case of the prevailing elephantiasis.' Ann Pacey in the *Daily Herald* noted that '*Zulu* emerges as a rare example of a thoughtful spectacular,' and Patrick Daly in the London-based listings journal *What's On* praised 'qualities which lift it out of the visual class and into – dare I say it? – the psychological one. For instance, it presents the Zulus ... as a race of dignified and intelligent warriors, whose strategy was at least equal to their prowess and showy aggressiveness. It offers British soldiers as subject to human failings as the rest of us, and as capable of rising above these failings as the best of us. It portrays battle as the confused, chancy and idiotic thing that it is.'

Daly's review shared with some other critics a sense of the film's sophisticated, revisionist approach to generic tradition. David Robinson in the *Financial Times* remarked that while *Zulu* 'recalls those sagas of Empire that were popular in the '30s,' it also demonstrated that the 'way the genre has been modified ... significantly reflects changing attitudes in the post-war cinema.' The differences included, he said, a 'new taste for documentary reconstruction [which] probably arises from the consciousness, which was not so acute in the '30s, that war is too serious a matter to be lightly fictionalised. It is an attitude everywhere explicit. Although the old clichés survive ... the light-hearted old swashbuckling approach is gone. The sense of shame in killing, of the waste when brave men must face each other in battle, is everywhere emphasised at the cost of old beliefs in the Errol Flynn brightness and glory of it all.' Gordon Gow in the popular film magazine *Films and Filming* echoed these comments and added some perceptive analysis of his own:

> Cutting through the spectacle-belt with a salutary bloodymindedness, Cy Endfield's *Zulu* takes an anti-heroic view of the kind of situation which used to be treated to flag-waving fervour ... an adventure story pervaded by an implicit sourness. Duty-bound and dubious, the British soldiers who stay at their post, when they could in reasonable conscience clear out and save their skins, are never glorified. Uniforms are dapper and strategy is shrewd, but there is fear and sorrow in every soldier's eye, and at length their collective attitude is summed up by a young lieutenant, new to combat, who surveys the blood-smeared vista of victory and declares himself 'sick and ashamed' ...
> At the same time, and without being two-faced about it, *Zulu* possesses what many a well-meant movie lacks: perspective. It is never so bigoted as to assume that the situation is simple; courage in itself is noted and acknowledged, but not with a crow of

This advertisement appeared in UK trade journal *Kine. Weekly*.

triumph: when Richard Burton speaks the names of the men who were awarded Victoria Crosses for their service in this action, he does so in tones more redolent of a lament.

While most critics were grateful for the absence of obtrusive 'love interest' and the rapid disposal of the Witts, some were distracted by the female nudity on display in the wedding dance. Raymond Anker complained in the *Liverpool Daily Post* that the 'cameras dwell so long on 500 shapely, half-naked Zulu girls doing a bridal dance that I began to wonder whether we were in for heroism or sex.' Alan Dent in the *Illustrated London News*, on the other hand, found that the sequence 'makes a superb and attention-grabbing opening ... The chanting music has its own kind of monotonous charm. The dancing has a dignity which is utterly lacking in those latter-day twitchings and twists of ours which basically imitate such African dances.'

One of the film's qualities which was often remarked upon (it is a favourite term of praise, particularly for British critics) was its sense of restraint, especially in relation to the overt patriotism expected of an imperial adventure. The *Sunday Mirror*'s Jack Bentley expressed his gratitude that 'Hollywood didn't grab the idea and turn it into a vehicle for US Cavalry hokum.' The *Daily Herald* commented that *Zulu*:

reconstructs a piece of British military history... with more integrity and restraint than most movie epics ever hope to achieve.

With the minimum of tub-thumping, the slightest hint of jingoism, the terrible slaughter is recreated in a style that invites sympathy with both sides and offers justification for neither.

One has the impression that many of the red-coated soldiers of the line had no idea who the Zulus were or why they were fighting them.

The *Daily Sketch* suggested that although the bare facts of the battle might have made 'for the biggest feast of flag-waving since the Coronation ... *Zulu* avoids all temptations. It is as straight and steely as a bayonet – a British-made epic of under-statement with the heroics left to speak for themselves.' Philip Oakes in the *Sunday Telegraph* felt that the filmmakers had 'chipped the high gloss off the heroics and concentrated instead on the plain mechanics of bravery. Strategy is made plain, the game is seen to be not only greater, but infinitely more interesting than the players.'

Many critics appreciated the film's 'realism,' meaning both its apparent period authenticity and the clarity and intensity of the combat scenes. Thus the *Evening News* complimented the filmmakers on 'the exciting battle scenes, filmed with rare coherence ... [and] the sense of period, the *feeling in depth*, that is conveyed.' The *Daily Express* noted that 'the men, those brave, red-jacketed men, are no longer sawdust heroes. They are real men, with real fears.' The battle scenes proved overwhelming in their vividness and immediacy

---

THE CATHOLIC HERALD — by Freda Bruce Lockhart

FILMS

SOME RATTLING GOOD HEROISM

NO doubt the fashion of stars becoming their own producers began as an economic expedient.

But as it proceeds, the star-producer concept develops closer and closer to that of actor-manager, with all the consequent identification and, at best, enthusiasm.

Stanley Baker is our latest British star to enter this ambitious field.

It is easy to see some of the factors which tempted him to make Zulu ("U", Plaza).

It is a good compact story of heroism — heroism which won eleven V.C.'s for the small detachment of a Welsh regiment who stood their ground unbelievably and so, I am given to understand, brought to an end the Zulu war.

Settings are spectacular and continentally topical, even if particular w...

Even Welsh patriotism encouraged the subject. The Zulu's savage sounds, from a clatter of spear on shields which was found to sound like a train, to a rather dusty-throated battle hymn, challenges a surprisingly (after the carnage) orderly rendering of "Men of Harlech".

A bunch of expert British character actors, characterise enough "little men" to hold the fort.

But there is one truly outstanding performance besides Mr. Baker's own expected good one. It is from Michael Caine.

Jack Hawkins and Ulla Jacobssen, as a treacherous, drunk...

Known on television for his authentic Cockney characters, Mr. Caine here turns in an excellent portrait of a Guards-type professional officer and gentleman. It is observed but not quite caricatured, and shows Mr. Caine to be quite ready to make the difficult transition from Cockney-type to full-range actor. It is pleasant to honour such an achievement.

The film is an honourable tribute to a gallant record. Its one...

THE ILLUSTRATED LONDON NEWS

OUR CRITIC'S CHOICE.

JAMES BOOTH IN *ZULU*.

Alan Dent writes: "One of the best of many good soldierly performances in "Zulu," the film of Rorke's Drift in the Zulu War of 1879, comes from James Booth. Mr. Booth, who is a graduate of the Stratford East-End school of acting, made his film debut as a particularly nasty and smooth young blackmailer in the better of the two Oscar Wilde films of some three years ago—the one with Peter Finch in the name part. He now plays, even more successfully, a malingering patient in the garrison sick-bay who shows himself capable of heroic fighting when this is called for. This character, Private Henry Hook, was actually one of the 11 men of the garrison who were honoured with the Victoria Cross for their defence of Rorke's Drift. The film, "Zulu," directed very strikingly by Cy Endfield, began its London career at the Plaza on January 22—exactly 85 years...

FILMS

Epic of courage

By F. H. SAMUEL

As I have visited Zululand, I was perhaps better able to appreciate the motivation of the thrilling new Stanley Baker-Cy Endfield production in Technicolor at the Plaza, Zulu ("U"). For every visitor to the vast Zulu reserve in Natal is soon made aware of the legends that have been proudly woven by these delightful folk out of the thrilling event that the film portrays—the gallant stand of a handful of British soldiers against several thousand Zulus at the battle of Rorke's Drift in 1879.

Without false heroics, Mr. Baker and a fellow-officer (an outstanding piece of work by Michael Caine) rally the men to superhuman efforts against overwhelming odds. The battle scenes are truly magnificent. All in all, an epic of courage and fortitude that stirs the senses...

JEWISH CHRONICLE

324 REVIEWS AND CRITICISM

This promotional article appeared in the April 1964 edition of *ABC Film Review*.

for many commentators. Dilys Powell in the *Sunday Times* complained that 'the U certificate benevolently allows children of the tenderest years to view the African dead and dying piled as if on a butcher's slab.' Keith Brace of the *Birmingham Post* also drew attention to the unusually graphic violence: 'In one harrowing sequence the British, in three alternating ranks, fire at assegai-thrust range until their feet are slipping in Zulu blood and flesh. The film is honest enough to present this as horror and to show the soldiers sick at the horror.'

Several reviewers discerned a distinct anti-war theme. Clive Barnes of the *Daily Express* found in this 'great epic film of battle ... a quality new to films of its bloodstained sort. Call it compassion.' He went on:

> But there is no flag-waving here. Glorious in small patches, yes. Yet also it is seen as a waste – a waste of men, and a waste of spirit ...
>
> The film is neutral. It doesn't talk about the rights of this or that or, more pertinently, them or us. It says there is a sort of shabby glory in battle, and it plays fair with both the glory and the shabbiness ...
>
> And when at the end Richard Burton, the unseen narrator, lists the honours won, and the camera idly picks its way among the dead and dying, I felt the film's great revulsion that killing people was wrong. Not good, not glorious, just plain wrong.

Even those critics who were not completely won over by the film, or expressed strong reservations about it on other grounds, generally made a point of acknowledging the technical skill with which it had been made. *Punch* conceded that, 'considering how little variety of incident there is to summarise ... it's surprising that it is so effectively gripping for well over two hours.' *The New Statesman* also applauded the visual spectacle and added a favourable word (surprisingly rare) for the sound department: 'Cy Endfield sends Stephen Dade's camera panning and scanning the small beleaguered bastion, tilting up to a slow ominous patrol of the mountain skyline around. Suddenly Zulus bristle on the ridge, disappear, emerge after minutes of tension in assaulting waves, are massacred to lie – corpse upon corpse – like some dreadful shoal of fish. The soundtrack is at times really distinguished.' Gordon Gow described the director's felicities of style at some length in *Films and Filming*:

> Filmically, Endfield would appear to have enjoyed himself quite a bit. Addicted to the panning shot (which admittedly never pans quite as far as you might expect), he gets in some splendid visuals on his African location, especially when the soldiers stand in a formal pattern awaiting the enemy, and when the dead and dying Africans lie in a heap at the feet of their sad-eyed conquerors. From the mountains and the sky, nature is constantly reproaching the ugly deeds of men; the first wave of attacking Zulus is presented in a composition that includes, right in the foreground, a tree loaded with blossom.
>
> Diverting details are plentiful, among them a shot of spears coming through a hospital door, which recalls one of Hitchcock's finer frenzies in *The Birds*, and for extra measure a cattle stampede with the camera underhoof.

The critic of *The Spectator*, Isabel Quigley, gave particular attention in her review to the aesthetics of large-scale combat situations:

> Battle, like all ritual, is photogenic; the actual tactics – groupings and formations, ways of defence, attack, feint and counterfeint – are, perhaps especially to the ignorant, fascinating and photogenic; 4,000 Zulus in full fig approaching on every side, in never-ending hordes, are fearsomely photogenic... it is this seeming *endlessness* of their number and attacks that makes the strongest impression... and for a film that's largely taken up with killing, it strikes me as decently unbloodthirsty.

The *Sunday Times*' Dilys Powell again demurred, however, considering *Zulu* 'a long film but not, I thought, boring... Not distinguished either, I'm afraid; except for some fine menacing shots of the African warriors (and they were heroic, too) drawn up on the hill-crest I have carried away few visual images – and after all a battle-film can be the occasion for superb cross-rhythms and cross-movements; I am thinking, for instance, of John Wayne's *The Alamo*.'

The film's presentation of the Zulus themselves was generally given favourable notice. 'The Zulus are not just a bunch of bloodthirsty savages,' pointed out the *Daily Mirror*. 'It is the noble savage at his noblest and his most savage and most disciplined.' *What's On*'s critic admired the fact that, 'although it is fairly obvious in which camp the film's sympathies lie, the Zulu is never made to look the screaming savage which other, less sensitive films, have tried to make him.' *The Observer* remarked on the seeming disparity between the two opposing forces: 'Beside the Zulus, blooming with health and thundering fearsomely on shields made of dried animal skins, the actors playing the British look touchingly underendowed physically and much more frightened of death; there is a marvellous shot when they are leaning against the barricades in sheer exhaustion, listening to the Zulus' war songs and wondering how to fight people who don't know the European rules.' Even the generally hostile *Monthly Film Bulletin* agreed that 'there should be a special credit for the handling of the Zulu hordes, presumably by 2nd Unit director Bob Porter.'

Among the principal cast, two actors in particular were repeatedly singled out for praise. Though Michael Caine has often pretended otherwise – for example, his protest in 1969 that 'the reviews for me were... well, sort of like that (as a matter of fact, all reviews for me are sort of like that)'[5] – most of his notices for *Zulu* were unstinting in their praise, as the following comments suggest:

'Michael Caine makes a screen debut [sic] that puts him right up in the front rank of Britain's best young film actors'
(*The Daily Cinema*)

'an outstanding piece of work by Michael Caine'
(*Jewish Chronicle*)

'For Michael Caine, actor, this, too, is victory … he has his best role to date.' (*Daily Mirror*)

'Michael Caine, well known on tv, makes a notable debut as Lieut. Bromhead'
(*Kine. Weekly*)

To some of the critics, Caine was a complete unknown. Others were familiar with his work on television and drew a sharply favourable distinction between his performance in *Zulu* and what was already becoming a stereotyped small-screen persona. Thus, Freda Bruce-Lockhart of *The Catholic Herald* noted that 'there is one truly outstanding performance … Mr. Caine here turns in an excellent portrait of a Guards-type professional officer and gentleman. It is observed but not quite caricatured, and shows Mr. Caine to be quite ready to make the difficult transition from Cockney-type to full-range actor. It is pleasant to honour such an achievement.' In a generally unenthusiastic review, the anonymous critic of *The Times* also conceded that 'there is one performance worth watching, that of Michael Caine as the untried lieutenant, cast right against type and proving conclusively that he can play something far other than his usual Cockney joker roles if only someone will give him the chance.'

Even those critics who felt that Caine was miscast generally found redeeming merit in his performance. John Coleman in *The New Statesman* considered that Caine '*looks* so staggeringly right' for his role (vindicating the reason behind Cy Endfield's casting of him in the first place). *Time and Tide* thought that 'despite the fact that he kept forgetting his accent, he played convincingly well,' while *The Observer* observed: 'There is an interesting

actor called Michael Caine who plays Stanley Baker's second-in-command; he is slightly wrongly cast as an upper-class officer, but he does it very well.' The only overtly negative comment about Caine that I have been able to find is by Alexander Walker in the *Evening Standard*. Walker found that 'the attempt to work up a little class battle between Stanley Baker, good as the tough artisan commander, and Michael Caine as a languid lieutenant gets nowhere because Mr. Caine can't keep up the accents and attitudes of an aristocrat.' This evidently stuck in Caine's craw and perhaps coloured his perception of the reviews generally. Walker later repeated the criticism in his book *Hollywood, England* and told one of the actor's biographers that, at the time of his original review, it became 'the cause of serious comic arguments whenever we met for months afterwards.'[6]

After noting that Caine had almost stolen the film from Stanley Baker, the *Daily Herald* went on to add: 'Grabbing the film from both of them is Nigel Green, as Colour-Sergeant Bourne, whose mutton-chop whiskers, bright blue eyes and rough but understanding attitude seem so absolutely right that one feels he has stepped out of the history books.' Green was the only actor to win more plaudits from the critics than Caine, being mentioned in glowing terms in virtually every single review, and never with a hint of negativity. For the *Liverpool Daily Post*, Green's work was the highlight of the whole show: 'standing out in a spectacle to which one must succumb, a performance that is masterly. The actor, Nigel Green, plays a colour-sergeant, and now I cannot think what *Zulu* would be like without him. The character is the perfect non-commissioned officer, and he plays it perfectly. This, one feels, is a real man of a real type at a certain historical period. *Zulu* is worth seeing for a number of reasons; it is worth seeing for Mr Green alone.' Green effortlessly swept the board of the reviewers' acting honours with his matchless interpretation of Bourne as 'the colour sergeant to end them all' (*New Statesman*). The following compliments represent only a small sampling of those he received:

'I shall remember many things. First, the astonishingly fine performance of Nigel Green – to me quite unknown – as the Colour-sergeant, a Kipling NCO brought to life with inflexible authority.'
(*Evening News*)

'To praise all the actors would be to offer as many medals as did Queen Victoria herself … the acting is superb. But perhaps a word should go to praise the gentle-hearted colour sergeant of Nigel Green.' (*Daily Express*)

'Other performances shine out from the muddle and misery of war against fearful odds … notably, Nigel Green as every tough but tender-hearted colour-sergeant compressed into one ramrod.'
(*Daily Mail*)

'The chest to pin acting's Military Medal on is really Nigel Green's – his paternal colour-sergeant is right in character *and period*.'
(*Evening Standard*)

'Mr. Nigel Green is excellent as the redoubtable colour sergeant (kindly but firm as an English nannie)'
(*The Tatler*)

'a performance by Nigel Green that makes all previous portrayals of the type look false'
(*Films and Filming*)

'there is a very good performance by Nigel Green as the colour-sergeant, a kind of military nanny, who coaxes an hysterical missionary (Jack Hawkins) into compliance as if he were soothing a bawling baby: "Now there's a good gentleman, sir…."
(*Sunday Express*)

By contrast with such extravagant effusions, comments devoted to some of the other actors often seem more dutiful than enthusiastic. Stanley Baker, for example, apparently impressed the journos more with his achievement as debutant producer than with his work in the seemingly thankless leading role, which tended to be passed over with token nods for his 'sturdy hero' (*Financial Times*), 'stony panache' (*New Statesman*) and 'suitably commanding' (*Sunday Express*) presence; though *Films and Filming*, having noted Baker's 'sincere and remarkably self-effacing' performance, added that he needed 'only to be informed that on occasions like this the omission of a reasonable haircut is carrying authenticity to extremes.'

Of the other performers, James Booth was regularly picked out as worthy of mention, albeit not always favourably. The *Sunday Telegraph* complained that Booth 'mugs away atrociously as a 19th century Dead End Kid who blunders into glory on the Veldt' and *The Daily Cinema* felt that that he had been 'allowed a little too much head as a trouble-prone ranker.' *Films and Filming*, however, thought Booth 'better than he has ever been on the screen as a "common" soldier drawn, for once, in depth,' and the *Illustrated London News* found Hook 'perhaps [the] best of all among the incidental characters.' Meanwhile, the ever-sceptical Alexander Walker remarked in the *Evening Standard*: 'James Booth is enjoyable as an artful other-ranker, but was "You're joking!" in use as sarcastic repartee in 1879?'

It is easy to see who took the brunt of negative criticism from comments such as the following:

'There are a dozen fine small performances, but for once Jack Hawkins, as an hysterical clergyman, fails to convince.'
(*Evening News*)

'Jack Hawkins is unremarkable as a drunken Swedish missionary'
(*The Tablet*)

'Jack Hawkins isn't what you'd call at home as a missionary' (*Sunday Times*)

'Mr. Jack Hawkins is woefully miscast as a pacifist missionary with bobbed hair and a weakness for gin'
(*The Tatler*)

'And I can't see why they used Jack Hawkins at all. He is wasted as a missionary.'
(*Sunday Citizen*)

To be fair, the trade papers found Hawkins 'strikingly effective' (*The Daily Cinema*) and 'agonisingly pathetic' (*Kine. Weekly*) – the latter meant as a compliment. Most reviewers preferred to ignore Ulla Jacobsson altogether or to be grateful that the film got her character out of the way early. The *Sunday Telegraph* remarked that she 'appears briefly to be ogled (a) by a Zulu warrior and (b) by a member of the licentious soldiery,' while *Films and Filming* described her 'doing very nicely' as 'the girl-most-likely-to-get-her-blouse-ripped.'

Other unfavourable comments tend to harp on one or more of several distinct themes: the film's supposed lapses into cliché and/or sentimentality; and its limited political perspective and failure to explore the historical context of the battle. The *Daily Telegraph*'s critic was initially delighted to find *Zulu* 'confirming my childhood impressions of masses of wild and naked blacks, howling horribly, raining down assegais on stout-hearted but inferior British forces. Alas, my delight was short-lived, the film, which concentrates on the defence of Rorke's Drift, making the mistake of relying too much on this sort of thing at the expense of character or story.' *Punch* also complained that 'such attempts as are made to show any interplay of character, or any character beyond the most superficial type-attributes, are fairly perfunctory.' The *Birmingham Post* reserved particular ire for the portrayal of the Welsh 'other ranks' as 'comic regional types' and the Reverend Witt as 'a caricature fanatic.' The 'battle of song' drew a number of brickbats even from critics well-disposed towards the film, such as the *Daily Mail*'s Cecil Wilson: 'Sometimes the drama is too theatrical to ring true, as when the Welsh diehards answer the Zulus' war cry just a shade too glibly with *Men of Harlech*.' This sequence was a gift for detractors, such as *The Times*' anonymous reviewer, who referred to 'the terrible inevitabilities (like the awful moment when the Welsh soldiers reply to the Zulu dawn-chant with "Men of Harlech").'

Perhaps the most thoroughgoing critique along these lines, and one of only two wholly negative British reviews I have found, came from *Manchester Guardian*'s Richard Roud, whose curmudgeonly review is worth quoting at length for its extreme one-sidedness, as if Roud had been determined to remain unimpressed:

Zulu, we are told, was suggested by an article by John Prebble. It must have been a very short article. There was a time when big, spectacular action films were action-full. Nowadays all that has changed…

There's nothing wrong with an old cliché, but oh, how slow it all is. Great pauses between each line, action and reaction following each other as boringly and as remorselessly as the clicks of a death watch beetle – and with much the same effect. The Zulus look terribly embarrassed as they are put through their paces, but then, so does Jack Hawkins as a brandy-drinking Swedish parson.

This is the kind of film where nobody ever seems to have given any real thought to what the characters do and say. Patrick Magee, for example, plays a middle-aged army doctor. He has apparently been in the service for at least 20 years, so one presumes this is not his first battle. And yet, the minute he has to exercise his function as surgeon, what does he do? He roars out, 'Oh, you butchers,' and mopes over the death of a soldier.

The sense of anachronism touched on by Roud – the implausible modernity of the film's attitudes and values – grated on many of the reviewers. Penelope Gilliatt of *The Observer* considered the film 'best when it's most like the *Boy's Own Paper*,' but felt that the 'liberal lines seem a bit out of period. Every soldier there must have called the enemy the fuzzy-wuzzies at the time, and it's like trying to graft a left-wing leaflet on to the Duke of Wellington to make us accept anything else.'[7] The *Daily Telegraph*'s Patrick Gibbs was more familiar with the facts of the battle than most reviewers, and as well as pointing out several of the film's discrepancies he complained that the 'attempt to fit in a Socialistic malingerer (James Booth) quite fails.' He explained: 'This putting of "retrospective views" into people's mouths is unhappy. The dying man who asks "why" or the officer who is "disgusted" hardly give to this Empire-building episode a convincing sense of period.' Isabel Quigley in

The Spectator found that 'Childish characterisation goes uneasily with a modern effort to look carnage in the eye and hate it.' John Coleman in the *New Statesman* argued: 'Morally, there are sops to all factions. Green's sergeant is absolutely in line with traditional heroics, barking and swaggering but deeply concerned with the welfare of his men and, of course, indefatigable ... On the other side, a modern sense of what is appropriate has prevented any revelling in the slaughter ... But none of this pandering to opposed prejudices – the BOP [*Boys' Own Paper*] and the CND – generates much in the way of likelihood.'

For the more sceptical, there seemed to be a contradiction between the film's attempts at authenticity and some of its invented details and dramatic contrivances. These reviewers were troubled by what they saw as divided intentions, its apparently split personality. *Punch*'s Richard Mallett recognised that *Zulu*'s 'detachment of tone, a refusal to glory in so much killing of the enemy' distinguished it from the traditional war adventure, but felt that the anti-war theme was not fully carried through in the treatment of the Reverend Witt. Brenda Davies in the British Film Institute's journal of record, the *Monthly Film Bulletin*, also found that: 'In spite of being concerned with long ago battles, *Zulu* is a typically fashionable war film, paying dutiful lip service to the futility of the slaughter while milking it for thrills ... whenever there is a pause in the action the script plunges relentlessly into bathos, with feuding officers, comic other ranks, and all the other trappings of British War Film Mark I, which one had hoped were safely obsolete. It seems a very poor tribute to the men who actually fought at Rorke's Drift to portray them on such a comic strip level.'

For other critics, attempts at factual accuracy and/or period authenticity were not enough: they wanted a better sense of the wider context of the battle. *Time and Tide* echoed the thoughts of many that *Zulu* stuck 'closely to the historical facts – too closely,' and asked for 'a larger panorama of the situation.' The *Sunday Citizen* commented that 'if the camera had lingered a little less on the fighting and a little longer in filling in the background of the heroes, I'd have called this film great.' Brenda Davies in *The Monthly Film Bulletin* criticised the script for its failure 'to set the scene and fill in the historical background. Worse still, in their anxiety to show that they are on the side of the angels, the writers make the whole defence operation appear to be motive-less and suicidal lunacy.' The *Sunday Telegraph*'s Philip Oakes argued that, during the Anglo-Zulu War itself, Rorke's Drift had been 'skilfully exploited for its propaganda value. Even now, 85 years on, cause and effect are never considered. What *Zulu* celebrates is courage – a virtue which history tends to cut down to size, but which still looks great on the wide screen.' Alexander Walker articulated the issues most forcefully in his *Evening Standard* review, portentously entitled 'Blood and spectacle – but I wanted history, too':

> *Zulu* arrives armed to the teeth to make a killing at the box-office, and it deserves to do so. But is it ungracious to regret that all the screen shows us nearly all the time is another kind of killing? ...
>
> For sheer scenic slaughter this is a giant of a film.
>
> But could we not have had a little history mixed in with the war-cries?
>
> Rorke's Drift was a face-saving success – rewarded by 11 VCs – in an aggressive adventure that made the Zulus victims of Victorian imperialism and cost the British army dear.
>
> But we hear next to nothing about this. The film takes up no attitude. The bravery at Rorke's Drift is stirringly commemorated: but it is as meaningless as Dunkirk would be if you knew nothing else about the war.

Other critics claimed that it was not just a history lesson that was at stake, but also a matter of politics. Raymond Anker said in the *Liverpool Daily Post*: 'I should have liked, too, some explanatory reference as to why we were building a bridge at Rorke's Drift; which means why we were fighting the Zulus; which means a wider canvas than Mr Baker has chosen. To-day, I can't help feeling, to say "This was heroic" is not enough.' Thomas Wiseman in the *Sunday Express*, comparing the film to 'the sort of illustrations you find hanging in military clubs,' felt that it 'would have appealed to those diehard Victorians who were convinced that the thing to give the natives (any natives) was a taste of British steel … Today we no longer feel one can assume automatically that the British were naturally in the right and that the reason why the Zulu attacked was sheer blood-thirstiness, which is the impression one gets from this film.' Keith Brace of the *Birmingham Post* suspected that Baker and Endfield 'were embarrassed when they looked into [the history] to find how meaningless the battle was … "Why? Why?" a dying British soldier gasps at the height of the battle: why indeed? We are never told, and the film falls back on a rather calculating use of bloody spectacle to sustain its length … Perhaps the eleven V.C.'s were awarded to divert attention from a nasty piece of imperialist blood-letting.' Stating the harshest case for the prosecution was, inevitably, Nina Hibbin in the Communist *Daily Worker*:

> It isn't a scrap of good having the imperialist-minded lieutenant (Michael Caine) admit in *Zulu* (Plaza) that he feels sick and ashamed after his first taste of battle.
> Or for the ruthless commander (Stanley Baker) to confess that he couldn't go through all that butchery again.
> It doesn't make sense dramatically, because we've just been entertained to a two-hour orgy of blood and slaughter.
> It makes even less sense historically, since the British Army didn't fight its colonial wars of the 1870s with the anti-war mood of the 1960s' audiences in mind…
> Once the carnage is over, there's a general sort of feeling that the Zulus are jolly fine chaps (for savages). The one point that is never even hinted at is that the land belonged to the Zulus and the British had no business to be there at all.

Surprisingly, only two British reviewers specifically linked *Zulu* to the contemporary international situation. The unsigned review in *The Tatler* felt that the film was simply insensitive in coming out at a time of political unrest: 'With all the uproar and unease there is in Africa at present, *Zulu* seems to me as untimely a film as it well could be. The battle … is doubtless a stirring piece of military history, but does anyone want to see it re-enacted in all its goriness just now? I salute the bravery of our red-coated soldiers … but as the mountains of dead Zulus pile up I experience nothing but horror.' Philip Oakes in the *Sunday Telegraph* cast doubt on the depth of the film's liberalism: '*Zulu* makes much of the mutual respect between the fighting men on both sides: the black and the white. Certainly it's progress of a kind but convenient, too, that in no way does it affect the apartheid creed of "separate but equal." It may be that I have that sort of mind but South Africa – where the film was made – thinks that *Zulu* is just fine.'

United States

The first American reviews of *Zulu* appeared in early 1964, reporters for the trade journals *Variety* and *The Hollywood Reporter* having attended the UK launch. Other magazines and newspapers ran their reviews several months later, to coincide with the US release of the film in June and July. Perhaps surprisingly, the overall balance of judgement tended to fall more decisively in the film's favour than in Britain, for out of the twenty-seven American notices I have consulted, sixteen were strongly positive, only eight mixed and three negative. The reviews to some extent recalled the British press response, but there were often key differences of tone and emphasis, and some critics raised issues that their British counterparts neglected entirely.

Many, for example, identified *Zulu* primarily with its executive producer, Joseph E. Levine – a well-known figure on the American film scene, whom none of the UK reviews even mentioned. As Levine's company distributed the film in his home market this was perhaps to be expected. Giving prominent mention to Levine also helped Americanise the film, perhaps in an attempt to remove the stigma of Britishness which compromised the appeal of many UK-produced pictures in the Stateside market. *Boxoffice* stressed the film's hoped-for transatlantic appeal: 'The picture already has broken records in England where Stanley Baker of *Guns of Navarone* and Jack Hawkins, currently in *Lawrence of Arabia*, are top stars who are also familiar names to U.S. patrons.' As *Zulu* was Levine's first venture into British production, this in itself made the film of interest to industry observers; certainly all the trade reviewers anticipated that it would enjoy his 'typically aggressive showmanship' (*Hollywood Reporter*), and that its box-office performance in the US and Canada would reflect the potential of its 'proven ingredients for bigscale exploitation' (*Variety*).

The trade papers enthused over the promotional possibilities attendant on its subject matter. *Variety*'s reviewer 'Myro.' pointed out that the wedding dance sequence was 'the basis for one of the promotional aids, already receiving exploitation locally via the introduction of the "Zulu Stomp" [sic] in dance halls and clubs.' In addition to plaudits for the film's technical qualities and the calibre of the performances, *Variety* commented that the film 'avoids most of the obvious clichés. It keeps the traditional British stiff-upper-lip attitudes down to the barest minimum.' *The Film Daily*'s Gene Arneel praised the film as a 'major production in the true sense ... an important nominee when they talk about the cinema as an art form,' and commended its 'sincerity of production concept and extraordinary professional follow-through.' However, Arneel's references to 'hordes of blacks [who] viciously descend upon a meagerly-manned British outpost,' and his tasteless observation that the camera's 'tendency to be overly concerned with the nakedness of the Zulu femmes [should] not arouse any prurient interests except on the part, could be, of Zulu males,' now seem, at best, ingenuous and insensitive.

James Powers of *The Hollywood Reporter* applauded 'the mechanics of staging the battle ... directed and edited so the spectator is sure at all times of what is going on, the ebb of success. Action moves from the grand scale to the intimate for variety in pace and to give the audience a chance to adjust and comprehend.' But Powers also drew attention to an aspect of

American Press Reviews

POSITIVE	MIXED	NEGATIVE
America	Cosmopolitan	Films in Review
Boxoffice	Cue	New York Post
The Film Daily	Film Quarterly	Saturday Review
The Hollywood Reporter	Los Angeles Times	
Life	Motion Picture Herald	
Los Angeles Citizen News	Newsweek	
LA Herald Examiner	New York Times	
McCall's	New York World Telegram	
New Republic		
NY Journal-American		
New York Daily News		
The New Yorker		
Playboy		
San Francisco Chronicle		
Time		
Variety		

the film which had entirely escaped the British reviewers: 'Endfield's direction gives both sides their due, so the story is not weighted in sympathy for white or black. He might, in writing and direction, have carried this insight a step further. If the Zulus had been personified as are the British, it would have given the picture an added dimension. *Zulu* is seen from the British point of view. It should be remembered that in today's world this is not the attitude of vast potential audiences.'

A similar uncertainty about how some sections of the audience might respond was registered by Ronald Gold in his review for *The Motion Picture Herald*. He found it 'difficult to identify with any of [the characters] or to root for their cause,' and suggested: 'Major objections to the film might be ethical ones.' Gold also elaborated on what he saw as important dramatic and thematic weaknesses:

The problem for the audience is not attention but belief. How, one asks, is it possible that so many Zulus get right up to the defenders' wall of sandbags and so few are able to clamber over it? How is it possible that when spear meets bayonet in hand-to-hand combat, the bayonet always wins? Surely the Zulus were better trained in hand-to-hand combat. How does Booth, cornered by a wall of flames, escape in time to appear unscathed in the next scene? These questions are not answered

visually, and they are likely to bother at least a portion of the audience.

A secondary theme in the film, symbolized by Jack Hawkins, as a missionary and Ulla Jacobsson, as his daughter, is the conflict between the 'man of war' and the 'man of God' on the relative merits of bravery and human life. Since the British have no 'moral' stake in the war against the Zulus, this question is certainly an arguable one. But the proponents of peace are outnumbered here, and the cards are further stacked against them by the portrayal of Hawkins as a fanatical drunkard, and of Miss Jacobsson as a prudish neurotic.

A number of the US critics, perhaps heeding the trade papers' remarks, tried to identify an audience for the film and to steer their readership in the right direction. Thus, the anonymous critic of *McCall's* magazine advised readers: 'Even if you hate war movies and flunked English history, Baker, Caine and those 4,000 Zulus will never let you forget how the British won this one.' The *Los Angeles Citizen News* tried gallantly to pitch the film at its female readers: 'despite the fact the film is attuned primarily to men's filmic tastes, it should have a certain appeal for the ladies since it has a surprisingly touching ending – one of almost poignant quality … Endfield's forceful direction often has a touch of greatness about it for he has made of *Zulu* a deeply emotional film of pathos, heartache, courage and great dignity.'

Most mainstream American reviewers were, like the British, thrilled by the film's spectacle. George H. Jackson in the *Los Angeles Herald Examiner* felt that it 'set a new benchmark in action epics … So strong, so compelling, so engrossing, so meticulous in the fields where it counts is this movie, that for years any new adventure film will be compared to it for impact.' Jackson also remarked on the way 'the story points up the fact that the Zulu of the period, 1879 were valiant warriors with leaders who understood the problems of warfare,' and noted how the film 'through the use of descriptive dialogue graphically tells the strategy of both sides.'

Strikingly, no-one on either side of the Atlantic questioned the publicists' claim that the production had genuinely employed thousands of extras. Thus, Nadine M. Edwards in the *Los Angeles Citizen News* remarked that, 'it is astonishing how the director was able to "handle" all the African natives – there seemed to be literally thousands of them and they all performed in a realistic (and frightening) manner.'

The more hostile notices could not escape a certain scepticism about what they evidently saw as Old World imperialist nostalgia. Arthur Knight of the *Saturday Review* noted scathingly that the British 'have a penchant for resurrecting previous wars in search of combat-inspired heroics,' and observed that *Zulu* 'must give them a special satisfaction.' Archer Winsten in the *New York Post* gave the film perhaps its worst American drubbing, with some quirky observations on its style and mildly malicious jibes at its main personnel:

The whole thing looks like a grand movie spectacular, even to the gallant singing of the Welsh soldiers (great singers, those), and the countersinging of the Zulus (strange sounds they make those natives). Both Zulus and Britons are got up in wondrous costumes, and the Technicolor-Technirama makes it resemble a musical even more …

More than anything else the picture reveals the artistic limitations of the people who made it. Writer, director and co-producer Cy Endfield, previously credited with *The Secret, Child in the House, Hell Drivers, Sea Fury, Mysterious Island* and *Hide and Seek* has never touched a memorable film.[8] And now that he has managed a big production, he proves why. And Stanley Baker, a capable actor, proves only that when he doubles as co-producer he knows how to give himself a lion's share of close-ups.

It's hard to believe that a battle of this size and fury could make you drowsy, but

after 138 minutes of it the lids get heavy and the mind does reel.

Like their British counterparts, several American reviewers could not forgive the film for its more traditional elements, particularly in characterisation. *Film Quarterly* remarked: 'It would be good to see one of these things in which some kid did not ask, "Why us?" and some veteran did not reply, "Because we're here."' *Cosmopolitan* complained: 'If the history books say it happened, it did. What couldn't have happened is that the actual event should have been peopled by such awful movie "types" – the bottle-loving missionary – the heart-of-gold sergeant – the brutalized goldbricker who turns hero – the comic relief cook who fails to understand that he must defend himself.' However some US critics compared *Zulu* favourably to the American Western, while others also referred to such fondly remembered imperial adventures as *Beau Geste*, *The Four Feathers* (both filmed many times), *The Lost Patrol* (1934), *The Lives of a Bengal Lancer* (1935) and *Gunga Din* (1939). *Playboy*'s anonymous reviewer could scarcely contain his enthusiasm:

Zulu is a lulu – a Technicolor, Technirama torrent of action that really is, like they say in the movies, colossal! Set in 1879, it's the old Lost Patrol yarn, with Britishers and Zulus instead of U.S. Cavalry and Sioux. Sioux what? Well, it's carried off here with more imagination, sweep and excitement than any similar saga ... Eleven Victoria Crosses were handed out for action at Rorke's Drift, and some kind of decoration should go to Cy Endfield who directed in the magnificent South African mountains, for the way he has caught the subtle shades of sunlight and skin, the manner in which he formed the long battalions that flow over the hills and through the grass, and his expert interweaving of close action and powerful panoramas ... *Zulu* is a treat for eye, ear and scalp.

Further upmarket, Whitney Balliett in *The New Yorker* also experienced some pangs of nostalgia for a lost tradition: 'One of the very few regrettable results of the collapse of colonialism has been the gradual disappearance of that noble counterpart of the American Western the colonial Western.' Balliett wondered if *Zulu* marked 'the beginning of a neo-colonial Western movement,' and commended its makers for having 'not only refurbished all the clichés of the genre but given them the sheen of high style ... their garrison never runs out of ammunition, and it is not saved by the cavalry. Sheer fortitude brings it through, and is rewarded by an admiring chanted salute from the Zulus themselves, who then retreat like departing tea guests into the hills that ring the encampment.' This critic also remarked, with wry indignation: 'It has already been pointed out that *Zulu* is in poor taste. But so are such invaluable relics as G. A. Henty and Rider Haggard and Kipling.' *Time* invoked 'the grand carry-on-lads tradition of *Four Feathers* and *Gunga Din*,' and felt that *Zulu* had actually 'improved' on history. The scene of the Zulus' final salute, the magazine suggested, 'alone explains, perhaps, why *Zulu* is currently raking in more pounds sterling than any other film in the history of British cinema. After a spate of "kitchen dramas" filled with whining social protest, *Zulu*'s bloodbath refreshes the spirit with its straightforward celebration of valor, tenacity and honor among men.'

Among the most perceptive accounts of the way the film not only revived a tradition, but also refined and developed it, came from Stanley Kauffman, distinguished critic of *The New Republic*. He thought that the film ultimately fell short of the highest standards that could be applied to works of popular art: comparing *Zulu* to the classic Cavalry Westerns directed by the veteran John Ford, Kauffman felt that '*Zulu* lacks the style, the sense of one man's vision that, at his best, Ford gives us.' However, he also appreciated the way the film built intelligently on expectations derived from earlier movies:

> We expect battle and recovery, interweavings of other stories, then more battles on later days – the usual pattern of the cavalry Western – but we are pleasantly surprised. Once we get to Rorke's Drift, after a tigerish battle-dance sequence in the Zulu camp, the film has Aristotelian unity. One battle (in several attacks), one day. Endfield's use of the long, long lines of Zulus rolling like copper tide down the mountains, the warriors filtering through the grass like fog, his relatively fresh figures-on-the-horizon shots, all deserve high praise. The picture is not free of action-film clichés: one bullet equals one corpse – nobody ever misses or merely wounds an opponent; and there is trite byplay in the barracks. But, barring the adagio opening, Endfield – aided by John Jympson's crisp editing and Stephen Dade's photography that is filled with mountain light and air – has handled matters so well that we concede the familiarities. In fact we welcome them as proof of how well the picture is being done: as if a good poem were being made out of very familiar vocabulary.

Paul Mandel's review in *Life* magazine also showed a close familiarity with generic tradition and an intelligent ability to distinguish the creative use of conventions from routine hackwork. Referring to the tendency of most films to distance themselves from the reality of hand-to-hand combat, Mandel told his readers:

> There have been lots of movies in which stalwart lines of perfectly disciplined Englishmen shouting "Front rank! Reload! Ready! Fire!" cut down wave after wave of screaming natives. *Zulu* manages to be very different. First of all the natives are disciplined too, and one quickly loses any illusion that this is anything like a western, where the Indians drop three to a shot and the cowboys are immortal. At any minute the Zulus may win this battle.
>
> Second, through a rigorous concern for keeping the moviegoer aware of how the fight is going, *Zulu* never dissolves into the amorphous battle ballets of most war movies, but remains understandable: when Baker finds the enemy attacking over one of his weakly manned barricades while sharpshooters in the hills pick off his men on another, he is frantic and so are you. The imminence of British defeat is so clear in *Zulu*, and its consequences so explicit, that you feel besieged yourself by those single-minded, shouting lines of able warriors.
>
> Best of all, throughout this mass carnage (it goes on for a day and a night – Zulus, unlike Indians, fight at night) the movie returns again and again to poignant, shocking details of men engaged in constant slaughter. There are men who go almost mad in a rage that grows from repeated killing. There are men who tremble. There are men who talk gently in the presence of death and there are men who rail, hoarse with thirst and fear, as the first cold wash of another dawn brings a promise of still more blood, more battle.

Few American reviewers seemed to be familiar with the details of the historical Rorke's Drift (not surprisingly, when the same could be said of many British critics, who might have been expected to know better). The *New York Daily News*' Kate Cameron, for example, referred to the film's setting 'during the British-Zulu wars in the 1870s, when Britain was fighting to maintain her hold on conquered territory in Zululand.' Other US critics wanted to know more about the history and, like several of their British colleagues, faulted *Zulu* for not telling them. William Peper wrote in the *New York World Telegram*: 'The details and strategies of the battle plus four or five cursory character studies are all there is to the movie. What the Zulus are fighting for, what the British and Boer attitudes are and what this battle meant to history is not discussed.' Peper did, however, note that, 'If nothing else, the movie is a startling demonstration of the profound advantage of the modern firearm, even non-automatic, in battle,' and suggested pointedly: 'The fact that Endfield and producer-actor Baker had the full cooperation of the South African government may explain why they kept their noses out of the battle's historical significance.'

Peper's was one of a number of American reviews that explicitly related *Zulu* to contemporary international politics. The anonymous film critic of *Newsweek* magazine attempted some historical analysis as well as topical comment. He acknowledged that the filmmakers had 'been faithful enough to the details of the engagement that the repellent nature of the fighting is inescapable. It was bloody, but like an abattoir. The victory was as inglorious as the Italian planes strafing the Ethiopians on their camels.' However he could not resist drawing parallels between the film's native warriors and their real-life counterparts: 'The long-range effects of the battle are evident even in the current picture, where the Zulu actors, playing the parts of their warrior forebears, carry only rubber-tipped spears, the Zulus having been "demilitarized" by the government of South Africa, where the film was made. True, Stanley Baker and his garrison are only firing blanks, but somewhere there is live ammunition in race-tense South Africa. Without wishing to be so, the film becomes a symbol of the current situation.' The review signed off with a suggestion that,

rather than making their 'quixotic gesture' of salute to the surviving British defenders, the Zulus 'would have done better with a telegram to the small-arms division of Remington Arms.'[9]

Perhaps the most idiosyncratic American opinion of *Zulu* appeared in a brief capsule review by Brian Sandenbergh in the Catholic-oriented magazine *Films in Review*. Uniquely of all commentators on the film, Sandenbergh felt that it was a 'denigration of the British past' and a virtual slander on British military and imperial tradition: 'the battle itself is staged so as to elicit sympathy for the Zulus, not the British. Indeed, one of the recipients of the VC is presented as an immoral wastrel.' Stanley Baker, he argued, 'portrays Chard as an incomprehensible kind of neurotic.' Saving graces for Sandenbergh seemed to lie only in ineptness: 'For a film to denigrate *successfully* those it pretends to be celebrating, it must have a subtler script than the one by Cy Endfield and John Prebble concocted for *Zulu*.'

But the critic who went furthest in questioning the morality and the political wisdom of *Zulu* was Bosley Crowther, long-time incumbent of the *New York Times* and one of the most prominent US opinion-formers. His review is worth quoting at length:

With so much racial tension and anticolonial discord in the world, a film on the order of *Zulu* seems strangely archaic and indiscreet.

Not that its vivid re-enactment of a bloody and senseless clash between a company of British soldiers and an overwhelming force of Zulu warriors attacking a remote mission station in southeastern Africa in 1879 is inaccurate or unprecedented ...

Indeed, if you're not too squeamish at the sight of slaughter and blood and can keep your mind fixed on the notion that there was something heroic and strong about British colonial expansion in the

19th century, you may find a great deal of excitement in this robustly Kiplingesque film …

But the question is whether such a picture, coming at this time, with tensions and discords so prevalent, is discreet or desirable. Is it a contribution to the cause of harmony to show so much vicious acrimony between black men and white, to wallow in blood-spurting slaughter, to make an exciting thing of firing rifles into the faces of charging warriors and sticking bayonets into them?

And is the ideal of the white man's burden, which this picture tacitly presents (for all its terminal disgust with the slaughter), in the contemporary spirit?

You decide.

Picking up the gauntlet was Moira Walsh in *America* magazine, whose review article was headlined 'Which *Zulu* Did You See?' Walsh directed her attention, not just to the film itself, but to the criticism it had received, especially at the hands of Sandenbergh and Crowther. How, she asked, could these two writers produce views of the film so completely at odds with one another? Their responses, she suggested, provided a prima facie case of what was wrong with much American film reviewing. She considered both critics guilty of 'unfair and irresponsible comment' on the film by confusing a genuine appraisal of its merits and demerits with speculation on its likely social effects (debate on whether film critics should concern themselves with such matters still continues today). Walsh added that Crowther's argument, taken to its logical conclusion, actively supported censorship.

I have generally refrained from adding my own voice to the reviews quoted in this chapter, or from expressing agreement or disagreement with them. It is only fair to say, however, that I am inclined to concur with the balance of Walsh's judgement on *Zulu*:

While conceding that it is very bloody and not without flaws, I thought it was an exceedingly good movie. It impressed me because I thought that, within its deliberately rather narrow framework, it was attempting to tell the truth about the episode, not the literal truth necessarily, but the artistic truth. What the film seemed to me to be saying, implicitly and through artful and unified use of all the various devices of film language, was: This is what it was like when two honorable forces – the British soldier doing his duty and obeying orders and the Zulu warrior defending his land and upholding his tribal traditions – met head-on as part of a much larger and less honorable historical movement that they could not comprehend or control. Explicitly the film offers no solution and makes no statement, pro- or anti-colonialist. It simply presents the facts in such a way as to force the audience to ponder the paradoxes of human courage in an unlovely context.

South Africa

The first published press response in South Africa came from the anonymous London correspondent of the *Cape Argus*, who reported from the London preview showing ('where the audience reaction was favourable') that '*Zulu* is a serious film epic which gives a reasonably authentic account of the battle of Rorke's Drift.' Predicting a success in the British market, the critic wondered – with good reason – how it would be received in official circles in South Africa itself:

It has still to be demonstrated that South Africans will, in fact, see the film with its countless shots of White and Black in close and gory combat. There is many a detail at which the censors will take at least a second look.

The overall emphasis, however, is on White heroism, as if the producers, Cy Endfield and Stanley Baker, were determined to show that those 11 V.C.s awarded after the battle were fully justified.

But the film will also set people wondering how many such awards might have been issued among the Zulu troops had their military organization been equally sophisticated. In spite of their numerical superiority, their long succession of onslaughts with shield against assegai are a stirring spectacle.

Unlike most British and American critics, the *Argus* reviewer was able to comment with some authority on matters of historical and geographical accuracy (or otherwise). Thus it was noted that the film 'may exaggerate the success of [the] attacks in actually breaching the defences and sending Zulus pouring through, only to be repulsed. But it looks realistic enough to bring the audience forward to the edge of their seats.' Reference was also made to the filmmakers' decision to shoot in the Drakensberg rather than on the site of the battle: 'Filmgoers who know no better will gain as rich an impression of Natal scenery as the South African Tourist Corporation could ever offer – but to those who do know it will simply not look right.'

When, nearly a full year later, two locally based journalists got their first sight of *Zulu*, they addressed similar concerns. Dora Sowden of the *Rand Daily Mail* (whose opinions on the local censorship restrictions on the film we have already noted) opened her review with the comments: 'In the history books, Rorke's Drift provides an episode after the battle of Isandhlwana. Here it is an epic – yes, a true epic, and what a bloodbath! ... no one can walk out of this reconstruction of the events of January, 1879, without being shaken to the marrow.' Sowden admired the performances and characterisations (more so than most Anglo-American critics had, with even a good word for Jack Hawkins' Witt), predicted stardom for Michael Caine and considered Nigel Green's Bourne 'a study in himself.' Adding favourable words for the photography and soundtrack – particularly the predominant use of natural sounds in preference to background music – Sowden echoed the frequent complaint that the film offered little understanding of history: 'Only a few side remarks indicate the contemporary situation – for instance, that 400 Black people perished with the White men at Isandhlwana, and that Boer and Briton were not seeing eye-to-eye.' Her main concern, however, was with the comparatively graphic nature of the violence: 'Seen on the curved Cinerama screen and in colour, the action is stirring enough to make the bloodlust rise in the most anaemic of us. It is no use telling oneself that it is all plum jam and mock battle. These men – Black and White – had their prototypes. This fighting was real.'

In the *Johannesburg Star*, Oliver Walker also drew attention to the 'switch of locale' but found largely in the film's favour: 'In the interests of dramatic pageantry the choice of the magnificent Drakensberg as a back-cloth has improved vastly on Nature and the facts.' Walker objected to the presence of the Witts and of Adendorff ('This little battle was an all-rooibaadjie [red-jacket] affair'), but considered the Chard-Bromhead conflict and other invented details to be 'pardonable licence.' He had praise for 'the many personal touches which enliven some of the most thrilling, bloody scenes of spears versus bayonets ever staged,' for the choreography of the Zulu attacks, and for 'the individual cameos of the soldiers, some bandaged in hospital, one a notorious skrimshanker (James Booth has a ball with his Victorian melodramatics), and the "titanic," pervasive calm of the bug-whiskered colour sergeant (Nigel Green presides magnificently as a butler at a grim banquet over the firing tactics of the defenders).' Walker concluded his review with a direct reference to the film's treatment by the local authorities:

I like, too, the touch of chivalry in the ending, not so much in the words exchanged between the lieutenants as in Chard's tribute as he stands against the mountain skyline amid the heaped, naked brown bodies of the fallen Zulus and plants a cowhide shield in the blood-soaked veld.

Strange that our censors by placing paltry restrictions on the showing of so notable a film to non-White audiences could not match that gesture![10]

Checklist of reviews consulted

United Kingdom

Anon., *CEA Film Report No. 1973*, 31 January 1964, p. 2417
Anon., 'Escapist,' *Sunday Citizen*, 26 January 1964
Anon., *The Tatler*, 5 February 1964
Anon., 'Stirring film of a gallant deed,' *Thames Valley Times*, 29 January 1964 Anon., *Time and Tide*, 30 January 1964
Anon., *The Times*, 23 January 1964
Raymond Anker, 'Fantastic but it's true – this story of amazing heroism,' *Liverpool Daily Post*, 24 January 1964
Felix Barker, 'I'd like to give *Zulu* a V.C. of its own,' *Evening News*, 23 January 1964
Clive Barnes, 'An epic worthy of 11 medals,' *Daily Express*, 21 January 1964
Jack Bentley, 'Epic stuff – and no Hollywood hokum,' *Sunday Mirror*, 26 January 1964
Ernest Betts, 'Cheers for the guts and glory boys!', *The People*, 26 January 1964
Keith Brace, *Birmingham Post*, 24 January 1964
Freda Bruce-Lockhart, 'Some rattling good heroism,' *The Catholic Herald*, n.d.
Bryan Buckingham, '*Zulu* will pack 'em in,' *News of the World*, 26 January 1964
Maryvonne Butcher, *The Tablet*, 25 January 1964
Graham Clarke, *Kinematograph Weekly*, 23 January 1964, p. 10
John Coleman, *New Statesman*, 24 January 1964
Patrick Daly, *What's On*, 24 January 1964
Brenda Davies, *Monthly Film Bulletin*, February 1964, pp. 23-4
Alan Dent, 'Coping with an impi,' *Illustrated London News*, 1 February 1964
Kenneth Eastaugh, 'On film – the battle in which eleven VCs were won,' *Daily Mirror*, 21 January 1964
Patrick Gibbs, 'African Antics,' *Daily Telegraph*, 24 January 1964
Penelope Gilliatt, 'So brave,' *The Observer*, 26 January 1964
Gordon Gow, *Films and Filming*, February 1964, p. 30
Nina Hibbin, 'A lovely war!', *Daily Worker*, 25 January 1964
Margaret Hinxman, *The Daily Cinema*, 20-21 January 1964, p. 6
Richard Mallett, *Punch*, 5 February 1964, p.210
James Monahan, *Housewife*, March 1964
Philip Oakes, 'Imperialists,' *Sunday Telegraph*, 26 January 1964
Ann Pacey, 'Zulus deserved a medal, too,' *Daily Herald*, 24 January 1964
Dilys Powell, *Sunday Times*, 26 January 1964
Isabel Quigley, *The Spectator*, 31 January 1964
David Robinson, 'Documentary Saga,' *Financial Times*, 24 January 1964
Richard Roud, *Manchester Guardian*, 21 January 1964
F.H. Samuel, 'Epic of courage,' *Jewish Chronicle*, n.d.
John Sandilands, 'Stirring, brilliant,' *Daily Sketch*, 21 January 1964
Alexander Walker, 'Blood and spectacle – but I wanted history, too,' *Evening Standard*, 23 January 1964
Cecil Wilson, 'A savage tale of Errol Flynnery,' *Daily Mail*, 21 January 1964
Thomas Wiseman, *Sunday Express*, 26 January 1964

United States

Anon., *Boxoffice*, 22 June 1964
Anon., 'How Eleven Victoria Crosses Were Won,' *Cosmopolitan*, May 1964
Anon., *Cue*, 11 July 1964
Anon., *McCall's*, June 1964
Anon., 'Thin Red Line,' *Newsweek*, July 13, 1964, p. 85
Anon., *Playboy*, June 1964
Anon., 'Grand & Gory,' *Time*, 10 July 1964, p. 96
Gene Arneel, *The Film Daily*, 11 June 1964, p. 4
Whitney Balliett, 'Redcoats and Pith Helmets Forever,' *The New Yorker*, 18 July 1964, p. 93
Ernest Callenbach, *Film Quarterly*, vol. XVIII, no. 1, Fall 1964
Kate Cameron, '*Zulu* – Men of War and Glory,' *New York Daily News*, 8 July 1964
Bosley Crowther, 'Screen: In True "Hold-the-Fort" Style,' *New York Times*, 8 July 1964
Nadine M. Edwards, 'Levine's *Zulu* Praiseworthy Film,' *Los Angeles Citizen News*, 17 July 1964

Ronald Gold, *Motion Picture Herald*, 24 June 1964, p. 74

George H. Jackson, '*Zulu* Impressive Adventure,' *Los Angeles Herald Examiner*, 17 July 1964, p. A-20

Stanley Kauffman, *The New Republic*, 20 June 1964

Paine Knickerbocker, 'The Barbaric Battle of *Zulu*,' *San Francisco Chronicle*, n.d. available

Arthur Knight, *Saturday Review*, 25 July 1964

Paul Mandel, 'War's Raw and Grisly Essence,' *Life*, 3 July 1964

Myro., *Variety*, 29 January 1964

Rose Pelswick, 'Stirring Action Movie,' *New York Journal-American*, 8 July 1964

William Peper, '*Zulu* Epic Battle Film But Significance Is Untold,' *New York World Telegram*, 8 July 1964

James Powers, '*Zulu* rousing action epic for blockbuster business,' *The Hollywood Reporter*, 3 February 1964

Brian Sandenbergh, *Films in Review*, vol. XV, no. 6, June-July 1964, p. 373

Philip K. Scheuer, '*Zulu* Carries On in *Geste* Tradition,' *Los Angeles Times*, 16 July 1964

Moira Walsh, 'Which *Zulu* Did You See?', *America*, 25 July 1964

Archer Winsten, *New York Post*, 8 July 1964

South Africa

Anon., '*Zulu* is serious epic film,' *Cape Argus*, 20 January 1964

Dora Sowden, 'Epic of the bloodbath at Rorke's Drift in Cinerama,' *Rand Daily Mail*, 29 December 1964

Oliver Walker, 'Bayonets and bullets beat spears,' *Johannesburg Star*, 29 December 1964

Notes

1 '*Zulu*'s Big Showmanship Campaign,' *Kine. Weekly*, 26 December 1963, pp. 10-11.

2 See 'The Press hail *Zulu*,' *The Daily Cinema*, 22-23 January 1964, p. 2. This trade paper noted: 'The initial Press notices for this spectacular Paramount release are studded with laudatory adjectives which augur well for the triumphant success confidently and justifiably predicted for this mammoth subject.' Critics Alexander Walker and Thomas Wiseman both subsequently complained (in *The Daily Cinema*, 28 February 1964, p. 3) that their reviews had been selectively edited for reproduction in trade advertisements, notably in a pull-out supplement to the same journal's issue for 19 February 1964 (from which several of the illustrations to this chapter have been taken).

3 Not being a gifted linguist, I have been unable to conduct a comprehensive survey of press responses to *Zulu* in non-Anglophone countries. However, the seminal French magazine *Cahiers du cinéma* included a brief, anonymous review in its survey of new releases, which offered the following, typically cryptic and poetic, comment: 'The piles of both dead bodies and sentimentality impede neither beautiful framing nor refined colour (red against black). Constant movement of the camera, however, prevents any distancing. What remains is one more English film over several fewer Zulus.' (*Cahiers du cinéma*, no. 161-2, January 1965, p. 153.) I am grateful to my colleague Angela Martin for her translation from the French.

4 Robert Shail, 'Stanley Baker's "Welsh Western": Masculinity and Cultural Identity in *Zulu*,' *Cyfrwng/Media Wales Journal*, vol. 1, 2004. For other accounts of the film's critical reception, see Sheldon Hall, 'Monkey Feathers: Defending *Zulu*,' in Claire Monk and Amy Sargeant (eds.), *British Historical Cinema* (London and New York: Routledge, 2002); and Chapter 9 of James Chapman, *Past and Present: National Identity and the British Historical Film* (London: I.B. Tauris, 2005). An incomplete collection of reviews and other press material can be found in the British Film Institute Library's microfiche on *Zulu*. Other clippings, including American and South African reviews, were sourced in the files of John Prebble and Cy Endfield, courtesy of Jan Prebble and Maureen Endfield.

5 David Austen, 'Playing Dirty,' *Films and Filming*, April 1969, p. 7.

6 Elaine Gallagher, *Candidly Caine* (London: Robson Books/London Weekend Television, 1990), p. 78. Gallagher adds: 'Walker stuck by his comment and Caine by his opinion, but across the years Walker has remained one of the few critics whose views Michael Caine respects.' In his book *Hollywood, England: The British Film Industry in the Sixties* (London: Michael Joseph, 1974; reprinted London: Harrap, 1986), Walker – one of the longest-serving and most acerbic of British movie reviewers, who died in 2003 – wrote of Caine's performance in *Zulu* that his 'East End vowels ... had come ruinously through his otherwise gallant attempt to play an aristocratic English officer' (p. 304).

7 In fact 'fuzzy wuzzies,' which dates from the later Sudanese campaign, would not have been used by the soldiers at Rorke's Drift; Bromhead's passing reference to the Zulus as 'fuzzies' is thus one of the film's more glaring anachronisms (though the more authentic alternatives would have been even more unpalatable to a contemporary audience).

8 Perhaps because the film's publicists did not want Endfield linked to his American past and the HUAC witch-hunts, press releases for *Zulu* tended to omit mention of his Hollywood-produced films; hence the absence from Winsten's list of Endfield's acclaimed *The Sound of Fury* (1950), which, had he known of it, might have altered his opinion of the director's abilities.

9 A later issue of the magazine included letters of protest at these last remarks from two British readers who accused the critic of Anglophobia. J.H. Brown of Glamorgan, Wales, commented bitterly that 'postwar history suggests that such an approach could well have proved fruitful. When British troops, defending Malaysia, a democratic, anti-Communist association of territories, are dying in fighting a U.S.-armed despot, we can, I hope, be forgiven for wondering who our friends are, and also who is crazy.' David Owen of London added a dig at both the Hollywood Western and American history, inviting *Newsweek*'s reviewer 'to compare the presentation of the culture and customs of the African warriors to the Hollywood cartoon-strip-type caricatures of the American Indian, although I do understand that many of these Indians speak with a Bronx accent owing to a shortage of the real thing. A legacy, perhaps, of a colonial past?' (Letters, 'Action at Rorke's Drift,' *Newsweek*, 3 August 1964.)

10 Stephen Coan informs me that Oliver Walker 'was also a novelist and wrote at least two novels dealing with Zulu history – *Zulu Royal Feather* and *Proud Zulu*' (email to the author, 20 April 2004). Walker's review was headed with a one-word capsule verdict: 'Bayete!' ('Thy will be done!')

This caricature by Norkin, intended for placement in newspapers and magazines, was included in the Campaign Book issued to exhibitors.

"NO COMEDIANS, PLEASE"

19

MYTHS, GAFFES AND SPOOFS

> There we were in the Zulu War. Only five left of an entire regiment. There was Idris Walters, Ivan Morgan, Sergeant Davis, me – and Ivor Emmanuel. Only five men left of an entire regiment, and all around us lay our dead and wounded comrades. Over the hill, two and a half thousand Zulus – you could hear them in the African night, playing on the drums. 'Come on,' Sergeant Davis said, 'come on lads, one more charge!' But we were tired and all we wanted was to go home. All around us lay our dead and dying and wounded companions. Our spirit was broken. 'Once more for Wales!' he said. Nobody moved, we were so tired and broken in spirit. And then Ivor Emmanuel began to sing: 'Men of Harlech rise to glory, Victory is hovering o'er ye...'
>
> The hope shone again in our eyes and the strength returned to our arms, and one by one we picked ourselves up from that blood-stained, sandbagged trench and over we went, over the top, toward the two and a half thousand All-Blacks. You could still hear them in the night, walking in the grass and playing those dreaded war drums. On we marched, and soon the air was filled with spears and assegais. Idris Walters fell to the floor, an assegai through his stomach. Still we went on, and still Ivor Emmanuel sang: 'Men of Harlech, rise to...' And the air was filled with rocks and boulders and assegais. I said, 'Who threw that?' 'A's-a-guy!' they said.
>
> On we went, through that night, on towards the Zulus. Still they played, and the air was filled with spears, and then a spear came straight through Ivan Morgan's chest. Down he fell, one by one we fell, until all that was left was me, Sergeant Davis and Ivor Emmanuel. We stood twenty yards short of the Zulus, and this big, huge assegai came straight through Sergeant Davis's neck. And as he fell he grabbed hold of Ivor Emmanuel and said, 'For goodness' sake, Ivor,' he said, 'sing something they know, will you!'
>
> (Max Boyce, *I Was There!! 'Live' in Concert*, MAX 1001, EMI Records, 1978)[1]

Zulu is, of course, responsible for propagating its own set of myths about Rorke's Drift. Not the least of these is the fabled Welshness of the 24th Regiment of Foot at the time of the battle, as discussed in the opening chapter.[2] But there are also a good many legends in circulation about the film itself. There is a lively, growing sub-culture of *Zulu* fans, many of whom communicate via the internet, where can be found evidence of many a misconception about the film. The preceding chapters should already have done much of the necessary work of correction, but for convenience' sake I thought it best to set out and refute here some of the more common fallacies. Here, then, in no particular order, are my top ten myths about *Zulu*:

1. **Stanley Baker financed *Zulu* with his own money:** Although, as a popular and successful actor, Baker was no doubt comfortably off by the time he made *Zulu*,

neither he nor Cy Endfield was rich enough to afford the almost $2 million worth of production finance needed for the budget (hence the more than five years from the project's inception to release). The money came from Paramount, via its relationship with executive producer Joseph E. Levine's company Embassy, which also provided development money. Baker claimed only to have financed pre-production research, such as the scouting of locations and budgeting the production costs.

2. *Zulu* was Michael Caine's first film: Caine had made small, often unbilled, appearances in at least seventeen feature films prior to *Zulu*. Bromhead was, however, his first featured role in a film made for the big screen. The credit line 'Introducing...' was often used on British and American films to designate actors who, while not necessarily making their debut, were being 'presented' to the public (i.e., offered as potential stars) for the first time.

3. "Stop throwing those bloody spears at me!" This apocryphal line of dialogue (usually recited in an exaggerated Caine-Cockney accent) is sometimes assumed by people who should know better to be spoken in the film itself. Its exact provenance is unknown to me, but it may have originated with the British comedian Jim Davidson (my sincere apologies to him if it did not). The other *Zulu* 'joke' involves a soldier being struck by three assegais in close succession and a disembodied voice shouting: 'One hundred and *eighty*!'[3] Needless to say, this is not in the film either.

4. *Zulu* is completely historically accurate: The film is faithful only to the broad general outlines and basic sequence of events of the Battle of Rorke's Drift. Many details, including all the characterisations, were wholly invented and many incidents embellished and fictionalised for dramatic effect.

5. **Chard and Bromhead were much older (or younger) than their screen counterparts:** Chard was 31 years old at the time of the battle, while Bromhead was 33. Stanley Baker was 35 when *Zulu* was made; Michael Caine had just turned 30.

6. ***Zulu* was filmed on the site of the real battle:** Permission was withheld to shoot at Rorke's Drift itself, and in any case the landscape there was found to be unsuitable for dramatic purposes. The film's location shoot was about 160 kilometres away, in the Drakensberg Mountains. Most of the interior scenes were filmed at Twickenham Studios, South London.

7. **Parts of the film were shot in Wales:** No motion picture camera was used to shoot any scenes or parts of scenes for *Zulu* in Wales.[4] The voices of the British soldiers as they sing 'Men of Harlech' were re-recorded by sound editor Rusty Coppleman on a hillside overlooking Stanley Baker's home town of Ferndale, South Wales, using the services of a local choir.

8. **The film employed 4,000 Zulu extras:** This was a myth the film's publicists and many of its participants were understandably keen to encourage. As noted previously, the company used a core of 240 warriors, supplemented by 100 dancing girls and 280 additional crowd for the mass wedding scene. For all other shots involving apparently large numbers of extras, cinematic sleight-of-hand was used.

9. ***Zulu* is soon to be remade by Mel Gibson, James Cameron, Steven Soderbergh and/or George Clooney:** Unless any reader has privileged insider information to the contrary, none of these gentlemen – nor anyone else, for that matter – has yet shown any interest in producing a remake

of *Zulu*. This claim is, of course, subject to revision in future editions of this book.

10. **The extras were paid for their services with wrist-watches and some of the Zulus can be seen wearing them in the film:** This is perhaps the most bizarre – and to me the most irritating – *Zulu* myth of all. One can only wonder at how such a fantasy was first started: the Zulus were

A schoolboys' favourite for four decades, *Zulu* was featured in an edition of 1970s comic *Battle Action*. The film was certainly not 'shot almost entirely in Wales.'

The Zulus' dawn chorus. Note the rubber-tipped assegais bending as they are beaten against the shields. (Jürgen Schadeberg)

paid government-approved wages of around £4 each per week, or $40 per month. Perhaps the warriors' decorative wrist bracelets have been mistaken for watches. Intriguingly, second unit director Bob Porter says that he once spotted an extra wearing a wrist-watch in some of his own footage, though it's not clear if this shot actually made it into the finished film. In any case, no-one to my knowledge has ever cited a single concrete example of this apparent gaffe, and I certainly have not seen any on-screen evidence myself. A prize of my choosing is hereby offered to any reader who can refer me to the exact frame on either the Region 1 (MGM) or Region 2 (Paramount) DVD which shows a Zulu wearing a wrist-watch.

This brings me to the next subject. Because *Zulu* has such an obsessive fan following (myself included: I look down on no-one), it has been subjected to more rigorous and minute scrutiny than is suffered by most films. This has been especially so since the availability of home video and DVD, permitting frequent playback, slow-motion and freeze-framing. Serious enthusiasts have examined every frame of the film for glitches in continuity, dramatic plausibility and historical authenticity. Indeed, these very different categories are often blurred and confused, so that many of the more pedantic nit-pickers (and there are quite a few) lump together instances of all three as if they were 'mistakes' of equal standing. I argued in the first chapter that when artists choose to alter the raw material of history for the sake of drama, the results cannot simply be regarded as 'wrong' because they differ from the factual record. Many such decisions have been made consciously, deliberately, and not just in ignorance (though I have also tried to establish that scholarship about the battle was not as advanced in 1963 as it is now, in large part because of the film's own influence in stimulating the growth of subsequent generations of scholars).

MYTHS, GAFFES AND SPOOFS 349

Chard's uniform shoulder straps and holster belt mysteriously disappear in this notorious continuity error.

MYTHS, GAFFES AND SPOOFS

Gordon Atkins and Ann du Pre, stand-ins for Jack Hawkins and Ulla Jacobsson, with cinematographer Stephen Dade.

With this in mind, mere disparities between the actual incidents of the battle, the uniforms, equipment and personalities of the defenders, the geography and layout of the location and so forth, and their representation in the film cannot be considered 'gaffes' or 'goofs' as they have so often been described. Nor can one properly include instances of questionable narrative credibility in the category of simple errors. Criticisms of this nature – such as the doubts expressed by some reviewers cited in the last chapter that a force of 4,000 attackers could have been successfully held off in the manner shown in the film – must necessarily be a matter of individual judgement and personal opinion rather than concrete fact. One internet website concerned entirely with the subject of 'Movie Mistakes' (http://moviemistakes.com/) has published a list of thirty-four 'errors' allegedly appearing in *Zulu* and nearly half can be included in these sub-categories of historical inaccuracy or dramatic contrivance.

If we are to take note of mistakes at all they must be genuine ones: unforeseen, unintended and largely unnoticed on the part of the filmmakers. This is, of course, an occupation for persistent party-poopers and habitual wet blankets, and genuine fans of the film may not want to be bothered by them. In fact, most of the following errors are so minor, of such little consequence and so barely noticeable except to very frequent and easily distracted viewers, that I am almost embarrassed to include them here at all. I do so only to placate those who insist that they do matter, and to put them (the alleged glitches) in their proper place. Some have appeared on internet postings; a number have not, and may well be receiving public mention for the first time here.

David Kernan (Private Fred Hitch)

David Kernan appeared in *Zulu* by mistake. 'I had a phone call from Thelma Graves, the casting woman. She said, they're very interested in you to play a part in *Zulu*. She sent me the script and it was the part of a slovenly Cockney private. I thought, that's imaginative casting.' At the time, the tall, well-spoken Kernan was appearing in the satirical BBC television show *That Was The Week That Was*, whose producer Ned Sherrin agreed to release him from his contract for six weeks' filming in South Africa.

'Dissolve, and the next scene is on the charter plane crossing the Black Continent. Stanley Baker, with all the charm he could muster – he wasn't at the front of the queue when charm was given out – saw me and said, "Who the fuck are you?" I said, I'm David Kernan. He said, "I didn't mean you, I meant Roy Kinnear!"' Stanley had apparently told Graves to book the *TW3* actor whose name began with a K. The late Roy Kinnear, another regular performer on the show, was a roly-poly comic actor about twice Kernan's girth and a foot shorter. 'I said to Stanley, should I get off the plane and go home? He said, "No, you'd better stay, but you couldn't be more wrong physically, could you? I saw a little fat man in this part." And that was how I got into *Zulu*. I've dined out on that quite a bit – I told the story on Roy Kinnear's *This Is Your Life*.' Perhaps as a consequence, David has always felt he was miscast in the film: 'Other people thought so too. It makes me hoot when I see it.'

In fact, another actor had also been offered the role of Private Hitch and had turned it down. Murray Melvin had been in *The Criminal* (1960) with Baker and spent two days in Cy Endfield's office discussing the role before deciding to accept an alternative offer from theatre director Joan Littlewood instead. According to Glynn Edwards, Melvin had been approached because 'they wanted a skinny little sparrow.' (Melvin's agent, Joy Jameson, says that he dropped out of *Zulu* to appear in Littlewood's *Sparrers Can't Sing*. However, both the play and film of *Sparrers* preceded shooting on *Zulu* and it seems likely that this was actually the stage production of *Oh! What a Lovely War*; as previously noted, Glynn Edwards had also had to choose between this and *Zulu*.)

With Edwards and Peter Gill, David was involved in the first few days' location shooting, but things did not go according to plan. Kernan and Gill ('the two naughty boys on the film,' as David puts it) found themselves submerged in freezing water in the depths of the South African winter, and told to push a pontoon across the river at the recreated Rorke's Drift. 'It was icy, coming straight off the mountains. Cy Endfield said [here Kernan adopts a very convincing Pennsylvanian accent] "You've gotta get in the river and push it, and do the dialogue while you're pushing it." But it was so cold we couldn't act.' The actors were pulled out of the river, given a medicinal shot of brandy, and told to jump back in the water. David refused. 'I said, I suggest you get some sort of rubber suit to put under our shirts. They postponed the scene for a bit till they got these rubber suits, then once again pushed us back in the river.' Most of this scene was later cut out in the editing. Despite these early experiences, David eventually warmed to the director. 'Cy was a very innocuous man; he didn't say much. He just left me alone. He wanted it technically to be perfect. I saw him many years later at a theatre. He seemed much nicer, more benign and jovial.'

David was born in London on 23 June 1938. He made his stage debut aged eleven in an opera at Sadler's Wells, playing a Black page. His other films include *Otley* (1969), *Up the Chastity Belt* (1971), *Carry On Abroad* (1972) and *The Day of the Jackal* (1973), but theatre, and especially musical comedy, is his forte. He starred in Stephen Sondheim's *A Little Night Music* for over a year in the West End, and in *Side by Side by Sondheim* in London and New York. This spun off into a television series, *Song by Song* (1978), showcasing the work of popular songwriters, and a 1998 stage sequel, *Sondheim Tonight*. David's other TV appearances include his own show for Scottish Television and for the theatre he devised and directed *Dorothy Fields Forever*. When we met at his London flat in November 2003, he was preparing to direct a new stage production.

Kernan keeps a framed copy of this portrait by Karsh on the wall of his London home.

Of his fellow players in *Zulu*, David got on 'terribly well' with Nigel Green. 'We were sort of an odd couple – we played tennis, probably that was the thing that brought us together. I remember that he'd have a go at me and say, "What are you doing piddling around on television, making fun of the Queen? You're an actor, you should just *act*! Don't bother about all this singing!" But, I said, that's what's paying the rent – I just do the work that comes in.' He has less fond memories of Stanley Baker, whom he recalls doing a lot of shouting, not necessarily directed at himself. 'I didn't get on with Stanley, and I didn't not get on with him – he just totally ignored me, as he did most of the supporting actors. It was not the happiest group, I have to say – partly because of the conditions, and partly because the hierarchy of Cy and the powers that be would always eat separately. We had a wonderful, jokey table of actors: Nigel Green, myself, Peter Gill, [second assistant director] Claude Watson. We used to crack a couple of bottles of white wine when the day's shooting was over and a lot of laughter would be ringing out of this dour dining room at the hotel. Consequently the only three [single] women on the shoot decided, that's the table to be on, because they're jolly. And I think it annoyed Stanley Baker slightly that they should want to be with the supporting actors.'

After shooting was finished, David bumped into Michael Caine in London. 'He said that he'd seen the film and was really excited by it, and I thought oh good, I'm glad it's worked well for you. At the time the supporting actors thought, it's a job, it's not very good, the script's not that great, and I can't believe that it's going to mean a great deal to the great British public. But it did, that was the extraordinary thing. You can never say what's going to be good or bad in a film until it's cut together, and I was staggered when I saw it. I realised it was a very exciting, cowboys-and-Indians sort of film.'

The opening screen caption reads 'January 23rd, 1879,' but the letter of dispatch is dated 11 February and the action of the film itself begins on 22 January.

The driver of the Witts' carriage as it leaves Cetewayo's homestead has mutton-chop whiskers, unlike the clean-shaven Reverend. (This was stuntman Joe Powell, doubling for Jack Hawkins).

The wrangler of the cheetah being hunted by Bromhead is briefly visible running towards a patch of trees in the background.

The river is easily crossed on foot and on horseback at the weir only a few yards from where the pontoon bridge is being built.

When Adendorff walks away from Chard and Bromhead (following his 'Grenadier Guards' line), in the background of one shot Bromhead starts to walk off screen right; in the next, closer shot he is still standing by Chard.

Corporal Allen's shoulder wound abruptly switches from the right side (where he clutches at the impact of a Zulu bullet) to the left side (where the wound is shown to bleed moments later).

Because there were only seven professional Black actor-stuntmen employed on the film, some of the Zulus appear to 'die' several times. Particularly noticeable for the frequency of their (dis)appearances are the bearded Simon Sabela and moustachioed John Marcus. Marcus is fought by Colour-Sergeant Bourne after being killed moments earlier, and he is killed several more times during the battle (for example, he is on the receiving end of Dalton's instruction to 'Pot that man, somebody!'). Look out also during the various assaults for the silhouette of the pointy-bearded extra, who appears (contrary to Adendorff's explanation of Zulu tactics) to be attacking both walls at once.

The trooper who passes behind Chard carrying an ammunition box is hit by an apparently silent bullet; he has a bayonet-less rifle over one shoulder, but when Chard picks it up a moment later, a bayonet is attached.

When Chard is wounded and crawls over to the wall of mealie bags, in several shots he is not wearing his full belt and holster.

When Hook bayonets a Zulu pinioned against a wall, the bayonet goes into the wall under the victim's arm, leaving a hole in the plaster.

During the battle of song (and elsewhere), the rubber tips of some of the Zulus' spears can be seen bending as they strike their shields.

The burnt-out hospital building appears to be intact in one long shot from the hillside during the final salute. (The shot was no doubt filmed earlier in the production schedule for the scene of the Zulus' first appearance above the camp, and it was probably decided during editing that no shots from the Zulus' position should be included in this early sequence.)

In the voice-over VC roll, Schiess is accurately described as belonging to the Natal Native Contingent. When he introduces himself to the Joneses earlier in the film, he claims to be a member of the Natal Mounted Police ('a peeler').

There are many other so-called gaffes described by various website contributors which, on further investigation, prove to be nothing of the sort. Viewers who care to direct their attention away from the foreground to the background action will be able to spot several unplanned incidents, such as a running soldier who trips over a tent rope, or another who bumps his head against one of the wheels of an overturned wagon. But people in life *do* sometimes have accidents, so these can hardly be called errors as such. Some eagle-eyed observers who have remarked on buildings behind characters seeming abruptly to disappear and reappear from shot to shot have evidently failed to grasp the principle that changes in camera angle often involve changes in optical perspective; or the fact that changes in the details of action from shot to shot may not necessarily imply poor continuity but rather creative editing, as director and editor construct coherent sequences out of a mass of often disordered raw material. There is a technical term for such creativity: *montage*.

Parodies and Tributes

Zulu very quickly worked its way into the consciousness of popular culture. A few weeks after the World Premiere it had already become the subject of affectionate parody. On 16 February 1964 a burlesque of the film was broadcast in the last-ever episode of the long-running (1958-64) BBC radio comedy show *Beyond Our Ken*, which included among its regular line-up of skits and spoofs a slot entitled 'A Film Worth Remembering.' Written by the late Eric Merriman, the show was a vehicle for the balding, avuncular Kenneth Horne; its other stock performers included Kenneth Williams, Hugh Paddick, Betty Marsden and Bill Pertwee (all of whom were carried over into the better-known successor series *Round the Horne*, which began broadcasting in 1966).

In the *Zulu* sketch, Horne played Lieutenant Chad, RE ('I don't care what your religion is!'), and Williams played Lieutenant Broomhead. Marsden played Margareta Witt, Pertwee the company sergeant and Paddick provided the voices for several roles, including the Reverend Witt and Private Hook. The following is a selection of some of the choicer moments from Merriman's script (any inaccuracies in my transcription are due to its origination in a poorly reproduced MP3 copy):[5]

ANNOUNCER: So to our drama of the week. Here is the thundering adventure story of the 2nd Battalion of the 1st Foot and Mouth, who held out against 4,000 Zulus at Rorke's Drift ... [music: *Soldiers of the Queen*] It's 1879, and a small contingent of soldiers are garrisoned at the Rorke's Drift mission station. They are the men of the famous Welsh regiment.

BILL PERTWEE: Atten-*tion!* Prepare for taking of the roll call! Jones!

NUMEROUS VOICES: Present! Present! Present! Present! (etc.)

ANNOUNCER: The regiment was commanded by the young, inexperienced Lieutenant Broomhead.

KENNETH WILLIAMS: You may wonder why I joined the army. There's usually some reason or other, and it's usually the other. Sergeant, where are Privates Hook, Line and Sinker?

[...]

HUGH PADDICK [as Witt]: We've just come from the camp of Cetewayo.

KENNETH HORNE: What are they up to?

BETTY MARSDEN: They're planning an all-out attack on your station, Lieutenant.

HP [as Witt]: There's no time to lose, you must evacuate immediately.

KW: I'll go and get my things!

KH: No, wait one moment. I say we should stay and fight it out.

KW: You're joking, of course?

KH: Come, Lieutenant, where's your get up and go?

KW: It got up and went.

[...]

KH: I'd rather put it to the men. Sergeant, call the men together.

BP: Platoon, fall in!

ZULU!—the Battle of Home's Drift... by Cummings

"...We only came out to make Zulu!"

These topical cartoons, commenting on current political issues, appeared in the *Evening Standard* in early 1964.

[sound of dozens of pairs of boots coming to attention]

KH: Now, lieutenant, I think you'll get your answer. Men, we're facing a desperate situation. We have a choice of two things. Either we stay and fight for the honour of the regiment or we run away like scared mice. I think I know you well enough to know what you'll do…

[sound of dozens of pairs of boots preparing to run away]

BP: Come back 'ere, the lot of you!

[…]

KH: We must make immediate preparations for attack.

BM: Lieutenant, what about me?

KH: You'd better do the same, I think. Oh, that is, I mean… I'm sure you can make yourself useful, Miss Witt.

BM: I will report to the hospital. I'm a qualified nurse, Lieutenant.

HP [as Hook]: Can I report in sick, miss?

KW: Hook, sling it!

[…]

KH: Well camp, there's nothing we can do now but wait. [dramatic music]

KW: [hysterical] It's the waiting I can't stand, the terrible, terrible waiting! Knowing that even now they're creeping up on us! [more hysterical] *I can't stand it! I CAN'T STAND IT!!*

KH: And neither can we, neither can we!

[…]

BP: Right men … here comes the first wave!

HP [as a very camp soldier]: Yoo-hoo!

BP: What are you doing, Private?

HP [camp soldier]: I'm waving back, Sarge.

KH: Here they come!

KW: Bugler, bugler, sound the retreat!

KH: What? You want to sound the retreat?

KW: Yes, I want to advance backwards!

KH: Stand by, riflemen! Alright, fire at will! [noise of gunfire]

HP [as Will]: Not at me, you great twits!

[…]

[the Zulus sing their war chants to frighten the soldiers]

KW: I can't stand it! *I can't stand it!!*

KH: Oh, I don't know, it's better than some of those Liverpool groups… Sing up, men!

KW [as Welsh chorister, singing]: "We'll keep a welcome in the hillside, we'll keep a welcome in the glen…" [sound of loud groans]

HP [as Hook]: That's enough. Look it's done the trick, they're running away!

The following month, March, just before *Zulu* began its national general release, Stanley Baker and James Booth appeared in their costume uniforms on the television variety show *Sunday Night at the London Palladium* to enact a ten-minute sketch with the show's host, the ever-popular Bruce Forsyth.[6] After forty years, Mr Forsyth cannot remember the details of the sketch, which he describes as 'a plug for the film being released,' though he guesses that 'Stanley as the officer was giving James a hard time in warding off those thousands of Zulus.'[7]

Nearly two decades later, the Monty Python team included an episode set during 'the First Zulu War' (sic) in their final cinema venture, *Monty Python's The Meaning of Life* (1983). John Cleese plays an imperturbable British officer calmly shaving during a full-scale Zulu attack, glancing up in irritation only when an assegai smashes his mirror. He calmly steps over piles of bleeding and dismembered bodies, stopping for an exchange of greetings with a severed (but still deferential) head, to inquire after a fellow officer (Eric Idle) whose leg has apparently been bitten off during the night by a tiger ('A tiger? In Africa?'). Graham Chapman is the avuncular, pipe-smoking surgeon who inspects the wound ('Been in the wars, have we?') and regretfully informs the officer that no, the severed limb ('Stings a bit') will not grow back.

Advertisers have also been alert to the instant recognition that *Zulu* iconography provokes in British audiences. Alan Parker, recently knighted for his services to the film industry, began his directing career in the 1970s by making commercials for cinema and television. 'We started to pastiche films that we'd liked,' he told fellow director Stephen Frears in the 1996 Channel Four documentary *Typically British*. Parker affectionately re-enacted the battle of Rorke's Drift in a studio for a two-minute Silk Cut cigarette advertisement (at a time when such things were allowed). As recently as 2003, commercials for the Royal Automobile Club featured brief, tongue-in-cheek vignettes of a film set apparently representing Isandhlwana, with actors dressed as wounded redcoats, surrounded by battlefield debris, and making such declarations as 'I wouldn't go anywhere without RAC breakdown assistance' and 'Get RAC to give it a thorough inspection first.'[8]

It is not only in a comic context that memories of *Zulu* have been deliberately evoked. Films depicting military conflict, especially those in which a small defence force is faced with a much larger antagonist, are now routinely linked to *Zulu* by critics, fans and even the filmmakers themselves.[9] Thus, reviewer John Patterson wrote of Ridley Scott's *Black*

Stanley Baker and James Booth join host Bruce Forsyth for a comic sketch on ITV variety show *Sunday Night at the London Palladium* **in March 1964. (Courtesy of Bruce Forsyth OBE)**

Hawk Down (2001) – set in Mogadishu in 1993, when a downed US helicopter had to be rescued at the cost of eighteen American lives and hundreds of Somalians – that it is 'basically a remake of *Zulu* with a tiny outfit hemmed in on all sides by a multitude of ululating savages.'[10] Scott himself, in his earlier film *Gladiator* (2000), had actually included war chants seemingly 'sampled' from *Zulu*'s soundtrack to evoke the Germanic barbarians ranged against the Roman armies in the opening sequence. In his audio commentary on the *Gladiator* DVD, Scott does not identify the source of the chants but explains: 'I wanted something really savage here rather than presenting a bunch of head-bashing barbarians, and just the sound of the chanting of these Germans [sic] suggests organisation and psychology, which psychology being to frighten the opposition. The Zulus in particular actually had this kind of psychology, so they would frighten the enemy before the enemy even saw them.' On the same commentary, *Gladiator*'s editor Pietro Scalia remarks to the director: 'You used the idea of the Zulus, their barbaric sound, as an initial contrast between the organised Romans and the psychological fear that the barbarians used with sound.'

"There was I in a three-an'-a-tanner seat watching Zulu . . ."

Other directors have also taken inspiration from *Zulu*. In an audio commentary on the Region 1 Special Edition DVD of the science fiction satire *Starship Troopers* (1997) – in which an interplanetary war ensues when a militarist (implicitly fascist) earth culture attempts to colonise a planet inhabited by fearsome but intelligent arachnids – one of the actors says of the sequence in which a platoon of soldiers in a small compound is surrounded by belligerent bugs: 'This is the *Zulu* shot!' In an alternative commentary track, director Paul Verhoeven states that he and his production team specifically looked at two movies to 'know how to shoot a scene like this': *Zulu* and *Gunga Din* (1939). Verhoeven's characteristically subversive irony, which undercuts the gung-ho action, arguably excuses the superficially offensive equation of giant insects with Zulus. A similarly wry sense of humour can perhaps be said to justify the scene in Neil Marshall's horror thriller *Dog Soldiers* (2002) in which British soldiers, holed up in a lonely farm house besieged by a pack of werewolves, compare their situation to that of the defenders at Rorke's Drift.

Perhaps the most notable recent homage to *Zulu* occurs in *The Lord of the Rings: The Two Towers* (2002), in which writer/director Peter Jackson modelled the scenes preceding the Battle of Helms Deep on the first half of Endfield's film. Jackson lucidly explained the thinking behind this in the documentary *From Book to Script: Finding the Story*, which accompanies the DVD Special Edition:

I think the trick with the battle scene is not so much the battle itself, but it's as much about the build-up to the battle. There's a movie called *Zulu*, made in the 60s, which depicts the defence of Rorke's Drift, which was where a hundred British soldiers fought against 4,000 Zulus. The first hour of the movie is just this slow, gut-wrenching kind of build-up to the first shot being fired, and once the shot is fired then all hell breaks loose. I always wanted Helms Deep to follow that basic pattern, which is establishing how the odds are so badly stacked against them, because it is a similar scenario of small defenders against overwhelming attackers.

Notes

1 This shaggy-dog gag inevitably loses something in translation from concert performance to cold print: not least Boyce's vocal sound effects for the Zulus' drumming, some expostulations in Welsh and, of course, the full sense and flavour of the assegai pun, which I have done my best to transliterate ('A's-a-guy' meaning 'That's the guy!'). This joke also turns up in the *Beyond Our Ken* sketch cited later. 'All-Blacks,' for the uninitiated, is a rugby football reference, not a racist remark.

2 While I have been engaged in writing this book, Paul Bryant-Quinn, a Research Fellow in the Centre for Advanced Welsh and Celtic Studies at the University of Wales, Aberystwyth, has been researching documents in Welsh relating to the Anglo-Zulu War. These include letters from soldiers and colonists as well as contemporary war coverage in the Welsh-language press, and are primary sources which have been largely overlooked by historians. I look forward to the publication of his findings.

3 Note for international readers: a reference to the highest possible score in a game of darts.

4 John McAdam, in his 'Observations on the film *Zulu*,' *The Journal of the Anglo Zulu War Historical Society*, no. 9, June 2001, claims not only that there is a 'sudden change of location to … the closest matching mountainous location in South Wales' for some exterior pick-up shots, but also that it 'must have been a small relief for the filmmakers to give a location credit as Wales' (p. 53). Needless to say, there is no such credit on the film because there was no such change of location.

5 I am indebted to Mark Lewisohn for locating (in the course of a telephone conversation with the author, 27 November 2003) the episode of *Beyond Our Ken* containing the *Zulu* spoof: Series 7, Episode 13, misleadingly titled 'Things to Come' in most reference sources. All archived BBC radio programmes are available for listening at the British Museum's Sound Archive at the British Library on Euston Road, London (contact website: http://bl.co.uk/cadenza/). A collection of 79 episodes (from the total run of 123) can be purchased in MP3 format from www.otrtoday.com/.

6 Forsyth recalls the sketch and his off-screen friendship with Stanley Baker in his memoir *Bruce: The Autobiography* (London: Sidgwick and Jackson, 2001). Writing to screenwriter John Prebble as the film began its record-breaking national release, Anglo Embassy's director Kenneth N. Hargreaves remarked that the sketch 'certainly did us no harm' (letter, 7 April 1964).

7 Letter to the author, 22 June 2004.

8 These ads (apparently shot on location in South Africa) were used to sponsor some of UK Channel Five's prime-time movies. I am grateful to Glenn Wade for loaning me his video recordings of the RAC commercials, broadcast during a screening of Richard Attenborough's *In Love and War* (1996).

9 In addition to those mentioned here, the 'movie links' page for *Zulu* on the Internet Movie Database lists a number of other films which supposedly contain 'references' to it, some of which I have not been able to check out for myself; I suspect most simply exhibit loose affinities rather than a direct influence. At time of writing, they include *Wizards* (1977), *Aliens* (1986), *Army of Darkness* (1993) and *Ghosts of Mars* (2001): see http://imdb.com/title/tt0058777/movieconnections. A now-deleted posting on the same website's Message Board also claimed that Big Audio Dynamite's song 'A Party' has 'sampled sounds from *Zulu*' (posted 13 January 2002).

10 John Patterson, *The Guardian*, 1 February 2002.

Members of the cast – looking a little heavier eight years on from the World Premiere – gather for a reunion press call to promote the film's 1972 reissue. Front rank: James Booth, Gary Bond. Rear rank: Jack Hawkins, Stanley Baker, Michael Caine.

"THEY'RE SALUTING YOU!"

THE LEGACY OF *ZULU*

> '*Zulu* changed my life,' [Stanley Baker] said the other day, inhaling deeply on his Gauloise. 'Neither I nor anyone else ever visualised what a success it would prove.
> 'I think maybe we struck just the right note at the right time. People wanted to be reminded of the greatness of Empire. Years ago, remember, we used to make that kind of film: *Clive of India*, *Disraeli*. And they were great. But then producers started trying to make films for America – like *Bonnie Prince Charlie*, which proved a disaster. With *Zulu* we just tried to make a good film. And it worked, dad, it worked.'
> (Roderick Mann, 'Mr. Baker beats the Jodhpur set,' *Sunday Express*, 10 January 1965)

Despite the enormous success of *Zulu*, the production team's attempts to follow it up with other African adventures were dogged by a series of misfortunes. A successor project was already in preparation even before shooting on the first film had commenced. As early as 1962, Baker and Endfield had begun making plans for an adaptation of William Mulvehill's novel *Sands of the Kalahari* – in which the survivors of a desert plane crash fight for their lives against each other, the elements and a colony of predatory baboons – and for a while contemplated shooting background material for the second film simultaneously with *Zulu*.[1] A formal financing agreement between Diamond Films and Joseph E. Levine's Embassy was not made public until a year later, when *Zulu* was almost ready for release and the *Kalahari* screenplay was still being developed, with several other collaborative projects also in the works.[2]

On the day of the World Premiere of *Zulu*, the British trade press announced that *Kalahari* was to be one of four more joint ventures between Embassy and Paramount.[3] *Kine. Weekly* commented approvingly that 'it is nice to think that the decisions [to make these films] will be influenced by the very fine job which has been done by Stanley Baker and Cy Endfield on *Zulu*, with the backing of Joe Levine and Paramount. They will certainly get a chance to do another.' The journal quoted Paramount vice-president George Weltner on the promise shown by the team:

Enthusing about the film, George said, 'If ever a picture was successful before the camera turned this is it, because of the careful preparation and the dedication to the property.' The producers, he said, had fashioned from a sincere story one of the most sincere motion pictures he had ever seen.

The industry, said George, suffered from 'too few.' Too few stars, too few directors and too few producers.

'In Stanley Baker and Cy Endfield we have two young people with talent and new ideas. Paramount will do all it can to assist and encourage them,' he promised.[4]

Joe Levine also promised to invest further in British production, leading Baker to remark that he hoped this would do much to help revive the moribund local industry with its many unemployed artists and technicians. He told *The Daily Cinema*'s diary columnist: 'It's good news for these British workers and the production boys as a whole that Joe's moving into the British studio field with his own productions.'[5]

As *Zulu* went into general release in March 1964, Bob Porter travelled to Namibia to begin scouting locations for *Sands of the Kalahari*. Baker positively relished the prospect of another shoot under tough physical conditions:

'It will be hot when we start filming,' he said with unconscious ambiguity. 'Worse than those mountains.

'But it's not a question of the tough life really. It's simply that the kind of film Cy ... and I want to make has to be made in the right place. And it's a damn sight more interesting than sticking in a studio.

'The days when a producer sits on his backside behind a desk and throws orders around are over. Today he's got to get his hands dirty.'[6]

Although Baker was also cast in *Kalahari*, this was to be in a supporting capacity, as the villain of the piece; Levine wanted bigger international names for the leads. They were offered to Richard Burton and Elizabeth Taylor, at the time the hottest properties in movies, thanks to their affair during the making of *Cleopatra* (1963). But Burton and Taylor did not come cheaply, she having the highest asking price of any star in the world. Perhaps Baker expected the couple to work for discounted fees in recognition of his many years of friendship with Burton, but if so he was mistaken. Taylor demanded $1 million for her services and Burton wanted $500,000 – together the equivalent of almost the entire budget of *Zulu* – and both asked for an additional percentage of the gross receipts. 'We just couldn't afford it,' said Baker ruefully as

production plans ground to a halt.[7] While talks began with Carroll Baker and Robert Mitchum to replace them, Baker flew to Johannesburg to star in another film produced under Levine's aegis, *Dingaka* (1965).

Having been postponed from September 1964, shooting on *Kalahari* was finally set to begin in March 1965, with Susannah York and George Peppard now heading the cast. But just as the cameras had begun to roll, Peppard too backed out. A number of explanations have been advanced for his abrupt withdrawal. Ellen Baker says that Peppard left in a huff because he was not permitted to carry his own gun with him on location. According to Maureen Endfield, 'He took one look at the baboons and fled. Also he didn't like the fact that we had a two-room apartment and he had only one room.' Others have suggested that he had lost confidence in Cy. The company was plunged into crisis until Stuart Whitman was hired at three weeks' notice as a replacement. Whitman, however, did not like the part he was offered and insisted on exchanging roles with Baker, meaning that the villain's role had to be expanded while what should have been the hero was reduced to a supporting part. (Despite this rigmarole, the sheer unexpectedness of the all-American hunter-gatherer becoming a near-psychotic monster works greatly to the film's advantage in dramatic terms.)

Under all these pressures, Endfield's working relationship with the crew broke down. He and director of photography Erwin Hillier stopped speaking to one another, Cy was nearly killed when a lighting rig almost fell on top of him, and in the last week of shooting he and Bob Porter, never the best of friends, had a calamitous falling out. 'The whole thing was doomed,' says Maureen Endfield. 'It was the kind of story that, if it were going to be made at all, needed someone like Burton and Taylor. I remember that when we had a preview screening Ellen Baker walked out, she was so disgusted; she felt Stanley wasn't right for the part he eventually played.'

In the interim, another dispute had arisen between Cy and Stanley over their next scheduled project, an adaptation of the South African novelist Wilbur Smith's best-selling first book *When the Lion Feeds*, which included scenes set during the Battle of Rorke's Drift (Smith had actually visited the *Zulu* set during shooting). According to Maureen, 'Cy suggested Stanley only be producer, which wasn't what he wanted at all. He wanted to act in it with Peter O'Toole, but Cy wanted Michael Caine and Terence Stamp, and Stanley wasn't very happy about it.' For $45,000 they had acquired the film rights to the historical adventure novel, which had been published early in 1964, around the time of *Zulu*'s release, and had sold 200,000 copies in the UK alone during its first year of publication.[8] But the project stalled later that year when the book was banned in South Africa; anyone in the country owning a copy was subject to prosecution. American showbiz journal *Variety* commented: 'Stanley Baker, who bought the film rights and who intended to start shooting early next year, is undecided what to do because he may have to go on location outside of South Africa. The author and publisher have lodged an appeal against the government, and future production of the pic depends on the outcome of the appeal.'[9]

Though the legal situation was resolved and pre-production resumed in 1966, when Baker, Robert Mitchum and Orson Welles were announced for the cast, the film was abruptly cancelled when Paramount was bought out by conglomerate Gulf + Western. Several other projects collapsed in its wake, including John Prebble's adaptation of John Weston's *The War Horses*, and films of two other historical novels: John Masters' *To the Coral Strand*, to be adapted by former blacklistee Dalton Trumbo, and Alexander Cordell's *Rape of the Fair Country*, set in the Welsh Valleys, which Cy planned to direct with Stanley, Dirk Bogarde and Jean Simmons. Paramount and Embassy had envisaged *When the Lion Feeds* and *The War Horses* as prestige roadshow presentations; the loss of these commissions was a major blow, and the Diamond Films partnership never recovered.[10]

While Baker and Endfield suffered this succession of disasters, other members of *Zulu*'s production team found better luck in returning to South Africa. Several worked on two local productions, *The Diamond Walkers* and *Tokoloshe* (both 1965), the latter featuring a second and final acting role for Chief Buthelezi; while associate producer Basil Keys, first assistant director Bert Batt, production

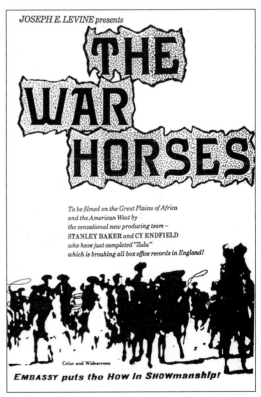

Trade advertisement from *Variety*, 22 April 1964, for a future collaboration between the *Zulu* team which never came to pass. (From a microfilm source.)

Bob Porter and Joe Levine.

manager John Merriman, unit manager Dawie van Heerden, continuity girl Muirne Mathieson, actor Gert van den Bergh and stunt performer John Marcus were all reunited on actor-director Cornel Wilde's fine adventure film *The Naked Prey* (1965). Baker and Porter temporarily went their separate ways after completing three films for the actor's Oakhurst company: *Robbery* (1967), *The Italian Job* and *Where's Jack?* (both 1969). While Baker acted in a series of international productions, Porter supervised several more films for Joe Levine – *The Idol* (1966), *Woman Times Seven* (1967) and *The Producers* (1967) – and later co-produced *The Last Valley* (1971) and *Golden Rendezvous* (1977), both of which involved yet more *Zulu* personnel, including action specialists Joe Powell, John Sullivan and Larry Taylor.

Son of *Zulu*

Ten years after *Zulu*, Baker, Endfield and Porter found themselves planning to return quite literally to the scene of past glory by reconstructing on film the Battle of Isandhlwana. 'I always wanted to make a sequel, of course,' said Baker in 1975, 'but I didn't want to make a *Son of Zulu*.'[11] After Endfield had begun work on the script using material researched for the first film, and Porter had made a location recce, the project was announced to the trade press in December 1973 under the title *A Washing of Spears*.[12]

Endfield collaborated on the screenplay for *Zulu Dawn*, as the 'prequel' came to be known, with Cambridge lecturer and writer Anthony Storey. According to Storey, Endfield provided the narrative structure and specific incidents – inspired in large part by his reading of Donald Morris's 1965 book *The Washing of the Spears* – while Storey worked out the detail of scenes and characterisations. Stanley, he says, did not interfere with the script but, with Cy, pitched it to a number of producers and potential financiers, some in South Africa itself.[13] Shooting was meant to start in 1974 or 75, but ill luck – of the worst possible kind – once again intervened.

'Cy was in his office waiting to have a meeting on the day Stanley found out he had cancer,' recalls Maureen Endfield. Though Baker was determined to battle on regardless, Porter knew that his illness would make the project impossible. He remembers pretending to have telephone business conversations in Stanley's hearing, with no-one on the other end of the line, in order to humour his friend's futile ambitions. Baker did, however, record the voice-over narration for a half-hour film about King Shaka, founder of the Zulu Nation, the proceeds of which were to 'be placed in a trust fund to be spent in the Zulu homelands,' though the film itself was apparently never made.[14]

Following Baker's death in June 1976, Porter dropped out and Endfield put the project on the shelf. That same year he met American producer Nate Kohn to discuss a commissioned script Endfield had written, a Western based on the life of the outlaw Belle Starr (this project ultimately came to nothing). When Kohn expressed an interest in developing a South African picture, Endfield gave him, in the producer's words, 'a free option' on *Zulu Dawn*. Feeling that he was not in good enough health to undertake such a large-scale movie, Endfield instead handed the

THE LEGACY OF ZULU

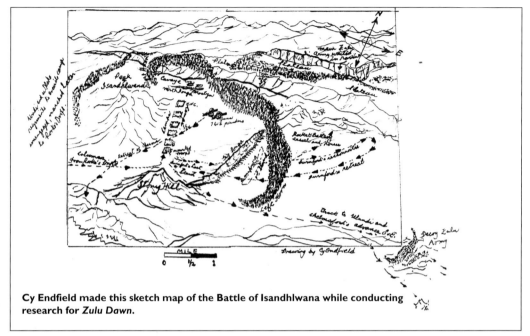

Cy Endfield made this sketch map of the Battle of Isandhlwana while conducting research for *Zulu Dawn*.

directorial reins over to Douglas Hickox, a friend of both his and Kohn's. Hickox had been third assistant director on *Sands of the Kalahari* and his own directing credits include *Entertaining Mr Sloane* (1970), *Theatre of Blood* (1973), *Brannigan* (1975) and *Sky Riders* (1976), along with a number of award-winning television commercials. 'Cy loved South Africa but he didn't want to devote two years of his life to being there again,' explains Maureen.

Kohn travelled to South Africa to raise finance and there joined forces with a local producer, Barrie Saint Clair. 'With a couple of others we formed a production company, Samarkand, to get *Zulu Dawn* made,' Kohn recalls. 'The money eventually came from a consortium of Swiss banks. The film was financed by advances on territorial pre-sales. There was no South African money in it at all, but it was a high-profile production at the time and so a lot was written in the press. It was the largest production made in South Africa to date: we had a crew of 250 and 6,000 extras at one time. The catering costs were astronomical. We had an agreement with Chief Buthelezi that we would only use genuine Zulus to play Zulus. We had a core of about 400 and brought in larger numbers when they were needed for the battle scenes. They were there for less than a week. We experimented with using 3-D polystyrene cut-outs, but we were shooting in Panavision to blow up to 70mm and they *looked* like cut-outs. So every Zulu you see is a real Zulu.'

Unfortunately, the producers had underestimated their initial budget of $8 million and the film ended up costing nearer $12 million. 'The banks had to put in more money than was originally envisaged,' says Kohn. 'It was always a few days or weeks late in arriving. We went through a number of budget-cutting exercises, such as reducing the production schedule from sixteen to eleven weeks. Some scenes we ended up cutting out were vignettes of characters we'd set up at the beginning of the story being killed in the battle. We had a few of those, like in the first film, but others were scripted and not shot. That gave it a more documentary-like flavour.' Kohn claims that authenticity was the keynote of the production: 'We went out of our way, more so than Cy had in *Zulu*, to be as historically accurate as we could – even down to having things like wagons and ammunition boxes constructed in the way they would have been at the time, without nails. Cy was more interested in the legend than in historical fact –

like the old John Ford line, "When the legend becomes fact, print the legend."¹⁵ He did the same with the Belle Starr story. We didn't have any of that romanticised stuff in our film.'

On seeing the completed 'prequel,' Cy Endfield was greatly disappointed. 'He thought at the time that he'd written a script that anyone could direct,' comments Maureen, 'but when it came out he wasn't happy with it. Douglas Hickox insisted on choosing very well-known people for the cast – Burt Lancaster and all these up-and-coming stars – whereas Cy wanted to use less well-known people: good actors, but not stars. He just didn't like the way Douglas went about it. He found the film dull.' Anthony Storey repeats a comment made to him by one of the producers – that Hickox was good at directing interiors but couldn't handle an army. 'The Zulu attack we see in the film is just a mad rush, not the disciplined buffalo head,' says Storey. 'That was Douglas.'

Other star names in the cast included Peter O'Toole, Simon Ward, John Mills and Bob Hoskins. Burt Lancaster played Irish cavalry officer Colonel Anthony Durnford, the role Baker would have taken had he lived; ironically, it was Lancaster whom Columbia had wanted to cast in *Zulu* as a condition of making the film back in 1960. Unit publicist Geoff Freeman, who worked on both films, believes that '*Zulu Dawn* tried too hard. It was quite political, whereas *Zulu* was a great, great story told in cinema terms. Also, Isandhlwana was a negative battle – we lost it. The feeling I get from *Zulu* is not the glory days of Empire but a group of men overcoming tremendous odds.' Other *Zulu* personnel who worked on the later film include Basil Keys, who advised the company on locations, and actors Larry Taylor (briefly visible as a grenadier standing by a cannon) and Simon Sabela, who took over Chief Buthelezi's former role as King Cetewayo, his dialogue spoken in Zulu and this time translated with subtitles.

Officially a US-Netherlands co-production, *Zulu Dawn* was first shown at the Cannes Film Festival in May 1979. It was released in the UK later that year by a small independent company, Tedderwick, and initially taken for international distribution by Warner Bros. and Orion, but in the event it was barely seen by theatrical audiences. It failed to return a profit and a number of those who

Some of the 6,000 Zulu extras who appear in *Zulu Dawn*.

Burt Lancaster as Colonel Durnford in *Zulu Dawn*.

worked on it did not get properly paid, including Storey. 'There are a number of territories where the film was never sold,' explains Nate Kohn. 'The major problem was that it didn't get a proper release in the US. It was sold to a company called American Cinema Releasing, which went bankrupt before they could release it. But we did a pre-sale to HBO [US cable channel Home Box Office], which was then just starting up, so it had a significant, substantial run on HBO around 1979-80.' In Britain the film also made a rapid television debut when it was shown by the ITV network at Christmas 1980. When finally given an American theatrical release in 1982 it was cut from 117 minutes to 98. Kohn, now a professor of journalism and communications at the University of Georgia, is currently engaged in trying to recover the rights in order to reclaim the original camera negative. 'The materials were in the possession of American Cinema Releasing. When they went bust the letter to the lab was in their name. Then the bank which gave the loan also went bankrupt. So I'm trying to get the materials released from the lab to get them restored.'

Asked to account for the film's disappointing box-office performance by comparison with its predecessor, Kohn says: 'There were several reasons, but the main one is that it's just not as good a movie! I wish that we'd told the whole story from the Zulu point-of-view: it would have made for a far more interesting film. It has a strong cult following, which always surprises me. But it came at the wrong time: historical epics were not in vogue after the Vietnam War. That was the time of the revolution in Hollywood, with people like Coppola and Scorsese coming to the fore, and people weren't interested in history. They still aren't, unless it's something like *Braveheart* or *Gladiator*.' Echoing these thoughts in an article for *American Film* magazine, Allen Barra offered an insight into the changing times: 'The irony is that, given the political climate of the audiences at the time these films were made, the story of the first battle [Isandhlwana] couldn't have been made in 1964, and the story of the second battle couldn't have been made in the late '70s.'[16]

Reflecting on *Zulu*

Zulu has come to be regarded somewhat ambivalently by film critics and historians, reflecting its mixed critical reception on release. Undoubtedly, if the Battle of Rorke's Drift were to be tackled by filmmakers today, the story would be told differently: more attention would surely be given to dramatising the Zulu viewpoint, and to providing a sympathetic focus for identification with non-White characters. It is also likely that opposition towards the politics of imperialism and the record of the colonial past would nowadays be expressed more explicitly, less ambiguously – though *Zulu* cannot, it seems to me, reasonably be accused of adopting a simplistic pro-colonial attitude.[17] In any case, there is little sense in demanding of a movie from the past that it embody the sentiments of today, though many observers have done so.

For some modern critics, the film is 'spectacular but mostly mindless'[18] or mere 'exploitative pulp,' exhibiting an 'unquestioned glorification of British heroism.'[19] Wayne Drew, introducing *Zulu* for a National Film Theatre season on 'Images of Welsh Culture and History,' described it as 'an immensely enjoyable, carefully crafted epic, but one which does not stand up to any but the most superficial political or social debate.'[20] But others have found the film worthy of revival in a more positive spirit. In a programme note for a screening at the Denver Film Festival in 1993, Howie Movshovitz of *The Denver Post* wrote:

> *Zulu* may be a great movie, in a class with the greatest films ever made. Its complexity of character and moral vision approach Renoir's *The Grand Illusion* and Endfield made the film with a spectacular sense of action and imagery. The film came out in 1964, but because of the title and the name of Joseph E. Levine, it was dismissed as either exploitative or racist. In fact it's neither. I can think of no other film that gives greater credit to people of another race and culture... As Endfield and his partner, actor Stanley Baker, imagined it, the fight was between two militaristic cultures. Only by implication is the film about imperialism or racism, because at the moment the two sides met, those concerns were extraneous to the strategies, the actual fighting and the class conflict between the two young lieutenants commanding the British troops. I find *Zulu* utterly fascinating, a film I can watch over and over because each viewing reveals new elements. The battle scenes are filmed with a wonderful eye for both geometry and drama.

Another American journalist, Stephen Hunter writing in *The Washington Post*, pondered both the aesthetics and the moral and political purposes of 'battle movies' in an article published shortly after the release of Ridley Scott's controversial *Black Hawk Down* (2001), a film widely compared (not always favourably) with *Zulu*:

> Battle movies usually eschew history. They ignore hindsight, larger meanings, the reality of armies as social institutions, the higher interpretation of policies, the wisdom or foolishness of the elderly who have decreed such a bloodfest into existence in the first place. They just put you in the thick and fast and try to answer a single question: What's it like? ...
>
> And ever so occasionally, the movies have gotten it right. The only masterpiece in the battle-movie genre is Cy Endfield's 1964 mind-boggler, *Zulu* ... [Endfield] captures completely the iffy quality of the fight. At no point does he allow an audience to believe in the inevitability of British victory; the battle is too fierce. It's what might be called a typical Western battle in the Third world: the Brits in their squares, locked in a kind of survival discipline, against warriors who rejected such tactics as cowardly and longed to get in close for the thrill of the kill.
>
> The issue was weirdly similar to the issue in Mogadishu in 1993: Will they tire of dying before we run out of ammunition? If it's the former, we win; if it's the latter, they do. Hundreds of Zulus died as they rushed through the rifle fire, and even when they breached the line, they could not stand against the determination of the well-trained British bayonet fighters, who found that four feet of Martini-Henry rifle tipped with 12 inches of steel was just as effective a close-quarter weapon as the assegai, the Zulu stabbing spear.
>
> Endfield also finds a quality missing from all too many battle sequences in millions of movies: that is, the utter physical labor of battle. It's very hard work to fight, which is why the young are so much better at it. His troopers emerge like footballers after an overtime – exhausted men, drained and emotionally flattened, smeared with dirt and blood, beyond the need to do anything but sleep for days. Almost no other film captures that soul-deep weariness.[21]

One can only speculate on the extent to which the enormous success of *Zulu* on its release in Britain was due, as has sometimes been suggested (and as Stanley Baker himself appears to confirm in the interview quoted as an epigraph to this chapter), to White audiences' reactionary nostalgia for imperial power. Following Indian independence in 1947, the 1950s and early 60s had seen the crumbling of Britain's colonial dominance, as one subject nation after another declared its independence. Between 1956 and 1968, more than thirty former dependencies, mainly in Africa, achieved self-rule – seventeen in 1960 alone, the year of Harold Macmillan's famous speech before the South African parliament: 'The wind of change is blowing through this continent, and whether we like it or not, this growth of national consciousness is a political fact.' Popular support for *Zulu* in 1964 could therefore easily be interpreted as an expression of the British public's feelings of loss and resentment at the post-colonial upheaval. However, such an explanation hardly accounts for the film's continuing appeal over four decades, or the extent to which its popularity straddles the generations.

In the absence of much in the way of direct testimony, it is difficult to assess how Black audiences have received the film. African-American film critic Jim Pines, a lecturer at the University of Luton, has told me of his distaste for the regular screenings of *Zulu* on British television at Christmas: 'I thought, why this? It seemed like a deliberate insult. *The Wizard of Oz*, fine, but why should *Zulu* be an annual ritual?' Mixed-race film historian Stephen Bourne ('a Londoner from a family which blends black Caribbean and white British ancestry') has argued that the very title of the movie added to the stock of racist insults often suffered by the children of immigrant parents.[22] He recalls how 'White British children were captivated by the film' and how this affected those belonging to racial minorities:

For them [White British children] it was like watching a Hollywood western in which the 'savage' plains of Africa stood in for America's Wild West. Stanley Baker took the place of John Wayne, and Africans stood in for Native Americans, brandishing spears instead of Tomahawks.

Zulu was released at a time when Black children in Britain were being exposed to BBC television's popular variety series *The Black and White Minstrel Show*, and Helen Bannerman's 1899 book *Little Black Sambo* was still being reprinted and used in schools and libraries. Perhaps unintentionally, *Zulu* added to this pool of racist propaganda. Black children who lived in isolation, in areas without Black communities, were particularly vulnerable.[23]

Other anecdotal evidence, however, suggests that at least some Black viewers were, to a degree, able to 'reclaim' their racial history through the film's presentation of their African ancestors. Stanley Baker's eldest son Martin, whose company makes documentaries for the music industry, has recalled how many of the African-American musicians he has interviewed have told him of their identification with the Zulus and their respect for the film's treatment of tribal culture. The *New York Times*' review of *Zulu Dawn* claimed that, in America, the original film had 'presented white British troops slaughtering such staggering numbers of Africans that trouble sometimes broke out in theatres in which *Zulu* was shown,'[24] though I have encountered no independent contemporary reports to verify this. But a White American student related to me his own father's experience of seeing *Zulu* with a multi-racial audience on its initial US release, in which different sections of the audience each cheered on their 'side.'

The film's honoured place in British popular memory can partly be gauged by its appearance in several UK polls conducted in recent years. It was voted number fifty-eight in *Empire* magazine's 1999 survey of its readers' favourite films, and achieved thirty-first place in the British Film Institute's *bfi 100* list of favourite 'culturally British movies,' as voted for by invited film-industry figures, critics, journalists and academics (actor Hugh Grant was among the celebrities who named it their number one).[25] Satellite TV channel Sky Premier's Millennium Movies poll, drawn from the votes of an estimated 60,000 subscribers, ranked *Zulu* eighteenth favourite overall: the second-highest place, after *The Full Monty* (1997), achieved by any British film. In a breakdown of votes by region, it achieved seventh and eighth position in Wales/West and the South West respectively, beating *The Full Monty* in those regions to be named their all-time favourite British film. In 2004, the cable station E! Entertainment Television polled 659 Members of Parliament on their own favourite films, receiving 140 replies; *Zulu* placed first among Conservative MPs and fifth overall.[26] Finally, Channel Four's *100 Greatest War Movies* programme (broadcast in May 2005), voted for by visitors to the station's website, put the film in eighth position.

Useful as they are, such statistics give little idea of how *Zulu* is actually regarded by its more dedicated adherents. One of the most valuable resources available to me while researching this book has been the internet website http://rorkesdriftvc.com/, particularly its Discussion Forum and Guest Book, which run to many pages of text contributed by the hundreds of regular and occasional visitors to the site. Though it is ostensibly devoted to preserving the memory and increasing understanding of the historical battle and the Anglo-Zulu War generally, website administrators Alan and Peter Critchley confirm that it was *Zulu* which initially stimulated their own fascination with Rorke's Drift and which likewise draws the vast majority of site visitors. 'From all the correspondence we've received it is undoubtedly *Zulu* which sparked people's interest in the subject,' commented Alan in one of his own postings. 'I was 20 when I first saw it, but age seems not to have any effect on the enthusiasm for either the film or the subject.' Peter adds that 'each time *Zulu* is shown on TV we (like the national grid) experience a surge in interest. New people find the website, and learn more about the subject.'[27]

These claims are confirmed by even the most casual perusal of the site's Guest Book; by my count, fully half of all the messages mention *Zulu* by way of explanation for their authors' interest in or awareness of Rorke's Drift. The following postings are a small but representative sampling from the five years of the website's existence:

'Having watched *Zulu* for about the twentieth time [I] thought that I would search the web – what an excellent site!!' (Philip Bale)

'I have just watched *Zulu* for the umpteenth time and thought I'd search the net for Bromhead, and up came this site!' (Roger Jones)

'I have been interested in the British campaigns in South Africa since watching *Zulu* when a young lad (like many people interested in the subject I guess).' (Richard)

'I have been a Zulu historian since I first saw the film in 1964.' (Peter Hopkins)

'Ever since the film I have always been interested in this particular battle.' (Richard Abbott)

'Due to my interest in history and due to the film *Zulu* I became fascinated by this African tribe.' (Hans Mortier)

'I have been studying the Cy Endfield movie *Zulu* in my Film Studies class and researching the events depicted in the film has sparked a new interest for me.' (Tom Legg)

'I have enjoyed the topic since seeing *Zulu* in my high school Victorian Era class.' (Tony Costello)

'I have been fascinated by the story of Rorke's Drift ever since I stumbled across the movie *Zulu* on TV one Saturday afternoon.' (Laura Knibb)

'I have long been interested in the history of Rorke's Drift, after having seen the movie *Zulu* as a young boy.' (John M. Salisbury)

'I have been a student of Rorke's Drift ever since I saw the movie *Zulu* in the early 1970s.' (Dan Perrine)

'I have always considered Rorke's Drift the greatest military encounter in all of military history but I have never encountered one person here in the States that knows a thing about it. It is certainly never covered in the history books here. I only learned of it initially from watching the film *Zulu*, which is just incredible.' (Sandy Ghosh)

Another poster, Andy Goodwin, surely got it right when he commented: 'Wow, it seems we owe a lot to a film. It seems to have made us thirst for more info, and maybe an old photo in an attic.' Many visitors have discovered through rorkesdriftvc.com a whole virtual community of like-minded buffs and fellow spirits, as Don Swait remarked: 'I never realized how many colleagues I have in the world who think the movie *Zulu* is one of the best ever made and the battle itself the most interesting from every point of view.' Through my own frequent website visits I have made contact with many dedicated fans and discerning experts who have enormously enriched and enhanced my understanding of both Rorke's Drift and the veritable subculture surrounding *Zulu*. I have also been consistently impressed by the enlightened approach taken by the overwhelming majority of its members: anyone expecting attitudes of gung-ho jingoism will no doubt be disappointed at the balanced reasonableness and wide knowledge which generally characterises the website's correspondence.

Some contributors have got in touch privately to describe the effect the film had on their personal and professional lives. Thus Peter Ewart wrote to me: 'I have to say that the film had such an impact on this 14 year old that it literally put me off cinema-going for life, as I felt that no other film would ever compare. I saw it many times in various cinemas in the 60s but by the end of my teens my cinema-going visits dropped off and have never been revived. A strange effect for a film to have! And for many years I thought I was almost the only person who remembered the film so affectionately!'[28] John Young, recognised as one of the leading experts on all manner of historical and military minutiae

Members of the 1879 Group attend the Annual Rorke's Drift Dinner in Llandrindod Wells, January 2002.

concerned with the Anglo-Zulu War, sent me this personal reminiscence:

> Personally, *Zulu* was the start of an odyssey for me, made even more entertaining by virtue of the fact my father had served in the South Wales Borderers.
>
> That film had a deep impact on me, and although I now watch once in a blue moon, it sparked a lust to find out more about the Anglo-Zulu War of 1879, and the combatants.
>
> My father, after we'd seen the film for the first time back in 1964, suddenly produced a tobacco tin containing little pieces of metal, some of which were obviously the remains of bullets. These he told me were from Isandlwana, collected by his father during the Natal Campaign of the 2nd Anglo-Boer War. The 'history' that I had seen on the screen was now coming to life in my very hands.
>
> That film made me what I am today, an amateur historian on the subject, who according to some others is a 'World's Authority' on the subject.[29]

Perhaps no historian has been as prolific in writing about the Anglo-Zulu War as Ian Knight, the author of many widely-read books who also maintains his own website ('You've seen the movie, here's the website').[30] 'Certainly, a lot of my own interest came from the film, which I saw as a boy,' he says. 'I then discovered a family connection with Isandlwana, which clinched it.'[31] Aside from his writing, Knight leads safaris to the historic battlefields and the film locations, and is convinced that *Zulu* is the prime stimulus behind this still-growing tourist industry. 'I have no doubt it is the biggest single factor in the UK in the interest in tours to the Anglo-Zulu War battlefields,' he told journalist Stephen Coan:

> 'I've been involved in promoting historical tourism from the UK to South Africa for 15 years now and, in that time, I can count on one hand the number of people whose interest had not, in some way, been stimulated by it …
>
> 'It is shown on mainstream British TV two or three times a year,' says Knight. 'And still – even though everyone has seen it! – pulls in audiences of two million viewers.
>
> 'One reason the film remains popular is that it has a very war-weary, anti-Imperial sixties sub-text which modern viewers can still sympathise with; it has none of the old unquestioning attitudes to Empire that make some of the thirties Hollywood films about the British in India uncomfortable viewing now.'[32]

Coan, an English-born journalist now writing for the South African newspaper *The Witness* (formerly *The Natal Witness*), experienced at first hand the interest created by the film when he joined one of Knight's tours. Of the seven British history buffs on the two-week trip, only one had not been initially inspired by *Zulu*. 'Without that film, it would be a forgotten war,' one told him. Another said: 'It's become part of the British psyche.'[33] Stephen himself admits that *Zulu* was his own first contact with the history, and that he emigrated to South Africa partly as a result of his childhood reading of stories of African adventure such as those written by H. Rider Haggard. He has since written a number of related articles for his paper, which four decades ago covered the shooting of the film in what is now KwaZulu-Natal.[34]

For some historians and battlefield conservationists the prominent role taken by a mere movie in stimulating public awareness is a matter for some irritation. Ken Gillings made his own feelings known in another posting on rorkesdriftvc.com: 'As an active member of the South African Military History Society … I am amazed at [the] amount of interest that the highly inaccurate film *Zulu* has aroused! The background scenery often spoils it for the numerous visitors whom I take to both Isandlwana and Rorke's Drift, because it was filmed in the Drakensberg mountains, several hundred kilometres from the battlefield.

Film archivist David Berry, television producer Steve Freer and the author with members of The 1879 Group's uniform section attend a fortieth anniversary screening of *Zulu* at the UGC cinema, Cardiff, November 2004. *(Glenn Wade)*

the film might have been expected – which adopted it for military exercises, as these other reminiscences demonstrate:

'Interesting, that when I joined the RN [Royal Navy], in '65, they showed us *Zulu* as an insight into leadership. Then when I joined the Australian Army in '78, we were shown *Zulu* for the same reason. Also at NCO schools, later. Especially Colour Sergeant Bourne.' (Tony Wood)

'I first saw *Zulu* as a training film when I was a recruit with 2Cmdo.' (James Logan)

'I joined the Royal Engineers in 1977 and within the first few hours we were watching *Zulu*.' (Steve Clough)

'I must say that as a young recruit in the Australian Army in the mid-70s, the motion picture *Zulu* was heavily used as *the* training example on the subject of leadership. One is heartened of course, that after 25 years of military service, I still look up to the Colour Sergeant as an inspirational leader of men.' (Lawrence Graystone)[35]

Nonetheless, it has whetted the appetites of thousands of visitors to these two famous sites.' Another website contributor, Melvin Hunt, offered a pragmatic justification of the film's liberties with the facts in view of its larger influence for the good: 'It doesn't matter that there are historical inaccuracies. It doesn't matter that Hookie was portrayed incorrectly and that the Zulus didn't really appear to salute at the end. The real facts emerged as the film spurred us all on to find out more about Rorke's Drift and the rest of the War. The popularity of everything Anglo-Zulu today, i.e., books, web sites, societies, visits to the battlefields, etc., stems from the film. It doesn't matter that there might be a remake. Nothing can detract from the original. It will always be around. Unsurpassed location, music, script... and great characters and acting.'

A number of the visitors to rorkesdriftvc.com have testified that, as well as inspiring many an individual to take an active interest in history, *Zulu* has also been put to practical use by numerous branches of the armed forces. David Cunniffe was actually serving in the South Wales Borderers at the time of its initial release: 'When the film came to a local cinema I seem to remember we were paraded as a Battalion to go see it.' It was not just the Welsh regiments – whose interest in

Those not in the services professionally have sometimes been inspired to form their own informal associations. In the UK there have been several groups of Anglo-Zulu War battle 're-enactors' whose main initial purpose was as much to emulate *Zulu* as to pay tribute to the historical combatants. Their members often purchase replica uniforms, play the roles of real-life figures, organise trips to the battlefields and recreate the scenes of heroic defence and disaster which they might otherwise only read about in books or see dramatised on the screen. Among these groups are the Die Hards, the now-defunct Rorke's Drift Club and The 1879 Group, of which I am myself a card-carrying member (though alas I cannot claim to have my own uniform). The 1879 Group was founded in 1998 by Maurice ('Mo') Jones, and currently boasts nearly four hundred members, about one quarter of whom are descendants of actual Rorke's Drift defenders. Its honorary patrons include Prince Mangosuthu Buthelezi and the Group is recognised by the Royal Regiment of Wales, representatives of which frequently attend its annual Rorke's Drift Dinner.

The driving force behind the Group is not hard to detect. At the age of eleven Mo assisted his father in the projection room of a cinema in Aberystwyth. One day, Dad told him to watch a 'fabulous film.' He saw *Zulu* while seated on a stool in the projection booth, watching it through the porthole, and in later life took over as projectionist. 'Sir Stanley has a lot to answer for!' he says. Another member, Danny Tully, has by his own estimate seen the film more than a thousand times. He watched every showing, every day, at his local cinema for several weeks on its first release, and came back early from his honeymoon to see it again.

But it is not just mature veterans who sustain the Group. At the 2003 dinner I was seated next to Christopher John, a bugler cadet in the Group's uniform section, who at the time was fourteen, going on fifteen. He saw *Zulu* for the first time at the age of seven when his Dad sat him down in front of the television to watch it. Since then he has seen it 'at least once every day' and has worn out three VHS tape recordings through constant use. Christopher knows the film's dialogue by heart and the story of Rorke's Drift itself in great detail, impressing his schoolmates with his knowledge of the subject. He wants to be a history teacher.

Notes

[1] '*Zulu* Partners Embassy, Anglo And Creators,' *Variety*, 11 November 1962, p. 5; '*Tropic Cancer* Like *Carpetbaggers* Covets Shurlock's Production Seal,' *Variety*, 26 December 1962, p. 4.

[2] 'New African Pic By Baker-Endfield For Jos. E. Levine,' *Variety*, 27 November 1963, p. 3. *Sands of the Kalahari* was eventually copyrighted by Endfield's company Pendennis, with Diamond's Robert Porter credited as associate producer.

[3] 'Lotsa Eggs But No Omelette?,' *Variety*, 22 January 1964, p. 3. The other films in the package were *A House is Not a Home* (1964), *The Idol* (1966) and *Imperial Woman* (which was never made).

[4] 'Long Shots,' *Kine. Weekly*, 30 January 1964, p. 4.

[5] Observer, 'Commentary,' *The Daily Cinema*, 27 January 1964, p. 3.

[6] William Hall, 'The Lush Life – by Mr. Baker,' *Evening News*, 7 March 1964. See also 'Films Made in South Africa,' *Variety*, 29 April 1964, p. 136.

[7] 'Balks When Burtons Ask % Plus $1.5 Mil,' *Variety*, 24 June 1964, p. 1.

[8] '*Where Lion Feeds* Goes To Embassy for Filming By and With Stan Baker,' *Variety*, 20 May 1964, p. 3. The passage set at Rorke's Drift (it unfolds in a subjective flashback) can be found in *When the Lion Feeds* (London: Heinemann/Pan Books, 1964), pp. 89-96.

[9] 'So. Africa Bans *Lions* So Film of Yarn Stalls,' *Variety*, 26 August 1964, p. 2. See also 'Ban on book stops film', *Evening Standard*, 4 September 1964.

[10] 'Embassy Roadshow Policy Set But Release Plans Are Not,' *Film Daily*, 16 July 1964, pp. 1-2; 'Baker-Endfield Back Filming In South Africa: It's for Par-Embassy,' *Variety*, 2 December 1964, p. 3. The same journal reported that *Sands of the Kalahari* had also been planned as a roadshow: see 'More Levine Pix Probable for Par,' *Variety*, 3 June 1964, pp. 4, 16.

[11] Alan Road, 'Zulu bwana,' *The Observer Magazine*, 17 August 1975.

[12] 'Baker, Endfield Team Anew On Africa Film,' *Daily Variety*, n.d. available.

[13] Anthony Storey's impressionistic first-hand account of this period in Baker's life, *Stanley Baker: Portrait of an Actor* (London: W.H. Allen, 1977), contains an intriguing report on a meeting with potential financiers for *Zulu Dawn*, one of them a Zulu (see pp. 95-7).

[14] Road, op. cit.

[15] This famous line of dialogue was spoken in John Ford's Western *The Man Who Shot Liberty Valance* (1962), written by Willis Goldbeck and James Warner Bellah.

[16] Allen Barra, 'The Incredible Shrinking Epic,' *American Film*, March 1989, p. 45. James Chapman includes a brief discussion of *Zulu Dawn* in his chapter on *Zulu* in *Past and Present: National Identity and the British Historical Film* (London: I.B. Tauris, 2005). See also Tiiu Lukk, 'Filming *Zulu Dawn* on location in South Africa,' *American Cinematographer*, February 1979; and Peter Davis, *In Darkest Hollywood: Exploring the jungles of cinema's South Africa* (Athens: Ohio University Press, 1996), pp. 162-7. Davis quotes extensively from a 1991 article written by producer

Nate Kohn, 'Glancing Off a Postmodern Wall: A Visit to the Making of *Zulu Dawn*,' but gives no details of where (or whether) it was published.

17 The expression of more modern attitudes would not, of course, necessarily make a remake of *Zulu* superior to the original. The pitfalls of imposing an anti-imperial viewpoint on material which will not support it are amply demonstrated by Shekhar Kapur's disastrous revisionist version of *The Four Feathers* (2002), which falls apart under the strain of trying to reconcile incompatible values.

18 Kenneth M. Cameron, *Africa on Film: Beyond Black and White* (New York: Continuum, 1994), p. 141.

19 Jim Pines, programme note for season 'Images of Empire: Colonial Surveillance,' National Film Theatre, London, 7 June 1986.

20 Wayne Drew, programme note for season 'Views of the Valleys: Images of Welsh Culture and History,' National Film Theatre, London, 17 March 1985. For further discussion of recent critical accounts of the film, see Chapman, op. cit., and Sheldon Hall, 'Monkey Feathers: Defending *Zulu*,' in Claire Monk and Amy Sargeant (eds.), *British Historical Cinema* (London and New York: Routledge, 2002).

21 Stephen Hunter, 'War is Hell, Battle is Worse: Like other films before it, *Black Hawk* is in for a fight,' *Washington Post*, 20 January 2002, p. G01.

22 Kathy Harris has told me that not only is *Zulu* her favourite film, but that she had named her cat after it. A White woman living in a Sheffield street with a number of Black residents, she recalls inadvertently offending her neighbours by shouting 'Zulu!' to call him in at night. Sheffield also boasts a rock band called Bromhead's Jacket.

23 Stephen Bourne, 'Secrets and lies: Black histories and British historical films,' in *British Historical Cinema*, pp. 8, 47. Some readers may, like me, recall playing games of 'Zulus and Englishmen' in the schoolyard (a popular alternative to the now even more politically incorrect 'Japs and Commandos'). In my own experience, such games usually didn't last very long, as (White) boys wanting to be Zulus far outnumbered those satisfied to be mere Brits and soon overwhelmed their foe, unlike the real battle.

24 Janet Maslin, *New York Times*, 11 July 1982, p. 39; quoted in Chapman, op. cit.

25 'Your 100 greatest films ever!', *Empire*, no. 124, October 1999, pp. 121, 130.

26 Jack Malvern, 'Dr Zhivago unites MPs in vote for favourite film,' *The Times*, 12 February 2004, p. 3. I am grateful to Peter Ewart for drawing my attention to this article. As its title indicates, *Doctor Zhivago* (1965) was the MPs' overall favourite film.

27 Posted 12 December 2001 and 23 April 2003 respectively. Subsequent quotations from website postings are undated for the sake of brevity. Topics concerning *Zulu* which are regularly debated in the Discussion Group include (in approximate order of frequency by my count): speculation on the prospects of a remake; the characterisation of the defenders; 'mistakes' and historical disparities; music and the Zulu chants; favourite scenes, lines and memories of seeing the film (see 'The First Time').

28 Peter Ewart, email to the author, 22 July 2003.

29 John Young, email to the author, 7 February 2002.

30 http://www.kwazulu.co.uk/. The website of the Royal Regiment of Wales also prominently features a 'Zulu' logo and maintains a 'Zulu Club.'

31 Ian Knight, email to the author, 10 February 2002.

32 Stephen Coan, 'The return of the redcoats,' *The Natal Witness*, 3 July 2003.

33 Stephen Coan, 'Anybody seen a film called *Zulu*?', *The Natal Witness*, 17 February 1998.

34 Stephen Coan, 'Beyond violence and death,' *The Natal Witness*, 20 February 1998.

35 Lest these testimonies give the impression that *Zulu* can be taken as nothing but an instrument of military propaganda, David Magee offers the reminder that it and *Zulu Dawn* 'deal sensitively with the plight of the humble foot soldier. Moreover, far from being an inane glorification of the imperial conflict, a sense of waste and common humanity is evident' (http://rorkesdriftvc.com/, posted 15 June 2003).

"A FINAL REDOUBT"

AFTERWORD

On one trip abroad during the writing of this book, I found myself on a plane seated next to a young American student who asked me what I did for a living. I told her that I write and teach film history. I don't think she meant to be rude when she replied: 'Tell me. Film history: what's the point?' She assumed that all film history was about explaining the background to the making of individual films. It isn't, but that was of course just the kind of project on which I was presently engaged. It's therefore worth attempting to answer that question: just what *is* the point of writing about the *making* of *Zulu* rather than, say, an interpretation and evaluation of the film itself, in aesthetic, social or political terms?

Not that I haven't thought about writing that sort of book too. Indeed, I have already mentioned an article of mine which seeks to defend the film against recent academic criticism that it is in some ways racist – for example, in its failure to provide rounded, individuated Zulu characters. Though some of my comments would need to be modified in the light of Prince Buthelezi's Statement at the beginning of the book (especially those concerning the use of tribal music), I still stand by the main gist of the argument laid out there.

At an early stage I had entertained the thought of incorporating such analytic material in the present volume, until it grew much too large for the inclusion of anything more than you will already find in it. I decided instead to present, as objectively as possible given the sometimes unreliable information at hand and the distance in time since the events, as thorough and detailed a history of the film's production as I could assemble. I hope and expect that, for many readers, especially those fascinated by every last bit of trivia concerning a favourite film, the variety of facts and anecdotes it has unearthed will have been justification enough of my project. But can such material offer anything to general readers not obsessed with this particular movie? Or, with my daily bread-and-butter in mind, to serious students of the cinema with broader concerns? What, indeed, *am* I doing here?

For a start, as both a historian and a critic I am interested in understanding how a film – any film – came to take the form that it did. This means, among other things, attempting to explore some of the contexts (social, political, industrial and commercial) within which the film was produced. With that in view, this book can be taken as a case study of *Zulu*'s historical 'moment' and the various pressures acting on it – forces which I have tried, as far as possible, to present in concrete terms rather than as vague speculations. I hope to have demonstrated how *Zulu* and its subsequent box-office success were enabled by a fortuitous conjunction of circumstances which include, for example: the readiness of major American film companies in the 1960s to invest in British-based production activities, especially large-scale pictures of international scope; the eagerness of the South African government to encourage foreign producers to use its facilities for location filming; and the British public's appetite for imperial nostalgia, coupled with its acceptance of a more sceptical, more questioning attitude to the colonial past than had hitherto prevailed in popular cinema.

But I have also been concerned to trace the progress of the artistic decisions that the filmmakers made in realising their project, and to advance some explanations for those choices. This will not necessarily help us in grasping the 'true' meaning of the film – there is no such thing – nor will it substitute for detailed analysis of the finished product, which can only be achieved by examining the images and sounds of which the film is composed. Film history is not the same as criticism,

First assistant director Bert Batt (left) with Stanley Baker and Jack Hawkins.

therefore, but it may aid the practice of criticism by making available to it a range of relevant background material. I trust that my readers will, at the very least, find themselves better informed when it comes to making interpretations and judgements of their own about *Zulu*, or when encountering those of other critics.

More than all this, however, studying the making of a film should lead to a greater appreciation of the sheer *effort* involved: not just creative effort (though obviously that is important too), but the practical, technical and logistical effort – the *labour*, if you prefer – necessary to put any film on the screen. Its particular nature and demands will of course vary from picture to picture, so the study of different films will yield different results and varied insights. I hope that *Zulu: With Some Guts Behind It* has conveyed something of my admiration for the accomplishments of all those involved in the production of *Zulu* and my gratitude, on behalf of all its many viewers over the years, for the pleasure the film has given me.

It is characteristic of the generation of film artists, craftsmen and technicians who made the movie not to seek special recognition, but to regard the successful completion of their work as its own reward. In a letter of 17 January 2002, responding to a query of mine about whether he was especially proud of the work he had done on *Zulu*, first assistant director Bert Batt made some comments which can justly stand as representative of this marvellous, self-effacing professional modesty:

> It was a great film to be associated with. I'm glad that I worked on it but not proud of it. I did the job I was paid to do and there's nothing to be proud in that ... We were a unit of professionals with all the tools to do the job. There was nothing special about it. I have a small mountain of photographs of the many films I worked on but not a single one of the four films worked on in South Africa.

I trust that this book will have given Bert a permanent memento of working on *Zulu*, and that it will serve as a worthy tribute to his skills and abilities, and to the equally admirable, if usually unsung, work of Bob Porter and Basil Keys, John Jympson and Rusty Coppleman, Joe Powell and John Sullivan, Stephen Dade and Dudley Lovell, and all those many others mentioned in these pages.

Postscript

While correcting the final proofs prior to publication of this book, I received news of the sudden death at 77 of James Booth on 11 August 2005. Aside from my enjoyment of his splendid performance as Hook, I treasure memories of the day I spent in his convivial company during the shooting of the documentaries for the *Zulu* DVD in 2002. I last saw James two years later, when we both, along with Joe Powell, attended an event at Woolwich Arsenal, at which he happily signed autographs for some of his many fans. On the day James died (peacefully, in bed), the chairman of The 1879 Group was writing to invite him to a ceremony for the rededication of the real Henry Hook's grave, to mark the centenary of his passing. I very much regret that James did not live to receive that honour, and that he never got to read any portion of this book. But perhaps it will act as a reminder to others of his talent and of his immense contribution to the film's lasting success. He will be much missed, and not only by those who knew him.

THE FIRST TIME

I began this book by describing my own first experience of watching *Zulu*. It is only fitting to end it by quoting, without further comment from me, those of some other viewers. Except where noted, all the anecdotes are reproduced from the website http://rorkesdriftvc.com/

I saw *Zulu* for the first time in the summer of 1964 at a drive-in. I was eleven. Coming as it did on the eve of my adolescence, the experience changed my life. I was enthralled by the film as a whole and electrified by Hooky, who to me embodied a state of grace and the ultimate in manliness. About halfway through the movie I started shaking, and I couldn't stop. I rode home in the back of the family station wagon trembling with arousal and exaltation. I felt that *Zulu* wasn't just a great work of art, but something special, something sacred. I stayed awake all night for the first time in my life, drinking vile black coffee and thinking about what I had seen. When dawn broke I went out onto the dewy lawn to look at the sky and became aware of a curious new sensation and the bodily process that caused it. My initiation into womanhood was all mixed up with images of masculine blood, red coats, and the thrusting of bayonets and spears.
(Diana Blackwell, http://jamesbooth.org/reviews/zulu.htm)

Of all the memories I am most proud of, seeing the items from the movie on display as the film was released for the first time in the town of Flint, Flintshire, North Wales many years ago, has to be the most treasured. From there at the age of eleven I gave my first one man show act on the Zulu War in front of my class. More than forty years later I am still there with Chard and Hook, et al. Each time I put on that red jacket and pick up my Martini-Henry to do a show I still get that thrill of 'being there.'
(Gwyllim Parry)

On my first visit to the cinema in the nearby town, a policeman had to be called midway through *Zulu* to expel some local youths, who had joined in with the African warriors' chanting-and-stamping routine so enthusiastically that a piece of ornamental cornice had come loose and brained the woman from the bike shop.
(Harry Pearson, 'The last great picture show,' *The Independent*, 15 May 1999)

I have enjoyed this movie from the first time I watched it. I was a 19-year-old warrior in Vietnam, 1966 and 1967, Pointman, Recondo Platoon, HHC, 2/502nd INF, 1st BDE (Separate), 101st Airborne Division. I have the greatest respect and empathy for the warriors on both sides of the battle at Rorke's Drift. I can watch this film over and over, and never get bored.
(Brien Richards)

Seeing the film in Cinerama on the big semi-oval screen in about 1972 when I was 12!!! What an impression it made. The music, the frightening approaching Zulus, the 'train' sound with their shields before you see them!!! Michael Caine looking absolutely knackered towards the end of the film added so much realism.... Seeing all those Zulus form a long line on the hillside before the attack.... Also the bit where Hitch gets hit by a bullet on the mealie bag.... Nasty, you could feel the pain he was in!!! So so much of that film has made a great impression on me, and the way epic cinema should be...
(Leigh Tarrant)

I saw *Zulu* when I was seven in 1977, on telly. I remember my dad telling me how good it was all during the day and after tea we went out to cut lettuce (we lived on a farm). My dad kept going on and on about it, and when we came home, the folks allowed me to stay up late and watch it. I was totally mesmerised, actually – and it's stayed my top film ever since.
(Richard Howes)

I saw *Zulu* when it first came out in London at the Ritz, Turnpike Lane. I guess I was 16 or a little older. The film just blew me away but would have been a lot better had it not been for an elderly couple of women, one of whom was hard of hearing, sitting behind my friend and I in the cinema. On a very regular basis the deaf one would ask her companion in a very loud voice, 'What he say?' and in an even louder voice her companion would repeat the last line delivered by the actor. This made my friend and I miss a lot of the script. However we both tolerated it until the part where in the middle of the battle Bromhead screams at the top of his voice 'FIRE'. And sure enough the deaf lady shouts to her companion, 'What he say?'

This was too much for my friend. He stood up and turned around to face the women and said in a VERY loud voice, 'He said F****** FIRE!' The silly women then mumbled something about there being no need to shout but remained quiet for the rest of the film. In the foyer later two other patrons thanked Mike for the action he had taken.

In his defence this was the first time I had known Mike to swear and this couple had ruined for us and others a classic movie. The folly of youth. Over the top maybe. I guess now that we should have left or spoken to the manager. We went back to see the film the following night and were made very much aware how much this inconsiderate pair has made us miss. However to this day when I hear Michael Caine shout 'Fire' you can guess what words go through my head and a smile crosses my face.
(Barry Iacoppi)

I first saw the movie *Zulu* while home on leave from the Air Force. I was preparing to go to Taiwan for a one year duty. My mother set me up with a blind date. I took her to the drive-in movie near our house (Niagara Falls, NY). I proceeded to watch the movie and not lay a hand on my date. She told my mother that she thought I was weird because all I did was watch the movie and not pay any attention to her. Needless to say, I never saw her again but have seen the movie so many times that I know the dialog. People in my office groan whenever they talk about a movie and I tell them that it may be a good movie but it is not as good as *Zulu*. I have actually had a Zulu Party where I introduce the uninitiated to the movie.
(David Wachtel)

I was a small boy of ten when I first saw this magnificent film. I thought then, as I still think now, how much I wanted to have been there with those brave soldiers, and if I had to die in battle, in what better company could I have been? I cried tears of pride when I heard the defiant, yet poignant rendition of 'Men of Harlech'; it still brings a lump to my throat and a tear to my eye even now, some thirty-nine years later.
(Michael D. Carroll)

In 1972 I first saw the film on television. At first I thought 'yeah, right', a small band holding off that horde. I was stunned to realize the story was true. I went out and bought *The*

Washing of the Spears two days later. Since then I have been an avid student of the Zulu War.
(Dan Norton)

Though I was aware of the movie *Zulu* when it was released in the theatres in 1964, I didn't get to see it until 1975. Up 'til then, I had no desire to see it, however, one night at work, some of the crew started discussing movies, and the manager, an unemotional and normally silent man, described the movie so energetically that his eyes glowed. That settled it; I saw the movie just a few weeks later (and again afterwards), and was blown away.
(swoeste, http://www.filmsgraded.com)

As you might imagine, the film was quite a big thing with Welsh boys of all ages in the 1960s: I particularly remember that it was one of the few of many films that my father took me to see for which we had to queue – this at a time of encroaching bingo and sweeping cinema closures. As this might suggest, the 60s weren't always that swinging in the Rhondda. Now, the 70s…
(Leighton Grist, email to the author, 19 January 2004)

I can well remember watching this film with my younger brother and my two (even younger) cousins – and when it finished making all three of them snuck down in their seats so we could immediately watch it a second time round! We exited the cinema to find two very frantic sets of parents waiting outside for their beloved offspring – and I received suitable punishment, I am sure!
(Martin Heyes)

I must have been five in 1964 when my friend and I went to see the film … When the film finished, my friend and I hid down low in the seat so that the usherettes with their torches could not see us, then we watched it all over again. Believe it or not, we tried the same trick to watch it again but got spotted by an usher and chucked out!
(David Alan Gardner)

In my youth, no other film came near it and it ruined me as a cinema-goer for the rest of my life, as nothing would ever equal it. I travelled miles on hard-earned pocket money just to see it when I learned it may be showing within 60 miles or so – all this in my teens on public transport, when I continued to attend the cinema, although for years I rarely met anyone with a similar opinion and I'm sure I sometimes invited ridicule when offering an opinion on it … Saw it around a dozen times in the 60s and once in the early 70s, all on the big screen of course. Have since seen it just once on video and of course it is simply not the same. Needs to be at the flicks.
(Peter Ewart)

PART IV: MORE GUTS

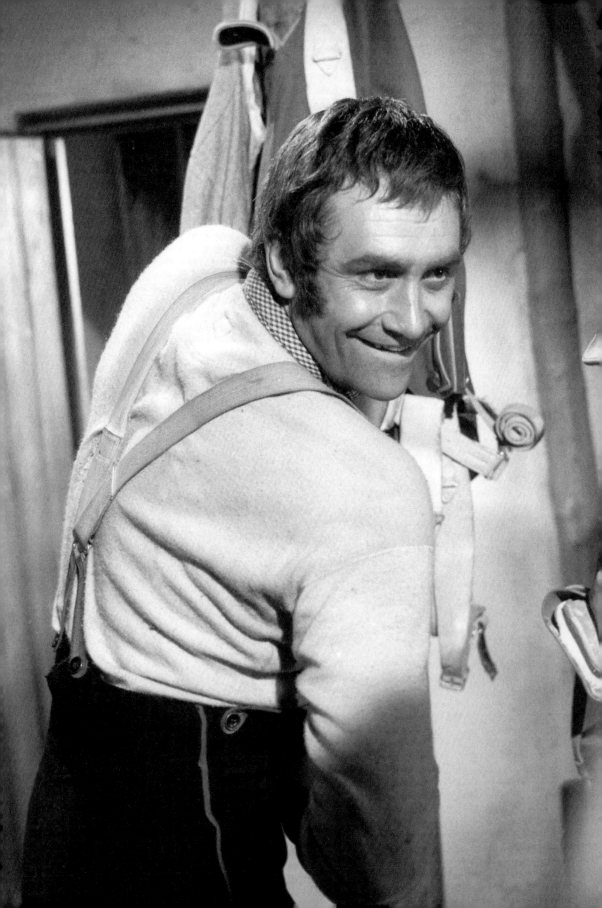

THE FILM FINANCES FILES

Included as appendices to the first edition of this book were two short chapters derived from material in the Paramount Production Files collection at the Margaret Herrick Library in Los Angeles, California. The documents located there provided a seemingly unique insight into the involvement of Paramount Pictures in the financing of *Zulu* and, through a complete set of daily Production Progress Reports, a record of some of the day-to-day occurrences encountered in shooting. However, an even more extensive set of primary documents has since been uncovered in the archives of Film Finances, Ltd, the British-based company that provided the production with its completion guarantee – essentially a form of insurance which, in the event of the budget running out or serious problems being encountered, ensures that the film will be completed and the investors' money protected. Among them were duplicates of much of the material I had located in the Paramount collection – including script drafts, budgets and cost statements, the Progress Reports and various types of correspondence – but also much more besides. In particular, the contributions of two figures directly appointed by Film Finances – its risk assessor, John Croydon, and the representative employed on location as an observer, Colin Lesslie – emerged very clearly, and their views on the film's pre-production and production periods respectively are the core of what follows. I have also retained some material unique to the Paramount Production Files (designated PPF) in order to provide as full and complete a picture as possible of the film from the financiers' viewpoint. It will be seen that many of the remarks made by Croydon and Lesslie are highly critical of the producers and of Cy Endfield in particular. To counterbalance these views, the next section will offer a more favourable portrait of Endfield written especially for this volume by his production assistant.

At a particularly fraught moment during production of *Zulu* on location in South Africa, Film Finances' representative Colin Lesslie wrote in one of his confidential letters, with evident exasperation: 'God! how I wish Stars would remain Stars and Directors remain Directors instead of all wanting to be Producers as well. They just haven't any sense of responsibility either to their backers or to the men who work under them.'[1] His experience throws into sharp relief the potential clash of interests between, on the one hand, the creative artists involved in filmmaking and, on the other, the managerial staff concerned with practical and financial matters. At some point, these two sides have to be reconciled and find a workable compromise.

Film Finances was first approached to provide a completion guarantee for *Zulu* in late September 1962 at the request of insurance brokers appointed by Anglo Amalgamated, the British company which was at that stage to be a production partner and co-distributor with Joseph E. Levine's Embassy. The film, with a budget of 1 million Rand (around $2 million or £650,000), was said to be less than two months away from the start of shooting on locations in

Pretoria, Transvaal Province, and near Durban, Natal Province.[2] The following month, Film Finances received copies of various documents pertaining to the preparation, planning and costing of the location shoot. They included details of arrangements for hotel accommodation and catering, estimates of sundry location, transportation and construction expenses, and especially the cost of hiring the services of 100 military personnel from the South African Defence Force and up to 2,000 Zulus (see Appendix).

The head of Anglo Amalgamated, David Deutsch, met with Film Finances' chief executive Robert (Bobby) Garrett in November 1962 to discuss the picture, whose start date had now been put back to the following April. Garrett was not at all optimistic, writing in a memo to his staff that 'it has been made clear that we were very far from keen on undertaking anything of this sort'. His objections centred on the large scale of the proposed film, along with the fact that it was mainly to be shot on a distant location, which meant that it would be difficult to keep tabs on its progress.[3] Nevertheless, Garrett agreed to put the proposition before the company's board for consideration. He acknowledged that there were a number of factors mitigating against his concerns, notably that most of the location shooting would now be concentrated at Mont-aux-Sources, a tourist spot in the Drakensberg Mountains, on a single set a short distance from the two hotels accommodating the principal cast and crew, thus reducing some of the logistical dangers; and the fact that a number of forms of fiscal protection had already been built into the deal.

The budget, to be shared equally between Embassy and Anglo, included a contingency fund in the event of cost overruns. Baker and Endfield had agreed to place their own salaries, of £42,500 and £12,500 respectively, in escrow, which could be drawn upon to meet the first overcost beyond the contingency if the need presented itself. Garrett noted that it had 'been explained to them that we will object to the control being solely in the hands of the principal actor and director and that we would expect to appoint a production supervisor. I also told Deutsch that we would not be agreeable to Stanley Baker having approval of director in case we felt obliged for any reason to remove Enfield [sic].' The next overcost up to £30,000 after the producers' salaries had been exhausted would be met by Anglo, 'possibly in partnership with Levine', in exchange for Film Finances giving up half its own fee. Only after this would the completion bond be drawn upon, up to a maximum of £225,000.[4]

The pre-production papers, budget breakdown, shooting schedule and a copy of the script were sent to Film Finances' risk assessor John Croydon, who delivered his report on 17 November. The schedule was now set to occupy '14 weeks – divided as to 10 weeks shooting in South Africa, with a little over 2 weeks allowed for travelling, packing and unpacking and weather contingency – completing with 2? weeks occupation of an unspecified studio'. The budget was '£648,641, including a production contingency allowance of £85,803 for the film to be shot in 70mm Technirama'.[5]

In eight pages of closely typed text, Croydon set down his detailed reservations about the proposition, which were such as to make it impossible for him to give it a firm recommendation. Croydon repeatedly compared the project to John Huston's 1951 film adaptation of Stephen Crane's novel *The Red Badge of Courage*, set during the American Civil War, and whose production history had been detailed in Lillian Ross's famous book.

> I feel quite certain that the basic idea behind this project is to make another *Red Badge of Courage*. However, it has the advantage that war stories have become popular and to that extent, the script lacks what I am sure was the degree of spontaneous, unconventional story telling which applied to *Red Badge of Courage*. [...] It has the stock cowards and heroes; a leavening of disreputable [C]hristianity; a feminine revulsion to war from an inarticulate virgin; massed movements by an overwhelming enemy and Technirama to give the exposition of blood and violence on a big screen. I suppose, that from a box office point of view, it is what is known in Wardour St. as 'infallible.' (So long as nobody wants me to see it once it is finished!)

To some degree Croydon's judgment reflected his usual aversion to location-based productions, partly based on the experience of previous such projects that had overrun their budgets. But his doubts this time also centred on the pedigree of *Zulu*'s co-producers, whom he considered inexperienced for the scale for the project at hand:

> Stanley Baker is undeniably a good actor, but I know nothing in his career which suggests that he would be a capable producer for a film of this sort. Cy Endfield when he first started to direct in this country, was a pretty safe bet to bring home a picture on schedule and budget, but in recent years he has tended to work in opposites. This, quite obviously, would be the biggest and most magnificent film he has directed and, like Huston and *The Red Badge of Courage* could represent an important cross road in his life, and to that extent, and from what I know of the man, I feel he will be quite ruthless in his determination to secure the best possible product.

However, Croydon considered that insufficient information had been provided about the director's proposed modus operandi. Endfield's schedule was presented in the standard form of a crossplot – a chart setting out the scene numbers to be shot on each day and the actors who would be needed. But it gave no firm indication of whether he planned to use wide, 'massed' shots (as his decision to use the widescreen Technirama format seemed to imply) or break each sequence up into the standard syntax of long shots, medium shots and close-ups (as the script directions appeared to suggest); it was therefore unclear how much time each scene was likely to require for completion. 'I do not know whether it is the intention of the director to take each and every individual piece of fighting and stage it as it is scripted, or whether he intends to pick it out of a much larger canvas of the fighting as a whole', Croydon noted. 'If this film were to be shot by conventional means I would be inclined to say that it was under-scheduled by at least 25%.' He also questioned the plan to shoot scenes out of chronological order in order to accommodate actors' work schedules, which would necessitate substantial redressing of the set including even the hospital having to be burned down and rebuilt; and the scheduling of all the Zulus' principal scenes at the end of the shoot, which 'virtually disassociates the encampment itself from these battle movements'.

Among Croydon's more general concerns were the plan to use only one main camera, a converted Technicolor unit, along with two supplementary lightweight cameras, for large-scale battle scenes that would appear to demand multi-camera shooting throughout (though he also noted that the choice of Technirama as screen format might have made that impracticable). He felt that the schedule – and the attendant daily running costs of maintaining a large, virtually self-contained production village – would most likely be exceeded, particularly because of the large number of people to be employed both in front of and behind the camera; how, he wondered, would the Zulus be controlled when shooting was at 'full stretch'? He noted that unknown factors mentioned in the production papers appeared not to be budgeted for: these included 'the question of change in colour of the terrain [due to varying patterns of rainfall] and traditional methods of feeding the native crowds'.

Croydon also saw the potential for a great many injuries, both minor and major, as 'even rubber tipped spears can cause some very nasty injuries, and blank ammunition can cause quite a lot of damage even when the exercise is under strict supervision'; but he noted that only one unit doctor and one nurse had been allowed for in the budget. He recalled his own past experience on the film *O.H.M.S.* (1937), 'when one soldier, in the heat of the moment, mistook one of his companions, simulating death, for a dummy and stuck his bayonet right through his body'. Where, he asked, 'is an allowance made for compensation to victims of this sort of thing?' He also wanted to know if the schedule, travel and accommodation arrangements and the crew's salary basis had been agreed or even discussed with the joint union location committee, which had to approve such matters.

Despite these and other reservations, Garrett was nevertheless persuaded to send Anglo Amalgamated a letter of intent setting out the terms on which Film Finances would be prepared to issue a guarantee of completion. Among the conditions set out was an increase in the budget so that the shooting schedule could be extended, along with sundry additional allowances.[6] The location schedule was increased from 62 to 75 shooting days and the studio schedule from thirteen to seventeen days; an additional week was allowed for travel; the period allowed for editing and dubbing was also increased, from twelve to fifteen weeks; and there were increased budget figures for various items. This raised the direct cost of making the picture from £493,488 to £553,200, excluding fees and salaries, which when added brought the total up to £688,672. The amount of Endfield and Baker's salaries to be placed in escrow was reduced to 50 per cent (£27,500 in total).[7] The principal recommendation that Croydon had made was the nomination by Film Finances of a representative who would join the film unit, report in detail on its operation and stay with the production until the end of shooting or preferably the delivery of the completed picture. Consequently, in confirming the offer of a guarantee, the company specified that 'a producer (without screen credit) will be appointed to the picture who shall exercise all the usual functions of a producer except that he will not concern himself with the script nor with the artistic direction of the picture unless the latter should appear to be seriously endangering the financial outcome of the project.'⁸ The person chosen for this role was Colin Lesslie, most recently the producer of *Tunes of Glory* (1960).

Anglo Amalgamated had by now dropped out of the deal and Embassy had taken over complete financing, while a new company, Diamond Films – jointly owned by Baker and Endfield – had been created to produce the picture. Shortly before shooting started a new distributor was found to release the picture outside the United States and Canada. This was the major Hollywood studio Paramount, which in turn took over financing from Embassy. Negotiations with Paramount began in earnest with a meeting on 24 January 1963 in Joe Levine's suite at the Beverly Hills Hotel in Los Angeles. Present were Levine, Cy Endfield and seven studio executives, including Paramount vice-president George Weltner. Another of the executives, Frank Caffey, subsequently wrote up the meeting in a memo that included a number of elementary mistakes: the film was referred to as *Zululand*; Endfield was referred to throughout as 'Sy Enfield'; Film Finances was referred to as 'British Filmways', and its representative was named as Colin Tapley rather than Coln Lesslie, who was credited with the production of *Paths of Glory* (1957) rather than *Tunes of Glory*. Nevertheless, Caffey listed the ways in which Endfield and Baker, having had their schedule and budget increased at Film Finances' insistence, were now seeking to reduce the projected cost by the equivalent of $300,000 (around £100,000).⁹

The director had outlined plans for savings in South Africa based on the resale of items such as props and construction materials, and from hiring most of the technical equipment from a local firm, S.A. Films, thus obviating the cost of transporting it from Britain. Technical expenses were to be kept to a minimum by using no large lighting equipment on location. Caffey noted with approval that the company had secured official South African government cooperation and the use of a 'mounted military unit' to be used as extras and as 'general police' for on-site security, communications and so on. Construction of the sets was due to begin on 1 February and it was noted that two 'extensive surveys [had] already been made into the territory, and the general planning is well along.' Endfield also intended to shorten the screenplay by the 'reduction of peripheral characters' in order to reduce the shooting schedule and the ultimate running time.

By March the script had been reduced from 171 to 138 pages (it was later cut again to 123 pages). Plans were being made to shoot some of the massed crowd scenes in Zululand, 100 miles away from the main location, to reduce the cost of transporting and accommodating up to 2,000 Zulu extras. In late February 1963, production accountant Arthur Hall was able to demonstrate savings amounting to £7,578 thanks to the deal made with S.A. Films, though Hall considered that 'the value of the contracts is considerably greater than this' as S.A. was supplying production services such as a projector and projectionist (for viewing rushes), office supplies, equipment and transportation facilities which had not been provided for in the budget.¹⁰ A revised production budget showed the estimated total cost now to be £666,554, including a contingency allowance of £82,241.¹¹

On the basis of these and other changes, John Croydon produced two further reports for Film Finances. He was, however, no more positive than he had been before, feeling that 'the script is impractical and the schedule ducks the issue'. Croydon still found no clear indication of the director's 'plan of campaign' and doubted that the picture could be completed in the time allotted:

> Many of the sequences are very difficult indeed to shoot. So much 'staging' is required. The picture is progressive in action and, therefore, certain sequences must be scheduled in chronological order, so that the destruction which happens inside the camp – the burning of the hospital for instance – must come at the right moment in the schedule, and this is only known [from the crossplot] by chronological progression of scene numbers, without any notation of the manner in which it will be achieved. [...]

Second Unit Filming in Zululand

The filmmakers had originally planned to shoot large-scale scenes of massed Zulu Impi movements at Mont-aux-Sources, involving a much larger number of Zulus than most of the shoot but for a limited time. Thus, between 1,250 and 2,000 additional extras were due to be brought in from local 'reserves' for a week, supplementing the permanent force of 250 Zulus based at the location. But in a letter of 26 February 1963 (the first correspondence in the Film Finances files to be on paper headed 'Diamond Films'), production accountant Arthur Hall suggested to associate producer Basil Keys that instead of bringing a large number of additional Zulus to the main production site, with all the transport and accommodation costs this would entail, it would be cheaper and easier to send a small camera crew to Zululand to shoot the mass scenes there.

Accordingly, before shooting on the film had started, location manager Bob Porter travelled north to make the arrangements for these scenes to be shot at Melmoth in the first week of June, utilising 1,500 local people as extras. The Zulus were paid a salary of £4 per week each, a figure stipulated by the Chief Information Officer for Bantu Affairs and Development that was ten shillings more than the company had originally intended paying them. However this was offset by a saving of £845 on the Zulus used at Mont-aux-Sources, which involved only 240 warriors instead of the 250 budgeted for. The shooting in Zululand was completed with a saving of £3,564 on the cost of extras and £1,700 on hotel and living expenses (Statement of Production Cost no. 10, 15 June 1963).

As it turned out, little if any of this footage was used in the finished film; but the surviving production stills used in this chapter testify to the impressive scale of the scenes Porter and his crew shot. Does the footage survive in a studio vault somewhere? Only time will tell.

I think there will be days when the unit will be concerned with 'setting the stage' and little or no shooting will take place. I think the amount of rehearsal for some of the 'stunt' action scenes will be lengthy, tending to reduce the amount shot each day. I think that second and third takes will be much more than a mere repetition of the action (mess will have to be cleared up and new rehearsals take place). All of these things will tend to slow the schedule, and I shall be extremely surprised if the schedule will be able to flow along at the pace indicated in this X-plot.[12]

Croydon was scarcely more positive about the revised financial provisions, casting a sceptical eye over virtually every entry in the new budget. He recommended calculating the likely overage for at least an additional month's shooting and deducting that figure from the contingency fund 'as certain to be expended'. The logistical scale of the film brought its own particular challenges, as Croydon outlined:

> On a location film of this sort, it is impossible to calculate the hazards before commencement of shooting. I think illness and accident will affect the schedule, perhaps resulting in emergency schedule alterations. The crowd movements, especially the Zulus, may take a great deal longer to work out and put into operation than has ever been envisaged. [...]
>
> As time goes on and the director's plan

for the thoroughness of the preparatory work that had been done at Mont-aux-Sources: 'The whole unit were very impressed too – even the real old-timers!' The key figure here was location manager and second unit director Bob Porter, who had set up the picture in South Africa. Lesslie was equally enthused by the permanent corps of 250 Zulus attached to the film, especially after, dressed in full costume regalia, they had performed a welcome ceremony for the crew and the soldiers who were to play the British troops:

> These Zulus really were *marvellous*! They all dressed up in the costumes they will be wearing and went through war dances and war cries etc., – all really very impressive. The 100 South African Defence Forces are excellent too – very smart soldiers and very co-operative.
> As I say, I really am extremely impressed. *Nothing* (anyway nothing I can think of) seems to have been forgotten or overlooked and to me everything now depends on the weather, the artists and Cy.[14]

of campaign begins to emerge, so the results of his work in terms of speed should be constantly applied to costs in a very accurate degree, so that were the film to start to run away with itself, red lights could begin to flash, thus giving us an opportunity to discuss, on the spot, what action could be taken to minimise costs, or at least confine them to contingency availability.

This form of control can only be obtained by our representative forming a very close liason [sic] with the production accountant and production manager, so that each and every variation of schedule can be instantly related to cost.[13]

Considering how profound were Croydon's doubts about the project, Film Finances' representative Colin Lesslie was altogether more upbeat when he joined the location in late March, just prior to the commencement of shooting. Throughout the production, Lesslie kept up a series of letters to Bobby Garrett and Embassy's Kenneth Hargreaves in London, along with daily telegrams to Paramount in Los Angeles with updates on the scenes shot, the amount of screen time accumulated and the extent to which the production was on, ahead of or behind schedule. His first report was full of admiration for the efficiency of the crew and

Lesslie was much less favourably impressed by Endfield, whose apparent lack of tact and diplomacy struck him as a potential problem from the outset; at least one crew member was subsequently to quit because of the director's rudeness and others threatened to do so. Endfield's ad-lib approach to filmmaking was also a matter of concern:

> He shoots completely off the cuff – nothing prepared or planned whatsoever either on paper or in his head. Always, *always* changing his mind. You will remember I told you some time ago in London that, although a sketch artist was allowed for in the Preliminary Budget, Cy said he didn't want one; nor did he make any use of the model set Ernie [Archer] built him. However at the time Stanley assured me Cy was planning on paper at home in the evenings but now I am convinced that this was not so. It is difficult, however, to push him too hard. Both Stephen [D]ade, the cameraman and John Merriman,

the Production Manager have worked with him before and both say that he is quite incapable of planning ahead and if you push him too hard it only confuses him. Already it is noticeable on the set that Stanley is a bit worried how slow he is making up his mind and is quietly trying to push him along but, obviously, for the sake of the picture, cannot push him too hard.[15]

Lesslie was also underwhelmed by the quality of the acting Endfield elicited from his players in the first few days of filming, with the exceptions of Baker's own performance and that of an apparently unpromising newcomer: 'I am very glad to be able to tell you that in my opinion and from the little he has done so far, Michael Caine as "Bromhead" is very good indeed. When he was cast for the part I couldn't see it but I think (and hope) I was wrong.'[16] When the first set of rushes arrived for viewing, Lesslie found his worst fears confirmed: 'The direction was amateurish to say the least; the small part acting horrible and the colour varying from excellent to terrible!'[17] He even had second thoughts about Caine's performance: 'Now I've seen more of Michael Caine as "Bromhead" I'm a little afraid that my original feelings were right after all but it's so difficult to judge here as the sound and acoustics are terrible in the hotel theatre.'[18] The view back in London was quite different, however: Kenneth Hargreaves told Bobby Garrett that he found the footage more than satisfactory, 'particularly the photography which is excellent. I am naturally a little perturbed by Colin's remarks about Cy and this is obviously a situation that he has got to watch very closely but I am hopeful that Cy will gain confidence as time goes on and I don't think we should allow ourselves to be unduly worried at this stage.'[19]

On location, it rapidly became apparent that weather was going to be a major problem. The shoot was timed to coincide with the South African winter, when the weather was supposed to be at its driest but when the days were short, so filming was scheduled for a six-day week. Variable conditions rapidly turned to unseasonably heavy rain which caused whole days or parts of days to be written off. In the first two weeks the company used up its total weather allowance, with four whole days rained off. Rain was not the only problem: even cloudy skies could prevent filming, as there needed to be continuous good light for story continuity. The schedule was further put back with the Easter holiday weekend two weeks into the shoot, when all work ceased for three days.

Lesslie's concerns mounted as filming progressed, even after the weather had begun to improve. A set visit from Joe Levine in mid-April gave him the opportunity to draw the executive producer's attention to Endfield's apparent reluctance to employ Bob Porter's second unit, which might have enabled the production to catch up on lost time. It was not easy to have two units operating simultaneously when shooting was largely confined to a single set but Endfield agreed to allow Porter to film action shots not involving the principal actors. However, he reneged on this following Levine's departure and, according to Lesslie, 'made what I think is almost a classic statement. He said "I wouldn't even let Willie Wyler direct a 2nd unit shot for me unless I had checked the set-up first"!!'[20]

Lesslie attributed the production's slow rate of progress partly to what he felt were the unwarranted ambitions of Endfield and Baker to make a more important film than, in his view, the material and the assembled talent permitted: 'This can never be the "great picture" Cy and Stanley are always talking about – nor will it win the "Oscars" they talk about either, but it can still be a very commercial "Western" set in South Africa and the answer to it all is in my opinion in the Zulus.'[21] Lesslie had hoped Levine would make clear to Endfield that 'instead of cowboys and "injuns", it's Zulus and soldiers and depends for its success on excitement and action and *not* on beautifully composed shots and Oscar-winning photography. If you want to win any Oscars, you've got to get a better cameraman, cast – *and* director than we've got!'[22]

Film Finances' major concern involved the seemingly excessive amount of coverage

Tom Gerrard (Lance/Corporal)

Among the credited British cast of *Zulu*, one actor is given but a single word to say throughout the entire film: 'Sir!' That actor is Tom Gerrard: he plays the blond Lance/Corporal who hands Chard back his pistol following the officer's visit to the infirmary, but otherwise appears mainly in the background and at the periphery of shots.

Perhaps there was a reason for Gerrard's being given so few lines. In one of his reports from the set, South African journalist Derrick Kain remarked: 'Tom is a Scotsman, and his big accent is so thick that you could almost cut it with a knife. He was formerly a circus clown and a trick diver in the high-diving act of a water carnival!' (D.N.E. Kain, '*Zulu*: A Film Completed,' *Personality*, 3 October 1963).

Gerrard's other credited work besides *Zulu* includes small roles in such films as *The Spy Who Loved Me* (1977) and *Dracula's Dog* (1978, released in the UK as *Zoltan, Hound of Dracula*), mostly as military types. He retired to Hove on the South East coast of England, where in 2005 he gave an interview to a local newspaper, *The Argus*, about his support of a campaign to have a blue heritage plaque placed on the former home of a survivor of Rorke's Drift, Private William Cooper ('Actor backs honour for real hero of Zulu battle', *The Argus*, 25 July 2005, pp. 22-23).

According to Gerrard, he was cast in *Zulu* through a phone call from his friend Stanley Baker, who asked 'Do you fancy filming in South Africa?' He shared a rondavel throughout the shoot with the other tall, blond newcomer, Michael Caine. Tom told the anonymous *Argus* reporter that the Zulus 'couldn't stop laughing when the tips of their rubber spears wobbled'. But one particular sequence had a very different effect on the crew, as he recalled: 'We stood there dumbfounded the first time the Zulus appeared on the top of the hill over our mock-up of Rorke's Drift and began chanting.

'The actor playing a South African scout [Gert van den Bergh] said: "You are listening to a thousand years of war."

'There was a sense we were doing something special and it turned out to be a great movie – one of the best action movies ever made.'

Endfield was shooting for a film intended to run no more than two hours. By Lesslie's calculations, 'at the rate of pages of script he was covering compared to the screentime he was getting' the director would most likely deliver a picture running around three and a half hours.[23] Lesslie was sufficiently alarmed at this prospect to inform Levine about it directly. Levine wrote personally to Endfield and Baker to make his position clear: 'Never in any of my conversations with you did I ever indicate that I wanted *Zulu* to run 3-1/2 hours. I think this would be disastrous and completely unnecessary.'[24]

To address his anxiety about the film's apparently running overlong and his concerns over whether some of Endfield's shots would cut together, Lesslie agreed that the film's editor, John Jympson, and his assistant, Jennifer Thompson, should fly out to the location to begin assembling the mass of footage.[25] With Jympson present on site to assess the material, Lesslie felt more confident that the editor might 'be able to make a good picture out of it at its correct length'.[26] Levine himself planned to make a second visit to South Africa at the beginning of June, possibly with Paramount vice-president George Weltner in tow, 'which I think would impress Cy and Stanley with the importance of *Zulu* to Paramount Pictures as well as Embassy'.[27]

Lesslie frequently took the opportunity to disparage both the film's producer-star and its director, writing that the crew 'don't like Stanley and are contemptuous of Cy: it's as simple as that.'[28] Of his own role, which largely remained that of an observer and advisor, Lesslie noted: 'I am ignored by both of them as much as possible anyway but very much the reverse by the rest of the unit.'[29] At one point he even compared the shoot to his wartime experiences: 'Being in this place is just like being a P.O.W. again – only between ourselves the company in Italy was more congenial! I know I'll never set foot out of this place until the day we finish – God help me!'[30]

Despite his antipathy for Endfield, Lesslie was reluctant to suggest that the director be replaced, as this would have further set back the schedule and probably resulted in the loss of several cast members, such as Jack Hawkins and James Booth, who had been contracted for only a fixed period of time. If they were forced to drop out because of a change of schedule, Lesslie doubted that 'name' actors of comparable stature could be found to replace them: 'we could never get a stronger star cast against the same old question we've had in the past – *WHO* is going to play second fiddle to Stanley Baker? I got Jack Hawkins to do it on the "old chums" act, I know, but in my opinion, I am not certain that he is of

sufficient weight even for the present cost.'³¹ (Hawkins was paid the same acting fee as Baker, £30,000 – far more than had been budgeted for the part before Hawkins was persuaded to accept it.)

Back in London, Paramount executive R.H. Harrison was concerned that the production was falling further behind schedule, even while the footage remained promising: 'roughly speaking 30% of the total scene numbers have been shot with 40% of the scheduled days used up. The production is shown as being eight days behind schedule. In fact it seems to be more.'³² No doubt rattled by the noises emanating from London and Los Angeles, Endfield was at last moved to write a lengthy letter to the studio's Jack Karp in Hollywood. The director explained that on his previous film, *Hide and Seek*, continuity clerk Muirne Mathieson had under-estimated the amount of screen time that had been shot to such an extent that the producers had obliged Endfield to shoot additional scenes to bring the picture up to length – footage that later proved to be unnecessary and was cut. When starting work on *Zulu* Endfield had reminded Mathieson of her 'stinginess in crediting film-time' with the earlier film but 'in consequence she has over-compensated on this one' so that 'our daily screen time has been over-estimated by a substantial percentage'. He noted 'a peculiarity in the script which makes the mathematical judgment of equating scene numbers shot to date with screen time credited to date an insufficient method of estimating how much more screen time will be finally produced'. It was perhaps this lack of clarity in the relationship between scene numbers and screen time that had moved John Croydon to doubt that the film could be completed in the allotted schedule. Nevertheless, the director argued that 'for many years now I have trusted my intuitions and found them to be far more accurate than stop-watches and progress-report estimations by script girls'. He estimated that the

'natural' length of this story is two hours plus. The 'plus' in this case means a maximum of twenty minutes. At the present writing I am more convinced than ever that this film will prove a genuine road show in first runs. If indeed it is so, then 2 hours 20 minutes shouldn't be too long. [...] The effect of the film is massive and it is not an easy job to bring it down to a precise two hour length, but the possibilities should be there if such is the ultimate requirement.

In any event I promise you that I am not shooting material that will be thrown out of the film. I am not speculating on either set-ups or story points. There are very great distances to be covered by great numbers of people, so that the demands for coverage on each scene are substantial. None-the-less, I wish to emphasise that *except for weather* we are actually beating our schedule.³³

The director also pointed out that he had reorganised the shooting schedule around the availability of Jack Hawkins and Ulla Jacobsson to remove the necessity of burning down and rebuilding the hospital set, as the original schedule had demanded. As for the delays caused by the weather, Endfield noted:

> We are approaching the South African winter, and as Joe saw for himself we lose the light here very early indeed. We were well aware of this, of course, and the schedule was based on this fact; but what we could not calculate was that we would lose so very much time in the early part of the schedule, when the shooting days were longer. This means we now have to make up for the loss of *long* bad days with much *shorter* good days. Again I would like to say that we are in fact doing this and even gaining time whenever we have the good weather, but the handicap is substantial.

In his estimation of the film's ideal length Endfield was proved right: its eventual running time was 138 minutes. Embassy and Paramount, however, were still concerned by Lesslie's projections that the film would run close to three hours. Following a 'high level conference' with studio executives, Levine cabled Endfield: 'Please examine script carefully and make every possible cut consistent only with maintaining importance of picture. Picture will not be released in excess of two hours.'³⁴ Stanley Baker responded to these and Levine's other concerns with an impassioned personal letter.

Whatever has been said, Cy was never 'reluctant' to use the second unit. Even while you were here this was being done extensively and the plans for transferring the main Zulu shots from here to Zululand

for second unit shooting were already established. I have just checked the number of slates that the second unit have shot to date and they amount to 124 not including yesterday's work. Compare this to the 281 shot by the main unit and I am sure you will have to agree that our second unit is working 'flat out'. Bob Porter is getting some very exciting stuff with his unit and we are all very thrilled with it, so the suggestion that Cy is in any way 'reluctant' to use the second unit is

ridiculous and in fact the reverse is happening. [...]

I can only tell you Joe that Cy and myself are not out to prove anything to the world through *Zulu* but have exactly the same interests in it as you do, that is to make a good picture of the right length that people will pay to go and see and therefore provide profit to us all. The unit is at the moment working most marvellously and in every department that matters, there is real harmony and unity of purpose. We did start having labour and union problems but both Cy and myself met the men and had a long, straight-from-the shoulder, talk since when there has been no trouble whatsoever in any shape or form. [...]

I hope you will come to visit us again as you promised when you will be able to see, and I will be able to tell you, first-hand what is happening. There has never been any crap between us and as far as I am concerned there never will be, but it is far easier for me to talk than write; maybe this is one of the results of reading other peoples' [sic] dialogue for so long, anyway, I am sure you know how I feel.[35]

The daily Production Progress Reports show that the second unit had not got into its stride until the third week, but most of the early scenes were relatively straightforward and small-scale, requiring little extra coverage. Once the company started on the battle scenes, Porter and his crew were employed more extensively. Paramount's Harrison noted: 'I have seen some of the second unit rushes and I must say that the action and the crowd scenes have been extremely well directed'.[36] To help recover the time lost to bad weather, the second unit was given more to shoot than originally planned, including scenes involving the Zulu army on the move, the cattle stampede and the wedding dance (later in the schedule, when much of the lost time had been made up, the first unit was able to 'cover' some of this material itself with extra retakes). In early June Porter travelled to Zululand to shoot the scenes of the Zulu impis and incidental background footage, little if any of which was used in the final cut of the film. But in having Porter handle this material Endfield effectively took a week off the main unit's shooting schedule, allowing Lesslie to report in a telegram to Levine: 'delighted inform you second unit done excellent work last ten days and their further agreed work should enable us commence studio shooting only three days behind original date planned. Although great pleasure to us all to see you here later do not now consider this exhausting trip necessary.'[37]

Lesslie filed no detailed location reports after 11 May, sending only brief telegrams with updates on the schedule and budget. This suggests that his conflicts with Endfield had gradually abated as shooting progressed; in one of his later communications there was even a rare compliment when he remarked on the 'excellent film [shot] so far'.[38] A minor crisis arose in June when it became apparent that the unit's arrival one week late into Twickenham Studios would create a clash with James Booth's commitment to another film, Ken Russell's *French Dressing* (1964). Booth would be unavailable for a week from 4 July, which necessitated either the recasting of his role or paying him an increased fee for the extension of his services beyond the agreed period specified in his contract, as well as the further extension of the studio hire. The extra expense was readily approved by Embassy and Paramount; according to Hargreaves, it would 'add approximately £5,500 to the cost of the *Zulu* studio shooting, but this does not seem a very serious matter in the light of the near certainty that less than half the contingency figure will require to be utilised'.[39]

On 26 June, the location wrapped after 81 shooting days: only six more than had been scheduled, despite the fact that fifteen days had been partly or wholly lost to bad weather. A further day was lost when the unit was unable to book a charter flight back to London; Baker and cinematographer Stephen Dade caught a regular flight while the rest of the cast and crew stayed an extra night and Bob Porter and Arthur Hall began the clear-up operation.[40]

Shooting resumed at Twickenham Studios and continued for twenty days, three more than scheduled. This was caused not only by Booth's unavailability but also by some of the interior sets having to be redesigned and construction not being finished in time. Post-production work was further extended from fifteen to 21 weeks; the last four were used for stereophonic sound re-recording at Pinewood Studios, which incurred additional costs in studio rental and sound-crew salaries. Even with these overages, the film was still completed substantially under budget. Its final negative cost, excluding interest, came to £625,445 ($1,751,246), with the completion bond along with Baker and Endfield's escrowed salaries untouched and less than half of the contingency used (only £34,563, leaving £47,678) – thus making the production officially under-budget.[41]

Bobby Garrett thanked Baker and Endfield with an official letter congratulating them 'on the most satisfactory manner in which the shooting of the production has been handled.'[42] Nevertheless he was convinced of Colin Lesslie's central role in helping to achieve this result, writing to him on 28 June, while Lesslie was still in South Africa:

> We have been very conscious that you were doing a fine job under what must have been most trying conditions. Ken has appreciated this too, and Paramount and Levine should be very grateful to you for not only seeing that they got the sort of length and shape of film they wanted but also for saving them something that at a guess might have been a six figure sum if you had not been there. Your information service also was first class.
>
> News has just arrived from the Palace that in the Battle Honours for Rorke's Drift 1963 you are to get the only V.C. with several bars![43]

Notes

[1] Film Finances Archive Realised Film Box 366: *Zulu*: Colin Lesslie to Kenneth Hargreaves, 13 May 1963; capitalisation as per original.

[2] Ibid: Morice, Tozer & Beck Ltd. to Film Finances, 28 September 1962.

[3] Ibid: memo from Robert Garrett, 7 November 1962.

[4] Ibid.

[5] Ibid: John Croydon, risk assessment, 17 November 1962.

[6] Ibid: Film Finances to Oakhurst Productions, 29 November 1962.

[7] Ibid: Cy Endfield to Bernard Smith, 14 December 1962.

[8] Ibid: Film Finances to Oakhurst Productions, 18 December 1962.

9 Paramount Production Files: memo from Frank Caffey, 25 January 1963.

10 FFA: Arthur Hall to Basil Keys, 26 February 1963.

11 Ibid: revised budget, 8 March 1963.

12 Ibid: John Croydon to Garrett, 8 March 1963.

13 Ibid: Croydon to Garrett, 16 March 1963.

14 Ibid: Colin Lesslie (undated), attached to letter from Kenneth Hargreaves to Garrett, 1 April 1963.

15 Ibid: Lesslie to Hargreaves, 31 March 1963.

16 Ibid: Lesslie to Hargreaves, 31 March 1963.

17 Ibid: Lesslie to Garrett, 8 April 1963.

18 Ibid: Lesslie to Hargreaves, 9 April 1963.

19 Ibid: Hargreaves to Garrett, 5 April 1963.

20 Ibid: Lesslie to Hargreaves, 25 April 1963.

21 Ibid: Lesslie to Hargreaves, 29 April 1963.

22 Ibid: Lesslie to Garrett, 8 April 1963.

23 Ibid: Lesslie to Hargreaves, 25 April 1963.

24 Ibid: Joseph Levine to Endfield and Stanley Baker, 7 May 1963.

25 Ibid: Lesslie to Hargreaves, 25 April 1963.

26 Ibid: Lesslie to Hargreaves, 29 April 1963.

27 Ibid: Levine to Lesslie, 9 May 1963.

28 Ibid: Lesslie to Hargreaves, 5 May 1963.

29 Ibid: Lesslie to Hargreaves, 29 April 1963.

30 Ibid: Lesslie to Garrett, 8 April 1963.

31 Ibid: Lesslie to Hargreaves, 5 May 1963.

32 PPF: R.H. Harrison to Jack Karp, 7 May 1963.

33 Ibid: Endfield to Karp, 10 May 1963.

34 Ibid: Levine to Endfield, 14 May 1963.

35 Ibid: Letter, Baker to Levine, 16 May 1963.

36 Ibid: Harrison to Karp, 14 May.

37 Ibid: Lesslie to Levine, 13 May 1963.

38 Ibid: Lesslie to Hargreaves, 10 June 1963.

39 Ibid: Hargreaves to Garrett, 14 June 1963.

40 Production Progress Report, 26 June 1963.

41 Statement of production cost no. 15, week ending 18 October 1963.

42 FFA: Film Finances to Diamond Films, 19 September 1963.

43 Ibid: unsigned (but probably Garrett) to Lesslie, 28 June 1963.

Michael Caine takes a well earned break from the action.

AN ASSISTANT'S SAGA

BY IAN FAWNE-MEADE

When I was researching the first edition of this book, one of the people I tried and failed to contact was Ian Fawn-Meade. Credited in the main titles of *Zulu* as assistant to the producers, Fawn-Meade was a close associate of Cy Endfield's from their days working together in the advertising industry. He had subsequently left the UK and now resided in America; a letter sent to the only forwarding address I had for him went unanswered. But in 2009, out of the blue, I received an email from Ian to say that he had read my book, liked it, and wanted the opportunity to offer his own side of the story. What he then produced was beyond anything I could have hoped for: a detailed chronicle of his professional association with Endfield and numerous fresh insights into the production gleaned from first-hand observation. As he goes on to explain below, Ian joined the *Zulu* location when shooting was halfway through, but remained with the project until the close of post-production. He also witnessed the aftermath of the film's release and Endfield and Baker's subsequent attempts to follow it up. The picture of the director provided in this account is a useful corrective to the decidedly unflattering one offered by Colin Lesslie in his correspondence with Film Finances. Who is to say where the ultimate truth lies?

Zulu and I really began our tumultuous affair late in1961. I was working as a young (23-year-old) television producer for the advertising agency Lintas, London. Commercial TV was in its infancy, and with no previous experience in the medium, the advertising agencies were totally unprepared. However, seizing an opportunity, J. Walter Thompson cleverly promoted a roster of British feature-film directors, who they said, would work exclusively for their clients.

The rush to find and use other film directors was on. (Only much, much later did the British film commercial industry give back its own, when new young filmmakers who started by making TV spots – Hugh Hudson, Ridley and Tony Scott, Adrian Lyne, et al. – went on to become successful Hollywood directors.)

So with a good level of comfort I worked with Jack Lee, Cliff Owen and John Schlesinger, among other directors, and, after I had admired a group of commercials he had directed for Players cigarettes, I started to work with Cy Endfield. He had directed those Players spots at a Mediterranean location for Douglas Rankin at Ogilvy, on behalf of Geoffrey Kent (later of Abercrombie and Kent). Certainly it was in Cy's commercial interests to befriend me. But during our first shoot together – a package of six commercials (total budget £16,000) – I quickly became awed by his creative talents. He was an enormously impressive personality, with a tremendously wide range of experience and interests. His intellectual curiosity was unique. No-one I had ever met, before or since, even came close to matching his extraordinary range

(Jürgen Schadeberg)

of abilities. His quirks were the fun part of his charisma. While he worked he wore white tennis shoes, and strode up and down behind the moviola, playing the flute as the editor and I struggled to cut the film. He mixed long, thoughtful silences with gesticulating outbursts. I was mesmerised. Once we had a cut, he moved on to his next job.

Over a short space of time Cy and I had thoroughly bonded, and he, his wife Maureen and I spent scores of hours together in their Thurloe Square house. As a group we dined at trendy restaurants and danced at the swinging 60s nightclubs. He took me to rehearsals of his West End comedy *Come Blow Your Horn*, starring Bob Monkhouse, at the Prince's Theatre; we toured the professional magic suppliers in Soho, worked on the commercials, and talked together in his basement office where he would pour out his philosophy on showbusiness, his ambitions and frustrations, laced with a large collection of Hollywood anecdotes – often funny, sometimes serious, gossip about everyone he had met or worked with: Marilyn Monroe, for instance, who worked for him when he was a magician ('Incredibly serious about her acting', he told me).

Together, we did a lot of work – at casting sessions, all night on Waterloo station complete with back projection, up a mountain overlooking Cannes, on the pier in Brighton, and of course on dozens of sets and in cutting rooms all over London.

Our first common ground was South Africa. Here I had something to offer. I had been to boarding school there (Kearsney College, Durban), then returned to South Africa to join my family when I finally I left school at Canterbury in Kent. As well as my first job, working for Lintas, Durban, as a copywriter/producer, I moonlighted, writing and acting for the national radio network and acting in weekly rep on stage in the Lyric theatre (fifteen shillings a performance – sneaking out of work for the Wednesday matinee, hoping no-one from the office was in the audience). For my Lintas salary of £25 a month I produced dozens of film commercials for the cinemas in South Africa and, when it started up, television in Rhodesia (after a fast-track experience in television production in Sydney, Australia, courtesy of Lintas). But more interesting to Cy, I had direct experience shooting outdoors with native Zulu actors in and around Zululand, using them in 16mm colour cinema commercials. These ran on back-projection screens, built into the rear of specially converted lorries. The trucks drove into the tribal areas and showed Laurel and Hardy and Three Stooges movies at night, to attract customers to the general stores. The commercials ran in between Hollywood slapstick. My simple tales of the sad women who couldn't get their wash clean enough when they beat it on the rocks only to find true marital happiness with Sunlight Soap must have made a puzzling mix. But we were a hit. Large crowds would begin to arrive from nowhere in the afternoon, crouch in the long grass, and then as darkness fell, would watch – and presumably wonder.

Never, ever, at any time did Cy bring up politics, or indicate any particular political viewpoint. It was widely known that, with no wish to name names, he had fled a McCarthy hearings subpoena. He had started in showbusiness with a magic act, made short subjects for MGM, was called up and made instructional films for the US Army, then worked his way up the Hollywood pecking order. He was extremely proud of *The Sound of Fury* – it was the only film he made that had a social point of view, but he was disappointed in the way it was received. After his flight to England he started all over again. According to Cy, at his first attempts at setting up his own feature films in Britain he was met by the constant refrain: 'You want to make a film here, there's only one way – two words: Tommy Steele.' In the face of the powerful film trade union, the ACTT – which bugged producers every time we wanted to introduce any fresh talent – he worked under an alias. He was sanguine, but unhappy about many of the movies he had made in Britain: *Mysterious Island* for Charlie Schneer and *Jet Storm* (about the then improbable possibility that someone would smuggle a bomb on board a passenger plane) were especially disappointing. With better movies, like *Hell Drivers*, he began to realise that actively working in feature films was the best way to position himself as a top director for the more lucrative business of directing TV commercials. He approached them as feature films, often making long (sometimes unusable) tracking shots. He sometimes drove the profit-conscious production companies to despair:

'I don't want to be like those guys who shout "action", keep their eyes on a stop watch, shout "cut" and then ask "How was it?"' As a producer I didn't care about his demands; we shot with the production

Servicemen of the South African Defence Force, who played the soldiers of B Company, 24th Foot, pose in their own uniforms with Cy Endfield and members of the cast.

companies on a fixed-bid basis. He knew the image vulnerabilities of advertising agencies, and tried to keep his fee (£400 a day) at the highest in town: 'You get more respect if you charge top dollar!'

It wasn't long before he asked me to read the screenplay of *The Battle of Rorke's Drift*, telling me how Duggie Rankin had brought him John Prebble's short story as a potential movie, and he and Prebble had written the script. At that point, it seemed over-laced with a strong Welsh influence. Several pages of dialogue were mainly in Gaelic, and I wondered aloud what Joe Levine (the potential backer) had thought of it. 'Joe doesn't read 'em', he said, 'but you should have seen him jump when I changed it to Zulu – "FOUR LETTERS!!! Could be the biggest goddamn movie title ever mounted in Times Square!"' Cy did his imitation of Joe complete with violent arm gestures. This Joe must be quite a character, I thought.

Inevitably Cy introduced me over dinner to his partner, Stanley Baker. They had made several features together, but Stanley was as different from Cy as anyone you could imagine. My first impression was how immensely brooding, almost threatening, he was. To me he seemed like a keg of gunpowder that was quiet while unlit, but with a spark might suddenly blow. He was socially very taciturn, but with a totally matter-of-fact directness and honesty that seemed unusual in an actor. Stanley was incredibly underrated in his acting ability, and I think, in a way, he was deeply concerned about not having the good looks and debonair appeal of the then-current crop of J. Arthur Rank leading male stars, á la Dirk Bogarde, who made picture after picture. Cy had caught part of that brooding aspect on film in all their movies together, and I think something about the Chard character rising above the British class struggle in *Zulu* gave him hope on that score. 'The leading actors are the princes of the business', he would tell me, 'those stars have it any way they want. And so do the guys that own them.' He so envied Jules Buck and his partnership with Peter O Toole. He talked about Anthony Mann and Jimmy Stewart. I believe Cy was hoping that an international *Zulu* deal with Joe Levine would propel Stanley into success in the States, and cement the kind of successful partnership that might give them both that bigger showbusiness momentum. Not that he wanted to go back to Hollywood, but he badly wanted that career achievement: 'Ian, get a star, and a lot of great properties in the drawer.' He advised me to hunt for stories, books, ideas – a rolodex of potential movie subjects that could be pulled out when the opportunities came.

Zulu was becoming more and more a reality. John Prebble would be driven to the house in Thurloe Square (where Cy had his office) and he and Cy would work each day on the fresh pages. I told him that I had absolutely no idea where Rorke's Drift was. On examination it turned out to be hopeless as a setting for the film but I recommended Durban (my home town, and the English-speaking city) as a base, and told him that the only two film studios (Alpha and Killarney) that had 35mm capability were both in Johannesburg. These sound stages only existed because they were owned by the two groups that had the cinema advertising franchises. Killarney was bigger, and had the best equipment. I eulogised about the Drakensberg Mountains and the wonderful Sani Pass Hotel, with great views of the mountain range, a spa, separate cottage rondavels, a squash court and a pool. Clearly my enthusiasm for the area was coloured by the romantic weekends I spent there with my Durban girl friend Barbara! But he questioned me more closely when I talked about the difficulties of shooting on location. I related how the crew of *Nor the Moon by Night* had struggled with the weather, but how they caught up by having Ernie Archer construct a British cottage set right there on location – the director, Ken Annakin, shooting the 'English' interiors in it, rather than doing those scenes after a company move back to the Rank studios in the UK. My actor friend Dennis Folbigge's partner, Gerry, worked as the set dresser, and gave us hilarious daily briefings. I had partied with Pat McGoohan – another very dangerous actor – and was thrilled at meeting

Belinda Lee. I told Cy that after the rain, which fell in buckets, the dirt roads turn to mush, and big trucks got bogged down; this had happened to me when I went to a rural location to record a mission choir for Swedish TV.

'Dit reent baaie in Natal' is the first phrase little English boys learn in their Afrikaans lessons. I told him 'Umbah gashli' is the useful *Zulu* phrase for good wishes – 'go well'. Zulu is a fascinating language full of tongue clicks and mouth noises. They used finger flicks as loud as pistol shots to call in their cattle. Somehow in Zululand sound seems to travel a long way, echoing off the hills in the still heat. I had seen Zulus on the hillsides near my boarding school at Bothas Hill walk away from each other and still continue their conversation, even as they drew farther and farther apart. To shoot their English scenes, the *Nor the Moon* producers had cast a young Durban actress, Joan Brickhill, to play Belinda Lee's sister, and I told Cy there was a pool of local talent there who would work for a lot less than the Equity members (another trade union I had difficulties with) in London – and save charter-flight space. But most emphatically, I warned him about the light. At that latitude there is no 'golden hour' – no long periods of low-angle morning and twilight sun which are the cinematographer's (and producers'!) delight. No staring up at clouds through a dark glass calling out, 'Stand by – not yet – couple of minutes' as the British sun emerges weakly through the clouds to softly light the shot. In South Africa, I told him, the sun comes up, and in a moment it is so high the actors have black sockets instead of eyes and squinting, ugly faces. Cy was a little dismissive about that. The most often repeated comment of Cy's in the industry was his famous response to the whining complaints of a crew member, desperately worried about how to set up one of his more impossible shots: 'Don't bother me with your production problems...' Cy could be tough.

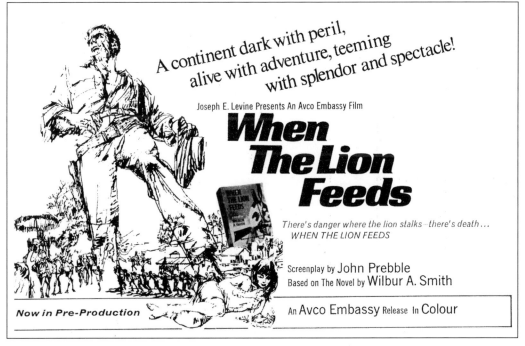

Trade advertisement for another of John Prebble's unproduced scripts for Joseph E. Levine, based on Wilbur Smith's novel, which includes scenes set at the Battle of Rorke's Drift. The artist's impression of the hero bears a striking resemblance to Stanley Baker, although Cy Endfield was said to prefer Michael Caine or Terence Stamp for the part.

Cy Endfield replies to future historian Ian Knight's query about the production of *Zulu Dawn*. He had to wait another three years for it to reach fruition. (Courtesy of Ian Knight).

JOSEPH E. LEVINE Presents the
STANLEY BAKER · CY ENDFIELD Production of

7. 10. 76

Dear Mr. Knight

I have only recently returned to London, where I found your letter of 10th August waiting for me.

To answer your queries re: 'Zulu Dawn' at this point in time I can say only that the prospect for going ahead seems gloomy. A combination of events — the passing of Stanley and the political difficulties in the part of the world where the shooting would have to take place — militate strongly against the project. I write this reluctantly, because I spent a year and half researching and writing the screenplay (The original 'Zulu' script was a 3 year stint).

Perhaps you can use the signature on this letter as your autograph item. Best wishes

Cy Endfield

39 THURLOE SQUARE
LONDON S.W.7.

DIAMOND FILMS LTD.

Directors: Stanley Baker, Cy Endfield (U.S.A.), E.R. Baker, M.B. Endfield

I was still on the periphery of the *Zulu* project – still a client. We dined with Maureen and the Bakers, Ellen and Stanley, at the White Elephant, talking about the trip. Both families were going, kids and all. They made up wish lists for the safari trek into the wild jungles of Africa: Fray Bentos canned steak-and-kidney pie (a Stanley favourite) and plenty of Mateus Rosé (as Stanley poured it into our glasses). But the diet requests had their practical side. Stanley told me that he always had a nervous reaction at the start of any production. His skin would break out, often with blemishes that were hard to cover with makeup. He didn't trust location food. Stanley and I became almost friends. He was a founding member of the White Elephant Club, the restaurant to see and be seen at by the cream of showbusiness, and he made me a member. 'He never gets a dime of profit out of it', said Cy with a sly grin.

Cy was very competitive with everyone and everything. I was smart enough never to challenge him. I once saw him fill in a whole *Sunday Times* acrostic crossword puzzle in one continuous sequence, without once lifting his pen off the paper. Beating Robert Shaw at table tennis was another triumph. He would raise his glasses up and peer closely at anything on paper. He was my professor in a free university course on the movie business, and I soaked it all up. Cy would never, ever tell me why their first choice for the second lead, Bromhead, was dropped. He was a young, handsome, well-known British TV actor and, I thought, was all set. Was it because he was on TV? Did Stanley think him too handsome? Too young? Cy didn't tell, and I didn't dare ask. I can say this: Stanley was in the driving seat of all the key personnel on that picture. He cut deals with everyone. Cy would argue hard, and Stanley could be persuaded, but while Stanley left creative control of script and shooting to Cy, he only wanted people around him he already knew and had a high comfort level with.

Both Cy and Stanley were thrilled to get Jack Hawkins. I was dismayed. He was my schoolboy hero, Captain of the Ship, Chief of Detectives, Stalwart Leader, Do or Die, etc. I simply couldn't visualise him in that simpering role. Why Jack Hawkins? 'Marquee weight', said Cy. 'Who in Kansas is going to pay $1 to see a Stanley Baker, Ulla Jacobsson movie?' It was painfully true. Jack was a wonderful asset, a sweet man, who kept a little tape recorder in his padre pocket to play back his lines just before each take. I asked him for an interview on my South African radio show and he agreed without hesitation. I knew, after I met him, that Jack was working cheap – probably helping Stanley out as a favour after their working together on *The Cruel Sea*. Ulla Jacobsson told me she took her part to expand her Bergman career into a more commercial arena. I thought her accent was at odds with Jack's, and I noticed that critics of Michael, saying (erroneously) that he didn't get a consistent upper-class accent, never mentioned this strange anomaly, or that the paler skins of the Jamaican extras inside the (Twickenham) hospital hardly matched the much darker tone of the Zulus on the roof!

One evening, Cy invited me to bring my current girl friend, Marylin Rickards, and go to the theatre with him and Maureen. I expected this would be an audience check on Bob Monkhouse, but this was to a different play, *Next Time I'll Sing to You*, and it featured a young cockney actor, Michael Caine. I was incredibly impressed, and said so. (More importantly, so was Marylin.) Cy told me he had been first suggested by Stanley for the small comedy role in *Zulu*. Michael was (and probably still is) a very, very funny man to be around. He had had a tiny part with Stanley in a Korean War movie, and he had apparently amused him no end during the shoot. Now things were different. At dinner, after the play: 'We're going to retest the role and try him for the Bromhead part', said Cy. And sure enough, a couple of weeks later, the decision was made. We went to a party and I watched Michael's reaction closely, knowing Cy was going to spring the news on him. He was there with Edina Ronay, a steady girlfriend. 'You got it.' Michael went absolutely speechless, slumping back into a sofa, transfixed. Cy gave that sly, merry grin he used when he pulled off a coup.

Joe Levine had given Stanley the 'If you get something good, let me know' routine when he was making a really bad biblical costume picture for him in Italy. It seems Joe had put together a great money-making formula, for example with *Hercules Unchained*:

a) Pick up period-costume Italian action movies cheap – give them a punchy title.
b) Revoice them with English dialogue.
c) Order a huge number of prints.

SENTIMENTAL JOURNEY
Nigel Green Speaks

Although I researched Nigel Green's life extensively for an entry I wrote for the *Oxford Dictionary of National Biography* (now available online), I had not come across any interviews with him. Until, that is, I was contacted by Australian reader James Peter Young, who wrote me 'a fan letter from Sydney' (his words, not mine!) in which he alerted me to a brief television interview included among the special features on the UK DVD of *Deadlier than the Male* (1966), released as a double-bill set with its sequel *Some Girls Do* (1969) by Network Distribution (#7952334). The interview was apparently conducted at Pinewood Studios in 1966 to help promote the spy film, about which Green had very little to say. More interesting are his remarks on *Zulu* and two other recently completed films, *Let's Kill Uncle* (1966) and *Tobruk* (1967), which are reproduced in full below.

Q: I know that sport plays a very large part in your life. Now how much of this is physical therapy as a result of a very serious accident that you had in, what was it, 1956?
A: I've always loved sport. I was born in South Africa and I didn't wear shoes until I came to England when I was five years old; I ran barefoot. I could swim when I was three – it was hot, you fell in the river and you swam. I was a small animal, you know? My brothers and I all excelled at sports, I've always loved them. But I took it for granted until I was paralysed – and then you really realise the value of physical fitness, which I try to keep. I do judo and swim, play tennis, golf and walk a lot.

Q: What belt are you holding in judo?
A: A blue belt. I'm very proud to be a middle-aged blue belt.

Q: Well now, from sport back to films. You've had some very good reviews from critics for many of your films, including *Zulu* and *The Ipcress File*, but of all these films is there any one in particular that gives you particular pleasure when you look back on it?
A: Well, *Zulu*, of course. Born in South Africa, I was brought up by a Zulu, because my father was very ill – that's why he had to leave South Africa. My father image was a Zulu. He was a huge, strong man who carried me on his shoulders and he made my toys for me. Going back to do it was a very sentimental journey, and I was very happy there. The part that John Prebble wrote was so superb that you wouldn't dream of changing a line. And the man was my chief petty officer in the Navy. It was so true, that men of real authority don't have to shout. We get so many square-bashing, shouting sergeant majors, you know, but the men of true authority have it in the eye.

Q: What's been the result so far of the seven-year contract that you've got with Universal Pictures in Hollywood?
A: Well, I went over and did two pictures straight away. *Let's Kill Uncle* – it's Grand Guignol and luckily old [producer-director] Bill Castle, who started with Cary Grant and all the old-timers, is a nice kind o' nut, as the Americans say, and we got on so well. He's very pleased with it and I hoped it'll be delightful when it comes out.

Q: And what's the other picture?

A: *Tobruk*, which is based on a true story of a Jewish commando unit called the PSIG – the Palestine Special Independent Group – who were escapees from Germany and Palestine and so on, and they could speak German fluently. They dressed in Rommel's Afrika Korps. uniforms and had German transport, which was stolen or borrowed or knocked together. They took a whole bunch of British commandos, pretending to be prisoners of war, in the truck right into Tobruk and blew up Rommel's fuel supply. That's the ... action, but it's an interesting character crossfire. I'm playing a colonel of the British Empire, the old British Empire: anti-Jewish, doesn't like anybody trying to prove anything new, like Israel. George Peppard is playing this German Jew who's leading the Jewish commandos, and I finish up full of admiration for him.

d) Distribute them for release in as many US movie houses as possible simultaneously, after a short burst of spot TV and newspaper advertising.

It had never been done before, but this way, 'He gets all his damn profit out before word of mouth kills it', said Cy.

So it was budget, budget, budget. Cy and Stanley had to get the picture made for under two million dollars. It was an almost unthinkable proposition, even in the 60s, when that was a lot of money. Everyone in the industry is kind to first-time picture-makers, and I am sure that Stanley went to all the suppliers – Berman's, Technicolor, the actors – pulled in favours and got sweetheart deals, all over town. With the contracts signed and the budget finally approved, Cy and Stephen Dade left for a recce of possible South African locations. There were two schools of directing at the time: the Hitchcock way (now being executed so successfully by Ridley Scott, et al) where sketched, shot-by-shot storyboard frames were the guide for each setup; and the John Ford way (whom Cy admired so much), where the director walks the location or the set to find the camera setup that enhances the required mood. That tilt up to the darkening cloud above the Drakensberg, as the bridge-building platoon of soldiers march off in the early *Zulu* scene, was pure John Ford.

This needed a lot of faith in the camera operator, long before the days of video replay. With the blimp wound over to be silent as it ran, the regular big Mitchell still had a large side viewer that gave an accurate look at the framing. The Technirama camera was no Mitchell; moreover, since small cranes could only support one person, Cy could only be held aloft for the rehearsal, He was sometimes worried that he didn't always get a good take, and he wanted to have some cover. With the optics of Technirama film stock running left to right (instead of the traditional up and down), panning shots could cause a judder if they were too fast. His relationship with operator Dudley Lovell was particularly bad, and this may have prompted him to cover more than usual on the big battle scenes. Dudley had his own problems. The camera was noisy, and it had to be muffled by a massively heavy sound blimp. It was a monster to move around, even on the dolly, and complicated to load and unload. The budget was too small: there were no generators and no brutes (10K arc lights), and the necessary reflectors poured heat down on everyone. But Cy knew when he had a good take with all the stationary set ups and the dialogue. Later, silent testimony to his efficiency, the 1,000-foot cans of unopened, unreturnable raw Technicolor negative stock lay piled up in our Thurloe Square office. They were begging to be made into a short subject.

In the event Cy and cinematographer Stephen Dade returned with Cy approving a Drakensberg site that had two hotels (Sani Pass Hotel was over budget!). They were ideally close to a wonderful valley location where Ernie Archer's set could be built. Cy positioned the build so as to have the curtain of the Drakensberg mountains as a magnificent frame-filling background whichever lens he chose. There was a huge amount of prep to do: the set had to be built, there were young soldiers from the South African conscript army to train, the Zulus to be taught, the making of all the props for the shoot, and gathering together enough period but practical guns that could actually fire. Many didn't work (the dioptre-lens shot of one rifle being loaded with a single shell in close-up, while the distance held focus, helped the firepower illusion). An army of local Zulus – men and women – were hired for the tasks. Notices were posted by the government warning of dire consequences for any race co-habitation. I think one of the penalties was seven lashes! Stanley's comment was funny – but unprintable. Cy recalled to me his excitement when the first, rag-taggle group of fifty Zulus in bare feet, dirty clothes and downcast faces arrived...then they put on the Zulu costumes and broke out into an immediate, totally ecstatic song and dance. Umbah gashli!

As the start of principal photography loomed, Cy asked me if I would get more

closely involved. In effect, I had seamlessly moved from agency TV producer to client of Cy, then friend of Cy and Stanley, and finally to assistant to them both on a major motion picture. Once the budget could start to be spent I came on salary (no cost to Cy or Stanley) and resigned my agency job. Wow! I was 24 years old, giving up the world of advertising and 30-second spots. We were making a huge feature film! I was going to Hollywood! Mmm... really? My salad days, and I was very green in judgement.

There were a couple of formal press parties to announce the shoot (displaying some of Ernie Archer's sketches) and the adventure began. The first dailies from the shoot were awful. The colour was pasty, and the film action seemed to stutter. Everyone was concerned, but a few weeks later I flew out to Durban and drove up to join the unit. I arrived on the day the unit began the first key dialogue scenes. I was a little surprised when Cy immediately ushered me into the cutting room, hastily constructed as an afterthought in the location office building, and asked Johnny Jympson to run an edited scene. It was the final redoubt, the deadly fire-and-load sequence. Even though the picture was anamorphically squeezed (the moviola rented from Killarney didn't have a CinemaScope lens) I was stunned by the power of the film. It was a vivid, gripping climax to the battle, the camera finally panning over the groaning, dying bodies of the Zulus. I couldn't contain my excitement – it was brilliant, unexpectedly brilliant! Cy grinned, and walked back to the set.

Inside the mealie bag storage room the shoot was going on, and Jack was about to do his drinking scene. Then his biblical quotation with Nigel Green and the young soldiers. Outside, Stanley was so involved in the production I saw him stitch squibs into the sacks for the bullet effects (against all the union rules). When the squibs fired in the take, corn poured out, totally unexpectedly, into the mouth of the stricken soldier. Gary Bond lay there as the corn trickled down on his face. Nobody moved – and there was no need for a retake. With luck like that, I thought, this is a dream come true. Then, as Jack peered out drunkenly through the slats of his little room, Nigel Green continued his masterful performance. I was elated.

Cy began to show me more of the early footage, pointing out that on arrival he had ordered in red dirt to cover the floor of the entire inside perimeter, and had pulled a brilliant coup. He had increased the sexual atmosphere of the dance sequence one hundred per cent by the inclusion of the little spears the girls carried – and, best of all in his opinion, he had headdresses made for them to wear: a very subtle, but modernising, cosmetic adjustment. One standout girl, with a spectacular figure, was always placed to the front, closest to the camera: 'Boy, they suddenly got very sexy.' He gave that sly grin.

The shooting moved into a steady work rhythm. Snow fell on the mountain ridge – you can just see it in the distance, as Chard exits the chapel hospital after his wound is treated. The set became quite cold, but the light held up day after day. Working in the cooler days was easier. Mornings began in the dark as ghostly figures, wrapped up, walked down from the hotel to the set. The unit began to come together like a well-oiled machine. Plenty of drinks at dinner each night and early to bed. Cy and Stanley had sensibly hired Bert Batt. He had worked in Natal

A POST-OFFICE PICTURE
Joe Levine on *Zulu*

Executive producer Joseph E. Levine was a master of publicity – a showman who knew how to promote and talk up a picture, even if he had very little direct involvement in the making of them. On a number of occasions he talked about *Zulu* and, as his voice was little heard in the first edition of this book, I thought it time to give him the opportunity to speak within these pages. Herewith are selected quotations from a number of interviews he gave in the mid-1960s, as reported in American newspapers and magazines.

When he thinks of *Zulu* with his [multi-theatre saturation treatment] in mind there are times when Levine seems on the part of actually shining like a supercolossal light bulb. […] 'I think of it,' Levine says, 'as a Cowboys and Indians picture. They used to make hundreds of them but nobody makes them anymore. The public wants one. Ten thousand frenzied savages charging all at once – actually we're only going to have two thousand of them but with three cameras it's easy to multiply. They tell me those fellows drink some kind of grass whisky – how would you like to be the cameraman filming *them*? I feel there's a need for this picture – no psychiatrists in it, no nuts in it, no dope peddlers in it. The real thing! I think you've got a post-office picture here. With some pictures you worry about the weather. […] But with a post-office picture if you advertise it right neither snow, nor rain, nor heat, nor gloom of night will keep the customers from tearing the box-office right off the front of the building. […] *Zulu*! I like that title. Six hundred theatres? Two *thousand* theatres – one picture in two thousand theatres all around the world on the same night.'

(Paul O'Neil, 'The Super Salesman of Super Colossals,' *Life*, 27 July 1962)

Zulu, made by Paramount from a script Joe had acquired because he liked the title, was presented to the exhibitors this winter with old-fashioned fanfare. […] 'Every bit of it is authentic,' says Levine. 'There's not one Zulu in it who isn't a Zulu.' […] As the exhibitors filed out [of the trade preview screening] they shook Levine's hand. 'Great picture, Joe!' 'You've done it again, Joe!' Bids came in fast from the exhibitors and Levine says the picture, which cost $1,750,000 to make, will gross at least $8 million.

Zulu was released in England on January 22, the anniversary of the historic battle of Rorke's Drift on which the movie is based. Levine flew over for the opening and was delighted with the crowds and critical acclaim. 'Everybody liked it but the *Manchester Guardian*,' he says, 'and it doesn't have much circulation.'

For the first time in a deal with one of the majors, Levine has the distribution rights to the U.S. and Canada; Paramount will distribute in the rest of the world. The two companies will then split the profits fifty-fifty. Unlike other independents, Levine always keeps firm hold on the advertising and promotion rights, which is fine by most of his producers. In fact, what they are really buying is his showmanship.'

(Katherine Hamill, 'The Supercolossal – Well, Pretty Good – World of Joe Levine,' *Fortune*, March 1964, p. 180)

> 'I'm very proud of *Zulu*, co-produced with Paramount. I had confidence in Stanley Baker, who stars and who made the film with director Cy Endfield. I got to know him when he was acting in *Sodom and Gomorrah* and I was attracted by all the preparation he had gone into on *Zulu*. They shot it in Africa for $1.65 million by Hollywood standards and did a wonderful job. I think it will outgross any picture I've ever handled; we'll get the cost out in England alone, where it's now running.'
>
> (Quoted in Philip K. Scheuer, 'Joe Levine Presents: $uccess,' *Los Angeles Times*, 17 May 1964)
>
> Levine cited *Zulu*, which has been seen to date by 75,000,000 people and ranks as one of Great Britain's all-time money-makers. 'Stanley Baker had an idea,' he said, 'to breathe life into a glorious chapter in British history.
> 'We took something from Britain's historical past, gave it a meaningful presence and it will be preserved for an illustrious future for succeeding generations.
> 'The idea originated with two men in England, they carried it across the Atlantic… and now showmen throughout the world are reaping its profits.'
>
> ('Men and Ideas Alone Essential to Films, Levine Tells Britons,' *Film Daily*, 15 June 1965 – on the occasion of Levine's CEA showmanship award)

on *Nor the Moon by Night* and knew the weather problems well. He was perfect, because Cy could sometimes fall into a kind of long, thoughtful silence when his idea wasn't immediately grasped by everyone. Bert was a tough, almost bullying kind of first assistant, and in my mind was another unsung hero of that shoot. His energy was boundless, and he stood no nonsense from anyone.

True, there had been low points, and there was sometimes a lot of tension on the set which erupted now and then. Stephen Dade pulled off a minor miracle, with only two little battery-powered inky dinks mounted over the lens. But the Technicolor camera was as heavy as hell, and Cy loved to shoot with a flowing style. It meant laying tracks on uneven ground, creating long trenches for the low-angle running shots, digging a huge pit for the stampede. When the first stampede was attempted the cattle didn't move a muscle. They had become too accustomed to the firing and yelling. A whole new herd had to be brought in. The running shots were very effective, but there was only one good long take without bumps, and Jympson had to have it flopped for both right and left attacks. I remember Ronnie Brandford's comment to me when we saw first saw the Players commercials: 'This man has a foot fetish.' But Cy's trademark feet shots made great cutaways.

But the worst moment was reported to me by both Cy and Maureen – an early crisis that occurred before I had arrived. Michael and a platoon of soldiers, working as a firing unit, was the sequence that caused the crisis. It was purely a problem of three-dimensional chess – where the line of soldiers fired, moved two paces, crouched to reload, allowing the group behind to fire above them, and the whole choreography over again. Apparently Johnny Sullivan (a brilliant stunt co-ordinator) and Bert Batt couldn't orchestrate the action effectively. It was a shambles. As usual, suggestions sprang from various sides, and the chaos got worse. Tempers began to flare. Cy made to intervene and, to his dismay, was warned off by Stanley who, according to Cy, said something to the effect, 'Cy, leave it to the guys who know what they're doing'. It was a wounding and particularly painful moment between them. Cy told me, 'I knew then, my whole authority was on the line'. He let the chaos peter out with nothing working… and – judging just the right moment – stood up, moved forward and repositioned each soldier, giving them each precise instructions on what to do when, and the rhythm they needed to move to. (Cy could move chess pieces at a world-class level.) Then, a simple command from Cy: 'Now, stand by [slight pause] – action!' The rehearsal was perfect. 'Now let's shoot and get on with it.' The scene was perfect again, and shot in one take. Cy's authority was never in doubt after that.

What I saw of Johnny Sullivan was spectacular. He worked tirelessly training and rehearsing the soldiers and the Zulu fighters. And he amazed me with his sheer athletic ability. He had a riding/speaking line – because I don't think an actor could have done it. Cy directed him to ride up to the camera fast, leading his whole mounted troop, then pull up his horse on the correct mark, deliver his line to Stanley and gallop off downstage right on the perfect line, all in one action. He did the whole thing at full gallop, reined to a stop using only one hand on the reins. He barely paused his action for a moment, delivered the angry line perfectly and then galloped off. Spectacular. He was as handsome as hell, and on one big production apparently fell madly in love on the set and went off with the leading lady – that isn't always good for a stuntman's career path.

The hospital fire, once it started, moved twice as fast as intended. Cy had to shoot the doorway scene fast because the set was burning too quickly. For once, Dade's sun-gun inky dinks gave a perfect fill light. We shot the roll-call scene the following morning as the first shot of the day, while the embers were still hot. The whole hospital set was gone, but there was just enough left of the burnt superstructure to be useable. Stanley thought the minimal look was great: 'You think I could stand this butcher's yard more than once?' As Nigel Green did his close-up I was holding my breath. He read the names, against the occasional crackle from the dying embers... an eerie moment. 'My God! He's going to steal the picture', was my thought.

The last sequence to be shot in Natal was the opening scene of the film: a long, slow pan across the damaged battle scene as the Zulus picked up rifles from the soldiers' dead bodies. We had a firm commitment to the charter flight, and I recall lying awake praying for the weather to be good so that the set could be wrapped on schedule and stay on budget. It was a perfect day and, I thought, a good omen for the rest of the production at Twickenham. Bob Porter was to stay behind and sell off everything he could, and supervise the restoration of the site to its former state. He had already spent days away in a distant location with the second unit camera, to get massed scenes of marching Zulus and so on. But I ran the movie last week and counted only sixty frames from that entire second unit shoot in the whole film – and that we crushed down darker to a night shot, adding some red tint. It wasn't entirely Bob's fault that there were no significant second unit shots elsewhere. Cy had no faith in his ability, but Bob and Stanley were close – however, the second unit camera used 35mm film, running two frames at a time left to right, to create a 70mm-size frame. With no blimp, as the claw pulled the pairs of frame through the gate, it made a horrendous loud noise like a machine gun. Run that camera on the set and Claude Hitchcock and his sound guys would have been thoroughly compromised. They were the other unsung heroes on the shoot – especially

when you can hear how low and intimately Stanley was playing his role: 'Bromhead, no need to make the Zulus a present of fire' – all in his sotto voce, captured perfectly, and not a single frame spoiled by shadow from the mike boom in the entire set of dailies. Remarkable.

I was already familiar with Twickenham Studios. I had frequently worked there because it was small, cheap and perfect for commercials. It was run by a helpful Italian, Guido Coen, but the stage was almost too small for the *Zulu* hospital sets. No room for tracking shots, just cuts, but in a way this actually helped the rhythm of the edit. It made the hospital rooms seem claustrophobic and the African landscape outside seemed so wide by comparison. Better still, we were going to have to set it on fire, in a highly safe and controlled way – and to accomplish that same task in Pinewood, Shepperton or Elstree would have been hugely expensive. I thought that I could mainly be most supportive in post-production. It was something outside Cy and Stanley's real interest, and how I had worked most with Cy on our commercials.

The Twickenham studio shoot gave us a proper fixed base of operations. There was a production office, we had an editing bay, a screening room, and a regular routine. There was steady progress where Cy and Johnny Jympson could fill in the edit in between takes on stage. Rusty Coppleman and his young lady assistant began to build his sound effects library. There was one excellent rifle ricochet sound effect which he doubled and redoubled to build the all important volley-fire sound. With no room or need for a crane, the camera stayed still. Stephen Dade had a full light pack, and I thought the scene where Jimmy smashes open the surgical cupboard to swig from the broken bottle was beautifully lit. But the end of the Twickenham shoot was the start of the problems I had with Johnny Jympson in post. This was his show, and he didn't want any young pup pitching in.

For the first time I saw the assembled early scene where Chard and Bromhead do a walk around the whole set. I had not seen it shot. Cy's plan was to play the entire dialogue – ending with the Witts' arrival – walking Chard and Bromhead around the buildings to reveal the whole perimeter to the audience, to give them a sense of the layout and then assault them with wave after wave of attack. I thought the editing of that sequence was very awkward. There were going to be pauses for the audience to catch its breath in between the assaults – the calf sequence, the water detail, Ivor Emmanuel and the singing contest and so on, but after each one – pow! – another ferocious clash. He explained this dramatic arc to me several times. But the early walk-around scenes were dreadfully short of cover and seemed to be cut overlong. Some overlapping dialogue would have helped overcome the lack of cover, I thought. I hadn't been in South Africa when they were shot, but I understand that the weather was bad, and possibly there was a sense of 'Let's move on' to catch up. Each day on the Drakensberg location Cy was surrounded by stationary 'producers' like Basil Keys, Colin Lesslie and so on. Colin represented the completion guarantor and others had other vested interests. These were all contractual commitments and people we had to have. Budget, budget, budget.

The 'breathing' pauses didn't seem fully cued to me, and I suggested to Cy that we copy David Lean (or was it Anne Coates – his cutter?) who artfully signalled these kinds of

pauses with forward-cut sound. In other words, for a second or two a sound effect, which seems out of place to the onscreen visuals when it is first heard, is then explained by revealing the source of the sound at the next cut. We had plenty of choices: the whistling wind and clanking in the water-break scene, animal noises for the dead-calf sequence, and so on. It just seemed a great way we could indicate a passage of time and also renew the audience's attention to detail, after the noisy and hectic clashes of battle. Johnny Jympson was totally dismissive. Cy came back to the set from the cutting room. 'He says we should have planned it', Cy said, 'and it's too late now.' I knew I had made a mistake by suggesting it to Cy and not talking it over first with Jympson. Salad days. Who was it who said you can achieve anything you like, as long as you don't want credit for it?

Joe Levine arrived in London. He had visited South Africa early in the shoot and, I understand, seemed very impressed by the magnificent location. Cy had everyone on parade: Karsh of Ottawa, the soldiers, the Zulus – quite a show. I never understood why a budget-starved picture had Karsh of Ottawa as stills guy. He was an elderly man, a slow, patient photographer (with a gorgeous young wife) who did magnificent portrait pictures. Luckily he wasn't in our budget, so obviously Joe had something in mind which I couldn't comprehend. More marquee weight? But now it was show time. We had a couple of rough-cut reels ready and rented a nice preview theatre in town. I owned a huge US Dodge car, complete with fins imported from Durban, and played limo driver while Joe and Cy sat in the back. Joe was short on time. (I learned later that Stanley was furious with Cy about this, accusing him of humiliating me.) I recall that one of the rough-cut reels was of the first attack, which had lots of action. As the reel played I suddenly became acutely aware (having seen it over thirty times by then – I counted) that they were, of course, totally undubbed. Several of the rifles didn't fire, and those that did sounded like sporadic pop guns. The Zulus gave only half-hearted shouts and grunts as they closed in[the cut and thrust was largely silent. It was a disaster. Joe was a showman, not a filmmaker. This, he must have thought, was his two million dollars' worth? Where was the money? As the lights went up you could have cut the atmosphere with a knife. A very long pause, and then one of his henchmen, Marty Rackin, said (this is burned in my brain – verbatim): 'Cy, you gotta get some human interest in there. You know, like a soldier sits under a tree and writes home... "Dear Mom", and then – wham! An arrow in the neck.' I thought Cy would explode. Instead, slowly, 'Well now Marty... throwing an assegai might be messy.'

I recall women swooning over Michael at the previews, and again at the opening night. But Cy and Stanley were both convinced Jimmy Booth would be the emerging star – and at that point I would have put both Michael and even Nigel Green way, way ahead of that probability. It was the one time I felt Cy and Stanley had made an error in judgement. And of course, South African actor Gert (Jamie) van den Bergh went on to big local success. His film career might have been ruined if it weren't for the sound editor, Rusty Coppleman, who saved all Jamie's original dialogue. During the dialogue looping session, I had winced at the terrible job a London actor was doing with his Afrikaans impersonation. I asked Rusty to go back to the original Nagra recording tapes. Despite the rush, bless him, he did, and he saved that wonderful rumbling voice: 'Who do

you think is coming to wipe out your little command? The Grenadier Guards?' In contrast, the London actor's impersonation and sync of Dennis Folbigge was perfect – and Dennis was a close friend who had taught me everything he knew about radio acting. 'Pot that man, somebody!' was pure Dennis.

Then came another extraordinary, memorable moment. We waited outside the Twickenham screening room for Lionel Bart to come for his music viewing. Stanley, Tommy Steele, John Kennedy (Tommy's agent), Vidal Sassoon (famous British hair stylist) and Lionel Bart would play regular poker at Alma Cogan's flat in Knightsbridge. Lionel Blair was there occasionally. Cy couldn't be allowed to play – because he could hand you a pack of cards to shuffle for as long as you liked, cut the deck twice and then deal you four kings! I didn't play because I had no money (and no skill). Lionel Bart was the whale. He had eight touring productions of *Oliver!* going at once: 'Eight thousand pounds a week', said Cy, with envy. Stunning – I was earning two thousand pounds a year! 'Just get Bernard Herrmann for the music', said Blair, facetiously, knowing he was Alfred Hitchcock's – and my – favourite film score composer, and probably the highest paid in the world. Naturally, Stanley had asked, and got, Bart to do the score for *Zulu*, and Joe Levine had been apprised and was no doubt thrilled by this coup – wasn't Bart currently the world's (and Broadway's) most successful composer? We waited; no Lionel. Then a pale, thin young man, with a North Country accent, walked up: 'Er – Lionel asked me to come and do a score for him. My name is John Barry.' It turned out that Lionel Bart was more entrepreneur than composer – and more lyricist than composer, if anything. 'He's a great organiser', said Cy, as if to excuse this mess. Later on, when Lionel gave us a tour around his vast and elegant new publishing-house offices in the West End, pitching for the music and album publishing rights, I was amazed that all the assistants were dressed in uniform. The set-up must have cost him a fortune. Seems he had missed out on the publishing rights for *Oliver!* and wasn't going to make the same mistake again.

Cy rushed back to the office to compose a cable to Joe Levine. He was concerned that advertising and press releases might be being prepared by Paramount with Lionel Bart being mentioned, and we waited for the inevitable, 'Who the hell is John Barry?' The cables went to and fro, but a couple of weeks later we assembled in the control room at CTS. I suggested it because it was a great sound stage I knew very well, having done dozens of music tracks there (from *Take It from Here* for the BBC to Captain Birdseye's theme song for me) with good friend songwriter Johnny Johnson, who owned part of it. An enormous orchestra started quickly to assemble: in music recording sessions no-one's pay time starts on the clock until the last musician is seated. A nod from John Barry, and we craned forward in the control room – not knowing what to expect. The players poised, watching with interest as the title sequence started to roll on the Technirama screen... a chinagraph mark moved across the frame indicating the first cue, the timpani bass drums began to throb, low at first, then louder, then the entire orchestra crashed in with the African-inspired opening theme. I felt my hair was standing on end. It was utterly magnificent! 'Bernie Herrmann!', I whispered to Cy, 'it's Bernie Herrmann!' Cy was dumbstruck, in awe... it was a truly wonderful moment, the highlight of the whole *Zulu* experience thus far. There wasn't a lot of music to record: Cy had a horror of music that mimicked the action of the scene, 'like a Disney cartoon', he noted. The final end-title music section was noteworthy. It was to start with the Welsh choir and then segue seamlessly into the score with the full orchestra picking up and playing the final, triumphant closing bars of 'Men of Harlech'. The choir tape ran and then, on cue, the orchestra came in – a hopeless mismatch. 'Er... what key is that choir in?', asked John Barry, tapping his baton to stop the recording. 'In the cracks', said one of the players – laughter – meaning no key you could find. He was right. The Welsh male voice choir hadn't used a key pipe. But with a little subtle blending, the problem was mushed over. I can still hear it, though.

We had real problems at Technicolor, who were to make the titles and create the visual post effects. Our little team going there was like a visit to a steel plant to make two nuts and a bolt. There were rooms of noisy, gurgling pipes and rows of giant film screens, all running prints of different films at high speed. The sound was deafening. The actors rushed across the screens, stopping, comically nodding and moving on – a kind of Chaplinesque movie hell. I could see how it would be really hard to get their interest, or their attention. But the colour work was outstanding. They were able to key in correctly on the red uniforms, and showed us a number of film strips with contrast and light variations to choose for each select. We could put real blue in the sky, and match all the takes for each sequence, almost regardless of the light conditions. We added a darker texture to the singing contest, some saturation with the water buckets and dust, but mainly tried to keep the film as an 'all in the same day' look.

Johnny Jympson and Cy had marked several dissolves. Here there was new technology. There was no need for an internegative (dupe of the incoming and outgoing shot, which often messed with the colour). Technicolor would use the new autodissolve whereby the printer would roll forward and backward on the negative so that each print was an original. The scenes would melt together: very effective as Michael takes off his cloak to shoot the leopard, then begins his stately journey back to the camp. But trouble came when we looked at the visual effects. The first one we needed was a binoculars'-eye view framing the closer shot of the galloping riders, as Chard hands them over to Ivor Emmanuel. 'Very wonderful things, these', says Ivor, looking down at the binoculars. No such luck. I was bitterly disappointed, expecting something with some soft edges and subtle turn-of-the-century engraved markings. The two conjoined circles were hard-edged and totally black, utterly incongruous and unbelievable. And we were in a tight time squeeze. 'Well', I said, 'that one is out.' Next effect to come was a 'paint'; that is, a matte painting of the entire Zulu capital – an establishing shot of hundreds of kraals to be carefully and seamlessly superimposed over the longest and widest shot of the actual dance, on the plain below the hillside. No way. I had no faith that Technicolor would make it look anything but fake. It didn't take more than a minute for me to persuade Cy that the shot stood on its own: 'Forget the paint, let's leave the scene as it was shot.' Cy agreed. We would gain some days, and Jympson nodded.

Nobody noticed, but If you look very carefully at that scene you can just see the construction frames holding up the back of the far-right kraals which that 'paint' was to cover up.

Despite our joy over John Barry's music score, we had a disastrous few days mixing at the MGM dubbing theatre. Then, just when Cy was in total despair, we moved into Pinewood's sound stage for the stereo mix. It was a huge theatre, and the projected picture was vast, at least as large as the biggest movie screen. We had never seen it so big. The giant console had three mixers working as a team – hundreds of exciting switches, meters and knobs. A big toy for grownups! From the moment the first reel ran, the detail and depth in the sound elements (which were actually audible for the first time) added an amazing, almost transformational ambience to the film; it made the picture seem to be in 3D. One by one each track was shifted to the correct part of each frame. Rusty Coppleman's 'train' was a brilliant tour de force (he actually used a train). The crashing rifle volley shots exploded with incredible unison and power, and a touch of echo. I thought Cy was going to jump through the screen – more arm-waving excitement. They did a mix down to mono, and that was the one used on the general-release version.

The initial screen length was way over three hours. Joe hammered Cy on the transatlantic phone: he had to take at least twenty minutes out. Cy groaned, until Joe explained that a lot of stateside screens on his distribution list would run the film continuously throughout the day, and could maybe squeeze another showing if it was shorter. He did the math. Say seven hundred screens, one more show a day, the total extra receipts that would generate – and Cy and Stanley's percentage of the extra net they could accrue (after the distributors' cut)... there was a pause. 'Let's cut it', said Cy. Goodbye to the arrival of the uniformed mounted reinforcements – the dialogue at the end, dialogue of the VC recipients, some of the comedy (I didn't think any of it was really funny) and trims to the battle scenes. It was big improvement to the overall film.

Later, we unrolled the graphics art sent over from Paramount for the newspaper ads and cinema posters. I was very disappointed, especially with the actual title word Z U L U. Where on earth in their culture were there any Zulu carvings to inspire such junk? They ran as was, because we had no say, and no-one really cared. After delivering the final negative our part was over. Then came the big day: the regular cinema opening after the premiere. I drove around Leicester Square that morning and telephoned Cy from a call box (still on that corner). 'Cy, you won't believe this –

there's a queue from the box office all around the corner of the street.' We had a hit.

To this day, I don't know why, once *Zulu* was an obvious London hit, we (Diamond Films) didn't pick up Michael Caine's three-picture option that – according to Cy – was in the standard contract. To Cy and Stanley both, Jimmy Booth was the find. A couple of years later I had lunch with Lewis Gilbert in his apartment in Cannes – where I was organising the Advertising Film Festival awards show – and he asked me the same question. Lewis (who directed it) told me he knew Michael was perfect for *Alfie*, and with that and *The Ipcress File* I knew with certainty he was the star Cy had been looking for, and lost. Michael was a natural: an extremely intelligent young man, careful to match his performance to the lens: small, subtle gestures in close-up (scratching his nose, adjusting his hat), bigger moves on the wider shots. I thought his laughter, with that desperate sense of relief at the line 'They're saluting you!' in the final moments of the Zulu retreat, was just masterly acting. He absolutely nailed it. I think Michael then had only two private demons he had to deal with. First, his eyelashes – they were very pale. Secondly, he didn't ever want to be out of work. I think this was a hangover from his years of family poverty – which must have been especially poignant when Terry Stamp, his roommate, got an Oscar nomination for *Billy Budd*. I can only imagine that Dennis Selinger (his agent) had his work cut out getting him signed for picture after picture. He told us he would be doing a television play when *Zulu* was released. Cy was horrified: 'Michael, there are two kinds of studio lighting in television – on or off. They'll shoot up your nose.' 'Well', said Michael, 'it'll pay for the Christmas presents, won't it?' Michael lived in 7 Albion Close Mews, just opposite me in 5 Albion Mews. I told him once how I had been followed by two giggling girls, mistakenly asking me for his autograph. Michael said, worriedly, 'You weren't rude to them or anything, were you?' Such is success.

Events turned sour after that. Cy, Stanley and I had a meeting with Joe Levine and his team at the Hilton Hotel. This was after the premiere, the parties, the triumph, the distributor lunches. (At one lunch, Joe said in his speech he had taken a chance with Cy, whose track record to that date hadn't amounted to much. Charming!) The picture was doing really well, and the future looked bright for Diamond Films. But this meeting was to be all business, the future of Diamond Films and Paramount. 'We see you as our guys in Africa', said Joe. 'What about a TV series? There's a lot of dough in television.' Cy and Stanley were crushed. Television? Africa? The meeting wound down, and after the usual congratulations and handshakes we regrouped.

It now all depended on *Sands of the Kalahari*. Diamond Films had optioned the book, a story of a plane crash in the desert, where the leading man turns on everyone who survives, makes a sexual conquest of the pretty flight attendant and morphs into the leader of a troop of baboons. Stanley was confident he could get his friend from their village, Richard Burton, and his new acting partner Elizabeth Taylor for the lead roles in this improbable plot. If we got Burton and Taylor for the lead roles in *Kalahari* Levine would kill for the picture, and if he didn't, someone else would. There was just one problem. Stanley and Ellen were close friends with both Richard Burton *and* his then wife. They had grown up together in Wales and shared a lot. But the First Mrs. Richard Burton was now the most publicly humiliated woman in the world. The tempestuous affair between Burton and Taylor during the shooting of *Cleopatra* was front-page news – and colossal box office. I assumed that to Ellen, any kind of intimate relationship between a world-renowned Hollywood actress and her married Welsh co-star must have seemed box-office poison. Supposing that idea caught on? So the screenplay unfolded thus:

Act One: the small, private little restaurant. Cy, Maureen and Ian are dining with Mrs. B (the scorned wife), Stanley and Ellen (the shocked, caring and compassionate friend). Ellen and Mrs. B, heads together, sit whispering at their own table throughout. Mrs. B is a middle-aged-looking, grey-haired, severe lady with a fierce body language and a strong Welsh accent. Ellen listens to her story, occasionally throwing mean glances at poor Stanley (one of his more uncomfortable nights). Cy, Maureen and I have the usual light-hearted gossip about our little circle of friends, not daring to use the words Elizabeth or Taylor or Richard or Burton.

Act Two: the party. The reconciliation for the sake of the family business? Richard Burton and Elizabeth Taylor are invited to Stanley and Ellen's fabulous Wimbledon home for an A-list party. This will be the public kiss-and-make-up where, presumably, Richard and Elizabeth will make some kind of accommodation with Stanley and Ellen and they will all live and work happily ever after. This has to be the hot ticket invite of the decade. The party is crackling with the electricity of the situation. I wish I had the guest list, but it is a who's who of London showbusiness power and money (plus a smattering of celebs from the States who happen to be in town). Richard arrives alone – well, with an elder brother. They are both drunk, and Richard lets it be known that Elizabeth is to join us soon – everyone smiles. Seems reasonable – after all, the world's biggest star (over a million dollars for *Cleopatra* – the biggest salary ever) needs to prepare her wardrobe to make a great entrance.

While we wait and wait for the world's number-one box-office star to arrive, I have a conversation with a likeable young man named Mike Nichols. His comment on the situation? He says to me, just a little too loudly, 'All golden lads and lasses must like chimney sweepers turn to dust'. 'Aaah', roars Richard, crossing the room towards us, 'the Bard!' Mike Nichols (just a little startled): 'Actually, it's Charles Dickens.' 'Never! Shakespeare, old man, I bet you ten thousand dollars it's Shakespeare.' And, turning to me, 'You! You'll join me in this little wager, won't you?' I don't have five thousand of anything, let alone five thousand dollars. I gently demur from this generous offer, forgetting that, drunk or sober, Richard Burton is probably the foremost expert on Shakespearean text in the world. (It's actually a quotation from Shakespeare's *Cymbeline*.) Luckily there's a distraction, and Burton's elder brother – an ugly brute of a man – then lurches at another even more famous guest. Burton shouts at him in fluent Welsh. This is not a language I am familiar with, but I suspect the translation would make a sailor blush. Elizabeth Taylor does not arrive; she really has no need. She can work with any director on any project she likes. Richard Burton leaves. Stanley gives us the news – they will not do *Sands of the Kalahari* at any price.

A week or so later and we get a publisher's note in the mail, telling us that they have sold the soon-to-be-released novel *The Flight of the Phoenix* to Jimmy Stewart. It's a story about a crashed plane in the desert, and how the disparate group of survivors come together to rebuild the plane. No-one turns into a camel, or seduces the female lead – there isn't one, it's a transport plane. Eventually *Sands of the Kalahari* is made after being passed by two more leading men, one of whom, George Peppard, actually gets as far as the location, and the picture is a miserable flop. Now we are in panic mode, *Zulu* is wrapping up and things are spinning out of control and Cy goes into overdrive. More bad news: the board game which Cy loved to play with the Zulus on location is of no interest to Parker Brothers. It's not new to them, and is in the public domain. Our idea of releasing it with characters from the movie on it is quashed.

We entertain Michael's roommate Terence Stamp and his model girlfriend, Jean Shrimpton. She is the most famous model in the world, and Terry is a handsome, young and successful actor. Cy gets a reply from Rank about their shared vision of doing *Precious Bane*. Rank not only owns the property, but had started pre-production before abandoning the project. They want £90,000 to release the rights, but Joe Levine sends back a strong wire saying he doesn't think American audiences have any interest in an 18th-century costume drama about a girl with a hare lip (for most of the movie). Jean Shrimpton with a hare lip seems lousy to me, too. Cy goes into hyperdrive and turns out a fresh script of his own, called *Night*. It is especially written for the pair of them. It's 24 hours of a tour de force set around a young sculptor and his lover. Terry asks for $12,000 from Cy, in a kind of goodwill gesture, for his investment in *Skater Dater*, a kids' picture built around the new US craze of sidewalk skating. Cy passes on the offer, and Terry passes on *Night*.

Jimmy Booth brings in a few pages of a script he is writing, based on an early episode in the life of Nelson. It is an adventure about his sailing up the Amazon. Cy dispatches me to the Reading Room at the British Museum, where I spend two or three fascinating days there, researching every contemporaneous document about early Nelson I can find, but other than the facts of his trip, I cannot locate anything that could be turned into Act Two (let alone Act Three). We try to get the rights to a short film based on a science-fiction story Cy has fallen in love with. A young boy turns into a chicken through a mixed-up experiment. (After all, we have several thousand feet of free negative sitting in the cupboard.) No luck: there is no reply from the publisher, and although Stanley is happy with the screenplay treatment (I get a young director on board) we judge it too dangerous to move without copyright approval. We consider starting a TV commercial production company and try and get Cliff Owen to join in with us, to get a group of directors to market. Cliff – a good friend – passes on the suggestion. He has more work than he can deal with.

The budget on *Zulu* closes, and my salary ceases. My rent is due, and I need a job so, I press the reset button and find that thirty seconds isn't such a bad length after all. I join Foote Cone and Belding as a TV producer (at £2,200 per annum). Cy and I start to make commercials together again. Life is sweet.

Post Script: A year or two later (I can't be sure of the date), Cy and Stanley take legal action in a dispute with Paramount over the profits from *Zulu* and their percentage. It was settled out of court.

Ian Fawn-Meade
Fosbury Village, Wiltshire
August 2009

DEFENDING *ZULU*

> Since publication of the first edition of this book, I have often been asked why I didn't add a critical analysis of *Zulu* – a review or 'reading' of the film itself – to my account of its production history. My answer has always been that an extended analysis of that kind belonged in a different sort of book and that, in any case, there wasn't the space: an interpretation which did full justice to the film would require a booklet along the lines of the BFI Film Classics series of monographs. I did, however, point people in the direction of an article I had written previously (before I started work on my own book) for inclusion in an edited collection, *British Historical Cinema* (edited by Claire Monk and Amy Sargeant, London: Routledge, 2002). But as that article is now more than a decade old, it seemed to me in preparing this new edition of *With Some Guts Behind It* that in I should make a second attempt at saying what I tried to argue there. The newly written chapter offered here draws substantially on the earlier one but also includes some fresh thoughts prompted by writers more critical of *Zulu* than the present author.

Why 'Defending *Zulu*'? For some readers the film will need no defence; for others, none will be possible. It has actually been described to me as 'indefensible' in a discussion on the social media website Facebook, and a number of contributors agreed. The reason for this is what are presumed to be the film's racial politics and also its position on British imperial history – in particular, the perception that *Zulu* endorses imperialism and all that goes with it. I hope it is clear from this book that I do not believe the film either to be racist or imperialist – certainly not in any straightforward, unproblematic way – but as a case can be made to the contrary I think it worth taking the time to spell out what can be said in its favour, as a response to criticisms that have often been made and will no doubt continue to be made. This, then, is my case for the defence.

Let's begin with the political context of the film's original release in 1964. The popularity of *Zulu* in Britain has led hostile critics to identify an ideological role for the film in the 1960s comparable with that of the Battle of Rorke's Drift itself for the Victorians. Following Indian independence in 1947, the 1950s and early 1960s bore witness to the crumbling of Britain's colonial power, as one subject nation after another declared its independence. Between 1956 and 1968, more than thirty former dependencies, mainly in Africa, achieved self-rule – seventeen in 1960 alone, the year of Harold Macmillan's famous 'wind of change' speech before the South African parliament.[1] Popular support for a film which represented the victory of a beleaguered White minority over an insurgent racial Other could thus easily be read as an expression of White British feelings of loss and resentment regarding the changing post-colonial landscape. The film's highly organised, fiercely belligerent 'native' forces could be seen as an objective correlative for the ascendant or newly independent African nations, and their defeat as appealing to reactionary nostalgia for imperial power and dominance over subject races.

It is no surprise, then, that for many present-day observers, *Zulu* is a pernicious misrepresentation: a film which, in selecting an atypical incident as the basis for an heroic epic, inverts historical reality, portraying the victims of imperialist aggression as themselves the aggressors, and the White imperialist forces as an oppressed minority. From this perspective, the film is at best 'anachronistic – a last desperate bid to mount an old-style imperial epic', or 'spectacular but mostly mindless'.[2] At worst, it is 'an epic step backwards [which] only reveals the racial conservatism of much liberal-inclined English movie-making'.[3] Jim Pines, the author of this last comment, later expanded on his judgement in a programme note produced to accompany a screening of *Zulu* as part of a 1986 National Film Theatre season entitled 'Images of Empire':

> In the context of Images of Empire, this colonial war adventure can only be seen as exploitative pulp – although in general most reviewers have shown an ambivalence towards the film's sheer force and impact ... What seems to be in play here is some notion of historical authenticity, which not only heightens the film's unquestioned glorification of British heroism, but also disguises its more unsavoury aspects, of which there are many. The tendency in colonial narratives to collapse African characters into a (typically menacing) mass is grandly exhibited here. And despite the film's apparently 'liberal' gesture, in acknowledging the magnificence of the Zulu warriors – in a romanticised way – the main thrust is clearly toward emphasising the militaristic and, more importantly, spiritual superiority of the hugely outnumbered British. Not surprisingly, the political issues surrounding the historical events, particularly the African point of view, is [sic] of little concern in the film. In the end, 'the whites and Zulus go their separate ways,' as Raymond Durgnat wryly puts it. 'Real understanding is attained through – apartheid, might one say?'[4]

More recently, in 2001 Christopher Sharrett published a substantial article on *Zulu* in the American journal *Cineaste*, one that professes to acknowledge the film's virtues yet constitutes perhaps the most sustained critical attack on it to date. Sharrett argues that *Zulu*'s 'liberal ideological veneer cloaks a reliance on a surprising number of generic conventions as well as some key historical distortions and omissions in order to perpetuate its own colonialist political agenda'.[5] It is important to address here the assumptions on which this argument is built. Sharrett seems to assume that the genre conventions deployed in the film – principally those of the Western and the war film, though he also links *Zulu* to the horror and science-fiction genres – are inherently conservative and repressive; that the use of these conventions necessarily conflicts with any attempt at a 'truthful' representation of historical actuality and perhaps with 'realism' in general; and that historical truth, insofar as it can be determined, should be the primary concern of any film which dramatises

an event from history. All three points seem to me highly arguable, and at times are even contradicted by Sharrett himself: for example, he demands historical accuracy from *Zulu* but wants to be spared even its token depiction of nineteenth-century attitudes and language ('fuzzies') uncongenial to a modern liberal sensibility.

On the matter of historical reconstruction, as I argued in Chapter 1 of this book, I would contend that filmmakers, like other artists, are entitled to as much latitude as they care to take in adapting the raw material of history to the demands of dramatic narrative. Their interests and responsibilities are those of dramatists, not historians. Nevertheless, the analysis of a film's 'distortions' of documented historical truth may indeed reveal the existence of an ideological agenda. As previously discussed, there is certainly plentiful evidence to support the common claim that *Zulu* 'gets it wrong' – often deliberately – in areas ranging from the appearance and characterisation of the main protagonists and the order of events in the battle, to details of uniforms, equipment and physical locations. Ironically, the fact that *Zulu* characterises the British participants – often unflatteringly – in greater depth than the Zulus left it particularly susceptible to objections from the descendants of the former. As noted in Chapter 5, Lieutenant-Colonel Sir Benjamin Bromhead, who had been a senior military guest of honour at the film's London premiere, wrote to the *Daily Telegraph* (28 February 1964) in protest at the portrayal of his great-uncle Gonville, while members of the Hook family have also had cause to voice their displeasure.

Within the sphere of historical reconstruction in the fiction film, it is necessary to distinguish between *accuracy* of detail and *authenticity* of impression. The latter is less a matter of strict fidelity to the recorded historical facts than of the achievement of dramatic verisimilitude – that is, a convincing illusion. This verisimilitude may depend upon one or more of the following: the fulfilment of viewers' expectations through adherence to established representational conventions; the reinvigoration of conventions which had appeared to be exhausted; or seeming to break through 'convention' to a more direct apprehension of (what we imagine to be) 'the truth', which may in itself lead to the establishment of a new set of conventions. *Zulu* works largely within the second of these three modes, drawing upon established generic conventions while adapting them to the emerging values of the 1960s.

One of the main criticisms made by Sharrett and others is that *Zulu* offers little or no historical contextualisation that would enable the uninformed spectator to understand the place of the battle in the Anglo-Zulu War or that of the war in British imperial policy. An introductory voiceover is often used in historical epics – *The Fall of the Roman Empire* (1964), for instance – to provide contextualisation of this kind. But the narration spoken by Richard Burton at the beginning of *Zulu* consists only of the opening paragraphs of a letter reporting the massacre at Isandhlwana, even fading out before the reading is completed as sound and image dissolve into the flames of the devastated battlefield. At the film's end, Burton reads the roll-call of Victoria Cross honourees, but all other immediately relevant data (such as the number and ranks of the defenders) is disclosed via action and dialogue, and then only selectively. The film suggests, for example, that the British casualty rate was higher than it was in reality, even though a body count reveals no more than fifteen British deaths actually depicted on screen. Beyond this, historical 'analysis' is scant. Even the – disputable – strategic importance of the post at Rorke's Drift, which was seen at the time as the last line of defence protecting Natal Colony from Zulu invasion, is not made explicit.

This sparsity of historical information can however be viewed as a symptom of *Zulu*'s equivocal character as an 'epic'. The battle it recreates was relatively minor in national or global impact; its principal value to Britain was as a much-needed diversion from the disaster at Isandhlwana. It did not announce the imminent rise or fall of a civilisation as many epics do (*The Fall of the Roman Empire* again being a relevant example). Nor does the film's narrative sweep over a broad geographical or historical span, as do those of most epics; indeed, the story is notable for its compactness, unfolding over less than two days and remaining largely in one place. Its visual spectacle aside, *Zulu*'s epic qualities are largely of the folkloric kind, in that it recounts great heroic deeds of the past for the admiration and moral inspiration of present generations. The battle constitutes material for an epic primarily because of the fantastically disproportionate military odds involved, and the extremes of courage and fortitude required of both the defenders and attackers.

Sharrett's article fails to mention the epic genre and while he is right to invoke the conventions of the Western and war film in his discussion, he draws the wrong conclusions from them. It is no more than a commonplace to observe that the American Western and the British imperial adventure resemble one another in many respects. Hollywood has produced any number of films in both genres sharing the same landscapes, themes, plots and personnel. In the mid-1960s, both the Western and the British imperial adventure were undergoing crucial transformations in response to a changing cultural and political climate, transformations of which *Zulu* is clearly symptomatic. The decade saw the appearance in America of the 'revisionist' Western, expressing an increasingly disillusioned view of the relations between White America and its indigenous peoples. Two key examples, released within a few months of *Zulu*, were John Ford's final Western, the bitter, pro-Native American *Cheyenne Autumn* (1964); and Raoul Walsh's last film, *A Distant Trumpet* (1964), the first sound Western to include subtitled translations of Native-American dialogue.

In Britain, *North West Frontier* (1959) was perhaps the last major production to endorse unambiguously the virtues of colonial rule – although even there, the British were shown to be embattled by the forces of Indian nationalism. The 1960s brought a cycle of 'post-imperial' British films – often, like *Zulu*, American-financed prestige productions – which conveyed a sense of the impending end of Empire or a more complex and ambivalent attitude towards it. These included *Lawrence of Arabia* (1962), *Khartoum* (1966) and *The Charge of the Light Brigade* (1968). Emerging alongside, and in some cases anticipating, them was a less distinguished, mostly low-budget series of colonial swashbucklers with native rebels as heroes: *Zarak* (1956), *The Bandit of Zhobe* (1959), *The Brigand of Kandahar* (1965) and *The Long Duel* (1967).[6]

The kinship between the Western and the British imperial adventure is matched by that between British and American examples of the war film. Jeanine Basinger has listed sixteen distinctive 'generic requirements' of the World War II combat film, as established in such pictures as *Wake Island* (1942) and *Bataan* (1943) and maintained or developed in the majority of subsequent U.S. and British war films.[7] All but one of these requirements are met directly or indirectly by *Zulu*. For example: Chard performs the role of 'a hero who is part of the group, but is forced to separate himself from it because of the demands of leadership'. The film features 'internal group conflicts' (between Chard and Bromhead, among the private soldiers, and between Chard and the pacifist missionaries the Witts); a 'faceless enemy' (in the sense that the Zulus are seen mostly from a distance and are not characterised in depth); and 'the need to remember and discuss home' (here, the Welsh privates' nostalgia for the valleys).

Significantly, however, the one generic element of war films missing from *Zulu* is 'propaganda, the discussion of why we fight and how justified it is'. At no point in the film do officers or other ranks discuss the political justification or strategic objectives of the war and the battle in which they are engaged. The remoteness of the Anglo-Zulu War, and the Victorian military-colonialist ethos, for 1960s audiences is one explanation for this omission. Another is that the film, following a common convention of the combat genre, presents battle from the point of view of the foot soldier – here, ranks no higher than lieutenant – rather than from that of generals, strategists and politicians. The loss of overview is compensated for in dramatic terms by a close identification with the ground-level participants.

The duty of lower-ranking officers and men was and is to follow orders, not to question them or determine the reasons for obeying them. Chard and Bromhead have received orders to hold their ground at Rorke's Drift, and most of their own discussions and disagreements relate to the most effective ways of achieving that objective. The film's one clear reference to the larger context of colonial politics beyond the characters' immediate situation comes in a brief, good-natured but suggestive exchange between Bromhead and the Boer officer Adendorff (Gert van den Bergh):

ADENDORFF
I'm a Boer, the Zulus are the enemy of my blood. What are you doing here?

BROMHEAD
You don't object to our help, I hope?

ADENDORFF
It all depends on what you damned English want for it, afterwards.

While barely commenting on colonial politics, the film does, however, repeatedly give expression to the subordinate ranks' sense of frustration and bewilderment at their very presence in Africa. Ordered to prepare defences in the hospital where he is confined, Private Hook (James Booth) wants to know: 'What for? Did I see a Zulu walk down the City Road? No – so why am I here?' As the soldiers wait expectantly for the first Zulu attack, the nervous, sweating Private Cole (Gary Bond) asks Colour-Sergeant Bourne (Nigel Green): 'Why is it us, eh? Why us?' and receives the stoical reply: 'Because we're here, lad – nobody else. Just us.' Later, mortally wounded, Cole repeatedly asks a similar question of Surgeon Reynolds (Patrick Magee) and is told, 'I'm damned if I can tell you why'. The precise object of the question 'Why?' is left deliberately vague. It may refer to Cole's own imminent death, the specific action of defending Rorke's Drift, or the European colonial presence in Africa; exact interpretation is left to the spectator. Equivalent rhetorical questions can be found in other war films of the period: in *Waterloo* (1970) a soldier repeatedly screams 'Why?!' to no-one in particular as he staggers around the bloody battlefield, the line echoing prominently on the soundtrack as the camera pulls back in a globalising helicopter shot.

Zulu's ambivalence concerning the British presence in Africa is further suggested by the soldiers' continuous visual prominence amid the African surroundings, where they frequently appear displaced and ill at ease. Much of the film's pleasure as spectacle derives from the contrasting splendours of spruce military uniforms, traditional Zulu (un)dress and massive, stark landscapes. Private Thomas (Neil McCarthy) comments on the contrast between the parched grasslands of South Africa and the greenery of his native Wales. In doing so, he draws the viewer's attention to the highly visible incongruity of red-clad White men in a geographical terrain in which they clearly do not belong and to which they are ill-suited. Frequent long shots take advantage of the towering mountain scenery surrounding Rorke's Drift (or rather the film's reconstruction of it in the Drakensberg, a landscape quite unlike that surrounding the

real mission), emphasising the smallness and vulnerability of the European outpost. The point is also made early on in the film when the camera tracks along a row of warriors in feathered costume to halt before the anachronistic sight of the Reverend Otto Witt (Jack Hawkins) and his daughter Margareta (Ulla Jacobsson) ensconced among them.

The Zulus, by contrast – heard before they are seen by the British soldiers via the eerie sound of assegais rattling against war shields, 'like a train in the distance' – seem to emerge from the land itself. They are first glimpsed arrayed on the crest of a hill overlooking the garrison, gradually appearing from behind it to fill and dominate the horizon. Throughout their assaults, the Zulus are able to take cover in gullies and dips in the land, seeming to blend in to the landscape as if part of it: 'I can't see a bloody one now.' 'They've gone to ground.' 'Oh.'[8]

A further key war-movie convention listed by Basinger is that 'the attitudes that an audience should take to the war are taught through events, conversations, and actions'. As we saw in Chapter 18, some of Zulu's contemporary reviewers lamented that the attitudes the film dramatised were those of the 1960s, not the 1870s, and there is some validity in this objection. Again, the issue here is questionable dramatic verisimilitude, not lack of fidelity to the known or assumed views of actual historical figures. The film's protagonists display none of the unashamed jingoism and casual racism, especially in the use of colloquial language, that one might expect to find among nineteenth-century soldiery (and which is evident in the testimonies of actual survivors of the battle, such as those collected by Ian Knight and Ian Castle).[9]

Instead, most of the White characters speak well of the Zulus. The Swiss Corporal Schiess (Dickie Owen) swiftly quashes a Welsh soldier's assumption that their foe is a 'bunch of savages, isn't it?' by praising the Zulus' physical capabilities. The Welsh are equally impressed by the Zulus' courage and stamina in the battle, remarking that 'they've got more guts than we have, boyo'.[10] Sharrett suggests that this is merely a form of imperialist self-aggrandisement: 'The emphasis on the superhuman skills of the Other makes all the more grand the white victory'.[11] It seems that for him the film is damned whatever it does.

The most derogatory comment we hear made about the Zulus, uttered by Bromhead about the native auxiliaries who died with the column at Isandhlwana ('Damn the levies man – more cowardly blacks'), is forcefully denounced by, of all characters, the Boer Adendorff. The White viewer is never encouraged to take a simplistically racist attitude towards 'the enemy' – at least insofar as such attitudes are not directly dramatised on screen. Viewers determined to read the film in racist terms can, of course, still do so: filmmakers may attempt to guide spectators' responses, but cannot hope to determine them. Thus another correspondent to the *Daily Telegraph* (also 28 February 1964), one Major F. A. I. de Gruchy, asserted that Rorke's Drift (the battle itself, not the film's recreation) demonstrated 'the eternal story of the British Empire, won often in the fields at odds of 100 to one ... the victory of quality against mere quantity.' De Gruchy gave no indication in his letter of actually having seen *Zulu*.

Another common criticism of the film (see for example Pines, Sharrett, and Knight and Castle) is that it fails to offer any Zulu or African perspective on the events depicted, since its drama is narrated almost entirely from the point of view, in the broadest sense, of the British soldiers. Subjective shots from White characters' literal (subjective) points of view are in fact given only, and then very briefly, to Chard during the battle (when he has to defend himself against two Zulu attackers) and in the wedding sequence to Margareta; but contrary to Sharrett's claim, the latter do not '[anchor] audience point of view and [embody] its sensibility', as the character never becomes sufficiently sympathetic to invite viewer identification.[12] A number of shots in the film do in fact show the British encampment from the Zulus' position in the hills surrounding the mission. We see, for example, Zulus training rifles they have recovered from the Isandhlwana battlefield on the British soldiers, and being ordered by their commanders not to attack the departing Witts. These are, however, brief inserts, insufficient to disrupt the spectator's predominant engagement with the British side. (I will mention one small exception to this pattern later.)

It is true also that King Cetewayo is the film's sole clearly individuated Zulu character, though his role is very small. Three other Zulu actors are credited in addition to Chief Buthelezi, but the few words of dialogue spoken by him and these others are not subtitled in English; they are instead translated to Margareta and the audience by the Reverend Witt. One possible rationale for this – although one that is open to debate – is suggested by Ian Knight and Ian Castle:

> The use of the single word Zulu as the [film's] title is intended to conjure up the potent myth, which dates back to the war itself, that the Zulus were the epitome of African savagery. To provide a Zulu voice within the film would have served only to dilute this objective, but it does reveal how inherently limited such a mythology is.[13]

In the film's screenplay, however (as discussed in Chapter 3 of this book), a young Zulu boy whom Witt has taught English and named Jacob (seen standing between Witt and Cetewayo and played by Daniel Tshabalala) *was* given a brief speech which would have supplied both historical information and a Zulu viewpoint: 'The great Nkosi Cetewayo is angry. He says the red-coated soldiers are already upon his land and wish to take all the hills between the Blood River and the Buffalo'. When news of the Isandhlwana massacre is received, Jacob renounces his designated Christian name and grins in triumph at his people's victory.

This restricted point-of-view, however problematic ideologically, nevertheless serves to strengthen the film's dramatic effectiveness. It enables the viewer to share without distraction the British soldiers' feelings of terror and entrapment at finding themselves in a situation not of their own making and beyond their control. *Zulu* can be compared in this respect to another, contemporaneous transatlantic group of films concerned with siege, or 'last stand', situations: *The Alamo* (1960), *55 Days at Peking* (1963) and, again, *Khartoum*. The effectiveness of siege narratives depends heavily upon the viewer siding with one set of protagonists over another, even if the antagonists are characterised in some depth (as is the case in *Peking* and *Khartoum*). The sense of isolation experienced by the soldiers at Rorke's Drift, and the construction of empathy with their fears – not in themselves racist – of an unknown, overwhelming and intimidating enemy, logically demand a concentration upon the besieged faction.

The pitfalls of more dispersed patterns of identification are well enough demonstrated by *Zulu*'s belated 'prequel', also co-written by Cy Endfield, *Zulu Dawn* (1879). A critical and commercial failure, the later film re-enacts the Zulu massacre of British forces at Isandhlwana on the same day as Rorke's Drift in the manner of the epic battle reconstructions which were also a feature of the 1960s international cinema; examples include *The Longest Day* (1962), *Battle of Britain* (1969), *Tora! Tora! Tora!* (1970) and *Waterloo*. Peter Watkins' 1964 docudrama 'reconstruction' *Culloden* for BBC Television, written by *Zulu* screenwriter John Prebble and based on his book, should also be located in relation to this cycle.

The greater scale of the Isandhlwana engagement and its more sprawling nature – as well as the fact of the Zulus' victory – demanded a different treatment from that of the Battle of Rorke's Drift in *Zulu*. Accordingly, *Zulu Dawn* intercuts among a large number of parallel plotlines and characters, including the kind of contextualising material on British colonial policy and the military aims of the war missing from *Zulu*. There are also scenes set in the Zulus' encampment without White characters present to 'mediate' the drama for a presumed White Anglophone audience. Zulu dialogue is given subtitled translation and the film features several sympathetically individuated Zulu characters, including King Cetewayo (played by Simon Sabela, who also appeared as a dance leader and stuntman in *Zulu*). Yet the result is diffuse and unwieldy, confused rather than enlightening, and almost wholly lacking in dramatic tension. *Zulu Dawn* is more explicit than *Zulu* about the egregiousness of European empire-building. By contrast, *Zulu*'s relative vagueness and indirectness, diffusing any commentary on imperialism into a more generalised, but also more resonant, sense of the British soldiers' displacement and disorientation, can be seen to work greatly in its favour.

It is doubtful that any unambiguously

anti-imperialist film could have been made about Rorke's Drift. Filmmakers wishing to make such a statement would surely instead have chosen the battles of Isandhlwana or Ulundi, where the Zulu nation was finally routed with even greater one-sided slaughter. *Zulu* is neither straightforwardly pro- nor anti-imperialist; it is, rather, *unconvinced* by the imperialist project. The opportunities for death-or-glory romanticism that its subject offers are for the most part emphatically refused, or admitted in only the most equivocal terms. The exchange of impressions between Bromhead and Chard, as they take stock when the fight appears to be won, presents neither triumphant self-congratulation nor the jocular banter of relieved survivors, but rather the officers' weariness and revulsion at their first direct experience of mass bloodshed and their discovery of their own capacity for violence:

CHARD
Well, you've fought your first action.

BROMHEAD
Does everyone feel like this, afterwards?

CHARD
How *do* you feel?

BROMHEAD
Sick.

CHARD
Well, you have to be alive to feel sick.

BROMHEAD
You asked me, I told you. (pause) There's something else. I feel ashamed. Was that how it was for you – the first time?

CHARD
The first time? Do you think I could stand this butcher's yard more than once?

Displays of fighting tactics are nevertheless a crucial element in the film's generic vocabulary. Like any combat film, 'anti-war' or otherwise, *Zulu* entertains its audience with the spectacular depiction of violent death. However, it seems to me the film is able to reconcile the unavoidable contradiction of offering pleasure based on violence while acknowledging its terrible human consequences. This is apparent not only in the dialogue just quoted but also in, particularly, the sequence of the final Zulu assault, at the end of which the camera moves slowly across a field littered with Black bodies to close in on the small group of White soldiers staring out at the carnage with a

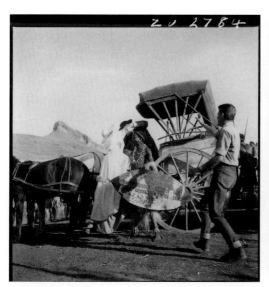

LOST MAN FOUND
Dickie Owen (Corporal Frederick Schiess, NNC)

The first edition of this book laid down a challenge for readers: I asked for anyone with information on Dickie Owen's present whereabouts to contact the publisher. In 1988, answering the latest of many fruitless inquiries about this mysterious, missing-in-action character actor, magazine columnist David McGillivray had commented of Owen, 'who as far as this column is concerned is a veritable Lord Lucan, I can only assume that he has a network of friends feverishly protecting his anonymity. He disappeared twenty years ago leaving nary a trace. Three appeals in these pages have failed to turn up as much as a left luggage receipt' ('Now You Know,' Films and Filming, June 1988, p. 47).

Two years after my book was published, however, there were several rumoured sightings – or rather, soundings. Someone claiming to be Dickie Owen called in to a late-night radio phone-in show and chatted at length about his career. I tried contacting the station to see if they could put me in touch with him, but never received a reply. Then, only a few months later, I received an email from Robert Vantan. He said that his wife, a reception officer at Deptford police station, had been dealing with an elderly gentleman involved in a civil dispute. Chatting while she assisted him, he had regaled her with stories about the time when he had been an actor, appearing in plays and films including Zulu. Aware that her husband was a fan, she called Robert from work to tell him that she was at that very moment with Dickie Owen! I asked that, if by any chance he called at the station again, my contact details be passed on. Three weeks later, Dickie did indeed reappear and subsequently left a message on my office answerphone, asking me to call him back late at night – he didn't go to bed until daylight... Thus it was that, shortly after midnight on 29 February 2008, I finally solved one of the great mysteries of filmdom.

Dickie and I talked for nearly an hour. It proved difficult to keep him on track – anecdotes spilled out, about his work in theatre as well as film and especially about his love of old music-hall songs: over the phone, he recited the lyrics of 'The Night I Appeared as Macbeth'. He was born on 26 March 1927, the son of a Great War veteran – his father spent fifteen months in the trenches. One of Dickie's first stage jobs was a two-week stint in a melodrama alongside the great barnstormer Tod Slaughter as 'Spring-Heeled Jack'. When Owen's fake beard fell off during a fight scene, Slaughter ad-libbed, 'I knew that fellow was in disguise!' Dickie is 6 feet 4? inches tall so often found himself playing policemen in such films as A Touch of Larceny (1959) and Three Hats for Lisa (1966), or in military roles, such as Chitty Chitty Bang Bang (1968) alongside Zulu's Larry Taylor. He appeared in The Young Mr. Pitt (1942), It Always Rains on Sunday

Dickie Owen with the author at the fiftieth anniversary screening of Zulu at the Odeon, Leicester Square, in June 2014.

(1947), *Passport to Pimlico* (1949) and *Inn for Trouble* (1960), provided battle noises for the epic *Solomon and Sheba* (1959) and was the voice of the titular gorilla in *Konga* (1961).

He played opposite Stanley Baker in *The Criminal* and *Hell Is a City* (both 1960) and they became friendly, leading to Dickie's casting in *Zulu*. He spent two months on location in South Africa but says that he was only paid for two weeks' work (his fee was £220). Given the money for a first-class air fare home after completing his part, he instead made his way to Durban, joined a shipping line as a waiter and kept the fare along with his per diem; he needed the money to get married on. In the Hammer horror *The Curse of the Mummy's Tomb* (1964) Dickie was clothbound, but on the first day of shooting as the mummy he 'became a daddy' and was given an extra scene as a present. For the sequel, *The Mummy's Shroud* (1967), Joe Powell's brother Eddie stepped into the bandages while Dickie blacked up as the bodyguard slave Prem and tackled Pharaoh's assassins with spear and shield, evoking memories of Schiess duelling Zulus with his crutch and rifle. Prem, he said, gave him his longest screen time in any of his forty-odd films.

Latterly offers dried up ('I never found an agent who understood me', he said) and Dickie slipped out of acting around 1970, for 'domestic reasons'. After his marriage broke up, his wife had taken their two young daughters to live in America; he went there to bring them back. He subsequently had a car accident which broke a leg and left him out of action for several months – shades of Schiess again. After that, he didn't want to resume acting and found other things to do, including taking over a furniture shop and becoming a taxi driver. In his early seventies he had a couple of heart attacks and 21 months before we spoke he had undergone an operation to remove a benign tumour from his brain. He told me that he is a great fan of Harold Lloyd and goes regularly to the BFI Southbank, but hadn't paid to go to a commercial cinema in 35 years.

I eventually met up with Dickie in person two years after our telephone conversation in July 2010, when we were both among the guests at the launch of a *Zulu* exhibition held at the London Film Museum in the former County Hall, also on the South Bank. Raffishly dressed in tweed hat and cravat, and clearly enjoying his emergence from obscurity, he entertained the packed audience with anecdotes which were always colourful, if not entirely verifiable.

mixture of disbelief, horror and sheer exhaustion. (In a seminar discussion I had about the film with undergraduate students, one said that the soldiers appeared disgusted with what they had done.)

Despite the absence from *Zulu* of a Black African perspective, compensation in the form of what might be called a 'Zulu discourse' is nevertheless embedded in the film in two ways: in the presentation of the Zulus' conduct in the battle scenes, and through the use of music. The film's visual depiction of the Zulus does not support Jim Pines' charge that *Zulu* reproduces 'the tendency in colonial narratives to collapse African characters into a (typically menacing) mass'. The Zulu forces are shown arrayed in clearly defined ranks and columns, making specific tactical manoeuvres with recognisable aims and objectives – thus also contradicting Sharrett's claim that 'the racial Other seems to have no rational strategy whatsoever'.[14] The Zulus are directed by their officers as an organised, disciplined army, and their military conduct is shown to be neither irrational nor inexplicable. The film's use of its Zulu extras is equally purposeful – in contrast with *Zulu Dawn*, in which, perhaps because of the larger numbers involved, the Zulus do indeed appear to swarm over the landscape in shapeless and disorganised masses, overwhelming the British positions through sheer force of numbers rather than tactical skill.

In its battle choreography, *Zulu* shows the Zulu forces to be fended off by the British by means of a superior position and weaponry and effective defensive tactics. The tactics we see enacted by *both* sides – the Zulus' 'buffalo formation' attack plan, as explained by Adendorff, their systematic assaults on the British positions, and the British soldiers' close-formation volley firing – are more orderly and structured than was apparently the case in the actual battle, which by most eyewitness accounts was something of a free-for-all. This gives the film's action scenes a representativeness beyond the reconstruction of a particular event: we see, in microcosm, the fighting skills as well as the weapons that won both the Zulus and the British their respective empires.

While courage and heroism are shown to be crucial to the outcome of the battle, only a partial or careless viewer could conclude that the film sees them on the British side only. Indeed, the Zulus' massed salute to the surviving British defenders before their final departure from the screen is, the film makes clear, as much a gesture of mercy or magnanimity on their part as of respect: the British fighting spirit having been effectively exhausted, Bromhead calls on the Zulus to get it over with and put the defenders out of their misery. Like the Zulus themselves with their final gesture, *Zulu* seems to celebrate and pay tribute to the qualities of courage and heroism for their own sakes – but without hyperbole, and without endorsing the imperialist context that provides the occasion for their display. The impression the film leaves is of a spiritual parity between the two opposing forces, not the superiority of one over the other. This is most effectively illustrated in a sequence which may be dismissed by detractors as merely sentimental: the exchange of battle songs prior to the final assault, as the Zulus' mourning and war chants are answered by the Welshmen's fortifying chorus of 'Men of Harlech'. The intercutting between them, in sound and image, is for me the film's most thrilling passage.

Of equal significance to the film's presentation of the Zulus is John Barry's sweeping symphonic score, which makes use of indigenous tribal music as the basis of its thematic structure. According to Cy Endfield's sleeve notes to the original *Zulu* soundtrack album (Ember NR 5012, dated March 1964), Barry 'used the themes of traditional Zulu music, elevated them with his musical skill into thrilling and dramatic musical effects to support and give character to some of the mighty moments from the film's dramatic content'. As discussed in Chapter 14, the massed dance in the early wedding sequence includes the music from which Barry derived the Zulu *leitmotif* for his score. The martial orchestration of this theme in *Zulu* contrasts with Barry's later reworking of it in a softer, slower, more melancholic mood for the second filming of Alan Paton's 1948 anti-apartheid novel *Cry, the Beloved Country* (1995), where it assumes an even more pointed significance, particularly for anyone familiar with *Zulu*. The theme was also adapted by Barry as a modern pop instrumental called 'Monkey Feathers', recorded as tie-in promotional material for *Zulu*.

This merging of Western and Zulu musical traditions in the *Zulu* score further symbolises the spiritual equality the film accords to the two cultures. Of course, the film's critics might argue that this is a further instance of its suppression of an authentic Zulu viewpoint – perhaps even a form of cultural imperialism, with a Western orchestra colonising Zulu music. But a reverse interpretation – that Zulu rhythms are infiltrating the European symphonic tradition – is equally feasible. We are dealing here with meaning at the *non-representational* level, where interpretation is especially conjectural. But it is precisely such ambiguities and resonances that give *Zulu* its unusual distinction. It cannot be reduced to a simplistic 'positive' or 'negative' message or statement, nor can its values be read off straightforwardly from a synopsis of its plot. As a product of White, First-World culture, *Zulu* could not possibly be expected to 'speak for' the Zulus; nor could its makers ever validly have claimed to represent the Zulus' viewpoint authentically. It accomplishes instead an impressive gesture of respect, much like that offered by Chard in its closing shot.[15] As the end titles play out over the image of a single Zulu war shield, erected by Chard as a kind of makeshift gravestone or memorial to the Zulu dead, a choral reprise of 'Men of Harlech' ultimately gives way to an emphatic orchestral restatement of the Zulu-influenced main theme.

Postscript

The above is a condensed, reedited version of the chapter first published in *British Historical Cinema* in 2002. In a review of the present book (mostly favourable) in the online version of *Cineaste* magazine, Christopher Sharrett – whose critique of *Zulu* is discussed above – expressed regret that 'critical interrogation' was not part of this book's project. But he also took issue both with my earlier article and with James Chapman's positive account of the film in his own book *Past and Present: National Identity and the British Historical Film* (London: I.B. Tauris, 2005). Sharrett remarks that my and Chapman's defences of the film are so much 'flowery special pleading', especially our insistence that the film should be seen in, and judged against, the context of its moment of production rather than with a political agenda establshed with the benefit of hindsight.[16]

Although naturally I disagree with Sharrett in this regard, I do think he may have a point that my argument, or at least some aspects of it, constitutes a case of special pleading. This is not to say that I concede much ground to *his* analysis of the film, but I can at least see where my defence might be found wanting. In particular, I'm now less certain about the use of music as one of the ways that the film characterises the Zulus. I'm taking into account here some criticisms of the film put to me by Elliot Ngubane and briefly discussed in Chapter 11: that the Zulu songs used were not authentic to the period of the story, nor did the lyrics make sense in their dramatic context. Of course, a Western Anglophone audience, fifty years ago or now, could not be expected to know this and even a non-expert Zulu viewer (one unlike Elliot, who is both Zulu and expert!) might be unaware of the 'deception' involved. But in a way that is the point: the songs are stripped of their original meaning and used merely as a form of musical local colour, to evoke an exotic sense of Otherness for an audience alien to the culture being represented. Western cultural imperialism may not be too strong a description.

Further to this point, none other than Prince Buthelezi – whose mother, as I have previously noted, served as consultant for the film's use of indigenous music and dance – notes in his statement printed at the beginning of this book that he had gone so far as to dissociate himself in writing from the film's inauthentic use of songs. Buthelezi's public position regarding the film has in fact shifted somewhat over the years. Sharrett notes in his review of the book that I might have been 'taken aback' by the comments in Buthelezi's statement that he might have wished for a dramatisation of the Battle of Isandhlwana rather than of Rorke's Drift. In fact I was not, as I had heard Buthelezi express this view previously; nor did I take him to imply, as Sharrett seems to have done, that his comment that the film being '*supposed* to pay tribute to brave people on both sides of the conflict' (Sharrett's emphasis) somehow means that in the end it did not actually do this. I have since had the opportunity to clarify Buthelezi's view of the film in a personal interview with him, and he has also recently gone on record (in the award acceptance speech reprinted following the present chapter) as expressing a more emphatically positive view of the film than he has ever done before.

These views were echoed in press interviews with the Prince marking the film's fiftieth anniversary, in one of which – while repeating the criticisms he has previously made of the use of songs and the failure to represent Cetewayo's reluctance to go to war – he is reported to have described *Zulu* 'as a notable piece of PR for South Africa's largest ethnic group'. He is also quoted as saying: 'Whenever I am abroad people always know about the Zulus ... In Washington I was invited by a senior official from the State Department fir supper. And *Zulu* was playing on the television – they never realised I was in it until then.'[17] In yet another interview, Buthelezi recalled the impact of his people's participation in the film:

'In a sense we forgot we were in this country at the time. Whites and blacks could mingle without any fuss. You might say it was a very small thing for this country, which was so racist at the time, [but] it was something of great significance for us,' said Prince Buthelezi.

'The film helped restore [our] pride about where we came from – about how our people resisted the mightiest army in the world at the time, even though we were poorly equipped with our cow-hide shields and spears,' he said.[18]

So Sharrett's highly arguable statement in 2005 that 'Prince Buthelezi's revaluation of the film, combined with the years of suffering a racist regime, may have dimmed his early, always slightly bewildered interest in *Zulu*' now seems to have been definitively refuted. That said, Prince Buthelezi is not the ultimate authority on how the film is to be regarded. It could reasonably be argued that his very participation in it gives him a vested interest in defending its reputation, whatever his reservations. So his statements should not alone be used to ward off criticism. An argument has still to be made.

I'll end by conceding a point to the opposition – and then snatching it back again. The best, most persuasive critique of *Zulu* that I have read has not been published. It is in the form of a dissertation written in 1996 by Ian Watson as his submission for a Master of Arts degree in Art History at Leeds Metropolitan University, a copy of which the author kindly sent to me after reading the first edition of this book (Ian's son was a final-year student at my own university, though not in my subject area). Entitled *Bare Black Breasts and Boys Own Battles: Images of Empire for White Working Class Lads in Mid-Sixties Britain*, Mr. Watson's thesis provides a thoroughly well-documented, theoretically elaborated argument for seeing the film, and especially the way it has been experienced by audiences, as the largely unconscious product of an 'image network' – a realm of pictorial conventions which have shaped the way in which imperial history and the racial Other (as well as gender and class) are constructed and perceived. This image network, in relation to *Zulu*, includes the conventionalised presentation in history books, comics and the cinema of non-Western landscapes and peoples, along with violent warfare, as a site of spectacle to be consumed by the Western viewer. The film's original audiences were themselves a product of this image network, having been exposed to it from an early age in their formal education as well as from the social experience of seeing films in the action-adventure tradition. Irrespective of the intentions of the filmmakers and their own conscious political disposition, audiences were thus quite unaware that their way of seeing and relating to the colonial Other – in *Zulu*, the Zulus themselves – was implicated in a discourse of domination. According to this argument (I trust that I am not misrepresenting it), *Zulu* cannot help but be racist and imperialist because the whole Western way of understanding the Other was and is the product of a racist, imperialist world view from which neither the film nor its spectators can be detached.

Such a totalising argument is hard to counter, though there is small comfort in Watson's apparent admission, in his closing remarks, that for all his deconstruction of the film's pleasures, he can indeed still take pleasure in a film he first saw at the age of eight (the same age I was when I first encountered *Zulu*) and now sees from a much more critical perspective. Indeed, as I understand it, his aim with the dissertation was precisely to understand, using sophisticated theoretical tools, the meaning of the film as a cultural experience for a working-class White British boy such as himself in 1964. But I'd like to pick out one small chink in his otherwise closely linked chain of ideas, one that relates to issues discussed earlier in this chapter. In the course of his discussion, Watson makes much of the film's denial of the Zulus' point of view – as we have seen (no pun intended), a common way of characterising *Zulu* as racist. He states:

> By use of shot-countershot we are helped in our identification by seeing what 'they' [the White protagonists] are seeing, and then seeing 'their' reaction to it. This is not something that is presented for the Zulus in the film. The all-seeing spectator is thus never allowed to identify with the Zulu gaze, not even by shot-countershot. We, the spectators, even in the scenes where the only characters on screen are Zulus, are not invited to 'see' events from their viewpoint.[19]

By and large, this is true. But there is one small exception to this general rule – one which allows, however briefly, the spectator to place themselves in the position of a Zulu character. Turn back the pages of this book to the very beginning and look at the pair of small frame blow-ups reproduced opposite the list of Contents. These images provide a good example, for readers unfamiliar with the vocabulary of Film Studies, of the typical shot-countershot pattern: Colour-Sergeant Bourne, at screen left, looks off right at the Zulu he is about to engage in combat; cut to a reverse-angle shot of the Zulu (played by stuntman John Marcus), positioned at screen right and looking off left to meet Bourne's gaze in the previous shot. These two frames are part of a brief sequence of shots showing this encounter amidst the melée of fighting at the North Wall. The sequence ends with Bourne bayoneting the Zulu (again off-screen right) and raising up to look around after delivering the final thrust (see the colour frame grabs in one of the plate sections). I mention this series of shots because I can recall quite clearly my own reaction to seeing them on my first viewing of the film. I shared (and felt the audience sharing) the Zulu's sense of intimidation when confronted by the formidable figure of Bourne holding his bayoneted rifle in the 'engage' position. In the reverse shots I could see the fear in the Zulu's face; but the shot-countershot principle also worked to show Bourne from the Zulu's approximate point of view. Fleetingly, I empathised with him – in my imagination I shared the experience of the racial Other in a way that, according to Watson's argument, I could not and should not have done. Just for a moment, the 'image network' was broken and I identified with 'them' as well as 'us'.

Notes

[1] In this speech Macmillan declared: 'The wind of change is blowing through this continent [Africa], and whether we like it or not, this growth of national consciousness is a political fact.'

[2] Martin Auty, 'Revolting natives', *The Movie*, no. 70 (1981), p. 1392; Kenneth M. Cameron, *Africa on Film: Beyond Black and White* (New York: Continuum, 1994), p. 141.

[3] Jim Pines, *Blacks in Films: A Survey of Racial Themes and Images in the American Film* (London: Studio Vista, 1975), p. 78.

[4] Jim Pines, 'Images of Empire: colonial surveillance', NFT programme note, 7 June 1986. The source of the quoted comment is Raymond Durgnat, *A Mirror for England: British Movies from Austerity to Affluence* (London: Faber and Faber, 1970), p. 82. Durgnat's condemnation depends on sophistry for its effect: if 'separatism' is substituted for 'apartheid' – the Zulus do, after all, *choose* to leave the battlefield – the connotation becomes significantly different.

[5] Christopher Sharrett, '*Zulu*, or the limits of liberalism', *Cineaste*, vol. 25, no. 4 (2000), p. 29. For letters responding to the article and Sharrett's reply, see *Cineaste*, vol. 26, no. 1 (2001), pp. 59-61.

[6] For a discussion of the colonial epic and adventure film in relation to the Western, see Sheldon Hall, 'Carry on, Cowboy: Roast Beef Westerns', *Iluminace: The Journal of Film History, Theory, and Aesthetics*, vol. 25, no. 3 (Fall 2012), pp. 103-25. This article includes a list of other comparisons of *Zulu* with the Western.

[7] Jeanine Basinger *The World War II Combat Film: Anatomy of a Genre* (New York: Columbia University Press, 1986), pp. 61-62.

[8] See Ian Knight, *Nothing Remains but to Fight: the Defence of Rorke's Drift, 1879* (London, Greenhill Books, 1993), p. 156, for similar observations.

[9] Ian Knight and Ian Castle, *The Zulu War: Then and Now* (London: Battle of Britain Prints International Ltd, 1993).

[10] The accounts of Anglo-Zulu War veterans collected in Knight and Castle's book include similar tributes to their foes' courage.

[11] Sharrett, '*Zulu*, or the limits of liberalism', p. 30.

[12] Ibid., p. 31.

[13] Knight and Castle, *The Zulu War: Then and Now*, pp. 255-6

[14] Sharrett, '*Zulu*, or the limits of liberalism', p. 29.

[15] The phrase 'gesture of respect' is used in the screenplay to describe this shot.

[16] Sharrett's book review has now been taken down from the journal's website, but the original page URL is www.cineaste.com/314zuluwithsomeguts.htm.

[17] Aislinn Laing, 'Why *Zulu* did wonders for my tribe', *Daily Telegraph*, 24 May 2014; accessed at www.telegraph.co.uk/news/worldnews/africanandindianocean/southafrica/. The interviewer's own understanding of the film seems in thrall to her realisation that it was 'produced long before the era of political correctness'. Laing states that *Zulu* is 'Littered with references to marauding "fuzzies" and "natives",' words used respectively once and not at all. She also seems unable to grasp that Bromhead's mention of 'cowardly blacks' on his own side was used in character and not offered as an example of model speech.

[18] Andrew Harding, '*Zulu* – the film which inspired UK and South Africa;, BBC News, 10 June 1964; accessed at www.bbc.co.uk/news/worlf-africa-27762901.

[19] Ian Watson, *Bare Black Breasts and Boys Own Battles: Images of Empire for White Working Class Lads in Mid-Sixties Britain.* (unpublished MA dissertation, Leeds Metropolitan University, 1996).

Preparing to shoot the Isandhlwana prologue. Note the soldier chatting with the Zulus; immediately behind him in the distance is first assistant director Bert Batt. Compare this shot with the finished version on page 241.

BUTHELEZI HONOURS ZULU

KZN FILM COMMISSION HONOURS PRINCE BUTHELEZI

In 2012, the newly established KwaZulu Natal Film Commission announced an annual award, 'celebrating pioneers, legends and veterans of South Africa's film industry', named in honour of Simon Sabela – the actor and director who appears in *Zulu* as the dance leader and a stunt performer, and who later became South Africa's first Black film director (see box in Chapter 10). At the Inkosi Albert Luthuli International Convention Centre in Durban on 20 July 2013, the inaugural award was presented to Prince Mangosuthu Buthelezi M.P. In his acceptance speech, Prince Buthelezi not only paid tribute to Sabela himself but also to *Zulu* and indeed dedicated his award to the film. I am grateful to South African journalist Stephen Coan for sending me the full text of the speech, which is reproduced in its entirety below.

I was somehow surprised when I received news from the MEC (for Economic Development and Tourism in KwaZulu-Natal, Michael Mabuyakhulu) that I had been nominated to receive the inaugural Simon 'Mabhunu' Sabela Film Award. I don't consider myself a film star.

Yet I did have the privilege of working with Simon Sabela when we acted together in the 1964 film *Zulu*, where Simon was one of the stuntmen. We also acted together in *Tokoloshe*. I subsequently worked on the BBC documentary *As Thick as Grass*, which recounted the Battle of Isandlwana. But my friendship with Simon was firmly cemented with that first film, *Zulu*. We spent many happy moments at the foot of the Drakensberg, which was the set of the film.

I therefore dedicate this award to that epic production, which became a milestone event, not only in cinematic history, but within the Zulu nation.

The film *Zulu* recounts the battle of Rorke's Drift, immediately after the Zulu regiments defeated the Her Majesty Queen Victoria's army on the 22nd of January 1879.

The success of *Zulu* was due in large part to director Cy Endfield's determination to accurately portray the pathos of the battlefield. To do this, he enlisted the help of thousands upon thousands of Zulu men who became extras.

It was remarkable at the time to engage so many extras. But what was more remarkable was that they were not emotionally removed from the work. Indeed, these men found themselves re-enacting the deeds of their own grandfathers. Somehow this drew the audience into what was, in the end, a very human experience.

The memories evoked by the film were recent in our national consciousness. They were part of the cultural narrative we grew up with and part of what shaped us as a nation.

It was therefore incomprehensible when a year after it release, *Zulu* was given a 'D' certificate by censors in South Africa, effectively barring black South Africans from watching the film. Particularly so when one considers that, decades later, *Empire* magazine listed *Zulu* as one of the 500 greatest films. I

Prince Buthelezi photographed by the author in London in June 2014.

was glad that a special arrangement was made to at least screen it for the thousands of extras, in places like Mahlabathini, Nongoma and Durban.

My portrayal of King Cetshwayo, my maternal great-grandfather, was not only a privilege, but almost inevitable once the idea was conceived. Cy Endfield and Sir Stanley Baker came to see me at KwaPhindangene to request my assistance in enlisting the thousands of extras for the Zulu regiments. They had already cast Mr Hubert Sishi, an announcer from Radio Zulu, for the part of King Cetshwayo. But when Endfield saw me, he was struck by the family resemblance, and persuaded me to play the role myself.

In a later production, titled *Zulu Dawn*, Simon Sabela played this role, and I admired the way he captured the dignity of the King. Simon was a truly gifted artist and his premature death somehow robbed the South African film industry. It certainly robbed us, his friends.

Aside from meeting Simon, *Zulu* gave me the opportunity to meet Jack Hawkins and Sir Stanley Baker, who was the star and co-producer. We too enjoyed a long friendship afterwards. I also had the privilege of debuting with Sir Michael Caine. We began our acting careers together. But while he went on to fame and glory, history and birth called me to the less acclaimed path of politics.

Three years ago, more than four decades since the making of *Zulu*, I was contacted by the London Film Museum which was organizing an exhibition of memorabilia, photographs, storyboards and costumes. International interest in the film, and in our nation's history, was reignited.

It is wonderful to see the pioneers, legends and veterans of South Africa's film industry celebrated. Since my appearance on the silver screen, there have been many internationally acclaimed South African productions, and South African actors and actresses have become significant players on the world stage.

I am grateful to have been part of this story. I accept this award with real excitement for what is still to come in the South African film industry.

In memory of one of the greats, Simon 'Mabhunu' Sabela, I thank you.

APPENDICES

COSTING DOCUMENTS

As well as extensive production correspondence, the Film Finances files on *Zulu* also contain copies of many documents pertaining to the financial arrangements involved in setting up the project. A selection of these are presented here for whatever light they may shed not only on the logistical considerations of such a complex, large-scale operation as the making of the film but also on working under the political conditions of the Apartheid regime.

The papers also provide evidence that the Zulus were paid for their services in cash and not in kind with the exchange of cattle, wristwatches or other such gifts. A letter from Basil Keys to Bernard Smith of Film Finances (29 November 1962) remarks of the projected costs of hiring the Zulu extras:

> The estimate for Zulus was made some weeks ago and we have since been informed that the R25 per month, i.e. 9/- per day, will be the sum of money we shall be paying to the 250 Zulus who are in our encampment.
>
> The other 14,000 man day Zulus who come from the Reserve locally will cost us 8/- per day and the women dancers a little less. There is no equality of pay for women in the Zulu nation!

Zulu Accommodation

While the troops of the South African Defence Force brought their own tents to the location site, 'barracks' had to be built especially for the Zulu extras intended to be present throughout the shoot. Bob Porter contracted with a local construction firm, Belvedere Timber Structures (Pty.) Ltd (Durban), to have the accommodation block built in such a way that when the structures were dismantled after filming, the materials used could be sold on to help defray costs. Profits from the sale were split 60/40 between the production and construction companies. This was one of the ways in which the film was enabled to come in under budget.

The safety and comfort of the occupants of the blocks were also considered a high priority. In a letter to Porter from Belvedere (24 October 1962), it was noted that the site was 'to be readily accessible and on levelled and drained ground' and that a fire-retardant chemical would be applied to the interior walls to ensure safety. The letter further stated:

> We have endeavoured to provide you with the most equitable amenities for your specified problem. The comfort of Zulus used to warm humid conditions being transferred to a high cold climate would appear to be of considerable importance, and necessitates the provision of a floor to protect against cold and damp. The high degree of insulation imparted by wooden walls and roofing may also be taken into account.

For the much larger force of Zulus needed for the ten-day second unit jaunt in Melmoth, tented accommodation was provided instead of built structures and the overall cost was much lower, despite the greater numbers involved.

Catering Arrangements

The realities of the Apartheid system are all too apparent in the separate arrangements offered by local caterers for the feeding of 'European' and 'non-European' staff (that is, White and Black members of the cast and crew). In a letter from Rupert Waite, manager of the Royal Natal National Park Hotel, to Bob Porter (10 October 1962), the provision of on-site food and equipment was offered on the following terms:

I will require a sum of £120 per week to cover my overheads at cost, for a minimum of 14 weeks. Thereafter I would charge 8/6d per person per day for the European Staff. This will include morning tea, lunch and afternoon tea as we have already discussed. The Zulu staff which you intend giving lunch on site would probably want a piece of bread, a stew [of] mealies and tea. This will cost 3/6d per person per day. [...] For the compound, a daily ration of mealie meal, brown sugar and tea; and meat three times a week, all to be prepared by their own cooks in their own cookhouse, a charge of 2/6d per person per day.

Similarly, a letter from Tony Allchurch (Pretoria) to Bob Porter (27 October 1962) set out the terms of the daily catering regime:

Further to our conversation at the Continental on the 26th October, I wish to confirm details as follows:-
 I am prepared to undertake the catering of the following approximate numbers:-

2,000 Non-Europeans for two weeks
600 Non-Europeans for a further week.
20 Europeans for one week (rehearsal)
50-60 Europeans for two weeks.
During this period we would have on site all the cooking facilities and staff.
Meals to be supplied on the basis:-

Europeans:
Liquid refreshment during the morning and afternoon working period, and mid-morning and mid-afternoon break for tea and sandwiches, etc.
Full course meal at mid-day or stated time for all European staff.

Non-Europeans:
Two light meals a day and one full meat meal and the issue of one quart of Kaffirbeer.
Utensils to be supplied by ourselves including plates, mugs and spoons for non-europeans [sic].
For information, the service for non-europeans will be split into units of 100 to 150.
This service can be supplied to Europeans at R1.40 per day (not R1.45 as previously stated); and non-europeans at 67$^{1}/_{2}$ cents per day. These figures are inclusive.

Hiring the Extras

Various costing sheets, all dated 17 October 1962, included sundry location, transportation, construction and accommodation costs for the military and Zulu personnel employed on the film by arrangement with the South African armed forces and government departments. The deal with the South African Defence Force involved the production company paying the regular wages and other benefits that the soldiers would have ordinarily received for the duration of their involvement in the picture. Their costume uniforms were not included in these expenses, whereas the costumes worn by the Zulus were included in the costs of their daily upkeep, along with their basic salaries.

SOUTH AFRICAN DEFENCE FORCE
Estimate: Pay Rates – Private Soldier.
5/6d. per day.
7/- Feeding. Given 'off the cuff' in Pretoria.
3/- Other allowances.
Allow for 9/6 per day [for]:
Marriage and children allowance
NCO's and Officers allowance.

Allowance for transportation to and from location.
Other transportation at camp.
Hire of tents.
Heating, lighting and cooking.
Ration collection.
Cost of Administration.
Total: 25/- per day per man.

80 men for 8 weeks (seven day week) is approximately 5,000 man days at £1.5.0.
per day   = £6,500
Contingency   = 500
                                         £7,000
80 men at £1.5.0. each per day   = £100

CAVALRY

I am awaiting written confirmation from the Commandant of the Police school regarding these figures:
50 men for 5 days @   £1.10.0. per day
(including horse):   £375
Estimate:
Cost of train –
Pretoria to Loskoff (return)   150
Loskoff to site (return) Busses/
Horse boxes.   150
Cost of camp. Rations for men
and horses.   350
                                         1,025
Contingency   75
                                         £1,100

It is understood that this Cavalry was only available for five days, which may, or may not, include travel to and from the site which must be checked. Maximum number of men and horses – 50.

Suggested method of travel from Pretoria (where Police Barracks are) to Mont-aux-Sources – train to closest railhead at Loskoff.

ZULU EXTRAS

Estimate:
250 for 6 weeks (seven day week) = 10,500
2,000 for one week
(seven day week)   = 14,000
200 Dancers.
250 Warriors.
150 Crowd.
Total: 600 for one seven day week = 4,200
                                    28,700
Add: contingency of   1,300
                                    30,000

COST:

(Including costume)
25 Rands per month each on a four week month = 63/- which is 9/- per day.
Estimate – Transportation:
Transportation of Zulu warriors to and from Reserve and location site
Cost of transportation for 200 dancers.
Possibility some transportation for part of 2,000 Zulus for one week.

ACCOMMODATION:

Cost of tents and/or temporary buildings (with resale value).
Blankets.
Catering and cooks (beer).
Heat, light, cleaning and sanitation.
Compound Manager and staff, Interpreters, Medical.
Estimate for above: Allow 11/- per man per day. (These figures should be quite generous and should include all Zulu bit parts and transportation).
Latest quotation from Rupert Waite [Royal National Park Hotel] on catering for Zulus is 6/- per day (16 Oct 62)
Total number of Zulus – 30,000. Total cost per head per day on above figures – £30,000.

Production Unit Salaries

The figures entered in the revised budget of 25 February 1963 represent the monies allocated in advance of production for salaries and other such expenses. They were not quite final in that a number of these figures changed before production was completed. It is worth drawing particular attention in the table below to the figures placed against the role of the Reverend Otto Witt, which along with a number of the other supporting parts had still not been cast at this advanced stage of pre-production (artistes cast after the budget had been prepared are indicated in square brackets). A sum of $50,000 (equivalent to £17,858) had been set aside for the role because it had been the intention to cast an American actor to add marquee weight and transatlantic appeal to the cast; Stanley Baker favoured Van Heflin, who was sent the script in New York (as noted by Paramount executive Frank Caffey in a memo to Jack Karp, 7 March 1963). However, when Jack Hawkins was cast – apparently through the intervention of Film Finances' representative Colin Lesslie, by his own account – he was given the same salary as Stanley Baker: £30,000. The completion guarantor stated, in an undated and rather convoluted note to Diamond Films, that 'you will not be liable to us for the guaranteed sum payable in respect of the services of Jack Hawkins as an artist in this film in excess of the sum provided in the budget for the artist to play that part which is to be played by Jack Hawkins'. In other words, although the fee was greater than the amount budgeted for, Baker and Endfield would not be penalised for this as an overage. According to the Statement of Production Cost no. 15 (18 October 1963), savings of £2,109 on other artistes whose roles were either deleted or reduced helped pay for this agreed additional expenditure.

	Cost Heading	Personnel	Budgeted Amount (£)
A	**Story and Script**		
	Adaptation and Screenplay	Cy Endfield	8,000
	Screenplay Collaboration	John Prebble	2,000
B	**Producer and Director Fees**		
	Producer(s)	Cy Endfield/Stanley Baker	12,500
	Director	Cy Endfield	12,500
C	**Production Unit Salaries**		
1	*Production Management & Secretaries:*		
	Production Supervisor [Associate Producer]	Basil Keys	7,500
	Production Manager	John Merriman	1,800
	Location Manager [+ 2nd Unit Director]	Robert Porter	4,180
	Embassy/Film Finances Representatives	Colin Lesslie	10,000
		Harold Huth	2,570
2	*Assistant Directors and Continuity:*		
	First Assistant Director	Bert Batt	1,915
	Second Assistant Director	Claude Watson	1,015
	Continuity Clerk	Muirne Mathieson	1,100
3	*Technical Advisers*		200
4	*Camera Crews:*		
	Lighting Cameraman	Stephen Dade	3,440
	Camera Operator	Dudley Lovell	1,380
	Focus Puller	Peter Hammond	1,037
	Maintenance	Brinley Jones	960

Cost Heading		Personnel	Budgeted Amount (£)
5	*Recording Crews: Floor and Location:*		
	Mixer	Claude Hitchcock	1,330
	Operator	D. Price [Derek Leather]	903
	Boom Operator	David Jones	1,007
	Maintenance	Fred G. Hughesdon	1,070
6	*Editing Staff:*		
	Editor	John Jympson	2,790
	Assistant Editor	Jennifer Thompson	1,415
7	*Stills Camera Staff:*		
	Stills Cameraman	Norman Gryspeerdt	1,445
8	*Wardrobe Staff:*		
	Wardrobe Supervisor	Arthur Newman	1,590
	Assistant	James Smith	800
9	*Make-Up Artistes:*		
	Chief Make-Up Artiste	Charles Parker	675
	Assistant (1)	Michael Morris	1,190
	Assistant (2)	Richard Mills	640
10	*Hairdressers:*		
	Chief Hairdresser	Bill Griffiths	900
12	*Production Accountancy:*		
	Production Accountant	Arthur Hall	2,533
	Assistant	Roy Skeggs	1,075
D	**Set Designing and Supervisory Staff:**		
	Art Director	Ernest Archer	3,920
	Assistant Art Director	Vernon Dixon	1,395
	Construction Manager	Ray Frift [Dick Frift]	1,666
E	**Artistes**		
1	*Cast:*		
	Lt. Chard	Stanley Baker	30,000
	Lt. Bromhead	Michael Caine	2,250
	Margareta	Ulla Jacobsson	3,000
	Witt	[Jack Hawkins]	17,858 ($50,000) [30,000]
	Cpl. Allen	Glynn Edwards	1,350
	612 Williams	Peter Gill	680
	Cole	Gary Bond	430
	Schiess	Dickie Owen	120
	Hitch	David Kernan	1,400
	Owen	Ivor Emmanuel	1,350
	Adendorff	[Gert van den Bergh]	700
	Dalton	[Dennis Folbigge]	280
	Sgt. Windridge	Joe Powell	1,500
	Sgt. Thomas [sic]	Neil McCarthy	550
	Co. Cook	Keith Stephens	120
	Stephenson	[John Sullivan]	30
	Byrne [character deleted]		120

	Cost Heading	Personnel	Budgeted Amount (£)
	Sgt. Gallagher [character deleted]	Larry Taylor	200
	Bugler	[Ronald Hill]	280
	Col. Sgt. Bourne	Nigel Green	1,320
	L/Corporal	Tom Gerrard	620
	Cetewayo	[Chief Buthelezi]	20
	Dabulamanzi		20
	Jacob	[Daniel Tshabalala]	20
	Red Garters	[Ephraim Mbhele]	20
	Zulu General		30
	Hook	[James Booth]	2,500
	716 Jones	[Denys Graham]	287
	593 Jones	[Richard Davies]	315
	Reynolds	[Patrick Magee]	1,500
	Orderly	[Michael Bishop]	50
	Howarth	[Dafydd Havard]	320
	Sgt. Maxfield	[Paul Daneman]	630
	Hughes	[Larry Taylor]	40
	Young Soldier		
2	Stand-ins and Doubles		4,661
3	Crowd	Location:	
		250 Zulus @ £12½ month	9,375
		1,250 Zulus @ £½ day	4,375
		Dancers	1,000
		Studio:	
		White	300
		Zulu	400
		White/Zulu Stunt Men	200
F	Orchestra and Composer		4,520

The Budget

Although the production budget was finalised before filming started, as the shoot progressed many cost items changed from their initial estimates due to schedule changes and other unforeseen contingencies. Production accountant Arthur Hall provided regularly updated statements of these revised costs, indicating for each item where the film was on, under or over budget and estimating the final cost of completion. The statement rproduced overleaf was issued during post-production, after the picture editing had been locked but before the final stereophonic sound dubbing had taken place. Nevertheless, it gives a good indication of just how efficient the unit was in remaining comfortably within the original budget.

Statement of Production Cost No. 15 (week ending 18 October 1963)

Cost Heading		Estimated Final Cost (£)*	Budget (£)	Over (Under) Budget
A	Story and Script	10,829	10,450	379
B	Producer and Director Fees	25,000	25,000	
C	**Production Unit Salaries**			
1	Production Management and Secretaries	31,719	29,496	2,223
2	Assistant Directors and Continuity	5,024	4,383	644
3	Technical Advisers		200	(200)
4	Camera Crews	8,659	8,397	262
5	Recording Crews	8,227	6,674	1,553
6	Editing Staff	8,775	6,895	1,880
7	Stills Camera Staff	2,289	2,029	260
8	Wardrobe Designer and Staff	2,652	2,609	43
9	Make-Up Artistes	3,107	2,840	267
10	Hairdressers	1,104	1,059	45
11	Casting	520	560	(40)
12	Production Accountancy	4,398	4,252	146
13	Projectionists	292	1,501	(1,209)
14	Other Staff	197	240	(43)
15	Foreign Unit Technicians	10,266	9,446	820
D	**Set Designing and Supervisory Staff**	10,700	10,337	363
E	**Artistes**			
1	Cast	84,883	74,850	10,033**
2	Stand-ins and Doubles	5,633	4,661	972
3	Crowd	15,078	15,713	(635)
F	Orchestra and Composer	3,895	4,520	(625)
G	Costumes and Wigs	8,341	6,750	1,591
H	Misc. Production Stores (Exc. Sets)	2,320	2,085	235
I	Film and Laboratory Charges	39,739	39,801	(62)
J	Studio Rentals	13,230	9,545	3,685
K	Equipment	16,631	14,995	1,676
L	Power	596	399	197

Statement of Production Cost No. 15 (week ending 18 October 1963)			
Cost Heading	Estimated Final Cost (£)*	Budget (£)	Over (Under) Budget
M Travel and Transport			
1 Location	65,600	66,020	(420)
2 Other	1,354	1,600	(246)
N Hotel and Living Expenses			
1 Location	45,720	47,601	(1,881)
2 Other	805	2,050	(1,245)
O Insurances	26,179	26,179	
P Holiday and Sick Pay Surcharges	4,589	4,672	(83)
Q Publicity Salaries and Expenses	15,988	13,339	2,649
R Miscellaneous Expenses	9,178	8,521	657
S Sets and Models			
1 Labour – Construction	7,520	5,875	1,645
2 Labour – Dressing	1,350	900	450
3 Labour – Operating	7,756	5,955	1,801
4 Labour – Striking	1,456	1,000	456
5 Labour – Lighting	6,737	5,240	1,497
6 Labour – Lamp Spotting			
7 Labour – Foreign Unit Labour	12,092	10,560	1,532
8 Materials – Construction	11,836	10,100	1,736
9 Properties	13,086	12,000	1,096
T Special Location Facilities	26,402	25,940	482
Total Direct Cost	581,762	547,199	34,563
Y Finance and Legal Charges	32,114	32,114	
Z Overheads	5,000	5,000	
Sub-totals	618,876	584,313	34,563
Production Contingency		82,241	
Total Production Cost	618,876	666,554	(47,678)
	($1,732,853)	($1,866,351)	($133,498)

* Estimate as at 18 October 1963.
** This figure is not an overage, but the agreed difference (£12,142) between the estimated allowance for the part of 'Witt' and the actual fee paid to Jack Hawkins, less savings (£2,109) on other artistes. (Note in original document. The role of Witt had been offered to American actor Van Heflin in March 1963.)

THE PRODUCTION SCHEDULE

This summary of scenes filmed on each day represents my very rough approximation based on the daily progress reports. It should be borne in mind that scenes were often filmed over several days, not always consecutively; additional retakes and 'coverage' were often done sporadically throughout the schedule. For example, the scene in which Chard outlines his plans for the defence to Bromhead and Adendorff is listed below as having been shot on Day 7; however, Endfield returned to it for retakes on Days 15, 17, 18 and 77. Similarly, the earlier exchanges between the three officers about Isandhlwana were spread over Days 8, 26 and 12 to 16 inclusive. The complex scenes of the Zulu assaults were even more broken up, often being filmed by both the main and second units on different days and thus difficult to record on this chart, which provides a loose reference guide only.

\multicolumn{4}{c}{Location Filming: Royal Natal National Park, South Africa}			
Day	Date	Principal scenes filmed	Notes from daily progress reports
-	25-27 March	-	Unit travels to location by charter flight from London and coach from Johannesburg. Wardrobe fittings for cast and S.A. soldiers.
1	28 March	River Scenes.	Bad weather: first day's work not completed. John Sullivan in charge of rehearsing 65 Zulus, soldiers and actors when free.
2	29 March	River Scenes.	Bad weather in morning. Sound crew record 'wild tracks.'
3	30 March	River Scenes.	Crowd: 16 Soldiers, 20 Levies, 2 Bearers.
-	31 March	-	No shooting: Sunday off.
4	1 April	River Scenes.	Bob Porter and Ernest Archer away sick.
5	2 April	River Scenes.	Peter Gill completes location filming.
6	3 April	-	No shooting: rain. First three days' rushes screened.
7	4 April	Planning defences.	Paramount announces participation as financier and distributor.
8	5 April	Camp: establishing shots; Witts arrive.	Doubles (Joe Powell, Judy Cadman) used for Witts. Crowd: 30 levies, 76 soldiers, 15 local men, 3 women.

THE PRODUCTION SCHEDULE

	Location Filming: Royal Natal National Park, South Africa		
Day	Date	Principal scenes filmed	Notes from daily progress reports
9	6 April	-	No shooting: rain.
10	7 April	-	No shooting: rain.
11	8 April	-	No shooting: rain. Brian O'Shaughnessy, cast as Stephenson but unable to shoot, leaves location to fulfil another commitment.
12	9 April	Adendorff arrives. Stephenson's horsemen.	37 horses used. John Sullivan takes over from O'Shaughnessy as Stephenson.
13	10 April	Stephenson's horsemen.	Bad light in afternoon.
14	11 April	Stephenson's horsemen.	Bad light in afternoon.
-	12-14 April	-	No shooting: Easter weekend holiday.
15	15 April	Adendorff reports.	Bad light all day.
16	16 April	Byrne (cook) at soyers; riders from the column.	
17	17 April	Thomas with calf; dawn shot of camp.	Official set visit by General Hiemstra, Errol Hinds (State Information), et al.
18	18 April	Owen and Thomas posted as sentries.	Joseph E. Levine arrives at location.
19	19 April	Soldiers hear 'train'; waiting at ramparts.	
20	20 April	Soldiers at ramparts; first volley firing.	'2nd Unit shot with 1st Unit in the morning and then left for the hills near Zulu compound to shoot linking shots of the Zulus approaching Rorke's Drift.' 280 Zulus used.
21	21 April	-	No shooting: bad weather all day. Car accident involving unit secretaries Caroline Murray, Penny Woolley. Joe Levine departs location.
22	22 April	Bromhead's ancestry; Bromhead shouting orders.	2nd Unit shooting linking shots of Zulus approaching Rorke's Drift. Crowd: 194 Zulus filming, 31 sick, 1 confined to camp.
23	23 April	'They're testing your guns.'	2nd Unit shooting linking shots of Zulus approaching Rorke's Drift.
24	24 April	Zulus on plain; sniper fire on North wall.	Further work on scenes 133, 141, 144, 149, 153 to be done by 2nd Unit.
25	25 April	Hitch and Allen wounded.	
26	26 April	First assault on North wall.	
27	27 April	Chard wounded; assault on North wall.	Bad light in afternoon; scene started but light went. 2nd Unit working with 1st Unit all day.
-	28 April	-	No shooting: Sunday.
28	29 April	Dalton at ramparts.	Bad weather all day. John Jympson and Jennifer Thompson arrive at location.

Location Filming: Royal Natal National Park, South Africa

Day	Date	Principal scenes filmed	Notes from daily progress reports
29	30 April	Cook assegaied; passing out ammunition.	
30	1 May	Chard's shaking hand; Chard shouting orders; Chard carried to surgery.	Charles Parker (make-up artist) leaves location; replaced by Richard Mills. Kerry Jordan completes role. 2nd Unit covering 1st Unit material.
31	2 May	Chard rescued by Schiess. 'Hold them!' 'Form two lines!'	Jim Harris (special effects) leaves location. Dennis Folbigge completes role.
32	3 May	Chard, Schiess and men fighting.	Bad light all day.
33	4 May	Sniper fire; officers' reaction to final salute.	Bad light in afternoon.
-	5 May	-	No shooting: Sunday off.
34	6 May	Schiess fighting Zulus; two lines volley firing.	
35	7 May	North wall fighting.	Joe Powell injures knee, sent to hospital. Dickie Owen completes location filming.
36	8 May	Zulus retreat from volleys; break for water; Thomas and dead calf.	2nd Unit shooting action shots and standing by with 1st Unit. Gert van den Bergh completes part.
37	9 May	-	No shooting: bad weather. Scene 243 (Schiess) to be transferred to studio.
38	10 May	Owen and Thomas on hill.	Bad weather until 2.00pm.
39	11 May	Assault on the hospital.	Bad weather in morning. John Poyner (property master) leaves location.
40	12 May	Roll call parade.	Bad weather until 2.30pm. David Kernan away sick.
41	13 May	Roll call parade; first assault on South wall.	Location visit by Paramount accountants David Schneider and Sam Bernstein.
42	14 May	Hospital evacuated; start of cattle stampede; Chard and bugler.	'Unit called early to shoot dawn shot, which was completed by 6.05am.' Sergio Strizzi (photographer) arrives at location.
43	15 May	Waiting for last assault; 'Men of Harlech.'	Bad weather in morning.
44	16 May	Night shots: Owen and Thomas.	Extended day until 7.15pm. Bad light in afternoon.
45	17 May	Final assault; redoubt volley firing.	Late start. Ivor Emmanuel and Neil McCarthy complete parts.
46	18 May	Hill: Zulus return to salute.	Joe Powell returns to work. Cast group photograph taken.
-	19 May	-	Sound crew recording sound tracks with Zulus.
47	20 May	Final assault repulsed.	Jack Hawkins arrives at location.

Location Filming: Royal Natal National Park, South Africa

Day	Date	Principal scenes filmed	Notes from daily progress reports
48	21 May	Flying platoon; Hitch and Allen at surgery; Windridge mounts roof.	89 Zulus return to Zululand (12 returned home previously). Ulla Jacobsson arrives at location.
49	22 May	Waking up; men's reaction to Zulus' final departure and relief column.	Bad light in morning. Yousuf Karsh (stills photographer) and 58 Zulu Dancing Girls arrive from Johannesburg.
50	23 May	Aftermath of final assault; store-room.	David Kernan and Glynn Edwards complete parts. Bad light; interior set used as cover.
51	24 May	Fighting on hospital roof.	2nd Unit shooting on Ext. Hill and Camp, doing pick-up shots of Soldiers and Zulus.
52	25 May	Fighting on hospital roof.	2nd Unit depart for Durban en route to Zululand.
53	26 May	Relief column arrives.	Rehearsals begin for Dancing Girls and Zulus. 42 horses, two cameras used.
54	27 May	Fighting on hospital roof.	Gary Bond, Daniel Tshabalala and Chief Buthelezi arrive at location.
55	28 May	Kraal: Zulus dancing.	Judy Cadman (make-up trainee) taken ill, returns home.
56	29 May	Kraal: Witts' conversation.	248 Mixed Crowd, 108 Dancing Girls, 100 Dancing Men, 119 Zulus filming.
57	30 May	Kraal: Cetewayo, Jacob and Witts.	2nd unit shots of hospital roof, camp and South wall directed by Stanley Baker.
58	31 May	Kraal: Red Garters arrives.	2nd Unit filmed matte shots of Ext. Camp.
59	1 June	Kraal: Witts leave.	2nd Unit worked at Kraal with 1st Unit then travelled to Zululand. Doubles used (Joe Powell, Ann du Pre).
-	2-3 June	-	No shooting: Whit weekend holiday. Karsh leaves location for Zululand.
60	4 June	Kraal: Zulu dancing; establishing shot.	Bad light in morning. Daniel Tshabalala, Chief Buthelezi, 87 Zulus return to Zululand; Dancing Girls return to Johannesburg.
61	5 June	Final assault: Chard and bugler.	'Weather good until 2.00pm, then smoke from veldt fires obliterated sun all afternoon.' 2nd Unit shooting in Melmoth, Zululand.
62	6 June	Chard, Bromhead and Witts at camp.	
63	7 June	Chard and Witts.	Ernest Archer (art director) and Dick Frift (construction) leave location.
64	8 June	Levies flee; Witt pleads for wagons.	Bad light; interior store set used as cover. Rushes car involved in accident.

THE PRODUCTION SCHEDULE

Location Filming: Royal Natal National Park, South Africa

Day	Date	Principal scenes filmed	Notes from daily progress reports
65	9 June	Bromhead hunting.	
66	10 June	Wagons over.	Arthur Hall (accountant) travels to Zululand to pay off crowd.
67	11 June	Witt inside store-room.	Bad weather; interior store set used as cover. 2nd Unit travel from Melmoth to Hluhuwe Game Reserve.
68	12 June	Witt inside store-room.	Bad weather in morning; cover tent built around ext. store set. 2nd Unit in Hluhuwe unable to shoot due to rain.
69	13 June	Witt, Cole and Bourne beside store.	Bad weather in morning.
70	14 June	Dawn effect; Witt, Cole and Bourne beside store; Cole at ramparts.	Early call (6.30am) for dawn shot, filmed by crew under Bert Batt (1st A.D.). Basil Keys (associate producer) leaves location.
71	15 June	Witt dragged from store.	Chita arrives at location. 2nd Unit shooting in Hluhuwe.
-	16 June	-	No shooting: Sunday off.
72	17 June	Witts leave camp.	Most of 2nd Unit return to main location.
73	18 June	Witts return to camp (deleted scene); burning of hospital.	Extended day for burning of hospital set (finished 8.55pm). 3 cameras and 2nd Unit used. Gary Bond completes location part.
74	19 June	Witts leave camp.	Karsh leaves location. Jack Hawkins and Ulla Jacobsson complete location parts.
75	20 June	Chard and Bromhead take stock after battle.	Bad light in afternoon. Sound crew record rifle shots, special sound effects, etc.
76	21 June	Zulu generals on hill; Zulu snipers deploy.	Bad light, intermittent sunshine. Tom Gerrard completes part.
77	22 June	Cattle stampede; Chard's final gesture.	Nigel Green completes part after recording soundtracks.
78	23 June	Bromhead hunting cheetah.	Chita completes part. Double: Jan Rossouw; stand-in: David Proctor.
79	24 June	Isandhlwana battlefield.	Bad light in morning. 106 Zulus, 64 soldiers, 20 oxen, snake and lizard used for battlefield. 2nd Unit filming cattle stampede.
80	25 June	Title and pick-up shots (kraal, camp, river).	Soldiers complete work. Stanley Baker leaves location for Johannesburg. Double: Joshua du Toit. Stand-in: David Proctor.
81	26 June	Pick-up shots (hills, river).	Michael Caine completes part. End of location filming by midday.

THE PRODUCTION SCHEDULE

Studio Shoot: Twickenham Studios, London (Stages 1, 2 and 3)

Day	Date	Principal scenes filmed	Notes from daily progress reports
-	27-29 June	-	Unit leaves location, travels to London by charter flight from Johannesburg.
-	30 June	-	No shooting: Sunday off.
82	1 July	Church surgery: Reynolds at work.	Start of shooting delayed because building of altered sets not finished.
83	2 July	1st Hospital Room: Hook, Margareta and men.	John Sullivan begins stunt rehearsals with five 'Zulus' on Twickenham Stage 2.
84	3 July	1st Hospital Room: Hook and Maxfield.	
85	4 July	2nd Hospital Room: Margareta and men.	Joe Powell completes part.
86	5 July	Church: Witt and Reynolds.	Jack Hawkins, delayed from earlier in week by French air strike, completes part.
-	6-7 July	-	No shooting: weekend off.
87	8 July	2nd Hospital Room: Chard, Margareta and Reynolds.	Two cameras used. Gary Bond completes part.
88	9 July	2nd Hospital Room: Margareta and men; Joneses firing.	Smoke effects. Actor Drewe Henley, on standby as 'Young Soldier', cancelled; lines later given to Richard Davies.
89	10 July	1st/ 2nd Hospital Room/ Corridor/Porch/Window: Margareta and men.	Smoke effects. Dickie Owen completes part.
90	11 July	1st Hospital Room: Hook and Williams firing from window.	Fire and smoke effects (special precautions). Ulla Jacobsson completes part.
91	12 July	Church: Reynolds under attack; end VC roll; Hook and Williams at ramparts.	Smoke effects. Jack Hawkins completes voice dubbing.
-	13-14 July	-	No shooting: weekend off.
92	15 July	1st Hospital Room: Margareta and men.	
93	16 July	1st Hospital Room: Hook and Maxfield.	
94	17 July	1st Hospital Room: Hook and Reynolds.	Firemen standing by all day. Patrick Magee completes part.
95	18 July	1st Hospital Room/ Church: Hook and men; Chard in surgery.	Smoke effects, trick bayonets. Stanley Baker completes part.
96	19 July	1st/ 2nd Hospital Room: Hook and men fighting.	Smoke effects.
-	20-21 July	-	Baker and Rusty Coppleman (sound editor) record Imperial Glee Singers performing 'Men of Harlech' in Ferndale, South Wales.

THE PRODUCTION SCHEDULE

Studio Shoot: Twickenham Studios, London (Stages 1, 2 and 3)

Day	Date	Principal scenes filmed	Notes from daily progress reports
97	22 July	2nd/ 3rd Hospital Room: Joneses fighting.	Smoke effects. Two cameras used. Joseph Levine arrives in London.
98	23 July	2nd/ 3rd Hospital Room: Hook and men fighting.	Smoke effects. Two cameras used. Rough cut screened in London for Levine and George Weltner.
99	24 July	2nd Hospital Room/ Reynolds' Room: Maxfield amid flames.	Fire and smoke effects. Two cameras used. Richard Davies, Denys Graham and Dafydd Havard complete parts.
100	25 July	2nd Hospital Room/ Reynolds' Room: Hook steals brandy.	Fire and smoke effects. Two cameras used. Paul Daneman, Peter Gill and Larry Taylor complete parts.
101	26 July	2nd Hospital Room/ Ext. Church: Hook close-ups and reaction shots.	Fire and smoke effects. Two cameras used. James Booth completes part. End of studio filming.

Post-production editing and sound recording
(Twickenham, Borehamwood and Pinewood Studios)

Day	Date	Principal scenes filmed	Notes from daily progress reports
	8 August	Kerry Jordan dubbing.	Additional voice tests for post-synchronised dialogue dubbing (ADR).
	9 August	Ivor Emmanuel, Glynn Edwards dubbing.	
	13 August	David Kernan, Peter Gill dubbing.	Work print screened for John Barry and Lionel Bart, attended by Cy Endfield.
	16 August	Neil McCarthy, Robert Rietty, Paul Daneman, Dafydd Havard, Roger Snowden dubbing.	Bob Porter leaves Mont-Aux-Sources location after completing clear-up of site.
	17 August	Michael Caine dubbing.	
	18 September	Fine cut (minus final sound dub) viewed by BBFC examiners.	
	21 September	Richard Burton records voice-over narration in Paris.	
	11 November	Start of four weeks' stereophonic sound dubbing.	
	16 December	BBFC grants 'U' certificate for UK exhibition.	
	3 January 1964	PCA grants Seal of Approval for US exhibition.	

LOCATION CALL SHEETS

Call sheets such as these were prepared by main unit first assistant director Bert Batt and second unit production assistant Alan Girney for each shooting day. They give an indication of the sort of logistical considerations the company faced during filming, and an insight into the daily life of a film unit (note the hotel entertainment in the evening). I have appended some of the remarks from the daily progress report for this day and a table of the number of days on which each cast member was on call (from which it can be seen that Michael Caine worked more days than any other actor).

LOCATION CALL SHEET NO. 31
DIAMOND FILMS LIMITED.

PRODUCTION: Zulu
SUNRISE FOR SHOOTING: 7.28 AM.
UNIT CALL: To leave both hotels at 6.15 AM. On site at 7.00 AM.
DATE: Wednesday, 1st May, 1963
LOCATION: Ext. Camp
SCENE NOS: 272 (pt), 186, 187, 188, 189, 262, 263, 279, 250, 251, 253, 279 (pt), 469 F, 254, 255, 256

ARTISTES	ROOM NO.	CHARACTER	LEAVE HOTEL	AFTER BREAKFAST M/UP HAIR	REQD. ON SITE
Stanley Baker	M.24	Chard	6.45	7.15	8.15
Michael Caine	M.37	Bromhead	7.45	8.00	8.45
Nigel Green	M.36	Bourne	7.45	8.00	8.45
Dickie Owen	M.38	Schiess	7.45	8.00	8.45
David Kernan	M.33	Hitch	7.30	7.45	8.30
Glynn Edwards	M.36	Allen	7.30	7.45	8.30
Neil McCarthy	M.39	Thomas	7.45	8.00	8.45
Joe Powell	M.1	Windridge	7.45	8.00	8.45
Tom Gerrard	M.39	L/Cpl.	6.45	7.15	8.00
Ivor Emmanuel	M.37	Owen	7.45	8.00	8.45
Larry Taylor	M.23	Hughes	7.45	8.00	8.45
Gert van den Bergh	M.19	Adendorff	7.45	8.00	8.45
Kerry Jordan	M.22	Byrne	6.00	6.30	7.00
Dennis Folbigge	M.18	Dalton	6.00	6.30	7.00
John Sullivan	M.1		6.00		
7 African Stuntmen	Fully dressed on site at 7.00 AM.				

STAND-IN
C. Bird for Mr. Baker   Via bus   6.15   7.30

SOLDIER STAND-INS
Chosen from Soldiers below.

SOLDIERS.
50 Soldiers   Those soldiers for M/UP and hair at 6.00 AM., including 5 Medical
                    Orderlies and Cooks.   The rest on Site at 7.00 AM.
5 Soldiers   Communications – 7.00 AM. on Site.
3 Soldiers   Working on Ammunition – 7.00 AM. on Site.

ZULUS.
To be fully dressed with Shields and Assegais on Site at 7.30 AM.

PROPS.
Ammunition Box for Dalton & Byrne as to-day. Chard's Cigar and Light. Stretcher for Byrne, Crutch for Schiess, Trick Bayonets, Ammunition, Spear for Byrne's back.

M/UP.
Continuity M/Ups for Dalton, Byrne, Schiess. Blood, Sweat, Grime.

WARDROBE.
Spear in Byrne's back, Chest and Rubber Protectors for Stuntmen, Continuity Bandages for Hitch, Allen.

FIRST AID.
Doctor to Standby during Fight Sequences.

GENERATOR.
To be started at 5.00 AM.

CATERING.
   BREAKFAST for Unit and Artistes from 6.15 AM. to 7.00 AM.
   UNIT. Breaks at 9.30 AM. and 3.30 PM. Lunch from Noon.
   ZULUS. Lunch and Breaks on Site.
   SOLDIERS. 58 Soldiers to Lunch on Site and Breaks.

TRANSPORT   MONT-AUX-SOURCES HOTEL
Car No. 1.   (Mr. Baker's) For Stanley Baker and Tom Gerrard at 6.45 AM.
Car No. 2.   For Dennis Folbigge, Kerry Jordan, John Sullivan, to leave at 6.00 AM.
Car No. 2.   (TO RETURN) For Glynn Edwards, David Kernan at 7.30 AM.
Car No. 3.   For Cy Endfield to leave at 6.00 AM.
Unit Coach   To leave with Unit at 6.15 AM. Howard Rennie in charge.
Unit Coach   To return for Dickie Owen, Larry Taylor, Michael Caine, Nigel Green,
               Neil McCarthy, Joe Powell, Ivor Emmanuel, to leave at 7.45 AM.

UNIT NOTES

WOULD MEMBERS OF THE UNIT KINDLY NOT ENCOURAGE VISITORS ON TO THE SET. THEY ARE TO STAY AT A STATED DISTANCE BEHIND THE BARRIER ROPES.

There will be a Film Showing to-night at the Royal N.N. Park Hotel at 8.45 PM. "TARZAN AND THE LOST SAFARI" with Gordon Scott, Yolande Donlan, Robert Beatty. In Technicolor.
Directed by Bruce Humberstone.

30.4.63   BERT BATT
           Assistant Director

2ND UNIT LOCATION CALL SHEET NO. 2

PRODUCTION: Zulu   DATE: Wednesday, 1st May, 1963

SUNRISE FOR SHOOTING: 7.28 AM.   LOCATION: Hill and Site

UNIT CALL: Leave Mont-Aux-Sources at 6.15 AM. On site at 7.00 AM.

SCENE NOS:

1st Shot: Hill overlooking camp. Action shot
2nd Shot: Action shot Zulu and Corporal

             6 ZULUS
             2 STUNTMEN – Chris and Osborne
             2 ZULUS for action shot
             1 SOLDIER

MAKE-UP: 6 Blood Capsules

PROPS: 6 Rifles
             24 Rounds .303
             6 Rounds .450
             2 Mattresses

SPECIAL EFFECTS:
             Trick Shield
             Trick Assegai
             Special Bayonet

             A. GIRNEY

Remarks from Daily Production Progress Report No. 30:

Charles Parker left with rushes car to Johannesburg. John Poyner, Property Master, away sick. Kerry Jordan has completed his part in the picture. 2nd Unit covering 1st Unit material. Set-ups: 8 (2nd Unit: 6). Scenes filmed: 273, 186, 187, 188, 189, 209, 262, 263, 265, 267, 278, 469A, 469E, 469F, 276 (pt). Screen time: 1.15 mins.

1.5.63   JOHN D. MERRIMAN
                                 Production Manager

Number of camera days on call:

Michael Caine: 71	Stanley Baker: 66 (as actor)
Tom Gerrard: 62	Larry Taylor: 58 + stunt rehearsals
Nigel Green: 56	Joe Powell: 56 + stunt rehearsals
Glynn Edwards: 47	David Kernan: 46
Ivor Emmanuel: 45	John Sullivan: 42 + stunt rehearsals
Neil McCarthy: 35	Ulla Jacobsson: 27
Dennis Folbigge: 26	Gert van den Bergh: 25
Kerry Jordan: 24	Jack Hawkins: 22
James Booth: 14	Gary Bond: 14
Paul Daneman: 13	Peter Gill: 13
Dickie Owen: 13	Dafydd Havard: 11
Patrick Magee: 7	Richard Davies: 7
Denys Graham: 7	Daniel Tshabalala: 6
Chief Buthelezi: 5	Ephraim Mbhele: 3
Harvey Hall: 3	Michael Bishop (uncredited): 3

CAST AND CREW

† Twickenham shoot only   * Uncredited

Cast

Lieutenant John Chard, RE	Stanley Baker
Reverend Otto Witt	Jack Hawkins
Margareta Witt	Ulla Jacobsson
Private Henry Hook	James Booth †
Lieutenant Gonville Bromhead	Michael Caine
Colour Sergeant Bourne	Nigel Green
Private Owen	Ivor Emmanuel
Sergeant Maxfield	Paul Daneman †
Corporal Allen	Glynn Edwards
Private Thomas	Neil McCarthy
Private Hitch	David Kernan
Private Cole	Gary Bond
Private 612 Williams	Peter Gill
Lance Corporal	Tom Gerrard
Surgeon Reynolds	Patrick Magee †
Private 593 William Jones	Richard Davies †
Private 716 Robert Jones	Denys Graham †
Gunner Howarth	Dafydd Havard †
Corporal Schiess, NNC	Dickie Owen
Private Hughes	Larry Taylor
Sergeant Windridge	Joe Powell
Stephenson	John Sullivan
Sick Man	Harvey Hall †
Lieutenant Adendorff, NNC	Gert van den Bergh
Acting Assistant Commissary Dalton	Dennis Folbigge
Company Cook	Kerry Jordan
Bugler	Ronald Hill
King Cetewayo	Chief Mangosuthu G. Buthelezi
Jacob	Daniel Tshabalala
Red Garters	Ephraim Mbhele
Zulu Dance Leader	Simon Sabela
Zulu Dancing Girl	Chastebell Nkosi*
Wounded Soldier	Joshua du Toit*

Orderly	Michael Bishop* †
Soldiers	Gordon Atkins/I. Bloch/F.W. Drndarsky/B. Fletcher/J.R. Gouws/Don McArthur/ Allan Perel/G.C. Poplett/David R. Proctor/G.F. Wolvardt/Ralf Zunckel*
Zulu stunt performers	John Marcus/Osborne Mbili/Franklin Mdhluli/Chris/Morgan/ Solomon*
Double (Jack Hawkins)	Joe Powell*
Double (Ulla Jacobsson)	Judy Cadman*
Double (Michael Caine)	Jan Rossouw*
Stand-in (Stanley Baker)	Charles Bird*
Stand-in (Jack Hawkins)	Gordon Atkins*
Stand-in (Ulla Jacobsson)	Ann du Pre*
Stand-in (Michael Caine)	David R. Proctor*
Narrator	Richard Burton
Voice dubbing	Robert Rietty/ Roger Snowden*
Extras	238 Zulus/108 Dancing Girls/248 Mixed Crowd

Cancelled:

Stephenson	Brian O'Shaughnessy
Young Soldier	Drewe Henley †

Crew

Director	Cy Endfield
Producers	Stanley Baker/ Cy Endfield
Executive producer	Joseph E. Levine
Associate producer	Basil Keys
Film Finances representative	Colin Lesslie*
Assistant to the producers	Ian Fawn-Meade
Production consultant	Douglas Rankin
Production manager	John D. Merriman
Location unit manager*/ Second unit director	Bob Porter
First assistant director	Bert Batt
Second assistant director	Claude Watson*
Third assistant director (S.A.)	Howard Rennie*
Continuity	Muirne Mathieson
Personal secretary to the producers	Caroline Murray*
Production secretary	Noreen Hipwell*
Unit secretary	E. Abbott*
Business manager	John McMichael*
Secretaries	Joan Dowie Dunn/Marguerite Green/Diana James/Susan Langford/Penny Woolley
Post-production secretary	Pam Tomling*
Production accountant	Arthur V. Hall*
Assistant accountants	Roy R. Skeggs/ Gillian Stone*

Story and Screenplay

Screenplay and adaptation	John Prebble/ Cy Endfield
Original story	John Prebble

Camera Department

Lighting cameraman	Stephen Dade
Camera operator	Dudley Lovell
Focus puller	Peter Hammond*
Maintenance	Brinley Jones*

Clapper/loader	Brian Ellis*
Grip	F.J. Williams*

Production Sound Department

Sound mixer	Claude Hitchcock
Operator	Derek Leather*
Boom operator	David Jones*
Maintenance	Fred C. Hughesdon*

Art Department

Art director	Ernest Archer
Assistant art director	Vernon Dixon*
Casting director	Thelma Graves*

Make-up Department

Chief make-up man	Charles Parker
Assistant make-up	Michael Morris*
Make-up staff	Judy Cadman/Bob Lawrance/Richard Mills*

Hairdressing Department

Hairdresser	Bill Griffiths*

Wardrobe Department

Wardrobe supervisor	Arthur Newman
Wardrobe assistants	James Smith/Charles Prime*

Stills Department

Production stills cameraman	Norman Gryspeerdt*
Special stills photographers	Yousuf Karsh/Sergio Strizzi*
S.A. stills photographer	Jürgen Schadeberg*

Publicity Department

Unit publicist	Geoff Freeman*
Publicity secretary	Maureen White*
Trailer scriptwriter	Esther Harris*
Trailer editor	Doug McCallum*

Special Effects Department

Special Effects	Ron Nicholson*
Special Effects	Jim Harris*
Special Effects	Roy Whybrow*

Editorial Department

Editor	John Jympson
First assistant editor	Jennifer Thompson
Second assistant editor	Nick Stevenson*

Construction Department

Construction manager	Dick Frift
Carpenter	E.T.H. Blake*
Carpenter	John Paterson*
Stagehand	Bill Savory
Painter	Bert Carr*
Rigger	Bill Savory
Plasterer	Jack Arnott*
Plasterer	J. Sherbourne*
Construction contractor	Dave Alexander*

Property Department

Property master	John Poyner*

Prop man .... Ron Hutchins*
Prop man .... T.J. (Tommy) Bacon*

Electrical Department
Chief electrician .... Jim Powell*
Electrician .... Arthur Green*
Electrician .... David Walsh*
Electrician .... Sydney George*
Generator operator .... P. Atkinson*
Electrical maintenance .... A.H. Monk*
Crane operator .... A.G. Holmes*
Property supplier .... Ernest Bisogno*

Stunts
Stunt director .... John Sullivan
Stunt arranger .... Joe Powell*
Stunts .... Robin Webb

Post-production sound and music
Sound editor .... Rusty Coppleman
Assistant sound editors .... Alan Strachan/Pamela Tomling/Len Walter*
Dubbing mixers .... J.B. Smith/ Stephen Dalby*
Stereo dubbing mixers .... Gordon K. McCallum/Ray Palmer*
Music composer and conductor .... John Barry
Choreographer (Zulu wedding dance) .... Princess Constance Magogo ka Dinuzulu*
Lyricists ('Men of Harlech') .... Ivor Emmanuel/Cy Endfield*
Orchestra leader .... Alec Firman*
Music contractor .... Sidney Margo*
Music recording engineer .... Eric Tomlinson*
Choir ('Men of Harlech') .... Imperial Glee Singers*

South African staff
Assistant location manager .... C. Hignett*
Location manager (S.A.) .... Joshua du Toit*
Assistant location manager (S.A.) .... Dawie van Heerden*
Construction firm .... Belvedere Timber Structures*
Costume designer (S.A.) .... Hilda Geerdts*
Property manufacturers .... Pam and Ken Coughtrie/A.J. Harborth*
Caterer .... Tony Allchurch*
Drivers .... Carl Howells/Mr. Elias*
Projectionists .... Mr. Dunbar/Mr. Wilcot*
Unit doctors .... Dr Fred Clark/Dr. Jack Danchin/Dr. Lane*
Unit nurse .... Anne Nickson*
Gaffer (South African crew) .... Corrie van Wyk*
Second unit crew .... T. Askew/Heinz Fenke/Alan Girney/Hank Martens/Jack Martin/
  Edu Masuch V. Whitten*
Miscellaneous crew .... M. Basson/R. Berry/R. Brown/P. Cauvin/J. Da Silva/M. Hoffbrand/
  B. Le Roux/ G. Martens/Bob Martin/F. Mentz/C. Syndercombe/G. Volans/G. Von Benecke*

Contacts in London
Production services .... Charles Cannon
Embassy Pictures' representative .... Kenneth Hargreaves
Travel agency .... Albany Travel Services Ltd.
Shipping agent for S.A. Films .... Brown Bros.

Company solicitors	Harbottle & Lewis
Insurance	Tufnell Satterthwaite & Co. Ltd.
Travel agency in South Africa	World Travel Agency
Agency for freight in South Africa	Ace Airfreight Services Ltd.
Costumiers	M. Berman Limited
Camera and laboratories	Technicolor Ltd.
Sound equipment	Location Sound Facilities Ltd.
Electrical	Mole-Richardson (England) Ltd.
Completion guarantor	Film Finances*
Laboratory contact	Les Ostinelli*

US staff

Paramount executives	Frank Caffey/Bernard Donnenfeld/R.H. Harrison/Jack Karp/Martin Rackin*
Paramount accountants	Sam Bernstein/Robert Garrett/A.A. Grosser/Donald Peverett/David Schneider*

Distribution staff

Paramount sales manager (UK)	Peter Reed*
Paramount circuit manager (UK)	Mike Ewin*
Distribution and publicity staff	Ann Bennett/Ralph Cooper/Theo Cowan/Martin Davis/Russell W. Hadley/Leslie Pound/Günther Schack/Jack Upfold/Robert Weston*
Distributors (US and Canada)	Embassy Pictures Corporation
Distributors (UK and World)	Paramount Pictures Corporation
Copyright	© 1963 Diamond Films Ltd.

BIBLIOGRAPHY

Listed here are all those books referred to in the text or consulted in the course of my research. Articles, reviews and news items from magazines, trade journals and newspapers, along with television programmes and internet websites, can be found cited in the notes at the end of each chapter.

General

Janine Basinger, *The World War II Combat Film: Anatomy of a Genre* (New York: Columbia University Press, 1986; second edition, Middleton: Wesleyan University Press, 2003)

Walter Bernstein, *Inside Out: A Memoir of the Blacklist* (New York: Alfred A. Knopf, 1996)

David Berry, *Wales and Cinema: The First Hundred Years* (Cardiff: University of Wales Press, 1994)

Anne Billson, *My Name Is Michael Caine* (London: Muller, 1991)

Melvyn Bragg, *Rich: The Life of Richard Burton* (London: Hodder and Stoughton, 1988)

Michael Caine, *What's It All About?* (London: Random House/Arrow, 1992)

Michael Caine, *The Elephant to Hollywood: An Autobiography* (London: Hodder & Stoughton, 2010)

Ian Cameron and Douglas Pye (eds.), *The Movie Book of the Western* (Studio Vista, 1996)

Kenneth M. Cameron, *Africa on Film: Beyond Black and White* (New York: Continuum, 1994)

Deborah Cartmell, I.Q. Hunter and Imelda Whelehan (eds.), *Retrovisions: Reinventing the Past in Film and Fiction* (London and Sterling, Virginia: Pluto Press, 2001)

James Chapman, *Past and Present: National Identity and the British Historical Film* (London: I.B. Tauris, 2005)

James Chapman and Nicholas J. Cull, *Projecting Empire: Imperialism and Popular Culture* (London: I.B. Tauris, 2009)

Steve Chibnall and Robert Murphy (eds.), *British Crime Cinema* (London and New York: Routledge, 1999)

John Cottrell and Fergus Cashin, *Richard Burton* (London: Coronet, 1971)

Lester David and Jhan Robbins, *Richard & Elizabeth* (London: Arthur Barker, 1977)

Peter Davis, *In Darkest Hollywood: Exploring the jungles of cinema's South Africa* (Athens: Ohio University Press, 1996)

Graham Dawson, *Soldier Heroes: British adventure, empire and the imagining of masculinities* (London and New York: Routledge, 1994)

Bernard F. Dick, *Engulfed: The Death of Paramount Pictures and the Birth of Corporate Hollywood* (Lexington: University Press of Kentucky, 2001)

Raymond Durgnat, *A Mirror for England: British Movies from Austerity to Affluence* (London: Faber and Faber, 1970)

Allen Eyles, *ABC: The First Name in Entertainment* (Burgess Hill: Cinema Theatre Association/British Film Institute, 1993)

Allen Eyles, *The Granada Theatres* (London: Cinema Theatre Association/British Film Institute, 1998)

Matthew Field, *Michael Caine: 'You're a Big*

Man…' *The Performances That Made the Man* (London: B.T. Batsford, 2003)
Eddi Fiegel, *John Barry: A Sixties Theme: From James Bond to* Midnight Cowboy (London: Constable, 1998)
Bruce Forsyth, *Bruce: The Autobiography* (London: Sidgwick and Jackson, 2001)
Elaine Gallagher, *Candidly Caine* (London: Robson Books/London Weekend Television, 1990)
Shelagh Gastrow (ed.), *Who's Who in South African Politics, Number 4* (Johannesburg: Ravan Press, 1992)
Kenneth Griffith, *The Fool's Pardon* (London: Little, Brown, 1994)
William Hall, *Raising Caine: The Authorized Biography* (London: Arrow Books, 1982; enlarged and reprinted as *Arise Sir Michael Caine* and *Seventy Not Out*)
Jack Hawkins, *Anything for a Quiet Life* (London: Elm Tree, 1973)
John Huston, *An Open Book* (London: Macmillan, 1980)
Leonard J. Leff and Jerold L. Simmons, *The Dame in the Kimono: Hollywood, Censorship, and the Production Code from the 1920's to the 1960's* (London: Weidenfeld and Nicolson, 1990)
Geoffrey Macnab, *Searching for Stars: Stardom and Screen Acting in British Cinema* (London and New York: Cassell, 2000)
Edward Mapp, *Blacks in American Films: Today and Yesterday* (Metuchen: Scarecrow Press, 1972)
Richard A. Maynard, *Africa on Film: Myth and Reality* (Rochelle Park, NJ: Hayden Book Company, 1974)
Colin McArthur, Brigadoon, Braveheart *and the Scots: Distortions of Scotland in Hollywood Cinema* (London and New York: I.B. Tauris, 2003)
Joseph McBride (ed.), *Filmmakers on Filmmaking: The American Film Institute Seminars on Motion Pictures and Television, Volume Two* (Los Angeles: J.P. Tarcher, 1983)
Patrick McGilligan and Paul Buhle, *Tender Comrades: A Backstory of the Hollywood Blacklist* (New York: St Martin's Griffin, 1999)
Claire Monk and Amy Sargeant (eds.), *British Historical Cinema* (London and New York: Routledge, 2002)
Robert Murphy, *Sixties British Cinema* (London: British Film Institute, 1992)
Brian Neve, *Film and Politics in America: A Social Tradition* (London and New York: Routledge, 1992)
Barry Norman, *The Movie Greats* (London: Hodder and Stoughton/BBC, 1981)
Jim Pines, *Blacks in Films: A Survey of Racial Themes and Images in the American Film* (London: Studio Vista, 1975)
John Prebble, *Culloden* (Harmondsworth: Penguin, 1967)
John Prebble, *Landscapes & Memories: An intermittent autobiography* (London: HarperCollins, 1993)
John Prebble, *Spanish Stirrup and Other Stories* (Harmondsworth: Penguin, 1975)
Paul Raby, Zulu: *The Truth Behind the Film* (York: York Publishing Services, 2009)
Jeffrey Richards, *Visions of Yesterday* (London: Routledge and Kegan Paul, 1973)
Jeffrey Richards, *Films and British National Identity: From Dickens to* Dad's Army (Manchester: Manchester University Press, 1997)
Jonathan Rosenbaum, *Placing Movies: The Practice of Film Criticism* (Berkeley, Los Angeles and London: University of California Press, 1995)
Jonathan Rosenbaum, *Movies as Politics* (Berkeley, Los Angeles and London: University of California Press, 1997)
Robert A. Rosenstone, *Visions of the Past: The Challenge of Film to Our Idea of History* (Cambridge, Mass., and London: Harvard University Press, 1995)
Lillian Ross, *Picture* (Harmondsworth: Penguin, 1962)
Anthony Sampson, *Mandela: The Authorised Biography* (London: HarperCollins, 1999)
Murray Schumach, *The Face on the Cutting Room Floor: The Story of Movie and Television Censorship* (New York: William Morrow, 1964; reprinted by Da Capo Press, 1975)
Robert Shail, *Stanley Baker: A Life in Film* (Cardiff: University of Wales Press, 2008)

Ella Shohat and Robert Stam, *Unthinking Eurocentrism: Multiculturalism and the media* (London and New York: Routledge, 1994)
Wilbur Smith, *When the Lion Feeds* (London: Heinemann/Pan Books, 1964)
Andrew Spicer, *Typical Men: The Representation of Masculinity in Popular British Cinema* (London and New York: I.B. Tauris, 2001)
Terence Stamp, *Double Feature* (London: Bloomsbury, 1989)
Peter Stead, *Acting Wales: Stars of Stage and Screen* (Cardiff: University of Wales Press, 2002)
Ian Stewart and Susan L. Carruthers (eds.), *War, Culture and the Media: Representations of the Military in 20th Century Britain* (Trowbridge: Flicks, 1996)
Anthony Storey, *Stanley Baker: Portrait of an Actor* (London: W.H. Allen, 1977)
Brian Taves, *The Romance of Adventure: The Genre of Historical Adventure Movies* (Jackson, MS: Mississippi University Press, 1993)
Ben Temkin, *Buthelezi: A Biography* (London and Portland: Frank Cass, 2003)
Tony Thomas, *The Great Adventure Films* (Secaucus, NJ: Citadel Press, 1976)
Keyan Tomaselli, *The Cinema of Apartheid: Race and Class in South African Film* (London and New York: Routledge, 1989)
Robert Brent Toplin, *Reel History: In Defense of Hollywood* (Lawrence: University Press of Kansas, 2002)
John Trevelyan, *What the Censor Saw* (London: Michael Joseph, 1973)
Robert Vaughn, *Only Victims: A Study of Show Business Blacklisting* (New York: G.P. Putnam's Sons, 1972)
Alexander Walker, *Hollywood, England: The British Film Industry in the Sixties* (London: Michael Joseph, 1974; reprinted London: Harrap, 1986)
Alexander Walker, *National Heroes: British Cinema in the Seventies and Eighties* (London: Harrap, 1985)
Stuart Ward (ed.), *British Culture and the End of Empire* (Manchester: Manchester University Press, 2001)
Ian Watson, *Bare Black Breasts and Boys Own Battles: Images of Empire for White Working Class Lads in Mid-Sixties Britain* (unpublished MA dissertation, Leeds Metropolitan University, 1996)
Tom Weaver (ed.), *Science Fiction Stars and Horror Heroes: Interviews with Actors, Directors, Producers and Writers of the 1940s through 1960s* (Jefferson and London: 1991)
John Willis, Saul Cooper and Laurie Bailey, *All About* The Heroes of Telemark (London: Rank Organisation, 1965)

The Anglo-Zulu War of 1879

A complete list of modern sources on this subject would be extremely lengthy. I list here only the works that I consulted in preparing the present volume.

David Clammer, *The Zulu War* (London and Sydney: Pan, 1973)
Saul David, *Zulu: The Heroism and Tragedy of the Zulu War of 1879* (London: Viking, 2004)
Michael Glover, *Rorke's Drift: A Victorian Epic* (London: Leo Cooper, 1975)
Adrian Greaves, *Rorke's Drift* (London: Cassell, 2002)
Alan Baynham Jones and Lee Stevenson (eds.), *Rorke's Drift By Those Who Were There* (Brighton: Lee Stevenson Publishing, 2003)
Ian Knight, *Nothing Remains But To Fight: The Defence of Rorke's Drift, 1879* (London: Greenhill Books, 1993)
Ian Knight, *The Sun Turned Black: Isandlwana and Rorke's Drift – 1879* (Rivonia and Sandton: William Waterman, 1995)
Ian Knight and Ian Castle, *The Zulu War – Then and Now* (London: Plaistow, 1993)
Ron Lock and Peter Quantrill (eds.), *The 1879 Zulu War Through the eyes of The Illustrated London News* (Kloof, kwaZulu-Natal: Q-Lock Publications, 2003)
Donald R. Morris, *The Washing of the Spears: A History of the Rise of the Zulu Nation under Shaka and its Fall in the Zulu war of 1879* (London: Jonathan Cape, 1965; revised and reprinted, London: Pimlico, 1989/1994)
David Rattray and Adrian Greaves, *David Rattray's Guidebook to the Anglo-Zulu War*

Battlefields (Barnsley: Leo Cooper, 2002)
Edmund J. Yorke, *Rorke's Drift 1879: Anatomy of an Epic Zulu War Siege* (Stroud: Tempus, 2001)

John Prebble's Bibliography

In order to research his original magazine article on Rorke's Drift ('Slaughter in the Sun,' *Lilliput*, April 1958), John Prebble visited the British Museum Library from 3 to 5 December 1957, and again on 25 and 26 January the following year. Included in his surviving files, access to which was graciously granted me by his widow Jan, are not just the twenty-six pages of typewritten notes Prebble compiled from the records he investigated, but also the actual request slips he filled in at the Library, which reveal what books and other materials he read, on what days, and even at which desk he sat while reading them (T6 in the Typing Room, for the curious). Because the notes were not intended for publication, with the exceptions of the official HMSO documents he did not identify the publishers. The list below is reproduced from Prebble's own notes, with the correction of a few obvious typos; further bibliographic data, where relevant and available, has been added in square brackets.

Narrative of Field Operations connected with the Zulu War, 1879 (HMSO, 1907)
Précis of Information concerning the Zulu country, etc. (HMSO, 1879)
Memorandum on Tactics in Zulu Warfare (HMSO, 1879 [? – Prebble's query])
Col. G. Paton [and F. Glennie, W. Penn Symons], *South Wales Borderers, Historical Records of the 24th Regiment* ([London] 1892)
C.T. Atkinson, *The South Wales Borderers, [24th Foot] 1689-1937* ([Cambridge] 1937)
2nd Battalion, 24th Regiment, Roll of B Company, Rorke's Drift, 22 January 1879 (1922, typewritten)
F.E. Colenso and E. Durnford, *[The] History of the Zulu War [and Its Origin]* [London: Chapman and Hall] (1880)
Edward Durnford, *Isandhlwana* (1879)
W.J. Elliott, *The Victoria Cross in Zululand [and South Africa and How it Was Won]* [London] (1882)
W.R. Ludlow, *Zululand & [and] Cetewayo* [London] (1882)
Sir Henry Hallam Parr, *[A Sketch of the] Kafir and Zulu Wars* [London: Kegan Paul] (1880)
D.C.F. Moodie, *[The] History of the Battles [and Adventures] of the British, [the] Boers, and [the] Zulus [etc., in Southern Africa from the Time of the Pharaoh Necho, to 1880]* [Adelaide] (1888, two vols.)
E.A. Ritter, *Shaka Zulu [The Rise of the Zulu Empire]* [London: Longmans] (1955)
Manual of Drill etc. for the Martini-Henry Rifle and Carbine (HMSO, 1876)
Daily Telegraph, January-June 1879
Morning Post, January-June 1879
The Illustrated London News, January-June 1879
Africana Notes and News, June 1957
Encyclopaedia Britannica, eleventh edition

Prebble grouped his notes in four sections, as follows:

(A) THE ACTION

Specific sources Prebble used for the events of 22 and 23 January 1879 were: Parr, *Kafir and Zulu Wars*; Elliott, *The Victoria Cross in Zululand*; Paton, *South Wales Borderers, Historical Records of the 24th Regiment*; HMSO, *Narrative of Field Operations connected with the Zulu War, 1879*; Atkinson, *The South Wales Borderers, 1689-1937*; the *Daily Telegraph* of 5, 6, 24 and 25 March 1879, and the *Morning Post* of 12 and 17 March. Lieutenant John Chard's Official Report and Chaplain George Smith's account of the battle are specifically summarised in Prebble's notes. Prebble also drew, or copied, rough maps of the location of Rorke's Drift in relation to Natal and Zululand, and of the layout of the mission station itself, including the direction of the Zulus' attacks, probably based on Chard's own hand-drawn plans.

(B) THE ZULUS

Detailed information on the history, customs, composition and conduct of the Zulus, including their dress, weaponry, command orders and fighting tactics, was derived from: the *Narrative of Field Operations* and *Précis of Information concerning the Zulu country, etc.*; Parr, *Kafir and Zulu Wars*; Ludlow, *Zululand and Cetewayo*; the *Daily Telegraph* (March 1879, but exact dates are unspecified); and, for background to Cetewayo's rule in the years immediately preceding the War, the *Encyclopaedia Britannica*. Prebble also sketched the Zulus' 'buffalo formation' method of attack (Adendorff's diagram in the dust in *Zulu* is very similar to the writer's sketch).

(C) THE BRITISH

Details of uniforms, arms and equipment were gleaned from: Paton, *Historical Records of the 24th Regiment*; the *Encyclopaedia Britannica*; the *Manual of Drill and Firing Exercises for the Martini-Henry Rifle and Carbine*; and *Africana Notes and News* of June 1957. From these Prebble learned the firing mechanism and capabilities of the Martini-Henry, and the correct drill, bayonet fixing and fighting methods, including the appropriate commands, for its use. He also drew sketches of the rifle and bayonet and the various positions adopted by the soldier using one.

(D) THE GARRISON

From Chard's Nominal Roll of 3 February 1879 and the 'official' regimental roll available in typewritten form in the British Library as *2nd Battalion, 24th Regiment, Roll of B Company, Rorke's Drift, 22 January 1879*, Prebble compiled lists of the names of the defenders of Rorke's Drift (the two rolls do not exactly tally, as scholars will know: see Chapter 14 of Adrian Greaves, *Rorke's Drift*, for a discussion of the discrepancies between the rolls). From Paton's *Historical Records of the 24th Regiment* Prebble made notes on the parts played in the fighting of most of the ten VC holders he then knew about. A further roll was compiled from the *London Gazette* (issue unspecified), which also identified the eleventh VC (Dalton). Pictures of Lieutenants Chard and Bromhead were described from *The Illustrated London News* (issues unspecified). A letter from the Rector of Bassingham in the *Daily Telegraph* of 7 March 1879 provided material on Bromhead's military lineage (see Chapter 7). General descriptions of the layout and surroundings of Rorke's Drift were derived from the *Précis of Information concerning the Zulu country*.

ACKNOWLEDGEMENTS

My first thanks must go to my editor and publisher at Tomahawk Press, Bruce Sachs, who was more than understanding throughout the three years it took me to research and write this book, not to mention the year or so to complete the revisions for the second edition. He has also been patient and supportive beyond measure throughout our ongoing friendship and professional collaboration, and has helped make many valuable contacts. Appreciation is also hereby expressed to the book's designer, Steve Kirkham, for his superb craftsmanship and attention to detail. Bruce and Steve deserve to share in whatever credit may be due for the book; any lapses or limitations it suffers are entirely the fault of the author. They also merit commendation for their extreme patience and forbearance with my nit-picking, procrastination and occasional tantrums (though I like to think they were all in the service of a greater good).

A number of people directly involved in the making and release of *Zulu* granted interviews on which much of the book is based. Jennifer Bates (née Thompson), the late Bert Batt, the late James Booth, Rusty Coppleman, Glynn Edwards, the late Geoff Freeman, Peter Gill, the late David Jones, David Kernan, the late Basil Keys, Robert Porter and Joe Powell were all interviewed in person. Others gave interviews by telephone: Pam Coughtrie, Richard Davies, the late Ivor Emmanuel, the late Mike Ewin, Denys Graham, the late Peter Hammond, Michael Morris, Dickie Owen, Andre Pieterse, the late Alan Strachan, the late Sergio Strizzi and the late Larry Taylor. Ellen, Lady Baker, Maureen Endfield, the late Doreen Hawkins and Jan Prebble discussed at length the work of their respective husbands. Several of those named above were also kind enough to read and offer useful comments and corrections on drafts of various chapters, or wrote letters giving additional help and information.

At a time of great political turmoil and personal bereavement, His Excellency Prince Mangosuthu G. Buthelezi graciously responded to my request for a formal statement regarding his involvement with *Zulu*. For invaluable help in translating Zulu songs, explaining Zulu culture and for providing an essential alternative viewpoint on the film, I am indebted to Elliot Ngubane and Paul Matewele, and to John Young for enabling me to contact them. I received welcome correspondence in response to a letter placed in several South African newspapers from David E. Arnold, Andy Coughtrie, Licia Dewing, Chris Dresser, Jeff Gaisford, May Hannah, Wendy Hittler, Darren Kirby, Don McArthur, John Murray, David Selvan, Peter Sheward, Jim Stockley, Gillian Stone, Roland Suhr and Tisha Watt.

I am extremely grateful to the many contributors to the Discussion Forum at http://rorkesdriftvc.com/ for all their exchanges of information and constructive argument which have given me such an insight into the Anglo-Zulu War and the whole '*Zulu* community.' In particular I would like to acknowledge Neil Aspinshaw, Arthur Bainbridge, Vaughan Birbeck, Colin Blackler,

David Colbourne, Simon Copley, Alan Critchley, Peter Critchley, Clive Dickens, Ian Essex, Steven Etchells, Peter Ewart, Edward Garcia, David Alan Gardner, James Garland, Peter Harman, Mark Hepworth, Martin Heyes, Mark Hobson, Andrew Holliday, Darren Holt, Melvin Hunt, Barry Iacoppi, Marc Jung, Greg King, Gary Laliberty, Andy Lee, Graham Mason, Alex Rossiter, Steven Sass, Eddie Saunders, Lee Stevenson, Robert Vantan, David Wachtel, Glenn Wade, Richard Waters, Kris Wheatley, Julian Whybra, John Young, and all those whose recollections of *Zulu* have been quoted or cited throughout this book.

I am particularly indebted to a number of fellow writers and researchers who have shared their own work with me or conducted additional research on my behalf: Diana Blackwell, James Chapman, Stephen Coan, Michael Coate, Henry Coleman, Allen Eyles, George Flaxman, William Hall, Ian Knight, Peter Krämer, Lawrence Napper, Brian Neve, John Oliver, Jonathan Rosenbaum, Robert Shail, George Smith, Jonathan Stubbs and Ian Watson. Steve Freer at BBC Wales made available video recordings of interviews he conducted for the television documentary *Stanley Baker: A Life in Film*. David Sharp at the British Film Institute granted me access to interviews conducted for the BECTU Oral History Project with the late Esther Harris, Dudley Lovell and Gordon K. McCallum. The staff of the Margaret Herrick Library in Los Angeles, including Barbara Hall and Kristine Krueger, arranged access to the Paramount Production Files. Barbara James Chapman and Charles Drazin invited me to participate in the project to explore the archives of Film Finances, Ltd, which allowed me to research additional material included in this second edition. I am also grateful to the staff of Film Finances' London office, whose hospitality made visiting there such a pleasure.

Among the many other people who have loaned materials, answered queries, provided contacts or suggested leads in the furtherance of my research are the late David Berry, Lionel Blair, Darrol Blake, M. Paul Bryant-Quinn, Wyn Calvin, Peter Charlesworth, John Clark, Henry Coleman, Nicholas Cull, Richard Dade, Peter Davis, Bruce Dettman, Guy Evans, Matthew Field, Michael Firman, James Fitzpatrick, Mrs Pat Greaney, Leighton Grist, John Havard, Joanne Hooper, Ian Hywel-Jones, Joy Jameson, Nate Kohn, Nicky Layouni, Geoff Leonard, Mark Lewisohn, Gavrik Losey, John McAdam, Murray Melvin, Dimity Morgan (née Dade), Patrick Newley, Lee Pfeiffer, Jim Pines, Stephen R. Pickard, the late Nosher Powell, Thelma Schoonmaker Powell, Peter Prichard, John Rowe, Sir Sidney Samuelson, Mike Siegel, Jackie Simons, Gary Slaymaker, Tony Sloman, Mari Stevens, Anthony Storey, Barry Taylor and Dave Worrall.

Since the book was first published, many people have written to thank me, share their thoughts on the book and the film, provide further information and offer helpful ideas and corrections. I am especially grateful to Richard Chatten for providing a long list of errata, most of which I hope to have addressed, and to other correspondents including David Allen, Malcolm Carter, Richard Conte, Janet Davis, Alan Gee, Ken Griffiths, Craig Grobler, Nick Haslett, Peter Hind, Patrick Humphries, David R. Johnston, Maureen Julia Jones, Tony Jones, Karl Lander, Rod Lodge, Graham Mason, John McAdam, Peter Mellar, Dennis Morris, Mark Moss, Roger Nash, Gene O'Brien, Derrick Smart, David Stephenson, Leigh Tarrant, David Todd, Ian Tootle, John James Wallace, Howard Watson and James Peter Young.

I am also grateful to the following individuals and their respective organisations: Alan and Angie Gibbs, Bill Howells, Christopher John, Maurice Jones, Brian Kirby, Roger Morgan, John Roberts, Danny Tully (The 1879 Group); Adrian Greaves (Anglo-Zulu War Historical Society); Katie Hart (BAFTA); Tony Watts (Bapty Limited); Vicki Mitchell, Tim Robinson (BBC); David Barrett, David Godfrey, Craig Lapper (BBFC); Rick Harley, Ann Millington (BECTU); Fleur Buckley, Bryony Dixon, Kathleen Dixon, Nina Harding, Janet Moat, Claire Thomas (British

Film Institute); Sarah Chadwick, Sam Copeland, Joe Phillips (Curtis Brown); Yewande Ojo, Cheryl Philbert (Equity); Christine Innes (The Golden Lion, Newport); Amanda, Robin Bray (Granada Television); the late Alfie Cox (Guild of British Film Editors); Toby Haggith, Sarah Rogers (Imperial War Museum); Barbara Entressangle (Limelight Publications); Philip Moores, Lancelot Narayan (Lipsync); The Magic Circle; Janet Lorenz (Margaret Herrick Library, Academy of Motion Picture Arts and Sciences); Kim Hoover (MGM Home Entertainment); Helen Wells (Pinewood Studios); Major Martin Everett (Royal Regiment of Wales Museum); Trevor Moses (South African National Film Archive); Andrew Wales, John Woods (Technicolor); the late Gerry Humphreys (Twickenham Studios); Keyan Tomaselli (University of Natal).

Hospitality during my various research trips was generously provided by friends including Stacey Abbott and Simon Brown, Sergio Angelini, Nick and Kaye Howe, Debora Mo, John Sylph and Virginia Walton, Cristina and Tor-Christian Pulido Ulvang, Michael Walker and, on a hastily arranged visit to Los Angeles, Paul Anderson, Joan Anderson, Sarah Crompton and the late Stan Routledge. All of them have also been helpful and supportive in ways too numerous to mention. Lastly, the first edition of this book was written while I was performing a full-time job as a lecturer in Film Studies at Sheffield Hallam University, with no time off for research. Thanks, therefore, to those present and past colleagues in the former School of Cultural Studies and the current Department of Humanities who held the fort, made my work bearable and offered encouragement for this project, especially Michelle Atherton, Catherine Constable, the late Gerry Coubro, John Cunningham, Sylvia Harvey, Frank Krutnik, Angela Martin, James McNichomas, Steve Neale, Shelley O'Brien, Matthew Pateman, Tom Ryall, Chi-Yun Shin, Neil Sissons and Suzanne Speidel. Chas Critcher arranged funding for my American research trip and Dave Waddington for subsequent research trips to London. To the many students who inquired about the book's progress or who have, since the original publication, discussed it with me or even read it, I also tip my hat.

Zulu was produced by Diamond Films Limited. Distribution rights are currently controlled by MGM/UA in the United States and Canada, and by Paramount Pictures Corporation in the United Kingdom and the rest of the world. It is available for purchase on DVD and Blu-ray in the US and Canada from MGM/UA Home Entertainment and Twilight Time respectively, and on all formats in other regions from Paramount Home Entertainment. The Paramount Blu-rays and DVDs include several documentaries and an audio commentary featuring Robert Porter and the present author. It is very good value for money and warmly recommended.

ABOUT THE AUTHOR

Sheldon Hall lectures in Stage and Screen Studies at Sheffield Hallam University and has written and taught on many aspects of the cinema. He studied Film and Literature at the University of Warwick and received his Masters and Doctorate from the University of East Anglia. A former freelance journalist, reviewing film and theatre for *The Northern Echo* from 1986 to 1997, he has published articles in such journals as *Cinema Retro*, *Empire*, *Film History*, the *Historical Journal of Film, Radio and Television*, the *Journal of British Cinema and Television*, *Iluminace*, *Picture House*, *Premiere* and *Viewfinder*. He has also contributed to internet websites including the BFI's *ScreenOnline*, *Oxford Bibliographies Online*, the *Oxford Dictionary of National Biography* and *in70mm*. He is the co-author of *Epics, Spectacles, and Blockbusters: A Hollywood History* (2010) and co-editor of *Widescreen Worldwide* (2010). Among the other books to which he has contributed are *The Movie Book of the Western* (1996), *The British Cinema Book* (2001/2009), *British Historical Cinema* (2002), *Genre and Contemporary Hollywood* (2002), *The Cinema of John Carpenter: The Technique of Terror* (2004), *Contemporary American Cinema* (2006), *Directors in British and Irish Cinema: A Reference Companion* (2006), *Journeys of Desire: European Actors in Hollywood* (2006), *Seventies British Cinema* (2008), *The Classical Hollywood Reader* (2012) and *The Return of the Epic Film: Genre, Aesthetics and History in the 21st Century* (2014). Sheldon provided audio commentaries for the Paramount Home Entertainment DVD and Blu-ray releases of *Zulu* and *Once Upon a Time in the West* and has broadcast widely on radio and television. Currently he is writing *Armchair Cinema: Feature Films on British Television* for publication by Tomahawk Press.

INDEX

100 Greatest War Movies 370
2001: A Space Odyssey 229
55 Days at Peking 47, 222, 246, 303, 310, 311, 434
6.5 Special 254
633 Squadron 222
8? 130

Abbott, Richard 370
Accident 118
Aces High 163
Adams, Leticia 257
Adendorff, Lieutenant Josef 14, 15, 17, 61-65, 92, 99, 100, 174, 340, 431, 433, 456
Adventurers, The (1951) 146
Adventurers, The (1970) 308
Adventures of Baron Munchausen, The 246
Adventures of Sir Lancelot, The 140
Adventures of William Tell, The 140, 153, 156
Affairs of the Heart 112
Africa Shakes 192
African Queen, The 171
Age of Kings, An 112
Airport '77 155
Alamo, The 325, 434
Alexander Nevsky 254
Alexander the Great 117, 221, 234
Alf's Baby 244
Alfie 143, 154, 422
Alice in Wonderland 112
Aliens 287
All Quiet on the Western Front 297
Allchurch, Tony 165, 449
Allen, Corporal William 19, 37, 92, 95, 104, 105, 266, 268, 274, 275, 353
Allen, Irving 129
American Ninja 2: The Confrontation 174
Amyes, Julian 140
Angels One Five 145
Angry Hills, The 117, 216
Anker, Raymond 322, 330
Annakin, Ken 161, 163, 406
Anne of the Thousand Days 107
Anouilh, Jean 140
Anything for a Quiet Life 149
Apache Drums 39
Apache Rifles 277
Archer, Ernest 55, 59, 167, 168, 393, 406, 412-413

Argyle Secrets, The 78
Arneel, Gene 332
Arnold, Edward 78
Aspects of Love 107
Asylum 97
Atkins, Gordon 230, 350
Atkinson, C.T. 31
Attenborough, Richard 83, 118, 145, 149
Attila (Attila the Hun) 129, 131
Attwood, Corporal Francis 91, 93
Auf Wiedersehen, Pet 155
Autry, Gene 190

Badel, Alan 291
Baker, Bob 97
Baker, Carroll 298, 362
Baker, Ellen 8, 115, 116, 118, 119, 122, 123, 124, 125, 126, 141, 145, 148, 157, 175, 189, 191, 194, 200, 201, 202, 254, 258, 295, 302, 362, 363, 408, 423
Baker, Martin 369
Baker, Stanley 1, 3, 5, 9, 10, 35, 37, 47, 48, 61, 67, 72, 74, 82-85, 87, 93, 94, 97, 99, 115-119, 121-124, 126-129, 131-133, 137, 138, 140, 141, 144, 146, 148, 149, 151, 152, 155, 156, 157, 161-163, 167, 171, 173, 178, 181, 183, 184, 185, 188-193, 195, 196, 199, 200-205, 207, 215, 216, 220-223, 227, 228, 230, 231, 233-235, 239-241, 243-248, 254, 256-260, 270, 274, 278, 281, 283, 286-288, 290, 291, 295, 296, 298, 301, 306, 307, 308, 315, 320, 321, 326, 327, 331, 332, 334, 337-339, 345, 346, 351, 352, 356, 357, 360-364, 366, 368, 369, 378, 388-391, 394-400, 403, 406-409, 412-413, 415419, 421-424, 437, 446, 451
Balcon, Sir Michael 128
Bale, Philip 370
Balliett, Whitney 336
Balsam, Martin 78
Bandit of Zhobe, The 430
Bannerman, Helen 369
Bare Black Breasts and Boys Own Battles 441
Barker, Felix 320
Barker, Lex 79
Barlow, Mrs Elizabeth 296
Barnes, Clive 324

Barnes, Susan 115
Barra, Allen 367
Barry Lyndon 97, 221
Barry, John 1, 122, 253-256, 295, 419-421, 439-440
Bart, Lionel 153, 154, 419
Bartok, Bela 254
Basinger, Jeanine 431-432
Bataan 431
Bates, Alan 153
Bates, Jonathan 240
Batt, Bert 144, 161, 173, 176, 189, 195, 200, 201, 223, 228, 239, 244, 363, 378, 413, 415, 463
Battle of Britain 144, 434
Battle of Rorke's Drift, The 46, 53, 127, 128, 406
Battle of the Bulge 219
Beat Girl 156, 254
Beatles, The 306
Beatty, Robert 286
Beau Brummell 163
Beau Geste 335
Beaumont, Binkie 156
Becket 168, 229
Beckett, Samuel 97, 112
Ben Casey 150
Ben-Hur 145, 229
Bennett, Constance 298
Bentley, Jack 322
Bergerac 155
Bergman, Ingmar 150, 409
Berkeley, Martin 79
Berman, Monty M. 35, 39
Berry, David 373
Beyond Our Ken 354
Bhekuzulu, Cyprian 183
Bhowani Junction 163
Biberman, Herbert J. 79
Bicycle Thieves 129
Bill, The 155
Billion Dollar Brain 288
Billy Budd 422
Birbeck, Vaughan 108
Birds of Prey 144
Birds, The 325
Birkin, Jane 122
Birthday Party, The 97
Bisogno, Ernest 172
Bitter Victory 156
Black and White Minstrel Show, The 369
Black as Hell and Thick as Grass 445
Black Cat, The 193

482 INDEX

Black Hawk Down 357, 368
Black Hole, The 254
Black Rose, The 163
Blackwell, Diana 108, 111, 381
Blair, Lionel 256, 257, 294, 295, 419
Blanket Story, The 193
Bleasdale, Alan 112
Blignaut, Paul 142
Blind Date 118
Blind Rage 47
Bliss of Mrs Blossom, The 155
Blood of Dr. Jekyll, The 97
Blue Max, The 244
Boccaccio '70 130
Body Heat 254
Bogarde, Dirk 137, 306, 363, 406
Bogart, Humphrey 119
Bond, Gary 107, 149, 307, 360, 413, 431
Bonnie Prince Charlie 145, 163, 361
Booth, James 58, 84, 97, 112, 123, 140, 141, 148, 152-155, 174, 206, 233, 235, 274, 275, 290, 291, 295, 307, 327-329, 333, 340, 356, 357, 360, 379, 396, 400, 418, 422, 424, 431
Borgias, The 47
Born Free 244, 254
Borowczyk, Walerian 97
Bottle Boys 291
Bourne, Colour-Sergeant Frank 16-19, 22, 31, 57, 61, 64, 65, 68-70, 90, 92, 94, 95, 100, 102-106, 128, 156-158, 173, 221, 275, 327, 340, 373, 431, 442
Bowen, Arthur 123
Boxer, The 193
Boyce, Max 345
Boyd, Stephen 140, 151
Boys from Syracuse, The 295
Brace, Keith 324, 331
Braden, Bernard 295
Brandford, Ronnie 415
Brannigan 155, 234, 365
Braveheart 367
Bredin, Patricia 295
Brickhill, Joan 407
Bridge on the River Kwai, The 145, 308
Bridge Too Far, A 143, 144, 223
Brigand of Kandahar, The 430
British Historical Cinema 8, 427
Broccoli, Albert R. 'Cubby' 129, 295
Bromhead, Lieutenant Gonville 1, 15-19, 21, 22, 26, 30, 32, 33, 35, 63, 64, 68-71, 90-96, 98-102, 105, 108, 137-144, 172, 269, 273, 295, 346, 353, 382, 409, 417, 429, 431, 433, 435, 439, 456
Bromhead, Lieutenant-Colonel Sir Benjamin 102, 295, 429
Brompton, Sally 43
Bronston, Samuel 47
Brosnan, Pierce 287
Bruce-Lockhart, Freda 326
Buchan, John 47
Buck, Jules 406
Buckley, Corporal 59, 61
Buffalo Soldiers, The 45
Bughwan, Dennis 220
Bulldog Breed, The 140, 144
Bullet for a Badman 310, 311
Bunting, Mrs J. 293
Burton, Richard 85, 116, 117, 124, 125, 127, 128, 156, 221, 234, 258, 260, 261, 262, 324, 362, 363, 423, 430
Burton, Sybil 258
Butcher, Maryvonne 319
Buthelezi, Chief Mangosuthu G. 2, 3, 53, 123, 162, 163, 168, 183, 185-189, 191, 192, 196, 201, 202, 207, 210, 212, 253, 278, 279, 363, 365, 366, 374, 377, 440-441, 445-446
Buthelezi: A Biography 186
Buttons, Red 298
Byrne, Louis 17, 19, 34, 68

Cadman, Judy 229
Caffey, Frank 391, 451
Caine Mutiny Court Martial, The 140
Caine Mutiny, The 140
Caine, Michael 1, 3, 32, 33, 88, 99, 102, 121, 131, 137-144, 148, 152, 154, 157, 158, 166, 173, 185, 192, 199, 201, 204, 205, 231, 239, 245-248, 260, 275, 286, 288, 290, 291, 294, 295, 297, 307, 321, 325-327, 331, 334, 340, 346, 352, 360, 363, 382, 394, 395, 402, 407, 409, 418, 420, 422, 424, 446, 463
Cameron, James 346
Cameron, Kate 337
Campbell's Kingdom 116
Canasta, Chan 88
Candidly Caine 127
Canutt, Yakima 221
Caprice 86
Captain Horatio Hornblower R.N. 116, 119, 138, 222
Captive Heart, The 234
Caravans 221
Cardiff East 205
Cardinal, The 303
Carmichael, Ian 83
Carpetbaggers, The 130, 298, 311-313
Carreras, Sir James 123
Carroll, Michael D. 382
Carry On Abroad 352
Carry On... Up the Khyber 234
Carstairs, John Paddy 163
Carve Her Name with Pride 163, 234
Cascando 97
Castle, Ian 24, 432-433
Castle, William, 410
Cetewayo (Cetshwayo) 11, 13, 15, 18, 22, 29, 37, 52-55, 98, 168, 186, 187, 193, 210, 211, 215, 353, 354, 366, 433-434, 441, 446
Chama, Sydney 119, 185, 190, 194, 196, 281
Changeling, The 122
Chaplin 254
Chaplin, Charlie 191
Chapman, Graham 357
Chapman, James 440
Charade 302
Chard, Lieutenant John 14-17, 21, 22, 26, 28, 34, 35, 56-58, 62-74, 90-102, 104-106, 115, 116, 118, 122, 173, 268, 269, 338, 340, 346, 349, 353, 381, 395, 406, 412, 417, 420, 431, 433, 435, 440, 456
Charge of the Light Brigade, The 430
Chase, The 254
Checkpoint 116
Chester, Hal E. 82, 88

Cheyenne Autumn 430
Chief Mamba and the Slave 192
Child in the House 82, 117, 334
Chiltern Hundreds, The 274
Chimes, The 140
Chitty Chitty Bang Bang 234, 436
Christie, Agatha 245
Christie, Julie 86
Cider House Rules, The 144
Cineaste 428, 440
Cinema of Apartheid: Race and Class in South African Film, The 193, 267
Clash of the Titans 245
Cleese, John 357
Cleopatra 128, 221, 234, 258, 286, 303, 362, 423
Clive of India 361
Clockwork Orange, A 97
Clooney, George 346
Clough, Steve 373
Coan, Stephen 142, 279, 372, 445
Coates, Anne V. 417
Cockleshell Heroes, The 219
Codron, Michael 297
Coen, Guido 417
Cogan, Alma 295, 419
Cohen, Nat 129, 295
Cole, Private Tom 18, 61, 66, 68, 97, 107, 148, 149, 431
Coleman, John 326, 330
Colonel March Investigates 81
Colonel March of Scotland Yard 81
Come Blow Your Horn 83, 140, 404
Compartment, The 140
Confederacy of Wives, The 155
Connery, Sean 82, 118, 140, 144, 222
Coppleman, Rusty 85, 203, 233, 240, 244, 247, 249, 253, 257, 258, 272, 346, 379, 417-418, 421
Coppola, Francis Ford 97, 367
Corbett, Harry H. 306
Cordell, Alexander 363
Corman, Roger 87, 97
Coronation Street 291
Corrigan Blake 112
Cotton Club, The 254
Coughtrie, Ken 172
Coughtrie, Pam 172
Courageous Moments in History 298
Cowan, Professor Edward 45
Cowan, Theo 286, 294
Crawford, Michael 83
Criminal, The 97, 117, 118, 138, 156, 245, 351, 437
Crimson Pirate, The 221, 222
Critchley, Alan 108, 370
Critchley, Peter 370
Cromwell 234, 287
Cross of Iron 223
Crowther, Bosley 338, 339
Croydon, John 387, 389-393, 397
Cruel Sea, The 35, 116, 118, 145, 146, 409
Cry, the Beloved Country 255, 440
Culloden 27, 45, 46, 127, 434
Cunniffe, David 373
Curse of the Mummy's Tomb, The 437
Cy Endfield's Entertaining Card Magic 83
Cymbeline 423

Dabulamanzi 13, 18, 19, 37, 65, 183, 185

Dade, Stephen 173, 196, 200, 216-220, 324, 336, 379, 393, 412, 416
Dalby, Stephen 248
Dalton, Commissary James Langley 17, 19, 23, 26, 31, 34, 52, 68, 174
Daly, Patrick 321
Dam Busters, The 297
Damn Yankees 259
Dances with Wolves 254
Daneman, Paul 112, 233
Danger Within 140
Dark Avenger, The 163
Daves, Delmer 46
Davidson, Jim 346
Davies, Brenda 330
Davies, Richard 61, 70, 141, 151, 233, 291
Davis, Peter 207, 208, 278
Day of the Jackal, The 352
Day the Earth Caught Fire, The 140
Day, Doris 86
De Sade 86, 87
Deadlier Than the Male 158, 410
Dearden, Basil 145
Death Drums Along the River 192
Death Watch 47
Deeley, Michael 122
de Gruchy, Major F.A.I. 433
de Havilland, Olivia 145
Deighton, Len 143
de Klerk, F.W. 204
de Lautour, Charles 82
Dementia 13 97
DeMille, Cecil B. 130
Demons of the Mind 97
de Neuville, Alphonse 26, 35
Dent, Alan 322
Deutsch, David 388-389
Diamond Walkers, The 174, 192, 203, 223, 363
Diamonds Are Dangerous 192
Die Another Day 287
Die Voortrekkers 193
Die, Monster, Die! 97
Dingaan 193, 277
Dingaka 121, 203, 240, 246, 362
Dingiswayo 193
Dinuzulu, Princess Constance Magogo ka 3, 186, 253
Dirty Dozen, The 223, 244, 287
Disney, Walt 163
Disraeli 361
Distant Trumpet, A 311, 430
Divorce, Italian Style 130
Dixon of Dock Green 140
Doctor in Distress 311
Doctor in Love 311
Doctor, The 193
Dog Soldiers 358
Donnenfeld, Bernard
Dorothy Fields Forever 352
Douglas, Kirk 151, 221
Doyle, Arthur Conan 245
Dr. No 129, 254
Dr. Strangelove or: How I Learned to Stop Worrying and Love the Bomb 302, 303
Dracula's Dog (Zoltan, Hound of Dracula) 395
Dresser, Chris 220
Drew, Wayne 368
Druid's Rest, The 116, 258
Drumbeat 254
Duel in the Jungle 171

Dullea, Keir 86
Dunkirk 297
du Pre, Ann 350
Durnford, Colonel Anthony 366, 367
Duryea, Dan 79

é Lollipop 193
Eagle Has Landed, The 144, 287
Easton, Captain Jock 221, 222
Edwards, Glynn 37, 56, 85, 119, 142, 155, 173, 174, 190, 199, 201, 211, 235, 247, 274, 275, 351
Edwards, Nadine M. 334
Eisenstein, Sergei 254
El Cid 47, 246, 249
Elizabeth R 47
Ellis, Brian 121
Elusive Pimpernel, The 145
Embers 97
Emmanuel, Ivor 123, 137, 157, 173, 175, 176, 188, 194, 201, 253, 257, 259, 286, 295, 345, 417, 420
Enchanted Island 302
Endfield, Cy 1, 3, 5, 31, 36, 37, 39, 43, 46-48, 51, 58, 63, 67, 74, 77-80, 82-88, 92, 97, 117-119, 121-123, 127, 128, 131, 132, 137, 140-142, 147, 151, 153, 156, 157, 161-163, 167, 172, 181, 182, 191, 192, 194-196, 200, 201, 204, 205, 211, 215, 216, 219, 220, 230-232, 234-236, 239, 241, 242, 244, 246, 248, 253, 254, 256-258, 260, 274, 283, 286, 289-291, 294-296, 298, 301, 307, 308, 320, 321, 324-326, 331, 333, 334, 336-339, 346, 351, 358, 361-366, 368, 370, 387-391, 393-394, 396-400, 403-409, 412-413, 415-424, 434, 445-446, 451, 456
Endfield, Maureen 10, 51, 77, 78, 80, 82-88, 139, 147, 166, 167, 172, 175, 181, 193, 194, 220, 295, 298, 362-366, 404, 408, 415, 423
Endgame 97
Enemy Mine 223
Englishman Who Went Up a Hill and Came Down a Mountain, The 246
Enigma 254
Ensign Pulver 310, 311
Entertainer, The 155
Entertaining Mr Sloane 365
Essery, G. Vernon 177
Essex, David 107, 155
Eva 118, 240
Evans, Clifford 291
Evans, Geraint 294
Evening in Byzantium 155
Evita 107
Ewart, Peter 371, 383
Ewin, Mike 301
Exodus 221, 234
Exorcist: The Beginning 288

Face of Fu Manchu, The 157
Faith, Adam 254
Fall of the Roman Empire, The 246, 430
Fallen Idol, The 145
Fantasia 303
Fassbinder, Rainer Werner 152
Fawne-Meade, Ian 294, 403-424

Fiegel, Eddi 254, 255
Fiend, The 97
Finch, Peter 153
Fings Ain't Wot They Used T' Be 153, 274
Finney, Albert 118, 153
Fire Maidens from Outer Space 297
Fish Called Wanda, A 240
Flash Gordon 221
Fleming, Ian 254
Flight of the Phoenix, The 424
Floyd, Keith 290
Flynn, Errol 321
Folbigge, Dennis 34, 174, 178, 406, 419
Forbes, Bryan 118, 145, 291
Ford, John 336, 366, 412, 430
Foreman, Carl 79
Forsyth, Bruce 356, 357
Four Feathers, The 335
Fox and His Friends 152
Foxhole in Cairo 140
Francis Drake 274
Frankenstein Must Be Destroyed 223
Fraser, Liz 142, 143, 295
Fräulein Doktor 155
Frazier, Colonel 201, 202
Frears, Stephen 357
Freeman, Geoff 162, 166, 177, 181, 185, 190, 200, 257, 286, 287, 289, 366
Freer, Steve 185, 373
Fregonese, Hugo 39
French Dressing 153, 400
Frend, Charles 116
Frenzy 240, 246
Friendly Fire 205
Frift, Dick 168
From Book to Script: Finding the Story 358
From Russia with Love 254, 306
From the Earth to the Moon 302
Frontier 107
Fry, Christopher 116
Full Monty, The 370
Funeral in Berlin 288
Futsh, Hazel 294

Galileo 97
Gallacher, Sergeant 68
Gallagher, Elaine 127
Game for Vultures 193
Games, The 122
Gardner, David Alan 383
Garrett, Robert (Bobby) 388, 390, 393-394, 400
Gawain and the Green Knight 158
G.B.H. 112
Geerdts, Hilda 168, 169, 170
Genghis Khan 222
Gentleman Joe Palooka 78
Gentlemen Prefer Anything 155
Gerrard, Tom 146, 231, 395
Get Carter 275
Ghosh, Sandy 371
Gibbs, Patrick 329
Gibson, Mel 346
Gielgud, John 156, 297
Gigi 149
Gilbert, Lewis 422
Gill, Peter 57, 140, 154, 156, 173, 205, 206, 235, 307, 351, 352
Gilliatt, Penelope 329
Gillings, Ken 372

484 INDEX

Girney, Alan 463
Gladiator 357, 367
Glass Menagerie, The 149
Glass Mountain, The 234
Glencoe 43, 45, 47
Gods Must Be Crazy II, The 193
Godzilla 129
Gold 192, 204
Gold, Ronald 333
Goldby, Betty 44
Golden Rendezvous 204, 221, 234, 364
Goldfinger 306
Good Woman, A 288
Goodlatte, D.J. 302
Goodwin, Andy 371
Gow, Gordon 321, 325
Graceless Go I 122
Graham, Denys 151, 233, 297
Graham, Sheilah 184, 190, 207
Grand Hotel 297
Grande Illusion, La 368
Granger, Stewart 163
Grant, Cary 302, 410
Grant, Hugh 370
Grant, Keith 256
Graves, Thelma 351
Gray, Charles 149
Graystone, Lawrence 373
Great Catherine 149
Greaves, Adrian 37
Green, Dr H.H. 156
Green, Guy 145
Green, Nigel 102-104, 138, 140, 144, 156-158, 173, 175, 221, 286, 291, 295, 327, 340, 352, 410-411, 413, 416, 418, 431
Greene, Richard 156
Grist, Leighton 383
Groping for Words 297
Gryspeerdt, Norman 287
Guinness, Alec 137
Gunga Din 335, 358
Guns at Batasi 148
Guns of Navarone, The 118, 222, 308, 332
Gwabi, Patience 294
Gypsy and the Gentleman, The 156, 234

Hadley, Russell W. 286
Haggard, H. Rider 336, 372
Hall, Arthur 391-392, 400, 455
Hall, Harvey 59
Hall, William 99, 139, 162, 185, 295
Hamill, Katherine 320
Hamlet at Elsinore 140
Hammer House of Horror 107
Hammett, Dashiell 79
Hammond, Peter 119, 170, 202, 218, 220
Hannah and Her Sisters 144
Harborth, A.J. 170
Hard Day's Night, A 240, 306
Hargreaves, Kenneth N. 286, 393-394, 400
Harlow 313
Harris, Esther 283, 284, 286
Harris, Richard 86, 118, 122, 151, 153
Harrison, R.H. 392, 397, 399
Harryhausen, Ray 83
Hathaway, Henry 149
Havard, Dafydd 35, 58, 233

Hawkins, Doreen (née Lawrence) 10, 123, 145
Hawkins, Jack 3, 35, 53, 118, 123, 137, 139, 144-149, 192, 288, 295, 307, 327-329, 332, 334, 340, 350, 353, 360, 378, 396-398, 409, 412, 432, 446, 451, 455
Hawks, Howard 145
Hayes, John Michael 47
Heart Within, The 274
Heatherton, Joey 298
Heflin, Van 389, 451, 455
Helen of Troy 117, 221, 234
Hell Below Zero 129, 244
Hell Drivers 81, 82, 88, 117, 167, 334, 405
Hell Is a City 118, 437
Hellfire Club, The 310, 311
Hellions, The 129, 153, 171, 174
Hellman, Lillian 79
Henty, G. A. 336
Hepburn, Audrey 302
Hercules 129, 130, 131
Hercules Unchained 130, 409
Heroes of Telemark, The 151, 152, 221
Herrmann, Bernard 419-420
Heston, Charlton 311
Heyes, Martin 383
Hibbin, Nina 331
Hickman, Darryl 298
Hickox, Douglas 87, 137, 365, 366
Hide and Seek 83, 334, 397
Hiemstra, General 201, 202
High Girders, The 45
Highland Clearances, The 45
Hill in Korea, A 140
Hillier, Erwin 362
Hinxman, Margaret 320
Hitch, Private Fred 19, 39, 57, 92, 95, 266, 311, 351
Hitchcock, Alfred 325, 412, 416, 419
Hitchcock, Claude 243, 244, 253
Hittler, Wendy 138
HMS Defiant 163, 205
HMS Pinafore 295
Hobbit, The 112
Hollywood, England 326
Hook, Private Henry 20, 21, 30, 58, 90, 92, 94, 97, 105, 107-111, 140, 152-154, 268-271, 291, 293, 311, 381, 431
Hopkins, Peter 370
Horne, Kenneth 354
Hoskins, Bob 366
House is Not a Home, A 313
Houston, Donald 128, 137, 295
How Green Was My Valley 122
How I Won the War 112
How the West Was Won 303
How to Undress in Front of Your Husband 129
Howard, Walter 39
Howarth (Howard), Gunner 20, 35, 58
Howes, Richard 382
Hudson, Hugh 403
Hughes, Private 58
Hughesdon, Fred C. 243
Hunt, Melvin 373
Hunter, Stephen 368
Hurd, Douglas 112
Huston, John 87, 144, 158, 223, 389
Huth, Harold 129
Hywel-Jones, Ian 290

I Know Where I'm Going! 249
I'm Not Feeling Myself Tonight 155
I-Kati Elimnayana 193
Iacoppi, Barry 382
Idle, Eric 357
Idol, The 364
If Only I Had Wings 112
Impulse 81, 82
In Darkest Hollywood 207, 278
Inflation 78, 88
Informer, The 80
Inkedama 193
Inn for Trouble 437
Inn of the Sixth Happiness, The 222
Innocent Bystanders 122
Ipcress File, The 1, 143, 157, 275, 410, 422
Iphi Ntombi 209, 210
Isabella and Ferdinand 47
It Always Rains on Sunday 436
It's a Mad, Mad, Mad, Mad World 303
It's All Happening 240
Italian Job, The 121, 144, 288, 364
Ivanhoe 221, 229

Jackson, George H. 334
Jackson, Peter 358
Jacob 53, 209, 433
Jacobsson, Ulla 53, 72, 149-152, 229, 232, 328, 334, 398, 409, 432
James, Clive 118, 138
James, Sid 187
Jameson, Joy 351
Jason and the Argonauts 156
Jazz Boat 153
Jazz Singer, The 155
Jet Storm 82, 83, 117, 128, 405
Joe Palooka in the Big City 78
John Paul Jones 221
John, Christopher 374
Johns, Mervyn 294
Johnson, Johnny 420
Jones, David 70, 121, 157, 163, 166, 220, 231, 234, 243, 244, 246
Jones, Maurice ('Mo') 373
Jones, Private 593 William 20, 21, 35-37, 59, 61, 291
Jones, Private 716 Robert 20, 21, 36, 37, 59, 297
Jones, Roger 370
Jones, Tom 194
Jordan, Kerry 34, 174, 178
Joseph and His Amazing Technicolor Dreamcoat 107
Journey's End 144
Joyce, James 155
Jurgens, Curt 83, 156
Jympson, John 190, 239, 240, 244, 246, 258, 260-262, 336, 379, 396, 413, 417-418, 420

Kafir and Zulu Wars 36
Kain, D.N.E. (Derrick) 139, 165, 168, 170, 174, 183, 227, 229, 230, 239, 395
Kane, Vincent 124, 187
Karloff, Boris 81
Karp, Jack 397, 451
Karsh, Yousuf 143, 189, 193, 288, 289, 352, 418
Katrina 192
Kauffman, Stanley 336

INDEX

Keaton, Buster 191
Keep, The 297
Kelly's Heroes 240
Kelly, Barbara 295
Kendall, Suzy 155
Kennedy, Charles 91
Kennedy, George Brown 91
Kennedy, John 419
Kennedy, President John F. 130
Kent, Geoffrey 403
Kent, Jean 274
Kernan, David 57, 137, 144, 157, 173, 174, 176, 191, 200, 201, 204, 215, 228, 257, 289, 351, 352
Kerr, Deborah 137, 151
Keys, Anthony Nelson 163
Keys, Basil 53, 162, 163, 172, 181, 183, 221, 228, 363, 366, 379, 392, 417, 448
Khartoum 43, 157, 222, 234, 430, 434
Khruschev, Nikita 289
Kick for Touch 205
Kind Hearts and Coronets 240
King and Country 234
King and I, The 259
King Kong 192, 254
King Lear 97, 153, 156
King of Africa 192
King of Kings 229
King Rat 254
King Solomon's Mines 171
Kinnear, Roy 351
Kipling, Rudyard 336
Knibb, Laura 370
Knight, Arthur 334
Knight, Ian 24, 35, 372, 408, 432-433
Knights of the Round Table 117, 163, 216, 229
Knowles, Patric 79
Kohn, Nate 187, 364, 365, 367
Konga 437
Korda, Alexander 116, 145
Korvin, Charles 79
Krapp's Last Tape 97
Kremlin Letter, The 158
Krupa, Gene 286
Kubrick, Stanley 97

Ladies Who Do 303
Lahr, Bert 298
Lake, Veronica 298
Lancaster, Burt 127, 366, 367
Land of Song 259
Land of the Pharaohs 145
Landscapes & Memories 48
Langlois, Henri 84
Lapper, Craig 268
Last Grenade, The 122
Last Safari, The 149
Last Valley, The 144, 221, 234, 288, 364
Lavender Hill Mob, The 240, 291
Lawrance, Bob 146, 229
Lawrence of Arabia 146, 148, 221, 229, 234, 303, 308, 332, 430
Lazenby, George 87
League of Gentlemen, The 146
Lean, David 145, 146, 148, 417
Leather Boys, The 303
Leather, Derrick 243
Lee, Belinda 407
Lee, Jack 403
Legg, Tom 370
Leopard, The 303

Les Misérables 223
Lesser, Sol 79
Lesslie, Colin 162, 387, 391, 393-394, 396-400, 403, 417, 451
Let's Kill Uncle 410
Levine, Joseph E. 47, 54, 83, 85, 86, 119, 121, 126, 129-133, 143, 154, 163, 175, 203, 276, 286, 289, 290, 295, 296-298, 302, 308, 309, 311, 313, 320, 346, 361, 362, 364, 368, 387, 389, 391, 394, 396, 400, 406, 407, 409, 414-415, 418, 421-424
Levine, Rosalie 129, 294, 296
Levy, Stuart 129
Lewis, Stephen 153
Lightstone, Leonard 298, 312
Lilliput 27, 29, 45, 46, 51, 127
Limping Man, The 81, 82, 256
Lion in Winter, The 254
Lion of the North, The 45
Little Black Sambo 369
Little Night Music, A 352
Little Shop of Horrors 240
Littlewood, Joan 140, 153, 154, 274, 275
Lives of a Bengal Lancer, The 335
Lizard in a Woman's Skin 122
Lloyd, Harold 191, 437
Logan, James 373
Lom, Herbert 83
Long and the Short and the Tall, The 140, 205
Long Arm, The 291
Long Day's Journey into Night 130
Long Duel, The 430
Long Ships, The 310, 311
Longest Day, The 93, 221, 434
Look Back in Anger 128
Lord Jim 148, 221, 229
Lord of the Rings: The Two Towers, The 358
Loren, Sophia 306, 312
Losey, Joseph 78, 80, 97, 112, 117, 118, 138, 154, 156, 244, 287
Lost Patrol, The 335
Lost World, The 245
Louise, Anita 298
Love Is a Ball 150
Loved One, The 240
Lovejoy 155, 297
Lovejoy, Frank 79
Lovell, Dudley 133, 189, 202, 217, 219, 239, 379, 412
Luther 97
Lyne, Adrian 403
Lysistrata 245

Macmillan, Harold 369
Mad Cows 240
Magee, Patrick 97, 117, 138, 233, 247, 296, 307, 431
Magnificent Ambersons, The 78
Magus, The 288
Majola, Ngofiza 170
Man Who Finally Died, The 156, 163, 216, 240
Man Who Had Power Over Women, The 155
Man Who Would Be King, The 144, 222, 223
Mancini, Henry 255
Mandel, Paul 336, 337
Mandela and de Klerk 204
Mandela, Nelson 279

Mandy 145
Mann, Anthony 406
Marat/Sade, The 97
March, Fredric 137
Marcus, John 201, 364, 442
Margo, Sidney 255
Markgraaf, Marius 142, 164, 193
Marmont, Patricia 158
Marsden, Betty 354
Marshall, Neil 358
Master Plan, The 81, 82
Masters, John 47, 363
Matewele, Paul 209, 211, 212
Matheson, Richard 86
Mathieson, Muirne 196, 246, 364, 397
Mattson, Arne 149
Maxfield, Sergeant 20, 36, 58, 61, 109-112
Mbhele, Ephraim 241
Mbili, Osborn 227
McAdam, John 31, 32, 34, 35, 37
McArthur, Don 230
McCallum, Doug 283
McCallum, Gordon K. 248-250
McCarthy, Neil 138, 173, 201, 245, 247
McGillivray, David 436
McGoohan, Patrick 82, 406
McGrath, John 140, 205
McLaglen, Victor 82
McLintock! 303
McMichael, John 122, 153
Measure for Measure 155
Melvin, Murray 351
'Men of Harlech' 39, 230, 248, 253, 256, 259, 295, 296, 328
Mépris, Le (Contempt) 130
Merriman, Eric 354
Merriman, John D. 162, 172, 272, 364, 393
Midnight Cowboy 254
Midnight Express 246
Midnight Hour 83
Midst Shot and Shell 39
Midsummer Night's Dream, A 149
Milinaire, Catherine 257
Mill, Lieutenant Robert 139
Miller, Mandy 82
Mills, John 366
Mills, Richard 229, 396
Milne (Millne), Sergeant Frederick 14-17, 56-58, 91
Minder 155, 275
Mister Moses 254
Mitchum, Robert 93, 362, 363
Mkize, Vimba 169, 170
Moby Dick 163, 221, 229
Modesty Blaise 154, 297
Mogambo 171
Monahan, James 321
Monkhouse, Bob 83, 404, 409
Monroe, Marilyn 78, 404
Monserrat, Nicholas 145
Monte Carlo or Bust! 163
Monty Python's The Meaning of Life 357
Moore, Roger 291
Morgan, Terence 274
Morris, Donald R. 31, 364
Morris, Michael 229
Morse, Glyn 115
Mortier, Hans 370
Movshovitz, Howie 368

Mthethwa, Themba 209
Mulvehill, William 361
Mummy, The 287
Mummy's Shroud, The 437
Murder on the Orient Express 229
Murphy's War 222
Murray, Caroline 175, 233
Mutiny 45
Mutiny for a Cause 47
My Child 193
My Great-Aunt Appearing Day 46
Mysterious Island 46, 83, 156, 167, 334, 405

Naked City, The 151
Naked Prey, The 163, 174, 203, 223, 313, 364
Narrative of Field Operations connected with the Zulu War, 1879 24
Nevada Smith 130
Neve, Brian 77, 88
Never a Cross Word 112
Newman, Arthur 168
Next Time I'll Sing to You 140, 297, 409
Ngaka 193
Ngubane, Elliot 209, 211, 440
Ngwanaka 193
Nicholas and Alexandra 149
Nichols, Mike 423
Night My Number Came Up, The 291
Night of the Demon (Curse of the Demon) 82
Night to Remember, A 234
Ninety Degrees in the Shade 155
Niven, David 163, 311
Nkosi, Lewis 277
Nolbandov, Sergei 115
Nor the Moon by Night 161, 220, 223, 406-407, 415
Norman, Frank 153
North West Frontier 430
Norton, Dan 383
Not in Front of the Children 112
Nureyev, Rudolf 86

O Lucky Man! 163
Oakes, Philip 323, 330, 331
Of Love and Desire 303
Oh No, It's Selwyn Froggitt 291
Oh! What a Lovely War 112, 149, 275, 291, 351
Oh, Boy! 254
O.H.M.S. 390
Oklahoma! 259
Old Boys, The 297
Oliver! 254, 419
Olivier, Laurence 116
On the Line 297
One Summer of Happiness 149
Open Book, An 223
Original Sin 205
Orkin, Harvey 260
Orphan, The 193
Osborne, John 128, 155
O'Shaughnessy, Brian 395
Osmosis 221
Othello 291
Other Man, The 140
Otley 352
O'Toole, Peter 118, 140, 153, 221, 363, 366, 406
Out of Africa 254

Owen, Cliff 403, 424
Owen, Dickie 67, 138, 436-437
Owen, Private 37, 39, 58, 68, 69, 92, 94, 147, 432

Pacey, Ann 321
Paddick, Hugh 354
Paisá 129
Palmer, Lilli 87
Palmer, Ray 248
Paper Lads, The 235, 275
Paris '90 83
Parker, Alan 357
Parker, Charles E. 229
Parker, Dorothy 79
Parr, Sir Henry Hallam 36
Parry, Gwyllim 381
Passage, The 221
Passport to Pimlico 437
Past and Present 440
Paterson, John 168
Paton, Alan 254, 440
Patterson, John 357
Pearson, Harry 381
Peper, William 337
Pepita Jiménez 122, 288
Peppard, George 362, 410, 424
Percy's Progress 155
Perel, Allan 230
Perfect Friday 122
Perkins, Anthony 298
Perrine, Dan 371
Pertwee, Bill 354
Peter Pan 155
Peters, Andrew 221
Pickard, Stephen R. 249
Pieterse, Andre 162, 313
Pines, Jim 369, 428, 433, 439
Pink Panther Strikes Again, The 221
Pink Panther, The 303
Pinter, Harold 97
Plain and Fancy 259
Play Dirty 144, 158
Please Sir! 291
Plummer, Christopher 140
Popsy Pop 122
Porter, Bob 8, 63, 66, 85, 119, 121-124, 126, 127, 133, 151, 157, 162, 163, 165, 166, 168, 169, 171, 172, 175, 177, 181, 185, 189, 201, 202, 216, 220, 221, 226, 228, 234, 253, 288, 325, 348, 362, 363, 364, 379, 392-394, 398-400, 416, 448-449
Pound, Leslie 286
Powell, Dilys 324, 325
Powell, Eddie 221, 437
Powell, Joe 103, 119, 142, 144, 157, 191, 201, 221, 222, 227, 228, 234, 253, 257, 353, 379, 437
Powell, Michael 249
Power, Tyrone 163
Powers, James 332
Prebble, Jan (née Reid) 9, 27, 44, 45, 47, 48, 51, 54
Prebble, John 9, 10, 13, 14, 22-24, 26-31, 36, 37, 39, 42-48, 50-52, 54, 57, 61, 67, 68, 74, 75, 91-95, 99, 100, 101, 108, 109, 118, 121, 123, 127, 131, 132, 162, 186, 241, 242, 257, 287, 290, 295, 307, 328, 338, 363, 406, 410, 434
Precious Bane 86, 424
Précis of Information concerning the Zulu country, etc. 24

Prendergast, Jack 254
Presley, Elvis 306
Pressburger, Emeric 249
Preston, Mrs K. 101
Prize of Arms, A 97, 118, 240, 274
Producers, The 364
Prokofiev, Sergei 254

QBVII 149
Quigley, Isabel 325, 329
Quo Vadis 229

Rackin, Martin 418
Ramsden, James 294
Randell, Ron 295
Rank, J. Arthur 406
Rankin, Douglas 46, 118, 127, 403, 406
Rape of the Fair Country 363
Ray, Nicholas 156
Reach for the Sky 156
Rebel Troop 47
Red Badge of Courage, The 389
Red Beret, The 116, 129
Red Garters 55, 241
Reed, Oliver 140
Reed, Peter 286
Reeves, Michael 86
Relph, Michael 146
Rennie, Howard 195, 220
Renoir, Jean 368
Rentadick 155
Requiem for a Heavyweight 140
Return of the Pink Panther, The 223
Reynolds, Surgeon James 17, 22, 26, 68, 96, 97, 106, 110, 268, 431
Richard III 116
Richard, Cliff 302, 306
Richards, Brien 381
Rickards, Marylin 409
Rietty, Robert 149, 401
Rio Bravo 311
Rio Conchos 277
Ritter, E.A. 31
Rivonia-Prozeß, Der 193
Road, Alan 181
Roald Dahl's Tales of the Unexpected 107
Robbery 121, 154, 275, 288, 364
Robbins, Harold 130, 154, 298, 308, 311
Robin and Marian 254
Robin Hood 223
Robinson Crusoe 122, 235
Robinson, David 321
Robinson, George 108
Rodgers, Richard 259, 295
Rohsmann, Dr Winfried 150
Rome – Open City 129
Romeo and Juliet 145
Ronay, Edina 142, 144, 294, 409
Ronay, Michael 294
Rorke's Drift 1879: Against All Odds 210
Rose Tattoo, The 149
Rosenbaum, Jonathan 88
Rosenstone, Robert A. 32, 43
Ross, Lillian 389
Rossen, Robert 79
Rossouw, Jan 142
Roud, Richard 328, 329
Rough for Radio 97
Round the Horne 354
Rule Britannia! 291

INDEX 487

Rumpole of the Bailey 297
Russell, Ken 153
Rutanga Tapes, The 193
Ryan's Daughter 229

Sabela, Simon 119, 185, 188, 192, 193, 226, 227, 281, 366, 434, 445-446
Sachs, Bruce 8, 259
Saint Clair, Barrie 365
Saint Joan 144
Salisbury, John M. 371
Saltzman, Harry 129, 143
Sandenbergh, Brian 338, 339
Sanders, George 117
Sandilands, John 320
Sands of the Kalahari 85, 121, 123, 124, 240, 246, 288, 313, 361, 362, 365, 423-424
Satan's Harvest 192
Saunders, Eddie 108
Saunders, James 140, 297
Scala, Gia 144
Scammell, Corporal 68
Scavengers 193
Schack, Günther 286
Schary, Dore 78
Schellhorn, Edward 275
Schiess, Corporal 19, 52, 59, 67, 68, 75, 268, 273, 353, 432, 437
Schlesinger, John 403
Schneer, Charles 83, 405
Schulberg, Budd 79
Scorsese, Martin 367
Scott of the Antarctic 240
Scott, Ridley 357, 368, 403, 412
Scott, Tony 403
Scrooge 287
Sea Fury 82, 117, 334
Sea Shall Not Have Them, The 156
Sea Wolves, The 223
Seagull, The 86
Secombe, Harry 123, 294
Secret of My Success, The 155
Secret, The 81, 83, 334
Selinger, Dennis 140, 294, 422
Sellers, Peter 306
Serling, Rod 140
Servant, The 97, 303
Setipana 193
Seven Against the Sun 174, 192
Shail, Robert 319
Shaka Zulu 209, 364
Shaka Zulu 31, 174, 193, 210
Shame of the Sabine Women 310, 311
Sharrett, Christopher 207, 428-430, 433, 439-441
Shaw, George Bernard 144, 145
Shaw, Robert 82, 140, 409
Shaw, Tommy 223
Sheridan, Ann 298
Sherriff, R.C. 144
Sherrin, Ned 351
Shirley Valentine 287
Shoeshine 129
Shout at the Devil 193, 204, 287
Shrimpton, Jean 83, 424
Shurlock, Geoffrey M. 273, 276
Side by Side by Sondheim 352
Simba 161
Simmons, Jean 137, 151, 363
Simon, Neil 140
Sinden, Donald 116, 295
Sinden, Jeremy 295

Sir Arne's Treasure 150
Sishi, Hubert 446
Six Wives of Henry VIII, The 47
Skater Dater 424
Skeleton Coast 193
Skinner, Cornelia Otis 83
Skull, The 97
Sky Above, the Mud Below, The 298
Sky Riders 365
Slaughter in the Sun 29, 30, 31, 36, 45, 127
Slaughter, Tod 436
Sleep of Prisoners, A 116
Sleeper's Den, The 205
Small Back Room, The 145
Small Change 205
Small Voice, The 221
Smiles of a Summer Night 150
Smith, Bernard 448
Smith, George 162, 188, 283
Smith, J.B. 248
Smith, Reverend George 15, 17, 22, 92, 93
Smith, Wilbur 363, 407
Soderbergh, Steven 346
Sodom and Gomorrah 119, 130, 415
Solo for Sparrow 245
Solomon and Sheba 437
Some Came Running 311
Some Girls Do 410
Sondheim Tonight 352
Sondheim, Stephen 352
Song by Song 352
Sound of Fury, The 79, 88, 405
South Pacific 259
South Wales Borderers, The 31, 37
Sowden, Dora 277, 278, 340
Sparrers Can't Sing 153, 351
Sparrows Can't Sing 153, 154
Speight, Johnny 140, 155
Spikings, Barry 122
Spy Trap 112
Spy Who Loved Me, The 395
Stamp, Terence 86, 140, 141, 154, 205, 257, 295, 363, 407, 422, 424
Stanley Baker: A Life in Film 186
Stanton, J. 275
Star Wars 229
Starr, Belle 364, 366
Starship Troopers 358
Steel Bayonet, The 140, 142
Steele, Tommy 121, 405, 419
Stephens, Robert 141
Stephenson, Captain 15, 61, 67
Stevenson, Lee 97
Stewart, James 406
Stiletto 154
Stiller, Mauritz 150
Stoppard, Tom 155
Storey, Anthony 87, 124, 258
Stork Bites Man 78
Stork Talk 240
Strachan, Alan 248
Strangers at Sunrise 192
Stravinsky, Igor 254
Strizzi, Sergio 287, 288
Suddenly, Last Summer 240
Sullivan, John 133, 144, 157, 201, 221, 222, 224, 230, 246, 379, 415-416
Summer Holiday 302
Sunburn 155
Sunday Night at the London Palladium 356, 357

Superbrain 88
Supergirl 249
Suspense 78
Swait, Don 371
Swiss Family Robinson 163
Sword of Sherwood Forest 156

Take It from Here 419
Tales from the Crypt 97
Tamarind Seed, The 221
Tandy, Jessica 145
Tapley, Colin 381
Tarrant, Leigh 382
Tarzan the Magnificent 221
Tarzan's Savage Fury 79
Taylor, Elizabeth 85, 128, 258, 362, 363, 423
Taylor, Larry 7, 58, 138, 144, 147, 173, 192, 234, 275, 436
Taylor, Rocky 235, 275
Teddy Bear, The 83
Temkin, Ben 186
Ten Commandments, The 302, 313
Ten Little Indians 245
That Time 97
That Was the Week That Was 351
That'll Be the Day 155
Thatcher: The Final Days 112
Theatre of Blood 365
Them 155
Third Man on the Mountain 163
This Is My Street 303
This Is Your Life 351
This Sporting Life 118
Thomas, Dylan 35, 261, 297
Thomas, Private 37, 68, 92, 101, 245, 432
Thomas MP, George 123
Thomas, Wyn 297
Thompson, Jennifer 85, 87, 146, 147, 156, 185, 201, 239, 240, 245, 253
Thorndike, Sybil 144
Those Magnificent Men in Their Flying Machines 219, 221
Three Hats for Lisa 436
Three Hostages, The 47
Tigers Don't Cry 193
Time for Singing, A 259
Time Without Pity 112, 244
To the Coral Strand 47, 363
Toboli, Mamsie 294
Tobruk 158, 410-411
Tokoloshe 187, 192, 203, 246, 363
Tom Jones 303
Tomaselli, Keyan 193, 267
Tomlinson, Eric 255
Top Secret! 222
Tora! Tora! Tora! 434
Touch of Larceny, A 436
Townsend, Sue 297
Travesties 155
Treasure of Monte Cristo, The 240
Trevelyan, John 267, 272
Trevor, William 297
Trials of Oscar Wilde, The 153
Trojan Women, The 97
Trumbo, Dalton 79, 363
Tshabalala, Daniel 53, 433
Tully, Danny 374
Tunes of Glory 391
Twin Peaks 155
Twisted Nerve 291
Twang!! 154
Two Women 130

Two-Headed Spy, The 140, 144
Typically British 357

u-Diliwe 192, 193
Under Milk Wood 35, 261, 291, 297
Undercover 115
Underworld Story, The 79
Universal Soldier 87
Untamed 161
Up the Chastity Belt 352
Upfold, Jack 286
Uys, Jamie 203

Valley of Song 297
Vanbrugh, John 155
van den Bergh, Gert 100, 174, 176, 364, 395, 418
van der Merwe, Chris 192
van Heerden, Dawie 171, 364
Vantan, Robert 436
Van Vooren, Monique 298
Verhoeven, Paul 358
Verne, Jules 83
Victim 223
Victor/Victoria 246, 287
Vikings, The 221
Violent Playground 116
Virginian, The 150
Vorhaus, Bernard 79

Wachtel, David 382
Waite, Rupert 449-450
Waiting for Godot 112
Wake in Fright (Outback) 107
Wake Island 431
Walkabout 254
Walker, Alexander 326, 328, 330
Walker, Oliver 340
Wall, Russell 8
Walsh, Moira 319, 339
Walsh, Raoul 430
Walter, Len 248
Wanamaker, Sam 259
Wanstall, Norman 248
War Game, The 46
War Horses, The 47, 363
Ward, Simon 366
Washing of Spears, A 364

Washing of the Spears, The 31, 364
Waterloo 149, 307, 431, 434
Waterman, Ivan 245
Watkins, Peter 46, 434
Watson, Claude 352
Watson, Ian 441-442
Way of the World, The 156
Wayne, John 325, 369
Weinstein, Hannah 80
Weiss, Peter 97
Welles, Orson 78, 363
Weltner, George 235, 286, 295, 296, 298, 308, 361, 391, 396
Weston, Bob 286
Weston, John 47, 363
What's It All About? 199
Wheels 155
When the Lion Feeds 47, 363, 407
Where Eagles Dare 222, 240, 245
Where Love Has Gone 130, 298
Where the Sea Breaks 44
Where's Jack? 35, 121, 288, 364
Whistle Down the Wind 240
White Feather 46
Whitman, Stuart 362
Who Killed Lamb? 122
Whoops Apocalypse 291
Why the Chicken 140, 205
Whybrow, Roy
Wilby Conspiracy, The 204
Wild Geese, The 219
Wilde, Cornel 364
Wilde, Marty 83
Williams, Private 612 (395) 20, 22, 30, 37, 39, 57, 109-111
Williams, Elmo 143
Williams, Emlyn 116, 258
Williams, Esther 78
Williams, Kenneth 354
Williams, Private 398 Joseph 30, 59, 61
Wilson, Cecil 320, 328
Wilson, Harold 122, 123
Windridge, Sergeant Joseph 17, 103, 106, 110, 172, 221, 222
Windsor, Barbara 154
Winner, Michael 88
Winsten, Archer 334

Winter Garden 97
Winters, Shelley 78
Wisdom, Norman 140, 163, 306
Wiseman, Thomas 331
Witt, Margareta 53, 54, 56, 59, 60, 61, 70, 71, 72, 73, 74, 149, 151, 268, 269, 271, 273, 354, 417, 432-433
Witt, Reverend Otto 15, 16, 18, 21, 32, 36, 52, 54, 55, 70-73, 92, 102-105, 144, 146, 148, 149, 269, 271, 328, 330, 340, 353, 354, 417, 432, 451, 455
Wizard of Oz, The 369
Woman Times Seven 143, 364
Wonderful World of the Brothers Grimm, The 303
Wood, Tony 373
World of Suzie Wong, The 222
Wouk, Herman 140
Wrecking Crew, The 158
Wrong Arm of the Law, The 140
Wyler, William 145, 394

Yesterday's Enemy 118
Yesterday, Today and Tomorrow 130, 312
York Realist, The 205
York, Susannah 124, 362
Young Mr. Pitt, The, 436
Young Winston 149, 222
Young, John 371
Young, James Peter 410

Zarak 430
Zorba the Greek 288
Zorro 122
Zorro, the Gay Blade 155
Zulu Dawn 31, 87, 122, 124, 137, 187, 193, 204, 209, 210, 234, 287, 364, 365, 366, 367, 369, 408, 434, 439, 446
Zulu: The True Story 188
Zulu War – Then and Now, The 24
Zunckel, Ralf 230
Zwelithini, Goodwill 186